Liberators, Patriot
Leaders of Latin Am

second edition

ɔm

ALSO BY JEROME R. ADAMS

*Greasers and Gringos: The Historical Roots
of Anglo-Hispanic Prejudice*
(McFarland, 2006)

*Notable Latin American Women: Twenty-Nine Leaders,
Rebels, Poets, Battlers and Spies, 1500–1900*
(McFarland, 1995)

Liberators, Patriots, and Leaders of Latin America

32 Biographies

Second Edition

JEROME R. ADAMS

McFarland & Company, Inc., Publishers

Jefferson, North Carolina, and London

LIBRARY OF CONGRESS CATALOGUING-IN-PUBLICATION DATA

Adams, Jerome R., 1938–
Liberators, patriots and leaders of Latin America :
32 biographies / by Jerome R. Adams.— 2nd ed.
p.   cm.
Includes bibliographical references and index.

ISBN 978-0-7864-4284-3
softcover : 50# alkaline paper

1. Latin America — Biography.   2. Heads of state — Latin
America — Biography.   3. Politicians— Latin America — Biography.
4. Revolutionaries— Latin America — Biography.   5. Heroes— Latin
America — Biography.   6. Patriotism — Latin America — History.
7. Leadership — Latin America — History.   8. Latin America —
Politics and government.   I. Adams, Jerome R., 1938– Liberators
and patriots of Latin America.   II. Title.
F1407.A33   2010   920.08 — dc22   2009049834

British Library cataloguing data are available

Front cover: Werner Horvath. *Garden of Revolution — Che Guevara.*
Oil on canvas. 27½" × 19½". 2002; sun art ©2010 Shutterstock

Manufactured in the United States of America

*McFarland & Company, Inc., Publishers
Box 611, Jefferson, North Carolina 28640
www.mcfarlandpub.com*

For Jan,
Beth, Matthew,
Daniel and Rebecca

Acknowledgments

When the first edition of *Liberators and Patriots* was published in the early 1990s, the youngest member of the family, Rebecca, was the one most excited by the prospect. Since that good day, Rebecca has grown up to be the one who provided professional editing of this second edition. It was a job earned partly by her trekking through Central America on more modes of transportation than Che Guevara ever used, and by guiding her father toward a better understanding of Latin American realities in the twenty-first century. The author would also like to express his gratitude for the patient, professional help of the denizens of Davis Library at the University of North Carolina at Chapel Hill.

Contents

Acknowledgments   vi

Introduction   1

1. Doña Marina (La Malinche): Mother of Conquest   5
2. Pierre François Dominique Toussaint L'Ouverture: Commander
   of a Slave Army   14
3. Simón Bolívar: Liberator of the North   25
4. Manuela Sáenz: Spirit of the Liberation   34
5. José de San Martín: Liberator of the South   47
6. Bernardo O'Higgins: Chile's Irish Liberator   60
7. Domingo Faustino Sarmiento: Educator of a Continent   73
8. Pedro I and Pedro II, Brazil's Emperors: Divine Right and Democracy   85
9. José Martí: Revolutionary Poet   96
10. Benito Juárez: Builder of Democracy   104
11. Pancho Villa: Political Warrior   114
12. Emiliano Zapata: Indian Reformer   120
13. Dolores Jiménez y Muro, Juana Belén Gutiérrez de Mendoza and
    Hermila Galindo de Topete: Women of the Mexican Revolution   127
14. Augusto Sandino: The Visionary versus the Marines   133
15. Juan Perón: Monarch of the Working Class   142
16. María Eva Duarte de Perón: Angel of the "Shirtless Ones"   151
17. José Figueres: At the Center of Latin America   161
18. Fidel Castro: Socialist Revolutionary   173
19. Ernesto "Che" Guevera: Existential Rebel   183
20. Bishop Romero: Modern Martyr   194
21. Salvador Allende and Augusto Pinochet: Ariel and Caliban   203
22. César Chávez: Hispanic Spartacus   231

Contents

23. Vicente Fox: Breaking the Political Mold   256

24. Néstor Kirchner Ostoic and Cristina Fernández de Kirchner:
    Peronist Pair   281

25. Daniel Ortega Saavedra: Sandino Redux   305

26. Luís Inacio Lula da Silva: Brazil's Diminutive Giant   329

27. Hugo Chávez: Elected Leftist   352

Chapter Notes   383

Select Bibliography   387

Index   393

Introduction

The second edition of this book crosses a wide chasm. The earlier biographies were almost all of individuals who were long dead, as were their adversaries and critics. The purpose of the book was to "bring Latin American heroes out of the shadow cast over them outside their own region," and the historians quoted were, for the most part, models of civility. Alas, those are no longer the guidelines of understanding. Modern Latin American leaders fairly leap from the headlines, or at least skulk about in the interior pages of national newspapers. They are derided by U.S. presidents and hanged in effigy in the streets of their own capitals. Everybody who "follows the news" can hold forth at the water cooler, describing the latest news about some Latin American scoundrel or, less frequently, some Latin American savior. Modern leaders' stories are told not by historians, but by journalists.

There are similarities, of course, in that some modern journalists, just like the scribes of long ago, take pen in hand not just to portray their subjects, but to lionize or vilify them. Indeed, modern news reporters divide themselves along with the populace as candidates for office assemble legions of voters just as Bolívar once scrounged troops to stand against the Spanish. This makes for loud and lively, if not altogether enlightening, discussions in which modern leaders have mastered both the fiery peroration and the memorable sound bite.

Another important similarity is that all of these figures were, and are, agents of change, nation builders. At the beginning of the nineteenth century, leadership generally meant driving out Europeans after three centuries of colonization. Here the emphasis was on freedom and equality. European monarchs had imposed economic strictures that thwarted development. Not until the Treaty of Utrecht in 1713, for example, was France able to trade with the Spanish colonies of Peru and Chile; students of Indian or mixed blood were never, until after independence, allowed to matriculate at the University of San Marcos in Lima.

After independence, leadership, perforce, meant dealing with less easily defined political issues. When leaders took up arms, it was usually against their own countrymen. And, today, the spectre of civil wars and military coups are engraved in the short-term memories of Latin Americans because civil wars were fought but a few years ago and, in too many cases, threaten to erupt tomorrow.

Octavio Paz, the Mexican philosopher whose father followed Zapata, has described the racial, philosophical, and political mixture that has shaped Latin America, where, he says,

> thought begins as a justification of Independence, but it is transformed almost immediately into a quest: America is not so much a tradition that continues as a future to be realized. Quest and utopia are inseparable ... from the end of the 18th Century to today. The quest includes, indeed requires, Iberian and mestizo, former slave and former clerk. Only by embracing all does it have meaning: the future must be imagined by us all to be built by us all, no more with imperial design, stamped in Europe, than imperialist design, price-tagged in the United States.

A future imagined by all has proved elusive. The inability of neighbors to cooperate destroyed the hopes of Bolívar and made his death especially bitter, although that has not stopped others— Pedro II, Martí, Bishop Romero—from articulating the dream. The deep divisions that once separated patriot from royalist now split socialist from free-market entrepreneur, agrarian reformer from plantation owner.

Patterns run through these stories. There is the recurring reminder of the native heritage in Latin America, a heritage that both extols the ways of the past and defends its right to tribal lands into the future. The native identity is an important aspect in the stories of Malinche and Juárez, Sandino and Zapata and affects profoundly the politics of modern Brazil, Mexico, and Nicaragua. One also sees a continuing compulsion to rebel against overwhelming odds in the cases of Manuela Sáenz and "Che" Guevara and, today, in that of Daniel Ortega.

There is also, sadly, a continuing refrain of betrayal, tales written in treachery, blood, and disillusionment like those of Toussaint L'Ouverture and Sandino long ago and, in the 1970s, that of Salvador Allende.

A much overlooked pattern has been the place of women in defining revolutionary values: Gutiérrez and her contemporaries and Eva Perón are voices that have been dramatized — soldaderas and Evita—but have not been listened to with sufficient respect. Indeed, not until Cristina Kirchner turned the image of Evita into the reality of the Argentine presidency had a Latin American woman taken executive control of such an important Latin American country.

Intertwined with many of these patterns is the role of the United States, which was developing its own foreign policy during the period 1800 (Toussaint's slave rebellion) to the present (Bishop Romero's plea to President Jimmy Carter). Over this period, U.S. troops failed to catch rebels like Sandino and Villa, and U.S. presidents were equally unsuccessful in understanding Latin American leaders. U.S. impositions have continued into the present, in the bright glare of international finance and the dark alleys of Central Intelligence Agency chicanery.

*　*　*

The second edition adds nine Latin American leaders, all presidents of their respective countries, to the twenty-three individuals of the first edition. Although several began their careers as leaders in the hard-knocks world of armed resistance or union organizing, all but one ultimately occupied the presidency by winning more votes than their opponents. As in the rest of the world, modern Latin American presidents prevail not because of clear, sweeping proclamations, but because their followers provide winning margins—sometimes razor-thin — in hard-fought democratic elections.

The obvious exception is General Augusto Pinochet of Chile, who led a bloody coup. In examining that example, the reader must consider the ignoble duplicity of the Nixon administration in the overthrow and killing of President Salvador Allende. Similarly, one cannot ignore the Reagan administration's Iran-Contra chicanery in trying to undermine the Sandinista government of Daniel Ortega. Even at the other, more civil, end of the spectrum, we can learn a great deal about U.S. foibles and Latin American eccentricities from Mexico's Vicente Fox and Argentina's Néstor and Cristina Kirchner. In each case, a Latin American president is steering a course through the shoals of U.S. hegemony. Thus Brazilian President Luís Inacio Lula da Silva is among those leading the independent development of an economy that is often compared, in size and dynamism, to those of India and China. And, of course, what observer of the 6 o'clock news has not either smiled or snarled at the antics of

Hugo Chávez, the Venezuelan president who continues to swim upstream, buoyed by a democratic majority. Finally, there is César Chávez, the Latin American who struggled to be accepted as a prophet in his own country, the United States of America. In each of these examples, it may be that the U.S reader, by examining Latin America, can learn something useful about his or her own country.

*   *   *

A final word about learning is in order. In Cali, Colombia, in 1964, that most ignorant of pupils, a callow Peace Corps volunteer — blinded by the lustre of his North American methods and instruments — met two teachers, Luís Espinoza and Raúl Adames. Neither was by trade a teacher; Luís worked for a European tire manufacturer, Raúl sold contraband. Their initial lesson was in their friendship, for Luís was a Conservative, Raúl a Liberal, and Colombia a battleground in which members of those two parties had been killing each other by the thousands for fifteen years.

We were neighbors. Although neither of them had finished elementary school, they knew a great deal. They knew about their own country, which they cheerfully shared; they had opinions about the United States' relations with its Latin American neighbors, which they modestly asserted; and they knew a very great deal indeed about the history of the United States — more, by conservative estimate, than would the vast majority of that country's high school graduates.

There is an embarrassing difference between how much Latin Americans know about the United States and how little curiosity flows in the other direction. The purpose of this book is to strengthen that flow.

*   *   *

The first 20 chapters are taken directly from the first edition, with sources noted in the text and in the bibliography. Full notes for Chapters 21 through 27 are in the back of the book.

1

Doña Marina (La Malinche)
Mother of Conquest
c. 1505–1530
(Mexico)

Doña Marina was an Indian woman whose life was deeply interwoven with Spanish conquest and settlement of the New World, a contradiction that has, for Mexicans, taken on historic proportions. Although she was flesh and blood, some view her as mythical. Although she was a slave, she rose to a position of leadership that is unique in the history of the New World. Without an army, she employed her wit to begin the conquest of a continent by leading Cortés to his destiny. In the words of Haniel Long, "she represents more than any one moment of history can hold."

Yucatan juts like a clenched fist from the Mexican isthmus to form the southern coast of the Gulf of Mexico. It is harsh country. Inland, broad plains of limestone over coral soak up rainfall so fast that vegetation is sparse; along the marshy lowlands of the coast jungles of mahogany and rosewood grow. It was here, using the offshore islands and safe harbors, that Spanish explorers stepped ashore on a mainland the extent and fierceness of which they could only imagine.

Accepting the theory that the New World was populated by way of the Aleutian archipelago, it is thought that nomadic people made their way diagonally across the great expanse of North America to reach Yucatan at least ten thousand years before Christ was born. Those arrivals became the Mayas, who built what historian Alfred Percival Maudslay calls "the highest culture ever attained by natives on the continent of North America." Art and architecture, and the educational structure supporting both, were highly developed. The Mayan fascination with time led to calendric measurement more precise than that devised by their European counterparts of the Middle Ages.

In fact, notes archeologist Elizabeth P. Benson, the Mayas enjoyed their Classic Period, from A.D. 300 to 900, during Europe's Dark Ages.

> They used a mathematical notation system more sophisticated than their contemporaries. They counted time past in hundreds of thousands of years, noted the movements of the planet Venus, and predicted eclipses of the sun and moon. Yet they never invented the wheel, that most basic of mankind's accomplishments, and they worked with only primitive stone tools and manpower. Technologically they were a Stone Age people. This combination of intellectual and esthetic sophistication with technical primitivism is the hallmark of the Mayan character.

Perhaps because they were peace-loving and unprepared to fight, perhaps because they were simply overwhelmed by the more populous Nahua tribes from the north, the Mayas began to die out after A.D. 900, leaving their temples to crumble with time and be overgrown by vegetation. Their less gifted descendants, the Maya Quiché, migrated southward toward the mountains of Nicaragua and Honduras. In the mythology of the tribes, the demise of the Mayan civilization is associated with the triumph of the warlike Huitzilopoctli over the civilized Quetzalcoatl.

The peninsula was next populated, still before the cultivation of grain or the smelting of iron, by the Toltecs, a Nahua tribe of considerable attainment, but a people destined to generations of subservience. Their masters were the fierce Aztec peoples farther north, whose government centered on the island city of Tenochtitlán. That city, in the great lake that then existed in Central Mexico, was the nucleus of today's Mexico City. The Aztecs, Maudslay tells us, "became the head of a military and predatory empire, dependent for their food, as well as their wealth, on tribute drawn from subject tribes and races. They were not a civilizing power."

Non-Aztec communities, long dominated and humiliated, hated their Aztec oppressors, a hatred that Doña Marina was instrumental in fanning and directing against the Aztecs. Absent such a strategy, the small band led by Hernán Cortés could never have conquered. Thus, responsibility for that conquest must be ascribed in large measure to the young woman who was originally known as Malinal.

Malinal (or, some suggest, "Malinulli") was the daughter of a *cacique*, a Cuban term for an aboriginal nobleman. She was born around 1505 in the village of Painalla in the province of Coatzacualco, at the north end of the base of the Yucatan peninsula. Historian William Prescott is convinced her father was "rich and powerful," and Marina herself was described by Bernal Díaz del Castillo, a foot soldier with Cortés, as "a *cacica* with towns and vassals."

When Malinal was young, however, her father died. Her mother re-married, bore a son, and was determined that her son be heir to her first husband's estate. To clear the way, she sold her daughter into slavery — at night, to prevent discovery. Malinal's mother took the body of a slave's child who had died and buried it, telling the townspeople it was her own child. Malinal was carried off to the town of Xicalongo. "Her early years," notes Jon Manchip White, "were singular and melancholy."

Malinal ended up in the possession of a cacique of Tabasco, and it is clear that through her earliest years she developed two important characteristics. Apparently because of her noble birth, she demonstrated a bearing and an education that commanded respect. She was chattel, perhaps, but high-born chattel. "She had a rare liveliness of spirit," suggests Antonio de Solis, "and natural gifts that accorded with the quality of her birth." A Spanish poet called her "a most beautiful Amazon."

Second, because she was well educated being moved around allowed her to develop her facility with language. She would learn Spanish, by all accounts, in a matter of weeks, and her principal value to Cortés was that she had learned Nahuatl, the tongue used throughout the northern, Aztec, reaches of the country.

Those characteristics made her more than a translator. As she was alternately cajoled, harangued, and threatened, she represented the new might of Europe in league with exotic, unpredictable allies and against awesome, innumerable enemies. "Cortés is discovering a new country," Haniel Long has her say in his fanciful portrayal of her life, "but I am discovering myself."

The man who would benefit from her self-discovery was, of course, Hernán Cortés, the archetype of the conquistador, the most *macho* of men. Like many great figures, Cortés was sickly as a child. Sent to university in Spain, he was undistinguished as a scholar and early aspired to a military life. After missing several opportunities to join expeditions, he arrived in the New World in 1504 at the age of nineteen.

He acquitted himself well against hostile Indians—whose crude weapons were inadequate against Spanish guns and crossbows—and was awarded an *encomienda*, a royal grant of land, and the Indians who were to work the land in feudal subservience. Cortés, although he prospered, was better suited for a more active life. His checkered record shows he was twice elected mayor of Santiago and once thrown into jail. When the governor, Diego Velásquez, ordered Cortés to take an expedition to the mainland in February 1519, Cortés' enemies tried to get the order rescinded. Cortés was forced to embark hastily. For the entire time Cortés led his small army through harsh territory and battle after battle, he was constantly attacked from the rear by Velásquez, who resented his arrogant independence and tried, in vain, to recall him.

On the mainland Cortés, in fact, declared himself captain-general and began communicating directly with King Carlos V. When his men mutinied, he had his ships burned so there could be no turning back. When Velásquez sent a troop to arrest him, Cortés captured its leader and bribed its men to follow him, obtaining gold for the bribery by short-changing his own men. If it can be said Malinal was discovering herself, Cortés was sculpting the role of conquistador with his bare hands.

It was after the Spanish won their first significant victory, at Tabasco, that, Malinal, among twenty women to be used as cooks, was given to Cortés by Tabascan caciques. Solis, an Argentine historian, imagines her lowly state, with her "humble clothing disguising her nobility." Díaz, however, who had been on two Mexican expeditions before joining Cortés, was there. He describes an extraordinary person: "One Indian lady who was given to us here," he writes, "was christened Doña Marina, and she was truly a great *cacica* and the mistress of vassals, and this her appearance clearly showed." The Tabascans were defeated in a brutal battle, losing at least eight hundred of their warriors, who at first thought Spanish horsemen and their horses were one and the same. They brought many gifts, cloth, gold, ornamented masks. "These gifts, however, were worth nothing in comparison with the twenty women given us," Díaz says, "among them one very excellent woman called Doña Marina, for so she was named when she became a Christian."

Although Díaz fails to explain, Indian women were commonly christened, a sacrament the Spaniards felt ameliorated their taking the women as mistresses, or, as in the case of married men like Cortés, their adultery. There were at least two priests among Cortés' troop, occasionally offering their advice on how to treat the Indians, sometimes "baptizing" tens of thousands of them in one fell swoop.

Thus Malinal became known as Doña Marina. The term *doña* (for a man, *don*) is placed before a person's Christian name as a mark of respect. Invariably, Spanish references to her are as Doña Marina. She is listed in the Codex Florentino and the Lienzo de Tlaxcala as "standing beside Cortés and translating his words or issuing her own instruction." The Spanish have taken her to themselves as if she had never been Malinal. After all, the bargain that the Spanish struck with their own conscience was that they would baptize and civilize and "protect" the Indians in exchange for the Indians' back-breaking labor in the mines or under the oppressive *encomienda* system. For the Spanish, Doña Marina was a crucial possession.

There is another view that is less benign. Originally, Indians referred to her as Malintzin, a term of respect associated with her position at the side of Cortés. The Spanish transliterated the Indian word to "Malinche." That is, Cortés was *El Malinche* and she was *La Malinche*. But among Mexican xenophobes, the term has come to be synonymous with betrayer. *Malinchismo* denotes the opening of Mexico to outsiders, those who have rendered Indian stock "impure" and have sullied Indian culture. Although she "showed an invariable sympathy" with "the conquered races," Prescott points out, Marina "always remained faithful to the countrymen of her adoption." Without her, he continues, it would have been Cortés who was conquered, for "her knowledge of the language and customs of the Mexicans, and often of their designs, enabled her to extricate the Spaniards, more than once, from the most embarrassing and perilous situations."

When the twenty women were brought into the Spanish camp, Cortés distributed them among his officers. Cortés gave Marina, described as "good looking and intelligent and without embarrassment," to his close friend, Alonzo Hernández Puertocarrero. Then, either because he recognized his mistake in giving her away—"women had always a great affection for him," notes translator J. Bayard Morris—or because he needed a trusted messenger for his audacious direct communication with the king of Spain, Cortés designated Hernández as bearer of his first missive to Carlos V. After Puertocarrero left camp, Cortés took Marina for himself.

There had been, and were, other interpreters, and their position was critical. The Spaniards—508 soldiers embarked with Cortés, plus about a hundred sailors and ships' masters—were lost on an uncharted plane of hostility, with hundreds of thousands of warriors surrounding them. "Communication" meant many things. First, the invaders, with a mule train and artillery, had to find the best route through inhospitable territory in their search for Moctezuma. Second, Indian communities had to be intimidated if possible, defeated if necessary, and, ideally, persuaded to march with Cortés against Moctezuma.

As soon as he had landed, Cortés was fortunate to encounter Jerónimo de Aguilar, a priest who had been captured by Indians, escaped, and had taken refuge with a friendly cacique of another tribe. He learned a language spoken in the south and was so assimilated into his Indian life that when spotted by Cortés' men, he was not recognized as a European. A European companion, in fact, whose situation was similar, chose to remain with his Indian wife and their sons rather than follow Cortés. Aguilar formed an important link with Marina. Before she learned Spanish he took Cortés' words and translated them into a language Marina understood, and she retranslated the words into the needed language, especially as they moved northward, where Nahuatl, the language of the Aztecs, was spoken.* Marina and Aguilar, writes Díaz, admiringly, "always went with us on every expedition, even when it took place at night."

Any interruption, any distortion, in Cortés' line of communication could be fatal. Before the Battle of Tabasco, an Indian interpreter had run off, joined the Tabascans, convinced them they could hold out, and helped direct the defense against Cortés. (After the battle, which took eight hundred Indian lives, the defeated Tabascans repaid him for bad advice, sacrificing him to their gods.) Communication meant psychological warfare as each Indian community tried to decide whether it benefited more by challenging Cortés' advance or by aiding that advance in the hope of throwing off the hated yoke of the Aztecs. Under these circumstances, Marina rose above the role of interpreter, to that of confidante and fellow strategist. Jon Manchip White describes her as "continuously at Cortés' elbow. In the eyes of the Indians they formed an inseparable pair.... Cortés consulted her on matters of general policy and on all matters relating to Indian psychology." According to Prescott, "she is said to have possessed uncommon personal attractions, and her open, expressive features indicated her generous temper."

Always surrounded, always outnumbered, Cortés had to communicate a variety of messages, sometimes simultaneously. He had to negotiate with the particular community that lay in his path while at the same time entertaining emissaries from Moctezuma. Even Moctezuma

---

Nahuatl is still spoken by more than a million Mexicans.

himself was of two minds, undecided whether this Cortés and his men were demigods sent by Quetzalcoatl, or mere flesh and blood, to be crushed like any other enemy. Moctezuma's ambassadors were often accompanied by Aztec artists, whose charge it would be to paint likenesses of the Spaniards. There had been other expeditions, Moctezuma knew, but this one was different, piercing like a lance ever deeper into his kingdom.

Cortés, shrewdly and with Marina's help, created a system of intelligence that embodied the advice of a contemporary, Niccolo Machiavelli, who warned in *The Prince* that "the lion cannot protect himself from traps, and the fox cannot defend himself from wolves. One must be a fox to recognize traps, and a lion to frighten wolves." This duality suggests why the Indians came to see Cortés and Marina as one.

Cortés was convinced, at least at first, that Indians believed his men — godlike shooters of lightning and eaters of human hearts—could not be killed. So he had his dead buried rather than let them be seen by Indians. In sight of a legation of caciques, Cortés made a show of "talking" to a horse to convey that horses were independent, rational beings. He had a cannon fired with a full load of powder to terrify his visitors with its noise and smoke. Deception and strength. Bluster and power. Advance and negotiation. All the time, Moctezuma was uncertain how to respond, and it might have been, historian R. C. Padden suggests, that Marina found out about and informed Cortés of Moctezuma's ambivalence. It was another weakness to be exploited, another stratagem to be employed.

Terror, intimidation, and bribery were augmented by continual, crafty negotiations conducted by Marina. She must have had a part in their strategic conception. Confrontations could not be prepared for, but occurred unpredictably along the trail. Delay could be deadly; allies had to be reassured and adversaried confused. These labrynthine considerations converged at Cholula, as Cortés confronted the fierce and brave Tlaxcalans.

They were his enemies, and he needed them as allies. Cortés described Cholula, holy to both Tlaxcalans and Aztecs, to Carlos V. It was, he said, "more extensive than Granada, and better fortified. Everywhere good order and good manners prevail. The people are full of intelligence and under standing. Their way of life is superior to anything to be found among the Moors."

Pondering his relations with the Tlaxcalans, Cortés was befuddled by their relations with Moctezuma. Díaz tells of watching five of Moctezuma's tax gatherers arrive unexpectedly. The officials studiously ignored Cortés and his men, walking past them — the officials were sniffing bunches of roses— to discuss the Spanish not with Cortés, but with the Tlaxcalans. Díaz was aghast at their "utmost assurance and arrogance." Moctezuma's men chastised the Tlaxcalans for providing the Spaniards with a place to stay. Cortés was insulted, but also somewhat abashed, and not at all sure what to do. "Doña Marina, who understood full well what had happened," Díaz writes, "told him what was going on."

Cortés made an instant, bold judgment, instructing that Moctezuma's men be captured. He then informed the captives that he, personally, was chagrined that they were captured, allowing two to escape, to take word back to Moctezuma. The Tlaxcalans, presumably, were impressed with Cortés temerity, and Moctezuma was both impressed and confused.

Cortés could trust no perception of his own and had to rely on Marina to see the truth. Were these people harboring so much hatred for their Aztec oppressors that they would ally themselves with Cortés, or was treachery afoot? Ambiguous attitudes were the most menacing. "The suspicions of Cortés increased," writes Cantu, "and he called the Indian woman Malinche to explain his apprehensions to her. She was ordered to mingle with the people to see what she could uncover."

Cortés himself, in one of the infrequent references he made to Marina in his letters to

Carlos V, told of her part at Cholula. "And being somewhat perplexed by this [the Cholulans' indifference and the Aztecs' arrogance]," Cortés wrote, "I learnt through the agency of my interpreter, a native Indian girl who came with me from Putunchan (a great river of which I informed your majesty in my first letter), that a girl of the city had told her that a large force of Moctezuma's men had assembled nearby, and that the citizens themselves, having removed their wives, children and clothes, intended to attack us suddenly and leave not one of us alive."

Díaz, as always, is more colorful. His account is of an elderly woman from the village who approached Marina, remarking that Marina was "young and good-looking and rich." Rather than be slaughtered in the imminent attack, the old woman suggested, Marina should gather possessions and seek refuge at the old woman's house, where, later, she could marry the woman's son. Marina pretended to accept the offer, as Díaz tells the story, but put the old woman off until night, warning her that Cortés' troops were on guard and would hear them. Marina then pumped the woman for more information, asking the ironic question, "If this affair is such a secret, how is it that you came to know about it?" The woman's husband, it turned out, was a Tlaxcalan captain who had, along with others, received gifts from the wily Moctezuma to help ambush Cortés.

Barrancas outside of the town were alive with Moctezuma's warriors. Planned was a monumental ambush. So confident of success were the Tlaxcalans, Díaz observes, that they were "laughing and contented as though they had already caught us in their traps and nets." Forewarned by Marina, however, Cortés took a townsman captive, interrogated him secretly to learn more of the plot, and then launched a preemptive attack. His troops killed three thousand Tlaxcalans while Moctezuma's warriors fled. Cortés fought his way out of the city "on horseback [with] Doña Marina near him."

Díaz offers this brief panegyric, the remarks of a soldier who recognized that his life was saved by the action of another: "Let us leave this and say how Doña Marina who, although a native woman, possessed such manly valor that, although she had heard every day how the Indians were going to kill us and eat our flesh with chili, and had seen us surrounded in the late battles, and knew that all of us were wounded and sick, yet never allowed us to see any sign of fear in her, only a courage passing that of a woman."

Fear was rational. The Indians' *macanas*—heavy, flat wooden blades with flint or obsidi.chips embedded in their edges—could sever the head of a horse. Javelins flew by the hundreds, many of them thrown a considerable distance by the use of *atlatls*, the cupped throwing sticks that extended an arm's length. The worst fate, however, was capture.

Capture meant sacrifice. The Spaniards, for all of their own ferocity, were appalled at the Indian priests, whose hair and animal-skin robes were matted with dried blood from sacrifices and who sliced their own ears in a form of worship, allowing the blood to coagulate in foul-smelling clots. Most shocking to the Spaniards, though, was the practice the priests had of cutting open captives' chests, sawing with an obsidian knife through the breastbone, to rip out still-beating hearts. The Spaniards and their allies knew — and would see confirmed before their expedition was ended — that such execution was the fate that awaited them if captured.

Cortés, whose troops were killing thousands in the name of the Christian god, was determined to end the Indian practice of sacrifice by destroying the temples in which it was conducted — tall, pyramidal structures that reeked like abattoirs. He ordered destruction of the temples, although for Marina this left the delicate task of convincing allies that such profane destruction was a good idea. Already fearful of Moctezuma's wrath, now they had their gods, too, to fear. Convincing the Tlaxcalans, Díaz notes, involved a complex process of threats from

Cortés, reminders of what Moctezuma would do to them if they failed to conquer, encouragement, and flattery. Marina, Díaz writes, "knew well how to make them understand."

In addition to threats and negotiations, there were sermons. Cortés and his chaplains did not neglect their Christian duty to seek converts—who would, presumably, make more steadfast allies. Díaz was amused by the proselytizing, explaining that both Marina and Jerónimo de Aguilar had become expert at portraying the story of Christ in a variety of tongues and "were so expert at it that they explained it very clearly."

So, with a diminishing band of soldiers and with Indian allies who were seeing their faith shaken and their culture demolished, Cortés pressed on toward the most formidable fortress in the New World, the Aztec capital of Tenochtitlán. Each village along the way was offered a choice of battle or alliance. At Cempula, when a great cacique, Xicotenga, considered a sneak attack, Indian friends of Cortés who heard of it considered the idea a joke, and failed to tell him. Marina made no such error, informing him in time for soldiers to capture seventeen of Xicotenga's spies. Cortés sent them back to their own camp, some without their hands, some without thumbs. Xicotenga threw his support behind Cortés, even arranging for one of his daughters to marry one of Cortés' officers.

In early September 1519, the expedition reached Tenochtitlán, a city that seemed mystical, with condensation rising from the great inland lake to give reality a quality no European had ever experienced. "Gazing on such wonderful sights," wrote Díaz years after the event, when he was blind and old, "we did not know what to say, or whether what appeared before us was real."

Tenochtitlán had emerged as dominant over the complex of settlements, including two other cities, built around an unusual geographical phenomenon. Four hundred and forty-two square miles were covered by trapped water, actually two shallow lakes, at 7,244 feet above sea level. In the distance were snow-capped mountains reaching more than 17,000 feet. The great expanse was formed by the heavy rainfall that, for the most part, was taken away only by seepage and evaporation. Where water was able to escape in streams, it stayed fresh, but another part of this inland sea was saline because salt accumulates in stagnant water over time. The Aztecs had constructed a system of dikes separating the clear and salt waters; causeways provided access to cities. Tenochtitlán itself had a population of 300,000 in 60,000 dwellings, mainly two-story houses of dull-red volcanic stone and lime-covered adobe. Scattered about were reed structures on stilts, islands, and floating gardens. The latter were formed by mats, heaped with mud and cultivated until roots intertwined into tangled, floating bases. Eminently fecund, these dreamlike gardens of flowers astonished the members of the expedition—as did the entire sight.

The expedition crossed Lake Texcoco on a "broad causeway running straight and level," Díaz writes. The soldiers passed "edifices of lime and stone that seemed to rise out of the water ... never yet did man see, hear, or dream of anything equal to the spectacle that appeared to our eyes on this day."

As Cortés approached the city, before he could decide how to deal with Moctezuma, he had to cover his rear. The still-angry governor, Diego Velásquez, had sent an eighteen-ship expedition to bring Cortés back to Cuba in shackles.

Therefore, Cortés had to halt his progress upon nearing Tenochtitlán in order to lead men back to the coast, fall upon the newcomers, capture their commander, and bribe the men into returning with him to Tenochtitlán as reinforcements. To effect the bribe it was necessary to use bounty already claimed by soldiers who had been with him all along, but Cortés was a determined man. "The shadow of a fern does not interest him," Haniel Long has his fictional Marina say, "nor does he pick up a blue pebble to look at it more closely, nor pass his fingers over the bark of a tree. Only what can be of use to him will he stay for. Me he loves because I can be of use to him."

Marina's use at Tenochtitlán was to help perpetrate the final treachery, the theft of an empire. While the Aztec federation that Cortés confronted was not as sophisticated as the long-departed Mayan culture, it was a functioning system that had extended its reach to the Gulf of Mexico and to the Pacific Ocean. The Aztec language was complex, their gods fierce, their buildings ornate.

The Spanish, especially the men who followed Cortés, were brigands, professional soldiers, some of whom fought with the brutal Gonsalvo de Córdoba in Italy and all of whom were interested in rape and plunder. "When our compatriots reach that remote world," wrote a contemporary of Cortés, "they become ravenous wolves." It would take another quarter of a century for the Spanish to begin to bring into subjugation this far-flung empire, and conquering Tenochtitlán was the key.

Ostensibly in Tenochtitlán as the honored guest of Moctezuma, with his Tlaxcalan allies camped on shore, Cortés and his men were isolated. The Tlaxcalans numbered about 2,000, while the Spanish, their number quadrupled by the reinforcements of Cortés brought back, were about 1,300 strong. Although Cortés knew Moctezuma was subject to conflicting advice, it was presumed that he was stalling until reinforcements could reach the city to crush the Spaniards once and for all. Moctezuma, a wily man, had served eighteen years as Aztec leader; he was in the ninth in succession of a line of powerful caciques. The principal burden of dealing with him was settled on the thin shoulders of Marina.

Cortés decided to invite Moctezuma to his quarters and there capture him, making him a prisoner in his own city. Marina first talked him into captivity and then tried to persuade him to surrender all his forces, yielding his riches and his kingdom to the Spaniards.

The longer Moctezuma delayed, however, and the longer he remained a captive, the less influence he had with his own people. He offered Marina bribes if she would desert the hated Spanish, perhaps saving herself in the process, but every day he was closer to his own destruction. Ancient Spanish paintings show Marina at Moctezuma's side when he was brought onto a roof to calm his people, who were restive, for Moctezuma had become a target of contempt. When the crowd below finally revolted, rocks were thrown and one struck Moctezuma in the head. He died three days later. Cortés was without his bargaining chip.

The resulting Aztec onslaught drove Cortés and his men out of the city with great loss of life as soldiers, weighted down with all the gold they could carry, were pitched from bridges and sank from sight. Cortés managed to save himself a sizable fortune by sending on ahead Tlaxcalans and horses loaded with gold ingots. Along the causeway of escape, Indians attacked from the sides from dugout canoes, and in the confusion Cortés was almost captured. It is known in Spanish lore as *la noche triste* (the Night of Sadness). Those soldiers who reached shore established a perimeter and listened through the night to shouted epithets and throbbing of drums, punctuated by the screams of sacrificed companions.

"But I have forgotten to write down," interjects Díaz in his chronicle of that terrifying night, "how happy to see Doña Marina still alive." She and several others had been guarded by a contingent of troops and their final escape was made possible, Díaz notes, with the help of Tlaxcalan warriors.

The departing Spanish were pursued, and the continuing fight was fierce. At the Battle of Otumba, 860 members of the expedition were killed or captured and sacrificed, and, at Tustepec, seventy-two more were lost.

As a result of this retreat, Spanish romantics have portrayed yet another side of their Doña Marina. The woman of *la noche triste,* the nurse to defeated soldiers, the comforter of Cortés, drying the tears that stained his lined face, has proved irresistible to Spanish chroniclers of the conquest. The Spanish imagination has raised Doña Marina to levels approaching those of Dante's Beatrice, Milton's Eve, Jason's Medea. She remains, asserts Haniel Long, "the simplest and clearest expression in history or mythology of the union and the disunion of man and woman." Marina and Cortés were one and opposed, united and at eternal odds. Analysts, depending on their points of view, have compared Cortés with Christ or with the Devil. Marina — La Malinche — had been considered, if not the Virgin of the story, the Eternal Weeping Comforter. Mexicans still see *La Llorana,* an important part of their mythology. *La Llorana,* according to Cecilio Robelo, is "a white ghost who utters prolonged and tearful laments on dark nights, who is the soul of Malinche, who walks in pain for having been a traitor to her country, helping the Spanish conquerors."

Marina's own fate was more prosaic, but, apparently, satisfying. Cortés returned to Tenochtitlán, this time with thirteen assault boats so his attack would not be limited to the causeways. He prevailed and became, in Spanish eyes, a hero, living to lead several expeditions to explore the isthmus of Mexico and Central America.

Marina bore Cortés a son, named Martín, for his grandfather. Díaz describes her accompanying Cortés on an expedition to Honduras that took her to her old hometown, where she met, and forgave, her mother and half-brother, whose greed had been the cause of all her adventures.

Eventually, Marina married Juan Jaramillo at the small town of Ostotipec, in the province of Nogales, and the couple is said to have had a daughter. Cortés attended the wedding and as a present gave Marina an estate at Jilotepec, fifty miles north of Mexico City. He later gave her a plot adjacent to her house at Chapultepec in Mexico City. Still later, Cortés gave Marina another plot, this one, in a small, ultimate irony, having belonged to Moctezuma. The Aztec heritage had already been reduced to choice plots of real estate.

Diego de Ordáz, a Spanish adventurer, reported seeing Marina, her husband, and young Martin in 1529. The line of Marina's progeny, according to Gustavo A. Rodríguez, extended at least until the death of a nine-year-old boy, Fernando Gómez de Orosco y Figueroa, who was born in Tlzapan on July 23, 1930.

2

Pierre François Dominique Toussaint L'Ouverture

Commander of a Slave Army

1743–1803
(Haiti)

One afternoon in 1799, Pierre François Dominique Toussaint returned to his villa after meeting with emissaries of Britain's King George III and U.S. President John Adams. The villa, at Gonaives, in the Haitian hills overlooking the Caribbean, was Toussaint's favorite, and the afternoon glare off the sea must have been like the attention being paid to a former slave by powerful nations—intense, a bit blinding, quick to fade. Not only had Toussaint been meeting with British and American messengers, his plans were also of great interest to the First Consul of France, Napoleon Bonaparte. Because Toussaint's tiny half-island was the focus of so much international concern, his task that afternoon was to decide how best to keep Europeans and Americans at bay while he tried to found the New World's second republic, the only one ever created by slaves. In battle, things were more simple. Toussaint earned his sobriquet at the head of cavalry when an admiring French adversary dubbed him "L' Ouverture" for his ability to break openings in enemy lines where least expected. *

Dealing with diplomats, Toussaint had learned that armed enemies were the least dangerous.

Toussaint L'Ouverture is thought to have been born on May 20, 1743. His father, Gaou-Guinou, was the second son of a chief of the Arradas tribe, taken in a raid by a neighboring tribe and sold at the port market at Ouidah, Dahomey, built by the French in the mid–1700s especially for the slave trade. It was a major exchange point on Africa's Slave Coast, part of a commercial system that would, in all, ship some 10 million Africans to the New World, counting those who died in transit and were thrown overboard.

Two months after his sale, Gaou-Guinou was unloaded at Cap François on the northern coast of the French colony of Saint Domingue, which slaves would later name Haiti. It is likely that in the slave society Gaou-Guinou was known by other slaves to be descended from Arradas royalty and treated with respect. Although slave languages were many and communication among them was kept difficult as a method of control, such was Gaou-Guinou's bearing that the Comte de Noé, his owner, mandated *liberté de savane*, which gave him both freedom and protection. He was also given land and five slaves and later baptized a Catholic. His wedding occasioned a plantation holiday.

A less romantic suggestion is that in northern Haiti many slaves were named "L'Ouverture" for the gaps in their front teeth.

14

Gaou-Guinou's freedom, under the careful French system of colonial law, did not extend to his children. Although the position of mulattoes would become ambivalent, there was no uncertainty regarding *noirs*. Children of freed slaves were slaves.

Toussaint was the oldest of several brothers and at least one sister, but was a sickly, moping boy, who was dubbed *fatras bâton* ("fragile stick"). Because of his weakness, he was relieved of herding, the job of young slaves, and was in and out of the plantation infirmary so often that he ended up working there under the tutelage of his godfather, an old slave named Pierre Baptiste. Baptiste had been taught to read and write by Jesuits and he taught Toussaint. The head of the infirmary, struck by Toussaint's ability to learn, put him to work in the slaves' dining hall.

Toussaint's education continued to be part European, part African. In the home, old ways were retained. The family spoke an African dialect, and his father taught him the uses of herbs (as an adult, Toussaint was a vegetarian). Toussaint began tending animals on the plantation. He was assumed by some slaves to have "magical" powers of the kind that still form, as "voodoo," an important part of Haitian culture.

Nature had left Toussaint weak, relatively short, rather ugly, and thin. He was surviving in a world that valued brute strength, and he compensated by being "diplomatic" with everyone.

It is possible that when Toussaint was about fourteen he witnessed — such occurrences were, after all, carefully prepared lessons — the burning of a fugitive slave, François Macandal. As a fugitive, Macandal had conducted his own, one-man guerrilla warfare, hiding in the bush, conjuring potions, and inducing other slaves to sneak them into their masters' food. Whole families had been killed.

Slavery was efficient only insofar as discipline was rigidly enforced, and revolts erupted right from the beginning. In 1522, just twelve years after King Ferdinand of Spain authorized African slaves as replacement workers in the mines of the New World, there was an outbreak on Hispaniola, an island about the size of Ireland that Haiti shares with the Dominican Republic. Before 1550 there were at least three more outbreaks of sufficient magnitude to be recorded. In the next two hundred years, until Macandal was burned at the stake, there were continual outbreaks under a series of renegade leaders who wreaked havoc on both Spanish and French plantations. Thousands of people, black and white, were killed, and any atrocity that could be conceived — exploding gunpowder in a slave's rectum, rolling men and women down mountainsides in spike-lined barrels — was perpetrated. In this way slavery maintained the rich commerce of the Americas, which, in turn, supported European societies that were defining what is now called the Enlightenment.

Yet within the slave system, Toussaint was well on his way, as it were, to working his way up. He married a slave, Suzanne Simone Baptiste, and adopted her son, Placide, whose father was a mulatto. Suzanne bore Toussaint two sons, Isaac and Saint Jean. M. Bayou de Libertad, Toussaint's overseer, had placed Toussaint in charge of livestock, and although the choice led to Toussaint's being used as an example of proper subservience, a model not universally popular among his peers, it was for Toussaint a step up. He then became personal coachman to Libertad and, eventually, steward of the plantation. When he was thirty-four years old, Toussaint was freed. The year was 1777.

By 1791, two years after the Bastille had become a symbol of freedom in France, slave unrest on Hispaniola was at the point of explosion. On the Saint Domingue end of the island rebellion was more difficult to quash because the rough terrain afforded so many hiding places. It is said that when Napoleon asked a lieutenant to describe the topography of Saint Domingue, the lieutenant took a sheet of paper and crumpled it into a ball. It is beautiful countryside, but so mountainous, with peaks rising to nearly 8,800 feet, as to leave only 13 percent of its land arable. Yet on that small portion of rich land, France had grown fat.

Before slave uprisings began to diminish productivity, the colony was instrumental in paying France's huge war debts, a point not lost on the newly installed republicans, who had their own expenses. About 1800, Haitian exports were valued at 27 million U.S. dollars annually, greater than what was produced by all thirteen American states combined. Napoleon was prepared to hold the Mississippi Valley in order to grow and ship the food needed to keep Haitian slaves alive — as long as the system remained efficient. Slave revolts, however, upset the bookkeeping. In 1799, Saint Domingue's plantation production was valued at 176 million francs; by 1801 it was one-third that figure because the work was not being done.

The first cracks in the facade of Haiti's strange society appeared along the line carefully constructed between white men and their mulatto sons. It was Louis XIV, the Sun King, who had done a bit of human accounting in 1674 and decreed that all children of slaves, regardless of whether either or both parents had been freed, were slaves. In economic terms, this assured that capital stock was not depleted. Colonial customs emerged, however, that mixed parental feelings of obligation with amorous drives and civil codes. What evolved were traditions that insured social conflict. At age twenty-four mulattoes would be freed, although at age thirty, they had to serve three years in the militia. In effect, the French plantation owners were providing military training for their offspring *cum* future enemies.

Mulattoes paid a special tax to maintain roads, but were supposed to humbly dismount upon entering a city's gates. Many were educated in Europe, where, posing no threat, they were widely accepted. They came home to oversee plantations and own their own slaves. Yet they were excluded from the professions and from public office. Laws prohibited a mulatto from praying in his father's pew, eating at his father's table, finding rest in the family crypt, and, especially, inheriting the family estate.

By the beginning of the nineteenth century, these contradictions had caused deep cuts, the scars of which remain today.* There was a pyramid of 700,000 to 820,000 black slaves; about 100,000 mulattoes; some 10,000 whites of different nations, extracting what they could of the colony's riches or shunted aside because of their low social status; perhaps 1,500 aboriginal Indians who had, by necessity, clustered in a few isolated areas; and, in charge, about 500 Frenchmen.

Mulattoes led the charge against the old régime. After the French revolution, Haitian mulattoes pledged six million francs and one-fifth of their property to help pay the national debt, a gesture for which they expected recompense. Thus on March 8, 1790, in the first flush of the Republic, the National Assembly resolved that mulattoes were entitled to seats in their colonial assemblies. So, in October, Vincent Oge, a Haitian mulatto, strode into the assembly at Cap François to demand that the pledge be fulfilled. The landowners refused. He pressed his case with two hundred armed mulattoes. The eventual outcome, in February 1791, was that he was broken on the wheel, screaming for mercy, along with seven other leaders of the insurrection. Nineteen others were sentenced to the galleys for life, and twenty-two were hanged.

At first, the slaves stayed out of the mulattoes' fight. But as the revolt spread, Toussaint, then forty-seven years old and steward of his plantation, became in effect the protector of his

---

*Few countries have divided people by color with such attention to detail as Haiti. An homme de couleur was free, while the generic mulatre was not. After the revolt began, however, who was to say which was what? Marron or chestnut, means in Haiti a domestic animal run wild, hence a slave — a noir — who had fled to the hills. There were inland marronage colonies. The law of Saint Domingue decreed that Negro blood "decreased" for six generations, after which it vanished. Today, however, an authentique is one whose lineage is untainted by "white blood."

benefactor, Libertad, the man who had freed him. By autumn of 1791, when the fires of rene-gade slaves could be seen in the hills at night, Toussaint informed Libertad that protection was no longer possible. Toussaint helped the family embark for North America and turned to find his place in the revolt.

That summer, a Jamaican slave named Boukman had been calling self selected leaders like Toussaint to clandestine meetings, moving through the northern hills where Macandal had operated thirty years before. Boukman inspired several strikes by factory workers, but found that such disruptions were easily put down. So, as fall approached, he held meetings to shape a new strategy. What followed was violence without bound.

Slaves wielding machetes, pruning hooks, stolen fowling rifles, pitchforks, and anything at hand that might be lethal "surrounded the houses, slaughtered the men, drank the rum, raped the women and fired the estates and cornfields," according to an account cited by his-torians Robert and Nancy Heinl. Particularly hated men were chopped to pieces or nailed up, alive, while their wives were raped. One counter-attack by whites was "overwhelmed by furi-ous slaves whose standard was the body of a white baby impaled on a spike."

The slaves' massive numbers sustained the revolt, for they fought largely with simple implements, often did not know how to fire captured cannon, and sometimes charged hos-tile fire convinced that African gods protected them. By the time Toussaint joined the revolt, the plain around the port city of Cap François was littered with bodies. Broad assaults led to hundreds being cut down at once, while the gallows and the wheel took care of those who were captured. A white man captured while fighting at the side of slaves was roasted by his white adversaries over a charcoal fire. Boukman was finally captured, burned to death, and beheaded.

While slaves besieged Cap François on the northern coast, mulattoes, some using arms hidden earlier by Oge, fought in the west and south. At the same time, there was a standoff between white Jacobins and royalists as the same forces that divided France fought in Haiti. Then, throwing fuel on the fire, the national assembly, some members of which were dismayed by Oge's martyrdom, decreed in the spring of 1791 that mulattoes be admitted to colonial governments.

In part, the enfranchisement of mulattoes fulfilled the Rights of Man. More pragmati-cally, however, the deputies knew mulattoes were the only trained republican troops able to withstand Haiti's climate. Because of the decree, however, colonial representatives walked out of the national assembly in Paris, and their brethren in Haiti continued to deny political rights to mulattoes. The situation was further confused by royalists, including priests, who recruited gullible blacks with empty promises of a black, royalist colony. As several permu-tations of alliance formed, the national assembly, faced with both rebellious slaves and irri-dentist royalists, threw up its hands and rescinded the decree. The color line for mulattoes, briefly erased, was redrawn, casting mulattoes against whites and blacks against both. Into this chaos came Toussaint.

"The rebel horde was made up of an assortment of tribes from all parts of the African continent," writes Stephen Alexis, "Congos, Senegalese, Dahomeans, Lybians, Abyssinians, Bambaras, Peuhls, Ibos, Yoloffs, Guineans, Aradas, Touregs, Moroccans. It was a mixture of humanity, of violent, unstable tribesmen who were as uncertain of themselves as they were of what they wanted.... And it was out of this heterogeneous mass that Toussaint was to forge a striking force, crush the enemy, and build up a nation."

Toussaint accomplished the task, it must be added, along with other leaders, mulattoes like Alexandre Sabes Petión — who would later provision Bolívar against the Spanish and the redoubtable mulatto known as "Candy." He did it with the help of his own lieutenants, the formidable Jacques Dessalines and Henri Christophe, who would later struggle with governing the social snake pit left to them. Together, they freed Haiti, Napoleon's prized possession, by making it so expensive to hold onto that even the man who would rule Europe could not bear the expense.

Toussaint's most important contribution may have been his personal dignity. He stepped into leadership alongside men like Biassou, who favored an orange costume of his own design that included a black, silk scarf, and Jean-François, who wore crimson velvet, gold braid, and a tri-cornered hat and declared himself "Grand Admiral of France." Toussaint continued to wear plantation garb: a white silk jacket, blue cotton pants, and a felt hat with the brim turned up.

The national assembly's idea of colonial government was to send an almost endless series of commissions to reestablish order, to redraw color lines, to punish rebels. Biassou and Jean-François, in exchange for freedom for themselves and a few hundred favorites, offered to betray the rest of their followers, whom they described as ignorant warriors uprooted from their African homeland. The Heinls point to this arrangement, which was accepted by the commissioners, as "a readiness to betray followers that students of Haitian politics would come to recognize." In the assembly at Cap François, however, landowners refused to recognize the deal, so slaves redoubled their violence.

The French response — signed by Louis XVI on April 4, 1792, within a year of losing his head — was yet another decree giving full political rights to mulattoes and free blacks. For enforcement, another commission was dispatched, accompanied by six hundred soldiers. In command was Etienne-Maynard Laveaux, who would become Toussaint's principal adversary.

A member of the commission was Léger-Félicité Sonthonax, whose antislavery sentiments and democratic beliefs made him profoundly distrusted by other governments with interests in the Caribbean. Because republican France had declared war on all monarchies, the English in Jamaica and the Spanish at the eastern end of Hispaniola were not eager to tolerate this penetration of their territory by such a democratic radical. On August 29, 1793, Sonthonax lived up to his enemies' worst expectations. Without authority from Paris, he declared all slaves free.

The British and Spanish immediately joined in an effort to destroy this threat to their own slave systems — at the same time seizing what they could of French territory. By early 1793, Biassou and Jean-François had thrown in with the Spanish. Biassou was named "Generalissimo of the Conquered Territories," while Jean-François was awarded the title "General and Admiral of the Reunited Troops." Both got new uniforms.

Toussaint, whose literacy and knowledge of medicine made him valuable, became secretary to Biassou. He was also given command of six hundred men, mostly mounted. Before long, Toussaint's command had swelled to four thousand and, making himself a colonel, he began to take orders directly from the Spanish at his headquarters at Marmelade.

By the autumn of 1793, the slave revolt had turned into a confused, extremely violent extension of the European wars. *Noirs* under Jean-François, Biassou, and Toussaint controlled the north; mulattoes established a lasting base in the south; the English took several port towns.

Toussaint began to build his reputation. "I am Toussaint L'Ouverture," he would announce to a conquered town. "My name has perhaps become known to you. I am bent on vengeance. I desire the establishment of Liberty and Equality in St. Domingue." Even as Toussaint's men confronted Laveaux's troops, however, Toussaint himself was in contact with the French commander. He had decided that the future of Haiti was better shaped against a background of the French Republic than the Spanish monarchy. In the spring of 1794, with Laveaux at the point of defeat, running out of ammunition and provisions, Toussaint switched sides. The Heinls write:

> Toussaint repaired to Marmelade. There, at the side of the Spanish commandant, he heard early mass. These devotions concluded, he mounted his horse, drew sword, unfurled the Tricolor and, at the head of his regiment and like-minded *noirs,* cut the throats of the Spanish garrison.

In one stroke, Toussaint had won the appreciation of the French, arrayed his forces against, rather than beside, one of the harshest slave systems of the New World, the Spanish; and, not incidentally, moved from beneath the command of Jean-François and Biassou to become his own man.

Through the spring of 1794, the Spanish were immobilized. Toussaint's army held the north, and his new allies, under an ambitious mulatto named Rigaud, held the south. Toussaint used the time to recruit and train; Rigaud plotted. In the meantime, the English were succumbing to an enemy that took no prisoners, yellow fever.

In July, the French and Spanish, each trying to stake out what was sure, agreed to split the ownership of the island, although Spanish troops were to remain and administer the eastern end in France's name. Biassou, idled, wandered off to Spanish southern Florida, where he died in a brawl. Jean-François retired, like a landowner, to Cádiz. Toussaint remained to fight.

Now his adversary was Rigaud. The mulatto commander had Laveaux, the French commander, wrestled from his office in Cap François and thrown in jail. As soon as Toussaint heard, he informed Laveaux's abductors that if the governor-general were not immediately released, everyone in the town would die. Laveaux was returned to his office. Immediately, he named Toussaint lieutenant-general, assuring the jealousy of every mulatto officer.

Toussaint was approaching a pinnacle as the most powerful man on the island. Laveaux himself had dubbed him "the black Spartacus" who, according to the prediction of Abbe Raynal in the sixteenth century, would one day avenge his people. On the horizon, however, there appeared more French commissioners. They included the fiery Sonthonax, who had been recalled to France, tried, and acquitted.

Real power was divided, uneasily, between Toussaint and Rigaud, and when the commissioners exiled several of Rigaud's lieutenants Toussaint's power was enhanced. In Toussaint's view, which tended toward the Olympian, that was not enough. It would be better, he thought, if the commission turned around and went back to Paris, leaving him to deal with Riguad. Indeed, eventually — and perhaps at Toussaint's instigation — both Laveaux and Sonthonax were elected to the national assembly in Paris. Laveaux sailed immediately, choosing France's violent political environment over Haiti's. But Sonthonax lingered, a white man, for all his republican intentions, administering a black society.

For a time Toussaint was preoccupied with trying to contain the British in their coastal strongholds, or put down mutinies of *noirs,* who were now called "cultivators" but were still prone to discontent when encouraged by royalist bribes. After a year, Toussaint ran out of patience and bundled Sonthonax aboard a ship bound for France. With the last French official finally gone, it is said that Toussaint was seen in Cap François, laughing. The scene was memorable, for Toussaint rarely laughed.

Now he was paramount. French authorities had named him *général de division,* and he was given Laveaux's old title, *général-en-chef des armées de Saint Domingue.* His two young sons had been sent to France to school. He commanded approximately 20,000 soldiers, as many as George Washington ever led.

With the Spanish at bay and French civil authority practically eliminated, it was still necessary to loosen the grip of the English on their coastal redoubts. The English, already devastated by yellow fever, found the nine hundred troops they had committed to Haiti fell far short of what was necessary. With the help of Rigaud — who commanded some 12,000 men — Toussaint forced the English to withdraw. The withdrawal, however, was allowed with honor. Toussaint remarked that republican France had never treated him with as much respect as had imperial England. The English, indeed, promised their support if he should crown himself "king of Haiti," but Toussaint declined.

Now Toussaint could concentrate on consolidating his power — after receiving yet one more commission from France. The spring of 1798 found the economy of the island, not surprisingly, in shambles. Toussaint was trying to revive agriculture by inviting *colons* to return to participate in a kind of feudalism, called *fermage,* conceived by his lieutenant, Henri Christophe. One reform under the plan was that only the slaves truly strong enough to work were to be sent back to the fields. In general, however, it was difficult for former slaves to understand and accept differences between feudalism and slavery.

The commissioners' benighted decision was to foment division in order to weaken the colony against the day that France might recoup its loss. Therefore, Rigaud was raised to equal rank with Toussaint.

So it was that Toussaint found himself at his villa at Gonaives, ardently courted by the English and Americans. The French had left the island with difficult problems, but Toussaint knew that Anglo-American intentions were hardly to solve those problems, simply to capitalize on them. As far as the great nations were concerned, all discussions, like those at Gonaives, turned on what benefit Toussaint and his slave army could be in the international struggle. Toussaint was no longer a slave in their eyes, but they still saw him as a pawn.

Toussaint is criticized for being indecisive. He did not, for example, simply declare Haiti independent and dare everyone to fight. He was encouraged to do so by the British envoy, Thomas Maitland. Toussaint, however, knew he was dependent on British and American manufactured goods — especially arms and ammunition — for a protracted war against France. Furthermore, what he did not need was to rush into the embrace of either Britain, which did not abolish slavery in its colonies until 1833, or the United States, which gave up slavery only reluctantly two generations later.

What Toussaint did was try to reach agreement with the mulattoes to strengthen Haiti internally. First, he made overtures to Rigaud. Then Toussaint called together mulattoes at the principal cathedral of Port-au-Prince, a mulatto stronghold. Combining accommodation with arrogance, Toussaint said that even though he understood their goal was to re-enslave *noires,* he would forgive them. If they would accept as their goal the rebuilding of the island's economy, all would be well.

Rigaud, however, was quick to make his intentions clear. Unwilling to accept alliance, Rigaud led an army northward in June 1799, crossing the bridge at Miragoane — along the traditional dividing line between southern and northern Haiti — and launching civil war.

Hispaniola is shaped like a giant fish, its mouth wide open, swimming westward. Rigaud was driving out of the lower jaw toward Port-au-Prince, which is flanked by the two jaws. Rigaud's march, once it became known, inspired uprisings among mulattoes in several central and northern towns. Toussaint's army outnumbered Rigaud's, but the south was well fortified after years of fighting, and mulattoes, now that the French were gone, saw themselves as destined for domination. They would resist interference by *noires.* The result was some of the bloodiest conflict in Haiti's history.

Toussaint himself took charge of the mounted forces that struck at the uprisings; he sent

Dessalines to subdue Rigaud's main force. So terrible was the feeling that the two sides adopted a particularly horrible method of punishment for captured leaders; they were stuffed down cannon barrels on top of grapeshot and literally blown to bits. Haitians had learned the technique from the British.

Toussaint's forces prevailed — with the help of the United States and after a brief interruption by France. Toussaint needed American shipping to maintain a line of supply, but he also asked U.S. naval forces to blockade and bombard southern ports controlled by Rigaud. The U.S. State Department, trying out its wings, complied, beginning what would become a long, troubled relationship between the two republics. As a result of the bombardments, Rigaud was squeezed into a corner by the spring of 1800. Dessalines was poised to deliver the final blow when Toussaint, in deference to the French, ordered him to hold back. Arriving was one more — the last — commission.

This commission had been personally dispatched by Napoleon, but that was of no importance to Haitians. Ostensibly, every commission from Paris had the goal of reestablishing Haitian productivity, but to Haitians that implied re-imposing slavery. The three commissioners landed at the Spanish end of the island and traveled overland to the frontier. At the border, Toussaint had them arrested and let them sit and cool their heels. He then ordered their release, saying it had all been an unfortunate mistake. One commissioner got the message, turned around, and went back to France. Another, a mulatto lawyer and landowner, also opted out of the proceedings, busying himself instead with seeing to his properties. The third, a European engineer, offered his services to Toussaint to help build the country. The commission was thus disbanded, a turnabout of the type that is said to have caused Napoleon to grumble that never again would he put epaulets on the shoulders of a *noir*.

Then Toussaint unleashed Dessalines, who drove Rigaud's forces into the sea. Rigaud — after a final battle in which his horse was shot from beneath him and bullets pierced his jacket and hat — sailed into exile to await the chance to return that Napoleon would eventually provide. In triumph, Toussaint entered Les Cayes and went on to Port-au-Prince. Having acquired a European flair, Toussaint instituted a practice of entering the local cathedral while the choir sang a *Te Deum*. Then he would deliver a sermon, sometimes on the theme of forgiveness. Sometimes, however, Toussaint was capable of ordering enemy fighters bayoneted and shot; the total grew to more than a thousand. Dessalines, made governor of the south, is estimated to have ordered some ten thousand more to be executed.

Toussaint returned to his headquarters at Cap François intent upon conquering the other end of the island, which was still being administered by the Spanish on behalf of the French. In Toussaint's way stood a French civil commissioner, who yielded, and a Spanish general, who did not. The general made it clear he would not give up without a fight. Toussaint's response, dispatched in January 1801, had two parts: one was a column of 3,000 men under a *noir* general, descending from the north; the other was a column of 4,500 men marching across the south and commanded by Toussaint's brother, Paul. Toussaint rode with his brother, and three weeks later, after weak resistance, Toussaint accepted the keys to Santo Domingo.

His pronouncement has the ring of being directed not so much at Haitians as at the world. "The measures of prudence and humanity which I have taken," the *London Times* quoted him as saying, "prevented the effusion of blood; and with very little loss I have put myself in possession of the whole island." The Olympian tenor of the proclamation was typical of Toussaint, and, in truth, he had put himself, not France, in possession of the island. The message did not escape Napoleon.

Toussaint stood where important forces were converging. The time was February 1801. Many nations had reason to dread Toussaint's slave army, with its record of retribution. Abolitionists, in fact, cheered Toussaint on as a "Negro Spartacus" and "the Napoleon of the Antilles"; he was the subject of poems, dramas, and news stories; William Wordsworth sang his praises.

No one was more acutely aware of what Toussaint represented than Thomas Jefferson, just elected and to be inaugurated the next month. Jefferson was ambivalent—as was his wont in matters related to slavery. On the one hand, the father of his own mulattoes feared a revolution in which, as Jefferson wrote to an abolitionist friend, "We shall be the murderers of our own children." On the other hand, Jefferson was a realist in affairs of state, and Toussaint's successes benefited the United States by distorting relations among nations. Jefferson knew that the threat of revolt by the slaves of other nations—Britain, Spain, Portugal—tied down their troops in Latin America, preventing mischief along still-contested North American frontiers. If Toussaint was a bad example for slaves in the United States, he was also a constant problem to France and other slave-owning nations, and Jefferson could not discount the possibility that Napoleon planned a thrust northward from New Orleans to reclaim the Mississippi Valley from Spanish interlopers.

Toussaint did not dally over his newly acquired power. He returned to Cap François, where, according to a fascinated *Times* correspondent, he "declared most positively that he is determined not to suffer any strong naval force belonging to the [French] Republic to enter his harbor. Several engineers are now employed by him in fortifying the different ports at the east end of the island; and at Port Plata they have thrown up a long range of battery and mounted all the guns of the English frigate 'Tartar,' wrecked there in 1795."

Thus barricaded, Toussaint sent a brief message to Napoleon. It was a simple report on civic affairs, but the tone of the message made it clear that the sender considered himself, in all ways, equal. Napoleon did not respond.

In late May, a *Times* correspondent reflected:

> It does not appear that *Toussaint L'Ouverture*, the Negro-Chief of Hispaniola, has deigned to make any communication to the French Government of the important incorporation he has made of the Spanish part of the Island. The Black *Chief-Consul* is not inclined to acknowledge the White superiority, even in *Bonaparte*, and is certainly a rival and independent Prince.
>
> The state of all the West–India Islands will doubtless experience a very considerable change from the establishment of a Negro Empire in that Archipelago. St. Domingo must either prove a neutral, independent power at the Peace, or be left at that period to be reclaimed by the Metropolitan Government in France. In either predicament the state of the slaves in all the Plantations, and West–India Commerce in general, will perceive the effects of it. The moralist will observe the experiment with anxious curiosity; but the statesman cannot contemplate it without serious apprehension.

The same spring Toussaint convened a "central assembly" to draft—or to approve his draft of—a constitution that named him *gouverneur-général-à-vie*. His government, however, was in reality an empty shell, its insides lost over a decade of warfare. It is estimated that more than three hundred thousand people had been killed; the white planter class had been reduced by at least two-thirds, mulattoes by one-fourth, blacks by one third. Haiti had to try to make productive a bottomless pit of hatred, ignorance, and uncertainty. Toussaint's military administrators simply could not cope.

Rumors continued that slavery, in order for the island to survive, would be restored. When troops threatened to rebel at Cap François, Toussaint assembled them in front of townspeople and ordered suspects to step forward. Then he told them to shoot themselves. Understanding the alternatives, they complied, raising pistols to their heads. At the same time, Napoleon was concluding the Treaty of Amiens, meaning that England would no longer interfere with his plans for the Indies. Now Napoleon and Toussaint faced only one another.

Toussaint professed his loyalty to Napoleon, whatever might be the impression left by his arrogance, but Napoleon was not convinced. Trusting only French generals, Napoleon assembled at several European ports an armada of sixty-seven ships with 21,175 French and mercenary troops commanded by some of France's best officers. Overall command was given to Victor-Emmanuel Leclerc, husband of Napoleon's sister, Pauline. Leclerc was named captain-general of the colony, and Pauline accompanied the force. Overlooking no detail, Napoleon also sent two of Toussaint's sons, taking them from their studies in order to convince their father that it was time to lay down his arms.

It is said that Toussaint, knowing of the approaching armada, rode to a hill to watch its approach, remarking, "We are lost. All France has come to Saint Domingue." His own army included 17,000 regular troops and an undetermined number of militiamen.

As the armada rode at anchor, a proclamation from Napoleon was sent ashore, telling all inhabitants of the island that "whatever your origin, or your color, you are all French, you are all free, and all equal before God, and before the Republic." While the island was "a prey to factions," Napoleon noted, he asked the people to "embrace the French and rejoice to see again your friends, and your brothers of Europe." So strong was his feeling of brotherhood, Napoleon declared, that he had sent Leclerc, his own brother-in-law, as captain-general.

Leclerc had specific orders and a timetable. With deadlines for each of three steps, Napoleon instructed Leclerc to talk his way ashore, secure major towns, and clear the interior of resistance. Promises could be made, but the point was to get men to lay down their arms and return to the fields. The tactics partially worked, isolating several of Toussaint's *noir* commanders, some of whom, confused, capitulated. Others, however, were not going to allow the French to take the island without a fight. Some put their stores to the torch and retreated inland, and many prepared to burn or blow up everything they could not defend.

Toussaint also, when the French secured the coastal towns, retreated into the rough interior of the island. He was declared an outlaw; people were warned to neither follow nor help him. Leclerc, however, was surviving on bluster. He would later write that at this point if Toussaint had been able to contact his scattered commanders "there can be no doubt that he would have been victorious."

Toussaint's sons were sent to him, but he was not swayed; he was convinced that the French were determined to re-subjugate all *noirs*. He told his sons he could not lay down his arms, so Isaac, saying he was a French subject, returned to Leclerc, while Placide, the older, whom Toussaint had adopted upon marrying Placide's mother, remained with his father.

The French advanced, some units led by mulatto officers, including Rigaud. Napoleon had instructed Leclerc to use the mulattoes if necessary, but, if not, to put them all on a ship and send them to Madagascar. Pockets of resistance were led by Dessalines, Christophe, and Toussaint. Dessalines, surrounded and with ammunition almost gone, earned the admiration of even his enemies by slipping his men through their lines in the night, leaving behind only the dead and wounded. Later, when Christophe and Toussaint were finally forced to open negotiations toward surrender, Dessalines, the fiercest *noir* of them all, refused to join them, fighting on.

After Christophe had given up, Toussaint went with four hundred mounted men to meet Leclerc at Haut-du-Cap. Leclerc waited, flanked by several *noir* officers who had surrendered. As Toussaint walked forward, his brother Paul, who had been at Leclerc's side, stepped forward to embrace him. Toussaint turned away. Leclerc asked Toussaint to betray Dessalines; he refused. After an uneasy dinner with Leclerc, Toussaint retired to his plantation at Ennery, near the villa at Gonaives.

As were other *noir* commanders, Toussaint was given nominal authority over a region, but within days he was summoned to another meeting with the French. Showing a lack of caution that suggests he had given up, Toussaint rode to the meeting accompanied only by two officers and an aide. He was captured, trussed like a subdued slave, and taken by carriage at night to Gonaives. At Cap François he was placed on board a ship with his family and valet. The ship was bound for France. Almost immediately, Napoleon signed decrees restoring slavery.

Toussaint arrived in Paris, where he was separated from his wife and family. Suzanne, given a pension after the Bourbon restoration, died in Paris in 1816. Toussaint was taken to an isolated fort in the Jura Mountains on the frontier between France and Switzerland. He was locked in a room twenty-five to thirty feet long and twelve feet wide. Its stone floor was almost always damp in the summer; in winter, a small stove was brought in to augment the fireplace.

It is said that Toussaint's harsh treatment might have been to make him disclose where he had buried 15 million francs, later killing the slaves who dug the hole. The story is as hollow as Napoleon's conscience. John Bigelow, an associate of William Cullen Bryant at the New York *Evening Post,* visited the fort and was struck by the structure's grimness. Seven centuries old, Bigelow wrote, the fort stood "upon the very summit of a solid rock about five hundred feet high." Bigelow concluded that the cruelty of Toussaint's treatment was caused by his having addressed a letter to Napoleon "from the First of the Blacks to the First of the Whites."

The two physicians who were brought in to certify Toussaint's death attributed it to apoplexy and pleuropneumonia, but it is likely that he was poisoned, perhaps by Napoleon's order. His body was found on April 6, 1803, lying on the stone floor.

Biographer Alexis allows himself a poignant smile in imagining the scene after the superstitious French jailer hurried out of the cell to inform others. He hesitated, Alexis writes, because "you can never tell, he thought, with these black princes.... To make quite sure, he went back and carefully locked the door."

3

Simón Bolívar

Liberator of the North

1783–1830
(Venezuela)

Spain, wrote Simón Bolívar, had kept its colonies "in a sort of permanent infancy." He described a vast colonial system that had bred three centuries' worth of Creoles who were given no part in the governance of their own land and of slaves whose only purpose was to extract wealth in the name of a distant monarchy. Peru, Bolívar wrote, was built on "two factors that clash with every just and liberal principle: gold and slaves. The former corrupts everything; the latter are themselves corrupt. The soul of a serf can seldom really appreciate freedom. Either he loses his head in uprising or his self-respect in chains." Bolívar's vision was of an "America fashioned into the greatest nation in the world, greatest not so much by virtue of her area and wealth as by her freedom and glory." To that end, Bolívar helped drive out the Europeans, but the Creoles he helped free rejected his vision and drove him to despair. Nevertheless, Bolívar's vision has inspired every Latin American generation for a century and a half.

Simón Antonio de la Santisima Trinidad Bolívar y Palacios was born July 24, 1783, just four years before the first abortive rebellion in Caracas. The revolt was in reaction to the monarchist struggles in Europe, to oppressive policies that kept Creoles from managing their own affairs, to the frustration of having to read Enlightenment ideas in banned books. Bolívar, the youngest of four children born to one of the most aristocratic families of the New World, was of that generation that finally tired of the oppressive practices of the Spanish Crown. Rather than profit from the colonial system — his ancestors through two centuries had been richly rewarded for service and loyalty in administering the orders of the monarch, helping build the port of La Guaira, laying roads, digging mines, and creating plantations— Bolívar followed a more torturous path.

He was orphaned early in life. Although biographers' dates vary, it seems certain his father died when Bolívar was very young and his mother before he had reached his middle teens. Nevertheless, Bolívar led what one biographer called a "spoiled and precocious boyhood" as a result of his family's wealth and the devoted attentions of slave women. Equally attentive were his tutors, including Andrés Bello, who would become a noted scientist, and Simón Rodríguez, a young dévoté of Jean-Jacques Rousseau.

Rodríguez began his lessons about the time Bolívar's mother died, and Bolívar later acknowledged the power of the Enlightenment ideas Rodríguez conveyed: "You have molded my heart for liberty, justice, greatness and beauty. I have followed the path you traced for me." Their relationship had its fullest effect for five years, and after Rodríguez returned to

Europe Bolívar sought him out. Thus Bolívar was both protected by great wealth and schooled, from childhood, in revolutionary notions.

Bolívar's training also included athletics, and about 1797, when he was fourteen, he was given military training for two years; he rose to the rank of lieutenant. When he was sixteen he was sent to Madrid to live with relatives and get further schooling. As a wealthy Creole he was introduced to people in the most privileged positions of the system he would later help destroy. In 1800, at the age of seventeen, Bolívar met María Teresa Rodríguez del Toro, a few years his elder, the niece of a Caracas merchant. Of their meeting, no biographer fails to note Bolívar's immediate and profound infatuation.

Impatiently, he waited two years before he could marry her and take her home, but within ten months of their arrival back in Caracas, in the tropical climate to which she was not accustomed, she was dead of yellow fever. Her death was crushing; six months after she died, Bolívar, restless and disconsolate, was back in Europe. He later wrote, explaining his single mindedness, "The death of my wife pushed me very early into politics." He would never remarry.

On this trip, Bolívar traveled to Paris, where, in the spring of 1804, he found Napoleon, whom he had admired, undermining republicanism by crowning himself. That Bonaparte would aspire to be "a Caesar" disappointed Bolívar, although he recognized the need for structure that was represented by Napoleonic law. The pomp of Napoleon's Paris also impressed Bolívar; he never lost his sense of wonder at the way cheering crowds sounded and would reconstruct the sensation again and again. In Paris, Bolívar was directed to the eminent German naturalist, Alexander von Humboldt. Humboldt, it is said, told Bolívar that a recent trip to Mexico had convinced him that the natural wealth of Latin America promised its peoples a great future — if a man dared lead them. In 1805 Bolívar went to Vienna to visit his old tutor, Rodríguez, with whom he set out on a walking trip to Rome. Admirers — and Bolívar, through his writing, did much to create his own myth — accept the dramatic story that while in Rome Bolívar took Rodríguez to the top of Mount Aventino. There Bolívar swore to God he would never rest until his homeland was independent.

After continuing on to Naples and spending more time with Humboldt, Bolívar, in 1806, went on to the United States. He traveled from Boston to New York, Philadelphia, the District of Columbia, and Charleston, observing the nation with its brand-new constitution. All this time, tremors of independence were being felt from Mexico to Argentina, and Bolívar saw the United States as the model for a united Latin America.

In 1810, after Bolívar had returned, Caracas cast its die. On April 19, the town council declared allegiance to the deposed Ferdinand VII of Spain rather than the dissolute Charles IV, placed on the throne by Napoleon and represented in Caracas by a Spanish captain-general. Ferdinand's restoration to the throne, of course, was but a convenient cause. It came too late if it was to be followed by restoration of the colonial system in America. Political freedom — and the commercial advantages it held — was not like some dried flower, to be saved between the pages of a book. For the group of independentistas to whose leadership Bolívar, then twenty-six, had risen, any monarchy represented oppression. In the summer of 1811 Venezuela declared its independence.

"Venezuela has placed herself in the number of free nations," it was announced. "'Virtue and moderation' have been our motto. 'Fraternity, union and generosity' should be yours, so that these great principles combined may accomplish the great work of raising America to the political dignity which so rightly belongs to her." The differences between the ideals of fraternity, union, and generosity, on the one hand, and reality, on the other, would become increasingly apparent. Even upon his return, according to historian J. B. Trend, Bolívar had to adjust. "The contrast between his ideals, acquired in Europe and from European books, [and] the actual conditions in South America which he found on his return came with something of a shock. Humboldt's glib and superficial view ... proved to have no foundation in fact."

The revolutionary junta sent Bolívar to Great Britain to solicit aid, and he was instrumental in bringing back to Venezuela the elderly Francisco de Miranda, a colorful character who had long advocated freedom from the Crown. Under Miranda's erratic leadership Creole armies were at first successful. Then human frailty and natural disaster combined to cloud the picture. First, Miranda came to consider himself a virtual dictator, rendering himself as unpopular in some circles of the New World as he was with the Crown. Second, earthquakes struck.

There were two severe tremors. The first was on March 26, 1812, a Maundy Thursday when churches were full. Entire towns were leveled; corps of troops were buried. Ten thousand people were said to have been killed in Caracas alone. Royalists shouted that it was the dissident towns that most suffered God's wrath for their opposition to the divine right of Ferdinand. They pointed to a Caracas church that bore the royal coat-of-arms on one of its pillars and was completely leveled — except for that pillar. Surely a sign, the royalists averred, angrily roaming the streets. Then, on April 4, another quake struck. Bolívar, too, took to the streets, arguing against the doomsayers and helping to dig out corpses. Rebel determination, however, was shaken.

Military setbacks followed with the result that rebel ranks were broken. In June, the rebel army was devastated in battle, and Miranda tried to flee. He was caught and turned over to the Spanish by Bolívar and other officers and gentlemen, whom the Spanish, in return for the favor, allowed to go into exile. The treachery was excused by Bolívar and his brother officers as justified in light of Miranda's excesses. Miranda would eventually die in a Spanish dungeon, but if honor was sullied, the rebellion's leadership was preserved. Bolívar fled first to safety on the island of Curacao.

From there he returned to the northern coast of Colombia, where his declaration from Cartagena suggests that his principal task was convincing Creoles that they, after three centuries of being told of their colonial inferiority, were capable of successful rebellion. They were, he declared, the equals of "those wretched Spaniards who are superior to us only in wickedness, while they do not excel us in valor, because our indulgence is what gives them their strength. If they appear great to us, it is because we are on our knees. Let us avenge three centuries of shame. War alone can save us through the path of honor." With such words Bolívar was able to gather about two hundred men, whom he led overland back into Venezuela. At Caracas, the Creole residents declared him "Liberator" and "Dictator." Then the Spanish once again drove him out.

During this brief campaign, in 1813, Bolívar helped codify another unfortunate practice of rebellion, one that ranks alongside treachery: retaliatory violence. Bolívar's decree, "War to the Death," warned royalists that they could "be sure of death even if you are indifferent. Americans: Be sure of life even if you are guilty." The declaration contributed to an atmosphere of rabid violence like that which had obtained in Haiti, and Bolívar is blamed for having condoned extreme violence. For decades, however, virtually every Spanish officer, surrounded by hostile Creoles, had demonstrated a taste for terrorism in order to keep adversaries, who were countless and usually invisible, at bay. Survival for Europeans had meant the enslavement of Indians and Africans, so it was but a small step to terrorizing rebellious Creoles. One of the practices the Spanish had perfected by Bolívar's time, for example, was the suffocation of captives. Bolívar responded with equal ferocity. Yet he made plain to the civilians who acknowledged his military leadership that his role was military alone. Once the war was won, he wrote, "I shall not retain any part of authority, even if the people themselves should entrust it to me."

In exile again, this time on Jamaica, Bolívar was protected, but not assisted, by the British, who were hewing a narrow line between protection of their own crowned head and development of new markets. Recognizing this, Bolívar argued that their long-term interests lay with eschewing support for old, European monarchies and supporting New World rebellion. "Europe itself, by reason of wholesome policies," Bolívar wrote in 1815, "should have prepared and carried out the plan of American independence not only because it is so required for the balance of the world, but because this is a legitimate and safe means of obtaining commercial posts."

Trying once more to return to the mainland, Bolívar was again chased out by royalist troops, this time to Haiti. There, he was more warmly welcomed than he had been by the British and he was able to get assistance from the government of former slaves. This new Haitian government, so feared in Europe and the United States for the example it set, formed an immediate ligature with Bolívar, and Bolivarian constitutions would all have a provision prohibiting slavery.

Bolívar, again, gathered an officer corps. His ability to continually recruit patriot armies suggests the attractiveness of his personality and the degree of his commitment. "Bolívar," writes J. B. Trend, "who had made himself into an army commander through sheer force of character and strength of will, never forgot his own men, and, for that, they adored him." With his nascent army, he landed again in the spring of 1816, on the coast of Venezuela. As he had promised, his first "official" act was to abolish slavery. The people hailed him. Again, they declared him Liberator, but they did not join his army. Royalists chased him back to Haiti.

Finally, in 1817, Bolívar was successful in making his return trip stick because he allied himself with an early practitioner of guerrilla warfare, Jose Antonio Páez. Unable to beat disciplined royalist troops in open battle, Bolívar needed time to build an army. By joining forces with Páez whose, rough, illiterate frontiersmen fought as effectively as had the farmers of New England forty years earlier — he got that time and much more besides. Páez, in fact, is directly responsible for the successful beginning of the wars of independence. Páez recruited peasants many of whom had at first fought on the royalist side as mercenaries — and turned them into a feared division of the patriot army.

Bolstered by Páez' men and instructed by his tactics, Bolívar stopped trying to march on cities and instead lived off the bounty of the countryside, keeping his own troops provisioned while denying supplies to the enemy. Tactics ceased being attack-and-retreat and were stretched into an effort at outlasting the royalists. Its legitimacy growing with every day and able to stay in the field, the army further benefited from thousands of mercenaries who began arriving from Britain and Germany. Under Bolívar's command, this reinvigorated army secured part of Venezuela, but avoided the strong Spanish force there and turned toward Nueva Granada, which was not as stoutly defended.

Bolívar's political philosophy was articulated at this point, early in 1819, in an essay written for the congress gathered at Angostura, Venezuela. Like pronouncements from Jamaica, these remarks expressed the ideals, set the standards, for the whole independence movement. "The continuation of authority in one individual has frequently been the undoing of democratic governments," he said, foreshadowing precisely the problem that would dog his later years. "Repeated elections are essential.... The most perfect system of government is the one that produces the greatest possible happiness, the greatest degree of social safety, and the greatest political stability." His goals for government would ring like bells over the continent, until, sadly, their pealing was drowned out by raucous shouting in the streets.

In the spring of 1819, however, those were ideas that ignited men's souls, and Bolívar led a patriot army of more than 2,000 men — roughly, 1,300 infantry and 700 cavalry — through the Orinoco jungles during the rainy season and up into the frozen passages of the Andes, which lay across his path to Nueva Granada. A portion of this army was recent European immigrants, some of whom had seen action in the Napoleonic wars. There was a full battalion of British troops. At thirty-six, Bolívar was the oldest commander; Francisco de Paula Santander, leading the forward contingent, was only twenty-eight.

At Paya, in late June, the patriots defeated a strong Spanish position and began their ascent. When they passed 10,000 feet the tree line was below them and they passed over narrow, treacherous, slippery trails, often in fog, beneath peaks that reached 14,000 feet. Men of the lowlands, they had never experienced such bitter cold. The feat came after San Martín's Andean crossing, but was through passes approximately a thousand feet higher. "Other crossings of mountains may have been more adroit and of a more exemplary strategy," remarks the Uruguayan José Enrique Rodó, "but none was so audacious, so heroic and legendary." Trend describes the crossing this way: "Bolívar, wrapped in a great scarlet cloak, was indomitable; but even the devoted aide-de-camp, O'Leary, almost gave up. Many died of exposure, including 56 of the English, and when the rest reached Socha (6th July, 1819) they had practically nothing on but their weapons. All the pack and saddle animals had died on the way."

With this army, Bolívar won three engagements in the middle of July against well-trained troops holding good positions. Then, with the Spanish rocked back on their heels, Bolívar pursued his advantage to a final victory at the Battle of Boyacá. The viceroy fled from Bogotá, and Bolívar rode, almost completely unattended, into the city. His entry, according to the official dispatch, was possible "after having overcome difficulties and obstacles much greater than could be foreseen ... and destroyed an army three times superior in number to the invaders." Victory was complete.

"After Boyacá," writes historian Guillermo A. Sherwell, "the campaigns of Bolívar were very swift, very successful and on a very different footing from his past campaigns. His enemies henceforth had to give up calling him the chieftan of rebels and bandits, and to treat him as an equal." Control of New Granada was assured; Bolívar was proclaimed Liberator — and before the year was out had to hurry back to Venezuela because officers and civilian politicians were plotting against him. It was a scene that would be repeated again and again. The Spanish could be defeated, but the Creoles could not conquer their wrangling for power or control their predilection for divisiveness.

The plans of both Bolívar and San Martín were enhanced by events in Spain. In Cádiz, the great army being prepared for embarkation by Ferdinand VII revolted on New Year's Day 1820. The Spanish were politically divided between supporters of the monarchy and adherents of the idea, embodied in the Constitution of 1812, of a constitutional system. The army, influenced by constitutionalists, declared itself more interested in staying home than mounting an expedition to re-conquer the colonies. Although Bolívar still faced at least 15,000 royalist troops in Nueva Granada and royal garrisons in major cities, his task was considerably eased. The commander of royalist forces in Nueva Granada, General Pablo Morillo, was ordered to negotiate; reluctantly he agreed and during 1820 the war in the north dwindled into discussion between equals. Late in the year, after Bolívar and Morillo met, Morillo described "one of the most pleasant days of my life in the company of Bolívar and various members of his staff.... Bolívar was wildly excited; we embraced again and again, and determined to put up a monument to the perpetual memory of our meeting."

Thoughts of a monument faded, however, when relations between the two sides, after Morillo had been recalled to Spain, deteriorated. The armistice was ended, and after two inconclusive engagements in the spring of 1821, the situation in the north moved toward its final resolution during the summer. It was the second great battle fought on the plain of Carabobo, south of Caracas, where Bolívar had won one of his early victories seven years before.

This time, Bolívar confronted approximately 5,000 skilled enemy troops in a strong position. From a hill, they covered with cannon and rifle the trails that were cut through rough, tall grass; a frontal assault was out of the question. Bolívar had 6,500 infantrymen, 1,500 mounted *llaneros* commanded by José Antonio Páez, and his faithful battalion of British, still with him, still willing to follow him anywhere. He first sent his cavalry around the enemy's flank over an obscure trail in a move that was supposed to be a surprise. The horsemen emerged from their two-and-a-half hour encirclement in plain view, however, and the royalists were able to wheel their artillery around to deliver withering fire as the cavalry found itself attacking over unexpectedly rough terrain. The day would have been lost for the patriots were it not for the British.

The battalion's determined attack cost it two-thirds of its nine hundred men, but it drew fire until the *llaneros* could reform, climb the final hill, and attack again toward the royalist rear. Then, with Bolívar leading a frontal attack, the three segments closed in, causing huge royalist losses in dead, wounded, and captured. The Spanish commander was chased with his few remaining troops to refuge in Puerto Cabello; within days, the Caracas garrison surrendered. The war in the north was essentially over.

The time, July 1821, had come for Bolívar and San Martín, who had just conquered Lima, to meet. The two had corresponded as their armies approached each other; San Martín had sent troops to help bring order to Ecuador's periodic madness, and now Bolívar was in Guayaquil trying to calm the excitable citizens of that city. Logically, the meeting should have paved the way for joint action, but that is not what happened. These were not logical times.

San Martín, unexpectedly, requested the meeting and sailed northward from Callao. He wanted to decide the proper government for Guayaquil — being pulled apart by forces favoring Peru, Colombia, or its own independent government — and to get reinforcements for his army. San Martín was also willing to discuss the idea of some form of constitutional monarchy for new Latin American countries, perhaps importing European princes for the purpose. He had been, after all, thoroughly chastened by his experiences in Chile and Peru; he was unable to point to any example of stable government and was uncertain whether any was possible under a republican form.

Bolívar, on the other hand, approached the meeting transfixed by his own grand idea, to create *Gran Colombia* out of New Granada (modern Colombia) Venezuela, and Ecuador and to weld a union of Latin American states that would be a model of strength against aggression from outside and of cooperation inside. He had reluctantly accepted the presidency of *Gran Colombia* from a congress assembled at Cúcuta — "I am not the kind of ruler the Republic wants" — and left Santander in charge of civic affairs while he journeyed southward to try to complete the war.

He wanted no part of winning a war against Europeans only to import European problems.

Like other Latin American thinkers, he saw Europe as fundamentally flawed. "The lessons of experience should not be lost on us," he had written. "The spectacle presented to us by Europe, steeped in blood in an endeavor to establish a balance that is forever changing, should correct our policy in order to save it from those bloody dangers."

Rather than the constant cross-border conflict that characterized Europe, he envisioned cooperation, the creation of an all-encompassing republic in order that "a single government may use its great resources [to] lift us to the summit of power and prosperity."

In his favor at this particular juncture, Bolívar had appearances. He was at the height of his apparent power, and as long as military, not political, solutions were sufficient, Bolívar was supreme. His triumphal entry into Quito—the one that had won him the affections of Manuela Sáenz—made it look as if he had gloriously completed his vision of creating *Gran Colombia.*

Despite sniping by local politicians and nationalist fervor that would soon break his union into pieces, Bolívar in mid–1821 stood head and shoulders above any alternative in Latin America. As if to press home this point when San Martín stepped ashore at Guayaquil, Bolívar welcomed him to "Colombian soil."

The two had never met, although they had exchanged cordial, general messages as they and their armies approached each other. San Martín, in fact, was reading messages from the fluent Bolívar right up to the time his schooner sailed into the Guayas River. At a banquet, Bolívar, never self effacing, toasted "the two greatest men in South America, General San Martín and me." There is a bit of irony in that Bolívar missed the chance to extend his characterization beyond continental boundaries: Napoleon had died three months earlier, so perhaps they were the greatest in the world.

The two men conferred in private, without even aides accompanying them, out of earshot and sometimes strolling out of sight of their solicitous lieutenants. History, as a result, does not record precisely what was said. Because, predictably, so much of what was written immediately after the meeting was written by Bolívar or his aides, there is the school of thought that Bolívar was somehow "superior." It is only certain, however, that San Martín was more humble. He looked at reality, while Bolívar tended to be constantly glancing in a mirror.

Probably the most crucial information exchanged in Guayaquil was that which arrived from Bolívar's minister to Lima. It was word of an uprising—of which San Martín was unaware—that had erupted as soon as the Protector left the city. The news must have confirmed everything San Martín had come to believe about the impossibility of stable government. Three days after his arrival, San Martín, disgusted with failure and apparently embarrassed by the gaudiness of the celebration, quickly and quietly left Guayaquil, sailed to Peru, resigned as Protector, went to Chile and traveled overland to Buenos Aires, and then sailed to Europe. He left, as it turned out, the remaining heartache to Bolívar.

The problem of clearing Peru of royalist troops remained. Bolívar sent a Colombian force for that purpose, but it was sent back, either because of Peruvian ingratitude or Colombian arrogance. It was difficult to tell with Peruvians, who tended to cover royalist sentiments with the thinnest of republican veneers. Whatever the reason, in early 1823, Bolívar sent the troops again, this time with Sucre at their head. Then Bolívar himself, at the insistence of Peruvians, went south, still looking for the last, great battle and determined not to slip into the bog of civil administration. "My repugnance to work in governmental affairs," he warned, "is beyond all exaggeration.... The Congress of Peru may count, nevertheless, on all the strength of Colombian arms."

The Battle of Junín on August 7, 1823, was a fitting last battle for the Liberator. It has been called the "Battle of the Centaurs" because it was fought entirely by cavalry with swords and lances. Before the battle, on a plain 14,000 feet above sea level in the Andes, Bolívar told 7,700 troops, "Men, the enemy you are going to destroy boasts that he has been winning for fourteen years. Thus, he is worthy of measuring his arms against yours, which have also shone brilliantly in a great number of engagements." The patriot victory was complete. The royalists retreated south where, after Bolívar had returned to Lima, General Antonio José de Sucre destroyed them on December 9, 1824, in the Battle of Ayacucho. When the news of Ayacucho reached Bolívar, he ripped off his uniform jacket and threw it to the ground, saying, "Thank God. Never again shall I have to command."

For eight months in 1825, Bolívar traveled through Upper Peru, which would form the country named for him, Bolivia. His last government effort was to write the constitution for the new nation, and, like his pronouncements from Jamaica and his Angostura remarks, the constitution is a testament to Bolívar's concern for a stable, republican government. Notably, the only thing the new republic rejected was Bolívar's provision for freedom of religion. "Should the state be the conscience of its subjects?" Bolívar asked, and the Bolivians gave their answer by requiring that the state be Roman Catholic.

More serious differences of opinion awaited him back in Colombia in 1826, where internal disputes and bankruptcy threatened, but the story was the same in every new republic. "His presence," writes historian Trend, "seemed necessary everywhere to inspire that loyalty and common sense without which his schemes would not work." Guayaquil and Quito left the union and, in January 1827, Bolívar returned to a Venezuela disenchanted with him and unable to live up to his requirements.

Bolívar rode into Caracas accompanied by Páez, but Páez was a dissident too. Bolívar spent six months trying to reorganize the government, working on agriculture and education and worrying over the budget; his thanks for his effort was a resolution asking that he never return to his native country.

He returned to Bogotá and Manuela Sáenz, the mistress who had been among his few devoted followers. Santander, privately, accused him of ruling "not constitutionally, but capriciously," and, indeed, Bolívar's mind was addled. His orders were often contradictory. Tuberculosis wracked his body, ingratitude was destroying his mind. His behavior only contributed to the widespread confusion. At the same time opponents were trying to hound him into exile, several town councils were declaring him dictator for life. If Bolívar was without direction, so was everyone else.

The attempt on his life in 1828 was a final ignominy. Saved by Manuela Sáenz, Bolívar hid beneath a bridge through most of the night, damaging his health and honor. As he spent the night beneath the bridge with the pastry cook, with whom he had escaped from the presidential palace, Bolívar listened to hoof beats on the cobblestones and shouts of "*Viva el Libertador,*" but he was never sure whether supporters or assassins were trying to draw him out of hiding. The coup attempt was never actively, overtly supported by more than a battalion of troops and a few officers, but it was clear that many more hung back, hoping for the attempt to succeed. Santander was at the root of it, and was at first condemned to death, although Bolívar commuted the sentence to exile. Still, he found himself condemning to firing squads men, including General José María Córdoba, who had been brave soldiers throughout the wars of independence. He despaired. "I shall go away to the country for several months," he wrote late that year, "to a place where there are nothing but Indians.... I can no longer abide such ingratitude. I am not a saint. I have no wish to be a martyr. Only the luck of having a few good friends enables me to withstand this torture."

The torture continued. In the south of Colombia, Popayán, an old royalist stronghold, revolted against the central government; Peru invaded Colombia; Venezuela and Quito left the union. Finally, the charge of being a monarchist was leveled at Bolívar. After sacrificing his physical and mental health for the cause of democracy, Bolívar was now subject to the same accusation that had been aimed at San Martín, that was thrown up to anyone who lost faith in Creoles' capacity for order.

The strain showed on Bolívar. In January 1830, returning to Bogotá from a trip, Bolívar was described as "ghastly pale." His voice was "almost inaudible." Addressing the congress, he pled: "The national treasury must claim your attention.... The public debt, Colombia's cancerous sore, demands that its sacred obligations be honored. The army, which has innumerable claims to the nation's gratitude, is in need of thorough reorganization. Justice demands codes capable of protecting the rights and the honor of free men. All this is for you to create.

"Fellow citizens, I am ashamed to say it, but independence is the sole benefit we have gained, at the sacrifice of all others."

In the spring, even as New Granada and Ecuador pulled apart, Bolívar, his tuberculosis having ravaged his health, tried to find peaceful exile. He rode off, accompanied by his long-time servant, José Palacios, and only a few others, seeking refuge on the northern coast of Colombia, on the sere, northern edge of what he had envisioned as a great political union.

Although General Rafael Urdaneta encouraged and aided by Manuela Sáenz — was successful in briefly leading pro–Bolívar forces back to power, Bolívar himself refused to return. He knew it would lead to bloody civil war. "In every civil war the winning side has been the more ferocious and energetic," he wrote, having learned the lesson that still eluded his countrymen. "From the beginning, no recourse remains to you except flight from the country or bringing despair to your enemies, because the response of your enemies would be terrifying. In order not to place myself between those cruel alternatives I have not dared take part in this rebellion, since I am convinced that our authority and our lives would not be saved without the cost of the blood of our adversaries, achieving through this sacrifice neither peace nor happiness, much less honor."

Bolívar stayed to die. "To the sepulcher, that's what my fellow citizens have meted out [for me]," he told the French doctor attending him, "but I forgive them.... I only wish I could take with me the consolation of their having stayed together."

He received, when he was not too weak to see them, a scattering of visitors, including one sent by Manuela Sáenz because he had not allowed her to accompany him. "Prepare yourself," she was informed in the winter of 1830, "to receive the final and fatal news."

The Liberator moved in and out of coherence. "They may take my kit aboard," he told aides who were not there in preparation for a voyage that would never be. In December, before he died, Bolívar had his last confession, and uttered plaintively, "Oh, how shall I get out of this labyrinth?"

4

Manuela Sáenz
Spirit of the Liberation
1797–1859
(Ecuador)

Manuela Sáenz created her own image; she was feisty, intelligent, indomitable, and outrageous. Her beauty was legendary, her intelligence freely and piquantly expressed, her spies feared. Her sexual fidelity to the Liberator was certainly stronger than his faithfulness to her. She never lost hope in the Liberation and never abandoned her will to fight, even when Bolívar, who was given to periods of depression, lapsed into despair. "Her passion for Bolívar is so explosive," writes a biographer, "that its sparks appear like luminaries in Bolívar's life." She was his "gentle, crazy woman." For eight years, Manuela Sáenz was at Bolívar's side, and when he went off to die she fought on without him.

Manuela Sáenz was born on December 27, 1797, to Simón Sáenz y Vergara and María de Aispuru, both of whom were reasonably affluent, but who were not man and wife. Simón Sáenz had come to Quito by way of Popayán, Colombia, arriving on horseback in the late 1700s. He was without money and with little to recommend him except his Spanish birth, which would open doors for him that were closed to Creoles. María de Aispuru, although a Creole, had no cause to make excuses for her background; her grandfather was Spanish (Vizcayan), an ancestry that biographer Alfonso Rumazo González says explained Manuela's "aggressiveness, compulsiveness, invincibility."

Although illegitimate, Manuela Sáenz grew up well provided for and could even count on a modest inheritance, something bastards had not always been allowed under royal law. Her illegitimacy, however, was a thorn she could not ignore; biographer Mercedes Ballesteros writes that to call her a bastard "lit in her angry character a desire for revenge that would never be extinguished."

Simón Sáenz prospered in commerce and was appointed to political office. He did not neglect his daughter, who frequently visited the home he shared with his aristocratic wife and their four children, Pedro, José María, Ignacio, and Eulalia. Manuela's relationship with her half-brothers and half-sister was mixed; they might have considered her beneath them. Later in life, the tragic realities of civil war that affected Ignacio and José María would rub off on Manuela.

As a youth, Manuela closely observed a black servant who was a few years older. From Jonatás Manuela learned the art of survival, the trick of pleasing everyone, most of all herself. "If she was sent to play in the street," Rumazo writes of Jonatás, "she returned full of news; if she was taken to mass, she prayed more than anyone, if with glazed eyes. She appeared to be shameless, laughing loudly. She detested work; she loved the sensational. For little

34

Manuela, she was an intimate friend, almost indispensable." Manuela learned to ride and to handle sword and pistol, preferring to ride astride a horse and to dress like a man.

Manuela's father was a staunch, unyielding royalist who was named a life member of the *cabildo,* the city council, after he had attained some prosperity in commerce. Sáenz was able to transform himself into a relatively big fish in Quito's small pond. A city of some 60,000 people at the time, Quito had a stagnant economy that was hindered by the city's being 9,350 feet above sea level and far from the sea. Politics were predictable; the city was royalist by default. In general, Ecuador did not have enough political will to protect its borders, which were periodically nibbled away by aggressive neighbors. Bolívar thought of Ecuador as part of his grand schemes because its borders conformed to the ancient Incan kingdom of Quitu, but within those borders there was little revolutionary ferment.

Nevertheless, after 1810 Ecuadorans were aware of revolutionary movements in other places, and they duplicated the unrest on a small, sometimes violent, scale. Manuela, when she was but twelve years old, watched from a balcony of her mother's house when soldiers brought into town shackled prisoners, rebels who were arrested after a short-lived "declaration of emancipation." The city government was even briefly overturned and her father jailed along with other royalists. Because of a brief flare-up in August 1810 — disembodied heads sent through the mail was one manifestation Manuela's mother took her to a country home for safety.

At the age of seventeen, Manuela was sent by her mother to the Convent of Santa Catalina, where young ladies were taught, among other things, the preparation of desserts. The convent, founded two centuries earlier, took in a few non-novitiates like Manuela. It had a scandalous history. The nuns enjoyed such worldly privileges as private maids, and were rumored to be under the influence of their Dominican mentors, who were described as "masters of sensuality." Manuela was untouched by such considerations, however, indulging in little more between prayers than surreptitious lessons in dancing and smoking. She was allowed out only once a month, on Sunday, after mass.

That, however, was enough time to meet a young army officer, Fausto d'Elhuyar, and soon Manuela was in love. Little is known about the affair; Manuela got permission to leave the convent one Sunday morning, met her young man, and simply did not come back. Manuela never spoke of what happened or where the young lovers were able to go. She was found and taken home, and before long a solution was found. She would be courted by Dr. James Thorne, a forty-year-old English physician and merchant.

In 1817, after Manuela and Thorne had been meeting at her mother's house once a month, never without a chaperone, they were married. She was not enthusiastic, calling the whole affair "supremely ridiculous," but the marriage stopped the gossip. Manuela was expected to be like other wives—chatting, sewing, praying, living an empty life in full — skirts but the opportunity for something more exciting emerged when Thorne decided in 1818 to take her to Lima, seat of the vice-royalty. There she met Rosa Campuzano, a society flirt from Guayaquil with a predilection for soldiers. Among those passing through Lima in 1819, in fact, was Manuela's half-brother José María. By then he was a royalist captain whose sympathies lay with the revolutionaries, and by December of the next year he would join San Martín, rising eventually to the rank of general.

Lima, of course, was the last prize of the wars of independence, caught in a vice. In August 1819 Bolívar entered Bogotá and drove southward. A year later, San Martín embarked from Valparaiso. Guayaquil declared independence on October 9, 1820, stealing the Crown's arsenal on the Pacific in the process. On July 10, 1821, San Martín quietly entered the city.

At the obligatory grand ball, Rosa Campuzano, who had set her cap for San Martín, was determined to shine, but Manuela was asked by Thorne not to attend. She obeyed, and stayed home until three weeks later, when she went to observe the parade commemorating the formal declaration of independence. With her dark eyes and long, straight, black hair, Manuela appeared in a blue silk, sleeveless dress. The dress, in Rumazo's enthusiastic description, "exhibited her amber bosom from which boastfully emerged incredibly graceful breasts that beckoned toward pleasure." She wore no jewelry.

Rosa Campuzano's play for San Martín was of fleeting success. Lima's society, always royalist to the core, settled back into the unwelcome business of defining itself under patriot administration.

In 1821, Bolívar completed the conquest of Venezuela and in 1822, General Antonio José de Sucre — who would become a firm friend of Manuela — helped free Ecuador. With San Martín's success in Peru, these victories set the scene for the Conference of Cúcuta, at which Bolívar's totally unrealistic dream, *Gran Colombia,* was accepted. What are today Venezuela, Colombia, Ecuador, Peru, and Bolivia were shaped into one unruly entity, and Bolívar was named president.

Meanwhile, in early 1822, Simón Sáenz played his role in destiny by arriving in Lima on business. Manuela decided, with Thorne's approval, to accompany her father back to Quito for a visit. She arrived about the time of the May 24 Battle of Pichinchá, after which Quito declared itself independent and a part of *Gran Colombia.* Manuela was introduced to Sucre and took part in the elaborate preparation for the triumphal entry of Bolívar.

June 16, 1822, has been lovingly documented — and embellished — by romantic biographers. The parade route was crowded with happy people; the sun was bright; aristocratic women rode to the parade route in sedan chairs borne by bare-footed slaves in bright colors and powdered hair. True patriots showed their enthusiasm for independence — no matter how recently acquired by — wearing simple muslin.

Bolívar — five feet, five inches tall — was splendid in uniform astride a white horse, at least from a distance. Up close, it was clear that although he was only forty years old, his face — described as "long, dark and ugly" with a prominent nose and lower lip — already showed signs of the strain of tuberculosis. He was, however, at the height of his strength in the popular imagination, in the eyes of a public that knew or cared nothing of his detractors, opponents, and critics. Masses were offered, banners were unfurled, line after line of troops marched by with bands playing. Manuela Sáenz, then twenty-six years old, was enthralled.

She watched from a balcony with the governor, wearing a crimson sash with the Order of the Sun, the highest decoration conferred by the new Peruvian government. The story is thus: She threw a laurel wreath. Bolívar looked up to see who threw it, and their eyes met.

Her white dress exposed her arms and shoulders and, of course, all the other endowments on which biographers have commented. It was the beginning of one of the most ardent love affairs of history. "Of the many women in Bolívar's life," writes historian Hubert Herring, "none held his loyalty and affection longer than she." After she saved Bolívar's life, he would refer to her, only half in jest, as "the Liberator of the Liberator." Even when she grew old, Giuseppe Garibaldi, the Italian adventurer, would describe her as "gracious and gentle"— and, still, "eccentric." General Daniel Florencio O'Leary, Bolívar's aide de camp, would write, quite simply, that Manuela Sáenz "looked like a queen."

At the ball that night, Juan Larrea, a friend, introduced them. The ball lasted until dawn; no one knew at what time they left, together.

For the next eight years, she would follow him, often arduously because he was a man at the head of an army, chasing a grand idea. She was often dependent upon him for support;

her mother's death left her some estate, but not much, and she was constantly at the mercy of Bolívar's largesse or loans from friends and acquaintances.

After their meeting, they spent twelve days together in Quito before Bolívar left for his fateful meeting in Guayaquil with San Martín; she did not accompany him, and he did not write. By early 1823, Manuela had begun her life of either being with Bolívar or corresponding with him. She became close friends with Sucre—they were two of the few people Bolívar could trust completely—and is thought to have had some influence with other generals as well, if only because no one could ever be sure how much influence she had with Bolívar. She was not shy about expressing opinions. It appears that her influence was limited to winning mercy for out-of-favor royalists who had been her friends, but she also operated a spy network. Her friends and her servants provided her with information, and with war a constant reality and distrust common, information was an important asset. Manuela never wavered in her candor, and Bolívar learned to appreciate that.

Her presence was not always appreciated. After she followed him to Callao, the Peruvian seaport, traveling behind in a stagecoach, patriot officers objected. "My general," one said to Bolívar, "we're about to go swordfight with the Goths and you're carrying on with women."

Manuela left for a while, returning to Quito, where her father was fatally wounded in one of the string of royalist uprisings that plagued Sucre's administration of Ecuador. Bolívar faced similar problems in Lima, so Manuela joined him there. Familiar with Lima's society, Manuela, with the help of her servant, Jonatás, collected information. Jonatás, a big woman in a brightly colored turban, worked the street for news. So helpful was Manuela's service, in fact, that O'Leary suggested she be named a colonel. When Bolívar complied, Manuela delightedly manifested her rank by wearing a blue military tunic with a red collar.

Manuela also acquired more direct military experience. By the middle of 1824, Bolívar had moved his army over a difficult trail to Cerro de Pasco, northwest of Lima, determined to finally stamp out royalist resistance. The 950-mile trek cost him 700 men to death and desertion while crossing the mountains. Manuela made the entire trip with the army and stayed at Bolívar's side to within ten kilometers of the enemy. At that point, Bolívar sent her back to be with the infantry.

The battle was a victory for the patriots, and when the royalists turned tail for Cuzco, seeking reinforcements among the friendly populace, Manuela joined in the pursuit. Maneuvering continued through August and into the beginning of the rainy season, both sides recognizing that the next battle would be important, perhaps definitive. The next battle, in fact, was the Battle of Ayacucho, which Bolívar missed, but Manuela did not. Bolívar had to leave the field because he needed to raise money to keep his army provisioned and because he was being implored to do something about the problems tearing apart patriot governments from Caracas to Bogotá.

Manuela stayed in the field with Sucre. Much has been made of the intimacy of their relationship—Sucre was twenty-nine at the time, Manuela almost twenty-seven—but all that is known for sure is that Manuela would be known after December 9, 1824, as having been "on the field at Ayacucho," a claim not even Bolívar could make.

The armies faced each other on a high Andean plain. The night before the battle men from both sides crossed to embrace brothers and friends. The royalists counted on at least 3,000 more men—more than 9,000 royalists against fewer than 6,000 patriots—and ten times the artillery, but when the battle was over, the royalists had suffered a humiliating defeat. At least 1,800 royalists had been killed, 500 officer's captured and 2,000 enlisted men taken prisoner. The rest deserted. The viceroy and several important generals were taken by the patriots.

Manuela rode alongside the reserve force, the commander of which was wounded. "Ayacucho marked the virtual end of the wars for Spanish American independence," notes Herring. As a bizarre remembrance, Manuela cut from a dead enemy soldier his mustache, making for herself a false mustache that she wore with a military outfit to costume balls. This, as might be imagined, was not universally appreciated.

Indeed, her place beside Bolívar was becoming the subject of censure, and some people suspected the Liberator would crown her. Over the next months, however, as Bolívar traveled back and forth across a disintegrating *Gran Colombia,* Manuela would have been the first to scoff at such speculation. She saw herself as having to fight for his attention in letters, or, when he was in Lima, to share him with admirers and sycophants—and other women.

Manuela dealt as well as she could with Bolívar's reputation as a Lothario. Upon finding a diamond earring in his bed in Lima, she gave him a tongue lashing that she knew would have but temporary effect; the cards were stacked against her. Bolívar was continually being seduced, as it were, by custom. Every time he entered a new town, for example, local leaders chose the prettiest girl for the honor of delivering a crown of flowers. If she delivered more, well, he was the Liberator. In Huaylas, for example, the damsel was Manolita Madroño, eighteen years old. When Manuela found out, she counter-attacked in a letter that, preserved through the years, still carries its original pout: "The disgrace is mine," she wrote. "Everything comes to an end. The general does not think of me. He has written only two letters in nineteen days."

Manuela was by turns furious or philosophical about Bolívar's amorous activities. His *quinta* outside Lima was legendary. Rumazo writes of Bolívar's being "solaced by Lima women who line up at the country house like a procession of love." Bolívar's private secretary blushed: "We are in a Babylon wherein all the beautiful women have been conjured in order to make us lose our heads." A visitor asked, "How many women loved him here? No one can be sure."

In the winter of 1825 Manuela despaired. A long separation could only exhaust his love, not hers. For his part, he tried to convince her that he loved her more for her spirit than her "delicious attractions." At such times their relationship was a study in the ambiguity that results from two strong personalities. Bolívar, for all his conquests, knew of the gossip and the need to preserve some modicum of propriety. He was, he wrote to Manuela, "determined to live up to my obligation to tell you of the cruel destiny that separates us from ourselves. Yes, from ourselves, since the soul that gives us existence, that affords us pleasure in living, flees. In the future, you will be alone, though at the side of your husband; I will be alone in the midst of the crowd."

When left behind, Manuela was forced to stay with Thorne—of whose jealousy and drunkenness she complained in letters—and then would rush to Bolívar whenever possible. She was convinced, with some justice, that her love was among the few things Bolívar, increasingly despised for his ambition, could trust. The accuracy of that belief would soon be proven.

In the autumn of 1826, Bolívar left Lima for Bogotá. Although in June the Panama Conference had given lip service to unity, everyone knew dissent was tearing *Gran Colombia* apart. Few trustworthy friends remained. On the road, Bolívar wrote back to Manuela, "You asked me to tell you that I love no one else. Oh, no! I love no one; I will love no one. The pedestal you occupy will not be profaned by another idol nor another image beyond that of God Himself." In November, he arrived in Bogotá; he had been away five long years and much had changed. A trip to his native Caracas would be his last, so intense had the hostility become.

At the same time—January 1827—Manuela was demonstrating just how far she was prepared to go in her commitment to Bolívar. In Lima, a Colombian division garrison there declared that it was terminating its allegiance to the Bolivarian constitution. Twenty-four hundred soldiers were in revolt. Manuela, determined to intervene, tried to reach the commanding general in person, but was turned back. Then she sent a message, which was intercepted. Frustrated, she took matters into her own hands. She rode at full tilt into the courtyard of the divisional barracks of the dissidents. She wore a man's clothing. Clutching the reins in one hand, she brandished a pistol in the other. She called upon the soldiers to remain loyal to Bolívar, and, as an inducement, she offered money.

For this dramatic gesture she ended up in jail, held for several days incommunicado at a convent and ordered to leave the country within twenty four hours. So determined was she, however, that she was able, while still in the convent, to contact supporters, who distributed bribe money on her behalf. The nuns, driven to distraction by her disruptive behavior, were forced to station a sentry, a nun whose orders were never to let Manuela out of her sight.

The governor who had ordered her jailed, according to the official bulletin, said that she and an accomplice had "not ceased trying to seduce, promise and spread bribes," the latter in considerable quantities. "With evidence implicating Armero and that woman, whose scandalous conduct has so insulted the public honor and morality, I called on her at four in the afternoon to say: You must embark within twenty-four hours." The alternative was prison.

Manuela left Ecuador by way of Guayaquil, embarking on the same ship with General José María Córdoba, a Colombian general who was one of Bolívar's principal critics. Manuela and the general crossed verbal swords. Her dislike of Córdoba would prove prescient.

By mid–1827, Bolívar was on his way back to Bogotá, periodically receiving gloomy messages that one or another capital had renounced membership in *Gran Colombia*. A revolt in Quito was put down with much bloodshed; not long after he left Caracas, dissidents had to be suppressed there. Depressed by the task of presiding over an embattled, shrinking government, he wrote to Manuela: "The ice of my years [he was forty-four] is melted by your warmth and grace. Your love renews a life that is expiring. I can't be without you; I can't voluntarily deny myself my Manuela.... I see you even though I am far from you. Come, come, come!"

Manuela was, as always, ready. She moved into a borrowed house a few yards down the street from Palacio San Carlos, the presidential palace. It was a fortuitous choice.

The atmosphere in the city, then with only about 22,000 inhabitants, was tense. Bolívar and his vice president, Francisco de Paula Santander, could not even speak to each other; rumors of plots surfaced constantly. This was the kind of environment, however, in which Manuela was at her best. Sexually, she would always have rivals, but in gall, audacity, and loyalty, she was without peer.

Juan Bautista Boussingault, a French contemporary, describes Manuela as "always visible." "In the morning, she wore a housecoat that was not without its attractions. Her arms were bare; she didn't bother to cover them; she embroidered, showing the most beautiful fingers in the world; she spoke little; she smoked gracefully. She imparted and received news. During the day, she went out in proper clothes. At night, she was transformed, wearing a bit of rouge, her hair artfully brushed. She was very animated and unafraid of making, from time to time, risqué remarks. Her self-possession, her generosity, were limitless." Manuela enjoyed her reputation for having "fought on the fields of Ayacucho."

Biographer Rumazo takes pains to suggest that Manuela was "a lady of State, who entered into politics, offered her opinion, made political suggestions, made decisions, unmasked enemies, made energetic determinations." The reality is less clear. Certainly, Manuela was only one of many voices, but she was not afraid to use that voice. She herself acknowledged, in pleading the case for some acquaintance, that if Bolívar decided to the contrary "I know well how much I can do for a friend and that certainly does not extend to compromising the man

I idolize." It was in laughing off suggestions of her power that Bolívar, perhaps defensively, called her "that kind, crazy woman." That anyone even suggested she might have influence, of course, affirms some measure of influence.

Manuela often presided at Bolívar's Colombian country estate, "La Quinta." Although the atmosphere of La Quinta was less carefree than that of La Magdalena, for Bolívar was less adored, Manuela still managed to be outrageous. Among the frequent callers when Bolívar was away were men rumored to be her clandestine lovers. She kept at the house a small bear, which delighted her and terrified unprepared visitors.

In one instance, however, she went too far in the eyes of many. At a particularly bois-terous La Quinta party a crude effigy was made and dressed to look like Santander, the vice president and Bolívar's adversary. The figure was set on a bench, facing a wall, its back to the boisterous, drunken crowd. A priest administered "last rites" and a firing squad was assem-bled. A young ensign, appalled at what was going on, refused to give the order to fire and was promptly arrested. Someone else gave the order, and the firing squad's bullets ripped into the back of the dummy.

Córdoba, the general who liked neither Bolívar nor Manuela, wrote to Bolívar to protest. Thanking him for his friendship and loyalty — thanks that would prove misplaced — Bolívar replied, "I know my friends and their craziness. But only the commander of the Grenadiers is to blame. The others have committed no legal wrong." Bolívar conceded, however, that the affair was "eminently shabby and stupid."

Of Sáenz he wrote: "As for the crazy one, what do you want me to do? You've known her for some time; after this event I'm thinking about making her go back to her own country or wherever. Moreover, I'll say that she has never meddled with the exception of asking favors, but she has never been accommodated except in the matter of C. Alvarado." Unrepentant, Manuela would always believe that the mock execution was clairvoyance.

After writing to Córdoba, Bolívar ignored the affair when he wrote to Manuela. He referred, rather, to having received her three most recent letters: "One ... pierces me with its tenderness, the other amuses me with your good humor, and the third convinces that you have suffered past, undeserved injuries." This was hardly a reprimand.

In August 1828, Colombians — some of whom had insisted that Bolívar assume total power — scheduled a great celebration of the Battle of Boyacá. Manuela was afraid. Alerted by her spies and conscious of the animosity surrounding Bolívar, she told him she did not think he should go to the masquerade ball. The ball, however, was dedicated to him, and she ran out of arguments to keep him away. One Marcelo Tenorio describes what happened:

Descending from an upstairs corridor toward the main ballroom about eleven o'clock, Tenorio found his way blocked by someone dressed as an old man in traditional Spanish garb. When Tenorio bristled at being detained, the man leaned close, lifted his mask, and said, "Don't you recognize me? In half an hour, at midnight, the tyrant will die." To drive home his assertion, the man pulled back his jacket to expose the hilt of a dagger. "There are twelve of us," he whispered. "Silence!"

Looking down into the ballroom, Tenorio could see Bolívar chatting with generals. Then, suddenly, Bolívar's attention was drawn to a clamor at the door. It was Manuela, described as "disheveled and dirty, but laughing uproariously," She was being denied entry, apparently because of her manly costume, a hussar's uniform. "I am Manuela Sáenz," she said loudly. It did not matter if she were Saint Manuela, she was told, *she* was not going to get into the ball without proper attire.

Bolívar, apparently embarrassed and hauling General Córdoba along with him, strode to the door, took Manuela by the arm, and departed. Tenorio heard someone gasp, "The tyrant has escaped." Later it was determined that a plot had been planned, the suspected mastermind being Santander, who innocently arrived at the party later. It was never known for sure, but widely suspected, that Manuela's timely disruption was also planned, to provide Bolívar with an exit.

Another plot was hatched almost immediately, for September. Again, to Manuela's dismay, Bolívar did nothing to prepare. Even when one group of conspirators gave itself away by bickering over who should be in command, Bolívar, hearing reports, brushed the story aside.

Then news of an assassination attempt was brought directly to the presidential palace by a lone woman who insisted on anonymity. After a servant had heard the woman's story, Bolívar sent his aide, Col. James Fergusson, to hear the woman out. She accused Santander, who was said to be condoning the plot without sticking his neck out, and also implicated General Córdoba. Bolívar did not believe her story, saying it was an unsubstantiated slur on a faithful officer, Córdoba, who had fought valiantly at Ayacucho. Fergusson, however, was beginning to believe the woman, and Manuela, always cautious, was thoroughly convinced. To their dismay, however, Bolívar did nothing, neither assigning extra guards nor even telling the sergeant of the guards of the warning.

Then, on September 25, a drunk artillery captain was overheard blurting something about a Masonic conspiracy to kill "that old man Bolívar, who is a tyrant." The captain was arrested, and other conspirators, apparently fearful that further delay would undo them, resolved to act that night.

At seven o'clock in the evening, the conspirators met at the home of Bolívar opponent Vargas Tejada. They knew the chief of staff of the Bogotá garrison, while not joining them, had agreed to absent himself by spending time at the house of a friend, effectively washing his hands of the affair — and waiting to see how it turned out. By ten o'clock, more than one hundred officers and civilians were on their way to arm themselves, although the vast majority got cold feet.

In the meantime — Manuela disclosed in a letter to old friend O'Leary in 1850 — Bolívar had sent for her early in the evening, and she had responded that she was ill. He sent a second summons, however, suggesting that she was less ill than he and that she should reconsider. As always, she went to him, pulling on a pair of boots over her slippers because the streets were wet.

When she arrived at his apartment, he was in the bath. He told her a revolt was planned, then tried to reassure her as she admonished him for being so casual. She calmed down enough to read to him while he was in the bath, and they went to bed without the guards being increased. As always, Bolívar kept a sword and pistols by the bed. He slept soundly.

About midnight, two groups entered the palace. One was made up of ten to twelve civilians led by a man named Augustín Horment; in the other group sixteen to twenty-five soldiers followed Pedro Carujo. One of the conspirators, Florentino González, wrote in his memoirs that successful overthrow of the government depended on the terror that "would result from the death of Bolívar, and in that moment, that end was supreme."

Horment's civilians killed three sentinels. Then the soldiers acted as lookouts while the civilians penetrated farther, breaking down two doors and disarming and wounding Lt. André Ibarra, officer of the guards. The band shouted, "Long live liberty." Behind the third door was Bolívar's apartment.

Manuela had heard dogs barking, then other noises as the conspirators made their way through the palace. Awakened by her, Bolívar sprang to his feet, seized a pistol and the sword, and started out the door. Manuela held him back and told him to get dressed. Then the two were unsure what to do next.

Should they barricade themselves? Deciding against that course, according to Manuela's account, Bolívar again thought to open the door, and again she had to stop him. Manuela reminded Bolívar that earlier he had remarked to a friend that the bedroom window was perfect for escape should it ever be needed. That was now the course they decided on.

Suddenly they realized that Bolívar's boots had been taken out for cleaning. Quickly, he pulled onto his small feet the boots she had worn. He started out the window, and once again she held him back momentarily while people in the street passed by. Then he dropped nine feet to the ground. Moments later, the bedroom door flew open.

Manuela confronted the assassins in the light of a lantern one of them carried.

"Where is Bolívar?" they demanded.

"In the council room," Manuela replied, a response that caused some consternation. Perhaps he and others were preparing resistance. Their concern was heightened by the fact that the one among them who knew the layout of the palace had lost his nerve along the way and deserted them. "Some believed me and some did not," Manuela wrote. "They saw the open window and the rumpled bed."

"Why is the window open?" they asked. She had opened it to hear the shouting outside. Why was the bed warm? She had been waiting for the Liberator, to wash his back.

Where was the council room? She did not know exactly, she had only heard them speak of it. She, after all, lived down the street. They insisted she lead them to the council room, but on the way they encountered the wounded Ibarra, and she delayed further by tending to his wound with her handkerchief. Have they killed the Liberator? Ibarra asked. No, she whispered, he lives. She insisted that Ibarra, wounded honorably, be lifted onto Bolívar's bed.

Outside, Col. Fergusson, the aide, clearly visible in the moonlight, shouted up to the window. He too, had been ill — so many at the palace were ill that Manuela referred to it as "a hospital" — and had heard noises. He was coming in. There was nothing he could do but endanger himself, she called back; stay there. He would rather face his duty honorably, he replied, and came ahead. He was dropped by a bullet in the chest. Carujo finished him with a sabre slash across the forehead.

In frustration after so much killing with still no sign of Bolívar, the assassins threatened Manuela, but one of their leaders intervened. Finally, however, the assassins were beyond restraint. According to historian Salvador de Madariaga, "The conspirators then vented their frustration and fury on Manuela, who was so severely beaten with the flat of a sword that twelve days later, on October 7th, she was still confined to bed." She was punched and kicked, all the while taunting, "Go ahead, cowards, kill me. Kill a woman."

Outside the window, the first person Bolívar met was his pastry cook, who had just left the kitchen on his way home. Together, the two hurried away, past a hostile sentry who thought, he recognized the pastry cook. The two were simply servants on their way home for the night. The cook hid Bolívar beneath a bridge, listening to the confused clatter of hooves above them, hearing shots fired and shouts of "*Viva el Libertador,*" which Bolívar was afraid might be a trap to draw him out of hiding.

Men from both sides were looking for him, but Bolívar, in his hiding place, could not tell who was who. When he finally dared go out, he was given a horse and escorted to the main plaza, where he was welcomed by a crowd, among which was Santander. Even then, Bolívar had to know — Manuela had repeatedly warned him — that he was surrounded not only by friends, but by others who had hung back, waiting to see whether the attempt would succeed.

Once he was safe, Bolívar undertook to rewrite history, erasing Manuela's role in saving him, exaggerating his own. He saw to it that the official *Gazeta* reported that he had tried to confront his attackers, but they outnumbered him. So, "being singlehanded against so many, he tried to barricade himself in his bedroom and, as it became impossible to resist any longer, he flew to the street." He reached the barracks of loyal troops, "where he was received with indescribable joy."

Historian Madariaga, for one, is appalled at the *Gazeta's* "omitting, of course, all mention of Manuela Sáenz." In addition, Madariaga adds, "the omission of his three hours of hiding is pathetic." Manuela later told O'Leary that when Bolívar finally got back to bed that night he was so overwrought that he alternated between asking about what had happened while he was in hiding and telling her to keep quiet so he could get some sleep.

Bolívar was uncertain what to do with the captured conspirators. At first, he agreed the time had come to pardon his opponents, try to calm the situation, and retire because of his widespread unpopularity. Then he changed his mind and ordered that the assassins be summarily shot. Troubled by his decision, Bolívar was counseled by Manuela not to lose faith in his mission, which required making an example of the assassins: "May God ordain that all your enemies die ... it would be a great day for Colombia ... these and others are sacrificing you with their enmity in order to make you the victim day after day. The most humane idea is this: that ten die to save millions."

Some confessed and others denied their complicity. The governing council decided that all who actually entered the palace were to be executed, and it was suggested that Manuela identify them. Bolívar, however, intervened. "This woman," he declared, "will never be the instrument of death nor the accuser of such shameful ones."

Manuela did testify, nevertheless, and although it was Horment, one of the leaders, who apparently said, "We're not here to kill women," perhaps saving Manuela's life, Manuela attributed the remark to Florentino González. González, presumably, had that turn of fate in mind while writing in his memoirs, "When he broke down the door of the bedroom, a beautiful woman stepped before us with a sword in her hand and an admirable presence of spirit to very courteously ask what it was we wanted."

If Manuela had saved Bolívar's life, however, she could not save his idea. Weakened by consumption — which was exacerbated by the night under the bridge — Bolívar vainly fought to prolong his dream. He commuted Santander's death sentence to exile — which infuriated Manuela — without winning Santander's adherents to his side. He condemned Córdoba to death, but he could not, as Manuela wished, execute all his enemies. Unrest cropped up like so many malevolent mushrooms; Popayán rebelled; Peru invaded.

At this point Manuela received a letter from Thorne, asking yet again that she return to his hearth. Her reply has often been cited as an eloquent expression of her spirit, her assertion to the entire world that she did not "live by the social preoccupations invented for mutual torment."

Give it up, she wrote, so I don't have to say no again and again. "Do you believe," she asked rhetorically, "after being the mistress of this general for seven years, with the security of possessing his heart, I could prefer to be the mistress of the Father, the Son and the Holy Ghost, or the Holy Trinity?

"If I feel anything it is that you haven't accepted any better your having been deserted. I know very well that nothing can unite me with him under the auspices that you call honor. [But] do you believe me less honorable for his being my lover and not my husband? Ah! I don't live under the social preoccupations invented for mutual torment.

"Leave me, my dear Englishman. Let's make a deal: in heaven we'll marry again, but on earth, no."

Manuela concluded with a devastating comment on the difference between the rainy nature of the English and the fiery soul of a Latin: "Monotony is reserved to your nation," she wrote, "in love, for sure, but also in the rest; who else does so well in commerce and sailing?

"Love affords you no pleasure, conversation no wit, movement no sprightliness; you greet without feeling, rising and sitting with care, joking without laughter, these are divine formalities, but I am such a miserable mortal that I have to laugh at myself, at you and at all your English seriousness.

"Enough of jokes. Formally, and without laughing, in total seriousness, truth and purity of an Englishwoman, I tell you that I will never be yours again."

The historical evidence is that the letter was closely edited, as friends apparently chuckled with Manuela over this final blow to her tortured ex-husband's ego. Furthermore, she sent a copy to Bolívar. He replied, in part, "The tone of the letter makes me love you for your admirable spirit — what you tell me of your husband is at the same time both painful and humorous."

After both had fought to suppress dissent in the south, Bolívar and Sucre met for the last time in Quito in March 1829. Bolívar then fell ill and eventually made his way back toward Bogotá, where Manuela awaited him at La Quinta early in 1830. He was a beaten man, his health destroyed, his will weakened. In the spring, Ecuador formed itself as an independent state, electing as its first president Juan José Flores, an illiterate. Bolívar's dream of *Gran Colombia* had gone up in smoke. Preparing himself for exile, he gave La Quinta to a friend in January, but stayed on until early March. Then he moved into a house lent to him by one of his generals, and Manuela moved into a rented house nearby.

On May 29, 1830, he rode by her house to say goodbye for what Manuela thought would be a brief interruption in their life together, an interruption like so many others. She thought it was just a matter of time before she would join him. His companions, including his long-time servant, José Palacios, waited outside while Bolívar talked to Manuela in the front hall. She did not know it was the last time she would see him. As the small group rode off, Palacios was weeping.

Hardly had Bolívar begun his trip north, however, when he got news of Manuela, who had become a rallying point for his supporters. If the fight was gone from Bolívar, it was not from Manuela, and that distressed him. "My love," he wrote, "I love you very much, but I will love you more if now, more than ever, you exercise judgment. Be careful in what you do, or, if not, the loss might be for us both, losing you." The danger was real; Venezuela declared that Bolívar was never to return to his native country; and, in the south, Sucre was ambushed and assassinated.

Manuela, quite simply, fought on. She found out that the new government was allowing, as part of a celebration in Bogotá, a fireworks display that included two effigies, one like Bolívar labeled "Despotism," the other a likeness of herself labeled "Tyranny." Military guards were assigned to protect the display before the celebration.

Manuela, predictably, was incensed. She dressed Jonatás and another female servant, Nathán, in military uniforms and sallied forth with them on horseback. Once again, her behavior sufficiently shocked the public consciousness that it made the official news. Sworn testimony portrayed the servants trying to disarm the guards. One witness said the attack was so fierce he ran to get a rifle to help defend the display. The three women were arrested, but not before they knocked down both the effigies and the elaborate fireworks. Jail merely added spice to their victory.

La Aurora, a newspaper supporting the government, described Manuela as a woman who "every day wears clothing that does not correspond to her sex and, similarly, allows her slave to insult decorum, and brags about her contempt for both law and morality." She had, *Aurora* gasped, "fired a pistol she carried, shouting against the government, against liberty and against the people." Manuela defended herself in a public statement, saying that while her detractors might revile her, they could "not make me take back one line of my respect for, friendship with, and gratitude to General Bolívar."

The conflict continued, even though Bolívar refused to be drawn back into it. Rumors that Europe's "Holy Alliance" would try to help Spain re-conquer its colonies heightened tension as General Rafael Urdaneta, a Bolivarian, sought to overthrow the new government. Neither Manuela nor the general was successful in luring the Liberator back from exile to lead their effort, and Manuela kept getting into hot water. "Manuela Sáenz is disturbing public tranquility with repeated scandalous acts," wrote the minister of state to the mayor of Bogotá in a bill of particulars, "that her servants have fixed posters in the streets; that she had tried to seduce with gifts the soldiers of the palace guard; and that she has committed other attempts, too, threatening public order."

A sentence to internal exile did not quell her, for she continued to turn up, spurring on dissidents. "Manuela was without doubt the soul of the revolution," writes historian Luis Augusto Cuervo—even when the revolution was over.

From afar, she agonized through Bolívar's final weeks in the autumn of 1830, informed by messages of personal emissaries, but unable to join him herself. He did not name her in his will, and, after his last confession, was not even allowed to utter her name because he was prohibited by church dictates from any mention of sin. When he died, she went to a small town and, like Cleopatra, caused a poisonous snake to bite her in a suicide attempt. Boussingault visited her, finding her with her right arm limp and swollen to the shoulder.

The virtual state of war between Urdaneta and Santander finally drove Manuela out of Colombia. In January 1834 she was told to leave, although she resisted so vehemently that it took a small squad of cadets and soldiers to force her out of her house. Because Guayaquil and Quito were at war her brother José María was killed in the fighting—she was exiled to Jamaica. From there, however, a steady stream of letters to Ecuador failed to win a visa to her native country because the government considered her too dangerous. Her reputation was too well known.

She wrote to Juan José Flores, the president of Ecuador, that he could not "ignore that a poor woman like me cannot do anything; but Santander does not think that way; he ascribes to me an imaginary valor." Flores did not think there was anything imaginary about Manuela's valor. When, after a year in Jamaica, she insisted on embarking for Quito she got as far as Guayaquil and the trail into the mountains; she was stopped by an official party. Her brother had been on the wrong side in the war, and the government was not going to allow Manuela back "in order to pursue her dauntless vengeance."

Without money, with only Jonatás and Nathán, she ended up just across the border in a miserable little Peruvian port called Paitá. She opened a small store—"Tobacco, English Spoken. Manuela Sáenz"—and after two years Flores informed her that Ecuador's legislature had approved her return. "How kind you are," wrote Manuela in reply, "The worst is that the damage is done; I will not return to my native soil since you know, my friend, that it is easier to destroy something than to make it new ... a safe conduct is not enough to revive my fond affections for my country and my friends."

Thorne sent her money, which she is said to have refused. When she was named in his will—he apparently was murdered—she refused any part of the estate. She grew fat from inactivity and was partly crippled by rheumatism; she was tired, outliving her beloved servants and eventually tiring of telling of her experiences with the Liberator. She was not, however, forgotten.

Ricardo Palma, the Peruvian writer, visited and told of her "strictly ceremonial" conversation. "In her tone," writes Palma, "was something of the high-born lady, accustomed to command, and to have done her will."

A ship's doctor, who stopped in Paitá when Manuela was more than seventy years old, remembered her having said that if "Bolívar had been French, he would have been greater than Napoleon." More to the point was the physician's own evaluation: "If that woman had been French and the lover of one of the Kings, she would also have figured in the forefront of events."

She outlived Bolívar by twenty-nine years. In December 1859, her rheumatic pains sharp and exacerbated by a pain in her throat, her temperature high, and her breathing labored, she could fight no longer. She was buried in Paitá, and her clothes and belongings were burned to prevent the spread of diphtheria. Also destroyed was a box she had kept containing letters.

5

José de San Martín
Liberator of the South
1778–1850
(Argentina)

"It has been said," writes Bartolomé Mitre, "that San Martín was not a man, but a mission." He was also an enigma, a victor who walked away from history. San Martín was "the other Liberator," who was overshadowed by Bolívar. Liberation of southern South America and capture of the viceroyal seat at Lima were not enough to save San Martín from lonely, impoverished exile, a widower adrift in Europe with his daughter, an outcast from the lands he freed from the European yoke.

José Francisco de San Martín was born in an isolated outpost because his father, a Castillian army officer who had worked his way up through the ranks before emigrating, was assigned there. It was a remote Indian settlement called *Tupambac,* "God's Estate," an experiment that exemplifies the creativity and intelligence of the Jesuits. The priests organized some thirty *reducciones* (settlements of Indians)—in this case Guaraní, converted to Catholicism—into a self-sufficient, productive community. Under the tutelage of the Jesuits, the Indians raised palms, figs, and oranges, and they were educated. When San Martín's father was appointed administrator at *Tupambac,* the building into which he moved had a fully stocked library.

It was the very success of the Jesuits in such projects, of course, that made them the object of hatred for royal administrators, who were usually incompetent and always jealous of their prerogatives. At the urging of such men Charles III expelled the Jesuits in 1767, and in 1770 Captain Juan de San Martín y Gómez was sent to *Tupambac* to take over.

So hastily was he dispatched that he had to leave his betrothed, Gregoria Mattoras, behind in Buenos Aires. His fellow officers raised enough money to send her along later, after the couple was married by proxy. Juan de San Martín eventually became lieutenant governor of the department of Yupeyú. "Much to the surprise of those accustomed to official rapacity," writes biographer J. C. J. Metford, "he did not abuse his position for personal gain, remaining a poor man for the duration of his tenure of office."

José Francisco was born on February 25, 1778 (although conflicting reports place the date over a range from early 1777 to as late as 1781). He was the youngest of three sons and had a sister, María Elena, who was probably younger. Money was short; in 1779 San Martín's mother traveled to Buenos Aires to try to obtain what was owed by her husband, and by about 1781 the San Martín family had been moved back to Buenos Aires. Finally, between 1783 and 1785, Captain San Martín took his family back to Spain.

Western Europe was at that time constantly at war, and until his death in 1796 the elder

San Martín supported his family at Málaga in military service. As an officer, he enjoyed certain prerogatives—as long as he could document that there were no Moors, Jews, or heretics in his family tree — and young José was accepted into Seminario de los Nobles, an aristocratic training ground for service to the Crown. All three San Martín boys became cadets at age twelve.

José de San Martín's military career was circumscribed by Charles IV's rather bizarre monarchy and France's expansionism. In 1793, at age fifteen, San Martín joined the Murcia Regiment. At that time, Spain still held, barely, the fort at the North African port of Orán. The fort had been under siege by warriors of the Bey of Máscara for two years, and the Murcia Regiment was sent in relief. After thirty days of fighting—through an earthquake—the Spanish surrendered; along with other prisoners, San Martín was allowed to return to Spain.

Shortly afterward, Charles made a feeble offer to help the deposed Louis XVI regain his throne, an offer that caused the Directorate to declare war. For the next two decades, San Martín would fight from one end of the Iberian Peninsula to the other, from the foot of the Pyrenees to Lisbon and, finally, Cádiz.

At first, Spanish troops scored successes over the poorly trained soldiers hustled into combat by the Directorate. In time, however, Spanish commanders, warring among themselves, were outmaneuvered. In early 1794, San Martín, among the forces being driven southward, was again captured. He was only sixteen.

Upon release, San Martín demonstrated abilities that were recognized in promotions up the line to second lieutenant in 1795. He had grown into a tall man, broad-shouldered and erect, with a pale complexion and "a remarkably sharp and penetrating eye." His hair was dark, his sideburns long. "His address was quick and lively," wrote an admirer, "his manners affable and polite." He was not given to the depression that would plague Bolívar — the younger Bolívar, a wealthy Creole student, took his sojourn through Europe about this time — but he would develop physical problems, including bloody coughing that would weaken him during strenuous campaigns.

When the short-lived Peace of Basel was signed in 1795, France pulled its troops out of Spain (but acquired the entire island of Santo Domingo), and hostilities abated. Then, in 1801, as Napoleon's Continental System sought to exclude English ships from friendly harbors, 30,000 French troops were sent to help the Spanish invade Portugal. Again San Martín was at war, this time storming the fort at Olivares.

After the action, San Martín finally found relative quiet — he was once stabbed and robbed, another time assigned to cholera-ridden Cádiz — with garrison duty. To improve his chances for promotion he changed regiments and rose to the rank of second captain.

After a second invasion of Portugal, San Martín was stationed back at Cádiz, which was in turmoil as the Spanish fought over whether they would be a monarchy — and, if so, French or Spanish — or a republic. At Cádiz, San Martín witnessed the chaos that characterized the Old World and felt the force of fresh ideas blowing in from the New. French ships were trapped in the port, chased and held there by the British after the Battle of Trafalgar. San Martín was called upon to help defend the Spanish administrator as he was threatened by angry mobs. Ordered not to let his men fire into the crowd, San Martín was virtually helpless as the king's deputy was dragged from hiding and, on his way to the scaffold, stabbed to death. San Martín had to escape to Seville. Biographer Metford suggests that "the affair made a deep and lasting impression on his mind and influenced his political outlook."

With the Crown debilitated, the junta of Seville took over civil administration of Spain and the Indies. The junta had the allegiance of the army, which tried to turn back French advances. In a cavalry charge near Andújar, San Martín so distinguished himself that he was promoted to the rank of captain. "This valiant officer," said the *Ministerial Gazette,* "attentive only to his superior's orders, engaged the enemy with such courage that he completely routed them." In July 1808 San Martín earned a gold medal and promotion to lieutenant-colonel at the Battle of Bailén, a Spanish victory.

San Martín, in service for more than twenty years and a veteran of countless battles, seemed to have reached the zenith of his career in an army conditioned to defeat. After an illness in late 1809 and early 1810, San Martín was appointed adjutant to his commander, and in 1811 he continued to serve through the frustrating effort the Spanish know as the "war of independence." After the French were driven northward, San Martín was present at the Spanish defeat at Tudela. The Spanish again, retreated southward, this time driven past Seville to the coast.

With their army essentially cornered at Cádiz, Spaniards fought among themselves. Partisans of the Bourbons preferred any monarchy to chaos; supporters of Ferdinand VII wanted a Spanish succession; republicans insisted on a constitutional monarchy. For his part, San Martín wanted more. He had met both English officers and Creoles, including Bernardo O'Higgins, the Chilean patriot. These men spoke of ideas, freedoms, causes, not tired European traditions. At this time, apparently, San Martín discussed the ideas of Locke and Montesquieu, and his dedication was raised a level, from obeisance to an unseen king to commitment to a political philosophy. He joined a clandestine cell, with O'Higgins. This fraternity would later, in America, be the Lautaro Lodge, a Mason-like organization with signs and passwords, named for the Araucanian Indian hero of a popular novel. It would be the vehicle of democratic ideas.

San Martín served in his last two battles, at Badajoz and Albuera, rising after the latter to become commander of a regiment of dragoons. The Spanish finally held Cádiz with the help of the English. San Martín, however, had turned his intentions toward America. It was the summer of 1811. Now thirty-three years old, San Martín requested retirement without pension and permission to travel to South America under the pretense that he had family matters to settle in Lima. This apparently reflects a conspiracy of military officers with democratic notions to enter the Spanish colonies. San Martín set sail, first for England, then Buenos Aires, where he arrived in early 1812.

Although discovered by Juan Díaz de Solis in 1516 — before Cortés landed at Yucatan — Buenos Aires was the least of the Spanish Crown's concerns. Direct trade between Rio de la Plata and Spanish ports was forbidden; all influence all communication, all commerce, trickled down from the west, from Lima through Upper Peru. Not until 1620 was Buenos Aires made a provincial capital, and then mostly to try to stop smuggling as traders developed the obvious, direct link with European ports. The city was made a vice-royal capital in 1776 and trade restraints were lifted, so industry prospered; but its independent nature was fully formed.

Early in 1812, San Martín disembarked in a city nearly two years into independence. Within six months he had married María de los Remedios Escalada y de la Quintana — at fifteen, she was twenty years his junior — the daughter of a prosperous, and independence-minded, merchant.

The revolutionary government commissioned San Martín to form a corps of mounted grenadiers. He instituted a strict code of conduct, well aware that patriot troops had sometimes carried the day with raw enthusiasm, but convinced that iron discipline would be necessary in the long run. "Soldiers are made in the barracks and on the parade ground" was the axiom he cited; the troop was drilled daily in the bull ring.

In October, word reached Buenos Aires that the patriot general, Manuel Belgrano had been defeated in the north. Then, amidst the anxiety caused by the defeat, a feud broke out between partisans of the administrative triumvirate and the legislative assembly. The city garrison, including San Martín's grenadiers, was called out to maintain order. Generally, the dispute was over which of several government alternatives should prevail. San Martín was among those wanting a clean, strong break with Spain, but factions continued to scuffle without resolution.

San Martín's first battle in the New World occurred a year after his arrival. Spanish troops had been disrupting river trade with the interior by sailing up the Paraná from their stronghold at Montevideo. San Martín took a contingent in pursuit and, when it appeared he would be outdistanced, he chose 120 grenadiers and left the others to follow. Near San Lorenzo, the Spanish put 250 men and some artillery ashore, giving San Martín his chance. He divided his small force and fell on the Spanish, losing 25 men, but forcing the surprised Spanish force to yield.

In the battle, San Martín's horse fell and rolled over on him and he would likely have been killed or captured had not a quick-witted soldier saved his life. The main Spanish force eventually had to turn back toward its base at Montevideo, and San Martín's small victory gave patriots something to cheer. "San Lorenzo," writes Metford, "was little more than a skirmish, but it had the effect of a great military victory. *Criollos* had proved themselves superior to Spaniards, even when outnumbered, and capable of tactical maneuvers in the best European tradition." No fewer than nineteen of San Martín's men who saw their first combat that day would later serve him as generals. After the battle, the patriot government deleted references to the king in official documents and took the royal image off coins.

In the bigger picture, however, change was more difficult. Towns and provinces of the interior both declared their independence from Spain and their freedom from control by Buenos Aires. Belgrano fought on although essentially defeated and disgraced; loyalists held out in the hope that Ferdinand VII would regain the throne with the help of his foreign allies. San Martín, meanwhile, was "rewarded" for his victory by being ordered home to command the Buenos Aires garrison by jealous leaders who wanted no more dramatic victories to overshadow their efforts.

San Martín's patron and apparent friend in the Buenos Aires government was Carlos María de Alvear, a member of the Lautaro Lodge and a witness at San Martín's wedding, but a formidable politician with his own agenda. In late 1813, Alvear helped obtain for San Martín 100 artillery pieces and 250 mounted grenadiers to relieve Belgrano. It appeared to be a hopeless task. As San Martín departed, one observer predicted, "The man is finished."

Arriving at the patriot camp, San Martín took command reluctantly, not wanting to embarrass Belgrano. His dual responsibility was to hold the Spanish, 5,000 strong, at bay while he rebuilt the army, beginning with the 600 men he got from Belgrano. "I have found here no more than the sad remnants of a routed army," he wrote.

More important, however, San Martín recognized that he was not where he needed to be. He founded a school for math and military science; he tried to rein in the fiercely competitive, independent chiefs who made up Belgrano's force; and then he requested to be relieved of the command. San Martín knew that Upper Peru—the "direct" route to Lima—was a dead end for the patriot army, which could not sustain a supply line over jungle trails. A 1,500-man expedition would later prove his point. He also knew, however, that the Spanish had the same problem in reverse. Their supply trains could not withstand harassing raids by guerrillas. San Martín's vision was toward the mountains, traversing 1,200-foot-high passes used by Incan invaders.

The goal was the same, Lima, but the method was to emerge on the central plain of Chile, take Santiago and Valparaiso, then sail with an invading force to Callao, Lima's port.

In September 1814, after an illness, San Martín was granted his request to be appointed governor of the province of Cuyo. Alvear, figuring he had San Martín in a weak position and wanting to destroy a rival, tried to replace San Martín with his own appointee. A popular outcry in Mendoza not only saved San Martín's job but cost Alvear his. Nevertheless, San Martín's position was widely seen as respectable retirement. Almost no one knew it was San Martín's carefully planned first step.

Slowly, he raised an army, imposed taxes, recruited seamstresses to make uniforms, and even found a monk, Luis Beltrán, who knew enough chemistry to direct the manufacture of explosives. María made the long journey to join her husband and gave birth to their only child, Mercedes, on August 4, 1816. For even his small family, because he was working at half-salary to help finance the expedition, San Martín had to borrow from the director of the revolutionary government, Juan Martín Pueyrredón. Pueyrredón, virtually the only leader in Buenos Aires who believed an attack over the Andes was possible, would remain a faithful friend and financier. "If I go bankrupt," he wrote to San Martín, "I will cancel my debts with everyone and come to you myself so you can give me some of the beef jerky I am sending."

In May 1816 the Congress of Tucumán "organized" the United Provinces of La Plata, although united was the last thing they were. Nevertheless, on July 9, shunting aside Ferdinand VII's apparent offer of a compromise, the congress proclaimed independence. Now the Spanish might invade any day, and San Martín, meeting Pueyrredón at Córdoba, got final support for his plan.

The threat of a Spanish invasion from Chile actually helped San Martín recruit, adding urgency to his words. Beginning with about 25 men from the Cuyo militia, he took in 1,200 regular enlistments, ordered slaves to enlist, fining their owners if they did not, and conscripted every Creole man between the ages of fourteen and forty-five. In addition, several companies of artillery and mounted grenadiers were sent from Buenos Aires.

Crucial to the invasion was military intelligence, and San Martín was something of a master of spies, who operated along the frontier, in Chile and up the coast to Callao and Lima. John Miers, an Englishman, observes, "The General was, from an early period, a great adept in cunning and intrigue." When spies from across the mountains fell into San Martín's hands, he made sure to send them back with greatly inflated estimates of his force, hoping to hold the Spanish off until he was ready. San Martín also met with the fierce Tehuelche Indians south of Cuyo, who agreed to provide safe passage. San Martín told them that his plan was to move his main army through the pass at Planchón, but that they were to tell the Spanish the route would be through the valley of Aconcagua. He assumed, correctly, the Indians would betray him upon receipt of bribes from the Spanish, and reinforced the game of mirrors by allowing interception of "orders" designating Planchón. All the time, of course, he intended to take a third route.

Meanwhile, in Chile, an army under Bernardo O'Higgins briefly established patriot supremacy, only to be beaten by the Spanish and royalists in October 1814. As a result, San Martín found his efforts hampered by the necessity of taking in refugees fleeing the battle at Rancagua. San Martín welcomed O'Higgins, his fellow Lautaro Lodgeman, and placed him in command of one of his divisions.

San Martín's Army of the Andes was ready by late 1816. He had prepared the way with misinformation, suggesting to the Spanish he was coming by each of six possible routes. The route he chose was the most direct, but he had spent months sending signals to his adversary, Marshal Marcó del Pont, that kept reconnaissance patrols constantly on the move and the defending army spread along a 1,300-mile frontier. He sent ahead a formal declaration of independence, making sure the officer who carried it gathered information about the pass at Uspallata during the trip.

On the morning of January 5, 1817, after a day of praying and parading and a night of feasting and dancing, the army, carrying an embroidered version of the blue-and-white flag adopted at Tucumán, lumbered toward the mountains, from which came the echo of a final ceremonial cannonade. Over more than two years, demonstrating the patience and persistence for which he would become famous, San Martín had built an army of 3,778 men, including 742 mounted grenadiers. They were supported by 1,392 auxiliary forces, from sappers, or field engineers whose specialty was hand-held bombs, to baggage handlers. Eighteen artillery pieces were slung between mules for the passage along mountain trails, through gorges, San Martín knew, which were so narrow they could be blocked by a handful of men.

There were 1,600 horses and 9,281 mules; the number of animals is the mathematical measure of the difficulty of the passage. The army would arrive with but 500 horses and 4,300 mules remaining. An English officer who accompanied the army, John Miller, wrote, "The intense cold on the summits killed many men." Although San Martín ordered an extra supply of garlic and onions, the only known remedy for *puna,* or vertigo, the sickening dizziness caused by the thin air of high altitude, the sickness affected virtually everyone. The crossing has been compared with feats of Hannibal, Napoleon, and, of course, Bolívar, who two years later would make his Andean crossing through passes a thousand feet higher.

Although royalists occupied the capital, San Martín counted on a friendly reception in other towns because Chile had harbored its own independence movement from 1781 and had been the site of a tax revolt as early as 1776. Del Pont, San Martín's spies informed him, would command 5,000 men, mostly mestizos and only 930 of them well-trained.

San Martín rode with O'Higgins and General Miguel Estanislao Soler, who commanded the main force. A secondary force, including the artillery, was commanded by Juan Gregorio de las Heras, and two other, smaller, forces rode flanking movements through separate passes. Deposits had been laid along the routes, and careful surveys had been made of the potential battle sites. All four forces were to be in place at their respective summits by February 1, 1817.

The main and Las Heras forces combined on February 8 and the march on Santiago proceeded at six points. Del Pont, already confused, now split into fractions. He had received reports of rebel advances at Los Patos, Uspallata, and Planchón, all of which had some truth to them. San Martín's main force, however, was marching up the valley of the Aconcagua River.

The army Del Pont sent to stop San Martín at had 1,500 men and five artillery pieces. In addition, he could count on those troops who were retreating in the face of San Martín's advance. Unsure of exactly what he faced and where he faced it, Del Pont held onto 1,600 men to defend Santiago. It would all be to no avail.

The defense at Chacabuco occupied the crest of a hill — a hill that San Martín's engineers had surveyed. San Martín knew of a narrow, rocky trail cut into the mountain and leading around the Spanish left. In addition, San Martín captured a reconnaissance patrol, effectively blinding the Spanish commander. Appraising the situation, San Martín sent Soler around the left flank to create pressure on the defenders' rear. O'Higgins was sent, by moonlight, to spring a frontal assault at daybreak, before the enemy was dug in.

At dawn, O'Higgins' men turned the defenders and set them to flight. Spanish officers, however, because Soler did not get into position in time, were able to establish a second line of defense. San Martín ordered O'Higgins to pursue and Soler to hurry.

Soler was not fast enough. The second time the Spanish established themselves, with two cannons, across a stream rushing through a deep arroyo. It was a formidable position, and O'Higgins impetuously attacked without waiting for Soler. San Martín, watching from an elevated command post, saw O'Higgins prematurely order an attack and be beaten back from the watercourse. Again hastening Soler, San Martín mounted and rode to help O'Higgins.

A furious assault by saber and bayonet — ex-slaves fought bravely — finally carried the position, but only after Solers flanking movement contributed to the royalists' disarray. Of the enemy, 500 were killed and 600 captured; the patriots' losses were 130 killed and about the same number wounded. The Spanish succeeded in getting 500 men away and, eventually, to Lima. Others retreated southward to royalist strongholds.

"I think we must now be more prudent and look to the future," San Martín wrote to his friend Tomás Godoy Cruz after the Battle of Chacabuco. "Let us not become conceited with our glories, but let us take advantage of the occasion to determine the destiny of our country calmly and on a sound basis." Such prudence would take its place in San Martín's personal history along with his reputation for careful organization, but it would often be seen as crippling timidity. Failure to pursue the royalists southward prolonged the war at least a year.

Del Pont was captured, along with his hated commander of slave labor in Santiago, as he tried to escape to Valparaiso to embark for Lima. After initial chaos as royalists' property was stolen and their shops pillaged, San Martín restored order. He turned aside the people's request that he proclaim himself leader, naming O'Higgins and extricating himself — almost — from the vicious internal politics that followed independence.

It proved impossible to dislodge royalists from a stronghold at Talcahuano in the south, on the Bay of Concepción, where they could be reinforced and provisioned by sea. Leaving the problem to O'Higgins, San Martín, ill and wanting to rebuild his army for the final push on Lima, left for Buenos Aires.

In May 1817, San Martín returned to Santiago in good health, but found the royalists still occupying Talcahuano while O'Higgins and Las Heras argued. San Martín agreed to a land and sea assault in November, but it was to no avail, encouraging royalists, who were waiting for rescue from Lima. Meanwhile, San Martín tried to build a new army. In effect, he had to shout his promises of cash and supplies over the racket of internecine fighting among Chileans. In addition, his association with the Lautaro Lodge led to the accusation that Argentines were trying to dominate Chilean affairs.

In the meantime, Viceroy Joaquin de Pezuela did not sit in Lima waiting for San Martín to arrive. He sent 3,300 troops by ship to the royalist stronghold at the Bay of Concepción. The viceroy intended a feint toward breaking the siege of Talcahuano, drawing patriot strength south. Then, with Santiago left undefended, the Spanish troops would suddenly re-embark for a sweep up the coast to Valparaiso before the patriots could return. The plan had one flaw: San Martín's spies in Callao told him.

With Chileans formally declaring their independence in early 1818, San Martín saw his chance to solidify their situation by exercising both caution and cleverness. "The preservation of the state," he said, "depends on our not risking any action the outcome of which might be doubtful. For the moment our plan of campaign must be the concentration of our forces in order to deliver a final and decisive blow." The viceroy's move gave San Martín his chance. Leaving Valparaiso fortified, San Martín marched south, but not too far. O'Higgins, at the same time, lifted the siege of Talcahuano and moved northward to consolidate with San Martín. They waited at Cancha Rayada as the Spanish, intent upon confrontation, were drawn in from the Bay of Concepción to follow O'Higgins. Four thousand Spanish and royalists moved north against seven thousand patriots.

There was contact between the hostile forces on March 8, 1818, and San Martín imme-diately ordered a cavalry attack. It achieved little on the field, but convinced the Spanish that the numbers were not in their favor. The Spanish halted their advance, but by now San Martín's army was swallowing them like an amoeba, threatening on three sides.

The Spanish commander, in despair, halted his advance and, not knowing what to do, prayed into the night. The second in command, disgusted with his superior's timidity, mounted a surprise night attack before the patriots had firmly fixed their defenses. The dar-ing Spanish charge took them suddenly into the midst of the patriot camp, and a shot wounded O'Higgins. The patriots broke and fled.

Witnesses to the rout reported all kinds of dire events: that O'Higgins was dead, that San Martín had committed suicide in disgrace on the battlefield.

Both leaders, in truth, returned to Santiago to reorganize. Las Heras had managed to save a flank of 3,500 troops, and — perhaps because they ran too fast to get shot — the patri-ots had lost no more than 120. Desertion, however, had thinned their ranks so that they, like the Spanish, were now about 5,000 strong.

On April 3, 1818, the Spanish army crossed the River Maipú and two days later assem-bled for a classic European-style battle on the plain outside Santiago. After an exchange of artillery fire, the patriots attacked the royalist right but were turned back. The Spanish, how-ever, overestimating the advantage they had gained, pursued, only to be turned back, then put to flight by San Martín's reserves. In the meantime, the patriot cavalry had broken the Spanish left. Victory was complete.

After the tension created by the Spanish night attack and the fear that Santiago might fall, the patriots were nearly delirious. An English observer wrote: "People embraced each other, laughed, wept and shrieked as if deprived of their senses. Some went literally mad, and one or two of them have never recovered their reason."

San Martín had taken the first, arduous step. "The victory of Maipú," writes Samuel Haigh, "left the cause of independence on so solid a footing as to deliver the mortal blow to Spanish power in South America." Neither San Martín nor the Spanish, however, yet knew that.

The next step required crossing not the mountains, but the sea. That was accomplished only with the help of English officers, those other veterans of the Napoleonic wars. Foremost among them was the almost mythical Scot, Thomas, Lord Cochran, Tenth Earl of Dundon-ald, who terrorized the Spanish navy all along the coast, conducting daring raids and allow-ing San Martín safe passage. "The importance of Cochran's contribution to San Martín's great design cannot be underestimated," notes Metford. "Although he failed twice to take Callao, he so terrified the royalists, that they were unwilling to risk their frigates on the high seas. This gave San Martín the necessary freedom to move his men into Peru."

But nowhere was San Martín moving until he could refinance the provisioning of an army and overcome the political infighting in both Santiago and Buenos Aires. Chile got a British loan, but O'Higgins was slow to pass along funds. Buenos Aires, as usual, was torn by dis-sension so San Martín was deprived of any help from Belgrano's Army of the North, with which he had intended to coordinate his assault on Lima. Leaders in Buenos Aires, in any event, had lost interest in Lima, wanting San Martín back to guard against an invasion rumored to be coming their way. Indeed, such an expedition was being mounted at Cádiz, but was brought low by yellow fever. In January 1820, moreover, a revolt forced Ferdinand VII, recently restored to his throne, to reinstitute the liberal constitution of 1812. Metropol-itan Spanish, preoccupied with their own problems, were lukewarm to foreign expeditions.

San Martín, frustrated by the lack of support from either government, withdrew a division to Mendoza, halfway between Buenos Aires and Santiago. Finally, an agreement for joint financing was signed in February 1819, but then the United Provinces government was deposed. At wit's end, San Martín resigned his command. He instructed Las Heras that the army's authority to exist had evaporated. He suggested the men elect a general to fight on. The men, predictably, decided to stick with the general they had, but two long years had passed since Maipú.

"[I]f the expedition to Peru is not undertaken," San Martín wrote to a friend, "every thing will go to the devil." Finally, in August 1820, he procured the last of what he needed — only to find that the docks at Valparaiso did not have the cranes he needed to load it.

Lima, South America's oldest vice-royalty, was there, waiting, fat from the wealth of silver mines, royalist by tradition, and this last fact troubled San Martín. Although Pizarro had been of an independent turn of mind, once burning the royal standard and Peru had been home to four Indian uprisings and two Creole revolts, Lima remained consummately loyal to the king. The city was not infested with patriots as Santiago had been, so there would be no internal revolt. In addition, there was so little trade with southern South America that San Martín's spies were of little help.

The viceroy could count on 23,000 regular troops, 7,800 in Callao and Lima, 6,000 in Upper Peru, and 9,000 spread from Arequipa in the south to Guayaquil in the north. Lord Cochrane, contemptuous of Spanish fighting ability, counseled attack. San Martín was cautious; his army would never number more than 14,000. On August 20, 1820, they set sail from Valparaiso.

To Cochrane's dismay, San Martín ordered a landing at Pisco, one hundred miles south of Lima. Critics still argue that Cochrane was right. San Martín, however, was negotiating, and so far killing had been averted. The viceroy, in line with the new liberal constitution his king was following, was ordered to seek an accommodation. One solution to avoid war was simply to set up a monarch in America who would send deputies to the Spanish parliament. San Martín was not interested. Recognition for Chile, asked the viceroy, and a halt to hostilities? San Martín accepted on condition that the viceroy pull his forces from Upper Peru and allow Britain and the United States to guarantee peace. The viceroy rejected the idea.

While the talks proceeded for two months, San Martín sent a force of 1,300 into the interior to recruit Indians, spread revolutionary propaganda, enlist deserters, and, if necessary, engage the enemy. The tactic worked in a defeat for the Spanish at Pasco, but the patriots then rejoined San Martín, leaving enough Spanish to slaughter Indians in revenge.

In late October, San Martín sailed again. Cochrane implored San Martín to be allowed to take Callao and march directly on Lima, but San Martín ordered the fleet to sail past Callao to the Bay of Ancón, just north of Lima. From there, he moved a bit farther north and set his camp at Huacho. There, he waited.

By early 1821, further expeditions into the interior had recruited more Indians and the blockade of Callao had begun to squeeze Lima's residents. San Martín still waited.

In May he sent an emissary to armistice talks, but only to gain time, to let the viceroy stew a little longer. The military commander of Lima, seeing the folly of trying to keep the city governed and supplied while defending it, decided not to wait, but to retreat. Leaving a garrison and supplies in Callao, he took the viceroy and moved his headquarters to the mountains. San Martín was invited to enter the city, but he declined.

Instead, he moved to Miraflores, halfway between Callao and Lima. He would later explain his enigmatic tactics in words as modern as todays: "I do not want military renown. I have no ambition to be the conqueror of Peru. I want solely to liberate the country from oppression. Of what use would Lima be to me if the inhabitants were hostile in political sentiment? ... The country has now become sensible of its true interests and it is right the inhabitants should have the means of expressing what they think. Public opinion is an engine newly introduced into this country; the Spaniards, who are utterly incapable of directing it, have prohibited its use; but they shall now experience its strength and importance."

Lima residents, with San Martín refusing to enter, were afraid of a slave revolt inside the city; outside city walls, moreover, hostile Indians could be seen setting up camp. Terrified, they again asked San Martín in. Again, he refused, although he provided troops for police duty. San Martín simply said he would not enter the city until its residents, once and for all, declared their independence.

On July 9 they did so, and the army marched in. Yet there was no triumphal entry, with San Martín, astride a white horse receiving garlands. Not until July 12, after commerce had been restored and governance reestablished, did San Martín, accompanied by a single aide, ride quietly into the city in the early evening.

He occupied not the vice-regal palace, but the home of the hastily appointed governor whom the viceroy had abandoned. When the people found out where San Martín was, they flocked to him. Captain Basil Hall, an English witness, wrote: "During this scene I was near enough to watch him closely; but I could not detect, either in his manner or in his expressions, the least affectation ... nothing which seemed to refer to himself; I could not even discover the least trace of a self-approving smile. His satisfaction seemed to be caused solely by the pleasure reflected from others."

On July 28, after a full dress parade, San Martín unfurled the flag he had designed, but other considerations were more complex. In Buenos Aires and Santiago patriots were eager to establish democratic processes; Lima was a royalist package, and in the unwrapping neither San Martín nor anyone else knew what to expect. Generations of slavery, both of Africans and Indians, an ingrained class system, and the departure of brain power with the vice-royal entourage all left the city's future unpredictable.

San Martín, who must have recalled the chaos of Cádiz, said, "Every civilized people is entitled to be free; but the degree of freedom which any country can enjoy must bear an exact proportion to the measure of its civilization." At the people's request, he proclaimed himself Protector of Peru.

He chose three men as administrators, including the wretched Bernardo de Monteagudo. Blame for many of Monteagudos misdeeds would fall on San Martín, and Monteagudo was so hated for his thievery and brutish behavior that he was exiled as soon as San Martín was out of the city. When he dared return, he was stabbed to death in the street. San Martín, indeed, was blamed for everyone's transgressions. *Limeños* followed the ignoble pattern of reviling the Protector they so ardently had sought.

In August, the Spanish, about 3,200 strong, came out of their mountain redoubt and assembled on the plain. San Martín was as the theater in early September when informed the Spanish were approaching the city. After standing in his box to call for the citizens' help, he took charge of the army — some 12,000 troops — and committed what would be seen as a woeful abdication of his power.

San Martín assembled his troops with a strong anchor in the hills on his left, but left a passage on his right, along the shore. The Spanish, trying to reach their companions holding the fort at Callao, had to pass through this gauntlet. As the Spanish moved along the shore, San Martín was asked, even begged, to attack. Cochrane rode up, furious at the thought of letting them escape. The troops were shouting that they wanted to fight. San Martín would not give the order. His lack of decisiveness in this and other instances might have been caused by the opium he used to treat his persistent illness.

After the Spanish passed, he said, "They are lost. Callao is ours. They do not have enough provisions for a fortnight and the reinforcements from the mountains will eat them all. Within a week they will be obliged to surrender or be skewered on our bayonets."

Although his evaluation was right, when the Spanish had to leave the fort San Martín again let them pass. By the time two pursuing forces were sent, one was badly beaten by the Spanish rearguard and the other exhausted its provisions and had to turn back. Callao finally surrendered, but San Martín had again, as after the Battle of Chacabuco, failed to press his advantage to destroy his enemy.

An American diplomat wrote to John Quincy Adams that "it occurs to me that San Martín ... prefers to continue his influence by protracting the military conflict ... rather than to put down the remnant of the royal troops and leave the country to the agonies of conflicting factions; or, in a few words, to make himself, as his own choice, King, Dictator, or Director." The judgment could not have been more wrong.

Cochrane took his fleet and sailed away (to appear later fighting for Brazil), and San Martín was left to govern Peruvians. His orders advanced education and founded the National Library. He abolished the various forms of Indian servitude and proclaimed the freedom of all children of slaves born after July 28, 1821. He abolished hanging, except for traitors, and the whipping of schoolchildren. He drew the enmity of the established church by recognizing freedom of worship.

For his efforts, San Martín was thanked with a coup attempt. His ministers were hated. Perhaps in desperation, he petitioned the British Crown for a likely relative to serve as a monarch, then convoked a congress to lay the idea of monarchy to rest.

How to govern unruly Peruvians would soon, however, be someone else's concern. Bolívar's army was descending from the north. Although San Martín had sent troops north to help Colombians under Bolívar's command, and Bolívar had ordered two Colombian battalions to Peru, misunderstandings had doomed both cooperative ventures. There would be no further attempts. The two generals were like oil and water.

The dispute ostensibly focused on Guayaquil, a malarial port in what is now Ecuador, the citizens of which could not decide whether to join Peru, become part of *Gran Colombia,* or be independent. Bolívar made the choice for them.

Bolívar and San Martín had planned to meet. San Martín wrote that "the stability of the destiny that America is rapidly approaching makes our interview necessary." Bolívar wrote that the two of them would march together like "brothers." Nevertheless, each surprised the other in July 1822, when Bolívar appeared unexpectedly in Guayaquil and San Martín sailed up the coast aboard a schooner. Their situations were hardly equal. Bolívar had a large army that was ready to march farther southward; he had just been elected president of Colombia. San Martín was having trouble administering the affairs of Peru, and his army was in disarray. He had, of course, lost his entire navy.

On July 25, San Martín sailed into Guayaquil's harbor. Bolívar preempted any discussion of Guayaquil's fate by welcoming San Martín to Colombia. The next day, when San Martín went ashore for formal discussions, there was an awkward moment when a laurel wreath was offered by a young girl. Bolívar required such pomp, but it embarrassed San Martín. He took it off; then, not wishing to appear ungrateful, he uttered a brief speech.

Immediately the two men went off by themselves for an hour and a half, out of hearing, sometimes, out of sight, of their lieutenants. According to an observer, they "emerged, frowning gravely."

The next day, before they met again, San Martín ordered his luggage put back on board. They would sail as soon as he could get away from a ball scheduled for that night. Then the two men met alone again, this time for four hours. Afterward, they were again silent. Both went to the ball that night, but at one o'clock in the morning, after dourly observing the festivities, San Martín summoned his aide, grumbled, "I can't stand this tumult any longer," and left. Bolívar saw San Martín off at the dock.

What happened? Despite later letters from the two principals and the recorded impressions of witnesses, what exactly transpired is unknown. We know, of course, that Bolívar was ambitious; he had a great design for the continent; he was a lover, in every sense of the word, of the grand. San Martín, the evidence shows again and again, was meticulous, careful, self effacing. "In conversation," wrote a contemporary, "he goes at once to the strong points of the topic ... [there is] nothing showy or ingenious in his discourse." A biographer observes, "His retirement was the greatest victory that man can achieve, for it was a victory over himself. He also had in him something of a saint." Perhaps San Martín himself disclosed everything in his disappointment when he wrote to O'Higgins after the meeting at Guayaquil: "The Liberator is not what we thought."

Disgusted with Peru, San Martín called an assembly for September 20, resigned, and left. (Bolívar's army would finish off the Spanish at Junín and, without Bolívar, at Ayacucho.) San Martín left six sealed envelopes. "I have fulfilled my promises," he wrote. "The presence of a victorious soldier, no matter how detached, is fearsome to states in the process of formation." Of San Martín's departure, Juan Bautista Alberdi declared that "as a final addition to a chest covered with Medals of Honor ... we must add a medal for modesty."

Chile was his respite. He lived outside Santiago with O'Higgins' mother and sister until, although ill, he had to flee when O'Higgins was forced out of office. San Martín then found relative contentment in Mendoza — he hung his portrait between those of Napoleon and Wellington — but he could not go to Buenos Aires because he had been declared a "traitor." He was reviled by English friends of Cochrane, who described him as limited in imagination, intellect, and daring.

In the winter of 1823 San Martín was informed that his wife was ill at her parents' home in Buenos Aires, but he could not go. She died in August. When he was allowed to make arrangements for her burial, he took their young daughter — "Child of Mendoza" was his affectionate name for her — and sailed into exile in Europe.

He settled first in Brussels. His Peruvian pension was slow in coming, but he eked out a living on income from property. Both politics and penury—for San Martín was both a famous democrat and poor—condemned him to a fitful wandering, carefully watched by chiefs of police. Between 1824 and 1830, San Martín's passport was stamped with forty-seven visas; between 1831 and 1849, there were another ten. Returning briefly in 1826, however, he found Argentina, rent by its usual problems, a poor refuge. Back in Europe, his brother Justo joined him, and he managed to keep Mercedes in private schools in Brussels and Paris. Her schoolmates treated the old general like "a beloved father." Mercedes married Mariano Balcarce, a man who briefly served Argentina until he, too, was forced back to Europe, reuniting the only family San Martín had. Eventually, an old friend provided San Martín with an income to keep him, at long last, comfortable.

When he expressed himself, even writing from Europe, his views attracted opposition as honey attracts foul-tempered bees. Writing to a friend, Tomás Guido, he despaired, "Liberty! Give a child of two years a box of razors to play with and see what will happen. Liberty! So that all honest men shall see themselves attacked by a licentious press, without laws to protect them, or, if there are laws, they become illusory. Liberty! So that if I devote myself to any kind of work, a revolution shall come and ruin for me the work of many years and the hope of leaving a mouthful of bread to my children.... I prefer the voluntary ostracism that I have imposed on myself to the joys of that kind of 'liberty.'"

San Martín praised the strength of Manuel Rosas, which won him gratitude from the despot (and forgiveness from Sarmiento), but calumny from Rosas' many enemies. His countrymen were more gratified when San Martín criticized the British and French blockade of Buenos Aires in the late 1840s.

But the tangle of European and Latin American politics dogged San Martín's path. When Louis Philippe fell in 1848, San Martín and his family had to escape from Paris to the countryside. On August 17, 1850, he died at his daughter's home.

6

Bernardo O'Higgins
Chile's Irish Liberator
1778–1842
(Chile)

The dramatic role of Bernardo O'Higgins in the drama of Latin American history is no more remarkable than that of his father, Ambrose O'Higgins, "the English viceroy." The elder, in fact, was a model for the younger, despite the fact that they were estranged by the younger's illegitimate birth, separated by the elder's overweening ambition, and made enemies by the radical difference in their political philosophies. That last aspect, of course, is crucial; while the father was a lifelong royalist, the son was a zealous democrat. Their sequential careers overlap the end of Spanish domination of southern South America, a reign that Ambrose O'Higgins did his best to perpetuate and Bernardo O'Higgins did so much to end.

Ambrose O'Higgins' family, not a wealthy one, sent him, probably with a cousin who was a priest, to Spain as a young boy to earn his livelihood. Such emigration was not as unusual as it might seem, the bond between the Irish and the Spanish being woven from the dual strands of their Roman Catholic religion and their common antipathy toward the English.

O'Higgins ended up a bank clerk in Cádiz in 1751 and embarked for the Americas, following a brother, five years later. His commercial ventures failed in the tightly controlled economy of the Spanish colonies, so he became a draftsman, designing forts along Chile's southern frontier, where the Crown held the fierce Araucanian Indians at bay.

In the winter of 1763 O'Higgins had an experience that almost led to the attention he coveted. He had returned to Spain to press for a better posting, but was disappointed. Returning to Chile, he was crossing the Andes when he nearly froze — one of his bearers died — along the frigid, windswept passes. He conceived of a string of shelters for travelers. The royal administration eventually accepted the idea. While O'Higgins saw it through to completion, his career was little improved.

In 1769, however, when there was an Indian uprising, O'Higgins, then in Santiago, jumped at the opportunity to volunteer. At the age of forty nine, he was made a captain of dragoons, the beginning of his military career. He rose to commander-in-chief of frontier forces and, at sixty-six, was named governor of the southern province of Concepción.

During this time, O'Higgins met Isabel Riquelme, the daughter of wealthy Creole landowner who traced his family's background to the Moorish occupation of Spain. Such loving, and necessary, attention to heritage was what would later drive O'Higgins to claim the spurious title of "baron of Ballinary." Isabel was a teenager, perhaps as young as thirteen or fourteen, when they met. She had a lovely oval face, straight black hair, light skin, and blue eyes. O'Higgins was an officer of the Crown, some forty years older. The relationship, which lasted several years, led to the birth in Chillán of their son in 1778, on August 20, the day of the feast of St. Bernard.

There was no question of marriage. O'Higgins, attentive to his career as a representative of the Crown, could not marry a Creole. He moved on, and Isabel later married a wealthy neighbor. After Bernardo's half-sister, Rosita, was born, Isabel was widowed in 1782. Her later liaison with another neighbor, which led to the birth of another daughter, Nieves, who was raised by her father, apparently hastened O'Higgins in his search for a foster home for Bernardo. Bernardo, however, remained steadfast in his devotion to both parents.

Little Bernardo, with curly, chestnut hair, was growing up to be as stocky, round-faced, and plain as his father. His early schooling was with Araucanian children, but when he was four he was taken to the estate of his father's friend, Juan Albano. Not until 1788, when Bernardo was ten years old, did he next see his father, briefly, when Ambrose had been named governor-general of Chile. About seven years later, when the father was named viceroy, Bernardo was shipped off to school in London.

This period of O'Higgins' life, biographer Jay Kinsbruner describes as "exasperatingly void of familial love." His financial agents cheated him, and his guardian, Nicolás de la Cruz, a son-in-law of Albano who lived in Cádiz, had little interest in his charge. O'Higgins got no instruction in life from his distant father. The long distance relationship between father and son Bernardo was known by the surname "Riquelme" was a poignant one. The son, unstinting in his respect, wrote his father long, adulatory letters. His father ignored him.

"My dearest father and benefactor," he wrote in January 1799, "I pray Your Excellency will excuse my using this term so freely, for I do not rightly know whether I may address you thus or not; but if I must choose between the two expressions, I will follow the inclinations of nature (having no other guide), for had I different instructions I would obey them. Although I have written to Your Excellency on several occasions, fortune has never favored me with any reply." Bernardo was then twenty-one, without a clue as to what his prospects for a career might be. His father had provided "no other guide" than a disdainful silence, leaving the son unsure even how to address him.

One man to whom Bernardo could turn in England was the enigmatic Francisco Miranda. The fiery Venezuelan was unsuccessful in his own attempts to lead democratic insurrections in South America—he would die in a royal dungeon for his revolutionary efforts—but his rhetoric was impressive to countless emigrés like O'Higgins. "Always bear in mind the difference that exists between the character of the Spaniards and that of the Americans," Miranda counseled his young admirer as O'Higgins left to return to the New World. "The ignorance, pride, and fanaticism of the Spaniards are invincible.... Do not forget the Inquisition, nor its spies, its dungeons and its tortures."

Indeed, O'Higgins' imminent return to America was watched by spies. Along with others of Miranda's circle, he had been identified as an insurrectionist, an enemy of the king and, therefore, an enemy of his father.

In the spring of 1799, O'Higgins returned to his guardian's house in Cádiz, where he was not welcome, in order to sail for home — only to have his ship captured by an English squadron blocking the port. Back he went to his guardian's house. In despair, he was giving up on seeking any help from his silent father. "I will not trouble you further," he wrote, "May God prolong your precious life for many years!" It was too late. Ambrose O'Higgins, always despised by jealous Spaniards, had been deposed as viceroy. In forced retirement, he fell ill and died. On his deathbed, however, he finally acknowledged his only son.

Bernardo O'Higgins landed in Valparaiso in September 1802. He had not inherited a great deal. His father, a reformer, had simply not enriched himself and had distributed what little he had to nephews and protégés. Bernardo was still the illegitimate son, and he was unable to change that as far as the royal records were concerned. He was welcomed home by cousins and old friends, but he had to be satisfied at probate with an estate, Las Canteras, and 3,000 head of cattle. At Las Canteras he installed Rosita and his mother and ever after kept them close.

His mother would take charge of two Araucanian orphan girls O'Higgins adopted and, later, his own illegitimate son, born to a mistress after the Battle of Maipú. O'Higgins, like his father, never married but rather kept a series of mistresses. Also, like his father, he never paid much attention to his son.

Biographer Stephen Clissold asserts that the denial of his father's honors and titles—and the resulting bitterness O'Higgins felt—was a godsend for Chilean independence. "Would a marquis," Clissold asks, "have fought so passionately to establish a Republic?" O'Higgins himself would write: "If it had been my lot to be born in Great Britain or Ireland, I would have lived and died on my estates. But father wished that I should first see the light of day in Chile, and I cannot forget what I owe to my country."

O'Higgins worked his Chilean estate for six years and made it prosperous. Then, in February 1808, a cleavage opened in Chile's colonial politics, and in March Charles IV was forced to abdicate, raising the stakes. The question of independence had to be discussed in the context of support either for Charles' son Ferdinand, or Joseph, insinuated onto the throne by Napoleon. In Spain, there was civil war; in Chile, there was ferment. O'Higgins was among those who wanted to break with all royalty but figured their best strategy lay in supporting Ferdinand for the time being.

On September 18, 1810, a *cabildo abierto* replaced the colonial leader with an independence-minded junta, and economic independence, especially trade with Britain and the United States, followed. The rock slide toward democracy gathered the weight of an avalanche. Elected a representative from Los Angeles, O'Higgins wrote to Juan Mackenna, a fellow Irishman and friend of his father who had married into the prominent Larrain family, "I have enlisted under the colors of my country ... never shall I repent."

Throughout this period, O'Higgins, still unsure of his place in life, played a secondary role. The dominant force in Chile was José Miguel Carrera, descended from conquistadors and everything O'Higgins was not. Carrera was dashing in appearance, favoring the colors of the Galician Hussars, with whom he had proved himself in the European wars. Carrera was followed slavishly by his brothers, Juan José and Luis. The Carreras were ruthless in their desire to lead, and the story of Chile's independence is written in the conflict between an honorable Bernardo O'Higgins and the dastardly José Miguel Carrera.

Seeking a clear direction, O'Higgins wrote to the independence-minded Mackenna. "If you study the life of your father," Mackenna replied, "you will find in it military lessons which are the most useful and relevant to your present situation, and if you always keep his brilliant example before your eyes, you will never stray from the path of honor." Ambrose O'Higgins had learned late in life to be a soldier and leader; now it was his son's turn.

José Miguel Carrera had his own ideas about leadership. In late 1811, only six weeks after returning from Spain, his troops surrounded a meeting of the new congress, which Carrera disbanded and replaced with a junta. Six weeks later, to consolidate his power, Carrera threw out that junta and named a new three-man group that included Mackenna and himself. Then, when the third member was out of the capital, Carrera prevailed upon O'Higgins to fill in. O'Higgins, whose most notable public service up until then had been a proposal to ban burials beneath church floors (because they were unsanitary), was reluctant, but agreed. Subsequently, having placed O'Higgins in an awkward position, Carrera ordered Mackenna arrested.

O'Higgins saw he had been duped, but all he could bring himself to do was resign, leaving Carrera's power uncontested.

Sensing O'Higgins' uncertainty, Carrera convinced him his course was honorable and even persuaded him to intercede with the third junta member, who was, in effect, in exile in the southern city of Concepción. O'Higgins agreed. He made the trip, became a mediator, and sent back to Carrera a proposal for power sharing. Carrera's response, in March 1812, was to reject the overture, claim all power for himself, and march south at the head of an army.

At long last, O'Higgins recognized Carrera's all-consuming ambition. He offered to lead an army against Carrera, but held his fire while efforts were made to avoid civil war. Carrera and his opponents talked and talked, into the rainy autumn, the indecision effectively cementing Carrera's power. Finally, O'Higgins, disenchanted, retired from public life and returned to Las Canteras. The stalemate was only broken in March 1813, when the royalists returned in force to re-conquer the colony.

The challenge reunited patriots. O'Higgins offered to serve Carrera, and they were soon joined by Mackenna, who came from the prison into which Carrera had him thrown. This was the real beginning of O'Higgins' rise to prominence; his star rose because of his bravery even as Carrera's plummeted because of his incompetence.

The Spanish moved north from their southern strongholds. As allies, ironically, they could count both on the Araucanians and the strong garrisons along the frontier, perhaps a thousand men in all, who were there to contain the Indians. The Valdivia garrison, 1,500 strong, had declared itself at the side of patriots, but switched sides and became the core of the royalist army. Three more towns quickly fell, and the royalists, now with 3,000 troops, grew stronger.

O'Higgins, quixotically, gathered one hundred sharecroppers and set out toward Concepción to do battle. His men were armed, for the most part, only with lances and swords. When he got word that his band was not only tiny but too late, he sent them home and rode with a handful of companions for the Maule River to join the main body of patriots. At the Maule, about one-third of the way between Concepción and Santiago, the patriots would make their stand. José Miguel Carrera showed up, arrogating to himself the title of commander-in-chief.

"Command," however, would prove an elusive function among patriot forces. Carrera procrastinated, and O'Higgins and others feared that the patriot troops, without a sense of leadership, would go over to the royalists. So O'Higgins seized command of a squadron of horsemen and launched a sudden attack on the royalists' advanced detachment, stopping it long enough to recruit among local townsfolk.

Then, his band slightly enlarged, O'Higgins led them under cover of darkness to Linares, where royalists were encamped. As dawn broke, the patriots rode into the town's main plaza, making as much noise as possible to give the appearance of a major attack. They were rewarded with a slew of captives, who were taken to the patriots' camp at Talca, where they, too, were recruited. Although there had yet to be a major engagement, O'Higgins leadership was providing successes that heartened the patriots and forged the beginning of his reputation.

O'Higgins fell ill just as confusion, as it so often did, took the field. Carrera arrayed his forces along the Maule, and a patriot advance guard —command of which passed from O'Higgins, in his illness, to another — was sent to engage the enemy's advance units. Another surprise attack was supposed to emulate O'Higgins' success. This time, however, six hundred patriots, advancing at night, crept quietly and ineptly into the middle of the royalists' main encampment.

At first, the mistake had great effect. Flustered royalists fired at each other in the dark.

When a troop of royalist cavalry realized what was afoot, however, it charged, turning the tide, which washed back over the entire patriot army. The cavalry drove toward patriot lines, and from there cowardly patriot officers were the first to flee. Mackenna stepped forward, arguing that there was still a chance to rally, but Carrera, intent on flight, overruled him and ordered a general retreat.

Confusion had not completed its work yet, however. When the royalist commander ordered a drive toward Santiago in pursuit of the retreating patriots, it stalled. The core of the royalist army, recruited from the southern island of Chiloé, was still unsettled by the patriots' night attack and refused to advance beyond the Maule. Every step northward, they said, was farther from home. They simply quit. The dismayed royalist commander was forced to halt pursuit and, finally, to turn back south toward Chillán to winter his troops.

Carrera, however, proved so witless as to cause one more disaster. With his troops reinforced, he swung back with a final attack on the royalists' rearguard, the result of which was nought but more casualties on both sides. Out of this dreary, bloody exercise in war only O'Higgins seemed to be able to prevail. As Carrera organized a siege of the town, O'Higgins, recovered from his illness, once again demonstrated such daring that he inspired a wider belief — albeit false — that the patriots' cause might succeed.

O'Higgins, recovered, was sent to recruit his own workers at Las Canteras. O'Higgins raised thirty horsemen and surprised the nearby Los Angeles outpost, crashing in on the troops at their leisure. The post commander was caught in the middle of a game of cards with the local priest. Local residents, impressed with this act of daring, joined the impetuous O'Higgins, who found himself in command of 1,400 men.

No other use could be found for the new troops, however, than to join Carrera's rain-drenched siege of Chillán. O'Higgins and Mackenna argued for a frontal assault, and Carrera finally acceded, but the attack demonstrated little besides the folly of motivating fighting men with strong drink.

At night, O'Higgins stoked five hundred infantrymen with brandy and occupied a rise before the town, where they set up cannons. Mackenna and Carrera, meanwhile, plied four hundred foot soldiers with brandy and dramatically led them across the Nuble River on the right. On the other flank, a cavalry troop, presumably sober, advanced.

As the sun came up, royalists sallied out to quiet O'Higgins' battery, and the battle was joined. At first, the brandy seemed a good idea. Spirited patriots put the royalists to flight; O'Higgins was in the thick of fierce fighting as his troop not only defended its position but counter-attacked, invested the city, and pressed toward its center.

The royalists, however, regrouped on the other side of town and turned on the patriots — who were by this time more drunk than fierce and more interested in the spoils of war than war itself. The distracted patriots never quite occupied the center of town, and when cannon shot exploded their gunpowder store they fled before a royalist counter-attack. Only nightfall ended the carnage, in which two hundred patriots were killed and as many wounded. Carrera called off the assault.

The patriots lost more than the battle. People in the countryside, earlier encouraged by O'Higgins' victories, were disheartened. Carrera, more bandit than statesman, had allowed plunder and reprisals against royalist families, further sacrificing respect. O'Higgins was nearly captured in a guerrilla skirmish after the battle, and Las Canteras was pillaged, its crops destroyed root and vine, its cattle driven off. His mother and sister were taken hostage and had to be exchanged for a royalist officer's family. Patriot strength around Chillán was sapped.

In October, reinvigorated royalists launched a surprise attack that surged across the El

Roble River and nearly captured Carrera, who spurred his horse away just in time. O'Higgins, wounded in the leg, bandaged it himself with rags and stayed to fight. He ordered that he be carried back to the front line, where, lying on the ground, he resumed command despite the pain. The contrast between the two leaders was not lost on their troops. After the patriots had fought off the attack, stories of O'Higgins' bravery circulated all the way back to the junta.

Nevertheless, junta members were unwilling to sack Carrera and risk being deposed in return. Furthermore, O'Higgins and several other officers informed the junta and Carrera that their support still lay with the commanding general as long as the royalist threat continued. Mackenna, however, was of another mind. He persuaded the junta to make the switch, and although Carrera resisted and the officer corps revolted, in the end O'Higgins, despite his own protestations, took command. On February 2, 1814, O'Higgins arrived at Concepción to find that desertions over the preceding four months had reduced the ranks to 1,800 men; provisions were low; ammunition was almost gone; uniforms were in tatters. "I dare not call it an army," O'Higgins wrote to Casimiro Albano, his boyhood friend, "as I can see nothing, absolutely nothing, in its equipment or morale that justifies that name."

The viceroy agreed. Encouraged by reports that the royalists, surrounded at Chillán but popular with local residents, were spoiling for an all-out fight, the viceroy sent reinforcements. The troops were to land at the Gulf of Arauco just south of Concepción to drive out the patriots once and for all.

The junta's defense plan called for O'Higgins to pull his troops back northward, where he could link with Mackenna's command. O'Higgins, however, vacillated, wanting to strike one more blow at royalists in the south before their reinforcements landed. When Carrera concurred with O'Higgins' misguided plan, the junta ordered Carrera off to Argentina on a diplomatic mission — on which he, along with a brother, was captured by royalists, suggesting a plot. Mackenna's troops, meanwhile, sank deeper into trouble.

The junta had been chased out of Talca, and Santiago was threatened. Mackenna could not rush to the defense of Santiago because that would leave O'Higgins isolated in the south. Mackenna began sending frantic messages asking why O'Higgins was delayed. "You, my dear friend," Mackenna wrote, "are responsible to your country for your present inactivity.... For God's sake, come, and all will be well." Finally, O'Higgins awoke himself and struck out northward, his troops ragged in appearance but so reduced in number as to be the patriots' hardest core of fighting men.

Even as he marched north, O'Higgins allowed himself to be delayed by royalist attacks on his rear. "These delays will be the ruin of us," Mackenna, who had been wounded, wrote to O'Higgins in frustration before the patriots finally consolidated their forces. Not until then, with a total of 1,500 infantrymen, 18 cannon, and several hundred mounted militia, did Mackenna feel confident — and O'Higgins finally understand — that they could defend Santiago.

Both armies then undertook a forced march to be first to reach the capital, and the result was a kind of tie. On April 3, 1815, both armies reached the Maule River and crossed it. The patriots set up a perimeter at a plantation called Quechereguas, which convinced the royalists they could neither turn their backs on the patriots to assault the city nor root the patriots out of their position. Neither could patriots advance, so a stalemate ensued and negotiations began.

At first, time was on the side of the patriots. The royalist army began to shrink as soldiers deserted. O'Higgins, on the other hand, was able to recruit and even to threaten the royalists' winter base at Talca. Eventually, however, negotiations led to the "Treaty of Lircay," a document neither side took seriously and both were ready to abjure at the earliest opportunity. Moderates greeted the treaty as an advance, but zealots on both sides continued to badger each other. Royalist troops, headed for embarkation, denounced the agreement and refused to board the ships. When their commander sent for orders from the viceroy, O'Higgins grew suspicious. He sent envoys to find out what was happening, and when they came back without an answer, O'Higgins lost patience and prepared to attack.

The royalists then unveiled a demonic plan. They still held the two Carrera brothers. Both sides knew that their release would serve to consolidate patriot opposition to the treaty, leading to such disruption that the royalists would gain an advantage. The patriots, however, including Mackenna, had to insist that as a point of honor the Carreras be set free. The royalists, happily, did so.

When the Carreras showed up at patriot headquarters, O'Higgins, as trusting as ever, welcomed them, although his officer corps was not so receptive. Sensing the chill, the brothers left for Santiago, where political leaders were outraged that these snakes in the grass had been allowed back among them. Sure enough, in late July the Carreras seized those political leaders, including Mackenna, and established another dictatorship.

O'Higgins, with his troops in Talca, 150 miles south of the capital, was outmaneuvered. His response was to demonstrate a naivete of monumental proportions. He thought Carrera might be induced to step down voluntarily rather than lead the country into yet another civil war. When O'Higgins suggested as much in a letter, Carrera put him off. In September, O'Higgins sought to force Carrera's hand by leading a troop of cavalry to the capital, but he took only 150 men, leaving the rest to contain the royalists. Carrera repelled this small force with little more than the back of his hand, and O'Higgins, charging into more than he had reckoned on, nearly got himself captured. O'Higgins then began to organize a full-scale assault on Carrera only to be informed by a messenger from the viceroy that the Treaty of Lircay was unacceptable. In addition, the patriots were expected to surrender forthwith.

This time the external threat healed Chilean divisions only after so much wrangling that the strengthened royalists were unstoppable. The diabolical release of the Carreras had paid off handsomely for the viceroy's strategy. Carrera threw the viceroy's messenger into jail and prepared to attack O'Higgins' position. O'Higgins sought accommodation, at least long enough to repel the threat. Carrera contemptuously rejected the overture. O'Higgins tried again. Carrera again rejected. O'Higgins then rode to Santiago to press his case in person.

Finally successful, O'Higgins tried to rally support to throw back the royalists, by now 5,000 strong, including well-trained troops. The patriots could muster no more than 4,000 men, counting ill-trained militia.

The final straw was that O'Higgins, in order to reach an agreement, had yielded command of those troops to the inept Carrera. Then Carrera refused, despite O'Higgins' repeated invitations, to take charge by going to the front. "I will be at your side," O'Higgins wrote, "serving as adjutant or in command of some division or small detachment — or simply with gun in hand." Carrera, however, hung back, making no decisions.

On September 30, the royalists marched against a patriot line along the Cachapoal River south of Santiago. O'Higgins was on the left, toward the town of Rancagua, while on the center and right, were divisions commanded by José Miguel Carrera's two brothers. The royalists broke through the patriot line and turned along the river toward Rancagua. O'Higgins moved his troops to meet the threat, expecting the Carrera brothers to join him. They did not. Juan José retreated with his division, taking refuge in Rancagua. Luís fell back.

O'Higgins' aides counseled him to fall back, too, joining Luís and leaving the other Carrera to destruction. O'Higgins would not take their advice. "It is because the Carreras are my greatest enemies that I cannot abandon them now," O'Higgins said. "Honor is more than life." When O'Higgins rode into Rancagua, Juan José embraced him and gratefully relinquished command. The patriots barricaded themselves in the central plaza, and on October 1 the battle was joined.

Had O'Higgins, at that point, been aware of an important bit of information, the patriots' tactics would almost certainly have been different, and probably more successful. The royalist troops were needed back in Peru. Their commander got orders to either strike a victorious blow or, failing that, negotiate a truce so he could remove his men to another front. The Spanish commander was convinced he had the strength for a quick victory and so launched his attack. O'Higgins fought back fiercely when he might have done better to string out the action, figuring that mere survival would have constituted the victory.

The royalists came on in a frontal attack, even though the narrow streets of Rancagua channeled them into the patriots' hellish field of fire. Some of the royalists' best troops were cut down in what Clissold describes as "an hour's fighting more intense than anything hitherto seen in Chile."

Thrown back, the Spanish commander reconsidered, but his lieutenants urged him on again. The royalists brought up artillery and blasted their way to the central plaza, but there the patriots fought back with bayonets, again repelling the attack.

O'Higgins knew, however, that his casualties were numerous, ammunition was low, and water — cut off by the enemy — was almost gone. A message was sent asking the main patriot force for help. A message came back promising help, but it did not come. O'Higgins was informed, however, that Carrera had a paid assassin in the camp, and should O'Higgins be successful in defending Rancagua he was to be murdered.

By the time the final assault came, the patriots had built barricades using their own dead. There was brief hope when a sentry espied, in the distance, a relief column. The royalists, surprised, swung around to meet the threat from the rear, and it looked as if the patriots were about to pull out a stirring victory. Then hope crashed into despair. The arriving troops, as suddenly as they had appeared, turned and retreated.

No longer was there room for hope. A spark ignited the patriots' powder store, and the invaders penetrated to the defenders' central trenches. The resourceful Juan José Carrera had kept himself a fresh horse and made good his own escape, but O'Higgins fought on alongside his men — the five hundred remaining. To try to break out, they drove pack mules ahead as moving cover.

As O'Higgins finally drove his spurs into his horse to climb the barricade and escape, his horse fell back, throwing him to the ground. Getting to his feet, he saw an aide killed beside him. A mounted royalist charged at O'Higgins, but was killed himself, allowing O'Higgins to swing into the saddle and rejoin his men. As the patriots fled, madness enveloped Rancagua. The attackers, crazed by the bitter resistance, killed prisoners and children and raped women, some in the cathedral where they had hidden. The house used as a patriot hospital caught fire and burned down.

With his troops now reduced to only two hundred soldiers, O'Higgins made for Santiago. He angrily asked why the relief column had turned back. Responses were several: the relief troops were inexperienced militia, untrustworthy in battle; O'Higgins had missed his chance to escape during the confusion; it appeared to be too late, that the patriots had surrendered.

It was October 1814. Following his mother and sister, O'Higgins went into exile in Argentina. A stream of refugees flowed over the Andes, using the shelters built there by Ambrosio Higgins years before. In Mendoza, San Martín welcomed O'Higgins, but knew the

Carreras were not to be trusted. When it became apparent they intended to use what was left of their army to take control of Cuyo, San Martín ordered them arrested and banished to San Luís, where they were closely watched.

The Carreras' capacity for evil, however, was inexhaustible. Arriving in Buenos Aires, they encountered Mackenna, whom they had earlier tried unsuccessfully to goad into a duel. Now Luís succeeded, and Mackenna died from a bullet through the neck. The Carreras slithered into a conspiracy with Carlos María de Alvear, the bitter rival of San Martín.

O'Higgins settled into a modest life with his mother and sister in Buenos Aires, where he was initiated into the Lautaro Lodge, and the secret cell of revolutionaries. Both O'Higgins and José Miguel Carrera presented to San Martín plans for the reconquest of Chile. When Carrera's was rejected, he petulantly left for the United States to try to garner support there. O'Higgins' plan, which called for a joint attack by land and sea, was also deemed impracticable, but he was extended an invitation to join the Army of the Andes. He was named a brigadier general in a force by that time grown to 1,500 trained men and 4,000 militiamen. His assignment was to complete by October 1816 a main training camp, which he accomplished, and at that camp the army grew to 4,000 trained troops by the beginning of 1817.

When the march began, O'Higgins was given command of the thousand men of the Second Division. As the army wended its way toward the Andes, a letter caught up with him from Juan Martín de Pueyrredón, the Argentine supreme director. The message had two parts: good wishes for O'Higgins' swift ascent to supreme director of an independent Chile; and a warning that Carrera was on his way to Chile on board a U.S. warship.

The royalists planned to stop the patriots near the village of Chacabuco, where a steep, rocky redoubt split the route to Santiago, one road passing through the village, the other rounding to the west. O'Higgins' responsibility was to lead his division — increased to 1,500 men — into the teeth of the royalist defense, up over the ridge toward the village. Miguel de Soler, meanwhile, would make a flanking movement to the right, along the longer route, so the two columns could coordinate a pincer like attack.

O'Higgins' men faced not only a tough fight, but a difficult climb, during which they lost two cannon over a cliff. Near the top, O'Higgins took command of one column, assigning the other to Col. Ambrosio Cramer, a veteran of the European wars. They attacked just as San Martín galloped up to join them. Observing from the rear, San Martín had seen the difficulty into which O'Higgins was advancing and had sent a message to Soler to hurry, before O'Higgins' division was ground up.

O'Higgins' columns drove the royalists off the ridge, and as they retreated O'Higgins pressed to pursue them. San Martín consented, but only after stipulating that a general engagement not be risked until Soler was in position.

O'Higgins carried on, thinking the royalists had retreated all the way to the village. He led his men down a narrow trail, discovering too late that the enemy was not so far off as he'd thought and that his soldiers, vulnerable by being stretched out along the mountain path, were threatened. He had overextended himself and could advance only at great risk; retreat was worse.

In the heat of midday, O'Higgins had led his men to within three hundred yards of the enemy, which opened fire with artillery to devastating effect. Cramer's experience, however, told him that as problematical as their situation was, Soler's appearance, when it finally came, would so alter the balance that the royalists would be forced to retreat. He advised a bayonet attack, contrary to San Martín's orders not to engage the enemy without Soler's division in place.

O'Higgins hesitated, then followed Cramer's suggestion. In two columns, with cavalry arranged in the rear, the patriots charged. O'Higgins and Cramer led their infantry into the royalists' right wing, leaving the left to the cavalry. The royalists were forced back, but were nevertheless able to repel the cavalry attack because a protective gully channeled the horses back toward the center of the patriots' line. While the royalists regrouped, O'Higgins swiftly changed his plan, reversing the roles of cavalry and infantry, and charged again.

The attack was successful on both counts. No longer stopped by the gully, the cavalry kept up with the infantry charge. Together, they overran the royalist artillery, chasing the enemy toward the village. When Soler's division finally appeared, the royalists were being driven all the way to Colima.

The Battle of Chacabuco was won, although Soler was furious that O'Higgins, by pressing his attack, had deprived Soler of a share in the glory. O'Higgins cut off Soler's tantrum and looked in the confusion for San Martín. He asked for a thousand of Soler's men — who, after all, were spoiling for a fight — to cut the royalists off before they could reach the port at Valparaíso. San Martín, wary of royalist reserves, demurred. Instead, O'Higgins rode by San Martín's side at the head of the patriot army as it marched into Santiago.

In February 1817, O'Higgins accepted the supreme directorship when San Martín, graciously and astutely, declined. San Martín was thus able to turn to the task of rebuilding and refinancing his army in order to continue on to Lima. O'Higgins was left to try to manage an obstreperous new republic. He confiscated royal property, founded a newspaper, and asked "patriots" to declare themselves but ordered that "non-patriots" not be harassed. Reprisals, nevertheless, cut to the heart of the new republic, and resentment, notes historian J. C. J. Metford, "eventually crystallized into a deep-seated enmity towards O'Higgins. It was one of the causes of the internal upheavals which for so long disturbed the peace and retarded the progress of the new Chilean state."

O'Higgins' association with the Lautaro Lodge was a problem, suggesting that the new nation would be managed by a cabal. The usual question of whether to continue Church privileges arose, deepening the conflict with a Church that had been divided on the question of independence in the first place. Many Chileans longed for the relative stability of the viceroyalty, a point that O'Higgins addressed in an 1821 letter to José Gaspar Marín:

"If Chile is to be a Republic," he wrote, "as is required by our oaths and suggested by its natural endowments; if our sacrifices have not been insignificant; if the creators of the revolution truly meant to make this land free and happy; then this can only be achieved under a Republican Government that is not just some variation of distant dynasty, but exists precisely because we shunned those cold schemers who crave a monarchy. How hard it is, my friend, to break old habits!"

Political problems, however, were no worse than military ones. San Martín's failure to follow and destroy the defeated royalists was an unmitigated mistake. By the time O'Higgins could assign Juan Gregorio de Las Heras, the third of San Martín's division commanders, to pursue and wipe out the royalists they had fled to their traditional strongholds in the south near the Bay of Concepción. Las Heras failed, so O'Higgins chastised him and took command himself, but could do no better. The patriots found themselves once again bogged down in the unsympathetic south trying to root out royalists. Then it was learned from spies that the viceroy was sending three thousand reinforcements with the purpose of once again breaking out and marching north to re-conquer the country. It was the same song, second verse.

Just as he had once moved an army northward to meet Mackenna, O'Higgins now hurried his 2,200 troops toward San Martín's main force of 4,400. Once again, the royalists followed. When the royalists got as far north as the Maule River, their commander, fearful of overextending, decided to dig in. His lieutenants, however, accused him of cowardice and insisted that the advance continue. So the royalists pushed on — until they saw the strength of the combined patriot armies and recognized their miscalculation. They tried to turn around toward better positions along the Maule.

San Martín saw the opening and sent his army racing to cut them off from the river. Outflanked, the royalists then turned toward Talca, and San Martín countered with a cavalry charge to keep them from reaching the town. The rough terrain and the royalists' spirited response, however, were too much for the horsemen, despite superior numbers. San Martín, still anxious to deny the royalists the town, next sent O'Higgins into the breach.

O'Higgins ordered an artillery barrage and then followed with an infantry charge, but once again the royalists' fierce reply turned the patriots back. As night fell, both sides contemplated their next moves.

The royalists' plan was dictated by desperation, and it prevailed. All of their leadership now conceded they had come too far. They were too weak either to hold Talca or to retreat in safety. While the commander continued to wring his hands, however, his lieutenants organized a desperate charge in the night into O'Higgins' command.

O'Higgins was caught flatfooted, his artillery still limbered, his cavalry unready, his division completely flustered. Although the royalists, hurried into action, suffered from some confusion of their own, greater was the panic of the patriots. O'Higgins did gather his wits and enough men to defend his position for a time, but a bullet broke his right arm. Bleeding and in pain, he was carried to the Lircay River to San Martín's retreating headquarters.

Losses on both sides were about equal in terms of soldiers, but the patriots had lost stores, equipment, and animals. They were thoroughly demoralized. An inferior force had routed them, and some patriot officers had behaved abominably, running for their lives.

The patriot command, falling back to Quecheraguas, learned that Las Heras' division was unscathed; the patriot army was still four thousand strong. San Martín, predictably, counseled a slow, solid effort at rebuilding. The fiery O'Higgins argued for making a stand at Quecheraguas. The physician attending O'Higgins' badly damaged arm, made worse by the rigors of retreat, recalled later that he reminded O'Higgins that the patriots could again escape to Argentina. "One case of exile is enough," was O'Higgins' reply. "As long as I remain alive and have a single Chilean to follow me I shall go on fighting against the enemy in Chile."

In Santiago, few Chileans were enthusiastic about following. Rumors had San Martín dead of a battlefield suicide and O'Higgins hopelessly wounded. Some patriots packed and began trudging into exile. A public statement from San Martín was of some help in restoring order, but supporters of the Carrera brothers were rapidly making the situation impossible. Luis Carrera insinuated himself into a position of leadership, causing frightened O'Higgins partisans to send a frantic message requesting that he return to the capital. He did so, and displaying his bandaged arm for emphasis he told an assembly, "I am not asking for money.... I only ask you to be whole-heartedly with us."

While San Martín returned to the front, O'Higgins supervised the construction of fortifications and hastened troops from Argentina and Valparaíso into town. When it appeared the royalists might skirt San Martín's forces and take the city, O'Higgins was advised to find safety at San Martín's headquarters. "No, I'll stay," he said. "If the enemy attacks, I will die at my post."

O'Higgins' efforts were toward the definitive Battle of Maipú on April 5. By the time he, himself rode out into the field with a thousand mounted militia, the battle was winding down. Fifteen hundred royalists and eight hundred patriots died in the battle. The patriots held more than 2,000 prisoners and had suffered a thousand wounded. Chile had won its independence.

Now O'Higgins had to secure independence from the depredations of the Carreras.

Pueyrredón, in Buenos Aires, was initially swayed by the Carreras' unctuous words and wrote to O'Higgins suggesting that the Chilean government pay them a pension. O'Higgins replied that Pueyrredón had "been taken in by the cunning and double-dealing of men who ought to be branded as outlaws." Pueyrredón soon learned for himself. When the Carreras tried their old tricks with him, Pueyrredón chased them into exile in Montevideo.

There, Juan José and Luís plotted to return to Chile, abduct San Martín and O'Higgins, and impose yet another dictatorship with José Miguel at its head. The two were no more adept at conspiracy than they were at warfare. They were arrested, in disguise, before reaching the Chilean border. "They have always been the same," declared O'Higgins, "and only death will change them."

They were not put to death, however, but languished in prison. The imprisonment had decidedly different effects on the two siblings. Juan José was repentant and wanted only to be allowed to return home. Luis, contrarily, decided not only to escape from jail but to shoot the governor and organize a guerrilla band. News of these audacious plans leaked to citizens of Mendoza at a time when royalists appeared to be in the ascendant, just before the Battle of Maipú. Panicked, they were in a mood to deal severely with the brothers.

In Mendoza at precisely that time was one of the few men whose hatefulness was a match for the Carreras: San Martín's trusted administrator, Bernardo Monteagudo, who would later be exiled, then stabbed to death by outraged Peruvians. Monteagudo persuaded the town council of Mendoza to execute the Carrera brothers, a punishment much more severe than the normal exile. Just four hours before a messenger rode in from San Martín and O'Higgins, the victors at Maipú, ordering that the brothers be spared, they were executed by firing squad.

News of the executions surely deepened the historic divisions of Chilean politics, but it was a drop in an already turbulent ocean of distrust. O'Higgins was adrift in that turmoil, blown from crisis to crisis.

O'Higgins was seen as having pardoned the Carreras only when he knew it was too late. An attempt was made on his life, getting as far as the courtyard of his mansion before its leaders were taken into custody. He was blamed for the murder of a Carrera supporter who was killed on his way into exile. Even the execution of José Miguel Carrera, captured, condemned as a common bandit, and shot in the same courtyard where his brothers died, did nothing to bring balance to Chilean politics.

O'Higgins was left surrounded by enemies. San Martín's labors to equip and build an army were crowned with the conquest of Lima; O'Higgins' reward was animosity. After Argentina reneged on its promises of support, it was O'Higgins who initiated the eminently successful naval fleet and who rebuilt the army to 7,500 troops; San Martín rode into Lima; O'Higgins was saddled with debt.

"Things have gotten to such a pitch that I even have the humiliation of having to find someone to lend me 500 pesos every month for my own needs," O'Higgins wrote to San Martín. A contemporary described O'Higgins' government as "hated by the entire population."

Improvements to the city required taxes. Church reform — although O'Higgins refused to try to confiscate church property — angered the faithful. Although he believed in the democracy envisioned by Miranda, O'Higgins manipulated politics as had the viceroys before him. Although he saw through the sycophants and scoundrels who surrounded San Martín, he was blind to those who closed in around him.

In his private affairs he was abstemious and plain. Another contemporary, describing his home outside Santiago, wrote that O'Higgins, "when here, sleeps on a little portable camp bed, and to judge by his room, is not very studious of personal accommodation."

In October 1822, two years after sailing off in high hopes of triumph, San Martín returned to Chile a broken man, deathly ill with typhoid and the target of harsh criticism. O'Higgins took in and protected his old friend and mentor, helping him recuperate before he departed for Mendoza and exile. Then O'Higgins was alone.

In early 1823, O'Higgins, in full uniform, strode into a rowdy congregation of dissident politicians clambering for his resignation. Civil war, again, loomed. Upon his resignation, the crowd outside shouted, "*Viva,* O'Higgins. We hold nothing against you," but even after he had stepped down he was feared lest his supporters revolt. Only outside Chile would he and his family be safe, so he took them to Peru, settling into a modest house outside Lima.

He was granted a staff position in Bolívar's army and caught up with the army in July 1824, arriving, according to an old English friend, "the same honest, kind-hearted, straightforward, unsuspecting character we always found him to be." O'Higgins saw no combat, but joined Bolívar back in Lima, where he attended the grand fete celebrating the Battle of Ayacucho. "In contrast to the be-medaled Colombian, Argentine and Peruvian generals," Clissold writes, "O'Higgins appeared in plain civilian dress."

For nearly two more decades, until he died quietly on October 23, 1842, O'Higgins observed the tortured politics of both Peru and Chile, which included an abortive war between the two. Memories haunted him, and he once had to disavow any intention of returning home. Chilean biographer Miguel Luis Amunátegui Reyes concludes. "In spite of everything, the Government of the Supreme Director was one of neither tyranny nor oppression, but an epoch of fertile labor, in which patriots first tasted the blessed fruits of liberty."

7

Domingo Faustino Sarmiento
Educator of a Continent
1811–1888
(Argentina)

Faustino Valentín Sarmiento Albarracín was born on February 15, 1811, within a year of Argentina's declaration of independence from Spain. This correlation between his birth and that of his nation was the beginning of a long association, parallel paths over which Sarmiento would insist, again and again, that he be allowed to play a role in shaping Argentina. The young nation would prove a boisterous schoolyard on which to impose Sarmiento's standards of civility, but he never stopped trying.

That Sarmiento, while still a boy, took as his own the name of the family saint, Domingo, was a bit of independence typical of him bred into him by his surroundings. He was born in San Juan, capital of the western frontier province of the same name, where the Tulum Valley separates the rich pampas from the towering Andes along Argentina's border with Chile. The town of San Juan — then inhabited by 3,000 people, mostly in adobe houses was founded in the mid-fifteenth century, a tiny outpost on the thinly populated periphery of a captaincy that was all but ignored by the Spanish Crown.

Sarmiento's biographers have stressed his mother's civilizing influence on him — so touchingly and thoroughly documented by Sarmiento himself — because his father was a rakehell. This is a bit unfair, because José Clemente Sarmiento had intriguing, if untamed, qualities. Although he was a financial failure — while his wife was a paragon of industry and organization — he was at his son's side at important times. Sarmiento himself, aware of the low opinion others held of his father, took pains to give him credit. Sarmiento's life, in fact, is a mirror not just of those virtues his mother embodied, but also of the unpredictability that his father manifested.

Both of Sarmiento's parents were reared in families that were prominent in the settlement of Argentina and Chile, although both had been left penniless. Paula Albarracín's grandfather was mayor of San Juan and her father a landowner. Her father's death when she was twenty-three, however, and her brothers' inability to make the land productive, forced the sale of the family holdings. The wealth to which young Paula had been accustomed simply disappeared. Undaunted — the story goes — she and a slave laid the foundation for what would be her house. Then she set up her loom beneath a nearby fig tree and made fabric to sell to pay the builders. Only after her house was complete was she willing to marry José Clemente Sarmiento Funes, a man who had reacted to his impoverishment by ignoring it. "It was a family," notes biographer Allison Bunkley, "not of normal, average people, but of eccentricity." The couple had fifteen children, nine of whom died. Sarmiento's only brother died at the age of eleven. Growing into adulthood were Sarmiento and five sisters. As a toddler, because his mother supported the family with her weaving, little Faustino was literally tied to her apron strings lest he wander off.

Her weaving and dyeing provided what little income the family had. José Clemente, mostly working as a laborer on nearby farms, had no luck that could be measured in money. He did have, however, certain flair, and Argentina's tumultuous times provided a wide stage. In 1812, when his son was still an infant, José Clemente made a modest name for himself by taking up a collection to relieve the plight of General Manuel Belgrano, whose revolutionary army was bogged down at Tucumán. José Clemente braved the scorn of royalists to raise funds, and as a result he was entrusted five years later by José de San Martín with bringing Spanish prisoners back to San Juan after the Battle of Chacabuco. Sarmiento's guarded comment "My father is a good man who has nothing more notable in his life than having given some service in a subordinate capacity in the wars of independence"—was condescending, but it revealed, at the very least, the son's recognition of his father's having lived up to a standard.

Sarmiento, meanwhile, was partly reared by uncles. In 1814, a forty-year-old uncle—a priest, later a bishop—took Sarmiento into his home, making him a kind of tiny acolyte and giving him his early education. This kind of education, seen at first as a bridge to formal schooling, would grow in importance when the formal schooling failed to materialize. Sarmiento's one stint in a regular school began two years later, when he entered, at about six years old, San Juan's first school, *Escuela de la Patria*.

Political struggles around Sarmiento would have more influence than education. In 1820 the province saw five governors take power. In 1821 Sarmiento's father took him to a more tranquil environment, the seminary at Córdoba, 250 miles away. Enrollment, however, was prevented by what Sarmiento later described as "sicknesses," without hinting that perhaps the normal sickness for a ten-year-old was plain old homesickness. Sarmiento returned to San Juan.

For the next several years, Sarmiento's father tried every trick he could think of to win his son a scholarship, "in order that he may, if possible," José Clemente wrote to the government in Buenos Aires, "be of service to America, and since my resources are on the threshold of beggary." It was to no avail.

The next step of Sarmiento's education was shaped by politics. Another of Sarmiento's uncles, José de Oro—a dynamic priest who served at the Battle of Chacabuco and held various political posts—was a vocal defender of the Church against anticlerical unitarists. In 1826, in the shifting sands of San Juan politics, Oro was exiled and took his nephew—fifteen years old and working for a civil engineer—with him.

Oro took up residence for a year in a cabin in San Luís province. An erudite man, he insisted that Sarmiento keep a journal recording their daily "dialogue between a citizen and a peasant." Sarmiento studied Latin and the Bible. Beginning the pattern of a lifetime, he founded a small "school," teaching fundamentals to rustic youths, including some older than himself. Again, however, his father reentered his life, appearing to inform Sarmiento that he had finally obtained placement at a school in Buenos Aires. Sarmiento resisted. He was growing into manhood and learning enough to teach. Why return? His father prevailed, but before they could get back to San Juan yet another revolt upset the political picture, erasing the school.

Sarmiento went to work in an aunt's store, continuing his self education. He kept records, ordered inventory, and was entrusted with buying trips, at the same time finding time to read at the counter when there were no customers. He delved into *The Autobiography of Benjamin*

Franklin, who had died about twenty years before Sarmiento was born. He read the classics and he was, almost, able to ignore the politics of San Juan.

A large region, including San Juan province, was then under the heel of Juan "Facundo" Quiroga, "the tiger of the llanos," whose name Sarmiento would make synonymous with Argentine barbarity. Sarmiento saw in Argentina's frontier crudeness an evil so profound as to affect every aspect of national life. It was a society, he believed, in which women were taught to provide the necessities while men were taught nothing except violence, handling horses, and throwing the three-pronged *bolo.* Children were little above animals. In the study titled *Facundo,* Sarmiento would write of Argentine boys: "When puberty approaches, they dedicate themselves to taming wild horses, and death is a minor punishment that awaits them if in one moment they lack strength or courage. In this youth first concerns are independence and idleness. Thus begins the public life of the *gaucho,* since his education is already over."

Given this disdain for the frontier, it was predictable that Sarmiento would have trouble with the frontier government. When the provincial militia impressed him into service, making him a sub-lieutenant in June 1828, Sarmiento sent a petition to the governor, explaining that he could not carry out his assignment because of responsibilities at his aunt's store. Therefore, he wrote, he was resigning his commission. He was promptly hauled, in uniform, before the governor.

Sarmiento later recalled the scene in romantic terms that not even his most enthusiastic biographers believe. The governor was seated on the patio and neither rose nor removed his hat. This offended Sarmiento, who at first refused to remove his own hat. The governor brought him up short with an angry admonition, however, and Sarmiento belatedly doffed his hat.

In the safety of his memoirs, Sarmiento described his and the governor's eyes meeting and flashing, as each tried to stare the other down. As Sarmiento remembered the scene, he won. The official resolution was that Sarmiento was clapped in jail. His family and friends told him he'd been foolish, but he figured he was being persecuted by Philistines. "This was my vision on the Road to Damascus," he wrote later, "of liberty, of civilization. All the ills of my country suddenly revealed themselves: barbarians!"

Un-chastened, Sarmiento came to trial. The court was surprised to hear him swear that others, too, were critical of the government. This raised proceedings to a more dangerous level, but when he refused to give the names of other dissenters, he was dismissed by a court that obviously did not consider the impetuous sub-lieutenant a threat. Sarmiento remembered it this way: "At the age of sixteen [he was seventeen], I entered jail; I came out with political opinions.... It was not difficult to choose among the parties.... Nourished on the books I had read, pre-occupied by the fate of liberty which the history of Rome and Greece had taught me to live, without understanding how to realize this beautiful idea, I threw myself into the partisan struggle with enthusiasm and self-denial."

He became a unitarist in a family of federalists, a family that would more than once bail him out of political trouble. In 1828, Juan Manuel de Rosas—"the Caligula of the River Plate"— consolidated power for the federalists. Only General José María Paz held out with a unitarist army in Córdoba, between San Juan and Buenos Aires. Although Rosas was unconcerned about Paz' stronghold, it constituted a threat to the *gaucho* leader Juan "Facundo" Quiroga. Quiroga held sway in the outlying provinces and wanted a clear road to Buenos Aires. So he led his *gaucho* army toward Córdoba, and riding as one of his officers was Sarmiento's father.

Sarmiento himself left his store counter to join Paz and was commissioned as a lieutenant. The bookworm had become a warrior, and in June 1829, at the Battle of Niquivil,

Sarmiento distinguished himself in battle. He carried the commander's orders through enemy fire to an officer who then accomplished a maneuver that won the day. Meanwhile, Paz' main federalist force defeated Quiroga in a major battle. These battles left the unitarists, however briefly, in a commanding position, while Sarmiento's father returned toward San Juan, part of a defeated army.

Sarmiento was then sent with a squad to destroy a federalist depot. He returned to discover that in his absence his comrades had been put to flight. He had no choice but to take flight himself across the countryside — where he ran into his father on the trail. His father, demonstrating a paternal concern that is also a commentary on Argentine politics, switched sides in order to be with his son. Then the two men, along with a few soldiers from Sarmiento's squad, rode off across the barren land, warriors in search of a war.

If the scene seems to have been written by Cervantes, there is more. The hapless group soon encountered on the trail Francisco Laprida, a respected statesman who had presided over the Congress of Tucumán. As the small group picked up information about more garrison revolts, more side switching, Sarmiento was impressed, as he later wrote, that "even a distinguished leader such as [Laprida] felt disoriented and confused by the chaos into which national life had degenerated."

Finally alighting in Mendoza, Sarmiento was given a staff job with General José Rudecindo Alvarado. His father accepted a unitarist commission, and the two comrades in arms awaited the siege that federalists were preparing. When the siege began, however, Sarmiento found it boring and endeavored to make his own action. He would sneak off to join skirmishers at the city's edge, and once was cut off on Mendoza's unfamiliar streets, requiring the help of his father to get back. A few days later, missing from his post again, Sarmiento was discovered by superiors and ordered to turn in his rifle. He was convinced his father had reported him in order to keep him out of trouble.

The siege ended with a rush, and Alvarado surrendered, but his troops would not, trying to fight their way out of the city. Sarmiento joined a detachment of San Juan soldiers, which, pausing at a waterhole, found themselves surrounded. There was an uneasy standoff until, as usual, confusion took over. The result was more brawl than battle because so many of the soldiers from both sides knew each other. "Over there were two Rosas brothers," Sarmiento would recall, "from the opposing parties, fighting over a horse; further on I joined Joaquín Villanueva, who was later lanced; I met his brother, José María, who had his throat cut three days later." One federalist who threatened Sarmiento before wheeling and fleeing had been a servant to friends of Sarmiento's family, a boy he'd once caned and who now saw his chance for revenge. Finally, Sarmiento was captured.

Other captured unitarists were being executed by firing squads, and Sarmiento awaited his turn. When the time came, however, a federalist officer spoke up for him, delaying the execution until Sarmiento's federalist relatives arrived and took him home with the simple agreement that he would not return to the war. Meanwhile, his father, following the federalist army in search of his son, was also captured and condemned to a firing squad. The story in his instance was that his sangfroid so impressed the enemy commander — legend has it José Clemente ordered dinner and wine while awaiting the firing squad that he, too, was sent home.

Between October 1829 and March 1830, Sarmiento was under a family imposed house arrest. He studied French, translating twelve volumes of the *Memoirs of Josephine,* but it became clear that old animosities in war-embittered San Juan would not allow such a peaceful respite. Fearing reprisals, Sarmiento fled briefly to Chile, but returned to become a lieutenant in the militia after San Juan unitarists again took the province. Then given a command in the regular army, Sarmiento found the stricter discipline satisfying and rose rapidly to the rank of captain.

"Discipline," of course, Sarmiento wanted to define for himself. Considering certain duties boring or beneath him, Sarmiento would sometimes simply wander off. Thus it happened that one day, when he was one of two officers in charge, he was absent at the time sixty federalist prisoners attempted to escape from a San Juan guardhouse. Sarmiento was blamed for the bloody retaliation by the small squad that stopped the escapees. Sarmiento's defense was that when he heard of the revolt, he hid, unsure of how serious the threat was. He did not emerge from hiding, Sarmiento said, until his executive officer assured him the "revolt" had been quelled. Sarmiento argued his failure was one of being too casual. Others called the offense cowardice.

The war, meanwhile, took a turn for the worse. Preparing to help in the defense of San Juan, Sarmiento saw the provincial government fall from within. Off he went, barely twenty years old, into exile in Chile once again. Juan Facundo Quiroga entered San Juan at the head of his troops and summoned Sarmiento's mother to his desk. He told her that if her son were caught he would be shot.

To support himself and his father, he turned to teaching, which served him well on the frontier. Observing the lack of education in this backwoods, Sarmiento began to tie the need for better schooling to his notions about politics. He was appalled at the rigid, ineffective formality of the pedagogy of the day. Rather than using the boring letter-by-letter approach, Sarmiento began employing a method of teaching syllables developed by English educator Joseph Lancaster, of whom Sarmiento had read. Lancaster taught poor boys in the London borough of Southwark, and Sarmiento found himself in a similar position. Like Lancaster, Sarmiento came to be criticized by the elitist old guard for this heresy.

Sarmiento saw all of Latin America as stifled by cumbersome thinking. Change had to be encouraged in an atmosphere of discipline; new methods were necessary. He would suggest in *Facundo,* in fact, that the entire foundation of civil order is laid in primary school, a notion gleaned from his reading of Locke, Franklin, and Rousseau, all of whom devised educational strategies that were interwoven with their political philosophies. When Sarmiento was asked later in his life if he could distinguish among his many works which was most important, he answered without hesitation: his basic reader.

Still unable to return to Argentina, Sarmiento and his father pushed on to another rural town, where there was no school at all. Sarmiento set one up, and, using money sent by his family, also established an alehouse. At this point one of Sarmiento's periodic romances led, in July 1832, to the birth of his first child. A girl, named Emilia Faustina, was taken to San Juan to be reared by Sarmiento's mother.

Sarmiento, his alehouse a failure and his family urging him to stay out of trouble, wandered on. "His amorous adventures were becoming more complicated and increasingly serious in their results," notes biographer Bunkley. He ended up at the sea, in Valparaíso, where he found work as a clerk and spent half his salary for English lessons. Chile was then awash with Argentine refugees, and Sarmiento followed his army buddies to a silver mine recently bought by his commander at the Battle of Niquivil. Sarmiento took to the miner's life with a flourish, adopting the distinctive dress and behavior, gambling and drinking with sufficient gusto to keep his wallet thin. Invited into polite society, he would show up looking like a lowly miner, and then amaze unsuspecting guests with his erudition. For nearly three years he enjoyed his role, as he put it, as "the miner they always saw reading."

Over the years, Argentine politics, although still in turmoil, calmed a bit. Rosas remained in power, although Quiroga had been murdered, easing the danger for Sarmiento to some degree. Quiroga was succeeded in San Juan by General Nazario Benavídez, who would become no less an adversary for Sarmiento but in 1835 yielded to Sarmiento's family in its request that their prodigal son, gravely ill with typhoid, be allowed to return. Benavidez, incorrectly as it turned out, saw no threat from a man, even a unitarist, at the point of death.

At home, however, Sarmiento's health and fortunes improved. Although penniless, he was well connected. Although a unitarist, his federalist family continued to protect him. For a while, he taught drawing and began practicing law, demonstrating real talent for neither. Finally, again with family help, he stepped onto safer vocational ground. In March 1839, Sarmiento founded a school for girls. He used capital invested by an uncle, Father Justo de Santa María de Oro, soon to be a bishop, and by the widow of the deceased bishop.

As headmaster, Sarmiento occupied a certain position in the town, and in the less oppressive atmosphere of the Benavídez government Sarmiento and his friends formed a salon. The governor saw no harm in literary discussions, occasionally appointed the headmaster to minor government posts, and even perceived no danger when Sarmiento, ever restless, proposed a weekly newspaper —completely apolitical, of course.

Sarmiento chose the name *El Zonda* and published the first issue in July 1839; his stated purpose was to publish for ten years. The paper lasted six weeks. Its comments on culture and morality were not the problem; its downfall was Sarmiento's biting satire. He wrote of the paper's having been attacked by "a little Cuzcan bitch [that] jumped out at it, seized it by the calf of the leg, shook it at will and sank its teeth into its flesh." The bitch was an unveiled reference to the wife of the governor, the man who had allowed Sarmiento to return from exile, who had supported his school, and who had allowed him to establish a newspaper.

Summoned to the governor's chambers, Sarmiento was told he owed a tax on his newspaper, and, when he refused to pay, saw the paper banned. He disconsolately completed his school's first year, during which he was for the second time refused when he proposed marriage to a pupil. To add to his problems, by late 1840 the civil war had begun to heat up again, and, after a successful unitarist uprising in a neighboring province, a nervous Governor Benavídez began rounding up unitarists. Other members of Sarmiento's salon took the hint and left San Juan province. Sarmiento refused to leave, was arrested, released, arrested again, and, finally, imprisoned. He was nearly lynched.

While Sarmiento was being held, federalist soldiers from a nearby encampment came into town one night on leave. As the liquor flowed, the soldiers thought a lynching might be amusing and gathered, along with a crowd, at the building where Sarmiento was held. They shouted for him to be brought out. When he refused to leave his room, the guard dragged out another prisoner, but the soldiers knew whom they wanted. Sarmiento was forcibly brought out to face an angry crowd, some of whom wore swords, some bayonets. Sarmiento was smacked with the flat sides of swords and prodded, and an officer ordered marksmen to report to the square to form a firing squad.

Sarmiento talked fast to buy time. Ducking under a porch, he scrambled to the other side to momentarily escape, but was recaptured. Eventually, his mother, informed of the ruckus, ran to the home of the governor and persuaded him to intervene. The next day, Sarmiento, accompanied by his father and a group of unitarists, was again on the road to exile.

Sarmiento would spend the next five years in Chile, essentially held at bay by Argentine federalists. During that five years, Sarmiento cemented his reputation as part of Argentina's "Generation of 1837," exiled unitarist intellectuals who attacked Rosas with their pens. Sarmiento's ardor would not subside, his style would not soften, and his predilection for trouble would never disappear. Argentine historian Antonio de la Torre describes Sarmiento as "a multiple personality ... of diverse spiritual tendencies, at times in conflict with each other."

Sarmiento reached Chile in November 1840. Although his father was allowed to return home, Sarmiento settled in Santiago. He was now thirty years old, but age had not improved his looks. A friend described him as having "a high forehead, slightly bald, his cheeks fleshy, loose and shaven." His heavy body was beginning to bend a bit, giving him more of a bull-like appearance than ever.

His first major essay, on the Battle of Chacabuco, was published in *El Mercurio* in early 1841 and immediately established his ability. Sarmiento defended San Martín as deserving equal consideration with Bolívar as a giant of the wars of independence. He used the article as a framework for his battle with Rosas, whom he labeled "a despot sworn to exterminate all the soldiers of the War of Independence." The essay brought Sarmiento attention, although it is unlikely that it was, as he immodestly recalled later, "irreproachable in style, pure in language, brilliant in its imagery, nourished with sane ideas, embellished by the soft varnish of sentiment."

Doors opened in the young — Santiago's population, it was then sixty thousand — politically volatile republic. Sarmiento was welcomed by Chile's conservatives, who controlled the presidency during the nation's early years. Most important to Sarmiento was his association with Manuel Montt. The two shared an interest in education, and like schoolmasters with a nation full of unruly pupils, the two men delighted in planning classes for the future.

El Mercurio editorials became Sarmiento's main forum, although other newspapers served as platforms for his ideas and invective. He founded a newspaper for strictly Argentine news, but closed it in despair when Rosas delivered a crushing blow to unitarists in early 1843. Sarmiento later described his Chilean sojourn: "Five years of work in the daily press of Chile, five newspapers, six hundred editorial articles, various university papers and works for the instruction of the people, and several books, ephemeral but full of the true love of liberty and civilization, must have left ... an awareness of the solidity of my convictions."

One of Sarmiento's pet causes was in the prickly area of Spanish grammar and usage. Sarmiento, despite his Romantic leaning, favored a modern, American Spanish, unfettered by "classical" terms, open to invention. It was a manifestation of his distrust of most things European. Not all of Sarmiento's arguments were so lofty, however. In late 1842 a personal remark directed toward a notorious nun of the day got him into a legal suit, charges and countercharges in newspapers, and, ultimately, an atmosphere of rancor.

Such was Sarmiento's style that even compliments carried a poison tip. He set the tone for generations of Argentine thinkers by viewing the United States as a place with bulging pockets and no culture: "The people of North America have no literature," wrote Sarmiento in June 1842, two decades before being introduced to Emerson and Longfellow, "but in the absence of literature, they have liberty, wealth, the most complete civilization, inventions, steamships, factories, shipping and sixteen million men who know how to read and understand what they read."

Literacy was the key. Montt, as minister of education, called on Sarmiento to write the decree for creation of Chile's first normal school, the first in Latin America. Sarmiento also planned its curriculum and taught, with one assistant, its courses.

In May 1845, the first installment of his study, *El Facundo,* or "Civilization and Barbarity" appeared in the Chilean press. This was the book that would crystallize Sarmiento's thought, posing Argentina's notorious *gaucho* as the symbol of all that was wrong with a continent. A second newspaper picked up the serialization, and, in July, *Facundo* was published in book form.

The book was written in haste and contains numerous historical and factual errors, but it was received as a torch against the darkness that threatened all of Latin America's brand-new republics. The *gaucho,* the man on horseback, was the focus. Personalist politics, the "gauchocracy," Sarmiento declared, was the enslavement of sensibility. "The constant insecurity of life outside the towns, it seems to me, stamps upon the Argentine character a certain stoic resignation to death by violence," he wrote. The book expressed Sarmiento's strong, if simplistic, belief in a Manichean duality: good and evil, knowledge and ignorance, violence and justice, "the two different phases that struggle in the breast of [Argentine] society."

The book was anathema to many, especially Argentines, but a source of fascination for others who were hungry for information about this strange continent. The French critic Charles de Mazade would call it "new and full of attraction, instructive as history, interesting as a novel, brilliant with images and color."

Sarmiento's reputation grew, as did his propensity for trouble. After several inconclusive love affairs, he was keeping company with a twenty two year old beauty, Benita Martínez Pastoriza de Castro. A native of San Juan, she was married to a very rich, very old, very sick man. In 1844, she became pregnant. A boy, Domingo Fidel, was born in April 1845 — just as *Facundo* appeared — and Montt concluded that it was time for Sarmiento go take a trip abroad.

Sarmiento was commissioned by the Chilean government to undertake a fact finding tour. Embarking in October, he sailed first to Montevideo, then under siege by Rosas' troops. Bartólomé Mitre, a unitarist, had serialized *Facundo* in his Montevideo newspaper. Sarmiento sailed on to Le Havre, arriving in May 1846 and ready to give vent to all his prejudice. Europe, after all, was all that was wrong with everything: "Ah, Europe! Strange mixture of greatness and abjection, of knowledge and stupidity at the same time, sublime and filthy receptacle of all that elevates man and all that holds him degraded, kings and lackeys, monuments and pest houses, opulence and savage life."

At first — before *Facundo* was published in Europe — Sarmiento was unknown. Thus in September, when he reached the heart of his discontent, Spain, he was widely ignored. "I came to Spain with the holy aim of verbally putting it on trial to give foundation to an accusation," he would write. By the time Sarmiento arrived in Barcelona, however, Mazade's review of *Facundo* guaranteed his reputation.

The next concern was his wallet. Sarmiento counted 600 pesos for the 700-peso trip back to Chile, but decided to head for England and the United States anyway. In England he met Americans who gave him a letter of introduction to Horace Mann, whom Sarmiento admired. Mann's ideas revolutionized public education in the United States, and Sarmiento began a life-long correspondence with Mann's second wife and collaborator, Mary Tyler Peabody Mann.

In the District of Columbia — where the Washington Monument was nearing completion — Sarmiento ran into a Chilean friend who agreed to help pay for the trip home. It was a fortuitous match, although it almost went awry; Sarmiento lost track of his new friend and had to chase him across Pennsylvania. "Great mental stress can be relieved only in one's own language," Sarmiento noted wryly, "and though English has a passable 'God damn,' for special cases I preferred Spanish, which is so round and sonorous for uttering rage."

Sarmiento returned to Chile in February 1848 after two years, four months abroad to find Benita a twenty-six-year-old widow. In May, they were married, and Sarmiento adopted little Dominguito. The family moved to Benita's estate at Yungay. For three years, Sarmiento remained at Yungay, writing and seeking ways to link himself with issues in his homeland.

Viajes en Europa, Africa y América was a catalogue of his fascination with practically everything, from signs in hotel lobbies to the future of religion. *Educación popular* was based on his official report. He then published the ill-fated *Arqirópolis,* dedicated to General Justo José de Urquiza, the caudillo of the province of Entre Rios and the only man capable of driving Rosas from power. The book drew only contempt; even Urquiza ignored it. *Recuerdos de provincia* was less cloying, but no less self-serving: "In school I always distinguished myself with an exemplary veracity," Sarmiento wrote, "to the extent that the teachers acknowledged it by making me a model."

In 1851 a door was finally opened toward home. Urquiza led his own and two other provinces into revolt, allying himself with the *República Oriental,* which would become Uruguay, with Brazil, and with unitarist exiles in Montevideo. The end of Rosas' long, harsh reign was in sight. Urquiza's forces invaded Uruguay in July and broke the siege of Montevideo in September. Commanding 17,000 Argentines and 4,000 Brazilians and Uruguayans, Urquiza turned toward Buenos Aires.

Sarmiento's first thought was to lead an army of exiles over the Andes to attack the western provinces, a plan that elicited no support. So, in September, Sarmiento, Mitre, and other exiles boarded a frigate and sailed for forty days to reach Montevideo. Sarmiento appeared at Urquiza's headquarters in the uniform of a lieutenant-colonel, a rank Urquiza accepted in light of Sarmiento's military experience. Sarmiento wanted a command; instead, Urquiza made him official propagandist.

Sarmiento bought a printing press that Urquiza said was too expensive and a uniform at which the general laughed outright. The cost of the press, Sarmiento explained, was the result of haste. The uniform, he said, was a fashion statement, to elegantly separate him from the common *gauchos* riding for Rosas. The press rattled along behind the advancing army, printing leaflets.

On Christmas Eve the army crossed the Paraná River and marched toward Buenos Aires, but rising like the dust was the inevitable rivalry between Urquiza and Sarmiento.

On the one hand, Sarmiento was popular in some, although surely not all, quarters. Also, Urquiza recognized that exiles like Sarmiento had fought Rosas for years, well back to the time that he, Urquiza, was allied with the tyrant. "I just came to meet the writers from Montevideo and Chile," he remarked derisively. "They did it all." Sarmiento insisted that anti–Rosas propaganda had been and still was crucial, which brought from Urquiza the rejoinder: "[I]n regard to the feats that you say the press accomplishes in frightening the enemy, the presses have been shouting in Chile and other places for many years and until now Juan Manuel de Rosas has not been frightened. On the contrary, every day he grew stronger."

On February 3, 1852, at the Battle of Caseros, Sarmiento left his press and entered the fight, once again distinguishing himself. The Battle of Caseros finished Rosas, who took flight with his British protectors on a gunboat to exile in England. In Argentine lore, the Battle of Caseros is symbolized by crossed pen and sword, but in early 1852 Sarmiento and Urquiza had the two instruments pointed at each other's hearts.

The split was not long in coming. Urquiza accused the unitarist Sarmiento of wanting "to make war on the governors." Sarmiento described Urquiza as just another caudillo; he refused to wear the red armband symbolic of the federalist cause. Sarmiento asked for and immediately got permission to return to Chile, losing no time in beginning to organize an opposition. Urquiza, for his part, set up a constitutional convention, persuaded governors to sign the cooperative Accord of San Nicolás, and set a date for a constitutional congress later in the year. That congress abolished internal tariffs, arranged for free congressional elections, and condemned local separatist movements. While Sarmiento sulked, Urquiza was trying to draw together an Argentine Republic.

Fourteen provinces ratified the agreement, but Buenos Aires, controlled by unitarists, refused and then seceded from a federation that had never been given a chance. Urquiza proceeded without the province. The result was the Constitution of 1853, shaped by the fertile mind of Juan Bautista Alberdi, which would stand as the charter of the nation until 1949. The constitution was drafted, improved, and ratified without Buenos Aires and without Sarmiento. While Mitre and other unitarists remained, Sarmiento fulminated from abroad, rejecting all offers of conciliation. Elected to a national convention, Sarmiento refused to attend. Mitre beckoned in vain, and Alberdi finally snorted that Sarmiento was a "caudillo of the pen."

In January 1854, when Sarmiento tried to return to San Juan, he was jailed, held incommunicado, tried for conspiracy and, finally, forced to flee back to Chile. A year later, he again returned. After a single-minded — if not monomaniacal — and fruitless attempt to persuade San Juan's Governor Benavídez to come over to his side, he trudged on to Buenos Aires, where he found a political home among unitarists.

Benita sold her estate in Chile and brought Dominguito to live in Buenos Aires, but the family's relationships deteriorated even as Sarmiento's political career emerged. Before 1855 was over, Sarmiento had been named editor of the newspaper *El Nacional* by Mitre and made director of public schools by the governor. He won elective posts as well, and established a successful experimental farm at Chivilcoy. After two and a half decades of contumacy and contumely, Sarmiento had arrived at his political destination despite an uncompromising nature.

Indeed, his acidic style of personal journalism was undiluted. Opposing editors— Urquiza supporters—countered, one challenging Sarmiento to a duel, a prospect Sarmiento ridiculed. He was accused of having poisoned Benita's late husband (although out of the country at the time) and won a slander suit. He got into a fistfight with another editor on a Buenos Aires street. When his old adversary, Governor Benavídez, was deposed, jailed, and shot in cold blood, Sarmiento published an article excusing the murder.

In 1858 Urquiza tired of waiting for Buenos Aires to find humility and sent an army to force it into the union. The provincial army, led by Mitre, was put to flight, and all that remained to Buenos Aires was to take advantage of a concession by Urquiza that the constitution might be amended and the national government restructured. Sarmiento was elected to the assembly drafting amendments.

Sarmiento's view of reforming the national constitution was to model it more along the lines of the constitution of the United States, expanding guarantees of civil liberties and freedom of the press, and, of course, strengthening central authority. He helped defeat a proposal to make Catholicism the official religion of the nation. The convention gave Sarmiento the chance to be seen as a responsible spokesman for provincial interests and he was soon elected to the provincial legislature. After Mitre was elected governor, he was appointed minister of state.

The barbarity that Sarmiento saw surrounding him, however, would not abate. In one of San Juan's periodic flare ups, a boyhood friend was executed. Sarmiento, already depressed by other setbacks, rejected appointment as emissary to the United States and in January 1861 resigned as provincial minister of state. Yet another civil war threatened in mid–1861, but after a battle at Pavón, Urquiza forces withdrew, not because they were beaten but because it was clear no Argentine could benefit from the endless bloodshed. Out of this morass Argentina would have to build itself.

The following year Sarmiento got his wish to be named the national government's administrator of San Juan, but he returned to a province enervated by war. His parents were both dead, his mother having died the previous November at the age of ninety-one. To add to his misfortune, Sarmiento left his wife and son behind in Buenos Aires, and there were rumors there — widely discussed and evidently substantiated — that Benita was unfaithful. Sarmiento himself had not been a model husband, and the tension between the two adults poisoned Sarmiento's relationship with his son.

Finally in a position of real administrative power, however, Sarmiento embarked on ambitious plans. He organized a more rational school system, and for the first time each department of the province was required to maintain at least one primary school. His administration founded agricultural communities, mapped the province, reorganized the militia, established an agricultural school, and drew up a proposal for irrigation. Then the smoldering civil war was enflamed anew.

This time Sarmiento's nemesis was Angel Vicente "El Chacho" Peñalosa, who, when captured, was summarily executed. His head was mounted on the point of a lance for display. This act of barbarity was laid at the doorstep of Sarmiento, the supposed advocate of restraint and civility. The controversy brought Sarmiento low again. Coupled with marital strife, the infamy overshadowed any successes of the past months, and Sarmiento lapsed into the sort of despair that had engulfed him before. Mitre, knowing of his problems, appointed Sarmiento envoy extraordinary and minister plenipotentiary to the United States.

Sarmiento arrived in New York in the spring of 1865, at the end of the Civil War. He established his office in New York City and founded a newspaper, *Ambas Américas.* The next year personal tragedy struck as a result of the seemingly endless fighting in the River Plate Valley. Captain Domingo Fidel Sarmiento was killed.

During this period, Sarmiento renewed his friendship with Mary Mann, who would translate *Facundo* into English. He met Emerson and discovered that Longfellow spoke "perfect Spanish." As in the past, neither political, pedagogical, nor publishing concerns kept Sarmiento, now estranged from his wife, from affairs of the heart. "Sarmiento," notes historian César Guerrero, "had women who loved him, who knew how to interpret his feelings, who understood little besides admiration for him, and who collaborated with him along the long road of this wandering civilizor and who did not leave upon his troubled heart some sediment of tenderness?" Returning from a voyage to Paris, Sarmiento met Ida Wickersham, who offered to help him improve his English.

"The most womanly woman I have ever known," wrote Sarmiento to a friend. They spent time together in Philadelphia, studying. Ida Wickersham was married, to a physician, but assured Sarmiento that their correspondence, especially if he wrote to her in French, would not be a problem. Through 1867, their letters (only hers exist) were torrid, and she carried on her end of the writing for several years, providing Sarmiento with details of the Chicago Fire, continuing to write after Sarmiento had returned to Argentina. Her last letter, in 1882, pleaded for some response: "I keep all your letters and reread them in detail. I could write if I knew you felt some interest in me.... Please, write and tell me of your life." By that time she was divorced and living alone in New York City. Sarmiento was embroiled in the affairs of his country and did not reply.

In 1868, Sarmiento knew his name had been placed in nomination to succeed Mitre as president of Argentina. Mitre was riding out a six-year term, during which there were no fewer than 117 local coups. Sarmiento had told his daughter when he left for the United States that the trip might be a device to isolate him from presidential politics, but he was supported by several generals and by Mitre. All he could do from abroad was wait and hope. Asked for his platform, he replied, "My program is in the atmosphere, in twenty years of life, actions and writings." On his way home, Sarmiento did not know until his boat entered the harbor at Bahía that he had won.

Along with Mitre, Sarmiento presided over a profound transition in Argentina that grew out of the country's natural strengths, a transformation that Sarmiento had helped to foster but that no one, once it was underway, could control. Awakening after decades of fitful, tormented wars, the country established a thriving sheep industry. Between 1830 and 1880 the number of sheep rose from 2.5 million to 61 million. The country also raised cattle and planted grain. While in the 1850s net immigration had averaged 5,000 people a year, by the 1880s the average was 50,000, peaking at 200,000 immigrants in 1889. Argentina's population grew from 1.1 million in 1857 to 3.3 million in 1890.

"Sarmiento initiated a period of bourgeois domination in Argentina," writes biographer Bunkley. "His presidency marks the advent of the middle and landowning classes as the pivot of power in the nation. The age of the gaucho had ended; the age of the merchant and the cattleman had begun. The aim of this group was stability, order, and material progress.... He had only to overcome the last vestiges of the old order to put his program into operation."

Alas, the last vestiges of the old order were not easily conquered. The caudillos, with Urquiza still in command of several alliances, persisted. A war with Paraguay raged on. In 1870, after Urquiza and his family were assassinated, the most virulent uprising of all, led by Ricardo López Jordán, raged. Even after Jordán's army was defeated and Jordán driven into hiding in Brazil, he returned in May 1873, overrunning Entre Rios and gathering followers.

Sarmiento blamed Jordán for an assassination attempt in August 1873 when two Italian seamen were hired to shoot Sarmiento as his coach carried him through the streets of Buenos Aires. An overloaded gun almost blew the hand off one of the inept assassins, and Sarmiento, by now quite deaf, did not even hear the blast.

In the end, the heavy-handedness that had characterized much of Sarmiento's writing did not serve him well as administrative technique. When a factional dispute split his own province of San Juan, Sarmiento issued a presidential decree that simply imposed his will, deciding the issue in favor of his supporters. In 1869, he imposed martial law in San Luis after a provincial leader was shot by a firing squad. Although presidents had issued arbitrary decrees before, Sarmiento's martial law was the first time this device had been employed, and even his old friend Mitre attacked the action as unconstitutional.

By the time the next presidential election came around, Sarmiento was glad to leave the wrangling to others; he had to call out the army to keep order. Tired, deaf, and thoroughly disenchanted, Sarmiento continued to be the center of criticism as if by national habit. Returning to the Senate, he was asked how, since he was deaf, he could debate. "I don't go to the Senate to hear them," he replied, "but for them to hear me."

In 1879 — after contemplating another run at the presidency — he made the mistake of resigning from the Senate to accept a presidential appointment as minister of the interior and head of the cabinet. His charge was to restore order to national debate. "The colt throws his ears back," he wrote confidently to a friend. "He will calm down, recognizing his old master. There will be government." Such confidence was unjustified, and he quit within weeks.

In 1883, Sarmiento wrote *Conflictos y armónias de las razas de América,* still trying to resolve the dilemma, as he saw it, of taking the best from various "races" while leaving old, European foibles behind. He continued to run for office and to lose to men of no reputation whatsoever. He founded *El Censor* to fight a censorship law and then, finally, gave up fighting anything at all. There was so much fighting all around that he was hardly being noticed, the worst possible fate for such a powerfully prideful man.

With Faustina, Sarmiento moved to a better climate in Paraguay, to a small house where his heart failed on September 11, 1888.

8

Brazil's Emperors

Divine Right and Democracy

Pedro I (1798–1834)
and Pedro II (1825–1891)

Prince Hal was Shakespeare's "rascaliest, sweet young prince," who eventually had to grow up, leaving behind Falstaff in order to become Henry V. Similarly, Pedro I of the House of Braganza, after a dissolute youth, was thrust into reigning over the largest country of Latin America. Pedro, however, was an anomaly — king of an independent nation, monarch of an emerging democracy. This unique scepter he passed on to his son, Pedro II, who proved better able to understand a country casting off the trappings of royalty. They were unusual men in a situation that has no historical parallel, and their roles were crucial. "History," writes Hubert Herring, "credits the empire with having held Brazil together; had it not been for the cohesive power of the crown, the nation might easily have split at its seams as did Gran Colombia, Peru and the provinces of La Plata."

On November 29, 1807, Portugal's insane Queen Maria I and the prince regent João VI fled their country, sailing down the Tagus and out to sea as Napoleon's army reached the hills outside Lisbon. Their choice had been to retain Portugal's long-standing ties to a selfish Britain, or succumb to Napoleon's jealous France. Five British men-of-war protected them and their entourage aboard 36 ships as they set a course for Brazil.

The trans–Atlantic maneuver had been planned and was not without precedent. Kingdoms were portable, and Portugal, in fact, a tiny nation with expansionist neighbors, had contemplated moving before. For three centuries the Portuguese had controlled Brazil, and the court was welcomed ashore at Bahía in January 1808.

Brazil is shaped like a mammoth, spinning top. Its shoulders bulge northwestward toward Colombia and the headwaters of the Amazon, 3,900 miles long, and northeast toward Africa, less than 2,000 miles away. The arid, impoverished northeast has historically sent its own rivers of poor people to work in the more prosperous states inland and southward, like Bahía and Minas Gerais. Forests and pampas have supported a rich agrarian economy and built great cities like Rio de Janeiro, where the royal family settled.

The arrival of the European court was a boon to Brazil; some reports say more than 15,000 Portuguese followed their government. The British, who had already built London into an international financial center on gold smuggled out of Brazil during the eighteenth century, now prospered from their relationship with this growing market. A few Irish and German settlers added their numbers.

Especially galling to the Brazilians, however, was the arrogance of the Portuguese, who made known their dissatisfaction with conditions, especially the lack of sanitation. This conflict between Creoles and Portuguese would continue through the reigns of both Pedros.

From the beginning, the relationship between gigantic Brazil and tiny Portugal was an odd one, like a huge organ grinder dancing on a monkey's chain. Portuguese navigators—from a nation of half a million people spread along the Iberian coast—were without peer. They had been to Labrador as early as 1474 and discovered Brazil before 1500. Soon after word of Columbus's feat, Pope Alexander VI was called upon to settle the argument between Spanish and Portuguese over who owned what. The pope drew the line of demarcation from pole to pole a hundred leagues (roughly, 350 miles) west of the Azore and Cape Verde Islands. The resulting slice of the New World did not satisfy the feisty Portuguese, who obtained, in the Treaty of Tordesillas in 1494, a line of demarcation set 370 leagues west of the Cape Verdes. Then they drove inland to take even more.

After 1500, when Pedro Álvares Cabral staked a formal claim to the territory, the Portuguese took advantage of Spain's fixation with the silver of Peru on the other side of the continent. The Portuguese pushed farther and farther inland, following gold prospectors and the ruthless, slave seeking *bandeirantes*. Unlike North American colonists, the Portuguese did not trundle westward with all their possessions and their families. Without women accompanying these interlopers, historian João Pandiá Calogeras points out, "racial crossing began early and broke down all barriers." The demographic result has defied precise measurement.

The geographic result, of course, was a huge colony. Portugal is just a bit larger than the state of Maine, and Brazil is about the size of the rest of the United States, including Alaska and Hawaii. Brazil encompasses almost half the land mass of South America. Its name, originally Terra da Vera Cruz, is from the *Caesalpinia*, which was commonly known as the brazil wood tree because its interior turns red like a coal, or *braza*, when exposed to air.

Economically, the metropolis prospered. After 1550, reaping the harvest of Brazilian plantations, Lisbon became the sugar capital of Europe. Politically, however, even control of this huge kingdom — Portugal also had to concern itself with India — did not prevent Portugal from being a mere pawn to European ambitions. Crown Prince João was more than glad to have found escape in the New World. Brazilians liked him, and *fazandeiros*, plantation owners, joined his court and built houses in Rio. In December 1815, he signed an edict giving Brazil dominion status within the empire. Matters of state, however, were not so easily avoided.

Napoleon had fallen the year before and Ferdinand VII, as a condition of his return, had been forced to accept the liberal Spanish constitution of 1812. This had as much effect in Portuguese America as in Spanish America; republican ideas were contagious. At the same time, however, the crowned heads represented at the Congress of Vienna (1815), tidying up the world after Napoleon, accepted the Brazilian monarchy for the first time. Thus, when Queen Maria died in 1816 and her son was crowned King João VI of the "United Kingdom of Portugal, Brazil and the Algarve [the medieval Moorish kingdom at the southern tip of Portugal]," he was promptly caught between demands on both sides of the Atlantic.

By 1820, there were in Portugal sporadic uprisings against "monarchial absolutism"; many of João's Portuguese subjects wanted a constitutional monarch. They also wanted their king to return, reducing Brazil to its former colonial status. João, for his part, wanted to stay in Brazil, so he countered with a proposal for a "dual monarchy." It was rejected. On April 21, 1821, João tried another ploy: a separate constitution for Brazil. This idea was rejected when the Rio garrison stepped in to break up the drafting assembly.

João had run out of options; he knew that if he insisted on staying in Brazil, the House of Branganza would lose Portugal. So, on April 24, pressed by his Portuguese supporters, by the British, and by his oldest son, Pedro, João grudgingly sailed for Portugal. To the delight of Brazilians, he took with him his shrewish wife Carlota, Ferdinand's sister, who had made clear her contempt for Brazilians and had tried to carve her own realm out of Brazil's southern tip — a region Argentines had come to think of as Argentina. On his way out, João robbed Brazil's treasury of money and jewels. To his twenty-four-year-old son, Pedro Antonio José de Alcántara, whom he left as regent, he is said to have counseled: "If Brazil demands independence, grant it, but put the crown upon your own head."

The evidence suggests, in fact, that João foresaw Brazilian independence and, knowing the Portuguese would not allow a dual monarchy, thought his return would at least assure that both countries would be controlled by Braganzas. When he died, he reasoned, the two crowns might be united with his son. Such a tidy plan was not to be. In Portúgal after João's death, the House of Braganza would fight with itself. In Brazil after João's departure, Brazilians would prove so independent as to reject Pedro's intention to serve as absolute monarch.

Biographers describe Pedro I in romantic terms. He was handsome, sentimental, impulsive, spoiled, and unschooled. Only irregularly was he seen in the presence of tutors. He was hated by his mother and ignored by his father, although he displayed a common sense and firmness that were likened to his mother's and an affability that he shared with his father. As a boy, he was allowed, even encouraged, to associate with lackeys at court and commoners— even in the street. Calogeras depicts Pedro I as "bold, inured to hardship, and adept in all sports, a marvelous horseman.... He could rise to heights of generosity and heroism, but was quite capable of falling into the opposite extremes.... As a consequence of his dissolute life and degraded companions he was ill bred, coarse, and rude, addicted to low jests and practical jokes." Although he had avidly supported the cause of Brazilian independence from Portugal's yoke, he was so vain and shortsighted as to imagine he could exercise absolute control.

Pedro's principal saving grace was his first wife, the plain but exceptionally well-bred (Maria) Leopoldina. "His wife was an asset," writes biographer Mary Wilhemine Williams. Leopoldina's father was Emperor Francis I of Austria, who was served by that most famous of statesmen, Prince von Metternich. Her older sister was Napoleon's second wife. In matters of state concerning South America or Europe, Leopoldina was at her husband's side, advising. She read extensively — among her choices was Malthus' *Principles of Political Economy*— and she managed to assemble a library that has been described as "the best in Brazil at the time." Interested in botany and geology, she sent samples of New World discoveries to learned friends in Europe. At court, she raised the level of discourse above Pedro's ribaldry.

She, too, supported an independent Brazil. Quite apart from her bloodline, her intelligence, or her political views, Brazilians lionized Leopoldina because she endeavored to understand them, to meet them on their own terms. She was seen in counterpoint to her predecessor, the despised termagant Carlota. "In Brazil," notes Williams, "to whose independence she directly contributed, her memory is still held in gratitude and respect."

The marriage of Pedro and Leopoldina in 1817 was not, alas, particularly romantic. It began well enough; although they never met before the wedding they had corresponded. She, two years older than he, was unswerving in her dedication. Both were equestrians and took long rides through the Brazilian countryside. When Pedro reviewed troops, Leopoldina, wearing the blue uniform of the dragoons and heavy silver spurs, would ride beside him. The couple had four children.

Physically, however, Leopoldina, despite blond curls, fair skin, and blue eyes, was not particularly attractive. She had a figure that has been charitably described as "sturdy." Calogeras remarks, "The princess lacked many of those feminine traits which appealed to a man of the type of Dom Pedro." Felix Reichmann calls her "totally lacking in sex appeal." The faithless Pedro focused his attentions on other women, but especially on Domitila de Castro Canto e Mello, who in 1824 gave birth to his daughter and whom he named, with crude irony, lady of the empress' bedchamber. Later, he elevated her to a marchioness.

Leopoldina did not suffer these indignities quietly. She openly quarreled with her husband and let her father know of her predicament. Brazilians in the street were aware of the indignities their queen suffered, increasing their hostility toward a king they did not like in the first place.

In 1826, Leopoldina fell ill and died two weeks before Christmas, delirious and ranting, apparently suffering from an infection following a miscarriage. The story circulated among her many supporters that their empress had been killed by a blow from the boorish Pedro during a violent argument.

Pedro's management of an unruly country was no better than his handling of marital affairs. "As a monarch he was less than nothing," writes Calogeras. In the Portuguese côrte, where members yearned for the old metropolis-colony relationship, antipathy for Brazil increased. Delegates arriving from Brazil were ridiculed. Pedro responded in letters to his father criticizing the côrte. There were attempts to reduce the status of Brazil within the partnership, and the côrte excluded Brazilians from all high military and political offices in their own country. As a final insult, Pedro was summoned to Portugal to "complete his political education."

Pedro hesitated, and Leopoldina was among those who persuaded him not to return. The Masonic Order, into which he would be inducted, also fed the flame of defiance. Petitions arrived from the provinces asking him to stay, not totally for love of Pedro—several municipalities in Minas Gerais were perfectly willing to let him go—but because of his tactical usefulness in the strategic battle with Lisbon.

Central to Pedro's decision to stay in Brazil was the advice of José Bonifacio de Andrada e Silva, who has to come to be known as "the patriarch of Brazilian independence." Bonifacio, a member of one of São Paulo's most distinguished families, had studied and taught in Portugal before returning to Brazil in 1819, when he was fifty-four. During his thirty years in Europe, Bonifacio counted among his friends Alexander von Humboldt, the German naturalist, Allessandro Volta, the Italian physicist, and Joseph Priestly, the English clergyman and chemist. He served as secretary of the Scientific Academy of Lisbon and earned a reputation as a leading mineralogist. Back in his native country, Bonifacio went to work on some very rough ore indeed in an effort to shape Brazilian democracy.

While Bonifacio devoutly believed in the need for Brazil's independence, he had been shocked by what he observed of the French Revolution in 1789. He was convinced that the monarchy must remain strong within a constitutional framework. Balancing those elements against each other in the tropical climate of Brazilian politics would test Bonifacio's wisdom and skill. The Masons criticized his efforts, as did other of Pedro's advisors, and, in fact, did Pedro himself. Bonifacio proposed social and economic reforms, like land redistribution and a higher standard of living for workers, which placed him on a collision course with the landed aristocracy. Liberals, on the other hand, objected to his defense of the monarchy. Bonifacio's contentiousness got him fired and exiled by Pedro, but, fortunately for the future of Brazil, he returned to a position of influence.

By early January 1822, Pedro could hold out no longer; he had to indicate whether he would yield, returning to Lisbon as demanded by the côrte, or stay in Brazil. Pedro's formal rejection of Portuguese authority is known to Brazilians as the "Fico"—I will remain. "As it is for the good of all and the general felicity of the nation," Pedro declared, "tell the people that I will remain." Portugal's military garrisons angrily demanded compliance with the order to return, but popular uprisings in support of Pedro silenced the garrisons.

Later that same year, on September 7, while traveling in the provinces, Pedro received a dispatch from Portugal telling him that the battle was not yet done. The *côrte* was annulling all of his acts as regent and declaring his ministers guilty of treason. Standing by the bank of the Ypiranga River, Pedro delivered his second dramatic pronouncement, the "Grito do Ypiranga." Drawing his sword, he said, "The hour has come! Independence or death! We have separated from Portugal!" Leopoldina wrote him at the time, "The apple is ripe; pick it now or it will rot."

These two pronouncements ushered in the brief period — Brazil's modest "war" of independence — that would end on February 28, 1824, when the last Portuguese garrison set sail for home. In Pará, Pernambuco, and Bahía there was brief resistance, but no more. Bonifacio recruited the Scotsman Lord Cochran, who had performed a similar service for Chile, to sweep Brazilian seas clean of the Portuguese navy. "The war of independence in Spanish America had lasted fifteen years," writes Calogeras, "the independence of Brazil was won in as many months."

On December 1, 1822, he was crowned Pedro I, "Constitutional Emperor" of Brazil. When the Portuguese garrison at Rio, 1,600 strong, rebelled, outraged Brazilians chased them across the harbor, where they were captured under a virtual state of siege. Pedro ordered the artillery they left behind trained on their hiding place, and a third of the soldiers switched sides. The rest sailed for home. Reinforcements, which met them en route, were of no help; Brazilians simply would not allow the fresh troops to get off their ships, so they turned around and sailed back to Portugal.

Pedro's battles, however, were only half over. He would later write to his son, "The time when princes were respected simply because they were princes is past." It was a lesson reiterated every day by Brazilians who wanted to breathe life into this odd notion of a constitutional monarch. When a constituent assembly, fired by the idea of designing some brand new form of government, opened in April 1823, Pedro's tolerance lasted only until November. The assembly went too far, so Pedro ordered it disbanded.

In its stead, Pedro appointed a commission to draw up a document that would serve as a legal foundation. The result Calogeras calls "a monument of political liberalism and well-balanced powers." Liberals of the day disagreed, wanting stronger republican institutions that made their own decisions. The country was left with ambivalence; a state in which the emperor's "moderating power" was no power at all if factions behaved immoderately. "The respect of a free people for their ruler," Bonifacio counseled, "should spring from the conviction that he is the leader capable of enabling them to attain that degree of well-being to which they aspire." Pedro I was not that leader.

An important political problem was that of the slave trade. Other new Latin American nations had immediately prohibited slavery, writing the prohibitions into their constitutions. In those instances, however, large slaveholders had often been peninsular Spanish, royalists who were defeated in the wars of independence. Thus slavery was toppled with other institutions of colonialism. In Brazil, slaveholders were supporters of independence and were helping to shape the new government. Slavery, therefore, was more imbedded.

Attempts to dislodge slavery were in vain. The British demanded in 1826 that by 1830 importation of slaves be ceased. The 1830 deadline was not met, and the issue divided Brazil as it did the United States, which had passed its own Missouri Compromise — assuring the continued admission of slave states into the Union — in 1820. Bonifacio was among those who argued for abolition. "He who lives on the earnings of his slaves lives in indolence," Bonifacio counseled, "and indolence brings vice in its wake."

The solution would not come for half a century, and, in the meantime, Pedro I's time was running out. It was always a source of resentment that Pedro's closest friends and advisors were Portuguese, not Creoles; Pedro isolated himself. His preferred venue was an army barracks. He submitted treaties to the legislature, but only after he had unilaterally ratified them himself. Expected to act as mediator of disputes among the far-flung provinces, Pedro argued with anyone in the room.

At his best, Pedro had risen to the drama of Brazilian independence. With cavalier gestures, he had been in the vanguard of independence. Nation building would require someone of more patience and wisdom.

On December 2, 1825, Pedro's youngest child was born, a son and heir. Pedro and Leopoldina had had two sons who died young — one in infancy; the other of pneumonia after the family was subjected to harsh conditions during their flight from a revolt in Rio. There were no more boys until — after three girls — the birth of Pedro de Alcántara, Pedro II, a child Brazil could rear in its own image.

Events quickly converged, as if on cue. João had finally recognized Brazil "to be in the category of an independent empire," but then, a few months later, in March 1826, João died. This left Pedro I to fight with his brother Miguel over who would take their father's throne. Brazilians wanted to keep Pedro in Rio, fearing that if he left they would become a second class partner in the kingdom.

Initially, Pedro thought he could control the throne in Lisbon by shipping off his eldest daughter, Maria da Gloria, in July 1827 to claim it and by naming Miguel regent. The plan did not work. First, Portugal split into a civil war between partisans of democracy and reactionaries who intended that Miguel rule as an absolute monarch. Maria da Gloria never got a chance to take the throne, and within a year Miguel had seized it for himself.

Pedro's plans for Brazil were no more successful. Taxpayers were incensed over the debt Brazil had to assume as a condition for recognition as an independent monarchy, adding to the hostility directed at Pedro as a person. He was blamed for the long, expensive, bloody war that failed to hold onto the Cisplatine province, which in 1828 became Uruguay. With his predictable contempt for public opinion Pedro only incurred further wrath by continuing his relationship with Domitila despite his 1829 marriage to a Bavarian princess.

By 1831, relations had so deteriorated that mobs were in the streets, and soldiers were deserting to join them. Disgusted and frustrated, Pedro scribbled out a note abdicating his Brazilian throne and embarked for Portugal, where he would continue the effort to make his daughter the queen. He was at least successful in that effort, but died in 1834, only thirty six years old. In the end, his greatest gift to Brazil was his departure, leaving behind as regent the five-year-old Pedro II and naming as Tutor the sage republican Bonifacio.

Pedro I demonstrated, according to biographer Williams, "a strong, deep affection" for his infant son. After the abdication, notes and letters were exchanged, a governess at first guiding the hand of "the crowned orphan," whose father would reply to "my beloved son and my Emperor." When his father died in 1834, Pedro II was nine years old. "They err," Bonifacio told him gently. "Dom Pedro did not die. Common men die, but not heroes."

Pedro II's sisters, Januaria and Francisca (Paula died in 1833), remained in Brazil with him, and among Pedro's closest friends was said to be one "Rafael," a black soldier who had been a favorite of his father. Rafael, whose rooms Pedro was allowed to visit, represented a kind of counterpoint to rigorous schooling, a thorough grounding in languages, the classics, and modern thought. There was an emphasis on reading.

He was taught, it is said, "to love labor as the foundation of the virtues, and to honor equally the men who toil and those who serve the state through political office." An elevated thought, yet early on Pedro was expected to don a uniform and review troops, and even as a child he received the credentials of arriving diplomats. His childhood papers, carefully preserved, demonstrate knowledge of the French revolution, of U.S. history, and of William Burke, the English conservative, all written in English. He translated Longfellow and Byron, and attained a working knowledge of fourteen languages, including Hebrew, which he mastered in order to study the Old Testament. To say, as biographer Reichmann does, that Pedro II was "totally different from his father" risks understatement. Reichmann adds primly, "His private conduct was impeccable."

His schooling, in fact, was characterized by strong religious influences, and a considerable moral example must have been set by his principal governess, Doña Marianna Carlota Verna de Magalhaes Continho, a widow who came to Brazil with her husband in 1808 to join the court of Dom João. Pedro's childhood name for her was "Dadama." Appointed head governess in 1831, Dadama was made a countess in 1844 and in 1855 opened her house to cholera victims, eventually dying of the disease after contracting it from her patients.

So important was Pedro's education that his relationship with Bonifacio became a political issue. Octavio Tarquinio de Sousa, a historian, dismisses objections about Bonifacio as "the hostility that invariably is felt toward superior men, above all when that superiority is felt as a result of the disdainful, even insolent, gesture." There was more to the hostile scrutiny of Bonifacio, however, than could be explained by his arrogance. There is the story of a European contemporary who made it his business to keep an eye on the comings and goings of the Brazilian court. Seeing a horse tied outside Bonifacio's residence, he asked if it belonged to Pedro. "Yes," came the reply, "it's the prince, José Bonifacio's assistant."

Bonifacio, clearly, had his hand on the hand that would be on the helm of Brazil's destiny, and the aging intellectual was determined to keep his grip firm. Bonifacio found in Pedro II "the fittest instrument," writes historian Manoel de Oliveira Lima, for his own republican goals. Bonifacio himself was "predestined" to shape the future of the continent's largest country. When Pedro I named Bonifacio to the task of educating his son, dissidents contested the nomination, saying the choice should rest with the legislature. Bonifacio—sixty-eight-years old at the time—held a seat from Bahía, but he took his case to the people. He published a "Protest to the Brazilian Nation and to the Entire World." The council of regency took the side of the dissidents, but when the matter was put before the full legislature on June 30, 1831, Bonifacio was eventually deposed as tutor, but not until, more than two years after the appointment, his mark on the development of Pedro II and the future of Brazil was assured.

The reason for Bonifacio's downfall was his conviction that the monarchy must remain strong. Liberals condemned this view, but Bonifacio's thinking was shaped, while in Europe, by France's example of republican chaos, and, since returning home, by the cases of Peru, Chile, and Argentina. From the time of Pedro II's birth, Brazil had threatened to fly apart from the same sort of centrifugal forces that afflicted Mexico. Revolts in the Northern provinces broke out in 1824, and mid–1825 brought the revolt of the Cisplatine province. Bonifacio argued that only a strong monarch could hold the nation together. Clinging to this opinion, Bonifacio saw his tutorial post terminated by the legislature in December 1833. He had to be removed forcibly from his office, after which he was imprisoned. Although acquitted in a criminal trial, Bonifacio was then driven to retire from politics.

Those who would get rid of the monarchy once and for all caused sporadic revolts, especially along the northern and southern borders, causing Pedro II's protectors to spirit him away from Rio seeking safety. Although democrats did not blame him personally, Pedro was the focus of their dissent just as he was the catalyst of monarchists' zeal. Brazil had grown to 4.5 million citizens in eighteen provinces— remote Amazonas and Paraná were formed during his reign—and it was by no means certain there would be a nation left to govern when he grew up. "While Dom Pedro's tutors were intent upon training him to be a good man and a good emperor," writes Williams, "the Brazilian regency was struggling to hold the country together — to preserve it for him to rule."

There were mutinies by soldiers who drove away civic officials and set up their own governments; there were republican rebellions, separatist movements, and conflicts between federalists and monarchists — with *moderados* in between. Civil war broke out in Rio Grande do Sul in 1835, in Maranhão in 1840, in São Paulo in 1841, in Minas Gerais in 1842, and in Pernambuco in 1847. From 1835, when he was only ten years old, there was pressure to bring Pedro II's minority to an end when he was fourteen in order to stabilize the nation. Another frantic proposal was to name his elder sister, Januaria, regent, although at the time she was only twenty-one and the minimum age for such an arrangement was twenty-five.

A national guard was formed to confront army mutineers, and in 1839 there was a move to grant the monarchy police powers. Conditions, however, did not improve. Creole unrest could only grow as long as the Portuguese controlled agriculture and commerce. In the spring of 1840, a legislative faction moved to end Pedro's minority and, after a parliamentary battle, succeeded in July. The coronation was held a year later.

At the time of his coronation Pedro was still very much an adolescent, a bit short and pudgy, with blond hair. He would grow to be six feet, three inches tall, and well proportioned; his hair and full beard would be brown. For all of his liberal education, it was noted of him that "an air of reserve discouraged familiarity." He was, as might be imagined, mature for his years. He immediately began opening and closing sessions of the legislature in full regalia, his costume including a scepter topped by a griffin, the symbol of the Braganzas.

"Yet in some ways," Williams writes, "the sovereign was but a child. His new dignity perhaps prompted him on December 2, 1840, to begin a diary which shows the naiveté of the average boy of fifteen. In his first entry he remarked that his birth was a historical event for Brazil. Then he solemnly proceeded to mention the coffee and eggs he had had for breakfast."

Almost immediately after the coronation, the regency began casting about for a wife. In Austria in April 1842, a betrothal contract was signed for Thereza, sister of Ferdinand II of the Sicilies. Metternich helped arrange the betrothal; Pedro gave his approval on the basis of a portrait. Thereza was apparently as close a relative as the House of Austria was willing to part with after the experience of Leopoldina. Thereza was related to so many of Pedro's relatives — including, of course, his irascible grandmother Carlota — that Pope Gregory XVI had to approve the marriage. On May 30, 1848, there was a proxy marriage and Thereza sailed; she was twenty-one, Pedro not yet eighteen.

Pedro went aboard her ship when it entered port. He had read the novels of Walter Scott and was thus familiar with scenes of romance such as to set a young man's heart throbbing. What he saw was a woman who was short, walked with a limp from a physical defect, and was "somewhat lacking in grace ... unquestionably plain." Besides, despite sound schooling Thereza was a bit dull.

The portraitist had fudged the truth. Pedro is said to have turned away in momentary despair and remarked to his former governess, "They have deceived me, Dadama." Twenty years later, when his daughters were both to be married to grandsons of France's monarch in exile, Louis Philippe, Pedro made sure they met their prospective husbands before committing themselves.

Yet Thereza was devoted to her husband, and he, in turn, was faithful to a fault. She came to be known as "the Mother of Brazilians." They had two sons, both of whom died while young, and two daughters, Isabel and Leopoldina. This family served as the sort of model that its predecessor could not; it represented intelligence, compassion, and gentility, giving Brazilians, members of a large and boisterous society, an important focus. The reign of Pedro

II was as effective as could be expected in a day when monarchies were ending, serving as an imprimatur on Brazil's republican birth. Pedro II and daughter Isabel were identified with the eventual, belated, end of slavery. When his time came, Pedro II was a paragon of graciousness as he sailed into exile.

Slavery was important to Brazil and suggests much of Pedro II's ambivalent role. Liberals won control of Pedro's education and brought him to power hoping he would lead their various causes, including abolition of slavery. Once he was monarch, however, Pedro had to deal with the realities of an unruly populace whose economy was inextricably entwined with slave labor.

After the mid–1830s, Brazilians gathered more power to democratic, if unpredictable, institutions, while stripping power from the monarchy. The power of the king's council was diminished, while elections were spun out to the provinces. In an atmosphere of untried institutions and uncertain allegiances, however, a clever monarch could hold sway. Pedro was not averse to ignoring the law, and there were many officers whom he would simply fire. As for the often raucous Chamber of Deputies—the law required voters to have some income but did not require them to have any education—its members were a rambunctious lot. Pedro suspended the Chamber of Deputies eleven times.

In addition, Pedro was constantly meddling in the affairs of ministers and of the aristocratic Senate, where members held life terms. His powers were weak, but his intellectual strength was great, suggesting that he could halt or delay undesired actions, but had a problem getting things to move. Politicians from across a huge nation offered a variety of challenges, and Pedro's *poder moderador* was no power at all if not reinforced by popular will. Manoel de Oliveira Lima has called Pedro II's regime a "dictatorship of morality."

By 1845, Pedro ruled a population of 7 to 8 million subjects, virtually all along the coast: a few hundred mestizos; 1 million whites, Creoles, and Portuguese; 1.5 million full-blooded Indians; and 5 million slaves. Except for the Spanish colonies of Puerto Rico and Cuba, Brazil and the United States were the only important places in the western hemisphere clinging to slavery. To the dismay of Pedro II, Brazil would hold on even longer than the United States.

It is often asserted that the slave's lot in Brazil was generally better than it was in the United States. Gilberto Freyre has pointed out that the long and deep relationship between Africa and Portugal—from the Moorish penetration of tiny Portugal to miscegenation in Brazil—has created the special "influence of the African, either direct or vague and remote." The ambiguity of the relationship was evident through seventy-five years between the rejection of slavery by other Latin American republics and Brazil's grudging acceptance of emancipation.

Attempts to end the importation of Africans through 1845 were largely brushed aside. Internal disorder, massive geography, and a lack of will prevented enforcement. After that year, when the law imposed by the British expired, imports soared. In 1846, 19,453 slaves were imported; in 1847, the number was approximately 50,000 and rising.

When the British insisted on switching enforcement of slavery law to British admiralty courts, and, later, when British ships began entering Brazilian ports in pursuit of slavers, much more was done to enflame relations with white Brazil than to diminish the growth of black Brazil. Not until 1850 were Brazilian authorities able to begin to staunch the flow.

Relations between a proud Brazil and a haughty, powerful Britain continued a broken course throughout this period. Brazilians were quick to chaff, and otherwise minor incidents related to British sailors deteriorated into a six-day blockade of Rio by British ships in 1862–63. These violations of Brazilian sovereignty forced Pedro, a private opponent of slavery and anything but a firebrand, to affect a public posture of nationalism. When angry Brazilians rattled their untried sabers, the scholarly Pedro drew himself to his full, impressive height and offered to go to war to defend his country's honor. "I am the equal of any other Brazilian citizen," he soberly announced.

The fundamental problem, however, worsened. It is not surprising that the Brazilian legislature recognized the belligerency of the Confederate States of America. Slavery was a powerful bond. By 1862, fully one-fourth of the Brazilian population, were slaves, some 1.7 million slaves in all. In 1870, one-fifth of Rio's 250,000 population, was counted as slaves. Pedro and others, frustrated by their inability to curb slavery through legislative measures, began in 1871 a fund to buy slaves' freedom, and Pedro once went so far as to buy a slave's freedom in the street.

Adding to Brazil's general malaise and Pedro's inability to govern were military fanatics along the country's southern border. Pedro's father had suffered a loss of prestige from civil war in the south, but now the threats were tripled from across the border with three neighbors. Juan Manuel Rosas, the Argentine tyrant so vehemently opposed by Sarmiento, drew Brazil into the problem created by his capacity for malice; Uruguay was chronically unstable; and, worst of all, Paraguay's Francisco Solano López, along with his son, turned Paraguay into an armed camp, a nation of fanatics who would eventually, through virulent, mindless warfare, seriously deplete the population of men.

Pedro II, a friend of Argentine President Bartolomé Mitre, the man who did much to restore his country after Rosas, insisted on going to the front in 1865 as the three allies fought to bring López down. "I want to go," Pedro announced when his advisors sought to restrain him. "If not permitted to go as Emperor, I will abdicate and go as a private citizen. Though I may not be permitted to go as a general, the quality of a Brazilian cannot be taken from me; I will enlist with a musket as a volunteer for the fatherland."

In July 1865, he departed for the front, accompanied by one son-in-law, later joined by the other. He "attended"—a term that suggests gentility, certainly not fierceness—the siege of Uruguayana. He opposed, in his humanitarian way, bombardment of the town, and, indeed, the battle was won without bombardment. His visit is said to have "stimulated allied solidarity" with Uruguay and Argentina, and he returned to Rio in November, unscathed.

This almost comical war record ought not disguise his determination, however.

When in 1867 a peace initiative was advanced by Paraguay, Pedro rejected it, with disastrous consequences. "For a time he stood almost alone in his demand that the war go on," writes Williams, "his was the responsibility for prolonging it." It dragged on in the face of insane determination on the part of the defeated, but unrelenting, Paraguayans. Paraguay's male population, almost literally, fought to the death.

The estimates of Brazilian losses range from 35,000 to 50,000 lives in five years of conflict. The war cost Brazil $30 million. Pedro's hair, light brown at the outset, was almost entirely white at the armistice. He was forty-four years old.

It was time for Pedro II to retire from the stage of history. In 1871–72 he made a trip, his first, to Portugal, then on to Europe and Egypt. He was nothing if not modest, carrying his own valise, his own umbrella. When Victor Hugo, weary of an endless stream of admirers, refused to accept an invitation to call on Pedro, Pedro called on Victor Hugo, who called him "the grandson of Marcus Aurelius" for the intelligence of his monarchy. If all monarchs were like Pedro, Hugo asked rhetorically, who could be a republican? In 1875 Pedro visited the United States, traveling from New York to California and back again.

The United States was rebuilding from the Civil War, and Europe was growing with the bulk of the Industrial Revolution. Brazil, Pedro knew, was entering its own difficult phase. "Very few nations are prepared for the system of government toward which we are headed," he wrote in a personal note in 1879, "and I certainly would be better off and happier as president of a republic than as constitutional emperor." Once again, however, despite the lofty philosophy he was disturbed by the political mediocrity he saw resulting from Brazilian elections.

He proposed progressive reforms, but his proposals were not joined by legislative force. Improved education was Pedro's principal concern — "if I were not an Emperor, I would like to be a teacher" — but he also wanted better irrigation in the northeast, a national school of agronomy, improved rail and telegraph lines, easier credit for investment. To rebuild the population after the war with Paraguay he wanted to encourage immigration.

Slavery was outlawed in 1888, while Pedro, very ill, was recovering in Milan. "Oh, what a great people, what a great people," he wired home, then, broke into tears. He wrote a sonnet to commemorate emancipation.

When he returned to Brazil in August, however, he found resentment over emancipation was strong and weariness with the monarchy widespread. "The Emperor of Brazil is personally popular," wrote the U.S. representative to Secretary of State William Seward, "not so the Empire." Biographer Reichmann adds that "at the end of Pedro's regime nobody came to his aid, although almost everybody respected him." Pedro's response, typically, was gentle: "[I]f Brazilians do not want me for their emperor, I will go and be a professor."

The professor's massive class was almost over. He was criticized as "soft" on Freemasons, those enemies of the Church, and was overwhelmed by antimonarchists dominating both houses of the legislature. Only Pedro's personal popularity stayed the inevitable.

Enter the military, politicized by the slavery debate, disaffected by the long war against Paraguay, surly because of a reorganization plan, impatient with rioting. General Manoel Deodoro da Fonseca, commandant and vice president of always troublesome Rio Grande do Sul, became the lightning rod for dissent. He was joined by a teacher at the military academy, Lt. Col. Benjamin Constant Coelho. The year 1889 was a long slide away from monarchy, and in November a republic was proclaimed.

Pedro's feelings were hurt when the revolutionaries held him in his palace, an insult for such a reasonable, gentle man. Although he said he wanted to stay in Brazil, he made it known he was ready for exile, and Deodoro informed him, "The country expects that you will know how to imitate, in submission to its desires, the example of the first Emperor." On the boat on November 24, Pedro's fourteen-year-old grandson suggested that a pigeon be sent back carrying a farewell message. Pedro wrote the note and attached it to the bird's leg, only to stand on deck and watch the pigeon beat its way against a strong headwind until finally, exhausted, it fell into the waves.

Soon after reaching Portugal, Pedro's beloved Thereza died, and he wrote in his diary, "I can only weep the happiness of forty-six years.... Nothing can express how much I have lost.... I wish that my daughter would come." His daughter came, but Pedro, visited by an endless stream of admirers, lived only two more years himself. He died at sixty-six in December 1891 in a Cannes hotel. A small placard outside his apartment said simply, "D. Pedro de Alcántara," but his countrymen remember him as Pedro the Magnanimous.

9

José Martí
Revolutionary Poet
1853–1895
(Cuba)

> I cultivate white roses
> In January as in July
> For the honest friend who freely
> Offers me his hand.
> And for the brute who tears from me
> The heart with which I live,
> I nurture neither grubs nor thistles,
> But cultivate white roses.

José Martí remains one of the most exalted figures of Latin America's wars of independence. He was a leader in the struggle to free Cuba, the last New World colony that Spain still clutched as the twentieth century approached. Yet he lived his life far from the fighting until that last, fatal moment when he thrust himself into the battle. Martí articulated revolution as a journalist, poet, and orator. Also, he was an ardent lover whose charms were known to many women, except, alas, his long-suffering wife. History cast Martí as an exile, condemning him to an odyssey throughout Europe and the Americas, circling, never settling on the island he sought to free. But his words, still heard, made him one of the region's most enduring heroes.

José Julian Martí y Pérez was born on January 28, 1853, into a Cuba as isolated and anomalous as the island is today. Half a century had passed since Haiti led the way, and between 1810 and 1824 the Spanish-American colonies had followed, making abolition of slavery a principle on which they formed themselves. Yet Cuba languished, along with Puerto Rico, as a royal colony with a slave economy.

There were independence movements in both Cuba and Spain, but dissent, even favoring modified autonomy as part of a commonwealth, was harshly put down by royal troops. Cuba lived in the preceding century because Mother Spain still dwelled there. The Martí family harbored no notions of independence and ignored politics in general. Everything was safer that way.

Don Mariano Martí y Navarro was a native of Valencia who served in the Royal Artillery Corps before emigrating to Cuba about 1850. He was a simple man, a policeman, sometimes a tailor of uniforms, sometimes out of work. He married Leonor Pérez, also of modest background, in 1852, when he was forty-seven and she was twenty-two.

José was born less than a year later. They had six other children, all girls. Life in the Martí home was one of constant economic strain, with Don Mariano periodically petitioning one government office or another to obtain a job. Martí was bright enough to have handled, while still a boy, the clerical tasks attached to his father's post as a policeman.

But if the home life of Martí was isolated from politics, school and the neighborhoods were not. The Havana school he attended — and where he won awards in arithmetic and sacred history — was directed by Rafael María de Mendive, whose tutelage included large doses of contemporary politics. Mendive's political activities made him a target of the authorities because the Spanish monarchy, threatened by republicanism at home and separatists on the island, clung to its final possessions with a blind tenacity. Royal interests were guarded by bands of armed roughnecks called "Volunteers." Much of the dissent emanated from small clubs, like Mendive's, who made public their literary aspirations, but kept secret their revolutionary publications. The mixture was one of art and politics, and the model was a strong one for the young Martí.

On October 10, 1868, when Martí was fifteen years old, there was an uprising in the small town of Yara. "The cry of Yara" would become a symbol of revolution. By the next year, the United States, which looked down on Cuba the way an anteater regards a particularly fat ant, threatened to recognize the insurgents as belligerents.

Mendive's school was a lightning rod in a charged atmosphere with revolutionary literature blowing through the streets. Much of it derived from the lack of accurate information. After every clash, Cubans' only source of news as to how each side acquitted itself had to be gleaned from propaganda sheets. One product of the tension was that combination of fire and arrogance for which defenders of the Spanish Crown have distinguished themselves. In January 1869, at a time the Crown was trying to mollify critics by recalling a particularly offensive captain general, a student was slain in Havana for not yielding the way to a Spanish officer in the street.

In response to indignation, someone, apparently the Volunteers, fired into a crowded Havana theater on opening night of a drama reputed to be unpatriotic. By exquisite coincidence, it was the next morning that Martí, days before his sixteenth birthday, broke into print. His dramatic poem told of Abdala, who sacrifices himself for the ultimate triumph of Nubia: "Oh, how sweet it is to die when one dies fighting boldly to defend one's country."

The poem was published in *La Patria Libre,* a democratic, cosmopolitan weekly conceived and edited — for one issue only — by a close friend and schoolmate of Martí, Fermín Valdés Domínguez. The publication was sponsored by Mendive, giving it the patina of advanced schoolwork, but Martí's parents were unimpressed. His father was, after all, an officer of the regime. Besides, when dealing with an enraged, dying monarchy, there is no such thing as a schoolboy's prank.

Mendive, who had been in a box seat at the theater, and whose mother-in-law was a part owner, was arrested, imprisoned for four months, and exiled to Spain. For the while, Martí was safe, but in the autumn, there was another disturbance. Some boys had the audacity to laugh during a Havana military parade honoring the birthday of the Spanish regent. One of the boys was the brother of Fermín Valdés. Officers searched the Valdés house and found the revolutionary literature of adolescents; Martí was implicated.

Most damaging, in the eyes of investigators, was a letter from Fermín and Martí to a third schoolmate who had joined the Spanish army as an officer. They accused him of "apostasy," a charge the authorities interpreted as mutiny. At their trial, both boys claimed authorship of the letter. But when the judge questioned them, it was Martí who delivered a speech proclaiming Cuba's right to independence. Fermín was sentenced to six months in prison. Martí got six years. He was sixteen years old.

From prison, he wrote to his mother and sent along a photograph showing him in a chain that stretched from his waist to his ankle. "I am sixteen years old," he wrote, "and already many old men have told me that I seem old. To a certain extent they are right, for if I have in its full strength the recklessness and effervescence of youth; I have, on the other hand, a heart as small as it is wounded. It is true that you suffer intensely, but it is also true that I suffer more."

His father, visiting him in prison, was shocked. He worked in a limestone quarry, where conditions were always harsh, and where men were sometimes blinded by the kilns. Using his position as a policeman — lowly, but one that put him in contact with notables — his father got Martí transferred to a cigar factory, where conditions were better and prisoners were only fastened to their work tables.

His mother was able to get his sentence changed to exile, and he was moved to the Isle of Pines. Until he was finally exiled to Spain in January 1871, Martí was confined for approximately a year. The harshness of his treatment was attested to by a recurring leg injury he carried for the rest of his life. It was a lesion caused by a blow from a chain, and, despite two operations, its pain returned periodically, sometimes debilitating him. By the end of his sixteenth year, Martí had been jerked from schoolboy revolutionary romanticism to the hard life of a nineteenth-century convict.

For some, the lesson learned would have been sufficient. Martí was not yet out of high school and could, eventually, have returned to Cuba. The alternative was one of the many émigré colonies that Spain's recalcitrance had sown around the world. The importance of his choice was made clear about the time Martí arrived in Spanish exile with publication of the *Book of Blood,* published by the exile community in New York. It listed the dates and places where 4,478 Cuban *independentistas* had been shot or garroted and suggested that more than 150,000 had been killed in the continuing civil war to free the last colony of the hemisphere.

A slight man, already in poor health because of his imprisonment, Martí took on a demeanor of pained sorrow. Upon hearing that eight Cuban students had been murdered by the Volunteers, he began wearing black. When his old friend Fermín Valdés saw him in Spain he described him, in the words of one Martí biographer, as "emaciated and melancholy."

Nevertheless, among émigrés he was introduced to more freedom of discussion than he had ever experienced. To continue his education, he enrolled in both secondary school and the university, in law, at the same time. He earned a living by tutoring and published in a Cádiz newspaper a fragment of what would be his first book, *The Military Prison of Cuba.* Although bothered, at times severely, by his leg, Martí spent some of his happiest years during this time. There were museums, the theater, art, the world of émigré salons a wider world than he had ever known. There was also a love affair — his brooding disposition seemed a particular attraction to women throughout his life — with the wife of a host. This predilection for the wives of hosts would follow him.

Martí spent four years in Spain. But although he was there when the king abdicated in 1874 and during the short-lived republic the following year, he was apart from these events, writing poetry, completing his high school studies, and readying himself for university examinations. Martí's intellect and rhetorical power would allow him to assert himself as a leader of the rebellion against the claims of fighters. He could make no pretense of being a military man, despite his record of endurance in prison. Nor did his social status or age entitle him to respect within the émigré community. So he formed his prospects from intelligence and literary style and cast his future with the rebellion.

In the summer of 1874 he passed the preliminary requirements for a law degree, and then took exams for a high school diploma in philosophy and letters. In late September and early October he took, almost back-to-back, examinations in Greek language and literature and in critical studies of Greek authors, in metaphysics and historical geography, in Spanish history and the Hebrew language. On October 20, he asked that a date be set for this final examination, and it was set four days later. He drew three topics at random and chose "Roman political and forensic oratory: Cicero as its supreme expression; speeches analyzed according to his works on rhetoric." He was given three hours by himself to prepare, then summoned to develop his thesis before a committee, which asked questions for thirty minutes. He took a grade of *sobresaliente,* outstanding.

Because he could not pay either school the necessary fee, Martí was given only certificates, not the diplomas he needed to guarantee work as an accredited teacher. Still ahead of him was a life of wandering, without independent income, and the lack of accreditation would continually hinder him.

When he decided to leave Europe, Valdés insisted that they spend some time in the museums of France and England. In December 1874, in Paris, a fellow poet introduced Martí to Victor Hugo, who was, like most intellectuals of the time, a supporter of Cuban independence. At Valdés' expense, Martí sailed from Southampton first class.

His eventual destination was Mexico City, where Martí was to be reunited with his family, but he arrived just weeks after Ana, a sister with whom he had been particularly close, had died. His family, he discovered, had not prospered, but had been held together with the help of benefactors and what the women could earn by sewing.

In Mexico at that time the political and literary climates were perfect for Martí. President Sebastian Lerdo de Tejada carried on *La Reforma,* the liberalization set in motion by his predecessor, Benito Juárez, who had died two years before. Too briefly, nascent democracy offered Mexico promises that would never be fulfilled. But in that fragile environment, Martí found a home writing columns for *Revista Universal,* owned by a Lerdo liberal. Martí adopted the pen name "Orestes," the son of Agamemnon and Clytemnestra who avenged his father's murder by slaying his mother.

Martí's wit won him immediate acceptance in Mexican literary society, requiring, to his apparent delight, that he occasionally clear away the chiffon in order to clear his head. One prestigious salon was presided over by Rosario La Pena, whose beauty and perfidy had reputedly driven one poet to despair and suicide. Martí, as ever, brooding, seemed at the point of falling gladly into Doña Rosario's gossamer net. But the vehemence of his ardor scared her off. Martí was not a man of half-measures, and in this instance his exuberance apparently saved him.

In his writing, Martí was a willing conduit for the Indian strength that flowed through *La Reforma.* The Indian peasant was the populist foundation of Mexican reform, and Martí thought he saw important differences between a natural, growing America and the aging, posturing Europe from which he had just come. Fundamental to Cuban independence, Martí would argue, was freedom for slaves, and during this time in Mexico he broadened as a thinker and as a moralist.

In this respect he broke from Latin American thinkers of his time who had given up on European scholasticism — medieval attempts to "prove" the existence of God — only to mire themselves in the fashionable European "logical positivism" — a modern conceit that science will get you where God can't. Martí, the chain-gang veteran and the Cicero scholar, would have none of this intellectualism. "Abstractions are proved by abstractions," he wrote contemptuously. "I have an immortal spirit because I feel it, because I believe in it, because I want it."

In 1876, Lerdo was toppled by Porfirio Díaz, *La Reforma* ended, and night again descended on Mexico. Martí, although allowed to continue writing, became, in the chill of the new conservatism, a foreigner. His writing had to be confined to Mexican affairs and could not stray toward criticism of the Spanish and their Cuban slave colony.

Martí's position was tenuous. He had become a favorite of Mexico City's *tertulias,* the literary clubs, but he had neither sought citizenship nor saved any money. With the change of government in Mexico, he was transformed, almost overnight, from a welcome friend to a suspicious alien. In early 1877, under the pretense that he was going to Guatemala, he sailed for Havana. He used the assumed name "Julian Pérez," his mother's maiden name.

In Havana he saw only the futility of a revolution now nine years old. It was suggested that he would be welcome in Guatemala as other Cuban revolutionaries had been. After arranging for his family to return to Havana, Martí returned to Mexico City, determined to go on to Guatemala. Before leaving the city, however, he asked Carmen Zayas Bazan, the daughter of another Cuban exile living in Mexico City, to marry him when he returned. Then, alone, without a job and without a country, he set out.

By now, Martí's reputation, in several respects, preceded him. For one thing, work was easier to find, and Martí began teaching straightaway. For another, as biographer Felix Lizaso puts it, "Everywhere, from Southampton to the Atlantic Coast of Guatemala, there had been a woman's soul to comfort him." It is said that a young Guatemalan woman pined away and eventually died of longing when she found out Martí was engaged. After nine months in Guatemala, he returned to Mexico City to marry Carmen and bring her back with him.

But the most significant aspect of Martí's reputation was his inability to resist a fight. The diminutive Martía—"frail little man of genius" as Lizaso—calls him who had paid for his views with imprisonment, hard labor, and exile, would not accede to authority. His opposition to slavery and his insistence on democracy made him important enemies, and this image lay at the root of his appeal. He had neither won fights nor gathered armies, but the popularity of his writing as champion of common people was such that Guatemala's elitist regime eventually forced him to leave.

Rather than go to New York City, his first inclination, Martí followed his wife's suggestion to return to Cuba in the autumn of 1878. Her parents had just gone back, and it appeared that the insurrection, after ten years, was ending. The government guaranteed increased freedom. The hope was short-lived. The royal mentality reverted to its ancient ways. The authorities would grant Martí only temporary certification as a teacher, citing the old fact that he had never acquired his degrees. He found work in a law office and taught part-time.

He also found some work as a journalist, but, as might be imagined, his writing was inhibited. He found a forum, however, as a speaker, and in the spring of 1879, he was asked to speak at a gathering of prominent people in Havana.

His speech contrasted two kinds of political philosophies. One, he said, makes demands of its contemporary adherents without violating the spirit of its founders, its first heroes. To this kind of philosophy, Martí tipped back his head and quaffed a toast.

The other kind, he continued, turns its back on its followers, refuses to hear their needs, and fails to give voice to the truth. Rather than drink to this kind of political philosophy, Martí whirled and smashed his glass.

The captain-general was told of Martí's remarks. A week later, he showed up himself to hear Martí deliver the principal address honoring a noted violinist as part of a contest for promising young musicians. Martí, true to form, called the truce between the Cuban authorities and the rebels "a lying transaction." The captain-general is reported to have said: "I do not want to remember what I have heard, what I did not think anyone would ever say in front of me, a representative of the Spanish government. I am going to conclude that Martí is a madman ... but a dangerous madman."

A Havana discussion group—a *liceo*—that had taken Martí in was censured by the establishment press. As a result of the news, he became more popular than ever. The attraction Martí's ideas had for Latin Americans outside Cuba was beginning to take hold among Cubans, who had never been allowed to read him. Then Martí's temporary teaching certificate expired, and his financial straits—Carmen had given birth to a son—grew worse.

His family's poverty, however, did not stand in the way of Martí's plotting. At the law office, as his employer nervously shifted clients to another room, Martí conducted strategy sessions. The authorities, meanwhile, had one eye on Martí and the other on fellow rebels Antonio Maceo, who was black, waiting in Jamaica, and José María Moneada, gathering an army in Oriente province at the eastern tip of the island, far from Havana and a traditional focus of insurrection. Calixto Garcia, only recently released from prison in Spain as a result of the truce, also plotted.

Finally, the authorities' nerves could stand it no longer. Martí was having coffee with a friend and fellow conspirator in September 1879, when a messenger called him away. He returned after a moment to tell his friend to stay and finish his coffee. He would not be returning.

Again exiled to Spain, he immediately traveled to France. By now his reputation was assured, so along his wandering route there were likely to be famous admirers, like Sarah Bernhardt in Paris. He went on to New York, where his writing in the *Hour* and the *New York Sun* would enhance his reputation as an observer of the cultures of both Americas.

In New York he enlarged his reputation in another way. Needing a place to stay, Martí was taken in by a Cuban émigré, Manuel Mantilla, and his Venezuelan wife, whose name, like that of Martí's wife, was Carmen. Carmen de Mantilla was a woman of great charm, and in the Mantillas' East 29th Street apartment she presided over the salons that Martí convened continually. Indeed, they cemented a relationship that left her, when Martí departed for Venezuela a year later, pregnant.

He began teaching in Caracas and founded a magazine that lasted two issues before running afoul of the authorities. In this case, Martí published a eulogy for Cecilio Acosta, whose record as a democrat had placed him in opposition to the despotic Venezuelan president, Antonio Guzmán Blanco. Guzmán made things hot enough for Martí that he was forced to leave hurriedly in mid–1881, after he had been in Venezuela less than nine months. His letter of farewell, which was published, increased his popularity among Guzmán's opponents, and Martí continued to write for a Caracas newspaper, but from New York.

In the judgment of Manuel Pedro González, a Martí biographer, "a less uncompromising attitude would have brought him wealth and social prominence." As it was, his attitude kept him out of work. Martí was the soul of a revolution that could not find its body. He returned to New York, where, in a testament to human compassion, Manuel Mantilla took him in again. Martí's wife and child were brought up from Havana and moved into the Mantilla apartment. Martí might have been satisfied with this arrangement, but his wife was not. After arriving in March, she took their son and returned to Havana and her family in November. That month, Carmen de Mantilla gave birth to a daughter.

Martí stayed in New York—save for brief trips to Mexico, Central America, and the Caribbean—planning, raising money, and recruiting fighters for a revolution that would not happen. He worked as a translator for D. Appleton and Company, the publisher, and he wrote about the arts, culture, and politics for newspapers from New York to Montevideo. During this period he recognized that a dangerous consequence of breaking the bonds of Spain would be avoiding the economic and cultural domination of the United States, with its "disproportionate craving for material wealth." The United States had hungrily eyed Cuba since buying the Louisiana Purchase from France in 1803 and the annexation of Florida in 1821. In 1823, John Quincy Adams had suggested that "laws of political as well as of physical gravitation" ruled the hemisphere and would bring Cuba into the U.S. sphere whenever it broke with, or was broken away from, Spain.

Living in the United States did nothing to ameliorate Martí's fears of such a fate. He saw the United States as exhibiting an unhealthy interest right across its southern neighbors. He wrote to a friend that he thought "my duty — inasmuch as I realize it and have the spirit to fulfill — it is to prevent the United States from extending itself through the Antilles and with that added momentum taking over our American lands. What I have done up to now, and what I shall do, is toward this end. It has had to be done in silence and indirection because there are things which, to be achieved, must be hidden; and should they be known for what they are they would raise difficulties too powerful to overcome.... I have lived inside the monster and know its insides."

When New York coachmen, mostly immigrants flooding into the country and working for less than a dollar a day, went on strike, Martí championed their cause against the private and government forces that sought to break their strike. He wrote that their goal was fundamental: "The employees, in mass, abandon the stables, demanding not higher salaries, nor seeking fewer hours, but because they are to be deprived of the right of association." Martí's defense of such causes has inclined modern adherents of several political stripes, from communists to reactionaries, to claim him. Thus today Cubans shout back and forth between Havana and Miami, each insisting that now, a century later, Martí would be on their side.

On which side one stood, Martí wrote, ultimately had to be made clear beyond words. He stated a personal principle when he eulogized abolitionist Wendell Phillips, whom he greatly admired. "An orator shines for his speeches," Martí wrote, "but he remains only for what he does. If he does not sustain his words with acts, his fame will evaporate even before he dies because he has been standing on a column of smoke." Martí would ultimately demonstrate how strongly he felt.

In Cuba, the rebellion had been dragged like great, empty cannon with broken wheels. There was never enough support among the Creoles to throw out the Spanish, yet the royal occupation was so clearly immoral that the insurrection struggled on. By 1894, relations among the rebels themselves were frayed from long wear; there were half a dozen strategies that many uses for every dollar raised, more frustration than could be measured. There was an apparent attempt to poison Martí while he was in Tampa trying to raise arms, ammunition, money, and men.

He went on to Key West, Mexico, and New Orleans. But although newspapers carried accounts of his efforts, for so long had Martí preached revolution and so many times had uprisings been put down that U.S. editors had increasing difficulty taking the movement seriously. In January 1895, however, the world, especially Spain, was shocked by a revelation. Perhaps the little man had not been standing on a column of smoke.

Because of confusion and dissension among the rebels, U.S. customs authorities discovered a shipload labeled "machinery" bound from Florida to Costa Rica that was weapons headed for clandestine unloading on the coast of Cuba. The authorities seized that ship and ordered that another, then two more, be searched. The proportions of the plot and the immediacy of action could not be determined; hence the seriousness of the situation could only be enlarged in Spanish imagination. Whatever was about to happen, it was bigger than people had realized.

Martí was chagrined. Like other rebel leaders, he was reduced to hiding from newspaper reporters.

But the news of aborted invasion had the effect of galvanizing rebel forces on the island and of increasing demands for support. In New York, Martí drafted a call to arms, a document owing more to romance than any understanding of military reality. The Spanish had been alerted, too. Nevertheless, Martí rhetorically charged. Émigrés were asked to mortgage their homes, if necessary, to raise new funds. Martí resolved to return to Cuba despite the setback, and he and an associate departed for Santo Domingo. There and in Haiti, at times on horseback visiting émigré enclaves, they searched for fighting men.

They got news of new outbreaks in Cuba and hastened their efforts. After so many years and so much death, it seemed that the time was finally coming to make it all count for something. "I called forth war," Martí wrote to a supporter. "With it my responsibility begins instead of coming to an end.... I shall raise the world. But my only wish would be to affix myself there, to the last treetrunk, to the last fighter, to die in silence. For me it is now time." As Martí and other leaders approached the point of landing, orders were for several small sorties to land at various points along the Cuban coast.

There was haste, and there was waiting. As Martí finally sailed slowly toward the coast of Cuba, he wrote to his daughter, María, in New York. The revolutionary was ever the pedant. He counseled her not to shy away, despite her tender years, from an effort to write a translation of a particular book from the French. He gave advice on style, and used his own experience as translator as an example. Above all, he said, write. "A page a day, my little daughter, learn from me. I have life on one hand and death on the other, and a nation on my shoulders, and see how many pages I write to you?" The letter held out the request, "Wait for me as long as you know I am living."

In Haiti, Martí and five other rebel leaders found out that a schooner captain hired to take them to Cuba had reneged. Nevertheless, with the complicity of Haitian authorities, they found passage on April 5 on a rundown German freighter that would put them off on a small boat near the coast. They went over the side the night of April 9 into a rough sea.

Reaching shore, the small band found the village of Cajobal, where residents, reluctantly at first, took them in. They made their way toward a rendezvous with other rebels, and Martí, spending his first days and nights as a soldier, seemed ecstatic. The others, seeing his enthusiasm, told him that not only had he been recognized as the official delegate of the Cuban Revolutionary party, but he had also been named a major general of the Army of Liberation.

The five first found a small rebel group, then, caught up with a column led by Maceo. There was Martí's first combat, in which he served as a medic. He sent a dispatch, as had been requested, to the *New York Herald*.

Martí was afraid, however, that for all his personal enthusiasm the revolution would again stall. He spurred Maceo to join forces with another column to mount a decisive assault. Maceo agreed, and the linkage was accomplished before the end of April. On May 19, the rebels approached the plain of Boca de Dos Rios, where they hoped to coordinate the efforts of both their cavalry and their foot soldiers. Spanish troops got there first.

When the battle was joined, Martí presented himself for orders in a battle that was quickly being dominated by the Spanish. Martí was ordered to the rear. Martí replied that he had encouraged the fight and was obligated to join it. When it was clear to the seasoned fighters around him that such an act was foolish, Martí spurred his horse toward Spanish emplacements. A friend named de la Guardia saw what he was doing and caught up to ride beside him. In the volley that ripped de la Guardia's horse from beneath him, Martí was knocked from his saddle.

His dead body fell too close to the Spanish lines to be recovered by the retreating rebels, and the Spanish refused to give it up until it had been demonstrated by the Spanish commander to his superiors.

When Martí's comrades got back to the rebel camp, they found an unfinished letter in which Martí, as always, was imploring, asserting his opinion, instructing, guiding.

10

Benito Juárez
Builder of Democracy
1806–1876
(Mexico)

For Latin America's former colonies, the last battle of independence was often followed by the first battle of civil war, and nowhere were centrifugal forces stronger than in Mexico, which is more than three times the size of Spain and Portugal combined. In addition, Mexico faced invasion by France, a determined effort not only to deprive Mexico of its independence, but to turn it into a bizarre, New World monarchy. No one did more to try to build the nation than Benito Juárez, warring with foreign invaders with one hand and building a nation with the other, maintaining his dignity all the while.

Benito Pablo Juárez was born on March 21, 1806, in a village of twenty Zapotec families in the mountains of Oaxaca, 250 miles southeast of Mexico City. In those mountains the viceroyalty, then dying, had never had much influence, although the Church reached everywhere. Juárez' father, godmother, and grandparents carried him to a nearby village, Santo Tomás Ixtlan, in order to find a church where he could be baptized.

Both parents were dead by the time Juárez was three, so he and his two older sisters went to live with their grandparents, who also died within a few years, starting Juárez on a round of uncles and friends who saw to the children's lessons. Juárez, who left a considerable body of writing, would recall that he bought his uncle the whip to be used when he had not studied hard enough. By his own evaluation, however, Juárez remained an indifferent student. It became clear that "only by going to the city could I learn."

To the city he went, although legend has it that the trip had extracurricular motivation. Juárez allowed himself to be talked out of his uncle's sheep, which he had been tending, by passing brigands. Rather than face punishment, he trudged twenty-five miles to the state capital.

There, he found lodging at the home where one of his older sisters, who had left her drunken husband, was working as a domestic. The owner, Antonio Maza, a produce wholesaler and perhaps a European, helped to polish the manners of the rough-cut boy and put him into school at the only place available, the seminary. His "patrimony" as a full-blooded Zapotec allowed him to study free.

At age fifteen, Juárez completed his studies in Latin grammar and had to refuse ordination. The idea of becoming a priest, he later wrote, was something "for which I felt an instinctive repugnance," an early indication of his view on one of the most bitterly divisive issues of Mexican society, the relationship between Church and state. Juárez knew, however, that Indian priests were trained just well enough to lead the faithful in prayer, but were not allowed to give instruction or to rise in the Church's hierarchy.

Still wishing to study, Juárez talked Maza into allowing him to stay at the seminary, but with a broader curriculum. When a secular school — Oaxaca's first, an example of the nation building going on opened — Juárez transferred. He eventually earned a degree in law, learning along the way Oaxaca's many lessons in politics. Away from the European affectations of Mexico City, the city provided a body of belief that convinced the young Juárez and others of the possibility of fulfillment of the nation's Indian heritage. Mexico remains a nation whose population is three-tenths racially and culturally Indian, six-tenths mixed, or mestizo, blood, and only one tenth European. Oaxaca was one of the places where Mexico's Indian consciousness has been defined.

Notions of independence were strong there. While Juárez was growing up, both of the priests of independence, Hidalgo and Morelos, fought important battles in Oaxaca. An Oaxaca contemporary of Juárez was Porfirio Díaz, who both helped shape Juárez' role in politics and built his own dictatorship. In the wild and wooly politics of Oaxaca — a disgruntled politician once took a shot at Juárez as he sat on his front porch — one of the lessons Juárez learned was to distrust "the enthusiasm of the crowd, which rarely examines events to their depths and causes, and always admires and approves anything that seems to it new and extraordinary."

During Juárez' early teenage years, the defeated vice-royalty was replaced by the abortive "monarchy" of Agustín de Iturbide and the inept dictatorship of Antonio López de Santa Anna. One of the many legends depicting Juárez' humility is the story of how Santa Anna — very European and a staunch guardian of church prerogatives — was once, during a visit to Oaxaca, served in a restaurant by a young Indian waiter — Juárez.

For Juárez personally, independence settled an important conflict between him and his benefactor, Maza. Although Juárez wanted a secular education, there was still pressure from Maza to follow the priesthood. Independence settled the issue: Juárez was spared the necessity of defying his benefactor when anticlerical rebels sent all bishops back to Spain. Juárez' military career, such as it was, was also resolved during this period. In 1829, when he was still studying law and teaching physics to help support himself, Juárez was drafted. Quickly, however, the Spanish, who had invaded Tampico from Cuba, were driven out. Four years later Juárez was briefly commissioned a captain during one of the periodic wars between clerical and anticlerical forces, a war that quickly passed over an issue that is still unresolved in Mexico.

Juárez' personality clearly inclined him toward teaching, but his lack of money led him to practice law. It was not a career without obstacles, for both the Church and politics were thoroughly mixed in with the courts. The influence of the Church, Juárez wrote, "Was almost omnipresent ... so they could indulge with impunity in every excess and every injustice."

In 1834, the young lawyer represented complainants before an ecclesiastical court. His clients claimed they were being overcharged for religious services. Juárez' argument prevailed, although he knew it was because the local authorities were liberals and he himself was a liberal deputy to the state legislature. The same authorities allowed him to get the offending priest banned from the parish. Alas, with elections there was a change in administrations, whereupon the priest not only returned to the village but had his accusers, and any who dared take up their case, jailed. Juárez returned to the village and was jailed. Released after nine days, he returned to Oaxaca a wiser man.

Despite this volatile environment, Juárez' political career advanced. He was thought of as a puritan, standing just over five feet tall in his customary black suit, and he did nothing to dispel the image of a bureaucrat picking his way along the difficult, always changing paths of Mexican politics. He had a reputation for thoroughness, and he nurtured it. He was called —

not always admiringly — "the little Indian," and he was willing to take on any administrative task, often turning the result to the benefit of his beliefs. He was appointed a judge and, eventually, president of the provincial court.

Mexico's internal struggles often ran parallel to the territorial ambitions of the United States. Where Americans saw their destiny manifest, Mexicans saw their territory being stolen. The United States was headed for San Francisco—founded by the Spanish in 1776 — and would absorb Texas and fully half of the land claimed by the Republic of Mexico along the way. In the Peace of Guadelupe Hidalgo, signed in March 1848, the United States paid $15 million, canceled all American claims against the defeated republic, and called home its troops. With a Prussian eye for detail, the United States filled in the Gadsden Purchase in 1853.

Throughout this turbulent period, Juárez' career was propelled by his administrative ability. While Mexican presidencies and personal ambitions rose and fell, somebody, quite simply, had to run the country, and one of those people was Juárez. In 1844, he was elected governor for the first of two terms. In late 1846 and early 1847, Juárez was one of nine men from Oaxaca to gather with other delegates in Mexico City — his first trip to the national capital — to revise the national constitution.

At that convention, the signal decision was made — to help pay the debt from the war with the United States— that part of the Church's property would be mortgaged. Secular-clerical conflict was again enflamed, and, Juárez recalled later, "I decided to go home and dedicate myself to the practice of my profession."

There was no escape, however. As the nation defined its democratic life, even Juárez' private life became an example, a model for people who had few models of modernity. In 1850, while he was governor, his two year old daughter, Guadelupe, died. In his grief, Juárez set an example by accompanying her body to a civic cemetery outside the city's walls to emphasize a liberal campaign encouraging hygienic burial. Conservatives considered such behavior blasphemous, although hygiene was not always possible in the traditional cemeteries administered by the Church, and Juárez wished to make his point.

"He is very homely," said his wife, Margarita, later, "but very good." Margarita, the daughter of Maza, Juárez' benefactor, was born just eight days after Juárez' twentieth birthday and married him when she was seventeen. Earlier, Juárez had sired two illegitimate children: a son with whom he maintained contact, and a daughter who became a drug addict and whose care Juárez entrusted to a long-time friend and his wife in Oaxaca. Tragedy also followed the large family — twelve children — born to Juárez by Margarita, and Juárez would bear countless domestic heartache's even as he wrestled with the republic's problems.

After leaving the governorship in 1852, Juárez became director of the Institute of Arts and Sciences, but within a year he was removed from the position by political opponents. Just weeks later, with Santa Anna back in power in Mexico City, Juárez was accused of inciting class warfare. As he prepared for a court proceeding in Ixtlan, he was arrested and ordered to Puebla, between Mexico City and the Gulf Coast. At Puebla, he was arrested by Santa Anna's son and taken to a wretched island prison off Vera Cruz.

In October 1853, along with his brother-in-law, Juárez was exiled, ending up in New Orleans. There he joined an émigré community, many of whom, like Juárez, had skin dark enough to make life difficult. The Mexicans were appalled at the slave markets they found among people fond of casting themselves as hemispheric leaders. There were conspiracies to return, but for the time being Santa Anna was propped in place by receipts from what Americans know as the Gadsden Purchase.

Finally, in June 1855, making his way across the country to meet with a rebel leader, General Juan Alvarez, Juárez was sidetracked in a typical display of his humility. On the trip, a rainstorm ruined Juárez' one good suit coat, so he showed up at the general's camp wearing the traditional white cotton shirt and pants of a Mexican peon. When an officer spotted him and found out that he could read and write, Juárez was made, apparently without his objecting, a corresponding secretary. Only later was Alvarez told that a letter had arrived at the camp addressed to "Sr. Licenciado Don Benito Juárez." Chagrined, Alvarez promoted Juárez to his staff.

After Alvarez' troops forced Santa Anna, once again, into exile, those who took power separated themselves over a kind of litmus test of liberality. Juárez was among the *puros;* others, more willing to compromise, were the *moderados.* Juárez fretted lest "the clerical-military" forces that Santa Anna had represented retain too much power. Juárez warned about politicians and generals who had "joined the revolution only to adulterate it." Juárez was most committed to what he saw as the necessity of controlling the Church. He supported the initiative to deny clerics seats in the national and state legislatures because, as he wrote later, they "believed themselves to be representatives in the congresses only of their class." Most of all, this was Juárez' chance to enact real reform.

When Alvarez moved into the presidency, and before Juárez returned to Oaxaca to resume the governorship, Juárez was a major influence on laws that ended the three decades of "the era of Santa Anna," laws that presaged *La Reforma,* the intellectual, social, and legal basis of modern Mexico. Although Alvarez allowed himself to be replaced by Ignacio Comonfort, a moderate, causing other *puros* to leave the administration, Juárez, who had been named by Alvarez minister of justice and public instruction, stayed. Seeing his chance to sculpt lasting reform, he acted fast.

"What most led me to decide to go on in the Ministry was the hope that I had the power to seize an opportunity," Juárez wrote, "to initiate one of the many reforms that society needed to better its condition, thus making use of the sacrifices that the people had made to destroy the tyranny that was oppressing them."

Special privileges for the military and the Church were among the most serious abuses Juárez wanted to stamp out. "I was occupied with working on the law for the administration of justice," he explained. "The revolution was triumphant, it was necessary to make effective the promises of reforming the laws that hallowed the abuses of the despotic power that had just disappeared. The previous laws on the administration of justice suffered from this defect: they established special tribunals for the privileged classes, making permanent in society the inequality that violated justice and that kept up a constant agitation of the social body."

Because of opposition by both Alvarez and Comonfort Juárez was not able to effect as sweeping a change as he sought: absolute elimination of all special courts for clerics and military personnel. "It was, then, very difficult to get anything useful done under such circumstances, and that is the reason that the reforms I effected in the law of justice were incomplete, limited as I was to the removal of the ecclesiastical exemption in the civil branch and being forced to allow it to remain in the criminal.... To the military was left only their exemption in crimes and misdemeanors that were purely military."

The law was published in November 1855, and the following spring another law established a process for breaking up the Church's great landholdings, allowing sale to tenants. Over the next two years, Juárez would help write the Constitution of 1857, which sought finally to separate Church and state and establish public schools. Then Juárez returned to Oaxaca, where he was elected governor with nine of every ten votes cast.

At home, he set in place other liberal reforms, but even as laws were enacted, traditions chafed. Comonfort was centralizing power, and defenders of the old prerogatives were reasserting their strength. The 1857 Constitution required civil officials to take an oath of allegiance to the state, but clerics threatened all who did with excommunication.

Late in 1857, although he had asked them not to, friends put Juárez' name forward for national office, and he was elected to the nation's second highest position, president of the Supreme Court, next in line for the presidency. In addition, at Comonfort's request, Juárez doubled as minister of the interior. That meant that in December, when Comonfort tried to seize supreme power, Juárez was caught in the middle again. Juárez stated his opposition, and Comonfort had him thrown in jail.

Then, although Comonfort was forced into exile, Juárez was not allowed to ascend to the presidency. Juárez and his supporters contended that it was his constitutional right, and Mexico fell again into civil war. His side by far the weaker, Juárez took a cadre of about seventy *puros* and fled the capital. For the next ten years, driven just ahead of would-be captors, Juárez represented constitutional government, but on the fly. "But where is he?" wrote a contemporary. "I do not know the bit of earth where he is right now, but ... in that corner will certainly be found the President."

Juárez was an exile in his own land. Defenders of the Church were determined that the *puros* meet their end. Liberal officials of the last regime also had to escape from Mexico City, sometimes in disguise. Juárez went first to Guanajuato, then Guadalajara, where he and his party were captured and threatened with being shot. They were freed only because confused, illiterate soldiers, unsure what they were fighting for, let them go.

On March 21, 1858, pushed toward the Pacific Coast, they saw in the distance an approaching band of Indians. The Indians had found out that the strange caravan was that of Don Benito Juárez, and they had brought wreaths of flowers in celebration of his fifty-second birthday. He was still their president.

On they went to Colima, where they were told the main constitutional army had been defeated. They labored on to New Orleans, where they caught a boat to Vera Cruz, a liberal stronghold. The government was finally off the road, and Juárez sailed into the port of Vera Cruz to a twenty-one gun salute. Margarita, then with eight children — ranging in age from infancy to fourteen years old — had arrived overland from Oaxaca, over difficult mountains.

Juárez was protected by governors defending their relative independence under federalism. In 1859 and again in 1861, Juárez issued decrees that institutionalized federalism and liberality, going for broke although he had no power. He had decided, he explained later, that this was an opportunity to speak his piece on the constitution and, at the same time, disestablish the Church once and for all. If he waited until he had real power, he reasoned, such views would cause civil war all over again. "Better one war than two," was his terse evaluation.

He decreed that all church property not used for worship was to be confiscated. This measure sought to correct an earlier, misguided reform that put church property up for sale, thus assuring that it would be bought up by the wealthy. The new decree was designed to put common land, *ejidos,* in the hands of peasants. He also decreed that the Church and state were separate, and while religious freedom was to be protected religion was not to spread its tentacles across state prerogatives.

In foreign affairs, more than decrees were needed. Mexico was in debt to almost every European capital that had a bank. Nations as powerful as Britain, France, and emerging Germany wanted their money and threatened to get it by taking customs receipts.

The United States, meanwhile, was sending mixed signals. Both the Union and the Confederacy wanted to buy Mexican commodities, but the Union also wanted to talk about a route to the West around the South. In the slave states, some leaders saw potential for added strength by acquiring northern Mexican states. Juárez found the former proposal troublesome, the latter odious.

To make matters worse, Juárez' representative in Washington, José María Mata, found himself dealing with mountebanks. Businessmen eyeing property in Mexico or just looking for opportunities there claimed expertise they did not have. Even President Buchanan had his eye on a piece of real estate in northern Mexico for a railroad right-of-way, and, more important, on the Isthmus of Tehuantepec, a narrow stretch across which an inter-oceanic railroad line might be built. When Buchanan had no luck with his representations to the government holding Mexico City, he turned to Juárez.

"I told him," Mata wrote to Juárez of Buchanan, "that I believed you would be willing to sanction any treaty that was based on principles of justice and was to the advantage of both countries." Mata had had enough of dealing with Washingtonians and wanted to return, but he counseled Juárez, "For my part, I consider it to the interest of Mexico to make those treaties, if in them the government of the United States binds itself to recognize and maintain in those routes the sovereignty of Mexico, and only in those treaties do I see a means of suppressing the rapacious spirit so prevalent in the southern states, precisely the ones closest to us."

Mata then made an eloquent statement regarding the future of relations between his country and the United States. "Perhaps I am deceiving myself," he wrote, "but I am convinced that Mexico is necessarily allied with this country, and that in order to preserve our independence and nationality it is necessary to adopt a policy that is based on fully liberal principles, that will serve the reciprocal interests of both countries, and that will permit the two peoples to come in contact with each other, so that they may know and appreciate each other better, and so that one country will lose its spirit of aggression and the other its mean distrust and absurd suspicion."

Without guarantees of Mexican sovereignty and dignity, Mata concluded, "in no case and for no reason should we consider the alienation of a palm's width of our territory."

Negotiations dragged on. U.S. military outposts spread across Mexico? The idea was out of the question for many Mexicans. Strengthen the forces of slavery? The notion was unacceptable to abolitionists. The figure of $4 million was discussed, with half going to settle American claims and half free and clear for Juárez' government. Was this a defensive alliance between the two countries, or a sale for hard cash? The "Treaty of Tehuantepec," which was never to be, did much to besmirch political reputations in both countries. Both the U.S. Senate and Juárez' cabinet — despite his support — rejected it. It was 1860, and the United States entered its own civil war. Half a century later the crossing would be built in Panama.

In March 1860 the siege of Vera Cruz was lifted as constitutionalist armies began to turn the tide. Toward the end of the year the civil war drew to a close. The successors of Comonfort fled into exile. It was the end of what Mexicans call "the War of the Reform." Juárez entered Mexico City, but his government was characterized by uncertainty. He expelled the ministers of Spain, Ecuador, and Guatemala, and the papal legate for their encouragement of reactionaries. Generals of the victorious forces arrested generals who had led the other side, and a kind of code emerged, born of necessity with almost constant civil war: if a commander had spared lives when possible, his life was spared.

The economy was in ruins. The design of a rational agronomy — a mixture of cash crops and sustenance — had to be ignored in the rush to satisfy creditors. Land redistribution would have to wait. The treasury was obligated to repay money stolen by commanders on both sides. The states took their cut of customs receipts before sending the diminished balance to the capital. Every month, the nation fell another $400,000 in debt.

Enter Maximilian. For four years, European arrogance would cause 40,000 Mexicans on both sides to be killed; 10,000 were wounded. Napoleon III, in an effort to prove himself his uncle's equal, provisioned and dispatched this "silly princeling," and Juárez was driven once again into internal exile.

In the autumn of 1861, Britain, Spain, and France signed an accord to collect their debts. The British insisted they held no territorial goals; the French and Spanish kept their own counsel. The divided United States was invited to join, but declined, coming up with absurd offers on its own. Confederates offered to return, in exchange for certain favors, California and New Mexico. The Union had in mind a $65-million purchase of mineral rights in several northern Mexican states.

In December 1861 and January 1862, matters were joined. Seven hundred British marines briefly landed at Vera Cruz. The Spanish invested the port city with 6,000 troops, and the French landed 2,500 soldiers and began to build troop strength by recruiting Mexicans. Juárez, in a gentlemanly if misguided gesture, gave permission to the invading commanders to move their troops inland away from the scourge of yellow fever along the swampy coast.

On May 5, a date that remains a proud symbol of Mexican history, the Battle of was fought. Puebla lies on the road from the coast to Mexico City. With heavy losses on each side, the French were defeated. For Mexico, however, satisfaction was short-lived.

During the rest of 1862, while Napoleon III sent more and more reinforcements, Juárez' government fought with itself. *Puros* worried about clerical power, demanding such measures as a reduction in the number of convents and a ban on sermons against the regime. With adversity at home and abroad — Juárez trying to prepare a second defense of Puebla — also had to deal with the death of a daughter and his father-in-law.

The French surrounded Puebla with 26,300 troops, including 2,000 reactionary Mexicans, in March 1863. Twenty-two thousand Mexicans loyal to Juárez fought back, holding out for so long they were reduced to eating dogs and cats. The French commander offered the Mexican commander the presidency if he would surrender. He refused, finally falling back to defend Mexico City against an onslaught of reactionaries commanded by Comonfort. When a supply train headed for the city was taken by Comonfort's troops, the capital was lost.

In May 1863, Juárez presided over the last session of the legislature. "Great has been the reverse we have suffered, but ... we shall fight on with greater ardor ... because the nation still has life, and strong sons to defend her." Once again Juárez fled the capital toward the wilderness of northern Mexico.

Maximilian and his queen Charlotte — he a Hapsburg without a throne, she a daughter of Leopold I of Belgium — arrived in Mexico in the spring of 1864. For them was established a system by which reactionary notables "elected" them, and they created the monarchy of Mexico, an idea previously considered by Agustín de Iturbide and Aaron Burr.

Driven north were constitutionalist armies, importuning all the while to the United States for arms. The times could not have been darker. In January 1864, a delegation claiming wide support asked Juárez to resign. Juárez refused, writing later that under those conditions, "in which power had no attraction, neither my honor nor my duty permitted me to abandon the power with which the nation had entrusted me."

When Juárez' party decided to travel to Monterrey, the delegation preceding him tried to welcome him to the city with a four-gun salute only to have opponents steal the four cannons and turn them on Juárez as he prepared to enter. Informed of this reversal, Juárez simply spent the night at a nearby ranch and resolved to try again the next day. "Pick up for me the clothes brushes that I left on the table where I was shaving," he calmly wrote to Margarita that night. "Remember me to our friends and many embraces for our children.... I am your husband, who loves you."

The next day, the governor of Monterrey, who was doing a thriving business in contraband with the Confederacy, made clear he was in no mood to receive Juárez. When an aide suggested that the presidential carriage proceed with haste, however, Juárez countermanded him: "At a trot," he said. "The President of the Republic cannot run." Before the day was out, however, Juárez, who had been prudent enough to keep the carriage waiting, had to beat a hasty retreat.

In late spring Juárez' last child was born, and in early summer his first grandchild. At the same time, although Juárez could claim no control over his own country, he began to garner sympathy outside his country. In the United States there was considerable contempt for this imposition of foreign power, which was precisely what the Monroe Doctrine was supposed to prevent. The American press identified Juárez' roving presidency with the true expression of the Mexican people. Victor Hugo, William Cullen Bryant, and Hamilton Fish, among others, added their rhetoric to his support. Nevertheless, by autumn 1864 he had been driven north to Monterrey — the irascible governor had earlier fled to the United States — and was forced to send his family first to Matamoros and finally to refuge in New Rochelle, New York. Juárez was so close to capture at one point that his coach was riddled with bullets, before he, too, fled to the United States.

American reporters eventually hounded Doña Margarita as a curiosity. She spoke no English and was defenseless, although a son-in-law did what he could to protect her. When she traveled to Washington and attended, as the wife of the Mexican president, some function, the American press made much of her wearing "jewelry" while her husband lived in poverty, narrowly avoiding capture. Then, two of their three sons died. Margarita made clear in her letters to Juárez that she felt responsible. Juárez feared for her sanity.

"Poor Margarita," Juárez wrote to his son-in-law. "How she will have suffered." He confessed to subordinates that he himself had trouble focusing: "You will appreciate all that I suffer," he wrote after the death of his son José, "from this irreparable loss of a son who was my delight, my pride, and my hope."

On March 21, 1865, while Juárez and his party found brief refuge in Chihuahua, local leaders insisted on celebrating his birthday. When glasses were lifted in a toast to his wife and children, Juárez wept.

Meanwhile, his forces in the field, because of inferior numbers and incompetent leaders, suffered defeat after defeat. What saved the day was Mexico's size. Maximilian's troops, although 35,000 strong, could not be everywhere. In addition, Porfirio Díaz, that other son of Oaxaca, proved a competent commander. When captured, he made a daring escape and set about raising another army.

Maximilian also had another problem: governing a population that included liberals. He issued proclamations that weakened the Church's position, stirring Mexico's oldest resentments. In December 1864, Maximilian confirmed the laws of *La Reforma,* losing the support of the clergy without gaining the adherence of liberals.

In the spring of 1865 the end of the American Civil War encouraged both sides in Mexico. Napoleon III had earlier suggested that American slaveholders colonize the Mexican state of Sonora, and now Maximilian suggested that Southerners bring their slaves into Mexico. Such schemes contributed to stories that Maximilian was losing his grip, and Mexican royalists began deserting his cause. On October 3, 1865, Maximilian decreed that "rebels" be shot, and within a few days a governor, a general, two colonels, and a priest died before firing squads.

Juárez also hoped to get help from the renewed republic to the north, a nation he now felt more comfortable dealing with. The response, however, was more of the same — the U.S. predilection for trying to buy what it needed. When his emissary in Washington informed him of the latest cash-for-acreage proposition in early 1865, Juárez replied: "The idea that some people have, as you tell me, that we should offer part of the national territory in order to obtain help is not only anti-national, but prejudicial to our cause.... The enemy may come and rob us, if that is our destiny, but we do not have to legalize that crime.... If France, the United States or any other nation should take possession of any part of our territory, and if because of our weakness we should be unable to drive it away, we should nevertheless leave alive the right of succeeding generations to recover it." Those remarks would be engraved on the memorial Mexicans built to Juárez.

By the end of 1865, Juárez had been driven out of the country, to El Paso, Texas, and was threatened by a rival for the presidency. The French controlled Chihuahua, just below Juárez' refuge. It was up to Maximilian to destroy himself. U.S. Secretary of State Seward, with the Civil War past, applied pressure to rid the continent of foreign intervention. Maximilian's wife, Charlotte, off in Europe trying in vain to rally support, was going mad. Maximilian faced desertions and the crumbling of an empire that had existed only in his mind. In the countryside, as French and reactionary forces retreated, harsh reprisals began.

It appeared that Juárez had won the war of waiting. "Impatient people," went a Juárez axiom, "are limbs of Satan." Díaz retook Oaxaca, and the constitutionalist Army of the North, augmented by volunteers from Canada and the United States, began to drive south. Juárez hurried along, too, so fast that he almost got himself captured while parading about in front of his troops, exhorting them. "I have received the sermon on what seems to have been my tomfoolery on January 27 at Zacatecas," he wrote to Díaz. "[But] there are circumstances in life in which it is necessary to risk everything, if one wishes to go on living physically and morally, and it is thus that I see the circumstances of that day. I got away with it, and I am happy and satisfied with what I did."

Republican victories continued in 1866, and the French forces that had propped up Maximilian's regime were recalled to take part in European wars in early 1867. It became clear even to Maximilian that the end had come, and he sent a messenger to Díaz, camped at Acatlan, requesting terms. Díaz refused to negotiate, and as the messenger waited out the night to return, Díaz paraded his troops beneath the man's window — in a circle in order to multiply their apparent number. Reactionary forces, without French leadership and arms, fell away before the republicans.

The last major battle was Querétaro, where reactionary forces converged on a plain north of Mexico City. They numbered 9,000. Arriving, battalion by battalion, were republican forces three times that number, including the volunteers from North America and Europe. They had been attracted, in the evaluation of an opponent, by the fact that Juárez was "not a man, but duty incarnate."

The republicans surrounded the reactionaries, and Maximilian was captured trying to escape at night. Imprisoned, he sent a message to Juárez asking for a meeting. Juárez replied that he could have his say at the trial. Pleas for Maximilian's life included those from Victor Hugo and Giuseppe Garibaldi.

The trial took place in a theater. Maximilian refused to attend. A seven number panel voted: three to banish, four to execute. On June 19, 1867, on the hill where he'd been captured, Maximilian and his two top officers were stood against a wall and surrounded on three sides by four thousand Mexican men at arms. As his final gesture, Maximilian stepped to the side and gave one of his generals the honor of standing in the center.

Knowing that Juárez had spoken of the day he might raise the Mexican flag over the National Palace, Díaz ordered a large flag sewn for the occasion be saved for Juárez' arrival. Juárez arrived late, delayed by rain, unable to pay his escort.

Margarita arrived with her five unmarried daughters and young Benito, her only surviving son. She brought the bodies of their two other sons. The family moved not into the national palace but into a hotel.

The task of rebuilding the country was too much for Juárez, as it was for everyone else. It was 1867, and he had stood for election in 1861. He called for elections, won easily, then had to satisfy himself with minor administrative victories while the army grumbled and priests won back the right to vote.

He suffered a stroke in October 1870, and his beloved Margarita died in their small house the following January. She was only forty-two years old. Juárez invited no one to her secular funeral, but respectful crowds lined the streets anyway.

Late in 1871, with Díaz, whom Juárez was probably holding at bay, and Sebastian Lerdo, Juárez' protégé, both impatient to succeed him, Juárez insisted on winning one more election. In July 1872 he went home from the presidential office complaining of chest pains. With forces loyal to both Díaz and Lerdo already forming in the hills, Juárez died in his bed, attended by one servant. Mexico's "Age of the Indian" was ended.

11

Pancho Villa

Political Warrior

1878–1923
(Mexico)

With Juárez gone, Porfirio Díaz did not delay long before overthrowing Juárez' successor and assuming dictatorial powers. He established a centralist government, imposed by an army that he dressed in uniforms copied from the French and Prussians. He turned back the clock.

The Spanish Crown had deeded virtually all of Mexico's land to fewer than five thousand colonists, and by the time Juárez became president half of the good land was owned by the Church. *La Reforma* certified some forty thousand transfers in an effort to redistribute the land to its original Indian owners, but when Juárez died the best land remained under control of the haciendas. The Age of the Indian was not an age at all, but a beginning; it had to be sustained. Díaz, however, used the land to enhance his power by distributing more of it to the haciendas. Large landowners were allowed to help themselves to both individual holdings and the Indian *ejidos,* farmed communally. To do this, Díaz chartered seventeen companies to survey traditional lands, allowing the companies to keep one-third of what they "found" uncharted and what they could "prove" unprotected by deeds. The legality of deeds was decided in Díaz courts; decisions were enforced by his ruthless rural police.

By 1910, after more than three decades of Díaz, more than 18 million acres, nearly one-third of the entire national territory, had been surveyed by Díaz' hand-picked companies and the land sold to new and old haciendas. Approximately five thousand Indian villages had lost their farms. Díaz, with his handsomely attired army, was seen abroad by leaders like 150 U.S. President Taft and German Chancellor Bismarck as a great leader. The foreign press described him as a hero.

Doroteo Arango, who would take the name Francisco Villa, was born on June 5, 1878, at the beginning of Díaz' regime. He is said to have weighed twelve pounds at birth. Although Villa was born in Central Mexico, he would claim as his domain the northwestern states near the Rio Grande, especially Chihuahua. It is a dry, barren region just below the land taken from Mexicans to form Texas, New Mexico, and Arizona. Roving country just below the belly of the United States, Villa embodied the dream of many Mexicans; he was an avenging cowboy, a pure, if rough, assertion of Mexican *machismo,* leaving in his dust the Colossus of the North.

At about the age of 17, while breaking horses on a hacienda, Villa killed the owner's son, who, according to legend, had molested Villa's sister. Villa fled to the hills and changed his name on joining the robber band of Ignacio Parra. When Parra was shot down robbing a stagecoach, Villa, who had become known as both intelligent and merciless, took over.

In 1908, when Villa was thirty-one, he retired from banditry, married Luz Corral, and opened a butcher shop in the city of Chihuahua. His markup was substantial: his men rustled the beef he sold. This picture of Villa as a bourgeois merchant in downtown Chihuahua might seem farfetched, but aspects of this image will recur. He was a simple, if exceedingly ruthless, man. Villa did not drink or smoke, and while he chased as many skirts as his shooting eye spotted, there was a bit of the burgher about him. He was stout, with spindly, bowed legs and pigeon toes. Even with his mustachio, when Villa wore a three-piece suit — which he sometimes did, even on horseback — he gave the impression of a German sausage salesman.

But friend and critic alike saw Villa as transformed on horseback. In the saddle, because of the disproportionate size of his torso, his five feet, ten inches seemed taller. The paunch disappeared, and so natural was his equestrian ability that at the head of his cavalry, *los dorados,* "the golden ones," Villa cut such a figure that he was dubbed "The Centaur." In 1910, as Mexico's definitive revolution toppled Díaz, Villa was recruited by landowners, the very men who would later want him destroyed. During the Revolution, however, landowners needed their own armies even as Italian princes had needed *condotierri,* hired warriors. Villa was hired by supporters of Francisco I. Madero.

Madero, of Jewish ancestry, was a man in the most tenuous of positions. With a coal black beard and an intense glare, Madero was known to his liberal admirers as "immaculate," "incorruptible," even a "redeemer." Although he suffered from the liberal intellectual's tendency to ambivalence, supporters saw him as offering the perfect alternative to the long, oppressive night imposed by Díaz.

Madero was no more a warrior than Juárez. The masses believed in him because he did not appear to be seeking every opportunity to exploit them and because he had, insofar as possible, stood up to Díaz. In the reorganization that followed Díaz' flight, Madero was rising to the top. But the reorganization itself was rough. Even after Madero won his electoral mandate, it had to be defended against those who were unwilling to change. Villa was recruited to defend Madero's ascension to the presidency. He would continue to fight Madero's assassins, carrying on the struggle not as a bandit, but as an instrument of politics, a general, a cavalry tactician.

Because the decade was filled with civil war, it was also filled with opportunity for warriors. At the point Villa was hired, he was commissioned as a captain who commanded but fifteen men. Before long he was a colonel, commanding several thousand.

While only a devoted student of Mexican history should be expected to follow the power shifts that occurred in the capital during the war, the essence of the struggle can be seen in the hinterland. Outside Mexico City, where there were fewer politicians, peasants wanted to prevent centralists from exercising control over the whole nation. Peripheral, peasant-led movements had their own ideas about independence and reform. They insisted on the former and felt themselves capable of shaping, without help from the capital, the latter.

Generally, elitists — however they characterized themselves — opposed the peasant movements. What made the Mexican revolution so drawn out, painful, and seemingly impossible to resolve was that it was struggle in the most fundamental sense — the taking of power from elites who abused it and turning it over to masses who had difficulty administering it.

Villa's place was in the countryside; Madero would articulate liberal ideas, and Villa would fight. Madero's betrayal and murder would bring despair to the faithful, but Villa would go on fighting. In the process, Villa would teach himself to be a tactician.

Although Villa's forte was as a cavalry leader, Mexico's expanse meant there was a need to move troops — and horses — in large numbers over great distances. So a friend of Villa,

Rodolfo Fierro, as unschooled as Villa, became a master of rail logistics, seeing to the coal that kept the trains running, moving thousands of troops, giving Villa's Army of the North a mobility beyond that enjoyed by many smaller European armies of the day.

Villa also was able to cope with another tactical problem of modern warfare. Because he could not count on sanctuary in mountain jungles, that traditional stronghold of guerrillas, Villa found himself pursued not only by horsemen but by airplanes. With airplanes, Villa was simply lucky enough to have been born before technology had caught up to him. Fleeing air pursuit, Villa's cavalry had only to cross mountains—over which the sputtering U.S. air force could not fly.

Villa's signal victory for Madero, and a victory for non-technological warfare, came at the border of the United States in the spring of 1911. Villa, along with Giuseppe Garibaldi— a grandson of the Italian hero who was attracted to the republican cause Madero represented — and Pascual Orrozco, commanded forces that captured stoutly defended Ciudad Juárez. The republican army attacked with little more than rifles, tin-can grenades, and courage. While North Americans watched from their side of the Rio Grande, the peasant troops rooted defenders out of the city and established Madero's claim to the presidency.

If Madero was grateful, however, his commander-in-chief, Victoriano Huerta, was less impressed. The aging Huerta was all spit-and-polish in the sunlight, if a drunkard by night, and he did not appreciate Villa's loose style of command. Villa, for example, followed a managerial philosophy of allowing his troops to raise considerable hell after successful battles. Huerta, a man whose courage and whose orders were not to be questioned, insisted that Villa follow directions sent from headquarters. Villa, dismissing them as administrative foolishness, did not always follow orders. Finally, Huerta ordered that his unlettered subordinate be arrested.

Villa considered the whole affair a bad joke, even when he was clapped in the guardhouse at Huerta's order. He awoke from this interpretation when guards stood him in front of a firing squad. Villa, finally realizing that Huerta had not been kidding, was talking very fast when Madero's brother, a personal emissary, rode up to mediate. Huerta was not mollified, however, and had Villa confined to prison in Mexico City, accusing him of insubordination, subversion, and looting. The first charge was undeniably true and the second ludicrous. As to the third, Villa reasoned, how else was he to pay his troops?

Under guard, Villa was taken to Mexico City on June 7, 1912. There, federal prisons had become gathering places for men who had lost their grip on power. Villa met a principal lieutenant of Zapata, Gildardo Magaña, a polished urbanite who had joined Zapata's agrarian revolution. Magaña, who had studied to be a priest, began teaching Villa how to read and write. It is uncertain how much Villa learned, for after six months, on the day after Christmas when the compound was filled with visitors, Villa put on a pair of sun glasses, tried as best he could to look like a lawyer, and walked out. He next turned up in El Paso, where a newspaperman stumbled across him and wrote the predictable profile of a pistol-toting bad man. Villa declined to dignify the story and refused to be interviewed.

The war raged on. In February 1913, reactionary cadets from the national military school seized the national palace and the federal prison, freeing two of Madero's principal adversaries. Fighting raged street by street. Because the fighting was confined to such a concentrated urban area, the damage within that core was the worst of any of Mexico's civil conflicts.

At the presidential palace, Madero's personal guard, the members of which had turned against him, burst into his office and began firing. A friend jumped in front of Madero, saving Madero's life but sacrificing his own. At that point the guardsmen hesitated, shamed by their own villainy, and were talked back into the hall by another Madero associate in the room as Madero wept over the loss of his friend.

Huerta played the unrest to his own advantage. Rather than defend Madero, Huerta grabbed the opportunity, reached agreement with the reactionaries, and, when Madero resigned a week later, ordered his arrest. Henry Lane Wilson, the U.S. ambassador to Mexico, called together the diplomatic corps to announce proudly that he had known Madero would be imprisoned and had encouraged it. Madero's downfall, Wilson predicted, would mean "peace, progress and prosperity."

Madero and his vice-president informed that they would be allowed to go into exile, left jail. They were in a carriage being escorted out of the city when they were stopped by a mob. Their guard stood aside, and both were killed. Huerta promoted the lieutenant and corporal who were in charge of the "guard," and both eventually became generals in Huerta's army.

Madero's faithful followers were both saddened and enraged. Villa, still in Texas, learned of events in the capital and reentered Mexico to begin gathering troops. Huerta, his alcoholism a severe hindrance, would not last much longer, but he clung to power while another coveted his place. This was Venustiano Carranza, a governor who dubbed his followers "constitutionalists" and who was able to recruit to his cause none other than Woodrow Wilson.

Wilson, a former university president, had vowed to "teach the Latin Americans to elect good men." Carranza, presumably, was his idea of a beginning toward that end. Wilson was also well aware that the Germans—who needed oil as much as Americans—had their talons in several Mexico City politicians. Part of Wilson's purpose was to minimize German influence in Mexico. For Villa, this unholy alliance between Wilson and Carranza meant a two-front war.

It took Villa no more than thirty days after his return to Mexico to gather 3,000 troops. They would follow him as long as they were well led and could count on plunder. Political idealism was at a minimum. They faced federal troops who followed their officers only because of regional prejudices, or because soldiering was the best available job, or because of naked fear. Federal officers shot troopers who did not fight to their satisfaction. There would be instances when Villa, about to execute captured federal officers, would have volunteers for the firing squad step forward from among the ranks of the captured federal troops. They wanted retribution, and Villa would give it to them. Then he would recruit the troops, for if Villa did not represent political ideals, he did represent a raw freedom, a kind of equality that common men understood. His pronouncements were simple promises that rang as true and were as easily fulfilled as any politician's promises.

Villa's army soon controlled all of the northeast except the cities of Torreón, Chihuahua, and Juárez, all three positioned along the long, north-south highway between El Paso and Mexico City. He took Torreón, closest to Mexico City, on October 1, 1913. Then he turned north toward Chihuahua, intending to take it and isolate Juárez, two hundred miles farther north, hard by the U.S. border. But he failed to take Chihuahua, so, rather than exhaust his resources; he circled the city and headed north for Juárez. On the way, he happened across a federal troop train on its way south.

As the train crossed the barren prairie, Villa's men stopped it and captured its passengers. Villa ordered the train backed up to a small station, where he sent a telegram north along the line to the commander of the garrison at Juárez. Engine broke down, Villa wired. A new engine and five box cars were needed. Then he sent a second telegraph message: A large force of rebels is approaching. What should be done?

The garrison commander took the sensible course, ordering the troop train to return to the safety of the garrison at Juárez. The train rolled into Juárez late on the night of November 15.

Many federal troops were shot down as they ran from the barracks in their underwear.

When the federal troops were able to gather themselves and counter-attack, Villa repelled them. Rather than prolong his attack, he pulled out of town and headed back south toward Chihuahua. There, the dispirited garrison, informed of events at Juárez, abandoned the city on November 29. Villa declared himself the governor of Chihuahua.

By early 1914, Villa and Carranza in the north and Zapata in the south had squeezed Huerta's federal forces into a narrow strip between Mexico City and the Gulf Coast at Vera Cruz. President Wilson, trying to help Carranza, had already embargoed arms shipments to Mexico and now took the final plunge to force out Huerta.

With a U.S. fleet already floating off shore to stop the Germans from delivering arms to the government, Huerta's agents made the mistake of arresting U.S. marines on shore leave in Tampico. Huerta's government in Mexico City, realizing immediately that it had picked up a rattlesnake, apologized. Wilson, however, had the excuse he wanted. He ordered the occupation of Vera Cruz. Huerta's government crumbled; Carranza entered Mexico City.

Neither Villa nor Zapata, however, accepted Carranza as president or, as he wanted himself known, "First Chief." They had fought, at the very least, to avenge Madero; certainly they wanted to establish the states' rights to govern their own affairs; and, ideally, they both wished to institute reforms. They had not fought to replace a drunken tyrant with a brazen opportunist.

Wilson liked Carranza—but then American presidents had liked Díaz—although both Villa and Zapata understood that the only reason Carranza was in the national palace was because of the efforts of his brilliant field commander, Alvaro Obregón. They kept their forces intact, and there was stalemate. A convention to settle affairs was called in November 1914. It broke down in acrimony.

Carranza announced to foreign governments that Villa's Army of the North—30,000 fighters at its strongest—constituted a grave threat to the republic. Villa replied: If my army is such a threat, why don't you and I jointly commit suicide to settle everything? Carranza did not reply.

No one was strong enough to hold Mexico City for long, and in December Villa and Zapata went there to meet each other for the first time. The two guerrilla leaders appeared ill at ease with each other. They agreed that Carranza was, in Zapata's words, a "bastard." They tossed off a celebratory drink of brandy together, Zapata downing his impassively, the exuberant Villa nearly choking because he was unaccustomed to liquor. Zapata left to lead his forces against Carranza troops occupying Puebla. Villa promised he would send Zapata arms, including artillery—a promise he was unable to keep.

When Villa returned northward, Obregón chased him. Their opposing forces would conclude the civil war in the north, writing the final chapter in terms of modern warfare. Villa was of the past. Obregón was schooled in the trench warfare that was defining warfare in Europe. Villa knew frontal assault by cavalry, the tactic of wars gone by. Furthermore, his troops knew only the frenetic pace of constant fighting; without the discipline of the saddle, they were at loose ends. As they moved northward, a trusted lieutenant simply detached the train car carrying millions of pesos of payroll for his own men, and rolled off.

In March and April of 1915, Villa met Obregón and his trenches and barbed wire and machine guns and artillery. On the plains outside Celaya, near where Juárez' troops had beaten Maximilian, Villa's cavalry charged Obregón's fortified positions. After two great battles, there was no clear victor. Villa was pursued northward, barely surviving. When part of his troops were encircled, their commander escaped only by leading his cavalry outside the ring, telegraphing federal officers conflicting messages, then attacking from behind in their confusion. Villa's troops were reunited at Chihuahua.

Villa was running out of places to retreat to. Wilson spread troops along the long border to keep Mexicans out and guns from going across. He guaranteed Carranza's troops safe passage over U.S. territory to flank Villa as he was driven northward. Cornered — and perhaps trying to embarrass Carranza Villa attacked the Texas town of Columbus the night of March 9, 1916. In response, Wilson sent General John "Black Jack" Pershing in pursuit — a caravan of 10,000 soldiers, 9,000 horses, and reconnaissance biplanes that could not fly high enough to get over Mexico's mountains.

Carranza complained that this was going too far; Mexican sovereignty was being violated. Wilson ignored him. The upshot — except for once again training U.S. officers, like Lt. George Patton, for other wars — was that Pershing had more trouble with Carranza's troops than Villa's. Indignant that their country had again been invaded, Carranza's officers were hostile. Pershing never even got a glimpse of Villa or his army.

"I do not believe these people can ever establish a government among themselves that will stand," Pershing wrote to a friend in frustration. "Carranza has no more control over local commanders or of states or municipalities than if he lived in London." For his part, Villa's manifestos, issued from traveling headquarters, characterized North Americans as "barbarians."

Pershing never got close. On March 27, 1916, not three weeks after the attack on Columbus, Villa was shot from behind, either by accident or by a guerrilla who, impressed into service, feigned an accident. The bullet hit Villa above the right knee, the first time Villa had ever been shot. He very nearly died. The whole time Pershing raged about the countryside looking for him, Villa was holed up, recuperating.

Villa retired and outlived Carranza, who was shot by his own bodyguard in 1920 and succeeded by Obregón. Villa found contentment as a member of the bourgeoisie, investing in real estate. But, in the end, the landed class got him.

It is unclear whether Villa's death was motivated by an old grudge, a recent aggravation, an old political hatred, or the threat that Villa, a natural leader, might reenter political combat. It is possible that Obregón was behind it. It is known that the ambush was planned and executed by a rancher who had never met Villa.

On July 23, 1923, Villa and six friends rode in a convertible to Hidalgo del Parral, Chihuahua, to pick up payroll for Villa's employees. Three men were in the back seat. Two bodyguards rode the running boards. Another man rode in the front seat, while Villa drove.

Eight men, who had carefully planned the assault, charged out of a house they had rented for three months, waiting. They poured pistol and rifle fire into the car.

As the car careened to the side of the street and stalled, Villa, like an enraged bull, was the only one able to get his pistol from its holster to get off a shot. As his friends died around him, Villa fired and killed an attacker with a bullet through the heart. Then he slumped across the front seat, twelve bullets in his torso, four in his head.

What is most overlooked about the man who called himself Pancho Villa is that he represented deep sentiments of large numbers of Mexicans. He was not a bandit, but a political figure who spoke for simple people, people whose politics should be regarded more, not less, seriously precisely because of the simple nature of their needs. They believed in him.

Mexican historian Pedro Vives obviously recounts with pleasure — and in dialect — the story of one peasant telling another of how Villa's body was dug up three years after being buried so the head could be displayed — "in order," says the peasant, "that the people not keep saying that he's still alive."

12

Emiliano Zapata
Indian Reformer
c. 1880–1919
(Mexico)

Estimates of Zapata's year of birth range from 1877 to 1883, making him the same age as Villa, although their stories are different in both style and substance.

Elders of tiny Anenecuilco elected Emiliano Zapata president of their council in 1909, when he was approximately thirty years old. His principal task was to represent the village in its claims to native lands, part of a widespread effort by Mexican Indians to reclaim land taken by Europeans and mestizos who drew up documents based on nothing but force of arms. The elders chose Zapata because he was from a family that had prospered through hard work, and because Zapata, except for a brief period in Mexico City, had stayed in Anenecuilco.

Although much of his past is unknown — he was the ninth of ten children, four of whom survived to adulthood — it appears that Zapata, for some teenage transgression, faced conscription into the army but was given the chance instead to work as a groom in Mexico City. It is said he returned to Anenecuilco embittered by the realization that too frequently horses lived better than Mexicans. But Zapata was not the first to have reached such a conclusion, and he was not the creator of a following. He was himself pushed ahead of the most powerful political movement of his day: the Indians' claims to their land.

Zapata's leadership consisted of balancing the efforts of regional chieftains like himself and of holding them together lest they lose heart and succumb to the bribery and threats of the central government. Because at the turn of the century new political ideas were finding expression all over the world, these unschooled, country people attracted leftist intellectuals who saw in them the natural foundation for widespread reform.

Reactionaries distrusted the Indian movements not only for their own force, but because of the way in which they focused the ideas of others. Zapata, for example, was rumored to have been influenced, while in Mexico City, by an anarcho-syndicalist who later led an abortive invasion of Baja, California. But the movement that propelled Zapata remained rural and indigenous; it was articulated as the "Plan of Ayala," land reform based on ideas that harkened back to those of Juárez and the *puros*.

In general, economists stress the importance of agrarian movements because they draw exceptional strength by mixing tradition with modern design. Scholars have documented scores of cases in Mexico where villages, independently of each other, asserted claims that were organized logically and were unsullied by personal greed. Peasants insisted that they could work the land more efficiently — with greater benefit to consumers and to the national economy — than could the *hacendados* who had stolen it. Today, Article 27 of Mexico's revolutionary constitution of 1917 is the foundation — or, perhaps, the unfulfilled idea — for agrarian reform. Article 27 directly resulted from pressure created by peasant movements like the one organized by Emiliano Zapata Salazar.

Unlike Villa, who made up a name for himself, Zapata bore a patronym and matronym that were part of history in Morelos, a small state just southeast of Mexico City. The name "Zapata" appears in records of the revolution against the Crown in 1810. Of José Salazar, his mother's father, there is the story of how he, as a boy, smuggled tortillas, tequila, and gunpowder through Spanish lines during the siege of Cuautla, a Morelos town that commands passage to both the south and west from the capital. Morelos's strategic location, in fact, would continue to be important to Zapata's efforts.

Throughout Mexican history, the state of Morelos — named for a revolutionary priest who insisted on the need to return their land to the Indians — has been important both because it is close to the capital and because it is agriculturally rich. It was in Morelos in 1869, when the state was chartered, that Porfirio Díaz ran for governor, hoping to begin his succession to Juárez' legacy. Díaz' defeat helped make Morelos' reputation for dissent and earned Díaz' enmity. By Zapata's lifetime, Morelos, still known for independence, was responsible for one-third of all sugar products in Mexico.

When Zapata was elected by the village elders, the specific dispute he was expected to help resolve was typical. Small farmers around Villa de Ayala claimed that their ancestral lands were infringed upon by a neighboring hacienda. The farmers were planting in this disputed margin, and the hacendado wanted to collect rent.

From this instance, one of many disputes, a movement took its name and grew. The Indians' ancient assertions conflicted with those of the landowners who supported Díaz' harsh dictatorship. Morelos, especially, smarted under the whip of Díaz' oppression, and when the dictatorship gave way to Mexico's revolution of 1910 — the world's first socialist revolution great, fundamental forces elevated simple men.

Francisco Madero emerged as the national "redeemer," and Zapata was linked to his future and lifted to prominence. What allowed Zapata to sustain himself; his military skills were, like Villa's, learned on the job. There was ample time, for the "revolution" dragged on and on in virulent civil war. First came the fight to overthrow Díaz and put Madero in office. In May 1911, two days before Villa and others took Ciudad Juárez to establish Madero's regime in the north, Zapata successfully led 4,000 guerrillas against 400 federal soldiers defending Cuautla, assuring control of the south. For Zapata, however, that was just the beginning because he represented a movement that required more than military success. It required reform, and Madero's tendency to ambivalence caught Zapata in a dilemma.

While newspapers characterized him as "Attilla the Hun," he faced the responsibility of leading reform even as he had led his peasant army. His troops were returning to their villages by June, leaving him at the head of no more than an idea. Furthermore, landowners, too, had supported Madero. Now they complained that claims were being made on their land. Indians were making the preposterous argument that their deeds were spurious, or at least antedated by native rights. Madero called Zapata to the capital to give voice to the landowners' fears.

When Zapata returned to Morelos, it was becoming clear that his fight was not with one side of Mexican politics — neither liberals nor reactionaries could make it without landowners' support — but with the entire Mexican system of land tenure. The Plan of Ayala, that is to say, represented a profound threat, and the government was not long in responding. That summer while Zapata — already the father of at least one child — was being married to Josepha Espejo in Villa de Ayala, he was informed at the reception that more than a thousand troops commanded by Victoriano Huerta, the most powerful general in Mexico, had entered Morelos.

The landowners wanted the state under control, and they found a willing champion in Huerta, the disciplinarian who had ordered Villa shot. Of the Morelos farmers his report asserted, "These people are all bandits." He had overridden Madero's efforts to mediate and was pursuing Zapata to execute him. Zapata had become, in the words of a landowner, "a constant menace to the interests of cultivated society."

Zapata fled, once bursting from the back door of a hacienda and dashing into the fields on foot as troops entered the main gate. Three days after his escape he was encountered, riding a mule, in the mountains of Puebla, eighty miles away. But the ferocity of Huerta's pursuit, rather than intimidating the peasants of Morelos, enflamed them, creating an idol. People who had called themselvles *maderistas* became *zapatistas*. By October 1911, Zapata commanded an army of 1,500 guerrillas and had pushed within fifteen miles of Mexico City.

During that autumn Mexico's agrarian revolution was defined more clearly than during *La Reforma* fifty years earlier. Zapata and his contemporaries wrote their program with a singleness of purpose that was unprecedented. "I am resolved," Zapata wrote to a friend with existential ferocity, "to struggle against everything and everybody."

A series of pronouncements informed the central government that its troops must be withdrawn from Morelos; "General Zapata" would keep order. The Plan of Ayala asked for small farmers to get the "justice they deserve as to lands" and that that justice be codified in a national agrarian law. Justice, the Plan of Ayala made clear, demanded expropriation of land from "monopolists."

John Womack, Jr., in his definitive biography of Zapata, notes the Plan of Ayala's "sense of history." Similarly, a Mexican psychologist suggests that Indian culture, as expressed in Juárez' and Zapata's leadership, has provided for a large proportion of the Mexican population "the necessary continuity of the psychic life in successive generations," a cultural assertion that cannot be broken.

Nevertheless, in early 1912, Huerta tried to end resistance with a strategy of "resettlement." If a village was deemed hostile, it was destroyed. The government identified outspoken opponents and burned their homes. In February 1912, Zapata's sister, mother-in-law, and two of his wife's sisters were taken hostage, and, for a while, the dissent subsided in a state tired of war. In a conciliatory gesture, the national assembly discussed a bill to prohibit further exploitation of Indian common lands, but took no action.

Then Madero's government fell, and Huerta took sole power. The possibility of conciliation ended. Huerta conceived of a bizarre plan to transport from the north as many as 20,000 field workers. The result would not be particularly efficient, he conceded, but at least the northerners would be less susceptible to recruitment by Zapata.

Some relief came in early 1913 with the inauguration of Woodrow Wilson, who was unwilling to recognize Huerta's government. As the closest thing Mexico had to a pacifier, Venustiano Carranza, safe in the north, announced his idea for a period of reconciliation. Huerta would have none of it. In a speech to Mexico City's exclusive Jockey Club, Huerta said that he would control Morelos using some "procedures that are not sanctioned by law but are indispensable for the national welfare." He predicted victory in about a month.

The effect was to force Zapata to organize a real army. Volunteering help was Manuel Palafox, a slightly built, short man in his late twenties with a pock-marked face. Palafox was a hustler whose instinct for survival had given him certain important managerial skills. He became the revolution's office manager. As the line was drawn between Huerta and Zapata, others from outside Morelos insinuated themselves into the movement. Morelos took on the characteristics of a government in exile.

Huerta's troops were able to take and hold the cities, but did not have the strength to reach into the countryside. In rural areas they could only destroy property, controlling nothing. When, in a typical maneuver, the government took Cuernavaca, the capital of Morelos, Zapata struck at the five hundred-man garrison in Jonacatepec, on the periphery of the state. Taking stores and guns, Zapata offered a pardon to any man who promised not to fight the revolution. The garrison commander joined Zapata and was put in charge of training troops and buying arms.

While Zapata's rebel government attracted outsiders, it was the planners, the intellectuals, who made their way to Morelos from the city. The fighters were natural leaders whose troops had known them since childhood. Close to Zapata was his older brother, Eufemio, a taller man whose black handlebar mustache was even more formidable that Zapata's. Eufemio had taken his share of a modest inheritance when their father died and drifted off to try his hand at business; he returned to fight.

One effect of local leaders' commanding his units was that Zapata sometimes had trouble in their seeing the greater scheme of things. Zapata commanded by persuasion and, if that failed, by threat. At one point "persuasion" meant threatening to rustle fifty cattle from a chieftain's territory if he didn't immediately send the six rifles Zapata had been asking for. His officers and men were continually being enticed to switch sides.

Socially and economically, the result of the warfare in Morelos was chaos. Fugitives from government oppression, forced to flee their villages, set up camps. Zapata's rebels encouraged the camps because they kept workers out of the fields. Morelos landowners had to contract with the government to keep one-third of their workers from conscription, registering them and arming them for self defense, in order to maintain production. Homeless children roamed the countryside, and at least one group of widows formed under the leadership of a virago known as "La China" and traveled from town to town, some dressed in feathered finery liberated from shops.

Women also fought. In 1911, a *New York Times* reporter noted their "spectacular part" in battle. Juana Belén Gutiérrez de Mendoza, a teacher, took up the cause of poor Indian children, founded a newspaper, and was imprisoned for criticism of the government. She eventually made her way to Morelos, joined Zapata's army, and rose to the rank of colonel.

As the war dragged on into 1913, atrocities committed by the Huerta government became so blatant that some members of the puppet national assembly threatened to walk out in protest. Huerta simply had the deputies arrested, all 110 of them, and assumed dictatorial powers. But Huerta was unable to bring the country to heel; it was too large, with too many armies rampaging in too many directions. When the government pulled troops out of the south to counter threats in the north, Zapata's forces would spill out into the neighboring states of Puebla and Guerrero.

Zapata was unable, however, to establish and protect a strategic axis between Acapulco, on the Pacific Coast, and Mexico City. The Plan of Ayala excited the imagination of leftist planners, but his peasant army could not secure enough territory to give his ideology a base. Supply lines for guns and ammunition — which ended as mule trails into the mountains— stretched for hundreds of miles. Any chance of winning lay in an alliance with Villa, Zapata decided by the autumn of 1913. Partly to demonstrate the strength of his southern army for such an alliance, Zapata focused on Chilpancinango, the capital of Guerrero, and took it. It was the first time he had been able to take a state capital.

In the spring of 1914, Wilson precipitated the fall of Huerta with the brief occupation of Vera Cruz. As Huerta's troops flowed toward that port on the Gulf Coast, Zapata's rebels flooded into the unguarded area left behind. For the first time, Zapata occupied the six district seats of Morelos; he laid siege to Cuernavaca. But when Huerta fled into exile the next summer, the government was left to Carranza, an old Díaz supporter widely recognized for the opportunist he was. Zapata's forces were still contained in Morelos and parts of adjoining states. Now the forces of Carranza, who was endorsed by President Wilson and who chose for himself the title of "First Chief," stood between Villa and Zapata.

In late 1914, Villa and Zapata agreed to meet in Mexico City. Womack cautions against equating the two forces. Villa, he notes, was "the very incarnation of irregularity." His supporters were "more a force of nature than of politics, the Villista Party was commotion rampant." Zapata's troops, on the other hand, demonstrated a discipline rare for any civil war. "If they plundered," Womack suggests, "it was not for fun, but on business."

Before the meeting Zapata was reluctant, apparently distrustful. Because neither man liked cities, they first met in Xochimilco, the site of the "floating gardens," and, more important for Zapata, closer to his territory. It was like a meeting of an ostrich and an ox. Their personal differences are evident from photographs and were remarked by observers. Zapata's sister traveled with him, and a North American observer speculated that "everything she had on her person could probably have been purchased for about $5.00 American money." Villa, contrarily, was the height of fashion, donning an English-style pith helmet. When they were induced to enter the capital and pose for photographers at the national palace, it was Villa who was coaxed into the ornate presidential chair, its carved eagle above his head. He wore an officer's uniform with braided cuffs and carried a billed military cap like the ones that Díaz made his officers wear so they would look European.

Zapata wore the clothes of Morelos—tight pants for riding, a waist length jacket, a huge sombrero. Photographs show Villa laughing. Zapata broods.

They could agree on their hatred of Carranza; Villa called him arrogant, Zapata called him a son of a bitch. But there matters rested. Villa was no help to Zapata in getting ammunition; he had trouble, despite his claims, getting it himself. Villa rode north; back to his anarchic, politically meaningless war and within months was defeated by Obregón at Celaya. Zapata went back to Morelos, to the last months of his revolution.

Carranza had earlier suggested alliance with Zapata, but Zapata regarded him a Cassius. "I see in him much ambition." Zapata wrote to an aide, "and an inclination to fool the people." In his refusal to compromise, critics began to see in Zapata a fatal egotism, but he persisted. "Revolutions will come and revolutions will go," Zapata told an emissary from Carranza, "but I will continue with mine."

Continue it did, tilting to the left as it went, although it is estimated that one-fifth of Morelos' population had been killed in the fighting against Huerta's oppression. Zapata stayed in the field, where he seemed more at home than dealing with the intellectuals planning the revolution. This meant he left headquarters affairs to Palafox, whose response to the heightened power was to abuse it, alienating field commanders by trying to impose control. When an informal delegation from Carranza arrived, Palafox, acting on his own, insulted men who knew something of agrarian reform themselves.

But Zapata's aides insisted that Carranza accept the Plan of Ayala and its explicit call for the return of Indian lands. And there questions of style exacerbated the dispute. In conferences and convention halls, as Mexicans tried to define themselves and their reborn country, there was a great deal of individual posturing, fiery speeches of hollow words. Zapata withdrew even further.

The Plan of Ayala was given whatever legal force Zapata could confer upon it in Morelos, but in the capital another law, "Article 8," was promulgated. It said that anyone opposing the revolution could have his land and property expropriated. But Article 8 went unenforced outside Morelos; the revolution bogged down in a three-way argument among Zapata, Villa, and Carranza over who was the most revolutionary.

In Morelos, Zapata's government, galvanized by the civil war and having attracted planners from all over, overcame old antagonisms among villages and implemented programs beyond land reform, suggesting a model for the whole country. Schools got redesigned curricula. Members of the graduating classes of 1913 and 1914 of the National School of Agriculture arrived (as they did in several states) to help with land reform. The political climate was such that in some places it was dangerous to appear non-rustic — without the white cotton outfits of campesinos.

But, meanwhile, Carranza's army occupied Mexico City. Although it withdrew, his dominance was made clear. His principal commander was Alvaro Obregón, who, no less than Huerta, intended to extend that dominance to the outlying states. To Morelos he assigned Pablo Gonzales, an orphan who had grown up in city streets, a sometime peddler who emigrated to the United States but returned to make a career in Carranza's army. He had never led troops in a significant battle, and one way of winning notice would be to break the back of Zapata's government. He rescinded all state laws and organized the systematic theft of sugar, timber, and other resources from the villages. He started to co-opt Zapata's field commanders. Into 1915, Carranza grew stronger.

Zapata's field commanders were trouble enough in their own right. One, a mystic, was convinced that God would ride with him and dictate whether Carranza forces should be allowed to pass. Another commander, who followed more traditional theology and tactics, threatened to shoot him. Zapata intervened, but when a patrol of the latter commander's men happened upon the mystic, they did, indeed, settle the dispute. They shot him.

Carranza had gotten Wilson's — that is, Pershing's — help in more or less pacifying the north. He then sought to prove he could control the south. In May, government troops took Cuernavaca, introducing the airplane, which bombed Zapata's troops. Zapata, arriving late for the battle, was nearly captured. Carranza introduced harsher and harsher measures, taking on the ugly demeanor of his predecessors. In Cuautla, a priest was hanged as a Zapata spy; in Jiutepec 225 prisoners were given a hasty military "trial" and shot en masse; in Tlaltizapan, which had served as Zapata headquarters, 286 people — 132 men, 112 women, and 42 children — were executed. By the end of the spring more than 1,200 prisoners had been sent by train to forced-labor camps in tropical Yucatan. Wilson's emissaries watched.

Zapata could have compromised, but his advisors insisted that he hold out for ideological purity. Field commanders, however, were inclined to blame purists for prolonging the agony. It was suggested that Zapata go into hiding to let Mexico City's always volatile political antagonisms take their toll on Carranza's government. Yet another suggestion was terror.

While it appears that Zapata held out against the idea of conducting a campaign of terror, he was forced to use only small guerrilla units — he could not risk a broad confrontation — and such a strategy must sacrifice control. His guerrillas tried to disrupt mills and factories and destroy rail heads. For every act of that kind, however, Carranza commanders ordered executions. Finally, in late 1916, Zapata's troops stopped a train and resorted to abject terror, killing four hundred soldiers and civilians.

Eventually Zapata was able to reorganize along traditional military lines, acquiring medical and engineering units. As late as 1917 it looked as if Zapata might prevail when Carranza forces were withdrawn from Morelos. The U.S. embargo on arms was lifted, and Zapata was able to reenter Cuernavaca. The concept of agrarian reform had been legitimated, at least to the point that it was under discussion in a constitutional convention.

Nevertheless, defections and intrigue continued in an environment now polluted by the black market prices engendered by World War I. In early 1918, Zapata lost Palafox, who for all his wild-eyed unpredictability had in many respects been the soul of the agrarian movement. He had alienated men with his insults, his intransigence, and his zeal, and, in the end, he lost his most important supporter by turning Zapata against him with a homosexual indiscretion. So infuriated was Zapata that he almost ordered Palafox shot.

At mid-year, Zapata, seeking some way out of his impasse, contacted Obregón to suggest that he revolt against Carranza. It did not work, and by the end of the year Carranza forces, again under the command of the former peddler, Pablo Gonzáles, drove back into Morelos. Gonzáles had learned to be cautious, and even a revolt against Carranza would now invite U.S. intervention. Zapata could do nothing but sit tight. North American journalists called it the end of Zapata.

But in the spring of 1919, he pulled one last trick. A Carranza colonel, something of a hot-shot cavalry officer named Jesús Guajardo, had sworn to meet Zapata face to face. Before that could happen, however, Guajardo was ignominiously clapped in the guardhouse for tarrying at the cantina after Gonzáles had ordered him into the field. Hearing of Guajardo's plight, Zapata saw his chance for a coup. He wrote to Guajardo: Why not switch sides?

There were spies everywhere, and the letter was delivered to General Gonzáles.

At first, Gonzáles used the letter to imply that Guajardo was a traitor; he humiliated him, driving him to tears of frustration. Then the general gave Guajardo the chance to redeem himself. He was instructed to play along with Zapata. A meeting was arranged.

Each was to arrive with a complement of only about thirty troops. Guajardo showed up with six hundred, including a machine-gun squad. Zapata and Guajardo talked, but Guajardo declined an invitation to dinner, saying he wanted to go back to pick up ammunition that had just arrived at his camp. They agreed to meet again at Chinameca hacienda, just thirty-five miles from Villa de Ayala.

At about 8:30 Thursday morning, April 10, 1919, Zapata rode down from his campsite with 150 men. He and Guajardo conferred at a small shop outside the hacienda. Because there was a report of Carranza troops in the area, they broke up the meeting and sent out patrols, Zapata riding with his patrol. When Zapata returned about 1:30 in the afternoon, all of Guajardo's troopers were inside the hacienda wall. The only Zapata trooper inside was an aide negotiating for delivery of 12,000 rounds of ammunition. Invited inside, Zapata said no.

A bit later, invited inside again, Zapata said yes. As he rode through the gate into the courtyard on a horse Guajardo had brought him as a gift, Guajardo's guard presented arms. Then they turned their sights on Zapata and fired. The aide, inside, rose from his chair and was immediately killed. Others, outside, were shot from their saddles trying to flee.

On his way back to Cuautla with Zapata's body draped over a horse, Guajardo stopped at Villa de Ayala to telephone ahead with the news. By the time the body was brought to General Gonzáles and dumped to the ground, it was after dark, but Gonzáles examined it with a flashlight. The general made sure the body was well photographed, although some of Zapata's people, even after seeing the photos, refused to believe Zapata was dead.

13

Dolores Jiménez y Muro
Juana Belén Gutiérrez de Mendoza
and Hermila Galindo de Topete
Women of the Mexican Revolution
1910–1920

At the turn of the century in Mexico, two ideologies converged to give impetus to the Mexican Revolution. Those forces were socialism and feminism, and while the former would not endure, the latter would impel Mexican women to create for themselves a unique and lasting place in their country's history. Because it was a popular revolution, a movement patched together out of many groups of intellectuals and poor people, the Revolution needed all the help it could get. There was much work to be done, and women played an important role. From the beginning, women were propagandists against Porfirio Díaz, and several were imprisoned for their words. When the shooting began, women, sometimes as leaders, fought and died beside men. Mexican women accompanied whole armies on the move by rail, on foot, and on horseback, foraging for food, keeping the soldiers in the field, and earning the respectful name, *soldaderas.*

Although their concerns were relegated to an undercurrent in the flow of a male-dominated society, Mexican women have long had their own pantheon of heroines. These exemplars were women who asserted themselves despite conditions that hindered their self-expression at every step. *Sor Juana,* for example, provided literary inspiration, while *La Corregidora* stood as a model for more combative, political instincts.

Sister Juana Inés de la Cruz, christened Juana de Asbaje y Ramírez in 1648, was the illegitimate child of a Basque captain and a Creole woman, the youngest of three sisters. Proving herself a precocious student, she was made a lady in waiting to the viceroy's wife. She left the court in 1667, when she was not yet nineteen, to enter a convent. In time, she entered another convent said to have a library of 4,000 volumes, probably an exaggeration since that would have made it the largest private library in the New World. In 1689, she published in Madrid her first volume of poetry and, in 1692, her second. Through her poetry, Sister Juana openly criticized the Spanish-Mexican cult of *machismo.*

Josefa Ortíz de Domínguez was the wife of a royal official, *Corregidor* Miguel Domínguez, in 1810, at the time Spain's colonial yoke was being broken. She conspired with and protected revolutionaries, and is best known for saving Father Hidalgo from capture.

These women head a long list of those who demonstrated revolutionary zeal, including Leona Vicario, a wealthy woman who joined insurgents in the countryside in 1810, and the saintly Beatríz González Ortega, who turned her school into a hospital during the Revolution of 1910.

That kind of feminine leadership formed a foundation for emancipation that began well before the Revolution of 1910. For reasons not completely clear, Mexican feminists began to register advances even under the regime of Porfirio Díaz, the dictator who managed to keep the great bulk of his country at heel. Anna Macías has noted: "When one considers that up to 1856 Sor Juana's dream of higher education for women had never been realized, the advances made by Mexican women between 1869 and 1910 were really remarkable and parallel other achievements of the Porfirian era, such as the building of railroads and a telegraph system."

Furthermore, it was during the series of civil wars that threw off Díaz' domination and shaped modern Mexico that women burst forth with a force that became legendary. "Women have taken a spectacular part in the revolution," wrote an anonymous *New York Times* correspondent in the issue of May 10, 1911. "With the first outbreak in Puebla in November, a woman of the family of Serdan made appeals to the people from house tops amid flying bullets to join the small bands fighting within, and was wounded.... At Casas Grandes, Patricinia Vásquez took an active part in the battle. In Guerrero, Margarita Neri, a wealthy girl and landowner, furious over excessive taxes, placed herself at the head of 200 laborers two months ago. She is now said to command 1,000 men under General Figueroa."

There was example after example, a flowering of feminism under the harshest condition, war. Society was profoundly changed. Of that change, Angeles Mendieta Alatorre writes, "For the first time, women sensed and understood an undeniable truth: they were able to marry for love and not out of necessity because their preparation offered them economic independence — the ability and the determination to make their own decisions."

This change had to be wrought in a society in which *hembrismo,* or "femaleness," had been coined as the term denoting the submissive obverse of *machismo.* The changing ground rules of sexual relationships were portrayed by John Reed, the U.S. correspondent, who wrote of the casual alliances—"six-peso weddings"—encouraged by the Revolution. But tradition persisted, as described by Reed in his account of the *soldadera* "Elizabetta," whom he encountered "trudging stolidly along in the dust behind Captain Félix Romero's horse and had trudged so for thirty miles. He never spoke to her, never looked back, but rode on unconcernedly. Sometimes he would get tired of carrying his rifle and hand it back to her to carry.... [He] had ordered her to follow him. Which she did, unquestioningly, after the custom of her sex and country."

That custom was radically, savagely reversed by stories of female officers and heroines among rebel forces, like *La Chata,* "Flatnose," and *La Corredora,* "the Scout." In Zapata's army there were several *coronelas,* like María de la Luz Espinosa Barrera, a motherless child of Yautepec, Morelos, who killed her husband's lover, then went off to serve the Revolution well for five years. There was Margarita "Pepita" Neri (mentioned by the *Times* correspondent above), who was described as somber, brave, and cruel, and who in reality came off the streets to better her position. She rose to lead hundreds of men, demonstrating a bestiality that could shock the toughest among them. And there was Jovita Valdovinos, daughter of a rebel chieftain, who demanded such perversities of her subordinates, it is said, that they were carried out only out of fear of what would happen if Jovita were disobeyed.

As colorful as these colonels and characters were, however, more lasting models for Mexican women include three whose intelligence and courage helped form the foundation for the Revolution and provided it with enduring values. They were Dolores Jiménez y Muro, Juana Belén Gutiérrez de Mendoza, and Hermila Galindo.

María Dolores Jiménez y Muro, born in Aguascalientes on June 7, 1848, remembered from her youth the end of Maximilian's abortive monarchy and Benito Juárez' hopeful presidency. A teacher, she wrote anti-essays for *La Patria* and *Diario del Hogar,* emerging as a kind of grande dame of the Revolution, earning for herself the description "virile, combative writer." So ubiquitous were Jiménez y Muro's writings—often under pseudonyms, sometimes male pseudonyms—and so shadowy was her life because of her revolutionary activities that historians concede the impossibility of gauging with certainty her full effect on the Revolution.

From 1900, Jiménez y Muro was active in the Precursor movement, made up of the earliest advocates of bringing to an end the long dictatorship of Porfirio Díaz. She worked on the staff of *La Mujer Mexicana* in 1905 and in 1907 joined the Mexico City group *Socialistas Mexicanos,* which included Juana Belén Gutiérrez, Elisa Acuña y Rossetti, and other female leaders. These women personified the intertwined forces of socialism, liberalism, and feminism. Those forces drew on ideas from around the world in a time of tremendous intellectual ferment, and the Mexican Revolution, as chaotic as it was, represented the combined eruption of those ideas.

In 1910, Jiménez y Muro helped organize the protest against Díaz' eighth term, and, for her effort, was jailed at Belén prison despite the fact that she was sixty-two years old. She was, in fact, placed in solitary confinement because in prison she continued to recruit. Upon her release, undaunted, she took part in 1911 in *el complot de Tacubaya,* an unsuccessful scheme hatched to put Francisco Madero into the presidency.

Important to the plot was its manifesto, a justification of the plot itself. The manifesto was an early articulation of revolutionary ideas. It restated and expanded upon a liberal program published five years earlier—and Jiménez y Muro was assigned the task of drafting it for publication on March 18, 1911.

The earlier statement had been a call for nationalist values and agrarian reform. Jiménez y Muro's proposals were more complex, forming a basis for later statements, including the drafting of a constitution at Querétaro in 1917.

Proposed was decentralization of school administration. Carranza later tried to affect this idea. Liberals were convinced of the need to free schooling from the clerical influences that mired education in Middle Age thought. Decentralization, as it turned out, did not work, the poorest states showing neither the capacity nor will to support their own school systems. The idea was another expression of Mexico's strong centrifugal tendency that pulls at national unity even today.

With a mentality that would be considered progressive in any city of the world today, the manifesto proposed lowering of tax values on urban rental properties in order to allow landlords to lower rents. Also envisioned was long-term financing for working-class housing. Included was that timeless proposal: higher pay for teachers. Other points called for an eight hour work day, the return of farmland to its original owners, a requirement that Mexican workers be hired by foreign-owned companies, and the abolition of monopolies.

In the spring of 1911, Jiménez traveled north to Ciudad Juárez to observe the assault on the city by forces led by Pascual Orozco and Pancho Villa, the attack that broke the tough back of the Díaz regime.

Returning to Mexico City, her dissidence was re-ignited after Victoriano Huerta—the man who ordered the murder of Madero—took the presidency in February 1913. Her views landed her back in jail for three months.

When Emiliano Zapata was told of the manifesto Jiménez y Muro had written, he remarked on the point calling for restitution of villagers' land—a principal goal of his own—and asked to meet this spinster teacher who wrote revolutionary tracts. Jiménez y Muro traveled to Morelos to join Zapata, who promptly named her a brigadier general. By 1916, owing to her allegiance with Zapata, there was a price on her gray head.

After Venustiano Carranza replaced Huerta in the presidency, however, Jiménez y Muro was able to exercise some influence over the drafting of the Constitution of 1917, when she was in her seventieth year. She continued to live in Morelos until Zapata was assassinated in 1919. She returned to Mexico City, where she died on October 15, 1925.

Juana Belén Gutiérrez de Mendoza was born in Durango in 1880. Her background and surroundings—the arid, rugged country northwest of the capital—were much like those of Villa, and she grew up hearing of the exploits of those who opposed the government. Her grandfather, she was told, was a poor laborer who died in front of a firing squad for his political dissent, a particular point of pride for the family. Her mother and father are variously described as Indian or mestizo. Her father, Santiago Gutiérrez, earned a meager living as a blacksmith, a horse-tamer, or a farm laborer. She was schooled as a typographer and in 1901 joined the Precursors movement, early critics of the Díaz regime and the foreign-dominated elitism it represented.

Her first publication was a small volume of poetry. Such a modest work was still the typical effort for a female writer in Mexico, although that condition was changing. While words of war, revolution, and patriotism were still largely the domain of men, women were being heard at a time when Mexico, in turmoil, needed new ideas. A feminist movement took form even before the oppressive, traditional regime of Porfirio Díaz had been driven from the scene.

In the spring of 1901, Gutiérrez, along with fellow teacher Elisa Acuña y Rossetti, founded *Vésper,* a weekly newspaper. It is said that Gutiérrez sold goats she owned to buy the press. Based in Guanajuato, the newspaper defended the serf like miners of the region and attacked the Church for its "religious obscurantism," the common charge that Roman Catholic priests, by claiming that only they held the keys to heaven, kept illiterate peasants in a kind of servitude. Unlike other dissidents, Gutiérrez did not just attack Díaz and his retainers, but upbraided the Mexican people for cowering before the dictator. So strong was Gutiérrez' commentary that a male anti–Díaz editor paid her the same compliment as had been paid Jiménez y Muro, calling her writing "virile."

Indicative of the times and of Gutiérrez' style was her publication of hundreds of copies of Kropotkin's *La Conquista del Pan.* Prince Peter Alexeivich Kropotkin (1842–1921) was a progenitor of communistic anarchism, a "pure" communism that did not allow individual moderation; his ideas were part of the swirl of socialist thought being discussed across Mexico. Gutiérrez also contributed to *Excélsior,* the publication of a Mexico City anti-re-electionist group.

The newspaper *Regeneración,* an important organ of anti–Díaz propaganda, described in 1903 the place of *Vésper* in the fight: "Now," wrote *Regeneración* in 1903, "when many men have lost heart and, out of cowardice, retired from the fight ... now that many men, without vigor, retreat ... there appears a spirited and brave woman, ready to fight for our principles, when the weakness of many men has permitted them to be trampled and spit upon."

Eventually, an infuriated Díaz struck back, and Gutiérrez was arrested along with male writers of several opposition newspapers. Three and a half years after the founding of *Vésper,* in 1904, Gutiérrez and Acuña y Rossetti were thrown into Belén women's prison. Gutiérrez remained behind bars for three years and was then exiled.

During the years of Gutiérrez' imprisonment and exile, the movement that initially had as its goal the departure of Porfirio Díaz broke apart into the factions that would eventually tear Mexico to shreds through years of civil war. A major personalistic fight was between the Flores Magón brothers and Camilo Arriaga, the oldest remaining leader of the Precursors. Gutiérrez and Acuña y Rossetti (as well as Francisco Madero, the future president) sided with Arriaga. In the spring of 1910, Gutiérrez traveled to San Antonio to be with Arriaga in exile. There they reestablished *Vésper.*

Mexico was now close to armed revolt, and Gutiérrez returned to publication, warning that simply driving Díaz out would not end despotism. It was a warning that would prove prophetic.

The scheme to bring Madero to power, *el complot de Tacubaya,* was conceived in 1911 by Arriaga. When the plot was betrayed and arrests made, Arriaga was jailed and not released until Madero took the presidency in May.

Gutiérrez, however, turned away from Madero as his regime proved unable, or unwilling, to shed itself of the *porfiristas* whom, she thought, were a drag on Madero's resolve to solve Mexico's problems. Similarly, Carranza's promises were, in her view, hollow. Gutiérrez then joined Zapata, the leader who was for many the only true beacon of social revolution. She founded *Desmontada,* trying to cut through all of the conflicting claims to leadership arising from all the personalist factions. With "the countryside bristling with old logs," she wrote, explaining the publication's name, "one must dismount." After all of the war, Gutiérrez charged, after all of the death, "for all of the so-called principles inscribed on the flags of combat" — with the sole exception of Zapata's agrarian reform — "there is nothing else that merits the name of 'principle.'" Finally, with the murder of Zapata, Gutiérrez' last hope for national reform was lost. Her spirit, however, was not extinguished.

She returned to Mexico City in 1920 after Alvaro Obregón had taken power. At the age of sixty, Juana Belén Gutiérrez de Mendoza had diminished in neither eloquence nor conscience. She published a biweekly newspaper called *Alma Mexicana,* and told an interviewer that, alas, her advanced age had not enabled her to blind herself to the needs she saw everywhere around her. She could not "retire," find a peaceful corner and ignore her struggling country.

"I have that right," she said, "but I don't have a corner. In all the world's corners lives a pain; in all the world's corners is coiled a treachery with open jaws, ready to swallow; and I don't have the indifference necessary to ignore it, nor the cowardice to flee it, nor the gentility to accommodate it."

Juana Belén Gutiérrez de Mendoza died in Mexico City in 1942.

Hermila Galindo was also born in Durango, in Lerdo, on May 29, 1896. In 1909, when only thirteen years old, she put the shorthand and typing courses she was taking in addition to her regular schoolwork to a revolutionary use. A dissident lawyer gave a speech in nearby Torreón, denouncing the Díaz regime. The discourse was so harsh in tone that the president of the municipal council took the original draft in order that it not be published. Little Hermila, however, had made a verbatim copy, which was passed along to Díaz opponents for their use as yet another broadside at the embattled dictator.

Five years later, still a teenager, it was her fate to once again cross paths with the Revolution. This time the episode was the beginning of a career. Her family had moved to Mexico City, and Hermila had continued to be a precocious student. She was chosen to deliver a welcoming speech for Venustiano Carranza, who was to make a triumphal entry into the city after the fall of the short-lived dictatorship of Victoriano Huerta. Galindo's intelligence impressed Carranza. He needed the moderating image of women around him to assuage the feelings of many Mexican women who feared that the revolution would come down hardest on the Church. Carranza could not know, however, that Galindo's revolutionary zeal would soon shock everyone.

Carranza, a landowner and former governor, stepped into the presidency only to begin betraying principles and people. Once in power he was perceived as too conservative by the people who had fought to put him in the presidential palace. But while others turned against Carranza, Galindo did not. "She steadfastly supported Carranza," writes Anna Macías, "after he was elected president in 1917, and remained loyal to him despite mounting criticism of his venality, duplicity, and bad faith as the supposed leader of Mexico's peasantry and urban working classes."

Support, however, worked both ways. If Galindo remained loyal to a despot, she also used her position in the administration to espouse feminist positions—positions more radical than anyone had imagined. "Emboldened by Carranza's support," Macías continues, "between 1915 and 1919 Hermila Galindo adopted advanced positions on divorce, sexuality, religion, prostitution and politics which shocked even secular oriented, middle class women with some education." While it cannot be said that Galindo's efforts bore immediate fruit, her force was a necessary and large part of the groundwork for women's advances that came later. Carranza, in fact, made liberalized divorce law a part of his program, and liberalization occurred in most Mexican states.

In January 1916, at the First Feminist Congress in Yucatán, a paper by Galindo called "Women in the Future" was so radical as to retain the support only of those delegates labeled "extremists." Its central argument was that a woman's sex drive was as strong as a man's, a shocking idea barely fifteen years after the death of Queen Victoria. Galindo's notion led her to the conclusion that girls and young women needed sex education classes in school. Even among most feminist militants, the conclusion was explosive, and its effect on Roman Catholic educators can only be imagined. Her ideas, however, found expression twenty years later during the presidency of Lázaro Cárdenas (1934–1940), when sex education was introduced to public schools.

Macías rendered this judgment in 1982: "Unlike her contemporaries, Juana Belén Gutiérrez de Mendoza and Dolores Jiménez y Muro, Hermila Galindo did not suffer imprisonment for expressing her ideas. However, she did have to face a great deal of hostility, scorn, and ridicule from both men and women for expressing unpopular views and for speaking up on a subject that still remains taboo in Mexico."

Similarly, at the constitutional convention at Querétaro in 1917, Galindo proposed giving women the vote. The proposal was rejected (liberals feared that enfranchising women would open a Pandora's Box of support for the Church), but it was the beginning of a period of incubation. Mexican women finally won the vote in 1953, casting their first presidential ballots in 1958.

As Galindo's feminist efforts diminished, her writing turned to politics, always a slippery slope in post revolutionary Mexico. Support for one candidate or another was sure to attract at least as many enemies as friends. In 1920, when General Alvaro Obregón succeeded to the presidency, Galindo was unwelcome in councils of power. In 1923, she married Manuel Topete and retired to a quiet life. Galindo lived to the age of seventy-nine, having sown ideas that would flower only in more enlightened times.

14

Augusto Sandino
The Visionary versus the Marines
1895–1934
(Nicaragua)

The life of Augusto Sandino bridges the gap to modernity. His name, of course, was made known during the long struggle between Nicaraguan *Sandinistas* and the United States. During his lifetime, however, his rebellion brought him into direct conflict with U.S. forces, including dive bombers, as they staged their long occupation of Nicaragua in a vain attempt to shape that tiny nation's political future. U.S. marines chased Sandino over mountain trails, attracting to his cause worldwide attention. Rebels, from communists in neighboring El Salvador to the Kuomintang in China, found Sandino representative of all struggles during that volatile period, 1925 to 1935. They transformed him into a symbol.

Augusto Sandino was born on May 18, 1895, in Niquinihomo, a village of about a thousand inhabitants. His father was Gregorio Sandino, owner of a modest farm. His mother was Margarita Calderón, a servant. His birth to a servant and a landowner imbued him with a sense of both cultures that would run through his political thought. Although both parents were *ladinos,* of mixed blood, his father exercised some power in the community, while his mother was "Indian" twice over, both by virtue of her family and her low status. Sandino's private letters and public pronouncements would suggest that such distinctions be destroyed.

For several years the young Sandino lived with his mother and was known as Augusto Calderón. When he went to live in his father's house he took advantage of the ample library, reading its classics and eventually deciding his name should be Augusto "César" Sandino. He went to secondary school in nearby Granada and then went to work as administrator of his father's farm.

Although the elder Sandino was a supporter of Nicaragua's Liberal party, Augusto showed no particular interest in politics. For years, the country's Liberals and Conservatives had tugged at each other without upsetting a system dominated by the wealthy and their foreign financiers. Had Sandino stayed at home, it is likely he would have been submerged in this traditional system.

But in 1920, when he was twenty-five, Sandino got into a fight in Niquinihomo and shot a man in the leg. He fled the country.

There was plenty of work in Central America for a man with Sandino's education, both formal and practical, and Sandino worked for fruit companies in Honduras and Guatemala as he made his way north. He settled in the Mexican oil port of Tampico, took a common-law wife who bore him a daughter, and settled into Tampico's turgid political environment.

Tampico was a magnet for foreign capital and foreign workers, the former representing a single conservative force, the latter bringing in radical ideas from all over the world. The ideas found a hospitable environment in Mexico, still in the throes of its peasant revolution, the Indian aspects of which attracted Sandino. In addition, nowhere in the hemisphere could Sandino have been more thoroughly schooled in the effects of U.S. domination.

Sandino was something of an intellectual explorer in this environment. Like Juárez, Sandino found cause to admire the Masons. Sandino also studied yoga and the beliefs of the Seventh-Day Adventists. Added to this eclecticism was a hint of mysticism, suggesting a range of thought that has caused some to admire Sandino's hunger for new ideas. Others simply dismiss him as weird.

On May 14, 1926, just before his thirtieth birthday, Sandino quit his job as head of gasoline sales for Huasteca Oil Company in Tampico. He took $500 in savings and his revolver back to Nicaragua. Crossing the border, he immediately found work at the San Albino gold mine in the Segovia Mountains, the area that would become the province of his army.

Sandino began lecturing fellow workers on the need for political change. His eloquence on the subject divided listeners into those who saw him as self-centered and voluble and those who were impressed by his willingness to explain his views to the least educated *peon,* just as long as he would listen. Sandino was able to recruit twenty-nine workers into his "army," using his own money to buy rifles and ammunition from a Honduran gun-runner.

At that time, Liberals in Managua were trying to take power from a Conservative regime that was propped in place by the U.S. marines. From 1912, Conservatives had been able to count for support on the marines' arrival whenever needed to protect their interests and the interests of U.S. investors. Historian Hubert Herring has described Nicaragua at the time as "the virtual ward of New York bankers." In 1916 the United States' authority to intervene in Nicaraguan sovereignty was guaranteed in perpetuity by treaty. Sandino considered the treaty an outrage. In one of his first pronouncements from his mountain headquarters he calculated that the $3 million that paid for the treaty, "spread among Nicaraguan citizens, would not have bought each one a sardine on a cracker."

Without identifying his band with the Liberal party — although no one mistook him for a Conservative — Sandino led it in a raid on the government garrison of two hundred troops at Jicaro on November 2. It was the beginning of Sandino's personal war.

The Sandinistas were repelled, and, although no one had been killed, there was a general loss of heart among his men after the raid. Sandino decided that what was needed was an alliance with Liberal forces, so he led his disheartened guerrillas down the Coco River to the Atlantic Coast. At Puerto Cabezas he declared his allegiance to "constitutionalist" forces gathered there.

But Sandino's arrival was not welcomed, either by Juan Sacasa, the Liberal pretender to the presidency, or by José María Moncada, his field commander, despite Moncada's having been a friend of Sandino's father. Also, as Sandino learned more of his would-be allies, he, too, cooled to the arrangement. They were, in Sandino's view, much too willing to collaborate with foreigners in general and the United States in particular.

The United States was in touch with both sides of Nicaragua's civil unrest, manipulating the Conservatives while covering all bets with Liberals. Sandino was aghast at the role the United States was able to play between the two sides. After arriving in Puerto Cabezas, Sandino watched in dismay as Liberals complied with a declaration of the commander of a small contingent of U.S. marines that the city would henceforth be a neutral zone. The marines were to gather up all arms, take them out to sea, and dump them overboard. What kind of revolution, Sandino wondered, throws away its guns? Reacting as fast as he could, Sandino and some friends recruited passing prostitutes to help them hurriedly grab up some thirty rifles and six thousand rounds of ammunition that had been stacked for disposal. Then they quickly left town.

Although the Liberals admired Sandino's resourcefulness—he was made a Liberal general—he had to insist to Moncada that he be allowed to keep the rifles. Clearly, Sandino's allies were planning a less aggressive strategy than he was. In February 1927, Sandino's force won an important victory by defending its position against government troops, his men proving themselves under fire and then falling on their attackers as they fled, recovering weapons and ammunition left behind. Then Sandino turned his men, now numbering two hundred, to an attack on the government garrison at Jinotega. They succeeded in driving off the defenders and occupying the town, if only briefly. Finally, joining forces with another rebel column, Sandino went to the relief of Moncada himself, whose troops had been stalled in a drive toward Managua.

At this point, however, Liberal heads were turned. Moncada was persuaded to sign a truce urged upon him by Henry Stimson, whom President Coolidge sent. As a part of the truce, Moncada offered Sandino the governorship of a northern state and $10 a day for each day he'd spent in the field if he and his men would lay down their arms. Sandino declined, saying he would fight on alone. He declared, in one of the existential telegrams from his headquarters that would become a trademark, "I will protest for my own satisfaction if there is no one to support me."

This was more than posturing. Despite the small size of his force and the fact that he was no threat to the capital, Sandino could not be ignored. He had demonstrated a capacity for leadership and the ability to learn military tactics. In addition, his voice, although solitary, carried out over the rubble of opportunism that characterized Nicaraguan politics. If he could not be silenced, there was always the chance that, eventually, he would be followed.

Moncada enlisted the help of Sandino's father to go to Sandino's camp to convince him to give up. After the two talked, however, the father wrote to his other son, Socrates, encouraging him to join Augusto. Socrates became his brother's liaison with supportive groups in the United States.

In 1927, the year the Liberals laid down their arms, the United States made a fateful decision—to commit its marines to building an independent armed force for Nicaragua, one that answered to neither Liberals nor Conservatives. It would be called the National Guard. At the same time, New York banks assumed the bulk of the debt Nicaragua owed British banks. Finally, there was a $3 million payment against the possibility that Nicaragua might be the site of a transoceanic canal. To make sure Nicaraguan finances were handled in a manner Washington considered prudent, the money would be disbursed—how much to retire debt, how much for international development—at Washington's order. Against this kind of domination, Sandino protested.

He established as his base San Rafael del Norte, taking as his headquarters the house where the telegraph office was located and as his intended bride the daughter of the telegrapher. Sandino met Blanca Araúz, nineteen years old, as she tapped the key for his many messages and pronouncements. Blanca's sister, swept up in the revolutionary spirit, arranged for a mass to be celebrated in honor of the safe return of Sandino's troops from battle. The men comported themselves properly, according to Sandino, except for "some salvos from rifles and machine guns." Sandino smoothed things over by paying for the mass.

From his headquarters Sandino kept up a running correspondence with his adversaries. He conducted a kind of continuing debate, salted with insults, with the marine officers in pursuit. He warned one marine captain that if he and his men contemplated venturing into the Segovia Mountains, which Sandino considered his domain, "make your will beforehand."

The marine officers generally had no trouble in replying in kind. Wrote this one, "Bravo! General. If words were bullets and phrases were soldiers, you would be a field marshal instead of a mule thief."

As the marines slogged through the mountains in search of Sandino, they were at the same time training the National Guard. Marine sergeants served as National Guard commanders. The idea — as durable as it was unsuccessful — was to train and equip a force that would be left behind after the marines had gone home.

Sandino either eluded these patrols or, at his choosing, ambushed them. Counterattacks chased Sandino to his mountain hideout, called *El Chipote*. Marine commanders would occasionally report to their superiors that Sandino's army, last seen disappearing into the undergrowth, had been "wiped out," but as long as Sandino and his men stayed deep enough in the mountains, they were safe. They were kept well informed by villagers.

In May 1927, Sandino married Blanca and prepared for his biggest attack, on the river port of Ocotal, in the heart of the Segovia Mountains. To taunt his enemies, he named a "governor" for the state of Nueva Segovia, allowed the nearby town of El Jicaro to be "renamed" Ciudad Sandino, and made it clear that just as soon as his troops took Ocotal he would appoint his own mayor.

Ocotal was defended by four hundred U.S. marines and two hundred Nicaraguan National Guard trainees. Sandino had eight hundred men. On his side, Sandino counted on surprise and stealth, infiltrating the town with spies and arming collaborators in the middle of the night. On their side, the marines had airplanes. Ocotal was a small beginning for modern warfare.

Sandino's awkward strategy might have prevailed against an enemy left to its own devices. But the planes and their bombs made the difference. When Sandino attacked Ocotal in darkness, the marines were able to hold out until morning, when two biplanes were called in from Managua. Dive bombing and strafing were introduced, and Sandino's revolution scattered for cover.

One marine was killed at Ocotal; at least fifty dead rebels were found in the streets, and it is assumed at least fifty more died in the houses or along the river or were carried away by Sandino's retreating troops.

The battle signaled the beginning of stalemate. Marine airplanes did not help them get into the mountains to drag Sandino out. But neither could Sandino come out when, within hours, he would be attacked from above.

President Coolidge called the Battle of Ocotal a "heroic action" by the marines. American critics, however, in phrases resembling those of the Vietnam era, called the use of bombs in a country with which we were not formally at war an "indecency" and "inhuman." The critics pointed out that marine body counts were likely to include civilians in a non war in which there were no "belligerents" but yet everybody *looked* like the enemy. The resulting charge and counter-charge turned Sandino, trapped with his troops in the Segovia Mountains, into an international celebrity.

In the eyes of U.S. policy makers, Sandino's notoriety made it imperative that he be stopped, so the giant's pursuit of the gnat began to take on epic proportions. Japan, involved on the other side of the world with sending its troops into Manchuria, was happy to have an example to throw in the face of the United States. International bullies shouldn't criticize each other, was the message. Sandino, meanwhile, was only too happy to be used as a global example.

Journalists who trekked into the mountains to interview Sandino found him wearing khakis or the type of clothes any bourgeois might wear for a day's hunting: checked jacket and high, lace-up boots. He did not wear a military uniform. North American journalists described him as short; Latin American writers saw him as of medium height. He was thin, with black hair combed straight back and delicate features, making him seem quite dapper. His day-in-the-country attire — topped by a ten-gallon cowboy hat that became his trademark — plus his natural gregariousness, made Sandino a kind of boulevardier of mountain trails. He and his troops wore kerchiefs of black and red, the colors of the international workers' movement — although while the troops' kerchiefs were cotton, Sandino's was silk.

In shaping his own image for the press, Sandino talked the way he dressed, with style. Replying to an associate who had asked for a photograph for a magazine article, Sandino cautioned that it be made "clear in any caption that I'm not a professional politician, just a plain artisan. My profession is that of mechanic, and up to my present age of thirty-three I have earned my bread, tools in hand."

Sandino argued that his goals were not earth shaking. He wanted, he said, the chance to negotiate the withdrawal of U.S. marines and the redrawing of the canal treaty. He wanted a hemispheric conference to discuss the sovereignty of Latin American countries. "A man who doesn't even ask his country for a yard of ground to be buried in deserves to be heard," he wrote, "and not only heard, but believed. I am a Nicaraguan and proud that Indian-American blood, more than any other, flows in my veins, blood that contains the mystery of loyal and sincere patriotism."

The Battle of Ocotal had shown Sandino that he could not confront marines with their airplanes overhead, and had demonstrated to the marines that they could not easily subdue Sandino. The tiny war became one of running battles and ambushes: a marine or two would be killed in the jungle thickness, or several *sandinistas* would be bombed when a patrol plane spotted horses tied outside a mountain cabin. Sandino captured arms and ammunition, dragging his dead away from skirmishes so the government could not count to what extent he had been weakened. The longer the conflict dragged on, the more bitter the behavior. A marine pilot, his plane downed by small-arms fire, was executed and hanged from a tree; a photograph of his limp body was sent to Honduran and Mexican newspapers. The marines carried the image in their heads.

When the marines could never quite claim that Sandino was within their grasp, the State Department grew impatient. Marine commanders alternated between predictions that his capture was not far off and admissions that he was unlikely to give up and, furthermore, enjoyed the support of the peasants. Sandino added to their dismay in the autumn of 1927 when from *El Chipote,* his now well-fortified hideout, he issued his "Articles of the Defending Army of the National Sovereignty of Nicaragua." Sandino's notion of sovereignty meant that while his area chiefs were forbidden from stealing from peasants, they were allowed to "collect forced loans from native and foreign capitalists" as long as they kept records. He declared that he was neither politically committed nor beholden to anyone, but he informed his soldiers they would not be paid until after the cause was triumphant.

The marines' response was an all-out attack on *El Chipote.* The mountain redoubt had taken on a heroic aspect, bolstering Nicaraguans' faith that perhaps the United States would not always win. The slang term *chipote* was coined to suggest "impregnability," as if Sandino could laugh down the mountain at his impotent adversaries; the word could be translated to mean everything from "myth" to "back-handed slap" to the lump resulting from a blow to the head. Used by Nicaraguans, however, the word allowed them to laugh at the United States.

In January 1928, the marines closed in on *El Chipote* even as Coolidge, accompanied by Charles Evans Hughes and Secretary of State Frank B. Kellogg, traveled to a hemispheric peace conference. At the conference, held in Havana, Coolidge testified to the United States' determination to get along with neighbors. A cynic might suggest that Coolidge's peace talk risked misunderstanding as he simultaneously cheered on efforts to subdue Sandino, who was given one last chance to lay down his arms before a siege was ordered. "The situation was getting tricky," Sandino would write afterward. "They were encircling us to prevent supplies' coming in, and the circle was constantly tightening." When the attack was sprung, it depended on air power. "During the sixteen days we were under siege," Sandino wrote, "the pirates' air squadrons paid us daily visits."

For sixteen days, four planes would appear in a wave, bomb, then be replaced by another wave. Two hundred horses were blown to bits. Cattle were killed by shrapnel. The stench of decaying carcasses became almost unbearable, Sandino wrote, and "the air was full of vultures for days. They did us a service by ruining visibility for the planes." When Sandino ordered a retreat, his men left behind straw figures topped by native sombreros. The planes continued to bomb the scarecrows.

The marines had shown they could destroy Sandino's refuge. Not so his image. American journalist Carleton Beals, visiting Sandino after he'd pulled out of *El Chipote*, described him in the *Nation* as "a man utterly without vices, with an unequivocal sense of justice, a keen eye for the welfare of the humblest soldier."

Despite such journalistic enthusiasm, however, the war dragged on with Sandino still unable to threaten Managua. U.S. planes continued to rain impersonal terror in the countryside, while small bands of Sandinistas inflicted what damage they could on isolated mines or defenseless towns. There the two sides stood.

Knowing he had to step up his capacity to make war, Sandino decided to go to Mexico for materiel and moral support. Before he left, Sandino tried to open talks with Moncada, who was elected president in the U.S. sponsored election of 1928. Moncada rebuffed him. Sandino departed overland for Mexico, leaving behind a confused army, uncertain whether his departure represented defeat. Almost daily, guerrillas were surrendering to a government amnesty.

Sandino traveled overland through Central American countries in the spring of 1929, sometimes greeted as a savior, sometimes treated like a pariah. Reaching Mexico, he cooled his heels.

The government of Mexico gave Sandino and his companions a house in Mérida, but otherwise studiously ignored him. He was free to make speeches and entertain reporters, but the materiel and spiritual support he sought from Mexico were not forthcoming.

He wrote letters to the Radical president of Argentina, Hipolito Yrigoyen, and to the Republican president of the United States, Herbert Hoover. Sandino was informed that his ideas dovetailed perfectly with those of the mystical Victor Haya de la Torre of Peru, whose dream of a united, Indo-Hispanic continent was attracting intellectuals. Sandino got news that a division of the Kuomintang army in China was named for him. But he could not get what he needed from the Mexican government.

After six months and a frustrating trip to meet the president and other national leaders, who yielded nothing, Sandino gave up. All he got was words from men who faced him squarely, but had their backs to the Rio Grande.

When Sandino returned to Mérida he and his associates began contacting real estate brokers. They drove in a caravan into the countryside as if looking for a permanent residence in exile. When the press, the spies, and the curious, all of whom had followed, were lulled into accepting the pattern of trips from which Sandino always returned, one day the cars did not come back. Sandino slipped back across the border carrying the only Mexican acquisitions that would aid him in his fight: two submachine guns disassembled and listed with customs as carpenter's tools.

The stalemate in Nicaragua in Sandino's absence had enabled the United States, by early 1930, to get closer to the day when the marines could live up to the promise of pulling out. Officers and noncoms had been busily training the Nicaraguan National Guard. The stated purpose was to create an apolitical peace-keeping force to replace army officers too inclined to take sides between Liberals and Conservatives.

Part of the State Department's strategy — anti-guerrilla strategies are timeless — was to "relocate" any Nicaraguan and his family if there was some indication he identified with Sandino or one of his regional chiefs. The result — such results are similarly timeless — was to spread from the towns where people were uprooted to wherever they were relocated stories of an impersonal, hostile government flailing blindly at a man officials insisted was just a common bandit. More thoroughly than he could have done it for himself, Sandino's message was being carried.

At the same time, no strategy of relocation could eliminate the necessity of capturing or killing Sandino. Only now the National Guard would have to do what the Marines could not. When Sandino returned to Nicaragua the frequency of raids increased, and in June 1930 Sandino returned to the fray himself by taking command of four hundred troops at El Saraguazca Mountain, not far from Jinotega, where he had led his first successful attack three years before.

The Guard was no more effective than the marines had been, but no less inclined to call in air support. Sandino was wounded in the leg. The battle was inconclusive, but the world read in an Associated Press dispatch of marine planes that "got away with bullet-perforated wings." Ineffective on the ground, badgered from the air, Sandino clearly still dominated the newswires.

Sandino let it be known that he claimed "control" of the rural areas of the northern states from the Atlantic to the Pacific. In towns, he said, his supporters watched and waited. He celebrated the fourth anniversary of the Battle at Ocotal by issuing a proclamation that spoke grandly of a kind of pervasive presence among the populace and a humane relationship among his troops. "I am in no way different from any rank-and-file soldier in the armies of the world," he proclaimed. "My voice is not arrogant, nor does my presence evoke terror as many might imagine. We have, however, fulfilling our duty as citizens, had the pleasure of seeing under our feet in humiliation a number of exalted chiefs and officers of the arrogant army of the United States, the would-be annihilator annihilated."

The bombast extended to calling Hoover "a rabid but impotent beast," casting aspersions on members of the Hoover administration, and suggesting that the wife of the U.S. ambassador to Nicaragua "now runs the Yankee legation in Managua." The earthquake that shook Managua in 1931, he said, was divine retribution. A world war, he predicted, would destroy most of mankind.

Sandino adopted a style of life as exotic as his pronouncements. In the mountains, moving constantly, he took, in the absence of Blanca, a mistress, Salvadoran revolutionary Teresa Villatoro. But by the spring of 1931, like a guilty husband, he proclaimed that although love ought to be unfettered he recognized social convention. He summoned Blanca to join him at his headquarters. Teresa left. Before long, Blanca was pregnant.

"My little Blanca," he called her in a letter, fondly describing "her .38 pistol and her .44 Winchester rifle." She shot up too much ammunition practicing, he complained gently, but admitted that "all I can do is permit her to do anything she likes."

In 1932, the State Department sponsored a presidential election as the final building block of its strategy. Sandino called for voters to abstain, but the appeal was unsuccessful. After the election, the State Department insisted, Liberals and Conservatives were to share power no matter which party's candidate won the presidency. The marines were to be pulled out, and democratic institutions were to develop under the watchful protection of the National Guard. Elected president was Sacasa, the man to whom Sandino had declared allegiance in his first days as a revolutionary. Sacasa, consolidating his government, bequeathed unusual power on one man, making him foreign minister in addition to his post as chief director of the National Guard. That man, educated in prep school and college in the United States and trained by the marines, was Anastasio Somoza.

Sacasa extended to Sandino the chance to cooperate with the new government. Sandino chose as his emissary Blanca, four months pregnant, who, despite being manhandled a bit by National Guardsmen, began the process of reconciliation. With the marines gone, a proclamation declared, "an era of basic renovation in our public life is opened.... In order to deepen this most noble tendency, the undersigned agree to make respect for the Republic Constitutions and basic laws the foundation stone of their respective political programs."

Amnesty was granted, and Sandino was authorized by the national government to control land in the valley of either the Coco or Segovia River to establish and advance his agrarian policies. In exchange for disarming the main part of his army, he was allowed to retain a personal guard. Sandino returned to the mountains.

But he was concerned about the strength and independence of the National Guard. This concern crackled through contentious messages between Sandino and Somoza. Sandino's regional chiefs let him know they needed ammunition because of attacks by National Guard patrols. Somoza opposed all such accommodations. Sandino, powerless, tarried in the administration of agricultural reform. Strong in his mind was the example of Zapata's reforms in Morelos. Strong must have been as well the example of Zapata's betrayal.

Sandino thought to organize a political party to enter national politics. Sacasa asked that he wait. So he did, turning back to his farming. In June 1933, Blanca gave birth to a girl and died. Sandino named the infant Blanca Segovia, left the child with her grandmother, and rode back into the mountains.

Fighting continued between government patrols and former Sandino soldiers. Sandino complained in messages to Sacasa that the National Guard was constantly provoking trouble, overstepping its bounds, demonstrating that the independent role on which Somoza insisted was "unconstitutional." Sacasa was powerless to intervene. Nevertheless, Sandino decided to go to Managua to argue his case.

He arrived on February 16, 1934, to confer with Sacasa and other administration officials, including Somoza. Somoza privately assured the U.S. ambassador that he should not be alarmed by the apparent hostility and that the ambassador would be informed of any plans Somoza might have. Sandino, meanwhile, embarked on a round of discussions with government leaders, one of whom informed the ambassador that Sandino, as flowing with ideas as ever, at times failed to make sense.

There is evidence, however, that Sacasa had no trouble understanding Sandino's suggestion that the National Guard be reorganized. The idea could not help but be appealing to the president since he could not control it any other way. His predecessor, Moncada, had feared the independence of the Guard, but only because he sought to control it himself. Preventing political control of the Guard, however, was the keystone of U.S. policy, notwithstanding the fact that that policy had created a monster.

On the morning of February 21, Somoza was noticed by the U.S. ambassador to be especially exercised over something, although he did not know what. That evening, Sandino and his father and several friends were expected for dinner at the presidential palace.

After dinner, Sandino talked on about exploitation of gold deposits in the Coco River basin, one of his myriad ideas. When it came time, about ten o'clock, for the guests to leave, Sandino shared a car with his father and Sacasa's agriculture minister, the man responsible for bringing Sacasa and Sandino together in the negotiations that led to peace. Sandino also invited to ride with him two old, trusted generals from the days of campaigning in the Segovia Mountains. The two generals sat in front with the driver, the other three in the back seat. In a car following was Sacasa's daughter.

The presidential palace was on a hill, and when the cars reached the bottom of the hill, where the street passed through a National Guard post, there was a car in the middle of the road, apparently stalled. Sandino's car stopped, and a National Guard sergeant stepped up to the car window in the dark. The two generals in the front seat reached for their pistols, but Sandino stopped them, saying his companions in the back seat were not fighters. Sandino and the two generals were arrested. Sacasa's daughter came forward to protest, but when it did no good she drove away back toward the presidential palace.

Sandino and his two companions were driven to the Managua airfield. National Guard officers would later say that their instructions came from Somoza, and that he had assured them the U.S. ambassador knew full well what was happening. They signed a conspiratorial document entitled "The Death of Caesar."

Sandino and his companions were told to stand together on the dark airfield, watching while soldiers took from the back of a truck a tripod mounted machine gun. The officer in charge of the squad, a Mason like Sandino, did not have the courage to stay to face what he was about to order. He gave instructions to his men to commence firing when they heard the sound of his pistol, then walked over the crest of a nearby hill, out of sight.

One of the generals with Sandino searched in his pockets for souvenirs to be taken to his family. Sandino, hoping to buy time while Sacasa's daughter alerted the president, asked for a drink of water. He was refused. He asked to be allowed to urinate. He was refused again. Then he, too, searched through his pockets for souvenirs until one of his companions stopped him, telling him to preserve his dignity and get it over with.

In any event, Sandino is said to have found nothing in his pockets, leading him, in the moments before the machine gun blasted all else into silence, to utter the frustration of rebellion. "Screwed," he said. "The politicians cleaned me out."

15

Juan Perón
Monarch of the Working Class
1895–1974
(Argentina)

Some parts of the life of Juan Perón read like a radio script, in which, of course, the radio actress Eva Duarte plays herself. There is about both of them a staged quality, contrived, so that in the end there is no sense of tragedy, no inclination toward pity for them, just a feeling that their audience —"the shirtless ones" was the melodramatic phrase — was used for corrupt purposes. Yet *peronismo* lives on, representing a strong force among Argentines, a political movement that has outlived the follies of its progenitor. It does so because Juan Perón touched a nerve among working people, one that had been ignored, if not oppressed, by Argentine elites. For that reason, Juan Perón deserves to be remembered.

Juan Domingo Perón was born on October 8, 1895, about sixty miles south of Buenos Aires, near the village of Lobos, where his father worked for a judge. Although some biographers portray Perón as having been born in an impoverished setting, a more sober judgment is that his parents, of predominately Spanish and Italian origins, were members of Argentina's growing middle class. Perón himself, as have other politicians, contributed to the image of poverty-stricken early days. Indeed, there is something in Perón's mythical background for everyone.

On the one hand, Perónist publicists claimed that his grandparents were friends of a colorful bandit, Juan Moreira, who operated in the southern part of the province. On the other hand, Perón himself claimed to an electorate dominated by Italian immigrants that his great-grandfather had been a Sardinian senator. To this claim there was attached speculation that the family name had been Peroni.

When Perón was five years old, his father, suffering hard times, moved the family to Patagonia, a barren province where Argentina and Chile squeeze together at the bottom of the continent. There the father found work as a hired hand. Later, he was able to move the family back to the province of Buenos Aires and to buy a sheep ranch near the Atlantic Coast.

When Perón was ten, he was sent to Buenos Aires to military school, where he proved a natural athlete and was trained as a horseman, a crack shot, a boxer, and a fencer, later winning the foils championship of the army. He grew tall, with a broad chest and shoulders. Striking was his smile and his dark hair, combed straight back, which accentuated his aquiline profile. These manly attributes would not discourage political opponents from whispering in later years of his "effeminacy."

One reason for the slur was, obviously, the jealousy of men not so endowed. In Perón's shadow, men found solace by mocking him. There was also the fact that there would emerge weaknesses in Perón's character. And in a country influenced by Spanish and Italian notions of male dignity, even a man who so carefully crafted his own image would not long be able to disguise such flaws. It is particularly embarrassing, of course, for the *macho* to need a woman to provide the drive for his leadership, and even Perón's supporters would have to concede that he would not have risen half so far without the intellectual and psychological toughness of his second wife, whom the crowds called "Evita."

Nevertheless, Perón's military career was relatively distinguished, considering that he served in an army at war only with its own civilian population. At the age of eighteen he graduated from military school as a second lieutenant and, soon afterward, completed officer training with the rank of captain. He went on to more military schooling and in 1929 was appointed to a post in the war ministry. While at the ministry, Perón also taught, developing sufficient background in military tactics to write four books.

Yet by 1930, when he was thirty-five years old, Perón was still a captain. In ensuing years, however, his résumé was enhanced with service at the Argentine war college and as an aide to the army chief of staff and to the minister of war. In developed countries, rapid broadening of an officer's experience is possible only in time of war; in Argentina, Perón was able to rise by virtue of participation in the coup that deposed Hipolito Yrigoyen, the grand old man of Argentine liberalism.

By 1930, the liberalism that once promised to organize Argentina's formidable cultural and economic strengths into political dynamism had withered. It had always been held suspect by the landed classes, and after independence in 1829 the tension between the cosmopolitan Buenos Aires and the agricultural provinces evolved into a corresponding split between industrialization and the interests of landowners. For a while, it appeared that liberalism would triumph, a necessity for Argentina's many graces to be accepted in the world community. Liberal ideas were written into the Constitution of 1853, and waves of European immigrant workers flocked to Argentina in the mid–1800s, filling, by 1880, the ranks of the Radical party.

But liberalism barely managed to struggle into the twentieth century. When Irigoyen was elected president in 1916, he proved to be the last hope. In 1930, Yrigoyen was eighty years old and senile, unable to keep his own aides from raiding the Argentine treasury. The military placed in power civilian puppets, but the end had been written for any hope of a two-party system in which a liberal opposition would compete for power. Captain Perón had learned the way government worked.

In 1936, now a lieutenant-colonel, Perón was assigned as military attaché in Santiago de Chile, the capital of Argentina's traditional Andean enemy. Perón, at once charming and devious, became a friend of the Chilean president, Arturo Alessandri — until Perón was discovered trying to buy Chilean defense secrets. Alessandri later told scholar Joseph R. Barager that when he found out about his Argentine friend's duplicity he called him into the presidential office and pointed out the window at Chile's most effective line of defense: the snow-capped peaks of the Andes. Perón was declared persona non grata in Chile.

Perón was ready for further training, so in 1939, with Europe dominated by warlike fascist states, Perón was sent to observe Italy's Tyrolean troops. He spent nearly two years studying military organization in several countries, including Germany and Spain. Argentina's upper classes were strongly drawn to European customs; commercial ties with Great Britain were important, and cultural ties with Italy, Germany, and Spain exerted strong influences. Argentine elites — like many of their counterparts in Brazil, Paraguay, and several other Latin American countries — saw totalitarian government, with its parallel excitement and control of the masses, as the answer for Argentina's future. Perón's own writings disclose his admiration for Alexander the Great, Hannibal, and Napoleon and his fascination with the views of the German officers he had interviewed.

In the late 1930s and early 1940s, banking on widespread sympathy, German agents operated openly in Argentina. At a hemispheric conference of foreign ministers in Rio de Janeiro in January 1942 — a month after the attack on Pearl Harbor — Argentina, with Chile, held out against the over-whelming sentiment of other Latin American nations and the machinations of the United States. Argentina and Chile insisted on retaining diplomatic ties with Spain, Germany, and Italy.

Argentina might have sustained this diplomatic position had the country's puppet civilian leaders shown any subtlety, any finesse. The regime would have become, effectively, a puppet of the Axis. But in 1943, after leaders' arrogance and corruption caused a popular outcry, an embarrassed military threw out the civilian government and took over itself. Perón was named administrative head of the war ministry.

The post was important for its control of personnel assignments. More important, Perón's mentor was Edelmiro Farrell, minister of war and vice president of the new regime. Perón would move up, a notch at a time, an understudy studying the lead role. Indeed, the man in charge of the new military regime, Pedro Ramírez, did not last long, mostly because he was yet another example of that enduring Argentine type, the clumsy general. While in power, however, he helped set the stage for Perón's approaching time in the spotlight. Ramírez reaffirmed the embrace between reactionaries and the Catholic Church, rescinding nineteenth-century prohibitions against Church teaching in public schools. Also during the Ramírez months, political parties were outlawed; leaders who signed a petition calling for the return of constitutional government lost their jobs. The internment of labor union leaders was continued. Finally, however, when U.S. and British agents presented evidence of Ramírez' continuing collaboration with Axis agents, the general had to go. Into his spot moved Perón's benefactor, Farrell. Into the vice presidency moved Perón.

Like the student who gets smarter than his teachers, Perón was augmenting his power by forging links beyond the officer corps. The most important base of his strength was his leadership of the vaguely secret, reactionary "Group of United Officers," but he reached out to workers as well. This was his signal contribution to the art of Latin American demagoguery. It would one day make him president when the officer corps turned on him.

Perón perceived that more was needed to take — and hold — leadership in the rough realities of Argentine politics than force of arms. He asked for and got directorship of the Argentine Department of Labor and Social Welfare (a subcabinet position newly created and thought to be powerless), then led the department into independence from the Department of Interior. That meant Perón was able to create his own bureaucracy, by virtue of which he got cabinet rank. He also got the undivided attention of workers.

The organized labor unions had seen their support among politicians wither. Disaffected, they saw in Perón an unprecedented chance for alliance, popular numbers added to military strength, held together by Argentina's fierce nationalism. The combination proved a heady one. Using Perón's rhetorical power for recruitment, the metal workers' union, as one example, grew from a nascent 1,500 members split off from other unions to 300,000 strong. The overarching General Confederation of Labor — to the directorship of which Perón appointed the elevator operator from the apartment building where he and Eva lived — would grow from a membership of 300,000 in 1943 to 5 million during Perón's presidency.

This ligature between labor and the military is significant in that elites of other Latin American countries have traditionally seen organized labor as something to be controlled, kept weak. This has ensured one kind of elite domination, but it fails to realize the potential of developing another. None, however, dare climb atop mass movements save those confident of their ability to stay there. Perón mounted the back of a workforce ready to regain strength achieved, then lost, under the Radicals.

Perón's rhetoric, style, and shrewdness led labor to a position without precedent in Latin America, in the process assuring his own position. Collective bargaining was carried out under Perón's auspices. Wage demands were satisfied, and workers were kept on the job. Should a union choose to take matters into its own hands, picket lines were dispersed and workers replaced. For this sacrifice of independence, unions won wage and salary increases in virtually all segments of the economy, including white-collar, agricultural, and maritime. Perón's most dramatic device was the "thirteenth month" of wages, a Christmas bonus. It was the vigor of the Argentine economy that enabled Perón to make good on his high-flown promises, but he would be the man on the balcony, raising his hands in victory and delivering the bounty. He would later write that he never learned how to be president, but his military training had taught him how to "lead."

The strategy even tended to neutralize those unions influenced by communists, and the case of the tough meatpackers union demonstrates Perón's flamboyant style. The union, run by Cipriano Reyes, was moving toward a strike when Perón's statements made it clear that he supported the workers. But Perón perceived that simple statements were insufficient to the style he was beginning to establish, so Perón left his office and was driven to the heart of the packing district, down at the docks along the La Plata River. There he met Reyes, threw his arm around the union leader's shoulders, and walked up the main street with him. When the strike was settled, Perón had won a valuable friend, one who would become a frequent visitor to Perón's apartment.

By late 1943, Perón was consolidating power. He lost no opportunity to enhance his image with the masses by grandly announcing social programs. In December, with the combination of flourish and cash that endeared him to common folk, he appropriated 500 million pesos for low income housing. It was about this time that he met Eva María Duarte.

It is harder to separate fact from fantasy with regard to Eva Perón than it is with Perón himself. Snobs on one side, zealots on the other, and Eva Perón's own flair for the melodramatic confuse the picture. Like Perón, she was from a small town south of Buenos Aires; she was illegitimate, poorly educated, and ostracized by people in her hometown even before she worked her way up to ostracism by Buenos Aires society. By virtue of pluck, wit, and beauty, Eva Duarte made herself an actress and commentator at a Buenos Aires radio station. By ingratiating herself with the right officers, she had gained entry to circles surrounding the power of the military dictatorship.

Then, when her contacts began losing interest and wandering away, she dramatized, on the radio, reforms instituted by Perón's department of labor and social security. Stories told of great improvements in common people's lives wrought by government programs. With either foresight or careful planning, this was done before she met Perón. It was as much a clever gimmick to make broadcasts popular with working-class people as a ploy to catch a rising star. Either way, it worked. Eva Duarte, even at twenty-three, had been taking care of herself long enough to recognize that good copy for her radio broadcasts might last longer, in Argentina's volatile politics, than a coup leader.

One version of how Perón and Eva met is that after he had given a speech at the dedication of a project, she approached with her microphone, narrating. She was next to him when an elderly woman approached and kissed Perón's hand, a show of emotion that drove Eva to even greater heights of praise. Perón overheard, was flattered, and turned to ask her name.

For some time, the two openly shared an apartment on Buenos Aires' Calle Posadas while their separate careers flourished. Perón continued to build support among workers; Eva built an audience.

Both his supporters and her audience saved Perón's career when opponents made their move in 1945. On October 10, amid increasing demands for a return to civilian government — and even calls for Perón to be executed — Perón was forced to step down from all three of the posts he had acquired or created. He was minister of war, secretary of labor and social welfare, and vice president. Perón's power, it was clear to many, far outstripped that of the president, his benefactor, who was indecisive and politically weak next to this master puppeteer of the masses. On the night of October 11, with his enemies calling for his head either figuratively or literally, Perón resigned. He did so, however, on a national radio hookup orchestrated by Eva. It is widely suggested that Perón, visibly shaken, wanted simply to save his own hide. Eva Duarte provided the grit to stage manage his departure so that Argentine workers would be sure to know they were losing their savior.

After the resignation, Perón met Eva back at the apartment. They drove to the river and rode in a launch through the small islands of the La Plata River delta to a resort used by Buenos Aires businessmen as a weekend hideaway. The spot offered quick access to safety across the border in Uruguay. But alert river patrols spotted the couple and they were arrested. That night, after first being returned to their apartment, Perón was placed aboard a gunboat and taken to the prison island of Martín García. All during his arrest, Perón, said to be shivering with the dampness, complained of his pleurisy. The same night, he wrote to the president, complaining of rain coming in at his cell window; he was moved to a more comfortable room. He also asked to be allowed to go into exile, and this night, as much as any time in Perón's career, fixed his reputation for weakness. He seemed unable to conduct himself with the dignity expected of a deposed leader. And on this night, wrote Argentine journalist María Flores, Eva, "in that moment of weakness, gained her hold."

Despite melodramatic claims that obscure just what Eva's effect was, it is certain that while Perón was held she went to the streets, working the doorbells of friends and potential enemies, cajoling the former and threatening the latter. If Perón was to be saved, he needed help. Those with influence were asked to exercise it. Those without it were invited to join her in the streets. Those who did not properly reply to her entreaties were never forgiven. Biographer John Barnes describes her as "a woman of incredible humourlessness, startling energy, and corroding rancor, who had an absolute inability to forget and forgive."

Instrumental in turning out the crowds that freed Perón was Cipriano Reyes, the leader of the meatpackers' union. Crowds, including a significant portion of roughnecks, began filling Buenos Aires' broad boulevards, shouting "Viva Perón." When the crowds were disparaged in a newspaper headline as *descamisados,* the shirtless ones—a reference not to their literal shirtlessness but their being without jackets in Buenos Aires' relative formality—Perón jumped on the term. He made a point to assure his followers that he welcomed the support of the shirtless. In fact, they would become putty in the hands of Eva.

In response to Perón's resurgent popularity, Argentine elites, including Perón's enemies in the military, simply missed their opportunity. They were indecisive, and when support for Perón mounted, they caved in. On October 17, a day that would live in the memory of *peronismo,* the General Confederation of Labor declared itself at the side of the crowds chanting "We want Perón." Perón was brought to a balcony of the presidential Casa Rosada and introduced by General Edelmiro Farrell, who had nurtured Perón's career and now saw it overwhelm his weak presidency. Here, Farrell told the huge throng gathered in the plaza below, was "the man we all love ... the man who has conquered the hearts of all Argentines."

Not quite "all," but Perón was where he wanted to be. Still complaining about his imprisonment's effect on his health, he told the crowd how he loved his *descamisados,* and how his poor little mother had also been worried about his whereabouts. From now on, he said, he wanted to be just one of the people. Dramatically, he took off his sword belt and handed it to the president. With teary eyes, he sent the crowd home.

A paradox was created. Both elections, to satisfy the middle class, Perón, and the masses, were needed. Political parties, prohibited by the military, were again allowed, and elections were scheduled for February 1946. Perón, whose first wife had died of cancer, married Eva Duarte.

As the elections approached, Perón's opposition again slept at the switch. Elites were convinced they would roll to a presidential victory, but Perón continued to play on themes most appealing to the masses, something the elites were unwilling to do. Then, on the eve of the election, the United States lent its support to Perón's opposition by issuing a 131-page pamphlet entitled "Consultation among the American Republics with Respect to the Argentine Government." Because of its cover, it was called "the blue book." For misbegotten tactics, the episode deserves a prize.

The blue book is credited to Spruille Braden, a former ambassador to Argentina who had been promoted to assistant secretary of state. Braden joined that long line of U.S. envoys, official and amateur, who overestimated their expertise in Latin American affairs. The book thoroughly documented connections between the Argentine hierarchy — especially Perón — and Nazi government officials. Perón condemned the pamphlet as an unacceptable intrusion into Argentine affairs. The majority of Argentines, already convinced that the United States was uncultured to the point of barbarity, roared its disapproval of the book. Perón turned the presidential race from one between him and his principal opponent to one between him and Spruille Braden. Of more than 2.7 million votes cast, Perón won 56 percent; in the Electoral College, his margin was 304 to 72; his supporters won overwhelming majorities in both houses of the national assembly.

Anyone sympathetic to Juan Perón and the role he played in Argentine history might prefer to end his story here, in 1946. He had served as catalyst for the workers' consolidation of power. His own power was formidable. He had organized the beginning of a corporate state. However, every system in which powerful classes, at the top, attempt to "balance" competing interests, tends, ultimately, to turn inward, ignoring international realities, resisting internal pressures.

Perón took people in, in every sense of that expression. The man who wrote that "the Nazis had the right idea" and called Mussolini "the greatest man of this century" offered his nation a grab-bag of duplicity and reforms, spurring the working classes to euphoria, rewriting the 1853 constitution, liberalizing divorce laws, and creating havoc with the economy.

During the presidential campaign, the Church sought to conserve its power with a pastoral letter that warned Catholics to beware of candidates who would separate secular from sacred education. Perón cast himself as the logical extension of the conservative, God-fearing, military government that preceded him. Although some Catholic leaders rejected Perón's vision of a "new Argentina," others fell in line. Perón placed the latter on policy-making councils.

After he was elected, schools adopted curricula that extolled the virtues of militarism, the fatherland, and Perón and Eva. Higher education was governed by its own set of rules, but the rectors of the six campuses of the national university were appointed by Perón.

The labor movement was controlled by Eva, who proved even more effective than Perón in communicating with the masses. In charge of the General Confederation of Labor was placed the man who had operated the elevator in the apartment building where the Peróns lived before their marriage.

Eva was also given control of news media in a country with a respected newspaper tradition. The once-proud *La Prensa* was hounded out of existence and *La Nación* was reduced to subservience. Other newspapers, with wealthy Argentines buying stock to assure control, were turned into *peronista* propaganda sheets.

Peronists in control of Congress impeached four of the five supreme court justices, and the chief justice resigned. Throughout the country, lawyers willing to assure the safety of Peronist programs took over the courts.

There were legitimate reforms. During Perón's presidency, a five-year plan called for improved electrification and, in fact, some forty-five power plants, large and small, were constructed.

Eva was head of a ministry of health that initiated relatively effective campaigns against tuberculosis and malaria, both of which were lethal diseases in Argentina because health care outside Buenos Aires was still rudimentary. Finally, the same plan that promoted electrification also called for female suffrage, and women helped reelect Perón to his second term.

There was an international acclaim that reassured Argentine masses that all they had been led to believe about Argentina's cultural leadership might be true. In 1947, Eva was sent on a well-publicized tour of Europe to meet Franco, to be received by the premier of France, to pay the obligatory visit to Italy, and, of course, to be received by Pope Pius . At home her charitable foundation — extolled by the poor, maligned by the grand dames of Argentine society who had lost their major public function — brought donations from hundreds of thousands of people.

While hardly "dismantling capitalism" as he claimed to have done, Perón straddled the cold war in foreign relations and returned substantial control of industry to domestic investors. Sixty percent of industry had been foreign-owned and 30 percent of profits had been flowing out of the country, mostly to British pockets. Gas and electric companies, telephone companies, and other enterprises, under threat of expropriation, were placed in Argentine hands.

More complex needs of the society were not so easily mastered. Perón's "system" of government, which he called *justicialismo,* was unsuccessful in harnessing the country's disparate forces. The term *justicialismo* suggested a middle path between capitalism and communism at the height of the cold war, but a wandering path it was. His five-year plan ran out of money, and, like so many revolutionary leaders in Latin America, Perón was unable to restructure the reality of long years of elite domination. His task was to distribute wealth and opportunity without destroying the economic structure that had produced wealth, without scaring off the elites whose domination was so resented.

Change, though, there was. Argentina's quasi-independent central bank was completely nationalized. The telephone system was expropriated from its American owners. The railway system was taken from the British. Steps like these cannot be overlooked in evaluating Perón's place in helping a proud, if confused, nation claim its rights. Perón was created by forces that surged from Argentine frustrations, and it is foolish to suggest that he was nothing more than a political Narcissus, manipulated by his wife and associates. The accomplishments, like the blunders, were his. But, in short, Perón's unsophisticated leadership, applied to a nation divided, managed to snatch defeat from the jaws of success. Change was not progress, but confusion.

Perón's path had been cleared by prosperity. His presidency began at the end of World War II, when Argentina sat atop grain and beef surpluses needed by a hungry Europe. Mounds of sterling reserves resulted from wartime trading. Resources were in place to boost Argentina into something like the position of Latin American leadership that its people thought was its destiny.

To handle Argentina's postwar trade cornucopia, Perón created, grandly, the Argentine Institute for the Promotion of Exchange. Typically, however, accounts were not precise. Income had a way of disappearing. Poor management led, eventually, to such paradoxes as the need in 1952, during Perón's second term, to "meatless days" in a nation accustomed to one of the highest per capita meat consumption rates in the world. Eventually it was discovered that ranchers, realizing that Perón's middlemen were taking a cut from producers' profits, scaled back production. The same happened to grain production. A national agriculture with so much promise was threatened with ruin.

In addition, the economy was not being infused with productive investment. Speeches portraying Perón as standing up for Argentine rights—a place on the United Nations Security Council, for example—satisfied national sensitivities, but did not build factories. Stress was on image. Peronist agents among labor unions in other Latin American countries were disruptive, meddling in politics, supporting conservatives, glorifying Argentina's leadership in the hemisphere. Meanwhile, unrest grew at home.

In September 1951, there was a coup attempt, during which some say Eva had to pull Perón from premature refuge in the Brazilian embassy so he could lead loyal army troops. In October, an abortive attempt by the General Confederation of Labor to put Eva on the ticket as vice presidential candidate had to be withdrawn. Eva, embarrassed, said she was really too young, anyway, to satisfy the constitutional requirement.

Capable of enflaming dislike in all directions, Perón was especially irritating to Great Britain. Close relations between the two countries are as old as Argentine independence, which the British were instrumental in winning. British interests in Argentina ran deepest in cattle and grain operations, and Britain financed and built Argentina's railroads. But as the British struggled to rebuild after World War II, a war in which many Argentines had flaunted their support for the Axis, Argentines engaged in what was seen as price gouging. British coal, machinery, and petroleum were shipped in return for Argentine leather, meat, and grain at exchange rates favorable to Argentina. When Argentina expropriated the railway system, a bitter dispute led first to Argentina's sterling reserves in England being frozen, finally to a price of 150 million pounds for the railroads.

In July 1952, an era ended when Eva Perón died. Great crowds of Argentine humanity had loved, if not Perón, this woman who seemed to understand them. Hundreds of thousands of Argentine working-class people thronged to see her lying in state; hundreds were trampled, eight of them to death. Her autobiography, *My Mission in Life,* was made compulsory reading for schoolchildren. Streets and schools were named for her. And with Eva gone, Perón's administration, already in trouble, increased its speed downhill. The former elevator operator was fired from his position over the labor movement. Eva's brother, Juan, was fired from his job as secretary to the president—and found in his apartment with a bullet in his head. The bullet, of the caliber used by military and police officers, was fired from too far away to have been suicide.

The Church, either because it questioned the morality of its choice or because it realized it had bet on the wrong horse, turned on Perón. Perón's response was typically clumsy. When two clerical emissaries were sent to the Casa Rosada, they found themselves hustled onto a flight for Rome. When Perón's thugs vandalized cathedrals, the crudeness of the acts sapped the last patience Argentines had with their precocious son.

Perón decorated the presidential residence at Olivos, outside Buenos Aires, and apartments in the city with mirrored bedrooms and installed garish bars. The world learned of his predilection for teenage girls. His favorite was a thirteen-year-old. Asked how he could besmirch the memory of Eva with a thirteen-year-old, his smug, insensitive reply was that he was not superstitious.

In April 1953, with his support disintegrating, with the economy shriveling, Perón did what he did best; he held a mass rally. Perón was a political leader who did as much as any in the hemisphere to demonstrate the effectiveness of rhetoric, to take Hitlerian speaking style and add television. The glossy magazines carried pictures of Perón as a virile, dynamic leader because that was what the people wanted to see. To his rally, held in Buenos Aires, hundreds of thousands gladly came. After his speech, they churned through the downtown streets, burning the Jockey Club, a symbol of patrician complacence, and destroying the headquarters of opposition parties. For another two years, before their enthusiasm waned to a level the military and the Church could jointly overpower, the masses insisted on Perón.

In June 1955, disaffected Catholics rallied where the workers' crowds had been, showing leaders of Perón's opposition that they, too, could count on numbers. By September, Perón was forced to flee aboard a gunboat along the same path that had seemed so close at hand a decade earlier. This time, the crowds would not save him. He wandered to Paraguay, Panama, Venezuela, the Dominican Republic, and finally to Spain, where he was taken in by his old idol, Francisco Franco.

The massive working-class discontent that propped up Perón did not subside, but floundered on in search of a leader. In late 1963, a visitor to southern South America could not help but be struck by the electric atmosphere that the absent Perón could still create by the mere possibility of his presence, even after eight years in exile. He was rumored to be on his way from Spain, and there was in conversations in the streets and cafés a sense of hope, or dread, an expectation that transcended ideas and programs. He was said to be flying first to the coast of Brazil, then down to Montevideo, then crossing the La Plata River in a decisive sweep back to power, without armies, certainly without programs, transported by expectations alone.

The governments of Argentina and Brazil, however, demonstrating international cooperation, turned Perón back the same day he landed in Brazil. He was bundled back to Spain.

In 1972, however, such was the state of Argentine politics that Perón was asked to return. He proved unable to achieve the gargantuan task of bringing order to a society split between the working classes and a military mentality, and died eighteen months after his return. Some considerable part of the disorder, of course, he had helped create.

He was succeeded by his third wife, Isabel Martínez de Perón, whom he had married in exile. Although she affected the style and dress of her fabled predecessor, Eva Duarte de Perón, she was no more able to solve Argentina's Gordian political problems.

Peronismo, with its shifting allegiances, its inclination toward mobs, its tendency toward complaints rather than consensus, remains deeply entrenched in Argentine politics. There are the old crowds and the sons and daughters of the old crowds, the old roughnecks, the old images. *Peronismo* might still represent as much as one-third of the Argentine electorate, a third with which the military and the oligarchs and the Church would rather not have to contend, a third that remembers that for all the corruption and confusion, working-class wages and self-esteem increased dramatically. It was a third that prevailed in 1989 to elect Peronist Carlos Menem president of the republic after too many dark years under the boot of the military.

Peronismo, its critics say, is political vulgarity, and Perón himself was an inept, cowardly demagogue. *Peronistas* still are able to argue, however, how well they both compare with so much that has befallen Argentina since.

16

María Eva Duarte de Perón
Angel of the "Shirtless Ones"
1919–1952
(Argentina)

Few women have ever been so vehemently damned and so passionately adored. Biographer J. M. Taylor, discussing "the myth" of Eva Perón, writes of the division of feeling, with one side convinced she was "an ideal of pure and passive womanhood incarnate," and the other side seeing her as "manipulated by specialists dedicated solely to the task." Eva Perón was unique. In a sense, she created herself, rising above abject poverty, driving herself relentlessly, boldly turning events to her advantage, molding an image of glamour, profoundly affecting Argentine reality. She encouraged her descamisados, her shirtless ones, toward a hope they could not otherwise have known. She was, remarks historian Hubert Herring, perhaps the shrewdest woman yet to appear in public life in South America."

Several authors have remarked upon the dusty, barren hopelessness of a small Argentine town like Los Toldos, where Eva María Ibarguren was born on May 7, 1919, with the help of an Indian midwife. It is thought that the Ibargurens were in Los Toldos because Eva's grandmother had followed the army there during the campaign to clear Buenos Aires province of Indians. For Eva and her family, one of the most depressing aspects of Los Toldos was that everybody knew everybody else's business. Eva was the fifth of five children born to Juana Ibarguren by Juan Duarte, a landowner and plantation manager who refused to let the children of his mistress take his name.

Duarte, after all, had three children by his wife, the sister of the mayor of nearby Chivilcoy. When he died in 1926, his family tried to prevent Juana Ibarguren and her brood from attending the burial. But Juana Ibarguren insisted. She had spent fifteen years as a cook on one of his plantations, and felt that, under the circumstances, he had really not been such a bad father. With a will that would later be shown by her youngest child — in fact, all her children did relatively well for themselves — Juana Ibarguren, plump, pretty, and determined, stood her ground at the cemetery gate. After a standoff, cooler heads prevailed. Duarte's wife was prevailed upon to allow Juana Ibarguren and her children to pay their last respects.

In 1930, Juana Ibarguren she would eventually refer to herself as "the widow Duarte," conferring a kind of legitimacy on her children — hired a truck and driver and removed her family to a larger small town, Junín. There, she would be under the protection of her new provider, Oscar Nicolini, who is variously described as a postal worker and a minor politician. Like Duarte, he was married, older than Juana Ibarguren, and a reasonably good provider.

Although Junín was a step up from Los Toldos, Eva had bigger things in mind. She wanted to be an actress, so, at the age of fifteen, she made up her mind to get to Buenos Aires, as bright a metropolis as there was to be found in the Americas in 1935. Argentina prospered as the rest of the world hurtled toward World War II. The center of Argentina, if not the world, was Buenos Aires. One night when Augustín Magaldi, a dashing tango singer whose troupe was appearing in Junín, returned to his dressing room, there was Eva, thin, dark-haired, and determined.

Magaldi was but the first of a string of men who helped Eva Duarte in her career, but what allowed her to succeed, without notable talent, was shrewdness, a flair for the dramatic, and an unembarrassed willingness to grasp the moment. By March 1935, after months of search as the Argentine winter approached, she had gotten a small part in a stage comedy with one of Argentina's leading actresses and, more important, one of the country's leading actors. He helped her find both a place to stay and further acting jobs, and Eva Duarte's career improved to minor dramatic parts that were as short-lived as her love affairs. In time, however, she maneuvered her way up from bit parts on the stage to the company of the military. Her success with Argentine army officers, some of whom were running the country, put her near, at least socially, the salons of power. She once astounded girlfriends by picking up the phone in her dressing room to place a direct call to the president of Argentina, a general. He accepted the call.

Eva Duarte's social connections were not lost on her first major employer, who gave her better and better parts in radio dramas, knowing full well that radio was controlled by the government. Eva Duarte was careful to include among her favored friends those officers who controlled radio communications, and as her contacts broadened; her salary grew, to a level unheard of for other radio actors. Fleur Cowles, a hostile biographer, pays perhaps unintentional tribute to Eva Duarte's capacity for survival by describing her as "doing a turn in a mediocre slot on a mediocre show with a mediocre audience at Argentina's leading radio station." That was precisely Eva Duarte's greatest strength, employing her limited resources in ways, and with results, others could only imagine. She did not waste time with anyone or anything that was not a leader.

By 1940, at the age of twenty, Eva Duarte was simply among the first of her generation to learn how to manipulate radio, a medium that was reaching the masses and that she would later employ to full political advantage. This was the day of primitive technology, and one of Eva Duarte's principal benefactors was the man who made a fortune by cornering the market on radio headsets. Another was a soap manufacturer who simply bought her a show of her own. Working-class Argentines, nonetheless, were transported beyond their own environment through all manner of programs. By 1944, at age twenty-four, she was playing the great empresses of Europe in historical radio dramas written specifically for her by Francisco Muñoz Aspiri. Movie parts followed.

None of her parts was the stuff of great literature; radio was a medium for the masses; her movies were decidedly Grade B. One detractor recalled that as an actress Eva Duarte was "cold as an iceberg." Nevertheless, Eva Duarte had shaped herself, on posters and in show-biz magazines, into someone who was a far cry from the impoverished little girl of the provinces. Her accent and grammar would always be ridiculed by the high born, but her words were being heard and read by hundreds of thousands.

In 1944, she met Col. Juan Perón. He was forty-eight, she was twenty-four. Suggesting the mythology that has been built around their relationship, biographer Fleur Cowles writes that she had heard at least seven different accounts of the historic meeting. It was most likely either at a gala party to raise money for earthquake victims, or at a neighborhood appearance of Perón, where Eva Duarte showed up with a microphone and crew to record his utterances. In the former instance, the rest of the story is that they stole away from the glittering affair to a riverfront tryst. In the latter instance the story goes that an elderly woman approached Perón, increasingly considered a hero to the masses, and kissed his hand, whereupon Duarte launched into dramatic description for her radio audience that Perón overheard and found flattering.

In any event, it seems likely that Eva Duarte would have engineered a meeting eventually, for there is general agreement that once the two met, she moved swiftly and surely to cement, as it were, the relationship. Within a very short time, they had adjoining apartments on Calle Posadas. Neighbors reported seeing Perón, a widower, in his robe, bringing in the morning delivery of milk, which attentive soldiers delivered to her door.

Perón at that point held three posts: vice president, minister of war, and secretary of labor, although his real strength derived from the loyalty he claimed among the officers who had, in 1943, overthrown the civilian government. Here, then, was the strongest protector of all for Eva Duarte. She immediately introduced him to Muñoz Aspiri, her script writer and image maker. Muñoz was named director of propaganda in the sub secretariat of information. Her mother's paramour, the erstwhile postal clerk, was named director of mail and telegraph.

For her part, Duarte, through her continuing radio broadcasts and her astute political maneuvering, became a conduit for information about all the good things the military government could deliver. Recognizing that the first information about benefits would associate her name with those benefits, she announced to her listeners the military government's initiatives. She interviewed common people who were beneficiaries of government policy. She put a human face on government institutions.

In doing this, she began speaking for herself, changing her role from that of observer, or reporter, to spokeswoman and, finally, to benefactress not just for the regime but for all of the country. On a program called "Toward a Better Future," she spoke as "the voice of a woman of the people."

As Perón's power grew, so did Eva Duarte's. The Office of Labor and Welfare, a Peronist power base created only a year before, ratified her ascension to head of the Radio Association of Argentina. This gave the association official recognition to represent radio workers at a time when the government was negotiating with competing unions for precisely that right. As an important token of her new post, Duarte was moved into a government office. She had climbed, thereby, from a radio actress to "the voice of Argentina" to an official mediator between the government and radio workers. Perón and the military, imitating the Spanish and Italian systems, were developing corporate fascism, in which labor groups, agricultural associations, industrial combinations, and so on have direct lines to policy makers. Eva Duarte was consolidating power within that system, implementing powerful moves that perfectly complemented those of Perón.

She was transporting herself from the demimonde of second-rate theater to the highest councils of power. Only five feet, five inches tall, she could be assertive in private with men who often bristled at this unexpected display of feminine will power. At the same time, she played a role of public passivity: "In an almost childlike way I live and dream each of the characters whom I portray," she told her audience of listener-citizens. "With this fresh and sincere voice I would like to proclaim how loyal I am to all of you.... It hurts me to think that I do not reach your ears."

By October 1945, however, opposition had mounted. Either because they were contemptuous of Eva Duarte's role in their government, or because they resented Perón's assumption of so much power, or for both reasons, the military officers who had brought Perón to a position of power, now wanted him out. Perón was forced to quit all three of his posts; Eva Duarte was immediately fired from her job on the air and, without Perón's protection, lost her semiofficial position as head of the radio association.

Adversity was to be Eva Duarte's metier. At this point, in fact, both critics and supporters alike say that Eva Duarte thrived on what seemed to be sure defeat. Her provincial toughness withstood the challenge when, by all accounts, Perón, the symbol of machismo, was ready to crumble. Argentine journalist María Flores writes that Eva, "in that moment of weakness, gained her hold." At the end of the day, they met at the apartment they shared.

"Perón was ready to give up," writes John Barnes, a biographer. "But Eva was not prepared to let him. First, she screamed at him, telling him to pull himself together and act like a man. Then she got to work on the telephone." Her calls went out to junior officers who owed their advancement to Perón. They came in small groups, according to Barnes, "leaving half an hour later pumped full of Eva Duarte's adrenalin." She spoke to labor leaders, reminding them that Argentine elites were no more accustomed to dealing with workers as equals than they were with assertive women. If Perón fell, their conduit to power would be gone.

Eva told Perón to go to his office to clean it out. Meanwhile, she induced labor leaders to raise a crowd and lead it to the government building where his office was located. She called her mother's old and close friend, Oscar Nicolini, who, as head of the mails and telegraph, controlled national radio. He was to set up a national hookup emanating from the steps of the building, she instructed.

Perón, hatless and in civilian clothes, emerged from the building to hold a carefully staged "impromptu" news conference. His statement included an edict that industrialists share profits with their workers, but only if "the workers are decided to defend your interests."

Later that night, the couple was found at their riverfront hideaway. Perón, convinced he might be shot for his role in the 1943 coup when naval cadets were killed defending the government, quaked with fear. Eva Duarte, apparently afraid of nothing, screamed obscenities. Perón was exiled to Martín García Island. Eva Duarte was set free. Historians have noted that the military committed a fatal and irreversible error by not having it the other way around.

Staying at a friend's house, she sallied forth to knock on doors, by turns threatening and cajoling former friends. At one point she was pulled from a taxi and set upon by thugs. "That was the worst aspect of my Calvary in the great city!" wrote Eva later, unabashed by the biblical comparison. "The cowardice of men who were able to do something and did not do it, washing their hands like Pilates, pained me more than the barbarous blows given me when a group of cowards denounced, shouting: 'That's Evita.'" "Those who did not reply favorably to her entreaties were never forgiven.

Labor leaders responded. A general strike was called for October 18, but the workers' zeal was not to be contained, and on October 17 a demonstration erupted. It was Perón who appeared on a balcony to the roar of the masses gathered in the main plaza, but it was Eva Duarte who put him there.

Five days later they were married. Perón was elected in February 1946, and as First Lady, Eva Duarte de Perón was uninhibited by tradition. "No woman had ever assumed the title in so official a manner, writes J. M. Taylor. "Attacks rained down on the presumption of a mere starlet of radio drama and cinema."

Eva Ibarguren, the illegitimate bumpkin, who had made herself Eva Duarte, the radio star, now, had helped win for herself a role as Eva Perón, the First Lady. Still, she aspired to an image the masses, quite literally, would sanctify as their "Lady of Hope," but that she would want to be called "Evita." She traveled throughout the country, refining that image, to the dismay of critics and to the delight of the masses. Her constant companion and confidante was Isabel Ernst, whose title was "Labor Secretary to the Presidency of the Nation." Muñoz Aspiri, the scriptwriter, turned his pen to this larger drama. Eva Perón, of course, was her own best director.

"A few days of the year I act the part of Eva Perón," she would explain later, with the help of a ghostwriter, "and I think I do better each time in that part, for it seems to me to be neither difficult nor disagreeable. The immense majority of days I am, on the other hand, 'Evita,' a link stretched between the hopes of the people and the fulfilling hands of Perón, Argentina's first woman peronista — and this, indeed, is a difficult role for me, one in which I am never quite satisfied with myself."

Just as she had presumed to be "the voice of the Argentine people," she shifted her speeches from explanations of government policy to her own expression of the people's needs. Her power grew with her independence; her agenda was long.

She wanted housing for working-class families; she initiated a child-care plan that included summer camps for middle-class children; she militated for safe drinking water; she wanted help for female immigrants from the interior; she promoted junior soccer, which included a medical exam that was for some children their first; she helped organize college-student housing.

When her efforts overshadowed government agencies, there was resentment. Either they were not doing their jobs, which caused resentment of her effectiveness; or they were doing their jobs, which caused resentment of her grandstanding.

Undaunted, at least in public, she would remark later, "I have discovered a fundamental feeling in my heart which completely governs my spirit and my life. That feeling is my indignation when confronted with injustice.... I think now that many people become accustomed to social injustice in the first years of their lives. Even the poor think the misery they endure is natural and logical. They learn to tolerate what they see or suffer, just as it is possible to acquire a tolerance for a powerful poison."

Withal, she was a controversial figure. She traveled — typically, without Perón, although with Isabel Ernst — on an exhausting round of personal appearances, her popularity growing as the Argentine working class convinced itself that here, for all her faults, was a champion. During 1946, she progressed from shouts of derision when she appeared at a February rally, to the title of "First Worker of Argentina" in July and, in December, to "Queen of Labor." During the December ceremony, in Tucumán, either seven or nine people (reports vary) were crushed to death in the enthusiastic crowd.

When the high-born matrons of the Sociedad de Beneficiencia, a snobbish charitable organization associated with the Church, said she was "too young" to be their president, she sarcastically suggested that maybe they would prefer her mother. Historian June E. Hahner notes that Eva Perón's "illegitimate birth was never forgotten or forgiven by the country's social elite once she achieved power." Power, however, allowed Eva Perón in September 1946 to take over the office of the Sociedad and make it the base for what became Fundación Eva Perón, the beginning of her empire. Importantly, she was sharing her power by empowering others. Before her first year as First Lady was over, she was making weekly feminist speeches.

Her views, especially in a traditional, male-dominated, snobbish society, were radical: "Although it is not fundamental in the feminist movement," she said, "the vote is its most powerful instrument.... 'Politics' is not an end, but a means."

"I think that men, in their great majority, above all in the old political parties, never understood this properly. That is why they always failed. Our destiny as women depends on our not falling into the same error."

She proposed a special tax on all workers — a device that would later be used to fund her foundation—for "fixing a small monthly allowance for every woman who gets married, from the day of her marriage."

As wily as she was determined, Eva Perón let no others scrape off any of the residual power that accrued to her efforts. She formed the Asociación Pro-Sufragio Feminino to win the vote for women, but when other wives of political leaders tried to form "sister" clubs, she rejected them, making public statements that their efforts were not to be confused with hers and that their funds were not to be mixed with hers.

Her appeal—and it was uniquely hers—was spiritual at its base, political in its expression, and intimately feminist: "Everything, absolutely everything, in this contemporary world, has been made according to man's measure."

> We are absent from governments.
> We are absent from parliaments.
> From international organizations.
> We are in neither the Vatican nor the Kremlin.
> Nor in the commissions of atomic energy.
> Nor in the great business combines.
> Nor in Freemasonry, nor in other secret societies.
> We are absent from all the great centers constituting a power in the world.
> And yet we have always been present in the time of suffering, and in all humanity's bitter hours.

She reclaimed her prominence in labor affairs. In early 1947 she met twenty-six labor delegations in one day. Her friendships included a number of Argentine image makers—publishers, theater people, and industrialists who understood the value of advertising to the leadership of a mass democracy. Reporters who went to her suite of offices described a consummate politician, listening to simple folk from the countryside who came to ask for housing or work, speaking with cabinet members who needed her help or could help her, moving among groups, being reminded of other appointments, distributing government largesse, demanding political quid pro quo. She sometimes dispensed houses to needy families; she often dispensed peso notes from a supply she kept ready on her desk.

Her power was manifest in two ways: directly, on her own; and indirectly, by influencing her husband. She served as president of an international conference on social security; she took a seat at the table for labor negotiations, dealing with striking bank employees, newsvendors, and railway workers. She held weekly meetings with labor leaders who were the mainstay of Peronist power. At the same time, she influenced Perón's selection of cabinet members. It is said that she would meet with "her" selections before they went into formal cabinet meetings, sometimes delaying their arrival so long that disgruntled military officers had already left.

"Thrilled or alarmed," writes historian Taylor, "Argentina watched Eva's growing contacts with organized labour, her activities in social welfare, her feminist initiatives, and her influence in the press."

In January 1947, she bought the newspaper, Democracia, and was widely credited with, or accused of, influencing the news coverage and editorial policy of two others. Newspapers in general had to respond to a blizzard of press releases about her nonstop, if contrived, activities. Critics, meanwhile, portrayed her as a threatening influence on affairs from the congressional to the social. When a compliant congress passed a Perónist law that prohibited insulting the presidency, newspapers could be, and were, closed for criticizing her. Radical Party opponent Ernesto Sammartino used his congressional seat to compare Argentina to a cart mired in the mud, stuck because it was being pulled by a mare. To escape arrest he fled across the river to Montevideo, joining other critics of the Peróns.

In 1947 Eva Perón raised her controversial image to the international level. She accepted an invitation from Francisco Franco, who had also been a "neutral" tool of the Axis during World War II. Such a trip, observes one biographer, was "thought by those who dreaded her growing consequence and magnetism to confirm all their fears."

The navy denied her a ship, so she flew. Five hundred thousand Argentines saw her off; 300,000 Spanish greeted her. It was a private trip, but she was accorded authority to sign certain agreements with European governments. She granted a shipload of wheat to Spain and approved a loan for the purchase of wheat and meat to France. She met, and was, of course, photographed with, Franco and French President Vincent Auriol. She was received by Pope Pius. In Switzerland, however, she was the target of tomatoes, which the anti–Perón press back at home chronicled with glee. As a result, two newspapers were closed.

When British royalty, presumably on the advice of Parliament, declined to invite her for a stay, she turned toward home and not only lunched with the president of Brazil, but attended a special session of the Chamber of Deputies convened in her honor. Friendly newspapers coined the term presidenta for her.

On the trip, she had collapsed from exhaustion, continuing over the advice of her physician. Detractors were suspicious, thinking the fainting Madona de los Humildes, as some called her, was just another public-relations trick. Indeed, after the trip, she gave up the flashy clothes and hats that had been her trademark and a new image emerged. She appeared in tailored suits; she went hatless, her hair pulled severely back into a bun; she wore simple dresses or a blouse and sweater. The collapse had been real. Eva's health was delicate all her life, as time would demonstrate.

She returned to Argentina on August 23, 1947, and Congress approved female suffrage shortly after that. It should be noted that this was six years before a similar empowerment was achieved in "revolutionary" Mexico. Congress also approved the nation's first law allowing divorce. Eva Perón was reaching the zenith of her power.

As president of the Perónist Women's party, she led legions whose electoral power was great and untested. The party was a springboard for women to run, successfully, for Congress. With government appropriations, private donations, and deductions from workers' wages, she created the Eva María Duarte de Perón Foundation of Social Aid. Incorporated in June 1948 and with a fund of 23,000 pesos after five months, its treasury held 2 billion pesos by 1952. She was able to fill warehouses of staples for low-income people at officially controlled prices.

Her family moved into positions of control as well. Brother Juan Duarte, an erstwhile soap salesman and ne'er-do-well, was first made inspector of government operations, then installed as Perón's private secretary. Her sisters and their husbands were handed sinecures in the courts and the ports, the schools and the mails.

How could this child of dusty, provincial streets find acceptance in the tight, arrogant society of Buenos Aires? "The oligarchy has never been hostile to anyone who could be useful to it," she wrote, with tough wisdom. "Power and money were never bad antecedents to a genuine oligarch."

Nevertheless, the military was resentful of her role and contemptuous of the evidence of mounting corruption in the regime. In 1949, the army refused to allow her into Campo de Mayo, a camp outside Buenos Aires, and it appeared there would be a confrontation between the Peróns and the military. The Peróns prevailed, for the time.

On January 9, 1950, Eva Perón collapsed at a public ceremony in the middle of a hot summer day. She was experiencing pelvic pain, fever, and vaginal hemorrhaging. Her ankles were badly swollen. It became known that for about a year sexual activity had been impossible. On January 12, 1950, a hysterectomy was reported to the press as an appendectomy. Although the end of her life was near, she drove herself obsessively, as if determined to make herself the martyr her enemies had mocked. Her personal physician quit in May 1950, after she flared up at him one day and slapped him after he admonished her not to work so hard. He later added that a reason for his resignation was concern over the increasing corruption in the administration.

Preparations for the coming election—Congress had repealed the prohibition against a president's succeeding himself—were under way. Despite increasing criticism of the administration and acrimonious distrust of her role by the military, labor leaders wanted Eva Perón to stand for vice president. On August 22, 1950, a cabildo abierto, a huge town meeting, was to be held. Labor saw it as the chance to announce that both Peróns would be on the ticket. Perón was ambivalent. Eva, who may have known she was dying of cancer, certainly understood the seriousness of the opposition to her candidacy.

Perón appeared on the dais without her, but the crowd would not that. The first speaker could not be heard over calls for Eva, and she was brought to the stage. Presumably very weak, always emotional, and witnessing the greatest outpouring of sentiment she had ever seen, she broke into tears. Knowing that she could not be a candidate, she said only, "I will always do what the people may say." Then her words wandered. "I prefer to be 'Evita' rather than the president's wife," she said, "if 'Evita' is said in order to alleviate pain in my country."

Disjointedly, she "proclaimed" Perón president. When Perón stepped to the microphone, however, someone shouted, "Let Compañera Eva speak," and when Perón ended his remarks that request was taken up by others. The moderator, a labor leader, insisted that she accept the vice presidency, telling her that she was "the only one who can and must occupy" the post. She took the microphone to beg for time. The crowd would not have it. They became unruly, perhaps suspecting that their Lady of Hope was in the control of the same old political forces that had for so long oppressed them. They began to clamor while shouted debates took place on stage. Perón, upstaged and irritated, wanted an end to the proceeding. Eva, pitifully, asked the crowd for a two-hour delay. She wanted to be allowed to make her announcement on the radio.

Immediately, newspapers reported that she had taken the nomination, and her candidacy was announced by the Confederación General de Trabajadores, the blanket labor organization that Perón created. Army commanders and units loyal to them grew restless. On August 31, nine days after the assembly, Eva Perón read an announcement broadcast at eight o'clock that night.

In her renunciation, she tried to describe a place at the head of her descamisados that ought to be distinct from an official position in the government. "This decision comes from the most intimate part of my conscience," she said, protesting too much that the decision was hers, "and for that reason is totally free and has all the force of my definitive will." She wanted it remembered "that there was at the side of Perón a woman who dedicated herself to carrying the hopes of the people to the president, and that the people affectionately called this woman 'Evita.' That is what I want to be."

Her illness worsened. When, on October 17, Loyalty Day, she made a public appearance, it was the first time in three weeks she had been out of bed. Then she underwent another operation, which was kept secret, and, in November, yet another. She still was able to record a speech from bed to be broadcast November 9. On November 11, a ballot box was brought to her hospital room for her vote in the first Argentine election allowing female participation.

In early December there was enough of a remission that she was able to take short drives around Buenos Aires with her husband. She made a Christmas speech and on Christmas Day met with reporters. Her agrarian plan was inaugurated, providing equipment to farmers and increasing the acreage available for crops. These last vital signs encouraged her followers to believe she would fully recover, but only a superhuman effort made that possible.

On May Day, 1952, she not only appeared at an assembly, she managed a short speech. Her last remarks, perhaps as she contemplated her own death, tended toward harshness, an insistence on judging others. Biographer Taylor describes "a definite element of violence in her rhetoric." Eva Perón herself had admitted that "all my life I have been prone to be driven and guided by my feelings," and the end was no different.

A week passed, and on her birthday she appeared on a terrace of the presidential residence, waving to the crowd. She was so weak, however, that she had to be held up. The Chamber of Deputies designated her "spiritual chief of the nation," and on May 23 she addressed governors and legislators at the residence. Again, there was violence in her message. It would later be publicly revealed that in spite of her condition, Eva Perón, hearing mounting criticism and fearing an anti–Perón coup, used Social Aid Foundation money and the good offices of Dutch royalty to buy 5,000 pistols and 1,500 machine guns to arm the workers.

Her last public appearance was at the inauguration ceremony for Perón's second term, June 5, 1952. A specially built support made of wire and plaster held up her thin, cancer-ravaged body in the open car as the couple was driven on the triumphal procession. "Like every woman of the people," she had written, "I have more strength than I appear to have." She managed to stand through the ceremony.

In bed, she began Mi Mensage, but never finished it. When U.S. publishers refused to publish La Razón de Mi Vida, Argentine workers called a protest strike for July 4.

On July 26, 1952, her death was announced at 8:25, two hours after it occurred, but Eva Perón's journey was not over.

There was a plan to convert the Buenos Aires monument to descamisados to a huge crypt, the largest in the world, and construction was begun. Her body, immaculately coiffed, a rosary in her hands, lay in state while two lines of mourners filed slowly past. "I never knew they loved her so much," Perón remarked to a friend after watching Argentines weep over the glass-covered coffin. "I never knew they loved her so."

Although Perón said she would lie in state "until the last citizen of the Republic has been able to see Compañera Evita," it proved impossible because of a rather bizarre scheme to embalm her for all time. The embalming process required a series of steps at certain times. On August 9, her body was carried at the head of a procession to the Congress. Two days later, she was pulled to the labor ministry on a gun carriage drawn by forty-five men and women dressed alike in white shirts and black trousers. Nurses and cadets swelled the ranks of mourners. Some 2 million people, kept in relative order by 17,000 soldiers, thronged the route.

There, at the labor ministry, her body was to remain, safe amid rumors that her enemies might "kidnap" her before the huge crypt was complete. Her book, La Razón de Mi Vida, was assigned to countless schoolchildren. Postal boxes were assigned and kept open for people to write to her. The pope was asked to make her a saint. On the radio, commentators continually recalled her birth date, her renunciation of the vice presidency, the day and time of her death.

In 1955, however, after Perón was deposed and hustled into exile in September, there was no rest for the body of Eva Perón. The value of the goods and assets of her various foundations, agencies, and funds were estimated at $700 million, a staggering sum. The tales of her opulence seemed to have been borne out. The site of the crypt, still under construction, was dynamited—deep had run the hatred and jealousy. Jorge Luís Borges, the literary giant, dismissed Eva Perón. "No one ever seemed capable of speaking of Eva Perón in dispassionate terms," notes historian Hahner. "Those who benefited from her large charity foundation glorified her. Others vilified her. But certainly no one ignored Evita." So high was the emotional tenor that the military was afraid Eva Perón's body would be used by Perónists as a mystical rallying point. One night, a squad of soldiers showed up at the labor ministry, and the body was taken away. No one knew where.

In June 1956, Eva Perón's body was found, hidden in a sealed wooden crate marked "radio equipment" and stacked in the basement of a government building. Its journey to that point had been a troubled one. An army officer in whose apartment it was briefly hidden had been murdered, leaving a pregnant widow. Hardly had this story come to light, when Eva Perón's body disappeared again.

There was, for some time, only a paper trail. All there was left of Eva Perón, the woman who had so moved the masses, was the signature of a priest who had claimed the body in January 1957. It was not publicly known where he had taken it.

In 1971, as Argentines continued to demonstrate their inability to form a stable, democratic government (the divorce law was repealed; the number of women holding office diminished), Perónists called for the return of their hero. Perón was living comfortably in exile in Madrid, married for the third time. Because of political pressure in Buenos Aires, it was disclosed, after a decade and a half that in a cemetery in Milan, Italy, was the coffin of "Maria Maggi," whom documents claimed to be an Italian citizen who died in Argentina and had been shipped "home." The body of Eva Perón was disinterred and shipped to Perón's house in Madrid.

The coffin was opened under the watchful eyes of Isabel Martínez de Perón, Eva's successor, Perón, and Dr. Pedro Ara, the embalmer. Her hair was dirty, and the end of a finger was broken off. Repairs were made.

Perón was returned to power in 1972 and after eighteen months died in office. He was replaced by Isabel Perón, who copied Eva's dress, hairstyle, and gestures—to little avail. Isabel had been careful to leave Eva's body behind in Madrid, but Perónists clamored for her return. Rumors flew that there had been mutilations. In 1974, Isabel Perón had Eva Perón's body shipped home to a televised reception, although the gesture was of no help in saving her stumbling regime.

In 1976, the body of Eva Perón was secretly taken to an exclusive Buenos Aires cemetery and enclosed in the Duarte family crypt. Eva María Duarte de Perón had finally found, in a way, acceptance.

17

José Figueres

At the Center of Latin America

1906–1990
(Costa Rica)

José Figueres, the five-foot, three-inch Costa Rican known as "Pepe," helped construct one of Latin America's most admired democracies. To supporters he is a Cincinnatus of the hemisphere, a patrician who tilled the soil, entering politics only to save the republic, an archetype of democratic moderation. Detractors, however, had a different image. He was labeled both Nazi-sympathizer and socialist and, finally, seen as a tragic Faustus, who sold his soul to the Central Intelligence Agency and to a hoodlum of international finance. The truth takes something from both portraits. Figueres was a man of wide interests who was always impatient for action. One of Latin America's most determined leaders, Pepe Figueres placed himself at the center of many storms.

It is a humorous irony that so desperate were critics to find fault with José María Figueres Ferrer, that they pointed out that he was conceived by his parents before they left Barcelona. So, although he was born on September 25, 1906, in the tiny village of San Ramón, Costa Rica, a few months after they immigrated, he would be called by some *el catalán,* as if he did not belong in their tiny country. San Ramón is in the coffee-growing hills northwest of San José. There his father, Mariano Figueres Forges, practiced medicine, specializing in electrotherapy, the use of electrical current to ease neurological and muscular discomforts.

José Figueres was the first of four children born to Paquita Ferrer Minguella de Figueres, and from the beginning he did things his way. The 217 schools in San Ramón were not good, a fact that put Figueres early on the road to self-education. As with Sarmiento, self-study would leave Figueres widely read, but without a degree. Because of his father's specialty, Figueres was interested in electricity even as a boy. He set up a small laboratory in his bedroom and enrolled in the International Correspondence Schools of Scranton, Pennsylvania, improving his knowledge of both electricity and English. By the time he was ready for high school; his father had taken the family to San José to establish a clinic.

The elder Figueres insisted, against his son's objections, that the youngster attend Colegio Seminario, where, according to a biographer, "the German priests were stern disciplinarians, and the curriculum ignored the sciences and discouraged free inquiry." The father wished his son to follow in his footsteps, but the son was showing signs not of the calm deliberation one associates with physicians, but the erratic temperament typical of some leaders. Young Figueres suffered from depression, tried to run away, and, it is said, attempted suicide. His father responded by switching him from boarding to day student. Still, after four years of the five-year secondary curriculum, Figueres peevishly dropped out.

In 1924, at age seventeen, Figueres went alone to Boston to study electrical engineering at Massachusetts Institute of Technology. When MIT conditioned its acceptance on his taking preparatory courses, Figueres had no patience for the idea. He left the school after six months and would later disparage "canned education." He turned, instead, to the Boston Public Library and charted his own course. When money from home was offered to help him return, he turned it down and stayed, working as an electrician for Salada Tea Company.

Moving to New York, he worked as a translator during the day and took classes in electrical engineering at night. In New York he was joined by Francisco "Chico" Orlich, a boyhood friend and scion of a wealthy family in San Ramón, and Alberto Martén, another boyhood friend. At the Liceo de Costa Rica, the three had been influenced by teachers who awoke them to political ideas. Those ideas now got full discussion as the three grew to maturity in New York City.

Figueres returned to Costa Rica at his father's insistence in 1928. With a stake provided by his father and the Orlich family, he established in San Cristóbal, south of San José, *Sociedad Agricola Industrial San Cristóbal,* a holding company that managed coffee plantations in four towns and used the capital to develop a down-at-the-heels farm. He named the farm *La Lucha Sin Fin,* Struggle Without End. Although only thirty-five miles south of San José, La Lucha took seven hours to reach on horseback. His brother Antonio worked the farm with him.

They developed the farm's former crop, maguey, the thick, broad leaves of which yield tough fiber for making rope suitable for heavy marine use. *Cabuya* fiber was processed to make gunny sacks for coffee beans. They brought in water through bamboo conduits with sufficient force for hydroelectric power. In building the business, Figueres also developed the area, introducing schools and libraries, recreation areas, better roads, telephones, and clinics. He became known as "Don Pepe," a respectful compromise between the informality of his education and the fact that he was the boss.

In 1934, Figueres married Henrieta Boggs Long, a teacher from Birmingham, Alabama, whom he met in San José. Although the Depression meant that sometimes they had to issue scrip in place of pay, Figueres' enterprises prospered. By 1942, as the war raged in Europe and Asia, San Cristóbal operated Costa Rica's largest rope-and-twine factory. Critics called Figueres paternalistic, although the leader of the Costa Rican Communist party, Manuel Mora, conceded that Figueres was not cheap with wages. Figueres called his workers "comrades," and argued that conflict between the classes was a useless concept in a developing country. Daniel Oduber, a protégé, wrote that Figueres was "a 'socialist' before it was fashionable to be one."

Figueres was drawn ineluctably into Costa Rican politics. The country had long been dominated by the "Generation of '89," men of the previous century who had encouraged democratic participation, but then, as they grew older, could not let go of the reins of control. Personal followings, the bane of Latin American politics, allowed Costa Rican presidents to alternate with hand-picked successors. Rafael Calderón Guardia epitomized this history.

In 1940, Calderón won the presidency with the full support of his predecessor, León Cortéz Castro. Upon taking office, Calderón cast himself as a populist, absorbing "New Deal" goals and the ideas of the recent papal encyclical, *Rerum novarum.* He instituted a social security system and proposed a minimum wage, an eight-hour working day, and adequate housing for working-class families. He reopened the University of Costa Rica, which had been closed since 1888.

There was a darker side, however. Liberals eventually began to grumble over his readmitting the Jesuits—expelled for poking their sharp minds into political affairs—and reintroducing religious instruction in the public schools. More seriously, The Calderón regime was accused of corruption.

Calderón also divided opinion by interning German and Italian residents. Costa Rica had declared itself on the side of the Allies in World War II, but Calderón took this declaration to the limit of his powers, and beyond. He confiscated the property of foreign owners despite their contribution to the Costa Rican economy. Figueres was among those coming to the defense of the emigrés.

In 1940, the year of Calderón's election, Figueres had helped found the Center for the Study of National Problems. He and colleagues like Orlich and Martén dubbed themselves the "Generation of '40." They were *centristas,* critical of Calderón, of the corruption that infused his regime, and, especially, of his alliance with the communist leader Manuel Mora, whose party enjoyed widespread support among banana workers.

In February 1942, by-elections brought matters to a head. Calderón forces were accused of ballot-box stuffing. As the nation seemed ready to topple Calderón's regime, however, his communist supporters saved him. Figueres, once called a socialist, was now labeled a "fascist" because of the center's opposition to the communists.

In this heated atmosphere there occurred, on the night of July 2, a crucial event. At a dock of the Atlantic port of Limón — which was not blacked out, as it should have been — a United Fruit Company freighter was being loaded when two torpedoes from a German submarine slammed into its hull. The ship sank in shallow water, and twenty-four workmen, most of them trapped below deck, died.

Without a visible enemy to confront, embarrassed by carelessness that had cost so many lives, and whipped up by Mora's communists, some people reacted with a protest march, demanding internment of "traitors." Twenty thousand angry Costa Ricans gathered at San José's main plaza, and in their march to the presidential residence they deteriorated into a rock-throwing, looting mob. Their targets were presumed Nazi sympathizers, but they ransacked Italians' and Germans' businesses indiscriminately, included in their binge a warehouse belonging to Figueres, and even stoned the church and school of Spanish monks. One hundred and twenty three buildings were damaged and seventy-six people hurt. Calderón never tried to calm the mob.

The church and the center pointed their fingers at the communists. Figueres blamed Calderón, whom he felt let the situation get out of hand. Figueres, outraged, bought time on the radio to speak his mind. He linked the government's inability to quell the riot with its weakness in protecting shipping. "The worst form of sabotage," he said acidly, "is an inept ally." Swept along by his own rhetoric, he widened his criticism to the government's social security program, charging Calderón: "You assure us of a decent burial and let us die of hunger."

As Figueres' harangue continued, police threw open the studio doors. The police chief grabbed his coat, but Figueres kept on talking. "The police order me to stop," he blurted. "I'll not be able to say what I think ought to be done, but I can summarize it in a few words: the government ought to get out!"

Figueres was held incommunicado. One defender insisted Figueres had only said "what the honest and conscientious citizens of the Republic are and thinking." Calderón, unassuaged, wanted Figueres exiled, but he stayed, stubbornly, in jail. Friends finally convinced him that to prevent confiscation of his lands he should accept exile.

He went to Mexico, where Martí had gone in exile. Also like Martí, Figueres sent his wife home to Costa Rica to give birth to their first child, whom they named Carmen after Martí's daughter. From Mexico Figueres sent home for publication his essay, *Palabras Gastadas,* sketching his ideas for Costa Rica's future.

Those ideas were expanded to Central America—in general then dominated by dictators—by his friendship with Rosendo Argüello, Jr., who had fled to Mexico from Nicaragua in 1936, when Antonio Somoza took power. Figueres and Argüello were among the authors of what came to be called the "Caribbean Legion," a plan to rid Central America of dictators.

Meanwhile, as Figueres looked abroad for enemies, the political situation in Costa Rica worsened. Calderón's heir was Teodoro Picado, who tried to make their politics more palatable by downplaying the alliance with the communists, fearing it risked losing the Church's support. Mora, in turn, put the best face on the communists by changing their name to *Vanguardia Popular*. The corruption did not cease, however, and criticism became more vocal.

In September 1943, the Center for the Study of National Problems invited people to submit ideas for postwar society, publishing them as *Ideario Costaricense*. Figueres' essay suggested eliminating personalism in politics by introducing a professional civil service. Never one to miss an opportunity for insult, Figueres referred in his essay to Calderón officials as "cut throats."

The presidential election of 1944 put such feelings to a test. The Popular Vanguard, or communists, using tough banana workers and encouraged by Calderón, formed *brigadas de choque*, bands of thugs. They disrupted gatherings of their opponents and broke into radio stations and newspapers. Their opponents bombed Mora's home. With emotions at a fever pitch, Teodoro Picado was elected.

Figueres' friends refused to accept the outcome. They sent Orlich to Mexico to induce Figueres to buy arms and to organize a revolution. Figueres shared their impatience, but was concerned about the safety of his employees, who were being harassed, and decided to return to Costa Rica.

His return sparked a demonstration, as thousands accompanied him from the airport to the downtown offices of *Diaro de Costa Rica*, a newspaper. Figueres grandly predicted a "Second Republic." More crowds welcomed him back to La Lucha, but he shunned further public displays, convinced that electoral politics were not the answer. He wanted fighters now, not voters, and began writing his views for the new weekly news paper *Acción Demócrata*.

Figueres rejected the notion of agricultural diversification, saying rather that Costa Rica should capitalize on its tradition of coffee growing. Diversification meant overlaying the economy with a new network of services, he contended, from roads to electrical lines. Why not, Figueres asked, heighten coffee production, bringing the cash necessary to import other goods? As for land reform, he declared that the important goal was to divide the profits earned from the land among all workers, not to subdivide the land into inefficient parcels.

His ideas attracted the intellectuals of the Center in a general blending of views among opponents of the regime. As a result of this blending, a convention was held on March 11, 1945, and *Partido Social Demócrata*, the PSD, was formed. It was the first time a Costa Rican party had grown around ideas, not around a personality. The platform demanded the vote for women and, to preclude fraud, creation of a separate "branch" of government to oversee elections.

The PSD made Figueres treasurer, but ignored his counsel. He believed armed revolt was the only lasting answer to Costa Rica's problems. At one meeting, Figueres, frustrated by his colleagues' talk, berated them for their timidity and ended his lecture by slamming his pistol on the desk. That, he told them, was the only way. After personally publishing a denouncement of the Picado regime without consulting other PSD leaders, Figueres quit the party. Martén and Orlich followed their impatient friend.

Spoiling for a fight, Figueres dispatched Arguello back to Mexico to buy guns with the more than $400,000 Figueres had raised. Arguello promised to match that sum. In a tragicomedy of errors, however, Arguello bought the guns, hid them, but then could not, despite bribes, get them out of the country. Meanwhile, Costa Rican by-elections simply strengthened the hand of Picado and Calderón.

Figueres rejoined the PSD, but still fought with its members. One PSD leader, taking a page from Figueres' book, staged his own coup attempt, but failed. Now, thwarted at the ballot box and in the field, the PSD sought accommodation with Picado, much to Figueres' disgust. Again, he quit.

To end this confused turning against themselves, the opposition called a mass convention for February 1947 at the National Stadium in San José. There, 2,000 delegates were to settle on an acknowledged leader. Figueres was nominated, and the choice was clear: Should the opposition follow the fiery ways of Figueres, or espouse moderation? Just before the convention was called to order, headlines told of the discovery by Mexican police of the clandestine guns; Arguello was arrested and the weapons seized. An embarrassed Figueres ran third in the balloting.

The convention settled on support for Otilio Ulate, a tall, engaging man whose lack of strong commitment to any one idea enhanced his value as a standard bearer for disparate groups. His opponent would be Calderón.

The election campaign, as always, was violent. Discussion often degenerated into street fights. Then, on July 20, 1945, a riot in Cartago galvanized the opposition. Although there were no deaths, many people were injured, and it was clear that Picado's government was not going to uphold public safety. Opponents of the regime protested by calling a strike, first in Cartago, then nationwide. Figueres welcomed the action, appearing one afternoon on a balcony of *Diario de la Costa* before an enthusiastic crowd in the streets below. With chalk on a huge blackboard, he printed "*HUELGA*" ("STRIKE"). Eight people were killed the first day. Ulate was forced into hiding.

Figueres was convinced there was no chance for electoral reform. By November 1947, he had disclosed to Ulate that he planned to equip and train an army in the countryside. Guns for the enterprise suddenly became available when an ill-begotten invasion of the Dominican Republic, launched from Cuba, failed. Two million dollars' worth of small arms were being held by the revolutionary government in Guatemala. The Dominican invasion had been backed by Cuba, Guatemala, and Venezuela, so a committee from those countries would determine how the weapons were to be allocated. Figueres argued that Costa Rica was next in line for revolt. To get the arms, Figueres signed a pact in Guatemala City on December 16, 1947. Parties to that agreement—the backbone of the "Caribbean Legion"—agreed to overthrow the governments of Costa Rica, the Dominican Republic (Rafael Trujillo), and Nicaragua (Anastasio Somoza). Now Figueres had his arms, if he could muster an army to use them.

On February 4, 1948, Figueres called together at La Lucha the seven who would form the cadre of his army. None had a military background, and they could hardly be described as centrists. Three were in hiding, suspected of having bombed the car of communist leader Mora. Two others had been part of the short-lived rebellion of the year before. One, Frank Marshall, had been a high school student in Germany in 1936 and was reputedly a Nazi sympathizer.

The election was held on February 8, and Ulate won, 54,931 to 44,438. However, Calderón thugs simply took matters into their own hands. A day after the election, many of the ballots, stored at a girls' school in San José, were burned in a mysterious fire. Two days after the election, there was a petition to cancel the result because of irregularities. Four days after the election, crowds were in the streets, claiming they had not been allowed to vote.

Each side blamed the other. Analysis seemed to make it clear, however, that Ulate, no matter how much cheating occurred, had won by at least 9,000 votes. Nevertheless, Calderón forces were understandably incensed when the director of the elections office dropped out of sight only to reappear at Figueres' side, a trusted officer of his army in the countryside. Costa Rica moved to the brink of civil war.

On February 28, one day before the deadline that would have reopened the voting in Congress, a special committee appointed by Picado decided, two-to-one, to declare Ulate provisional president. Calderón refused to accept the committee's judgment.

He insisted that Congress reopen the voting. As the congressional debate restirred the controversy, police were dispatched to the home of an Ulate supporter, where there was a small meeting. After a heated exchange in front of the house, police shot and killed one of the men at the meeting. Although another national council of reconciliation was hastily convened, the die was cast. Figueres waited in the countryside, his small army ready. "Don Pepe did not have to make a revolution," notes biographer Ameringer. "One was delivered to him."

Figueres' plan was to descend from the mountains, block the Inter American Highway, and create an occupied zone in the southern part of the country, near the border with Panama. After airlifting in arms and equipment, he would take San Isidro, then fall on Cartago, southeast of San José. Figueres thought that the taking of Cartago would break the government's will.

The Costa Rican army numbered about three hundred men, not well trained and owing little allegiance to either Calderón or Picado. When Calderón tried to take command of the army, Picado refused, then failed to take charge himself, while Figueres grew stronger.

On March 11, thirty of Figueres' men took San Isidro de El General, a small town with a dirt airfield. They captured three DC-3s, a type of aircraft none of the rebel pilots had ever flown. Despite that fact, two planes were immediately flown to Guatemala for arms and ammunition. Figueres, commanding what was barely an army, had an air force. Back came the planes with six hundred rifles, a few machine guns, ammunition, and seven Dominicans and Hondurans ready to fight. The "Caribbean Legion" had landed.

Three days later, Figueres took Frailes. With the government turning his right flank and growing in strength, he had to immediately retreat into the mountains. Another rebel force was at La Lucha, meanwhile, headed by Alberto Martén, who was second in command. Martén, knowing he could not withstand the predicted government assault and afraid to bury the weapons entrusted to him, placed the weapons in trucks and lumbered away over dirt roads. That clumsy retreat turned out to be just the right thing to do. Fearful that he would be run down by faster-moving government troops, Martén established a perimeter at El Empalme, on the Inter American Highway. The chance tactic turned out to be perfect; the rebel forces had their "northern front." Government troops destroyed La Lucha, which was left undefended, but they went no further. Businessmen were making a revolution.

Figueres began daily broadcasts to the tiny nation, opening each one with Beethoven's Fifth Symphony, a sort of theme for the rebels. His army, as volunteers reached it, grew to seven hundred, including a priest, Benjamin Núñez, the rebels' rifle-toting chaplain. In San José, saboteurs knocked out three-fourths of the electricity for the city and guerrilla activities in other places suggested that support for the rebels was widespread. By all appearances, San José was surrounded.

On March 20, however, a week after Figueres made his move, Picado responded with what force he had. Three hundred banana-plantation laborers, rallied by the communists, drove the rebels halfway out of San Isidro before a counter-offensive regained the town for

Figueres' army. At Empalme, a government attack on the rebels was thrown back after only forty-five minutes.

Picado panicked, and hastily flew to neighboring Nicaragua to ask Somoza for help. Somoza, fearful of both the international rebels commanded by Figueres, the Caribbean Legion, and of Picado's communists, offered support only if Picado would betray the communists. It is unclear whether Picado refused the aid under those conditions, or, treacherously, accepted. Nicaraguan troops were later reported seen in Costa Rica, but were of no effect.

Figueres kept up his propaganda war. He issued a First Proclamation of the Army of National Liberation, spurring Costa Ricans to join in sabotage to hasten the government's fall. "We are on the way," he boasted. As if to corroborate his claim, a more determined government attack on Empalme was again thrown back. Figueres then ordered, of all things, an air raid. One of his DC-3s zoomed in over the palms of San José, and from it a bomb was dropped into the courtyard of the presidential residence.

In search of a truce, the archbishop of San José traveled to the rebel encampment, but Figueres would have none of it. Instead, he issued a Second Proclamation. Those who accused him of being "reactionary, bourgeois or retrogressive," he said, did not know him. His victory in the civil war would signal the beginning of a "war against poverty ... the greatest good for the greatest number."

In San José, confusion reigned. Figueres' lofty pronouncements made it unclear who the rebel leader was. After all, it was Ulate — in hiding in San José — from whom the election had been stolen. It was Figueres, though, who was at the center of the maelstrom. Confusion was exacerbated by the fact that Figueres was surrounded by Caribbean Legion friends who spoke of a utopian Caribbean, cleansed of dictators. On the other side, Picado's army was strongly supported by those other utopians, communists. Picado was also counting on help from the communists' arch-enemy, Somoza. The United States encouraged Somoza to help only if Picado would disavow the communists' support.

In early April, Figueres prepared for a final blow. He moved on Cartago, just south of San José, while at the same time sending a parallel force to take Puerto Limón on the Atlantic.

The rebels entrusted with occupying Limón — whom Figueres called "the Caribbean Legion," a name that had not actually been used theretofore — did so easily. To take Cartago, however, Figueres needed the help of nature. For maximum mobility, Figueres had each man carry his own supplies. The army set out walking, moving at night along narrow trails. As they neared San Cristóbal Norte, dawn threatened to expose them as they crept past government emplacements of artillery and machine guns. Recognizing the danger, Figueres hid his men in the forest until, in the early morning light, a fog bank descended on the mountains. Hidden by the fog, the men moved silently past the danger in what became known as "the phantom march."

At Llano de los Angeles, they hid until nightfall. Padre Núñez baptized a local baby while they rested, and when darkness came they moved in three columns to easily take Cartago. Securing nearby towns, the rebel army was joined by the Caribbean Legion approaching from Limón.

On April 13 was the showdown. A government force advanced on Cartago from the south along the Inter-American Highway. The two forces met at Tejar, and the rebels prevailed in one of the most fiercely fought battles of the civil war. In forty days, the war had taken two thousand lives.

Figueres delivered his terms at the Mexican Embassy to a small group that included foreign mediators. He called for unconditional surrender and demanded that Congress appoint him, Martén, and Fernando Valverde Vega, another of "the original seven," as first, second, and third designates to oversee the restructuring of the government. Ulate was left out in the cold. A conflict that cost two thousand lives, Figueres calculated, had been for more than just a change of presidents.

Padre Núñez took over negotiations, which boiled down to a standoff between Figueres and the communist Mora. They met on a cold, overcast night after ten o'clock on April 15 on the rise at Ochomogo. Figueres assured Mora that the rebellion was a revolution for social and economic reform.

Mora offered to join forces to stave off a rumored invasion from Nicaragua. Mora finally gave up, at least partly because he feared continued division would invite a Nicaraguan invasion. Indeed, on April 17 Somoza ordered Nicaraguan National Guardsmen to be flown to Villa Quesada, thirty-five miles inside Costa Rica, but when Picado read a statement that the Nicaraguan incursion was unwelcome, the troops were withdrawn.

The rebel army entered San José on April 24, and there was a victory parade four days later. Figueres wore a khaki uniform without military adornment; the guns and jeeps of the conquering army were decorated with flowers. "Arms bring victory," Figueres proclaimed. "Only laws can bring freedom."

Ulate claimed the presidency, and on May 1 Figueres agreed. Importantly, however, a governing junta, with Figueres as its head, would hold power for at least eighteen months, two years if necessary. Then there would be elections for an assembly to write a new constitution, and Ulate would take over for a four-year turn. "Don Pepe was now free to make his revolution," writes Ameringer, "but he had only eighteen months, possibly two years, in which to do it."

The junta that Figueres headed included old friends Orlich and Martén. The junta's resident radical was Núñez, who served as minister of labor and social welfare. Figueres' protégé, Daniel Oduber, was secretary- general. "We are a government of the middle class," Figueres said. Ethical standards were to be the foundation of the new, and succeeding, governments. A merit system was written for civil personnel. Social progress was to be made possible without communism.

Such goals, while noble, rang hollow until Figueres underlined his intent. Over the loud complaints of elites, Figueres took the startling step of nationalizing Costa Rica's banks. He called it "the democratization of credit." He also shocked elites by declaring a 10 percent tax on wealth. Although definitions of taxable wealth were poorly drawn and administration of the tax was weak, it served notice as to how deep the Figueres revolution was intended to reach. Elites resisted, lied about their holdings, boycotted, and turned to the junta's enemies for relief.

Almost immediately, as an economy measure, the junta fired three thousand government workers, including some teachers. There were accusations of a "Caribbean reign of terror," with Figueres cast as Robespierre, replete with charges of torture, unjust impoundment of wealth, and dismissals of junta opponents from government jobs. Figueres, it was claimed, recovered damages for destruction of his plantations—which in several cases was severe— amounting to ten times their true value. Figueres did, in fact, emerge from the revolution with a sizable bank account.

Before the end of the year, however, in another marked departure from Latin American practice, Figueres and the junta disbanded the army. Only civil police were retained to keep order.

Disagreements still ran deep. Opponents said Figueres was disavowing promises. Ulate, anxious about his long-promised presidency, organized an electoral sweep in the December

8 election of delegates for the constitutional assembly. Thus, the junta, which kept its most important promise to allow elections, was summarily swept aside in them.

In addition, Figueres' old Caribbean Legion pals detected cold feet because he did not immediately mount an offensive against neighboring dictators. Nicaragua was supposed to be next, but Somoza was strong, and Figueres had his hands full with Costa Rica. Costa Ricans complained about Legionnaires who were encamped, with Figueres' protection, in Costa Rican bases.

Caught in this verbal crossfire, Figueres suddenly found himself under armed attack. On December 8, when the junta was but seven months old, Somoza launched an attack on La Cruz, Costa Rica, in an attempt to return Calderón to power. Figueres, of course, had no army, but a volunteer militia pushed Somoza's soldiers back. Sixteen Costa Ricans were killed.

Trying to calm continuing criticism from domestic opponents, Figueres addressed the constitutional assembly in January 1949, describing himself and Ulate as on parallel paths for Costa Rica's ultimate benefit. Convention delegates were unreceptive. It was bluntly suggested that he retire, like Cincinnatus, to his farm. Another delegate suggested that his rebel army turn in its arms. He responded to the former suggestion by saying he would not be dismissed like a bandit, like a Costa Rican Pancho Villa. To the latter suggestion, Figueres invited anyone who had the nerve to come and take the weapons.

His popularity was not enhanced. He was not popular enough to win an election and not strong enough to rule by fiat. In March, with the junta ten months old, Figueres persuaded Ulate to agree to extend its life. In the interim, he reasoned, elections would be held in October and the new constitution would take effect in November. Thus Figueres would have several months to work his way with newly elected officials.

The strategy had its problems. Figueres was a man who could alienate friends, so working with adversaries was not easy. In addition, events were moving much too quickly. Figueres was infuriated when a split among his oldest friends on the junta pitted conservatives against radicals. It led to a half-hearted coup attempt — Figueres dramatically offered to settle differences with his fists — that collapsed of its own lack of support in half a day. Despite the brevity of the revolt, six lives were lost.

Democratic debate proved no more effective. Figueres submitted to the convention a draft constitution that envisioned state control of the economy and social systems. Conservative delegates spurned the proposals. Piqued, Figueres told Ulate to go ahead and take over the government; he had had enough. Ulate, though, recognizing chaos when he saw it, declined. Nevertheless, conditions convinced Figueres to withdraw his request for extension of the junta's life. He had exhausted his already limited patience. The two leaders agreed to submit a single slate of candidates for national elections in the fall of 1949. Like it or not, Figueres said, "destiny" had cast them together.

One final insult to Figueres' pride, however, remained. The compromise slate of candidates submitted by a caucus of Ulate and Figueres representatives failed to include Figueres as candidate for first vice president. Figueres, beside himself with anger, threatened to divide the country by running against Ulate for president. Ulate supporters responded with a proposal to prohibit junta members from ever running for office. This would have blocked Figueres from the presidency later, so, to prevent that, he agreed to a compromise slate and gave up on being first vice president. Figueres' ambition had been profoundly frustrated, but the compromise was not in vain; the October elections were fair and unmarred by violence.

The Constitution of 1949 retained old guarantees and included new programs, like social security and a code protecting workers' rights. The convention delivered the constitution on November 7, 1949, and the next day Figueres turned over the government to Ulate.

Figueres "retired" to four years of being appointed to international conferences. He came to symbolize, in those days of the cold war, "the democratic left." Figueres was widely identified with Victor Raúl Haya de la Torre of Perú's *Alianza Popular Revolucionaria Americana*, or APRA, and with Rómulo Betancourt of Venezuela's *Acción Democrática*, or AD. Luís Muñoz Marín of Puerto Rico, the author of "Operation Bootstrap," was another friend. In the United States, Arthur M. Schlesinger, Jr., Chester Bowles, and Norman Thomas asked Figueres' opinion. He may have been the eye of a storm in his own tiny country, but Figueres was avidly courted in the hemisphere.

In March 1952, he announced his candidacy to succeed Ulate, but a question remained as to whether he could unite a following. On a dais, after so many years of lecturing abroad, he was a bit pedantic. He tended to lecture, to talk down to his audience. In the end, however, the informal style that had served him so well in building his business had not left him. Away from the lectern, his personality shone through; he related to crowds when he was among them. Banana workers, remembering the civil war, never took to him, but *campesinos* did.

A sad aspect of the campaign was that he and his wife, Henrietta, were divorced just before the election. Less than two years later, while he was president and on a speaking tour to the United States, he would meet Karen Olson, a Dane who was a naturalized U.S. citizen. He was forty-seven years old; she was twenty-three and studying for her doctorate in sociology at Columbia University. They married quietly in Costa Rica in February 1954.

The election was delayed from May 31 to July 26 to register women, who were newly enfranchised, but on July 26, 1953 — the same day Fidel Castro stormed the Moncada barracks — Figueres won with a 65 percent majority, 123,444 to 67,324 for his opponent, Mario Echandi. Figueres' party, the PSD, won 30 congressional seats, the other three parties a total of 15.

He was now president of the only democracy in Central America, and evidence of that fact was everywhere about him. He was host to Rómulo Betancourt of Venezuela, who, already in exile in Havana, had fled to Costa Rica because he was unwelcome after Fulgencio Batista's coup in Cuba. Figueres was also host to twenty-two assassins on their way to Nicaragua to kill Somoza. These circumstances, portrayed in headlines, did not endear Figueres to nearby dictators.

There was, as well, pressure from the left: Jacobo Arbenz of Guatemala had begun expropriating the property of United Fruit Company, which had extensive holdings in Costa Rica. To follow suit, Figueres said it was time for a gradual departure of United Fruit Company. "The gradual and judicious withdrawal of the economic occupation would be the rectification of one of the gravest errors, or anachronisms, prevailing in the American hemisphere," he said. He went after a 50–50 split on profits like the arrangement Betancourt had achieved with foreign oil companies in Venezuela. He also wanted to eliminate the company's tax avoidance on imports of equipment and supplies.

In June 1954, he signed a contract enabling the government to take over the health services the company had provided. The company also agreed to higher taxes, although the rate was 30 percent, not the 50 percent Figueres sought. He settled for a daily minimum wage of $2.40, although the workers wanted more and struck to get it.

Figueres' government designed other programs, but progress was slowed after 1954 when coffee prices declined. Still, his international reputation grew. After repelling yet another Somoza-sponsored invasion in January 1955, Figueres was portrayed by Adolf Berle, an old Roosevelt hand, as a hero in Washington. Figueres suspected, however, that while he was being praised in some Washington circles he was being targeted in others. He blamed the Central Intelligence Agency for backing Somoza.

Figueres remained a target for critics, both domestic and lethal. Throughout 1956 he was criticized by Costa Ricans for spending so much time abroad. Then, in the spring of 1957, assassins contracted by Rafael Trujillo of the Dominican Republic were arrested in San Juan as they calculated the best time and place to strike.

When his term came to a close, Figueres hoped to hand the presidency to his old friend "Chico" Orlich. That, of course, was the way Costa Rican politics had always worked, the very system Figueres had helped to dissolve. So there was justice of a sort when, in February 1958, Mario Echandi, beaten by Figueres four years earlier, made a comeback with the support of old Figueres antagonist Otilio Ulate. Echandi also beat the indomitable Rafael Calderón, trying his own comeback.

So the country underwent peaceful change, but Figueres was once again a prophet with less honor in his own country than in international assemblies. In the spring of 1958, after riots dogged the path of U.S. Vice President Richard Nixon's South American tour, Figueres was called upon to testify before a subcommittee of the U.S. Congress. Nixon's delegation had been jeered and spat upon in Montevideo, and Nixon was briefly trapped in his car cavalcade by a stone-throwing crowd in the streets of Caracas. "People cannot spit on a foreign policy," Figueres told the subcommittee, explaining that Nixon merely represented his country, which Latin Americans felt had turned its back on the hemisphere. "If you talk human dignity to Russia," Figueres asked, comparing two dictatorships, "why do you hesitate so much to talk human dignity to [the people of the] Dominican Republic?" Figueres' words were published throughout Latin America.

He remained one of the best-known Latin American spokesmen for the Latin American idea of progressive democracy. He watched with satisfaction when Rómulo Betancourt was elected president of Venezuela in late 1958, and he excited hostility in Cuba in 1959 when he dared to support the United States in the global cold war.

International pride, however, leads to international sins. To propagate his ideas, Figueres used the Institute of Political Education in San José, an arm of his party, now called *Partido de Liberación Nacional.* The institute was a font for progressive democratic ideas, inviting lecturers, publishing essays, and generating discussion. Like all such institutions, however, it needed funding. So, in April 1959, when Figueres was introduced to Romanian refugee Sacha Volman, an answer appeared to be at hand. An avid anticommunist, Volman opened doors for Figueres, flattering his already sizable ego. Volman seemed to know everyone, and suddenly, Figueres was more popular than ever before for lectures. His name was linked with that of Richard Nixon, of Nelson Rockefeller. Funding flowed.

Because it was a time of heightened conflict in the Caribbean and Central America — Cuba sent insurgents to Panama; Costa Rica invaded Nicaragua — never was the dissemination of democratic ideas more necessary, in Figueres' view. Unfortunately, that was also the view of the CIA, which turned out to be the source of the funds Volman provided. Figueres knew this, and when the facts were made public in 1960 the institute was branded an ignominious tool of U.S. policy, the policy Venezuelan mobs tried to spit on.

Figueres' ego was salved a bit the next year when President John F. Kennedy, in announcing the Alliance for Progress, remarked, "In the words of José Figueres, 'Once dormant peoples are struggling upward toward the sun, toward a better life.'" It soon was reiterated, however, that Figueres' words, while convenient for quotation in speeches, went unheeded in the formation of policy.

For example, Figueres insisted that Rafael Trujillo ought to be "the first target" of overthrow in the Caribbean. The advice was ignored. Kennedy focused on that double-whammy of U.S. fears: a Latin American, communist dictator — Fidel Castro. In April 1961, Figueres tried to warn Kennedy away from what became the fateful Bay of Pigs invasion, but was unable to do so. Then, when Trujillo was assassinated by Dominican officers on May 30, 1961, Figueres' involvement with tainted U.S. policy became more pronounced. The assassination was carried out with the complicity of the CIA and, perhaps, Figueres, whose Institute of Political Education was then harboring a rival Dominican, Juan Bosch. There seemed no end to the entanglements.

Figueres' was a lonely voice crying out for moderation in the midst of excess. "Latin America is now in a grave economic situation," he told a U.S. college audience in 1962, "which is being converted into a serious political situation."

Although he was able to help Orlich win the presidency in 1962 perpetuating the important, ordered succession of Costa Rican presidents that continues to this day — and in October 1963 he began a lectureship at Harvard University, Figueres' fortunes were in decline. In November 1963, Kennedy was shot. Figueres traveled from Kennedy's college to Kennedy's funeral, walking sadly along Pennsylvania Avenue behind the caisson, dwarfed by the throng and the tall, gaunt figure of General Charles de Gaulle next to him.

Figueres, however, like Sarmiento, could not step out of the arena. Unable to help his one-time protégé, Daniel Oduber, win the presidency in 1966, Figueres slid deeper into his role as handmaiden to U.S. policy. In 1967 *Ramparts* magazine revealed that "the J. M. Kaplan Fund Inc.," was yet another funnel for CIA money — a funnel pointed, once again, toward Figueres' Institute of Political Education.

In 1970, after regaining the presidency for himself with 55 percent of the vote, Figueres found that the world had become a complex thing indeed. A Central American border dispute required his service as comediator alongside the oldest of his antagonists, Nicaraguan dictator Anastasio Somoza, the man he had once vowed to depose. To make matters worse, in the middle of Figueres' term the notorious international financier Robert Vesco showed up in Costa Rica. Vesco was eager to escape extradition to the United States for prosecution of his alleged crimes, and he was willing to pay for his stay. Vesco's investments in Figueres' interests would once again stain Don Pepe's reputation, fueling his critics' antipathy and embarrassing his supporters.

Figueres' career was like that, never avoiding controversy, never shirking involvement, never shunning risk. He insisted, as if compulsively, on returning to the center of the storm, and for that, Figueres is still admired. He died at his San José apartment on June 8, 1990, of a heart attack at the age of eighty-three. He was eulogized by the *New York Times* as "Costa Rica's Fierce Pacifist."

Fidel Castro

Socialist Revolutionary

1926–
(Cuba)

Fidel Castro took up arms to shape the first socialist revolution in Latin America that was made to last, a revolution the United States failed to prevent and could not erase. As a result, Castro has remained a hemispheric pariah as far as the United States is concerned, although Latin American democracies have long since learned to live with Cuba. In recent years, Cuba has become even more unusual, a socialist island ever more lonely as it is deserted by its European retainers.

Fidel Castro's father was Angel Castro y Argiz, a Galician and soldier in the army sent to suppress the Cuban insurrection of 1898. Without formal education, he built a small farm in Oriente province into a prosperous cattle ranch of more than 23,000 acres. The plantation—two and a half years after the father's death—would be broken up by the revolution. Angel Castro's first wife, who died, bore him two children. He married Lina Ruz González, the mother of seven more of his children, after Fidel was born on August 13, 1926. Because the parents of Lina Ruz de Castro were also natives of Galicia—a coastal province at the northwest corner of Spain that once was an independent kingdom Castro is said by some to be *puro gallego,* a Spaniard on an island of Creoles.

Because neither of his parents had gone to school, there was no thought of sending Fidel until, the story goes, he threatened to burn the house down. He was sent to live, not altogether happily, with godparents and enrolled in a Jesuit school. Later, he was moved to the prestigious Colegio Belén in Santiago, the provincial capital. Oriente is a province noted for its independent turn of mind, prosperous and isolated at the eastern tip of the island—far from Havana, the corrupt urban "leech" of Cuba's agrarian riches. Santiago would serve as political classroom for the young Castro, just as its Moncada barracks would provide him with the first laboratory to test his theories.

Castro was athletic and unusually tall. He graduated from high school with a citation in the yearbook for "defending with bravery and pride the flag of the school." He went to Havana to study law in 1945.

At the university, campus politics were practiced with a zeal that bordered on thuggery. While Latin American campuses have traditionally sheltered critics of their governments, and while student activism typically includes rock throwing, Havana University was in a league of its own. Campus leaders, for example, oversaw the organized sale of black market textbooks. During the time Castro was at the university, several students were murdered, and although no convincing evidence has ever been adduced that he played a role in the deaths,

Castro earned a reputation for toughness in a tough environment. If, as it is said, he carried a pistol while a student, he was not alone in the practice.

More substantial evidence describes Castro's role in the events of the spring of 1948. Castro and two fellow students were sent by campus organizations to Bogotá to an international convention of university students. Thus, they were in the Colombian capital on April 1 when Jorge Eliécer Gaitán, a popular leftist, was murdered on a downtown street. Enraged followers of Gaitán tore his assailant to pieces and the ensuing riot became known as the *bogotazo,* an explosion of mob violence. Castro and at least one of his fellow Cubans appear in reports resulting from a special investigation; they distinguished themselves in a chaotic situation for having done their best to fan the flames of chaos. That Castro played any direct role in the beginning of the riot or contributed to its aftermath — decades of virulent clashes between Colombian Liberals and Conservatives has never been demonstrated and seems naive. Yet it is clear that Castro, even as a student encountered no revolutionary conditions he wouldn't try to improve upon.

Indeed, while he was still at the university, Castro took part in an abortive attempt to overthrow, by seaborne invasion, Dominican dictator Rafael Trujillo. The idea of overthrowing Trujillo was supported by Venezuelan authorities and, at first, Cuban President Ramón Grau San Martín. But pressure from the U.S. ambassador to Cuba subtracted Grau from the equation. Nevertheless, a tiny expeditionary force set out from the coast of Cuba, and when a coastal patrol boat closed in, Castro dove over the side to escape. Another legend was born in that Castro is said to have swum to shore without letting go of his submachine gun.

With revolutionary politics as his principal extracurricular activity, Castro also found time to marry. He and Mirta Díaz-Balart, a philosophy major, were married in the autumn of 1948 and honeymooned in Miami. A son, Fidelito, was born on September 1, 1949.

Castro graduated the next year. With two partners, he began practicing in Havana, a city with political and juridical systems known for their corruption and an economy tightly controlled by sugar interests.

The sugar economy prescribed all other conditions in Cuba after the Spanish were driven out. The royalty was ended, but reality lingered on. And into the twentieth century Cuba's sugar economy was increasingly dominated by North Americans. Absentee landlords thus made themselves heirs to the feudal system that had evolved from the hemisphere's last slavocracy. Thousands cut cane to put sugar onto a world market that paid richly in foreign exchange for the owners to buy imports. Plantations were already becoming vertically integrated — controlling not only growing, but grinding, transportation and distribution as well. American capital and organizational skills accelerated the consolidation, linking the system with railroads, and building a one-crop economy without rival anywhere in the colonial world. This system flourished in the 1920s, but when it began to slow it dragged all else with it. By the 1950s, it had slowed considerably. By that time about one-third of Cuba's population was destitute despite the fact that the island's per capita income was third highest in Latin America. The lights of Havana's casinos created a glow over the city that could be seen clearly from hovels without hope of electricity.

Political solutions to the imbalance, however, were not apparent. Many, if not most, politicians were for sale. Cuban government had staggered since the U.S. army and the Platt Amendment had left Cubans to their own devices early in the century. The most egregious example of Cuban self-governance was President Gerardo Machado, of whom Castro heard as a child. Machado's skills at leadership earned him the sobriquet "the butcher" before he was overthrown by the coup that eventually elevated to the presidency Fulgencio Batista.

By contrast with Machado, Batista's first term was enlightened. When he retired to opulence in Miami in 1944, Batista was followed by two civilian presidents, and it appeared that Cuba might have righted itself in the sea of democratic practices. When national elections were again scheduled for June 1952, Castro intended, as a member of the Orthodox party, to run for congress.

His law practice was successful, although the cases he accepted tended toward those with social implications, not high fees. He had joined the *ortodoxos,* which began as a splinter group but was built to a substantial populist force by the charismatic Eduardo "Eddy" Chibas. The enigmatic Chibas brought his own career to a bizarre end by shooting himself in the head at a radio studio at the end of an emotional speech, but the party continued. Castro had found a political niche and was confident of election.

In late 1951, however, Batista returned. He led a second successful coup, terminating any chance of continued reform by democratic processes. Deprived of his seat in Congress, Castro took the Batista government to court. He petitioned a special court, charging that Batista had violated the Cuban constitution written in the 1940s. Had the court accepted the petition and found Batista guilty on all counts, he would have faced jail terms adding up to something over a century. Castro also brought suit in the Court of Constitutional Guarantees, claiming, understandably, that the coup was illegal. The Court of Constitutional Guarantees, in an opinion that both recognized Latin American realities and prophesied the island's future, dismissed Castro's complaint, acknowledging instead that revolution "is the font of law."

Castro took the court at its word. The following year, on July 26, 1953, he led nearly two hundred men and several women in an attack on the Moncada barracks in Santiago. Simultaneously, seven others staged a coordinated attack on the small garrison at Bayamo, on the highway about sixty miles west of the city. From the outset, the plan was shot through with mistakes.

The Santiago attack was to have two waves. The first wave, led by Castro, intended to emerge from the cover of a carnival crowd to take the main sentry post and occupy the nearby civic hospital and the palace of justice. But as they rolled up to the gate in a caravan of cars and trucks, they saw a government patrol, by chance, emerging from the guardhouse. The ensuing firefight alerted the garrison, and the few rebels who succeeded in taking the hospital were quickly isolated and surrounded.

The second rebel wave, more heavily armed, got lost in the streets of Santiago. Its caravan drove around helplessly until it was too late.

When Castro signaled retreat from the attack on the main fort, his brother Raúl was able to extract his squad from the palace of justice, but no one could cover the escape of nineteen men and two women trapped at the hospital. The assault at Bayamo was no more successful. Fidel Castro's first attempt as a guerrilla was a dismal failure.

In the assault on Moncada, three rebels were killed and approximately one hundred captured. Sixty-eight prisoners were summarily executed. Fifty rebels, including Fidel and Raúl Castro, escaped. The inchoate revolution had won nothing but its name, the 26th of July. For days after the attack, as government troops hunted down the rebels, residents of Santiago including parents of captured rebels— were subjected to grisly reports, smuggled out of prison and into the streets, of torture and slow death. The stories were not all true, but they were strong enough to embarrass even a populace accustomed to political savagery. The archbishop of Santiago was pressed to intervene, and his efforts tempered the government's fury, although it is less certain, as some stories suggest, that he was personally responsible for saving Castro's life.

Some of those who escaped were hiding in the woods, and they came out, cautiously, hoping to face prison rather than execution. Castro and two others were spotted and captured at the home of a sympathizer—fortunately, for them, by a junior officer who disapproved of the slaughter that had already taken place. Castro was first brought to trial with several others, and he insisted on speaking in his own defense.

One morning as the trial began, however, he was not in the courtroom. The judge was told Castro was too ill to continue. In his cell, Castro, fearing that he would be killed, managed to smuggle out a note, which one of the defense attorneys plucked from her coiled hair in the courtroom. He was not sick, Castro wrote, but being forcibly detained. His trial was postponed.

The incident illustrates the porous nature of the Batista regime. When a jailor was ordered to poison Castro, he refused. So weak was the Batista government, so shot through with corruption and ambiguity that it was incapable even of carrying out its own nefarious tactics. It was in Batista's prison, in fact, that Castro began his climb toward prominence. Only one of many opponents of the Batista regime, Castro used his rhetoric to climb to a position of pre-eminence. Had Castro, as the twenty-six-year-old leader of the Moncada assault, been one of the five dozen rebels executed, the hemisphere would doubtless have changed less over the past thirty years. But had a less determined person been captured, one less capable of turning imprisonment into a forum, so, too, would history have been different.

Castro's trial was held at the civic hospital; it drew a standing-room- only crowd of nurses, another example of the regime's lack of control. Although the trial was closed to the public and press accounts censored, full news, including Castro's remarks, carried across the island. His own lengthy closing statement, polished by editing, was published and distributed widely as the first formal suggestion of what Castro had in mind for Cuba. He spoke of a "return" to the Constitution of 1940, free elections, and made his assertion, "History will absolve me."

He was sentenced to fifteen years on the Isle of Pines, where Martí had been sent. Reaching the island in October 1953, Castro organized in the barracks what came to be known as the "Abel Santamaría Academy," named for a fellow rebel who was captured in the Moncada attack and tortured to death. Castro was sole lecturer, other prisoners his pupils. The authorities clapped him in isolation.

Yet his ideas—written in lemon-juice "invisible ink" between the lines of letters, or smuggled out in match boxes—were communicated, largely through the efforts of Haydée Santamaría, Abel's sister, and Melba Hernández. "No weapon, no force," he wrote, "can overcome a people who decide to fight for their rights." As many as 20,000 copies of his prison pronouncements were printed and circulated.

Early in Castro's imprisonment Mirta served as a link between her husband and the rebel movement. When she had trouble supporting herself and young Fidelito, however, her brother, in the time-honored tradition of Latin American politics, used his position to help. He simply had her name added to the payroll of Batista's interior department. Checks were issued regularly. When this was discovered and publicized, Castro took it as a reproach to his ability to support a family and as an accusation of hypocrisy. His family, after all, was sustained by the very government he sought to overthrow. His relationship with Mirta deteriorated, and before he left prison she had filed for divorce; she took their son to the United States.

Batista, without significant opposition, perpetuated his regime with an "election," but by the spring of 1955 he was under pressure manifest by a vote in the Cuban House of Representatives to grant amnesty. Families, including Lydia Castro, a sister, had begun to demonstrate at the main gate of the Isle of Pines prison camp. Batista relented and pardoned the July 26 rebels, who, as they rode the train back toward Havana, were greeted by occasional crowds of sympathizers.

Several veterans of the Moncada assault, almost immediately after they were released, left for Mexico City to await Castro. At first, Castro stayed using his popularity to give his opinions to Havana reporters, but the attention was a mixed blessing. Eventually access to the news media was choked off by Batista supporters, and Castro found himself under the scrutiny of government agents. Following Raúl, he went to Mexico City.

In the Mexican capital the small group of Cubans was joined by a short, ill-kempt Argentine, as intense about politics as he was loose about his personal habits. He was knocking about the continent in search of a cause, and the Cubans had one. With their guttural Caribbean pronunciation, they were amused by the slow, Italian-influenced accent of this newcomer. They were taken with his use of the affectionate "che," a common term at the bottom of the continent, and so dubbed Ernesto Guevara with the name, and it stuck.

The Cubans, given new life by the Latin American tolerance for rebellion, rented a farmhouse and underwent combat training by a veteran of the Spanish civil war. Long marches through the volcanic mountains toughened them for a war the dimensions of which they could only try to imagine. Castro went to the United States where, like Martí, he spoke to émigré groups seeking support. After each discourse, a wood-and-papier- mâché machine gun would be passed around for donations.

Help was welcome from anywhere. Although Castro was then denouncing the *ortodoxos,* accusing them of collaboration with the Batista regime, Castro supporters were accepting donations from the Authentic party — whose funds bought the yacht used for Castro's miniscule invasion — another anti–Batista group. There was, in fact, relatively broad opposition to Batista, which would later lead to the accusation that Castro "stole" the revolution.

The Cubans in Mexico were closely watched by both Cuban agents and Mexican authorities. Once when Castro's car was stopped in Mexico City and the stock of weapons it carried confiscated, he replaced them only to be stopped again, losing the replacement arms. When, finally, arms and ammunition were gathered and stored aboard the *Granma,* eighty-two men, along with their provisions, crammed themselves on. The plan was to arrive on the south shore of Cuba on November 30, 1956.

Castro planned to coordinate the arrival of his small army with an uprising in Santiago. Then, gathering provisions hidden near their landing point, they would link up with another hundred men at arms and establish a base in the Sierra Maestra. However, tactics at first seemed as ill-fated as they had been at the Moncada barracks. Against all advice, Castro insisted on telegraphing his punch by repeatedly boasting that his force would invade before the end of the year. So Batista's army was prepared. In addition, he ignored warnings that the planned uprising in Santiago was unlikely to occur. Indeed, the uprising was immediately suppressed, the waiting troops were too far back in the mountains to make the rendezvous, and the yacht arrived late, past the designated point and too overloaded to be beached. The boat was finally anchored off a swamp, and its hapless expeditionary force waded ashore carrying what it could. Batista's army and air force attacked.

Although the rebels made it from the coast into the mountains, they were immediately surrounded. Castro reacted by splitting his force to avoid the capture of everyone. But one group of fourteen was trapped and promised treatment as prisoners of war if they surrendered. When they surrendered, they were shot. Radio stations in Havana reported that the entire invasion force had been wiped out and Castro killed.

In fact, the rebel forces were splintered, and for the second time in his short military career, Castro was forced to flee for his life. With two companions, he wandered, trying to regroup what was left of his forces. Others also wandered, living on sugar cane. At one point Castro and his two companions hid from a group of men they could see, but could not identify. It turned out to be Raúl and two others—who had seen them and were trying to hide. Eventually, as stragglers from the *Granma* gathered themselves again, Castro's army numbered twelve men.

Theodore Draper has suggested that at this precise point Castro distinguish himself by having the iron will, not to say madness, of a revolutionary hero. Rather than escape from the island in order to start again, Castro clung to the Sierra Maestra like a tick to a dog. The men with him, mostly city-bred and unaccustomed to living off the land, were reduced to hunger, wandering, confusion. They were largely without arms. Men who were with Castro during those months recalled that when they rested, complaining of their plight, they would look over at Castro, who was not paying attention but gazing at the sierra, planning.

Within six months, he had learned the mountains that would be his refuge for two hard years. Castro's strategy, like Sandino's, was shaped by the terrain and his weakness. He claims to have won the war with five hundred guerrillas, and even more objective estimates confirm that his forces never exceeded about eight hundred fighters at their strongest. He was able to win by virtue of his own tenacity and because of the corruption of the Batista regime, unable to rally either people or army to its own defense. Guerrillas picked off army outposts, disappearing back into the mountains to await the next opportunity, to sustain themselves, and to train the recruits that filtered in from the farms and out of the city.

Castro, meanwhile, kept himself accessible. Foreign correspondents, in a stream led by Herbert Matthews of the *New York Times,* legitimated Castro's rebellion by according him a forum with their interviews. When Batista functionaries claimed Castro had been killed, there he was, with Matthews, in a photograph in the *Times.* One CBS correspondent became so enthralled with Castro's homilies that he became a spokesman for Castro's ideas, and the network had to pull him off the assignment.

As he had from prison on the Isle of Pines, Castro built a constituency, national and international, by issuing pronouncements from the sierra. From prison he had promised a return to the Constitution of 1940. Now he predicted a future of promise without bounds. Because Castro dealt in generalities, the U.S. State Department, sensitive to American business interests on the island, saw Castro as no threat. The 26th of July movement seemed nothing more than one of many pairs of hands pushing at the side of Batista's toppling structure.

Opposition was varied. In March 1957, four months after the *Granma* landing but independent of Castro's direction, Havana students attacked the presidential palace to assassinate Batista. The attempt was unsuccessful, but students who escaped fled to the mountains of Central Cuba, creating another "front" there, or made their way to Castro's forces in the western sierra.

In May, a trial was held for the twenty-two men captured from the *Granma* and one hundred more people accused of participating in the failed Santiago uprising. The three-judge panel — reflecting Cuba's deep ambivalence — split. Two judges insisted on freeing the defendants. Manuel Urrutia,* speaking for the court, held that the defendants had the right to rebel against an unjust regime.

In the autumn, naval personnel at Cienfuegos revolted. Batista ruthlessly bombed the base into submission, ending the uprising and creating even more opposition.

Meanwhile, Castro's small army eluded air strikes and attacked only when victory was assured. The same month as the Cienfuegos revolt, it mounted its first successful raid against a small garrison on the south coast. Vital to Castro's force was that it preserve its unity. The

---

Castro would later reward Urrutia for his courage by making him the first president of post revolutionary Cuba. Then he would dump him as one of the first thrown overboard when the revolution began its swerve to the left.

rebels had time, and time had to reveal that they were the only opposition force able to hold itself together without being killed, captured, or co-opted. Even Cuba's traditional, Soviet-oriented communists—later to be so closely examined for their influence on Castro—was at that point condemning Castro as a "putschist," a selfish bourgeois who sought power for himself. So toothless were the communists that Batista felt safe appointing them to his cabinet.

Not all threats to the rebels were external. Fighting alongside Castro was Eutemio Guerra, who was a spy, disclosing the band's position whenever possible. Then Guerra's superiors assigned him a bigger job: assassinate Castro. He planned to shoot Castro at close range with a pistol, discouraging pursuit as he escaped down the mountainside with two hand grenades.

As Guevara later told the story, one frigid night in the mountains Guerra asked Castro to lend him a blanket. Castro replied that because he only had one blanket they would both be better off sleeping side by side, sharing their two coats, the blanket, and their bodily warmth. They did so, Guevara wrote, while either lack of nerve or absence of opportunity prevented Guerra from carrying out his assignment. After later betrayals, Guerra's purpose was discovered, and he fell to his knees, asking quick execution. The request was superfluous, but Guevara notes that the revolution saw to it that Guerra's two sons were provided an education.

In the spring of 1958, the rebel army had accumulated sufficient numbers to launch a column of fifty-three fighters. Led by Raúl Castro, they moved into the Sierra del Cristal, broadening the attack, although the rebels were still confined to the southeastern end of the island. It was a significant expansion, and Batista's generals, trying to crush the rebels before they strengthened themselves further, tried to surround them. During the summer, soldiers were sent around the island, landing on the south coast to push upward, into the Sierra Maestra toward the main body of about three hundred rebels. The strategy nearly worked, but Castro withdrew into a perimeter less than twenty miles across and fought off the attack. Counterattacking, Castro took government prisoners. He turned them over to the International Red Cross. His small army had achieved a military respectability that meant Batista's defeat eighteen months later.

With bolstered confidence, Castro sent Guevara and Camilo Cienfuegos at the head of 150 rebels aimed toward the island's waist, tightening the pressure on Havana on the north coast. They captured two towns and more government troops in sometimes bloody fighting; both sides knew that the end was near for one or the other. In the south, the Castro brothers increased pressure on the garrison at Santiago.

Then came the end. Batista staged an election, but it was window dressing for a deserted building. On New Year's Eve 1959, Batista flew into exile, and Guevara and Cienfuegos led their troops into Havana three days later. Ironically, Castro, at his camp, heard the news on the radio. He had just successfully negotiated the surrender of the Moncada and Bayamo garrisons at Santiago, against which the 26th of July movement was forged five and a half years earlier. He and Raúl led their troops across the island toward Havana, entering the city on January 8. Castro rode into the city atop a tank with his son, who had been in school on Long Island, riding beside him.

Some insight into Castro's attitudes upon his entering Havana is gained from a letter hung on the office wall of Celia Sánchez, who was rewarded for her revolutionary work with a position in the new government. Enlarged and framed, the letter was sent to her by Castro during the Sierra Maestra campaign. He described watching government troops firing rockets made in the United States at the home of a friend. "I swore to myself," he wrote, "that the Americans were going to pay dearly.... When this war is over, a much wider and bigger war will begin for me."

At first, Castro insisted that his role would be only as head of the armed forces. His choice for administrative positions included both communists and men who had proven themselves as administrators under Batista. It was clear, however, that regardless of their titles or backgrounds they were not the ones sought by the crowds. Those people, spilling over with requests so long suppressed, went to Castro and his rebel soldiers, whose beards identified them with the future. The result was total confusion.

Castro, with enemies not only from the deposed regime but also from among other Batista opponents, kept closest to himself the men and women who had been with him in the mountains. Beyond them, he counted on those who had supported him from the cities. Neither represented a strong cadre of administrators. By mid–February 1959 he had decided to name himself prime minister. He began replacing cabinet members. The principal qualification for service became loyalty to the prime minister.

In the immediate aftermath of the revolution there were approximately six hundred executions, a modest number by some standards in Latin America and elsewhere. Trials were often hastily arranged, sometimes held in public arenas and televised.

But revenge did not substitute for solutions, and the island's economy was in shambles. Some Cubans, opposed to Castro's takeover, tried to keep it that way; saboteurs and snipers cropped up, trying to frustrate reorganization of the island's resources. In addition, an exodus of middle and upper-class Cubans had already begun. While it relieved antagonistic pressure on Castro, it also threatened to strip the economy of both capital and managers. It is at this juncture that Castro is accused of failing to return Cuba to the democracy that was struggling to find itself in 1952. Doing that, Castro knew, risked perpetuating U.S. domination, something he was determined to change. He persisted, and what followed was change of enormous proportions, creating equally enormous problems.

U.S. President Eisenhower, more concerned about the communists in Castro's administration than he had been about those in Batista's, recognizing the vulnerability of American-owned sugar plantations and following the precedent of every president since James K. Polk, was belligerent. Early in 1959, Eisenhower threatened, unless Castro disavowed his increasingly leftist orientation, to reduce American imports of Cuban sugar. Castro, anxiously trying to consolidate power and stifle opposition, accepted Eisenhower's challenge — and the aid eagerly offered by communist governments. The resulting strain in U.S.–Cuban relations quickly became a severe break.

For a few weeks, there was ambivalence as neither side could get used to setting policy in a situation unique in the four and a half centuries since the hemisphere had been colonized. Castro came to the United States in April and addressed newspaper editors. In May, at a meeting of Latin American ministers in Buenos Aires, he proposed a $30 billion "Marshall Plan" funded by the United States. Then he returned to Cuba and nationalized agriculture.

Oil refineries met the same fate. Before the revolution, U.S. and British refineries had processed petroleum from Venezuela, but after Castro took power the supply began to dwindle, threatening the already precarious state of the economy. Cuban requests for oil from Venezuela and Argentina were to no avail. The alternative was to bring in crude oil from the Soviet Union, but when the first tanker arrived, the refineries refused to accept it. Castro nationalized the refineries, and by the middle of 1960, Nikita Khrushchev was blustering that the Soviet Union would protect its new Cuban ties with "rocket firepower."

More immediately necessary, however, was to prop up the Cuban economy with Soviet-bloc transfusions of money, goods, and management. The resulting advice was not always helpful. Advisors from land locked East European countries sometimes misunderstood island conditions, planning warehouses inland while imported food rotted at the dock. Guevara joked about Coca-Cola that was like syrup, toothpaste so hard it could not be squeezed from the tube. Exacerbating Cuba's domestic disarray — pockets of armed resistance persisted in the interior — was the United States, which busily organized international disapproval.

Castro had difficulty coping, and was inclined to paper over the problems with political poses. Wearing army fatigues and probably longing for the simpler problems of the sierra, Castro often reacted to problems by driving off to the countryside, the scene of his military successes, to make pronouncements. Agrarian reform, he declared, was crucial to answering Cuban economic problems, but rewriting ancient laws of land tenure was no easier in Cuba than it had been anywhere else in Latin America. In May 1959, when the Castro family's holdings were nationalized, brother Ramón and sister Lina were outraged. Ramón later joined the government to administer agricultural reform in the eastern end of the island, but other land owners were not so easily mollified.

The long-term idea was that sugar had to be replaced by a variety of crops. Cane-cutters had to be released from the feudal characteristics of the sugar economy, which locked Cuba into dependence on erratic, occasionally glutted, world markets. For the time being, however, sugar brought in dearly needed cash, so the symbol of the revolution became pictures of government, business, and professional people, machetes in hand, toiling in the fields. "Fellow *macheteros,*" Castro was fond of saying at the beginning of hortatory speeches that went on for hours. Those who failed to demonstrate revolutionary fervor he called "scum." Self-exiles were "worms."

Then, on January 3, 1961, the United States and Cuba broke diplomatic relations, and the United States instituted an almost total embargo on goods shipped to the island. In the spring, impatient with this hemispheric upstart, the Kennedy administration trained, transported, and gave logistic support to an army of refugee invaders. The Bay of Pigs invasion failed. "We regarded him as an hysteric," remarked Arthur Schlesinger, Jr., the historian and advisor to Kennedy, explaining the United States' hysterical policy.

The next year, Khrushchev moved to make good on his bluster, dispatching ships loaded with missiles for emplacement on the island. Kennedy called the bluff with a naval quarantine, which succeeded in turning around the Soviet ships. To Castro's humiliation, the drama played out well above his head; it was clear that in the largest sense Cuba's place in international politics would be determined by the superpowers.

Judgment of Castro's place in the contemporary affairs of the hemisphere has never lent itself to objectivity. Differing opinions will be heard in the exile community in Miami, in a Havana schoolroom, in a poor *barrio* of another Latin American country, languishing under another Batista.

The most lasting criticism is that Castro and his army of the Sierra Maestra "stole" the Cuban revolution from other anti–Batista groups and, since, have driven away or imprisoned opponents. Cuban poet Armando Valladares, released from prison in 1986 after twenty-two years, writes of having met inmates who were the very Cubans "who helped the Revolution come to power, students, professionals, *campesinos.*" Valladares, who was imprisoned for criticizing the government, tells of brutal torture for those who refuse "political rehabilitation."

Have Castro's policies improved the lot of Cuba, which had the highest per capita income in Latin America in 1959, in comparison with other Latin Americans, which, in the aggregate, owed U.S. banks roughly $350 billion in 1986? Judgment has always amounted to a balance. Some shake their heads at the rationing caused by shortages; others point to the new classrooms and the virtual elimination of illiteracy. Some call Castro an adventurer in the serious world of international relations; others see him as an expression of realities too long denied.

Domestically, as early as 1970 Castro pointed out that while Cuba's population had grown from 6.55 million people in 1958 to 8.25 million, the nonworking population had been reduced, by his measurement, from 686,000 to 75,000. During that time, he claimed, spending on education had tripled, the number of public school teachers increased fivefold. The number of scholarships, not counting for children in kindergartens or the revolutionary *circulos infantiles*, had been increased from 15,698 to more than a quarter of a million. But at the same time, he conceded, 300,000 to 500,000 Cubans had already fled the island. Individual departures, although severely restricted, continued, and when in 1980 the port of Mariel was opened 120,000 Cubans left their homeland.

Internationally, despite having had to yield in the past to Soviet direction on the large questions, Castro managed to play a revolutionary role other Latin American rebels could only imagine. He made himself pariah or hero, depending on one's point of view, providing soldiers and civilian workers to revolutionary governments from Angola to Nicaragua. He has given ideas teeth. In exile, Martí warned of U.S. domination; Castro embodied anti–United States sentiment. In the mountains, Sandino sent down proclamations; Castro shipped arms and soldiers. "We will never get on our knees at the feet of imperialism to beg for peace," he said in a typical speech in 1980. The speech, marking the twenty-seventh anniversary of the Moncada attack, was aimed at encouraging the Sandinista government of Nicaragua.

Such public pronouncements, over a period approaching three decades, have shaped our image of Fidel Castro. But a private moment recorded by the Colombian novelist Gabriel García Márquez affords another view. Márquez describes Castro standing at the dock, seeing off a Cuban expeditionary force bound for Angola. The troops were sailing on a rusting freighter, one so old and ill-equipped that fifty-five gallon drums holding water and fuel were lashed to the deck. Hatches were locked open so air could circulate and the fumes from fuel, crudely stored below decks, would not collect and blow up the ship. Castro looked at the woebegone example of international revolution and offered a historical observation: "Anyway," Castro told the troops, "you'll be more comfortable than the expeditionaries on the *Granma*."

Over the years—and into the twenty-first century—Castro blended the mythology of the *Granma* with the realities of modern, often repressive, politics. Against a steady drumbeat of criticism for his harsh treatment of domestic opponents, Castro rallied an impressive array of international defenders. His personal stature grew with every year he withstood the verbal assault of U.S. presidents and ranting television commentators, and his influence increased among the cohort of emerging leftist leaders in Latin America. By the late 1980s, when Cuba's principal international benefactor, the Soviet Union, crumbled under the weight of its own exaggerated importance, Castro had attained sufficient security to withstand—better than many former Soviet bloc countries—the USSR's collapse. Even the pope—John Paul II—smiled as he shook hands with Castro during a 1998 trip to Havana in his long-anticipated attempt to open Cuban church doors wider.

Most importantly to his regime's survival, Castro pulled Cuba's economy past the shoals of the long U.S. embargo and several punitive immigration measures imposed by Congress. In 2000, free-trade exponents finally prevailed on U.S. policy to admit the export of foodstuffs to the island, improving the diets of 11 million Cubans and the balance sheets of Midwestern farmers. And, in 2008, when Fidel Castro, gravely ill, turned over executive power to his younger brother, Raúl, the winds of appeasement and accommodation blew even softer. Whether history, as Castro had claimed more than half a century before, would "absolve" him, he could be sure the hemisphere would always remember him.

19

Ernesto "Che" Guevara

Existential Rebel

1928–1967
(Argentina/Cuba)

Ernesto Guevara, two years younger than Fidel Castro, also grew up in a middle-class family, although one with decidedly more liberal politics. Guevara's mother, Celia de la Serna de Guevara, was an active dissident in Argentina. Although she protected her frail, asthmatic son, it may be presumed that she transmitted her revolutionary idea that events can be controlled, that things can be made better. Guevara acted on that idea not in the schizophrenic political environment of his native country, but in Cuba. It seems clear, however, that had Guevara not met Castro in Mexico City he would surely have made some other revolution in some other place, as, in fact, he would die trying to do in Bolivia.

The family of Ernesto Guevara de la Serna moved from Rosario, where he was born on June 14, 1928, to Buenos Aires when he was two years old. They hoped the new environment would relieve his asthma, but the condition persisted, and his sister Celia would recall their father sleeping with his tiny son's head on his chest because his breathing improved with his head elevated. When the tortured breathing that would plague Guevara all his life continued, the family moved again, this time when he was four, settling in Alta Gracia, in Córdoba province. Finally, his health improved.

Because of the asthma, he at first did not attend school, learning at home from his mother. Later, Celia de Guevara would drive him to school 248 the days he was able to attend, directing his brothers and sisters to get his assignments when he was forced to stay home.

There were four other children, two brothers and two sisters, in a closely knit family. Both Ernesto Guevara Lynch, a civil engineer, and his wife were of old colonial families, his partly Irish in origin, hers Spanish. What was left of inherited lands, however, had been sold, and the family's economic status was firmly middle class. That combination — patrician heritage and middle-class reality — had produced political views that were strongly expressed. Although weakened by asthma herself, Celia de Guevara was an ardent socialist, vociferous enough to get herself jailed briefly in 1964 in Argentina's always volatile politics.

The family's political tutelage didn't end with Celia de Guevara. An uncle, the family poet, contributed to the children's political education by traveling to Spain during its civil war, a war that divided world opinion as no other war had. He returned to write a book, *Spain in the Hands of the People,* which Ricardo Rojo, a long-time friend of Guevara, credits with helping to begin Guevara's leftward trek. Such was the political involvement of Guevara's family that in the 1950s, even as Guevara fought in Cuba's Sierra Maestra mountains to overthrow the Batista government; his second cousin was serving as Argentina's ambassador to that government.

Early in life, Guevara began a practice — on foot, bicycle, and motorbike — of observing Latin America, like a Darwin examining the subjects for whom he would later adopt a universal theory. Refusing to let his asthma interfere, he toughened himself playing rugby in school and first, while still a schoolboy, walked about Argentina, later embarking on longer motorbike and motorcycle trips. In 1950, his letter to the manufacturer of the "Micrón" motorbike served as a testimonial used by the company in its advertising. Under a picture of the twenty-two-year-old Guevara was his endorsement for a machine that could carry him "4,000 kilometers through the Argentine provinces." The next year he and a friend set out northward into Chile on motorcycles, working at odd jobs as the need arose.

On these trips he cultivated, if that is the proper term, his ability to eat when food was available, to do without when necessary. His rugby teammates nicknamed him "Pig" because of his careless disregard for manners, but he began to take on something more like the digestive system of a snake. He would eat prodigious amounts of food when invited to table — and when he knew there was a period of abstinence coming. When times were lean, he bore them, apparently happily, by eating almost nothing. It was as if he were schooling himself in survival.

Although good in mathematics, Guevara confounded family predictions that he would follow his father's career as an engineer. He chose medical school, taking a particular interest in tropical diseases and focusing on leprosy. He was also interested in archeology, the study of Latin America's ancient Indians.

In his travels he indulged these interests, visiting in Peru, for example, both Macchu Picchu, an ancient settlement, and a leper colony. The trips, however, always seemed to find their principal justification in adventure, in survival. Leaving Peru, Guevara and a friend went on to Colombia, were deported, and ended up in Venezuela. Then, while his friend stayed behind in Caracas, Guevara hitched a ride on a transport plane carrying thoroughbreds to Miami. He later told friends he survived in the city on Cuban *café con leche*.

He returned to Buenos Aires to complete medical school, crowding into one year, as had Martí, a heavy load of classes, as though there were many pursuits more important than school. He graduated in the spring of 1953 when he was twenty-five years old. As soon as he was able he was declared unfit for military duty because of his asthma he set out, by train, to rejoin his friend in Venezuela.

As Guevara continued his travels, he was intent upon observing the Indians in the highlands, silent, sullen, and often stoned on *coca*. He rode with them, standing in the backs of trucks to better scrutinize them, declining the privileged seat in the cab that was offered because of his European appearance. Among his observations was that the Indians were suspicious of him; although politically unorganized themselves, they seemed unreceptive to outside ideas. It was a lesson later driven home. Nevertheless, at the time Guevara was traveling, it was popular to believe that Bolivia provided fertile ground for revolution because the political consciousness of its miners, it was thought, could be mixed with the peasant strength of its Indians. He would return to test precisely that theory.

In Bolivia, Guevara met Rojo, an Argentine political refugee. As a tattered band of students traveled about Latin America without apparent aim, Rojo convinced his new friend to go to Guatemala, where it appeared a new day was being built. Guatemala, Rojo convinced Guevara, was where the model revolution was in progress. There, struggling since World War II to overcome the dominance of U.S. interests, the archetype of which was the United Fruit Company, a series of revolutionary governments had labored to survive. Guevara abandoned the idea of putting his medicine to work for lepers and decided he would work, instead, for revolutionaries.

Guevara and a companion struck out up the isthmus by ship, foot, and thumb. They stopped in Costa Rica, where José Figueres' liberal government provided sanctuary for political exiles, some of whom belonged to the romantic "Caribbean Legion," democratic activists in a hemisphere dominated by military dictators. At sidewalk cafes, Guevara met Rómulo Betancourt of Venezuela and Juan Bosch of the Dominican Republic.

He also met escaped Cuban survivors of the 26th of July raid on the Moncada barracks. Rojo recalled: "To both Guevara and myself, it seemed that these excited young men were living a fantasy. They talked of summary executions, dynamite attacks, military demonstrations in the universities, kidnappings, and machine-gun fire; and they talked in a way so natural that it made our heads spin.... It was from them that Guevara first heard about Fidel Castro."

Guevara reached Guatemala just months before the CIA directed coup that ended the ten-year experiment. Because he refused to join the Communist party, he was denied a license to practice medicine, but stayed to work in the bureaucracy. He did not leave the country until the government of Jacobo Arbenz was at the point of collapse. Guevara watched the Arbenz government let itself get thrown out in the summer of 1954 by a small, rag-tag army conscripted by the Central Intelligence Agency and organized in Honduras—then as now a jumping-off point for U.S. policy. The government fell, in Guevara's view, because internal dissent and confusion prevented a concerted counterattack.

During the final days, Guevara was informed by an Argentine diplomat that his name was on a list of people to be executed by the new regime. His participation in the revolutionary government, although short-lived, had made at least enough of an impression to mark him for death. This was the first instance of Guevara's unfortunate capacity for sticking up, as short as he was, like a lightning rod. He tended to give full rein to his contempt for anyone less committed than he, and it was not a characteristic easily overlooked. He took refuge in the Argentine embassy, but declined the chance to return to Buenos Aires. He chose safe-conduct to Mexico City.

There he made a paltry living selling books door-to-door or as a street photographer, working in the latter enterprise with a Guatemalan with whom he shared his apartment. In Mexico, Guevara married Hilda Gadea, a Peruvian woman of Indian-Chinese extraction he'd met in Guatemala. Rojo called her "an unselfish companion of the exiles." When their daughter was born in February 1955, she was named for her mother.

Hilda was a friend of several Cuban expatriates waiting in Mexico City for Castro to be released from prison. Among them, Guevara found a spiritual home. When Guevara was again given the chance to return to Argentina, as Perón finally was driven out, for the second time he declined. He stayed in Mexico City and was introduced to Castro one summer night in 1955. Talking into the morning, Guevara threw in his lot with the planned invasion. In November 1956, although Castro excluded other foreigners, Guevara took his place with eighty-one Cubans on the *Granma*. His asthma exacerbated the seasickness that afflicted everyone, and Guevara was ill throughout the voyage.

Immediately upon landing, Guevara later wrote, he was put to a test. Batista forces were instantly upon them; would he remain the force's physician or take arms? Under fire from the air and ground troops, the small force was confused and split up. Guevara and several others saw as their only escape a field of sugarcane. He had to decide whether to concern himself only with the wounded, or to fight. "At my feet were a pack full of medicine and a cartridge box," he wrote. "Together, they were too heavy to carry. I chose the cartridge box, leaving behind the medicine pack." He was wounded in the neck and chest before staggering to relative safety with his comrades, several of whom were even more severely hurt.

Batista's troops set the cane field afire, but Guevara was among the survivors who made it until nightfall and escaped.

He continued in a dual role, acting as doctor to the rebels, occasionally caring for wounded Batista troops, and, out of necessity, even becoming a dentist. But Guevara's bravery — a seeming lack of concern for safety despite having been wounded twice — attracted notice. The Cubans were impressed that exceptional courage was being shown by a man who was fighting not for his own country, but theirs. During the battle at Uvero, an early, successful clash that did much to build rebel confidence, Guevara volunteered to recover some rifles lost by nervous rebels under fire. Castro began to trust Guevara in a guerrilla war in which commanders were also teachers, confessors, kind uncles, and harsh judges all rolled into one. No one was a professional soldier, so as raw recruits straggled in from the city, they had to be motivated and reassured as well as trained. Eventually, Guevara was given command of a column.

Guevara's importance to the Cuban revolution, however, was not as a fighter. Guevara himself kept his record as a warrior in context. He wrote of returning to one battle site from which he had been forced to take to his heels: "There I found a piece of my blanket tangled in the brambles as a reminder of my speedy 'strategic retreat.'" Like Archilocus of Pylos, Guevara's contribution to the lore of battle was more lyrical than tactical. His diaries reveal the everyday drudgery of living off the land, learning all that could be learned from the peasants, fighting an enemy that had more of everything except will.

If Guevara was compelled to rebel, so was he obsessed with the idea of recording everything, from inventories to emotions, in his diaries. That writing is relatively free of the leaden dogma that characterizes much communist "literature." In the case of twenty-five months in the Sierra Maestra, his diaries, edited after victory, provide one of the most complete chronicles of guerrilla warfare. His descriptions of battles, his observations of both enemy and ally, his expression of his own and others' feelings, all distinguish Guevara as neither a great leader nor a great warrior, but as a simple human being experiencing the kind of warfare only imagined by the many who would rebel, but do not.

"That night the weapons arrived. For us it was the most marvelous spectacle in the world: the instruments of death were on exhibition before the covetous eyes of all the men.... A few days later, on May 23 [1957], Fidel ordered new discharges, among them an entire squad, and our force was reduced to 127 men, the majority of them armed and about 80 of them well armed.... There remained one man named Crucito who later became one of our best-loved fighters. Crucito was a natural poet and he had long rhyming matches with the city-poet, Calixto Morales. Morales had arrived on the *Granma* and had nicknamed himself 'nightingale of the plains,' to which Crucito ... directed in mock derision at Calixto, 'I'm an old Sierra buzzard.'"

From the moment the rebels landed —"disoriented and walking in circles, an army of shadows, of phantoms, walking as if moved by some obscure psychic mechanism"— until they entered Havana, it was Guevara who gave voice to the revolution. From rebel headquarters, Castro issued pronouncements, declarations, manifestos. But as supreme commander he was kept safe during battles. It was Guevara who recorded the terror. "His name was Armando Rodriguez and he carried a Thompson submachine gun," Guevara tells us from precise notes and shared experience. "Toward the end, he had such a terrified and anguished face whenever he heard shots in the distance that we called that expression *cara de cerco*, 'the face of the surrounded.'"

Movement, distrust, constant vigilance: these, Guevara lectures, were the cardinal requirements of successful guerrilla tactics. In the early days the rebel army risked extinction, eating raw crabs, making reed straws to suck water from tiny pools among the rocks, drawing weak sustenance from sugarcane. If hunger did not incapacitate them, disease was the next risk. Guevara contracted malaria. If the army outside the sierra could not penetrate the rugged terrain, spies were always possible. Guevara recounts the story of Eutemio Guerra, the peasant who worked his way into the rebel force, betraying the rebels' position three times while awaiting his chance to assassinate Castro, a chance only narrowly missed.

When fifty new men, many recruited in Santiago, were marched in, it took weeks to determine whether they had the mettle, mental and physical, to remain. "A few other boys left us," Guevara writes, "a fact that was to the advantage of the troops. I remember one of them had an attack of nerves, there in the solitude of mountains and guerrillas. He began to shout that he had been promised a camp with abundant food and anti-aircraft defenses, and that now the planes harassed him and he had neither permanent quarters, nor food, nor even water to drink. Afterward, those who stayed and passed the first tests grew accustomed to dirt, to lack of water, food, shelter and security, and to continually rely only on a rifle and the cohesion and resistance of the small guerrilla nucleus."

Guevara's notes also record his sense of personal development. At first he felt conspicuous, as if his nickname, *el argentino,* were the Cubans' way of isolating him. Although he was willing to risk his own neck, he tended to be tentative in command. He was reprimanded by Castro for not being assertive. Then, a delivery of weapons, distributed on a strict merit system, assured him of his worth when he was placed in command of an automatic- rifle squad. "In this way," he recounted, "I made my debut as a fighting guerrilla, for until then I had been the troop's doctor, knowing only occasional combat. I had entered a new stage."

In late 1958, Batista's generals made a last attempt to destroy the rebels before the staged elections planned for November. The army moved into the sierra and encircled Castro's army, but fell far short of the victory needed. "After two and a half months of steady skirmishing," Guevara wrote in a kind of gleeful accounting, "the enemy had a thousand casualties—dead, wounded, captured and deserters. They had abandoned to us six hundred weapons, including one tank, twelve mortars, twelve tripod machine guns, and an impressive quantity of automatic weapons, not counting an incredible amount of equipment and ammunition of all sorts, plus four hundred and fifty prisoners, whom we turned over to the Red Cross at the end of the campaign."

When the time came for what would be the rebels' final offensive, Guevara marched his column toward Santa Clara, the railroad center for the central plain, under difficult conditions. Without trucks, through a cyclone, under fire, twice surrounded, the column staggered into Las Villas province, new territory for the guerrillas. Guevara conceded that closer to Havana the peasants were not as sympathetic as they had been in Oriente. In mid–October, he reached the relative safety of the Trinidad-Sancti Spiritus mountain range. His mission was to upset the elections.

With Camilo Cienfuegos, another column commander, Guevara directed the decisive battles up to and into Santa Clara, a city of 150,000. The battle for the city Guevara sketched, including the story of a soldier he encountered in a rebel field hospital during the battle.

It was a man, now mortally wounded, whom Guevara had earlier found disarmed and asleep "at the height of a battle" and whom Guevara had ordered "with my customary dryness, 'Go to the front lines barehanded and come back with another gun, if you are man enough.'" In the field hospital, from his makeshift bed, the man reached up, "touched my hand and said, 'Remember, major? You sent me to find a gun at Remedios.... I brought it here.'" The soldier died "a few minutes later. It seemed to me that he was pleased to have proved his courage. Such was our Rebel Army."

Victory was more complicated. The administration of a thoroughly dependent, undeveloped, historically exploited island economy and the design and construction of a new society were problems considerably more intractable than beating Batista's army. The infighting; the counter-revolutionary sabotage; the difficulty of understanding, then improving, the economy; the embargo by the United States these were not battles the men of the Sierra Maestra could win with automatic weapons. Guevara, ultimately, retreated from those wars and sought once again the kind of war he understood.

Guevara brought to Havana an easy grace that captured imaginations in a way the looming figure of Castro did not. As director of the National Bank, Guevara signed new money, simply, "Che." For admirers, the signature signaled revolutionary flair, but for Guevara, it completed a journey. He had been dubbed "Che" in Mexico City by the same Cubans who would isolate him in the sierra as *el argentino.* Now the name fluttered like a banner.

To Castro's dead-pan, long-winded *jefe máximo* of the new society, Guevara played a kind of intelligent jester—committed, but with a sense of humor. He made light of the new leadership's inability to manipulate the economy the Yankees had left behind. Coke tasted like bitter syrup and toothpaste turned so hard it could not be squeezed from the tube, Guevara admitted. But, patience, socialist morality would prevail. What was needed at the moment was style, and he was the embodiment of that style.

In mid–1959, six months after he and Cienfuegos had led their troops into Havana— and about the time five new cabinet ministers were being forced to resign—Guevara was sent abroad as a kind of traveling spokesman for rebellion. He cut a rhetorical swath for three months from Yugoslavia and Egypt to Ceylon and Japan. As far as international sympathizers were concerned, Guevara was a fetching symbol, with his beret, his scant beard, his good looks, and his ability to turn a phrase.

In December 1959, heading a trade mission to East Germany, Guevara met Haydee Tamara Bunke Bider, the attractive daughter of a college professor. Two years later she would visit Cuba on his invitation. To whoever was watching, it would have appeared the natural consequence of the meeting of two attractive people committed to the same ideas. It would eventually be revealed, however, that this was an early piece of an international jigsaw puzzle, a puzzle that would only be understood after Guevara and "Tanya the Guerrilla" were both dead.

In Havana, after the hardships of the mountains, Guevara slipped easily into the role of international celebrity, compensating at the banquet table for the years of deprivation in the sierra. His friend Rojo, who had not seen him since before the *Granma* expedition, found him well fattened. The breast pockets of his khaki shirt, however, still bulged with asthma medicine, and his face was bloated from cortisone. Also, his old friend was now cautious enough about assassination attempts that he carried in his Jeep a cigar box filled not with his favorite Cuban cigars but with U.S. made fragmentation hand grenades. Rojo found all Havana in preparation for the invasion that would come in February 1961 at the Bay of Pigs. During the invasion, Guevara, already bearing scars in the neck, chest, and foot from the sierra campaign, managed to get wounded again by dropping his automatic pistol and shooting himself in the cheek.

In addition to being a major in the army and directing the National Bank—and serving as chairman of the committee directing the new Bank of Foreign Commerce—Guevara was chosen to direct industrial development. Schooled as a physician and having shown aptitude as a guerrilla, he was a prime example of how the Cuban revolution's enormous possibilities had to be realized by people outside their fields of competence.

Castro created an all-powerful Instituto Nacional de la Reforma Agraria, or INRA, and it was from that fount that all policy was to flow. Guevara's industrial development office was a part of that structure. Edward Boorstein, an American economist who went to Cuba, wrote: "You could see and feel in the halls and offices of the INRA headquarters in Havana that it was a revolutionary organization. Here were not the prim, old-line functionaries of the National Bank or Treasury, but bearded rebels in uniform, carrying arms. The working hours were not the 9-to-5 of the ordinary government worker. They were the irregular hours— the nocturnal hours— of the guerrilla fighter. Meetings could start at midnight and last till daybreak."

Guevara had remarried, a Cuban woman, Aleida, and happily adopted the practice of working on administrative matters until midnight, then sitting, talking with friends and drinking *mate,* the traditional tea that Guevara made from herbs brought to him from Argentina. Guevara warned his colleagues that they were being observed by their fellow Cubans, who would be quick to notice signs that old, corrupt ways might be allowed to return. If style was important, it had to convey frugality and honesty.

There was also a hidden side. It is important to recognize that virtually from the day he walked into Havana from the sierra, as he assumed his role of public spokesman, worked as a member of the cabinet, went home to visit his family, received awards from other nations, and spoke at lecterns from New York to Punta del Este, Guevara's hand was in subversion. As he did tricks for his many admirers with one hand, the other was out of sight, making rebellion.

He hung an oilcloth map of Argentina in his bathroom, the better to contemplate revolutionary options in his native land, and in 1961–62, he helped establish a "revolutionary focus" in the northern mountains. Using Cuban fighters, it was led by an Argentine friend, Jorge Masetti, who was known as *El Segundo* to recognize Guevara as the principal leader. By the spring of 1964, it was wiped out, casting Guevara into grief over the loss of friends, but not convincing him that the Cuban model could not be transferred. While the world was transfixed by the missile crisis in 1962, Guevara was supporting another rebellion in the mountains of Peru, a movement eradicated by 1965. In both instances, a reasonably efficient, trained, motivated military found and destroyed the rebel forces, but Guevara was still convinced his design would work. He envisioned an axis of rebellion from Peru through Bolivia into northern Argentina. "Violence is the midwife of new societies," he assured Rojo.

In public, Guevara became a spokesman for hope. If the United States would not buy Cuban exports, the socialist nations would have to. Guevara went to Europe, to Asia. With his eagerly reported statements in the press, he became the embodiment of the notion that the Cuban revolution could be exported.

Eventually, however, after the trade agreements were signed and the loans extended, words began to have a hollow sound. His capacity for talking rather than for listening, made enemies at home among confused, pressured cabinet members. He was a bit too quick with opinions that rolled over delicate relationships.

In 1964, while Guevara's public image was maintained, changes were occurring. His inability to accept others' ideas, his arrogance, isolated him in the cabinet. If at lecterns from Geneva to Algiers he was the toast of international rebellion, in Cuba he was an annoyance. There was the impression that a breach had been opened between Guevara and Castro although the reality was that the two were clandestinely planning subversion on two continents.

In April, after arranging to send Cuban troops to help Congolese rebels, Guevara wrote in a private letter to Castro that "the time has come for us to part." Guevara went briefly to Africa with the troops, but reality directed him back toward his old interest, revolution in Latin America.

Divesting himself of his rank and Cuban citizenship, he wrote, not altogether accurately, "Nothing legal binds me to Cuba.... The only ties are of another nature; those that cannot be broken as appointments can." From then on, Guevara wrote, he would "carry to new battle-fronts the faith that you taught me, the revolutionary spirit of my people, the feeling of fulfilling the most sacred of duties: to fight against imperialism where it may be. This comforts and heals the deepest wounds."

What bound him to Cuba was both illegal and secret: logistical support and volunteers for his revolutionary adventures. Guevara dropped from public sight, but he and Castro remained inextricably joined. With his wife expecting their fourth child, Guevara said publicly that he wanted to work in a factory, to absorb himself with the simpler tasks of building a new economy. It was widely interpreted not that he was going underground, but that he was being banished to some minor post.

His mother, in a letter he would never see, written only weeks before she died of cancer, asked why Cuba's revolutionary leaders spent so much time winning the sympathies of the people rather than improving government. "It seems to me true madness," she wrote, "that with so few heads in Cuba with ability to organize you should all go cut cane for a month as your main job when there are so many and such good cane cutters among the people." His plans, she suggested, meant "that the madness has turned to absurdity." With the tenderness of a mother and tenacity of an old socialist, she insisted that if he was unappreciated in Cuba he should go back to Ghana or Algeria to do revolutionary work. "Yes, you will always be a foreigner. That seems to be your permanent fate."

At the time Guevara was assembling 125 Cuban fighters to join Congolese rebels, but the six-month expedition was a failure. The Congolese annoyed Guevara with their corruption and lack of willingness to fight. He urged Castro to drop Cuba's support, and, undercover, returned to Cuba.

In October 1965, six months after Guevara had last been seen in public, Castro made public his letter renouncing his responsibilities in Cuba. He was still not seen in public, however, and the effect, for his many admirers, was mysterious, romantic.

In fact, plans were well advanced toward a Bolivian "focus." A network of supply and information was established by operatives from Cuba, including the East German woman, the one known as "Tanya." Posing as an Argentine national, she adopted several covers and was able to broadcast advice-to-the-lovelorn over a radio station — sentimental messages that carried codes for Guevara's guerrillas, whom she would later join. Castro, Guevara, and their intermediaries made contact with Bolivian communists, although the effort was half-hearted and never risked allowing the divided, Moscow-oriented party to interfere. Bolivia was the keystone in a potential series of revolutionary enclaves in Argentina, Paraguay, and Peru, and neither Castro nor Guevara was prepared to let European party dogma get in the way of Latin American design.

"Once again I feel between my heels the ribs of Rosinante," he wrote to his mother and father in the spring of 1965. "Once more I hit the road with my shield upon my arm. Almost ten years ago today, I wrote you another letter of farewell. As I remember, I lamented not being a better soldier and a better doctor. The latter no longer interests me; I'm not such a bad soldier."

Into Bolivia traveled a man carrying the passport of Ramón Borges Fernández. The passport, one of two the man carried, showed he had flown from Havana to Prague to Frankfurt to Brazil to La Paz. The man was portly, clean-shaven, wearing heavy horn-rim glasses, and bald. His occupation was identified as "businessman." Guevara had transformed himself, as his mother said, into yet another foreigner.

Using the code name "Ramón," Guevara was headed for a remote farm in Nancahuazú. Eight stalwarts of the sierra who had accompanied him to the Congo were with him. Out of Nancahuaz operated seventeen Cubans, all officers of the Cuban army, and three Peruvian veterans of the unsuccessful revolution there. To them they would gather twenty-nine Bolivians—as in the Cuban experience some city people, some peasants—and depend on a small, fragile network of operatives in the city. It is unlikely that Guevara knew Haydee Tamara Bunke Bider was a double agent. While working for him, she was also employed by East German security forces—and, in turn, the Soviet KGB. Apparently, her role was to keep an eye on Guevara and Castro, who had a marked tendency to make revolution on their own, independent of Moscow, as they were doing now.

"A new stage begins today," Guevara wrote on November 7, 1966, upon arriving at the safe house in Nancahuazú. He had last been seen in public in March 1965, and it amused him greatly that when his driver found out who his passenger was the shock almost killed them both. "While heading toward the farm on his second trip, 'Bigotes,' who had just discovered my identity, almost drove off a cliff, leaving the jeep stuck on the edge of the precipice. We walked about 20 kilometers to the farm." Five days later he reported, "My beard is growing and in a couple of months I shall start looking like myself again."

But nothing would ever be the same. Nancahuazú was in the middle of a vast, rugged wilderness that would have swallowed the entire island of Cuba. The land was uninhabited for great stretches, and the guerrillas wandered aimlessly. They had to hide even from hunters for fear of discovery. What natives they did encounter spoke an Indian dialect the guerrillas had not planned on. The peasants, unlike those of the Sierra Maestra, were often hostile and informed on them. Government broadcasts capitalized on the fact that so many of the guerrillas were foreigners. Government troops, on the other hand, were largely natives of the area, recruited nearby, defending their homeland, able to communicate with their countrymen. And whereas Batista had cowered in Havana, Rene Barrientos, the Bolivian leader whose own background was a humble one, would fly out to inspect his troops with a machine gun slung jauntily from his shoulder. He once landed within 250 yards of where Guevara lay hidden.

Less than four months after Guevara arrived in Bolivia, the first of his fighters was lost, not to hostile fire, but to the hostile environment. Exhausted from marching over the mountain terrain, he slipped and fell from a rock into a treacherous stream and was carried away. Once again Guevara's diary was the chronicle of the effort, but this time it was written mostly in despair. "Nothing new from La Paz. Nothing new here."

Simply holding the group together was a burden. There were continual arguments with the Bolivian Communist party over who was in charge. To join Guevara was to defy the party line. "I spoke to the entire group, giving them 'the facts of life' on the realities of war," he wrote on December 12. "I emphasized the one-man command system of discipline and warned the Bolivians of the responsibility they took in violating the discipline of their party in adopting another line." After listening on the radio to a Castro speech broadcast from Cuba that referred to their tiny, isolated fight, Guevara wrote: "He referred to us in terms that obligate us even more, if that is possible."

Yet very little was possible. In February 1967 a second rebel drowned. By March, with the group almost as large as it would get, about forty fighters, he despaired. "The men are getting increasingly discouraged at seeing the approaching end of the provisions, but not of the distance to be covered."

On March 23, there was a seductive success. An ambush killed seven government soldiers and a civilian guide and captured mortars, radios, boots, and eighteen prisoners. "A major and a captain, prisoners, talked like parrots," Guevara wrote in a tone that conveyed elation.

Guevara heard on the radio that the government still denied guerrillas were operating in the country. Then he heard that their base camp had been discovered. Two deserters were captured. Military attachés from Argentina, Brazil, and Paraguay had flown into La Paz to observe. Was this the continental revolt Castro had promised?

Barrientos ordered bombing raids and declared, yes, Guevara, the feared Guevara, was there with the guerrillas, but now he was dead. Another Bolivian leader said, yes, and not only was Guevara dead, they were all dead, all of them. Guevara listened to the radio and hung on.

Guevara treated his prisoners humanely and released them after trying to give the impression he headed a well-organized, efficient, and large force. On April 10 another ambush caused nineteen government casualties; the government, in retaliation, suspended activities of the Bolivian Communist party. Then Guevara heard that sixteen U.S. Special Forces "advisors" would train a Bolivian battalion, something rebels never had to deal with in Cuba. He wrote: "We may be witnessing the first episode of a new Vietnam."

What he was witnessing was the beginning of the end. On April 17, the group, forty-five rebels, was inadvertently split, a mistake, caused by the rugged terrain that would prove fatal. Five days later a clash killed four guerrillas and wounded several others in Guevara's reduced group. Two more clashes followed. "It will take time to transform this into a fighting force," he wrote, adding hopefully, "Although morale is rather high."

The government, perhaps getting reports on both halves of the guerrilla army, estimated it at twice its size, but kept up the pressure. Guevara who figured by early May the rebels had killed twenty-three soldiers, placed his hopes on a miners' revolt and accelerated help from the Communist party. Neither occurred.

His analysis for May: "Total lack of contact" with the other half of the group. "Complete lack of peasant recruitment." Guevara called for a "National Liberation Army," asking Bolivians "to close ranks, to weld the tightest unity without distinction of political colors." It had all the effect of a manifesto issued by Sandino.

Guevara was trapped, cut off. He was satisfied with the government's acknowledgment it was he, in fact, who led the guerrillas. The thought of retreat, leaving Bolivia, never occurred to him. "I am now 39," Guevara wrote on June 14, "and am relentlessly approaching the age when I must think about my future as a guerrilla; in the meantime, I am 'complete.'"

In early July, Guevara's group decided to stop a truck on the road near tiny Samaipata — but another stopped behind it. Then a third driver stopped to see what was happening, and a fourth because the road was blocked. The episode would represent the final, exuberant cry of the guerrillas. They finally got around to going into town, capturing two shocked local policemen and the chief of the post. "Then they took over the barracks and ten soldiers in lightning actions," Guevara cheered. "The action took place before the whole village and many travelers in such a way that the news will spread like fire."

The news spread across the world, but the guerrillas left town without taking medicine Guevara needed for his asthma. Denied a safe zone and forced to constantly move, Guevara fell too sick to march. He had to hold himself on horseback and be floated across streams on rafts. Nights in the mountains were cold. When their tape recorder was lost so was their ability to capture radio messages for decoding. Their comptroller in La Paz absconded with a quarter of a million rebel dollars. Caches of arms were discovered. Deserters led the army closer.

"July 27: My asthma hit me hard." On August 26, "Everything went wrong." Guevara's mistakes were exacerbated by the army's increasing efficiency. "August 30: The situation is becoming desperate." The jungle was so thick that the macheteros in front could not keep going at the altitude they were forced to travel.

On August 31 the other, separated, column was caught fording a stream and wiped out, the East German woman along with them. Even before learning of their demise, Guevara wrote in his monthly analysis, "It was, without doubt, the worst month we have had so far in this war."

In late September, a village official apparently warned the army the guerrillas could be found near Alto Seco, a dot on the map at 1,900 meters, and on September 26, after climbing to 2,280 meters, Guevara's group was cut to pieces by a pursuing army patrol.

September analysis: "It would have been a month of recuperation and it was just about to be, but the ambush in which they got Miguel, Coco and Julio ruined everything and we have been left in a dangerous position.... The army appears to be more effective in its actions, and the peasants do not give us any help and are turning into informers."

Nevertheless, on October 7, Guevara wrote, "We completed the 11th month of our guerrilla operations in a bucolic mood." After resting, "the 17 of us set out with a very small moon. The march was very tiring and we left a lot of traces along the canyon.... Altitude 2000 meters."

On October 8, Guevara fought his last fight. He and his remaining sixteen men were trapped in a shallow canyon. Guevara was second in the guerrilla column when it made contact with a Bolivian ranger patrol. In the lead, a Bolivian miner returned the patrol's fire and the guerrillas tried to retreat. They were unable to scramble their way back up the slope or to make their fire effective. Guevara was hit in the legs, and the miner, Simón Cuba, carried him. Guevara was hit again.

Cuba propped Guevara against a tree and tried to defend him until he was cut down. Guevara tried to fire his machine gun with one hand, but was hit yet again, in the leg. Then a bullet hit his trigger, splitting the gun's stock and knocking it from his hand before ricocheting into his right forearm. He was defenseless and captured.

Although bleeding, Guevara was not mortally wounded. He spoke to the two officers in charge, a captain and a colonel. They had him placed on a makeshift stretcher and carried to the village of La Higuera, where he was set down in an empty room of the schoolhouse. They left. Decisions had to be made.

Was Guevara, the international figure, to be taken to Vallegrande for medical help? If so, should he be given preference over wounded soldiers? The colonel was on the phone. The decisions would be reached in La Paz.

The next day, Guevara was sitting on the floor of the schoolroom, propped with his shoulder against the wall, when the captain and the colonel returned. The captain walked behind him. With a machine gun, he fired a burst, hitting Guevara four times in the neck and upper back. The colonel fired his pistol once into Guevara's heart.

His body was taken to Vallegrande and displayed on a table in a public laundry.

20

Bishop Romero
Modern Martyr
1917–1980
(El Salvador)

In Latin America, oppressive governments have always sought the complicity, or at least the docility, of the Roman Catholic Church. During colonization, the Spanish king, commissioned by the pope, was secular head of the Church; he counted on priests to do his bidding. From the beginning, however, some priests answered to a higher law, standing at the side of the oppressed. Father Bartolomé de Las Casas won the title "Protector of the Indians" in the early sixteenth century; the Mexican priests Hidalgo and Morelos led the Mexican rebellion; Jesuits have periodically been at odds with kings and *caudillos,* and, in modern times, some priests, compelled by their understanding of Christianity, have gone into the hills to join guerrillas. Archbishop Romero, by inclination a conservative man who opposed public demonstrations of dissent, was cast into the middle of the continuing civil war in Latin America's smallest country. That war was being fought over ancient and fundamental questions of land tenure and the exploitation of workers, but Romero could have remained safe in his priestly vestments. He chose, as a matter of conscience, to step into the line of fire.

Oscar Arnulfo Romero y Galdámez was born on August 15, 1917, in Ciudad Barrios, in El Salvador's highlands near Honduras. It was a small town without electricity, reached only by foot or on horseback, in an area where Indian blood was dominant. His father, Santos, from a nearby village, was sent to Ciudad Barrios by the government in 1903 to serve as postmaster and telegrapher. He operated both services out of a modest stucco home on the plaza and married Guadalupe de Jesús, who bore him eight children, one of whom died in infancy. Santos, who also sired several children outside the family, augmented his income by growing cacao and coffee on twenty acres outside of town.

Oscar was the second oldest child. He was of medium height and rather wiry, and had his mother's prominent chin. Throughout his life, his nature seemed to balance between frailty and tenacity, fatigue and a fearsome temper. As a boy, he delivered telegraph messages in the town and learned how to operate a telegraph and read Morse code. He attended the small school overseen by a single teacher, learned to play the flute and harmonium, and, at the age of twelve or thirteen, was apprenticed to a carpenter.

According to Romero's principal biographer, Father James R. Brockman, S.J., the youthful Romero himself broached the subject of studying for the priesthood, to the dismay of his father. His brothers and sisters were not surprised, having noticed their brother visiting the church on his own. He went off to the seminary at San Miguel, but left during the Depression to work in a gold mine near Ciudad Barrios, perhaps to help pay the medical expenses of his ailing mother. Two brothers also worked at the mine.

The Depression weighed hard on El Salvador, a country barely twice the size of New Jersey and dependent on coffee exports. It is a country that never has rested easily, although at times it has been kept quiet by agreement among the dominant families. At other times it has been split by civil war. From 1913 to 1930, fueled by high coffee prices and administered by a relatively stable government, El Salvador progressed. But coffee prices crashed in 1930, and the next decade witnessed a harsh civil war that installed a dictatorship; the 1940s gave birth to another war to unseat that dictatorship. So its history continued, the army and national guard by turns taking power and mediating between conflicting elites.

In 1937, after three years' absence, Romero returned to his studies and was sent to the national seminary run by Jesuits. Seven months later, having proved himself a scholar, he was sent on to study in Rome. Romero was in Rome at the outset of World War II. While there, he learned of the deaths of his father — and the subsequent loss of the family farm to creditors— and of a brother. He was ordained in the spring of 1942 and intended to stay in Italy to earn a doctorate, specializing in "ascetical theology." But the war made it impossible, and he returned to say his first mass for friends and relatives in January 1944.

His first parish was in a small mountain village, but he was soon called to the city of San Miguel to serve as diocesan secretary. Because others in the family were unable to take care of her, his mother lived with Romero until her death in 1961. His diocesan duties included editing a weekly, and Romero developed into something of a stylist; his homilies, when saying mass at a small colonial church in San Miguel, were broadcast over a local radio station. However fluid his style, Romero's view of the Church was staunchly conservative. Protestants complained when he refused to let them use the cathedral to honor the nineteenth century patriot Gerardo Barrios because Barrios had been a Mason. Brockman dryly notes of Romero's position in the community: "By refusing Christian burial to Masons, he alienated various families."

In the mid–1950s, Romero participated in a month of devotions conducted by Jesuits, whose role in the Salvadoran civil war would be pivotal. "Romero had had at least indirect exposure to Ignatian spirituality through his Jesuit teachers in San Salvador and Rome," Father Brockman writes. "There is nothing quite like making the exercises themselves, however. Some clue to their effect on him is the phrase from the exercises that he later took as his Episcopal motto: *Sentir con la iglesia*, To be of one mind with the church."

Father Brockman, himself a Jesuit, recognizes that the "effect" of Jesuitical training must be, by turns, extolled or explained. This is especially true in the context of Latin America. Founded by Spanish soldier-turned-priest Ignatius Loyola in 1534, the order has trained some of the sharpest minds of the Church. Yet it has also earned for itself a reputation that inspires the second definition of Jesuit: "one given to intrigue or equivocation."

The Jesuits' predilection for "intrigue" has continually put the order's members at loggerheads with governments. In 1767 — after French Jesuits refused absolution to the king's enlightened mistress— the strain became so severe that Charles III of Spain expelled all Jesuits from Latin America. Other priests declined to defend or protect them, and Jesuits were literally packed up and shipped back to Spain.

Also of significant effect on Latin America and on Romero was a series of liberalizing influences on the church. These began with the conferences of bishops in Rome from 1962 to 1965 that are known collectively as Vatican II. Latin was joined in the liturgy by parishioners' own languages; lay members were given more of a place ceremonially and administratively in the life of the Church; the hierarchical mentality of the traditional Roman Catholic Church was modified, softened. The Church opened up, and the new atmosphere was perceived by many as a threat. The liberality was seen by conservatives as blasphemous. Reformers looked to a new spirit of cooperation.

To apply the principles of Vatican II, Latin American bishops convened in Medellín, Colombia, in 1968. New principles for the Church, in Latin America, would apply side-by-side with very old, very oppressive economic and social conditions. Decisions made at Medellín were especially radical because they signaled change in an environment of oppression. The conference at Medellín allowed communication among those priests whose most leftward inclinations have come to be associated with the term "liberation theology." That term encapsulates the notion that the Church belongs firmly at the side of the poor and must accept, as a legitimate worldview, the Marxist interpretation that maldistribution of wealth creates class conflict.

In 1967, as these ideas were beginning to spin about in discussions, Romero was transferred — despite parishioners' petitions to let him stay — from San Miguel to the capital, San Salvador. He was given the title of monsignor and named secretary-general of the national bishops conference. In the spring of the next year he was named executive secretary of the Central American Bishops Secretariat.

Romero was known as thorough, contemplative, and conservative. When he was named auxiliary bishop in May 1970, the elaborate ceremony marking his elevation was seen by some as an example of the Church's historic "triumphalism" — which so often placed clerics at the shoulder of oppressors, softly assuring the oppressed that their kingdom was in heaven. Romero's conservative reputation had much to do with his continuing progress within the hierarchy.

By coincidence, the day after Romero's elevation to bishop 123 priests convened in San Salvador to discuss the implications of Vatican II and the Medellín conference. Because liberalization was so painfully controversial, about half of the clerics in the country indicated their opposition to change by staying away. "To a person schooled in a vision of life in which one must accept suffering and seek peace and harmony at any price," writes Father Brockman, "such ideas involve a considerable readjustment of attitudes and preconceptions."

By autumn of 1970, reflecting the pressure of his new position, the tensions within the clergy and the country, and the fact that a priest's life under such circumstances is filled with demands, Romero was ill. There would be rumors that his sickness was more than physical, that he was mentally ill. He went to the home of a lay friend, whose family cared for him. He remained virtually isolated at their home for weeks.

When he returned, his responsibilities were multiplied. He was named, in May 1971, editor of the archdiocesan publication. He moved it, editorially, toward being more conservative, avoiding the ferment of Medellín altogether. Two years later, Romero's conservatism put him at the head of an assault on new ideas as they were written into the curriculum of a Jesuit high school. Parents were complaining; here were liberal ideas, awakening ideas, foisted on the sons and daughters of the upper class. Romero warned against "false" ideas and "demagogy and Marxism." The liberality of Medellín should not be taken too far, Romero wrote.

Again, in late 1971 and 1972, Romero was forced by poor health to take time off. It was as if there was a battle within as to whether he could withstand the rigors of a public life, especially in a forum so torn by dissent. At the end of 1972, to place his steady, conservative hand on an institution drifting leftward, he was named rector of a Jesuit seminary. Among the transgressions noted was that seminarians were taking philosophy courses at a nearby secular college and playing volleyball in gym shorts. Romero's attempts at reform — there were severe problems of finance and management — were less than successful, testing his resilience to criticism.

The Church's internal wrangling affected him personally in 1974, when Salvadoran bishops elected him their delegate to a synod in Rome. He first accepted, then resigned and was replaced by Arturo Rivera Damas, a bishop identified with the liberal wing of the Salvadoran clergy. Seeing his mistake, Romero then changed his mind again and decided he wanted to be the delegate after all. The matter was left to the Vatican hierarchy, which picked Rivera.

In December, Romero was named bishop of Santiago de María. This made him, rather than an "auxiliary" in the archdiocese of the capital, a bishop in his own right, with his own diocese, his own flock. He was a contemplative man, but now he was being drawn toward daily contact with parishioners and the priests who felt responsible for them. He was nearing the conflict that divided Salvadoran society, and the proximity would change him. Instrumental to the well-being of many people, especially in his diocese, was a land reform bill being discussed by Congress. Although weak and eventually watered down even further, the law signaled the possibility of change. Opposed to the law were the well-organized associations of Salvadoran businessmen and landowners. Supporting reform were peasant organizations, many of them put together with the direct participation of priests.

Confrontations were usually one-sided and always brutal. Soldiers would enter a town where a peasant organization was being formed. The officer in command would search for "weapons and subversive literature." The search would lead to the town's church, where sacred places, the sacristy or catafalque, would be opened (sometimes shot open). Articles, not excluding communion wafers, would be scattered. Priests who helped the peasant organizations were condemned as communists, making the soldiers, like Inquisitors, the "true" representatives of the Church. There was that twisted hatred peculiar to the mentality that heaps anticommunism on top of religious zeal. It bore bitter fruit. Soldiers, conscripted from the villages and barrios, were expected to carry out all manner of atrocities.

On November 29, 1974, six people were killed and two of their widows beaten. Men were stripped naked and humiliated by national guardsmen and police. On May 7, 1975, a priest and three of his friends were arrested, blindfolded, taken into San Salvador, and beaten. A "subversive" pamphlet was found, or planted, in the priest's mass kit. On June 21, 1975, five campesinos were shot and hacked to death, their homes ransacked. The last of these atrocities occurred in Tres Calles, a town in the diocese of Bishop Romero.

The bishop went to the national guard commander and wrote a letter to the president of El Salvador, Col. Armando Arturo Molina. Still deferential to authority, Romero, referring to the mass he said for the slain men in Tres Calles, said he regretted that protest songs had been sung. He did not believe, he said, in public expressions of dissent.

At about this time, in May, Romero had been named a "consultor" to the Pontifical Commission for Latin America, an important vehicle for information and opinion about the region to the Vatican. Made up mostly of Vatican officials, the commission includes one member and three consultants who are Latin American bishops; Romero, Brockman notes, had received "singular recognition." The experience forced him to contemplate and express his understanding of the forces acting on his country and the region. Later that year, after traveling to Rome, he set down his views. Although he conceded that the Salvadoran government was oppressive, Romero was still convinced that the place of priests was alongside authority. He criticized dissenting priests as "politicized." Brockman notes Romero was "blind to his own political stance in support of the government.... That only a year and a half later his closest helpers would be those whom he pronounced suspect in this document is proof of a radical shift by then in Romero's viewpoint."

Indeed, the beginning of the transformation was imminent. In the summer of 1976, Romero, in order to learn more of plans to strengthen the land reform law, instigated a study. The priests who conducted the study were critical of the government's proposal, calling it weak in the face of centuries of injustice. No social progress was possible as long as a relatively few families owned the vast majority of arable land, forcing the bulk of the population to work as day laborers. Romero took the results of the study to the president. Nothing happened. The proposal, in fact, as weak as it was, eventually was emasculated by Congress in response to the complaints of landowners, who saw even slight change as a threat. Romero was learning realities. The lessons would get harsher.

At the outset of 1977, a new archbishop was needed for the archdiocese of San Salvador. Luis Chávez y González, at seventy-five, had served as the tiny nation's only archbishop for thirty-eight years. On a scale of such considerations in the tense, antagonistic environment of El Salvador, Chávez was a liberal. He had looked to the well-being of believers, not just the wealthy. So his departure was welcomed by elites. A possibility to replace him, however, was Bishop Rivera, who was even more liberal. Rivera was popular with the masses and the clergy of the capital and just as unpopular with their adversaries. The choice of the Vatican, where Salvadoran divisions were well known, was Bishop Romero. His conservatism, presumably, would provide stability. Romero knew his elevation was not universally popular and wrote to priests of the diocese that he hoped to serve in a "spirit of cooperation."

At the same time as Romero's elevation, the political atmosphere of El Salvador was growing hotter. In the weeks before Romero was to take over as archbishop, the government had thrown out of the country two seminarians and four priests — a Colombian, an American, a Belgian, and a Salvadoran — accusing them of organizing peasants. Their treatment in captivity ranged from relatively gentle to cattle prods. The two seminarians and the Salvadoran (actually a former priest) were Jesuits, and traditionalists' hostility was directed at foreign priests and Jesuits.

Contributing to the atmosphere of crisis were preparations for a presidential election in February. The establishment of El Salvador had decided to exchange, as president, a colonel for a general. Elected was General Carlos Humberto Romero, former minister of defense and public security. The fraud was massive.

The election was held on a Sunday, and two days later Romero took over as archbishop. When Salvadoran bishops visited Molina, the out-going president, to present their new archbishop — whose elevation Molina had not even noticed — they got a lecture on how the Church had been misguided by new and dangerous ideas. While Romero returned to Santiago de María to bring his belongings to the capital, crowds protesting the election fraud gathered in San Salvador's Plaza Libertad. On Sunday night, one week after the election, the crowd was ordered to disperse, and when more than a thousand refused to leave troops opened fire. Many people took refuge in the church on one side of the square, where they were trapped until Rivera and Chávez helped negotiate their release. Romero hurried back to the capital.

The shootings and beatings, sometimes of priests, continued. Priests were thrown out of the country or, once out, prohibited from returning. On March 4, troops surrounded the home of the parish priest of San Martín, just east of the capital. Townspeople protected him, so the troops ransacked a house where four seminarians lived and left. On March 12, as another priest drove to say Sunday mass in the small town of Aguilares he was shot and killed. With him in the car were a fifteen-year-old boy and a seventy-five-year-old man. They were also killed. The priest killed that morning was Rutilio Grande, a Jesuit and an old friend of the new archbishop.

Father Brockman suggests that the assassination of Grande radicalized Romero, and it certainly drew the archbishop fully into an unholy war that would over the next three years kill hundreds of people, mostly farmers but also ten priests. Romero's thinking, his growing anger, can be seen in retrospect in his public statements, his homilies and pastoral letters.

Although his first pastoral letter dips into an unreal placidity — "We are passing through a very beautiful Eastertide" — it begins to focus on what he will see as the Church's mission. Delivered on April 10, 1977, less than a month after Father Grande and his two companions were killed and as the country was convulsed by civil unrest, he draws on the ideas of the Medellín conference. He concurred that the Church must be "truly poor, missionary and paschal, separate from all temporal power and courageously committed to the liberation of each and every man....

"The church cannot be defined simply in political or socio-economic terms. But neither can it be defined from a point of view that would make it indifferent to the temporal problems of the world. As Vatican II puts it: 'The mission of the Church will show its religious, and by that very fact, its supremely human, character.'" Romero linked the church's evangelical function to "human advancement." He would tread nowhere; he made clear, that the words of the popes and of Jesus Christ and the apostles did not lead. But, following them, he would bring Salvadorans "to have a clearer idea of the liberation that the church promotes."

Romero was offering a dialogue, he said, but with the offer came a moral warning. "From the perspective of our identity as a church, we also realize that our service to the people, precisely because it does not, as such, have a political or a socio-economic character, must seek sincere dialogue and cooperation with whoever holds political and socio-economic responsibility. The church does not do this because it has some technical competence or because it wants temporal privileges, but because the political community and other elements of society need to be reminded that they are at the service of the personal and social vocations of men and women."

Four months later, on August 6, he delivered his second pastoral on the holiday celebrating the Savior as the national patron saint. While the message of the Church is a message of hope, he said, "It is not an innocent hope that the church proclaims. It is accompanied by the blood of its priests and campesinos; blood and grief that denounce the obstacles and the evil intentions that stand in the way of the fulfillment of that hope. Their blood is also an expression of a readiness for martyrdom."

At the time, the streets were filled with accusations, in government controlled newspapers and crudely printed flyers, that priests were part of a conspiracy. Increasingly, Romero himself was the target of vituperation. He responded that the mission of the Church "comes alive in an archdiocese that, out of fidelity to the gospel, rejects as a calumny the charge that it is subversive, a fomenter of violence and hatred, Marxist, and political. It comes alive in an archdiocese that, out of the persecution it is undergoing, offers itself to God and to the people as a united church, one ready for sincere dialogue and cooperation, a bearer of the message of hope and love."

Romero pointed out that the accusations leveled at activist priests had some historical precedent. "From the beginning of Jesus' public life, these denunciations brought in their train frequent attacks upon him. They brought personal risk and even persecution. The persecution was to go on through the whole of his life until, at the end; he was accused of blasphemy and of being an agitator among the masses. For these reasons he was condemned and executed."

Because of his place at the center of a storm, observers outside the country began to recognize his courage. Early in 1978, Romero received an honorary doctorate at Georgetown University; later that year British ministers of Parliament and others nominated him for the Nobel Prize for peace.

In August 1978, again on the national holiday, Romero went straight to the heart of matters. His third pastoral was coauthored by Bishop Rivera and opposed by Salvador's four other bishops, who thought the message too radical. "The Church," they wrote, "which is the extension of the teaching and salvation of Christ, would be wrong to remain silent when faced with concrete problems.

"The testimony of the Second Vatican Council, always the point of reference for the teaching of Pope Paul VI; its application to Latin America through the documents of Medellín; the recent popes; many Latin American episcopates; and our own tradition in the church of El Salvador; show us that the church has always made its presence felt when society clearly seemed in a 'sinful situation,' in need of the light of the word of God and the word of the church in history. This prophetic mission of the church in the defense of the poor, who have always had a special place in the heart of the Lord, numbers among its apostles in Latin America such men as Fray Antonio de Montesinos, Fray Bartolomé de Las Casas, Bishop Juan del Valle, and Bishop Antonio Valdivieso, who was assassinated in Nicaragua because of this opposition to the landowner and governor, Contreras.

"To these eloquent testimonies of the church, both universal and local, we join today our own humble voice....

"We realize we risk being misunderstood or condemned, through malice or naiveté, as inopportune or ignorant. It is, however, our honest intention to dispel the inertia of the many Salvadorans who are indifferent to the suffering in our land, especially in rural areas."

The principal goal of this pastoral letter was to defend priests' work with community organizations, seen by landowners as threatening. Romero and Rivera saw them as not only necessary to the dignity of the common people, but instrumental for social progress. For the church, they were an extension of its ministry. And, yes, that meant that priests and Catholics must work side-by-side with communists. So complex was the issue that the two bishops issued with the pastoral letter three appendices for Salvadorans to study.

Salvadorans must analyze for themselves, the letter continued, the national situation. "The first conclusion of any impartial analysis of the right of association," they offered, "must be that groups in agreement with the government or protected by it have complete freedom. Organizations, on the other hand, that voice dissent from the government — political parties, trade unions, rural organizations—find themselves hindered or even prevented from exercising their right to organize legally and work for their aims, just though these may be....

"The church is aware of the complexity of political activity. However, and we repeat, the church is not, nor ought it to be, an expert in this sort of activity. Nevertheless, it can and must pass judgment on the general intention and the particular methods of political parties and organizations, precisely because of its interest in a more just society."

Of violence, the bishops spoke a truth that is still, for the most part, only whispered in Latin America. "The most acute form in which violence appears on our continent," they wrote, "and in our own country, is what the bishops of Medellín called 'institutionalized violence.' It is the result of the unjust situation in which the majority of men, women and children in our country find themselves deprived of the necessities of life.

"To those who hold economic power, the Lord of the world says that they should not close their eyes selfishly to this situation. They should understand that only by sharing in justice and with those who do not have such power can they cooperate for the good of the country, and will they enjoy the peace and happiness that come from wealth accumulated at the expense of others."

A year later, on August 6, 1979, the killing continued. Nothing had changed. "In El Salvador," Romero wrote in what would be his last pastoral letter, "new kinds of sufferings and outrages have driven our national life along the road of violence, revenge and resentment." Latin American bishops had recently met in Puebla, Mexico, ten years after the Medellín conference to renew their commitment to the social and economic change envisioned there.

But Romero returned to a nation tortured. His unflinching view of the torturers was what made him so dangerous.

"Analysts of our economy point out that, if it is to function well, it needs a large and cheap labor force. Producers of coffee, sugarcane and cotton, which go to make up the agricultural export trade, need unemployed, unorganized campesinos. They depend on them for an abundant and cheap labor force to harvest and export their crops. On the other hand, the agricultural and cattle-raising sector of the economy is the one that pays the most taxes to the public treasury — which is one of the reasons it has the greatest influence upon the government.

"And still today many industrial and transnational corporations base their ability to compete in international markets on what they call 'low labor costs,' which, in reality, means starvation wages."

Romero also attacked the shibboleth of "national security." Citing the statement issued at Puebla, Romero denounced "this new form of idolatry, which has already been installed in many Latin American countries. In this country it has its own particular way of working, but substantially it is identical with that described at Puebla: 'In many instances the ideologies of National Security have helped to intensify the totalitarian or authoritarian character of governments based on the use of force, leading to the abuse of power and the violation of human rights. In some instances, they presume to justify their positions with a subjective profession of Christian faith.'"

This frail, introspective man, against all predictions, had turned into the conscience of Latin America. Vilified in slanderous publications, he had even received death threats, he told his parishioners. Yet he kept up his attacks, knowing they were against men whose predilection for the most obscene forms of violence was well documented. "The omnipotence of these national security regimes, the total disrespect they display toward individuals and their rights, the total lack of ethical consideration shown in the means that are used to achieve their ends, turn national security into an idol, which, like the god Moloch, demands the daily sacrifice of many victims in its name."

Leaving no doubt as to the profundity of the change he felt was needed, Romero continued. "The church sincerely believes that without such changes the structural bases of our whole malaise will remain. The full liberation of the Salvadoran people, not to mention personal conversions, demands a thorough change in the social, political and economic system.... I realize that some terrorist activities induce a state of mind in the powerful that hardly favors serenity and reflection. But they ought to overcome that preoccupation and generously lay down the basis for a democratic evolution, so that the majority of the population may participate equitably in the national resources that belong to all."

During the summer of 1979, the archbishop brought together representatives of the democratic opposition to the government, seeking "a dialogue." In October, the government was overthrown. The coup was led by younger officers. In place of the fraudulently elected General Romero was established a five-man junta of three civilians, including José Napoleon Duarte, and two colonels.

Speaking to the governing board of the National Council of Churches in New York City in November, Romero said, "Violence is the outstanding characteristic of my poor country at the present time. Full of anguish, I must agree with the final document of Puebla: the 'muted cry' of people pleading for a liberation that never came is now 'loud and clear, increasing in volume and intensity.' It comes from blood-stained and tragic experience. At the base of all violence is social injustice, accurately called 'structural violence,' which is our greatest social evil now." He told the governors that in the first half of the year there had been "406 assassinations and 307 political arrests, all due to this violence."

Returning to El Salvador, he found leftists withdrawing their support from the junta and he supported them, agreeing that the junta was unresponsive to the country's greatest needs. In January 1980, Romero accused the defense minister of being an obstacle to reform and asked that he resign.

He was critical, as well, of U.S. assistance. To such criticism, a State Department spokesman blandly insisted that weapons were critical to land reform; they were used, he said, for "protection and security provided by the Salvadoran military for the new owners and the civilian technicians and managers helping them." The archbishop was not convinced. He wrote to President Carter in February 1980, asking that he rescind an effort to arm, equip, and train three Salvadoran batallions. "Instead of favoring greater justice and peace in El Salvador," he told Carter, "your government's contribution will undoubtedly sharpen the injustice and the repression inflicted on the organized people, whose struggle has often been for respect for their most basic human rights.

"The present government junta and, especially, the armed forces and security forces, have unfortunately not demonstrated their capacity to resolve in practice the nation's serious political and structural problems. For the most part they have resorted to repressive violence."

He got a reply from Cyrus R. Vance, the secretary of state, assuring him, "We share are-pugnance for the violence provoked by both extremes." The letter came in March.

Virtually every public utterance of the archbishop had become an event. He had inflamed the judges of the country by suggesting that they had sold out to the oligarchy. In his sermon on March 23, 1980, his last sermon, he referred to the army's "genocide against the Salvadoran people." Speaking to the common men who filled the ranks of the army — and inciting them, some said, to mutiny — he pled, "You don't have to comply with the orders of your superiors if they oppose God's laws. I implore you to cease the repression

The next evening, as he had promised, he was celebrating an evening mass in memory of the mother of Jorge Pinto, editor and publisher of El Independiente and a man who had been persecuted for opposing the government. All day, Romero, sixty-two years old, had been preoccupied with arrangements for Palm Sunday, the following Sunday. But he kept his promise to say the mass, going to the chapel at Divine Providence Hospital because his own Metropolitan Cathedral was filled with dissidents taking refuge there from the authorities. The same thing had been happening in churches all over the country. At the chapel, Romero led the congregation in the 23rd Psalm — "and I will dwell in the house of the Lord forever" — and chose as the Gospel reading the Book of John — "Whoever wants to serve me must follow me."

His homily, which had gone on for about ten minutes, concerned the return of Jesus. He was associating that with the concept of justice. "This is the hope that inspires us Christians," he said. "We know that every effort to better society, especially when injustice and sin are so ingrained, is an effort that God blesses, that God wants, that God demands of us."

A red car with as many as four men pulled up at the chapel's main entrance. As Archbishop Romero talked on, standing behind the altar and facing the congregation, a man walked into the back of the sanctuary, took aim, and fired a .22-caliber bullet that entered his heart and lodged in a lung. It seems, somehow, particularly obscene that the assassin apparently was not an enraged Salvadoran, but a hired killer, skilled in the use of his weapon, able to murder professionally, with a single, small-caliber bullet.

The archbishop pitched backward. There might have been other shots fired to intimidate the parishioners as the red car sped away. Several people fell on Pinto to protect him. As the archbishop lay dying, a nun knelt and softly kissed his forehead. He whispered, "May God have mercy on the assassins."

Salvador Allende and Augusto Pinochet

Ariel and Caliban

1908–1973
1915–2006
(Chile)

The term "compromise" is not some civic abstraction, but the lifeblood of societies. In Chile in the 1970s, however, one of Latin America's most advanced societies dissolved into molten conflict, crushing democracy in the process. The nation's vibrant political left — principally communists and socialists, but also a portion of Christian Democrats and including members of the military — was sure of its vision for the future. That vision, however, frightened Chile's political right, a combination of traditionalist oligarchs, and the majority of the Chilean officer corps, as well as powerful interests in U.S. industry and government. Caught in the ensuing vice was about a third of Chile's electorate, the nation's moderates, with nowhere to turn. Chile was wrenched from its course as a leader of Latin American political progress and cast into a maelstrom of killings, torture, and tragedy from which it is still recovering.

* * *

Salvador Isabelino Allende Gossens was born July 26, 1908, in Valparaíso, on the Pacific coast. He was given the same Christian name, Salvador, as his father, an official of the national government. The younger Allende's nickname was *Chicho*, according to his friend, follower, and biographer Eduardo Labarca.[1] As a child, Labarca knew Allende as "Uncle" and later joined Allende's youth movement, supported his government, and fled into exile after the 1973 coup. Allende spent considerable time with his father as child and teenager as the elder traveled about the country on various government assignments. Indeed, the elder Allende's occupational travel led the entire family through something of a nomadic existence.

During his earliest years, Allende was taken care of by his nanny Rosa Ovalle, "Mama Rosa," and his mother, Laura Gossens Uribe de Allende, both of whom he idolized. "From the moment of his birth," Labarca wrote, "Chicho lived surrounded by women — his mother, his nurse, sisters — who lavished caresses, kisses, and affection on him."[2] Allende had an older brother and sister, Alfredo and Inés, and a younger sister, Laura. Salvador and Laura — both of whom bore the same Christian names as older siblings who died in infancy — were close as children, and they remained close as he rose in the world of politics. Brother Alfredo, however, drifted off into a world of his own. An amateur boxer when young, he continued as a boxing referee but otherwise lived a solitary life with his mistress in Santiago. Salvador, too, was a competitive athlete when young, as a boxer and as a swimmer.

A strong influence on young Salvador's life, though he died twenty-five years before his grandson's birth, was his paternal grandfather, Dr. Ramón Allende Padín. His grandfather was held up by the family as a shining example of honor, social and political activism, and determination. An advocate of keeping the Roman Catholic Church out of civic affairs, Grandfather Ramón set the pattern for men in the family by joining the secular Freemasons. His church-state views were all the more remarkable in that his ancestors were royalists and thus closely aligned with the church. Politically, Grandfather Ramón was a founding member of Chile's progressive Radical Party.

As for the future president's relationship with his father, Labarca has written that it was "complicated." His father's service as a soldier in Chile's civil war of 1891 and his knowledge of political and governmental affairs obviously nourished young Salvador's later career. Yet Labarca described Allende's father as aloof, shunning tradition at least to the extent of ignoring its restrictions. The elder man, a spendthrift who evidenced a sharp eye for the ladies, was "different from his father — and from the son who would become president — in that *Don* Salvador didn't see himself on a transcendent mission. He loved a party, he could shine, and he was unaffected ... *Don* Salvador was widely admired, although not, apparently, by his son Chicho. Why? Mutual incomprehension? The son's reaction to the frivolity of his father, the party animal?

"There was probably a cocktail of factors, including, especially, resentment over his father's infidelities. But for all his love of the highlife, *Don* Salvador had a strong sense of family and was surely not an absent father. Just as his son would later, he had time for both great causes and tiny details. They exhausted his energy, as they would exhaust his son, the pace of running after beautiful women and taking wing into several orbits."[3]

Labarca's biography is a kind of scorecard for the youngest Allende's *affairs du coeur*, from *chilenas* to *cubanas* to *colombianas*. In Labarca's telling, the women were all beautiful and always shared his leftist political dreams. One Allende paramour was the daughter of Jorge Eliécer Gaitán, the Colombian leftist whose assassination set his nation on a path of violence from which it has never recovered. Labarca presented them all as *deslumbrante*, or "dazzling," and only poorly hidden from public view by Allende's indulgent circle of friends. This appreciation for the well-turned ankle, Labarca speculated, was why Allende, though a gregarious man, rarely spoke of his father later in life: the two were so much alike.

An important similarity was that both father and son married strong-willed women who enabled their promiscuity and protected their careers. "As a married couple," Labarca wrote, "Allende's parents fit the stereotype of the time, the Masonic husband and the pious wife. But Laura Gossens de Allende wasn't even close to being the wife who dedicated herself solely to her children and saying her rosary. She had studied in a well-considered North American secular school founded in 1880, Santiago College — 'the prestige school of the moment' — where she learned English. She also spoke French. She had, in fact, an ability with languages that her son did not especially inherit. She provided the practical side that her husband couldn't quite manage, and even managed affairs of his office."[4]

A large part of Allende's youth was spent in Tacna, a formerly Peruvian town, where his father was sent as an administrator for the national government. At the time, Chile was intent upon protecting its citizens' investments after its army had conquered the region. In the War of the Pacific, from 1879 to 1883, the Chilean army invaded Peru and Bolivia to take for itself the nitrate-rich area just beyond Chile's northern border. The war forever eliminated Bolivia's coastline and established Chile's dominance over a large area taken mostly from Peru. The prosperity made possible by the conquest paid for formation of the Radical Party, bringing to the fore an element of political thought far more progressive than either of the two traditional parties ever imagined. From then on, Chilean politics reflected the conflicting ambitions of the three parties and the military.

Growing up there provided for young Allende a certain international perspective. He observed the wide economic gap between the Peruvian conquered and Chilean conquerors. With few playmates, he and his sister Laura became close, and when Allende was ten years old, the family moved again ... and then again. For a time they lived in the frigid southern reaches of the country before the father was assigned back to Valparaíso, where Allende was born but had never lived.

Finally in an urban setting, Allende began to show a new side of his personality, that of a dandy, charming friends in the manner of his father. He and his brother were sent to a secular boys' school in Valparaíso, while his sisters went to a Catholic school. Laura would go on to study law at the university, but for all of the children, their time in Valparaíso was filled with unusual educational opportunities. Their father's position in the government and his flair for making friends meant that the family was often in the company of distinguished visitors, from professors to poets to a president.

In 1920 a signal political event gave direction to Allende's—and Chile's—political future. Arturo Alessandri, "the Lion of Tarapaca," was elected president. Alessandri stamped his personal style and moderate-to-conservative philosophy on the nation, leading the Chilean middle class into an expanded role in electoral politics. Importantly, Alessandri was only able to fulfill his promises of reform after young military officers dramatically demonstrated their support. One of the officers' less-than-subtle tactics was to crowd into the observers' galleries of Congress; once there, they dramatically demonstrated their support for Alessandri's proposals by rattling their swords in their scabbards during debates.

By 1925, a new, progressive constitution had been enacted. "But the army," wrote historian Jordan M. Young, "had tasted power." In 1927 Alessandri was succeeded by Col. Carlos Ibáñez del Campo. He was democratically elected but brought to the presidency a military, and decidedly undemocratic, style. Ibáñez "took control of the nation and gradually eliminated opposition until nearly all the powers of government were concentrated in his hands. By 1930, Ibáñez was a dictator as the Chilean Congress voluntarily gave up its rights...."[5]

However, some Chileans, especially students, were not so disposed to give up their rights. Among them was Salvador Allende, who had ended up in medical school after a period of uncertainty as to where he wanted to be. A few years earlier when Allende was graduating from high school, his father's career had taken a detour. After irregularities were discovered in the affairs of his office, the elder Allende was transferred temporarily back to Tacna, in the north. The family went with him.

In Tacna, 17-year-old Salvador, though an honors graduate and qualified for other career choices, joined the army. Perhaps he was frustrated and simply eager to strike out on his own, but he was posted to the cavalry. After six months of training, he was assigned as a junior officer to Tacna, too. This was the frontier where he had grown up, but much had changed as Peruvians militated for the return of their land and sovereignty. Allende, after contemplating remaining in the cavalry, decided to give up his commission and enter medical school in Santiago. In school he excelled in his studies and filled the rest of his time with the extracurricular activities of boxing and Greco-Roman wrestling. He also renewed his interest in competitive swimming. Intellectually, Allende had found his career as a physician and focused on the lack of health care available to poorer Chileans. Socially, he saw himself as a bit of a tough guy, quick with his fists and attractive to the ladies. Politically, he was a confirmed socialist.

And, along with other Chilean leftists, Allende was spoiling for a fight to rid the nation of Ibáñez's oppressive presidency.

Following the example of his father and grandfather, Allende, at 21 years old, became a Mason. Following his heart, he ran for, and was elected, president of the medical students' organization. That led to election as vice president of the national Student Federation. Even before graduation from med school, Allende was practicing enough to contribute to his family income, which had been lately diminished by his father's failing health. In addition, according to biographer Labarca, the young Allende "took time for the life of a young man about town." He moved out of an aunt's house where he'd been staying as a student and rented his own apartment. In 1931, at 23 years old, Allende was jailed and briefly expelled from school for participating in a street demonstration against the Ibáñez government.

The politics that attracted Allende reflected the competing forces that had been at play since Chile's beginning. Liberalism periodically emerged and was shoved back into its seat by the conservative establishment. All the while the military, or, at least, portions of the officer corps, might be found on either side. Even Chile's Irish liberator, Bernardo O'Higgins, was forced into exile in 1823 because of his liberality after only six years. O'Higgins had ideas about social reform that were repugnant to the young country's mercantile class, so he was thrown out. Conservatives then dominated Chile for a century until Alessandri's emergence in 1920 gave hope that reformist days had returned. When the harsh regime of Ibáñez exploded that dream, Chile's left was outraged. Their demonstrations forced Ibáñez — weakened by an economy in the throes of the Depression — into exile. Medical doctors like Allende were prominent in those demonstrations. A testament to the euphoria that followed Ibáñez's overthrow was the Chilean military's establishment of a Marxist government in 1931. It lasted 12 days.

The next year, Alessandri was returned to the presidency for another six-year term, and Allende graduated from medical school. He opened a practice in Valparaíso. His political activism had been elevated from organizing students to helping found the Chilean Socialist Party in 1933. By that time Allende was becoming known for his views on the deplorable state of health care for the poor. He was convinced that there was a political solution, and in voicing that opinion he was identified as a subversive. Brought before three trials in military courts, Allende was ultimately sentenced to five months of internal exile in the port city of Caldera. The court also prohibited him from joining the staff of any public hospital.[6] After being thwarted in attempts to practice medicine on his own, he finally got a job at a Santiago hospital performing autopsies. By his count, Allende cut up, over one year, 1,500 cadavers. Throughout, he would recall, he was reminded of the tragic conditions that preceded those deaths. Biographer Labarca wrote: "[T]he young doctor Salvador Allende would never be as he had been. The imprint on his mind and his soul would be deep and would project itself into every step of his future life, marking forever his view of the world, his humanity, and his behavior."[7]

In 1937, Allende was elected to the Chamber of Deputies as a Socialist, benefitting from an electoral swing to the left. Such were the times — in Germany, Adolf Hitler was rising — that Chile's leftward tilt was briefly interrupted by an abortive coup attempt from the right. A number of Chileans who admired Hitler's nascent Nazi party forcibly occupied several government offices in Santiago. They were harshly routed — 62 people were killed — by police.[8] In the next year's presidential election, Chilean leftists banded together in a Popular Front movement that was an unwieldy alliance including members of the Radical Party, communists, and socialists. Their candidate, Pedro Aguirre Cerda, was narrowly elected. He named as his minister of health Salvador Allende.

*   *   *

Only weeks before the cabinet appointment, on the night of January 24, 1939, Allende met his future wife, Hortensia Bussi, because of an earthquake. Bussi was the daughter of a captain who had turned his hand to farming after retiring from the merchant marine. Well-educated and very pretty — Labarca described her as of "legendary beauty" — she had persuaded her reluctant father to pay for her university education in Santiago. Through family and friends, she had become absorbed in the politics of the left. The night of the earthquake she had gone with a friend to see a Deanna Durbin movie, and when the temblor struck, they both moved quickly outside — onto Santiago's broad Alameda — surrounded by crowds of frightened people. As the danger subsided, she and her friend would have drifted off with the dispersing crowd, but she remembered that she'd left her gloves in the theater. She went back inside to retrieve them as her escort waited at the curb. There, he spotted in the crowd a friend and fellow socialist, Allende, who had just left a Masonic gathering. As she emerged from the theater, the friend introduced them. Bussi's appearance was striking, Allende's not so much. He wore his signature heavy, black, horn-rimmed glasses. The three went to a café.

Allende and Bussi, known as "Tencha," soon shared an apartment, and before long she was pregnant. He said nothing about marriage, and she was too proud to break the silence. Eventually, friends and relatives prevailed upon them, and they were married in a civil ceremony in September 1940. Their first-born was Carmen Paz, but the delivery was troubled. She grew up "silent and timid, observant, intelligent, and with limited use of her left hand."[9] She required physical therapy for years. The next, Beatriz, known as "Tati," was born in 1943. As they both grew up, Tati took her older sister under her protective wing. But Beatriz was also troubled. Guided by a lively intelligence and loving spirit, she took to politics with the enthusiasm of her parents. She worked at a hospital in Cuba and was trained there in guerrilla warfare; she married a Cuban and was pregnant with his child, a son, when her father was overthrown and killed. Tati could never escape a tragic history of bulimia and anorexia, and finally, depressed and dieting, she committed suicide in 1977. Her memory was preserved by Carmen's having named her daughter after her beloved, protective sister. A third daughter, María Isabel, was born in 1945, and the girls cemented a family tradition of Saturday lunches at their parents' home, whether in Santiago or at the house they bought at the beach. Their extended family filled a large table around which the talk was, unsurprisingly, politics. That Allende was something of a pushover for his girls was demonstrated in his crumbling whenever one woke up in the morning to say she did not feel well enough to go to school that day. Allende, who was, after all, a doctor, would write the excuse.

Lest this picture of familial bliss prevail, however, Labarca, who was a friend of the whole family, drops into the middle of his 400-page biography a story. The story avoids names, but the conclusion that its protagonist was Allende is inescapable. Allende was, like so many politicians, known for his amorous conquests, and Labarca's story is of a man's liaison with a younger, lower class woman who bears him a child. When the man refuses to leave his sweetheart to make an honest woman of her, the working class girl refuses to give up the child. Her brother, pistol in hand, goes to reclaim his sister's honor, but is thwarted by the police. The father of the child and his sweetheart go to court to try to claim the child, but the judge finds in favor of the mother. Only later, very quietly and extra-judicially, does the mother give up the child to the sweetheart to be reared, presumably, by upper-class foster parents.

The politician-as-stud, far from unknown in other cultures, finds a particularly comfortable place in Latin America, and Allende's reputation was well known, including by many who recognized the harm it did. Labarca, for example, was not blind to the social prejudice inherent in Allende's choices. With a withering view of society and politics, he wrote: "As a young congressman of the nascent Socialist Party, [Allende] met leaders and militants of modest origins and even simple proletarians. Among socialist women there was an abundance of nurses, primary-school teachers, municipal functionaries, employees of the post office or some other ministry, or the wives of workers and clerks. Some were attractive, and with one or the other Allende initiated further meetings. Nor was there any scarcity in those circles of painters, sculptresses, poets, actresses, singers...."[10] When election to the presidency created logistical problems for Allende's philandering — because government cars were recognized by Chileans in the street — he worked it out. His security men borrowed private, unrecognizable vehicles.

It seems that Allende's priapic pursuits were unaffected by his political fortunes. One of his continuing affairs was with Gloria Gaitán, the daughter of the martyred Colombian leftist, Jorge Eliécer Gaitán. As late as July 1973, three months before Allende was overthrown, Gloria Gaitán wrote to her mother in Colombia that she was pregnant and Allende was insisting that she bear the child. But as such stories made their way into public gossip, the ones who suffered most were his family. Labarca summarized the pain it caused his wife this way: "Tencha was alone, her familiar surroundings shaken, but she knew how to make something of nothing. She was a buoyant and singular woman."[11]

*   *   *

Allende held the post of minister of health until 1941, the year he visited the United States for the first time and was elected secretary general of the Socialist Party. That same year, however, Aguirre died, and his awkward coalition, already rent by internal disagreements, fell apart. Nevertheless, the marriage of convenience between the Radical Party and leftists worked to hold conservatives at bay and prevent Ibáñez from returning to office. Radical Gabriel González Videla was able to win the presidency by again winning the support of Chilean communists. Alas, when the grateful González named three communists to his cabinet he soon had to fire them all for malfeasance. Political zeal was not always matched by administrative competence, making Allende's abilities all the more evident. He built a national reputation and in 1945 was elected to the seat in the Chilean Senate that he would hold for 25 years.

The left-right tension that was crippling political cooperation only got worse after World War II. Chile struggled with labor unrest that included a particularly damaging strike by coal miners, and politicians lined up on both sides. In 1948, González Videla, the same man who had won the presidency only with the help of communists, shepherded through Congress an anti-communist measure called the "Law for the Permanent Defense of Democracy." It made the Communist Party illegal and erased communists' names from voter rolls. That June, Allende rose in the Senate to take his place, he said, in "the eternal attempt to define in words what exists only in one's heart and mind, to explain the inexplicable divide between those who would build a world by cutting through granite and those who have hidden all the tools."

Allende quoted from a declaration that he and other Chilean Socialists had prepared to describe the differences between themselves and Chilean Communists despite their shared goal of elevating the prospects of the working class. "Socialism does not formulate absolute principles built upon abstract, universal truths," he said, "nor does it affirm itself in metaphysical concepts.... As in nature, all history is subject to the law of constant change ... [and] the entire world has entered upon a period of social revolution....

"Within capitalism cannot be found the solutions to the many problems that derive from general discontent: the conflict between merchants and the suppliers of primary materials; the periodic crises that indicate the internal contradictions of the present system of production and exchange; the relative poverty of the great majority of the working population; or the obstacles that are imposed upon the great mass of able men with the tragic consequences of their material and moral misery."[12]

In November 1951 Allende announced that he would run for president. His principal opponent was the old dictator, Carlos Ibáñez del Campo. It might be said that another opponent was his own fiery personality. During a particularly heated exchange in the Senate, Allende almost came to blows with another senator. They were separated, but not before there was a challenge to a duel. By that time, Allende had already announced his presidential candidacy, and his supporters were worried that the other senator, Raúl Rettig, might squeeze off a lucky shot and leave them without a candidate. Their seconds took them to an appointed spot on a moonlit night, and they both fired wildly enough to satisfy their honor without risking anyone's life. The clandestine event — dueling was illegal — was memorialized by a satirical poem and otherwise forgotten, or nearly so. Half a century later, and only a year before his own death, Rettig revealed in an interview that the mutual anger was really the result of Allende's belief that Rettig was a rival for a lady's affection. And even that motive was unfounded, Rettig said. The woman in question was only a go-between between him and *yet another woman*. Allende, in his breathless quest for the affections of the woman of the moment, had gotten it all wrong. Allende's 1952 presidential campaign was less of a farce, but Ibáñez still won by a comfortable margin.

In 1958, Allende ran again. This time a newspaper columnist accused Allende, champion of the working class, of sending his daughter Carmen — the timid, withdrawn one whom the whole family protected — to a bourgeois private school. Once again, there was a confrontation, though corroborating witnesses would never speak in public. Press reports suggested that Allende, furious, confronted the columnist in the street and exhibited the considerable skill he'd acquired as a competitive boxer. Although no one came forward to confirm the fight, the columnist dropped out of sight for some time after the incident while his face recovered.

Although Allende's second presidential race was again a losing cause, his popularity was increasing significantly. However, electoral results also exhibited that Chileans were digging ever deeper their division into three irreconcilable political camps. In the middle were moderates, who were totally unable to control the radical wings of the left and right. Friction grew worse, abrasions grew deeper, and hotheads were determined to fight each other with the rest of the population as spectators. Allende's 1958 opponent was the old conservative war-horse Alessandri, who won with a bare 31.6 percent of the vote. Allende tallied 28.9 percent. Moderate Eduardo Frei was third with 20.7 percent. Two other candidates split the remaining 19 percent.

* * *

The Alessandri presidency was tormented by earthquakes, sparse harvests, and crippling inflation, all of which set the stage for the next presidential campaign. In addition, however, it was during Alessandri's term that Fidel Castro's rebels triumphed in Cuba, changing forever the hemisphere's political profile. Allende and his wife made a well-publicized trip to Havana, whereupon Ernesto *Che* Guevara presented Allende with a copy of his book, *Guerrilla Warfare*, with the inscription: "To Salvador Allende, who is trying to do the same thing by other means."

Allende got his third try at other means in 1964, but Frei rose to the top with an impressive 59.1 percent of the presidential vote. Allende also bettered his performance, taking 38.9 percent. It appeared, however, that Frei, the moderate, was going to lead Chile along a path between its left and right wings. Although economic troubles continued, Frei used his term to begin the important process of encouraging the Chilean Congress toward nationalization of the country's copper mines. Chile was the world's second biggest exporter of copper, most of which came from five big mines that shipped most of their production to the United States.

Thus Allende's prospects were uncertain. Sister Laura's political career was flourishing—she was re-elected to her Santiago congressional district—but the possibilities of a nation-wide win were difficult to predict. Having lost three times, Allende had to be concerned about being pushed aside by opponents in his own party or in any left-wing collaboration. As always, the Chilean left was divided. Allende's own nephew, Laura's son, was director of the collection of firebrands known as *MIR*, the *Movimiento Izguierdista Revolucionario*, or Leftist Revolutionary Movement. Laura, in fact, had expressed sympathy for at least some of the MIR's radical positions. In Labarca's accounting, "Allende's candidacy was seen as doubtful. Within the leadership of the Socialist Party, Allende was in the minority. Under those circumstances, as a tactical consideration and perhaps to free himself from Chilean intrigue, Salvador Allende took a trip. The distance may have contributed to Chileans' missing him and calling him back."[13]

However, in March congressional elections, Chilean voters showed that—far from pining over Allende—they were instead shifting back to the right. Frei's middle-of-the road Christian Democrats—whose presidential vote in 1964 was 56 percent—lost ground. They had to give up majority control of the 150-seat Chamber of Deputies. Radicals, the erstwhile middle-class party that had been leaning to the left, also lost strength, dropping to third place among the traditional parties in congressional seats. The beneficiary of those results was the conservative National Party, which won 21 percent of the vote, up from 13 percent four years earlier.

Just when it appeared that Frei and the CD would bolster the Chilean middle, the old divisions were widening again. The Chilean Communist Party—legal again and the largest Latin American communist party outside Cuba—moved up in the polls. Allende's Socialists, whose ideas were farther to the left than the communists', also gained strength in the popular vote (though not in Congress). Allende was re-elected to his seat in the 50-member Senate—where he retained considerable status—but it was undeniable that he was a leader of a confused following. Furthermore, all Chileans were acutely aware that countries around them were being subjected to military dictatorships when they were unable to resolve their political differences.

Finally, there was one more troubling aspect of Chile's congressional elections: apathy. When the parties fought, many voters were turned off. In 1969, Chile had 3.25 million registered voters, but nearly 30 percent of them abstained from voting. While abstention is a common Latin American tactic to show disapproval of "the system," Chile's rate had gone up more than 10 percent in just a few years, despite the fact that voting was legally mandatory. Casting a blank ballot invited a fine. So general discontent had to be added to the rightward political momentum. None of those considerations was a propitious sign for a Socialist candidate who'd run for president, and lost, three times before.

Allende tried to bolster his image when about 100 squatter families staged a land raid in the southern town of Puerto Montt. Police were called; the squatters threw rocks and brandished clubs; and police responded with gunfire. Eight people were killed and 30 wounded. Allende showed up with Senator Julieta Campusano of the Communist Party. Allende told the press that he believed the police had turned machine guns on the squatters without provocation. The deaths were the fault of the Frei administration, Allende charged. Frei could only respond that some in his government had made mistakes.

Allende's real target was the Christian Democrats' presidential candidate, Radomiro Tomic Romero. Allende, along with the communists, accused Tomic of failing to acknowledge the importance of the killings in Puerto Montt. Tomic was already being criticized by some Christian Democrats for being far more liberal than Frei, and a few were leaving the party as a result. If those views seemed contradictory, no one was more confused than Tomic himself. He contributed to his own fate by precipitately withdrawing from the race altogether in April, and then, before the summer was over, jumping back in. In the meantime, observing from the sidelines that many Chileans didn't like any of the candidates, the venerable former President Jorge Alessandri, now 73, threw his tattered hat into the ring. He became the candidate of the right-wing National Party. Allende, busily recruiting support wherever he could find it, sought out dissidents and joined a coalition of socialists, communists, and Radical Party members who were forming *Unidad Popular*, or Popular Unity.

In October, as if Chile were reminding the world that it was still Chile, two army regiments rebelled. The uprising only lasted a day, but it was the first military threat to the government in 35 years, a gloomy portent of things to come. A month later there were rumors of another military revolt being planned, and Frei had to declare a state of emergency in one province.

Ironically, through it all Chile's economy was doing well, despite a drought that had reduced farm production. The government was able to announce that a flourishing copper market would contribute to a balance of payments credit of $135 million, the highest in the nation's history. In addition, Frei, who had promised in his own campaign that he would demand a bigger cut of copper profits for Chile, assured his countrymen that the nationalization of copper production was on schedule. Chile was also strengthening ties with Bolivia, Colombia, Ecuador, and Peru by signing the Andean Pact, the basis for a Latin American common market. Despite such valedictory announcements, however, the left protested that change was too slow. On the right, conservatives grumbled that it was too fast.

By December 1969, Allende and the Socialists had cemented their bonds with four other parties, including the communists, and *Unidad Popular* was almost ready for the campaign. Its probable candidate was Chile's poet laureate and sometime diplomat, Pablo Neruda. There was still internal wrangling, however, and a chance that Allende would be the standard bearer. In fact, at a January convention that went well into the night with a lot of pushing and shoving among delegates, Allende's forces managed to move all other candidates out of his way. Allende was going to make his fourth run at the presidency atop a jerrybuilt agglomeration of dissidents.

That night, however, if Allende allowed himself any thoughts of glory, he was suddenly dismayed when he got back to his apartment to find a note from his daughter Beatriz. In a Cassandra-like prediction, Beatriz, whose own life was so troubled, foresaw disaster. What had up to then been relatively benign discussions between wings of the leftist parties, she wrote, eventually would boil over into open warfare. "Beatrice referred to the debate between the pacific and the armed wings of the movement and expressed her belief that the socialist revolution in Chile would inevitably be one of armed conflict."[14] By that time, Beatriz was deeply involved in her support of guerrilla groups operating in Latin America and steeped in Castroite mythology. She was right about the coming armed conflict, but not the direction from which it would come.

In June 1970 there was a suggestion of things to come when Edmundo Pérez Zuvojica, a former minister of the interior, was machine-gunned in his car in Santiago. The murder was blamed on the radical leftist *Vanguardia Organizada del Pueblo*. Almost immediately, nine male and three female members of the organization were surrounded in the early morning hours in Santiago. As police closed in to take them, one was killed, perhaps while he was carrying a white flag. The noose of tension that surrounded the presidential campaign tightened. Supporters of different candidates poured into the streets in several cities and in the ensuing confrontations with police two students were killed and more than a hundred arrested.

At the same time, rumors were flying that the top military officers would never accept an Allende victory, but Allende's private secretary, Ozren Agnig, later told a more complicated story. On the eve of the September 24 election, Agnig wrote, he was at the house where Allende was staying with a small group of friends. Agnig went to the door when a five-man delegation of officers, led by a general, arrived unannounced. Those officers, Agnig said, offered a deal to avoid what they saw as the probability that Alessandri, the conservative, would win. Their idea was to stage a pre-emptive coup. According to Agnig, Allende blurted indignantly: "General, never, ever in my life have I heard anything of such towering madness.... It shocks me beyond measure that a general of the republic would lend himself to such an infamous maneuver."[15] The next morning, with no one quite sure which officers supported which candidate, the citizens of Santiago awoke to find tanks parked throughout the capital near government buildings.

By that time, the Nixon administration knew well which candidate it did not want to win, and it was straining at the leash to stop Allende, as a later investigation by the U.S. Senate discovered. "The political crisis—replacing the mechanisms of political democracy with direction by the military—a military coup—appeared only to be possible if an *economic collapse* were provoked.... U.S. Ambassador Korry informed his superiors that he was sending a warning through an intermediary: 'Frei needs to know that we won't allow Chile to receive even a screw or a nut under Allende. Should Allende assume power, we will do everything in our power to condemn Chile and Chileans to the greatest privations and miseries, a policy designed over the long run to exacerbate even the worst that can happen under a Communist regime in Chile. In consequence, if Frei believes there can be some alternative to total ruin, one of seeing Chile absolutely prostrate, that is an illusion.'"[16]

Allende won a plurality of the vote, with 36.3 percent, polling 1,075,616 votes. It was apparent that, in addition to the votes of communists and socialists, Allende had also attracted a number of disaffected bourgeois voters from the Radical Party. Finishing second was the conservative National Party's Alessandri with 1,036,278 votes, or 34.9 percent. Radomiro Tomic Romero of the Christian Democrats—the man in the middle and the choice of the U.S. State Department—won 824,849 votes, or 27.8 percent. Abstaining were a bit more than 16 percent of the electorate, down almost half from the number of abstentions in the congressional election.[17]

It was the culmination of Allende's persistence through four campaigns, and the flowering of work by thousands of Chileans. Historian Jordan Young noted that the victory was a long time coming. "[A]lthough Allende was the first Marxist to win a country's presidency in a democratically conducted election, Marxist and Communist elements had achieved occasional prominence in Chilean government and politics for at least four decades."[18] At a triumphant post-election rally, Allende called himself "the first president of the first authentically democratic, popular, national, and revolutionary government in the history of Chile."[19]

The victory still had to be ratified by the Chilean Congress because Allende had not won a majority. Traditionally, Congress had given its imprimatur to the plurality winner, but this election had no precedent. There was no certainty Allende could count on a congressional majority. "Allende's popular-front coalition contained the bourgeois Radical Party, which had not and never would agree to a real 'transfer of power from the old ruling groups to the workers.'" Trying to reassure moderates, Allende was telling everyone who would listen that he would not destroy Chilean institutions. "To secure the votes of the major bourgeois parties—the Christian Democrats and the Nationalists—in a runoff election in Congress in October he publicly pledged to leave the military and the police intact, not to reduce the size of the army, and not to appoint any officers who had not graduated from the bourgeois military academies. He also agreed to outlaw any independent workers' militias."[20]

This national conversation was taking place above the crack of rifle fire and explosion of homemade bombs. Bombings rocked two Chilean supermarkets, the house of a conservative congressman, a bank, and the Santiago headquarters of Ford Motor Company. Trying to calm fears, Allende promised "a multi-party government, a nationalist, popular, democratic, and revolutionary government that will move toward socialism. Socialism cannot be imposed by decree. It is a developing social process." He cited what he hoped were goals common to all Chileans, stressing that "we must recover our basic resources that are in the hands of foreign capital, essentially American—copper, iron ore, nitrates, which are in ... the hands of American monopolies." Then he added the thin disclaimer: "We are not going to imitate either the Soviet Union or Cuba or China. We are going to look for our own way.... Our aim is not to isolate Chile. On the contrary, our aim is to tie Chile to all the countries in the world, seeking in the commercial field Chile's best interests."[21] Allende was, of course, telling Chileans that he could be all things to all factions. Again and again, Allende insisted that the country was not in peril of a left-wing debacle. That meant, he told *The New York Times*, he was not interested in "a Socialist regime tomorrow. Socialism cannot be imposed by decree. It is a developing social process."[22]

Then, just a few days before the up-or-down vote in Congress, *Le Monde*, the French newspaper, reported that 83 U.S. military officers were seeking visas to enter Chile. The Frei administration asked Washington to explain why so many visas were necessary and was told it was all perfectly innocent. "Bald-faced lie!" was Agnig's evaluation of Washington's explanation. "Our authorities knew perfectly well that this was elements of the CIA sent to our country with the mission of capturing Salvador Allende before October 24."[23] Allende blamed his conservative enemies within Chile. "Never before," he charged, "has any political group acted as has the right. Nor has any called upon extremist organizations ready to use any means, including the CIA. But they have gone even farther." Referring to intelligence reports, Allende continued: "At a meeting, it was said that there is a Chilean army officer who could be bought for half a million dollars. They also said it was a lot cheaper to eliminate me."[24] The Frei administration denied the visas, and a U.S. investigatory commission would eventually confirm the Nixon administration's maleficent intent.

On October 24, the Chilean Congress—150 deputies and 50 senators—assembled. Eighty seats were held by Allende supporters, 75 by Christian Democrats, and 45 by backers of Alessandri. They confirmed Allende as victor. The president of the Christian Democrats promised Allende his assistance; Alessandri's supporters vowed the opposite. To the November inaugural celebration, at least 60 countries sent representatives, including Cuba. Although President Nixon had declined to send a telegram of congratulations, the State Department's assistant secretary for inter–American affairs showed up for the ceremonies.

*   *   *

From its very beginning to its premature end, the Allende presidency was fraught with feverish activity. Within days of the inaugural, Allende confirmed the worst fears of the right by re-establishing relations with the Castro government. By the beginning of December, he had expropriated three large manufacturing companies, two of them U.S.–owned. When there was a run on Chile's bank deposits, Allende, accusing his opponents of causing a "wave of economic terror," promised to guarantee deposits. Convinced that his adversaries were plotting to assassinate him, Allende sent daughter Beatriz to carry a personal message to Castro to inform him of the delicacy of the situation in Chile. Castro replied with four pieces of advice: The first two were to try to convince technicians to stay in Chile and to sell copper for only dollars. The other two suggestions proved impossible to follow. Castro warned Allende "not to act in a manner so revolutionary as to give counterrevolutionaries a pretext for crippling your economy" and to "maintain good relations with the military until you have time to consolidate your popular forces."[25]

As for complying with the fourth admonition, however, Allende tried. During a parade mounted in Santiago to initiate his term. Allende suddenly called General Augusto Pinochet to the reviewing stand. Pinochet's presence, Allende told the crowd, was "proof that the Armed Forces would maintain the Chilean tradition."[26] That remained to be seen, however, and that afternoon at a cocktail party Pinochet held himself aloof from Allende's blandishments. He later described himself as "very laconic" as he accepted Allende's effusive congratulations on a recent promotion.[27] Their relationship was a cat-and-mouse game from the outset, though no one could predict which was the cat and which the mouse.

What both Allende and Pinochet knew, however, was that the big dog of the hemisphere, the United States, was watching their game. There was much at stake. "At the time Allende assumed office, more than one hundred U.S. corporations had established themselves in Chile," wrote three American journalists. "Among these were twenty-four of the top thirty U.S.–based multinational corporations. These included the major auto producers, four of the biggest oil companies, Dow and DuPont chemicals, International Telephone and Telegraph (ITT), and other big industrials. In recent years, the ranks of the industrials had been joined by multinational banks and corporations operating in the service sectors."[28] The total assets of all those companies were close to $1 billion, and the Nixon administration was prepared to defend its constituents' investment.

According to National Security Decision Memorandum #93, issued a few weeks after Allende's election was confirmed, plans were afoot, as Nixon put it, to "make the Chilean economy scream." Nixon and his national security advisor, Henry Kissinger, were intensely aware that in addition to all the U.S. companies operating in Chile, the United States bought four-fifths of all Chilean copper. If Allende was at its helm, they intended to isolate Chile. "All new bilateral foreign assistance was to be stopped," the memorandum directed. "The U.S. would use its predominant position in international financial institutions to dry up the flow of international credit or other financial assistance. To the extent possible, financial assistance or guarantees to U.S. private investment in Chile would be ended, and U.S. businesses would be made aware of the government's concern and its restrictive policies."[29] The Cold War was at its most frigid when Nixon and Kissinger served as devoted tacticians.

Of course, plans to destroy Allende's presidency went tragically beyond economic isolation. Two days before Congress confirmed Allende's ascent, Chilean Chief of Staff René Schneider — who had earlier refused to command a coup against Allende — was assassinated. His car was ambushed, and he was shot several times at close range, dying three days later. In such an atmosphere of terror, Allende made a special unit for suppressing riots a part of the regular police force. Immediately, the opposition newspaper El Mercurio complained. Opponents resigned their seats on corporate directorships, students demonstrated — with at least one killed — both for and against the new regime. Allende asked for "a climate of democratic coexistence, discarding all forms of aggression," but he also briefly closed the office of United Press International, the international wire service.

The carnage continued. In June, a former high official of the Christian Democrats was assassinated, shot to death in a car with his daughter, who survived. Allende condemned the killing, but the Christians Democrats blamed it on the "climate of hate, defamation, and violence" occasioned by Allende's election. A non-partisan commission called the killing the predictable result of political conflicts "that have spread hatred in the life of Chile."[30] The killers were identified as two brothers, left-wing extremists who themselves were later gunned down — submachine guns in hand and grenades stuck their belts— in a shootout with police. Such was the continuing mayhem during Allende's first year in office that Christian Democrats, whose pledge of cooperation with Popular Unity had been crucial, withdrew their support. Some left-leaning Christian Democrats quit the party to support Allende, but to little effect. Allende only turned his efforts further leftward. With the support of communists and others, he tried to reform the constitution to allow a unicameral legislature, to be called the Assembly of the People. The bill failed, and his opponents in Congress also foiled his effort — in the dark tradition of Latin American presidents— to change the law so he could unilaterally suspend Congress and rule by decree during emergencies.

Allende's promises frightened the right and his accomplishments failed to satisfy the left. Even as he reviewed the changes of his first year, leftist university students rioted, calling for greater Marxist influence in administering the national university. Housewives marched, banging empty pots, to protest rising prices and the absence of food on supermarket shelves. In December 1971 the Christian Democrats rallied 60,000 protesters at Santiago's National Stadium. Four days later Allende supporters turned out only a third of that number.

*   *   *

When its gears were first engaged, however, Allende's industrial plan — orchestrated by Pedro Vuskovic, his economics minister — worked. Some of it was built on ideas advanced by the Frei government, which had nationalized more than a fifth of a list of potential takeover targets. Allende continued down that road, taking over banks and further controlling copper production. Allende accelerated land reform, also begun under Frei, who had called for nationalization of all irrigated plots of more than 200 acres. Out in the countryside, however, the pace of reform was too slow for the landless and too fast for the landed. Allende's police were forced to arrest leftists who were encouraging land raids, while owners of large plots wailed that the situation was already out of control. Dramatically, the administration announced plans to buy three foreign banks— American, Italian, and English — and to acquire the Bethlehem (Pennsylvania) Iron Mines Company. Every takeover increased the acrimony.

In order to be able to claim that Chile was buying, not seizing, assets, the Allende government simply devalued them down to bargain prices. "President Salvador Allende announced September 28 [1971] that he would deduct $774 million in 'excess profits' from the book-value compensations paid to the U.S. copper companies Anaconda Company and Kennecott Copper Corp. for nationalized copper properties. Since the net worth of U.S. copper interests in Chile was estimated at only $550 million, the deductions—if they were, as expected, upheld by a five-man indemnification tribunal — would mean that the companies would receive no compensation." At the news, the Nixon administration pronounced itself "deeply disappointed and disturbed."[31] Only a week earlier, however, National Security Adviser Henry Kissinger had pledged in a newspaper interview that the United States would not impede Chile's development by choking off access to international capital markets. Allende, pressing full-steam ahead, presented to the Chilean Congress a list of 150 more Chilean companies to be nationalized.

For all the furor, the economic climate improved, and social programs, including free milk for children, were implemented. Allende hoped to sustain progress by broadening the consumer base. He mandated higher wages for workers at private companies and created public jobs with government-financed projects. Demand, he hoped, would follow. In fact, during Allende's first year in office, industrial growth was up 12 percent, and Gross Domestic Product was up by 8.6 percent. Inflation dropped from 34.9 percent to 22.1 percent. Unemployment was down to 3.8 percent. Then, however, as increasing demand outstripped productivity, inflation quadrupled what it had been under Frei, and things fell apart.

An early sign of democratic revolt came in January 1972. Provincial by-elections to fill two congressional seats went to opposition candidates. To no avail was Allende's attempt to counteract his diminishing popularity by his administration's announcement in one of the provinces—on election day—that 200 large farms were being turned over to the people. There were economic signs as well. Copper production, now in Chilean hands, fell, and profits dropped as world prices collapsed. Payments to nationalized U.S. companies were in arrears, and in New York a court froze assets of the Chilean copper monopoly until a suit brought by Anaconda could be resolved. In sum, events were overtaking rhetoric. Allende's pronouncements were drowned out by the din of reality.

Moreover, as investigations would later confirm, executives of U.S. copper companies and ITT were in close contact with the U.S. State Department, plotting feverishly. They insisted on clandestine action to exploit internal unrest. Barrio residents were already clashing with police, protesters were marching, and by September Allende was moved to say that if the discontent did not abate, he would call on his supporters for strong-arm support. "President Allende charged September 2 that there was a right-wing 'September plan' to overthrow his government. He asserted that any attempt at a coup would be met by a nationwide general strike and occupation of plants and buildings by workers."[32] The president had the month right, but the "plan" took a year to mature. During that year, Allende refused to temper his rhetoric or modulate the pace of reform. Behind closed doors, Christian Democrats moved from rejecting Allende's methods to supporting the idea of a coup.

Allende had no answer for Chile's economic tailspin, and a nationwide truckers strike added to the urgency of the situation. The truckers were followed by 17 professional organizations, from doctors to taxi drivers, and then by bank employees. Food shortages continued. Allende could do little but shuffle his cabinet, and at the end of 1972 he flew off on a trip to Mexico, the United States, the Soviet Union, and Cuba. He did not bring back any answers, and the Socialists in Congress had to head off a law that would have returned some Chilean companies to private ownership. During the congressional debate, more groups peeled away from Popular Unity.

By early 1973, matters met in a whirlpool of economic and political crises. There were public revelations of U.S. chicanery. There was public dismay over dwindling food supplies. There were complaints that Allende's controls—the government took over wheat sales and placed the army in charge of distributing essential goods—amounted to rationing. *El Mercurio* editorially accused Allende of imposing a dictatorship. Although several nations, from Argentina to China, made credit and aid available, it was not enough. When negotiators from Chile and U.S. companies tried to resolve differences over expropriation, their meetings ended in bitter recriminations.

Political factions on both left and right split themselves into even finer segments with mutual accusations of betrayal. So directionless was the opposition that even military officers who might be disposed toward a coup despaired of Allende's opponents' being able to put together a new government. When conservatives and moderates did manage to paste together a coalition for the March congressional elections, its candidates were not particularly successful. "The opposition ... retained its Congressional majority in the March 4 elections," wrote historian Sobel, "but President Salvador Allende's Popular Unity coalition (UP) showed surprising strength, gaining seats in both the Senate and the Chamber of Deputies."[33] Allende was being spared outright defeat by the incompetence of his adversaries.

That incompetence stretched as far as Washington, since the United States' clandestine efforts to bring Allende down were similarly ineffective. Those efforts were revealed in a report by a special subcommittee of the U.S. Senate. After a two-year investigation by its staff, the subcommittee, headed by Idaho Senator Frank Church, disclosed a shameful record of undercover activities perpetrated by ITT, the National Security Council, the White House, and the CIA. While details of the tawdry affair need not be belabored, it was made clear that Harold S. Geneen, chairman of the board of ITT, twice offered the U.S. government a million dollars to help subvert the democratic process in Chile. Testimony related to the offer — which Geneen later admitted — came from William V. Broe, director of CIA operations in Latin America: "The money was offered at a July 1970 meeting and was intended to finance a CIA effort to stop Allende."[34]

Subsequent revelations showed that the United States, contrary to its public stance of supporting Chilean democracy, had channeled $20 million into trying to sink Allende's career beginning in 1964. Most embarrassing to the United States, however, must have been that its efforts at fraud, deception, and international tyranny were so ineffective in 1970, so outrageous in the eyes of the world when revealed in 1973, and yet served as no more than a prelude to the Nixon administration's scurrilous association with the Pinochet regime well into the 1990s.

After the 1973 congressional elections, Chileans continued to conduct their political efforts in the street. In April, Allende called out police to control disruptions initiated by both left and right while denying that his intent was to stifle legitimate debate. Strikes disrupted the economy as owners of bus companies demanded higher fares and copper workers higher wages. By the middle of the year, the cost of living had risen by 238 percent. In late June, the army had to put down a revolt by its own troops. Allende declared a state of siege — allowing rule by decree — but suspended it in a few days. When his cabinet stepped aside for reorganization, Allende vowed not to appoint military officers, who were said to be making demands for patronage. The new cabinet arrived, tilting decidedly to the left, but the entire exercise was like recruiting a crew for the Titanic. In late July, after his top naval aide was assassinated, Allende tried to restore some semblance of balance. He agreed to a meeting with the president of the Christian Democrats. They spoke of what could possibly be done to avert civil war, but the meeting was inconclusive. Within the week 60,000 truck, bus, and taxi owners were on strike. Another military uprising, this one involving the crews of a cruiser and destroyer docked at Valparaíso, was snuffed out, but the military demanded that Allende open his cabinet back up to military appointees. The streets were alive with strikes, demonstrations, bombings, and terror.

* * *

One description of what happened next came from Allende's friend, aide, and admirer Ozren Agnic, who had arranged for a meeting with Allende at La Moneda on September 11, 1973. He was to go by car to the capital, but his driver woke him early to tell him to turn on the radio. At first, Agnic thought the news was nothing more than a repeat of earlier, brief uprisings, so they started out for Santiago. However, when their passage was frequently delayed or rerouted by military convoys, he grew concerned about the safety of his employees at the banking ministry. He would later learn that by that time the army, without firing a shot, had already captured Concepción, the country's third largest city. Two hundred and seventy people were imprisoned.

Arriving at the capital, it was clear Agnic wouldn't be able to get into La Moneda. In fact, no one was supposed to move because of a curfew, so he awaited events at his office a few blocks from La Moneda. On the radio were announcements from the military interspersed with recorded music. Eventually, Agnic would be able to hear and feel the vibration as the Chilean air force attacked with air-to-ground missiles. "Anguish, pain, and a feeling of impotence kept me from thinking clearly," Agnic wrote. "I could only think about the president, surrounded by a few men protecting the constitutionality of his government.... Who, besides those few committed defenders of the regime at La Moneda and a few surrounding buildings were able to put up a defense? Where were the '15,000 Cuban soldiers?' Where were the 'strongly armed bands' so frequently denounced by Frei, Pinochet, and others? The moment belied such nonsense."[35]

Allende continued to argue his case to the last moment, talking on the phone with party leaders, trying to hold his opponents at bay. Across town, Pinochet was taking no chances on letting a politician talk his way out of a predicament of his own making. "This guy is gaining time," he snapped impatiently. "We're making ourselves look weak. No, don't accept anything parliamentary. Parliament is empty dialogue. Unconditional surrender. If he wants to come here with Sepulveda [commander of the National Police], or with the Minister [of the Interior], and surrender; if not, we're going to bomb right away. Tell him."[36]

The one-sided battle for La Moneda lasted seven hours. At first, there were a few shots fired and a lot of phone negotiations. Photographs show Allende in his office, holding a submachine gun. He wore a helmet tilted at a bizarre angle, completing, with his scholar's horn-rim glasses, a most unmilitary image. To demands that he surrender Allende replied, "I will not resign. I will not do it.... I am ready to resist by any means, even at the cost of my own life so this will serve as a lesson on the ignominious history of those who have strength, but not reason."[37] Daughter Beatriz, pregnant, went to La Moneda as did at least one of Allende's many close female friends. After they had left came the bombardment — including of the presidential residence — and the final assault. Anibal Palma, Allende's minister of housing, was captured at La Moneda and executed there. Allende was shot to death.

The absurdity of the end gave birth to many mysteries. Were not the 200 Cubans working with Allende's administration supposed to defend him? Could the army be believed in its claim that Allende, cornered in his office, committed suicide? Tencha fled first to the home of the Mexican ambassador in Santiago and then flew to asylum in Mexico. At first she believed her husband had committed suicide. Then she changed her mind. She had talked to people who saw the body at La Moneda, and they told her they had counted 13 bullet holes in his body. A correspondent for the Cuban news agency, *Prensa Latina*, reported that Allende died fighting.

The new regime insisted that Allende shot himself — twice! — under the chin with the AK47 automatic rifle found beside his body. The body was studied and the claim corroborated by a Princeton University professor. The Cuban representative to the United Nations, however, took a broader view. He stood before the Security Council and said: "The trail of blood spilled in Chile leads directly to the dark dens of the Central Intelligence Agency and the Pentagon."[38] The official U.S. position, unsurprisingly, was that the United States had not known the coup was coming, but then various spokesmen kept stepping on each other's lines. Jack Kubish, an assistant secretary of state, told the Senate Foreign Relations Committee that a U.S. office in Chile had, in fact, been informed of the imminent coup 10 to 16 hours before its launch.

Biographer Labarca concluded that Salvador Allende had lived in two worlds. One was the world of his daughter Beatriz, who had been trained in guerrilla tactics and how to fire submachine guns and bazookas; this was the world of friends and hangers-on, who goaded him to excess. The other world was that of his daughter Isabel, "who had never even shot a pistol;" of moderate politicians who were disposed to negotiation. On his last day, the two worlds in which he lived were the ones in which he died: "With the machine gun in one hand and a telephone for negotiating in the other, submitting to the people even as he was firing from the window of his office, the President on that day was Chile's revolutionary split-personality incarnate, even at its hour of catastrophe."[39]

* * *

With Allende dead and thousands of his followers being rounded up, taking command of Chile's government were the four top officers of the military branches. At their head was Augusto José Ramón Pinochet Ugarte, whose name would become synonymous with state-orchestrated terror.

Pinochet was born on November 25, 1915, in Valparaíso. His father, Augusto Alejandro Pinochet Vera, a native of France, had worked on and around the docks of Valparaíso since before he was 14 years old. He belonged to a family from the coastal province of Brittany that has been described as one of "fishermen, merchants, smugglers, and roughnecks that worked along Spain's Pacific coast during the days of the empire."[40] Young Augusto's first job in Valparaíso was with the English merchant company Williamson Balfour, and he later was a clerk in the customs office. Still later, as a fireman, Pinochet Vera demonstrated considerable bravery. However, he was remembered by friends mostly for his solid, if somewhat dull, character. "A balanced man," wrote biographer Gonzalo Vial, "honest, laconic, austere, hard-working, a man with a clear, precise routine, who loved his family and was without ambition."[41] His wife, the future dictator's mother, was Avelina Ugarte Martínez, born in Santiago. At the age of nine, Avelina was sent to a school operated by nuns when her widowed mother remarried. Her stepfather, Francisco Valette, another French immigrant, took the small family to Valparaíso. They had only recently arrived when Avelina, described as "out-going and of strong character," met the elder Pinochet and was engaged to marry. Doña Avelina would live until 1986, "assisting," as biographer Vial put it, "her oldest son's brilliant military career."[42]

Augusto Pinochet was born a year after his parents married, a tough time for Valparaíso because World War I had reduced shipping. His father would provide, nevertheless, for six children—three boys and three girls—born over a six-year period. Young Augusto was sent to a series of small schools, by turns parochial, secular, and military. It was a proper tutelage, though it did not prevent him from taking up smoking from the time he was nine years old. "He was an average student—neither outstanding nor lazy—and his complexion, according to his own description, was fair, more 'gringo' than Chilean, a result of the Ugarte side of the family."[43] His parents' religious beliefs portrayed a clear choice between the rewards of heaven and the everlasting fires of hell.

In 1931—the year Allende was jailed for participating in demonstrations against the presidency of General Carlos Ibáñez—Pinochet, then 16 years old, got his first taste of politics. The race to be Ibáñez's successor was between the conservative Juan Esteban Montero and Arturo Alessandri, the latter seen in those days as a dangerous liberal. Pinochet was encouraged to attend a meeting of some of Montero's youthful supporters on the theory that Pinochet would be sympathetic. Pinochet quickly concluded, however, that such groups were mostly interested in street confrontations with Alessandri supporters. The whole idea left him cold. Politics was unseemly, and not for him.

In fact, it should be said that there was not much in the Chilean political arena for a young man of a military bent. Many Chileans were so disgusted with Ibáñez that they began militating for a "civic movement" that might prevent such a man from returning to the presidency. The political confusion continued, however, as Ibáñez's immediate successor was run out of office by a barracks revolt. Its leaders put in place a "Socialist Republic" that lasted all of twelve days. The 1932 election of Arturo Alessandri was supposed to bring an end to the madness, despite Alessandri's having himself been deposed twice and exiled once.

Pinochet went off to military school in 1933, at age eighteen. It was a career choice filled with uncertainty because many of his classmates could point to family legacies of fathers, uncles, and grandfathers who followed military careers. They were headed for the sort of respect and financial security that was limited in a traditional society. But Pinochet's course, apparently, had been set by his family; there was little discussion. His mother, he recalled later, took him to the school, where "she left me with my suitcase and departed without a backward look."[44] In addition to his classes, Pinochet was on the wrestling team and, in the European tradition, was trained in fencing. He graduated as an infantry ensign in 1937.

The life of a young officer was not one of material comfort. Very early in his career Pinochet had to take six months' furlough to add to his army income by working for his father.[45] Over the next ten years, however, he rose through the ranks of the infantry to captain. Pinochet became known as a man of relatively Spartan habits, drinking little and eating in moderation, partly as a result of a bout with hepatitis when he was just out of military school. Pinochet also built a reputation for keeping his eye on the task presented to him, his ear attuned only to superiors' orders. There was neither time nor inclination for anything else, especially analytical thinking. "Reading Pinochet's diaries," Vial wrote, "it is surprising how national events of the first magnitude went almost unnoticed by military officers. The formation of the Popular Front, the successful presidential campaign of Pedro Aguirre Cerda (1938), that of Juan Antonio Ríos (1942), and the rupture of diplomatic relations with Germany, Italy, and Japan (1943) are hardly mentioned.... Of much more interest are events that embroil the army, like the massacre at Seguro Obrero (1938), the big race riot (1939), the unsuccessful uprising against Aguirre Cerda led by General Ariosto Herrera."[46]

He joined the Masons, though biographer Vial was at pains to reassure the reader: "If Pinochet was a Mason, it was only nominally, especially after he was married (in 1943) because his wife, as we'll see, was a devout and traditional Catholic.... Perhaps membership provided a measure of protection; it was common among officers who were not well connected politically or socially and helped them ascend through the ranks throughout their careers."[47] His marriage was to Lucía Hiriart Rodríguez, of Basque and French descent, and her upper-middle-class family provided Pinochet with solid social and political connections. Her father was a lawyer and a Radical Party member who served as senator and, briefly, minister of the interior. The Pinochet's first child, Lucía, was born in late 1943.

Pinochet's father died the next year after having traversed some financial hard times. The two had remained close, however, and when the elder Pinochet was formally condemned for having had business dealings with Axis powers during the war, his son fought to have his reputation restored posthumously. The process took a full year, but was in the end successful.

Persistence was a hallmark of Pinochet's personality. "Captain Pinochet, with twelve years of service, had learned a basic truth of a military career: the chain of command, modeled in the army on the German tradition, meant that prudence required that one hide — without lying — one's own thinking with regard to anything philosophical, religious, political, or socioeconomic.... The old ways could be trusted; the new were suspect."[48]

With the end of World War II, however, new ways were ascendant. The political left was no longer so burdened by romantic notions arising from the Russian Revolution. Now, hard-eyed organizers trained in and dispatched from the powerful Soviet Union took the field. Communists helped to organize strikes and ran strong in Chilean municipal elections; their leaders were enough of a threat that they were being arrested and held in remote jails. In October 1947, some 500 "leaders" were arrested and a portion of them transported to an abandoned saltpeter factory in Pisagua. The prisoners put up no significant resistance, so the task of the army detachment guarding them was to provide shelter and food and to hold them until their cases were resolved. The unit was under the command of Captain Pinochet.

In January of the next year, the path of Captain Pinochet would cross— almost — that of Salvador Allende. Allende traveled to Pisagua as a member of a delegation of leftist legislators visiting internments. When a spokesman for the delegation telephoned the guard unit's headquarters to request permission to visit the encampment, Pinochet refused. Not only was he having no grandstanding by politicians, he was acquiring a certain, if grudging, respect for the internees. He came to admire their uncomplaining discipline and their ability to make the most of their imprisonment. They established an "academy" for younger party members. They showed obvious skill at recruiting outsiders to their cause, a skill that made them, of course, especially dangerous. In general, Pinochet was learning of the communists' humanity — as long as they did not go too far toward subverting the state he served.

Over the next four decades, Pinochet rose from captain to division general. He was provided training in several fields, including a period in law school. He was posted to several cities and earned assignment abroad as a military attaché. He served as an instructor in military schools. And, eventually, he learned the lesson of every officer in a peacetime army: rank is hard to come by when one's superiors are neither killed nor shamed in battle and live out their tenure to retirement. Progress through the ranks required playing politics in competition with dozens of others of the same rank, clawing one's way up the side of a steep, narrow pyramid. "It is significant to note that Pinochet showed enthusiastic personal admiration for three of the most brilliant field-grade officers of the day ... and that they rewarded him with the ultimate prize, their confidence, and appointed him to a secondary, but important, role, that of 'adjutant.'"[49]

Pinochet needed look no farther than the armed forces of Argentina, Brazil, or Paraguay for examples of what generals do when they are all dressed up in their epaulets and there are no foreigners to fight. Generals of the day either overthrew presidents, whose incompetence often made them easy targets, or they defended incompetent presidents by pointing weapons at their fellow citizens. Even Ibáñez's dictatorial regime, which incurred the wrath of the left and middle of Chile, was admired within the officer corps whence he sprang. "Other young officers of the epoch remembered the old *caudillo* with a certain benevolence. They appreciated his improvements in pay and equipment for the Army and the other armed forces and that he had eventually regulated —for good or ill— professional problems that had been irritants for decades: 'sweeping the chimney' [of retirees], making promotions, and providing oversight. Pinochet neither glorified him nor criticized him. Only once, in an unguarded moment, did he almost reveal his secret opinion: "The dictator transformed himself into ... a good person."[50]

In the late 1950s— with Alessandri yet again in the president's chair — Pinochet was serving in the north of Chile. It was a difficult time for him. His year-old daughter, Jacqueline, fell gravely ill, and, fearing for her life, Pinochet had to go out in search of a competent doctor. His wife was not happy in the arid, barren region, which she found depressing. Pinochet, however, had been appointed commandant in Antofagasta, meaning he was stuck there. So he waited, biding his time, following orders, playing officers' politics, and awaiting the next opportunity. Superior officers had "acquired unlimited confidence in Pinochet for one simple reason. The lieutenant colonel always, without discussion, followed orders."[51]

Back in the capital, things were happening. Chile was opened to the possibility of progressive government by the election of Eduardo Frei in 1964. There was more spending on social programs, using income from high copper prices, Alliance for Progress funds, and a flourishing economy. The generals, however, found reason to grumble because none of the benefits were coming to them. Frei, in fact, fired the army commander, Bernardino Parada, after Parada came to him with a plan for modernizing Chile's army. What few military improvements were possible seemed to be going to the navy and air force. When Britain's Queen Elizabeth visited came to visit and was lunching [in November 1968] with Chilean dignitaries at an exclusive riding club outside Santiago, the discussion turned to what military hardware might be helpful. The queen "noted on a paper napkin Chile's request for British armaments: two missile frigates, two submarines, 20 Hawker Hunter fight planes, and a nuclear reactor, a total of $280 million ... nothing on the list was for the Army."[52]

By the late 1960s, Pinochet's career was elevating him to the point that he would be involved in such high-level discussions—as long as he remembered his place. He was appointed assistant director and professor of geopolitics at Chile's Military Academy and promoted to colonel. In a bizarre incident, the promotion was delayed for months because several leftist senators, including Allende, had him mixed up with another "Pinochet." That one, Manuel Pinochet—no relation—had incurred their wrath as commander of the detachment assigned to guard a copper mine during a strike. In a brutal confrontation, seven miners had been killed. It took weeks to clear up the confusion and get Pinochet's career back on track.

Pinochet's training was now including diplomatic duties, including thirty days of traveling and training in the United States. The U.S. military was then deeply and fatally mired in the jungles of Vietnam, and Pinochet, an admirer of the U.S. effort, sought a way to express his solidarity with U.S. soldiers. Though he knew nothing of combat, he imagined a worldwide battle against communism, with himself a part of it. During his trip to the United States, he had his driver stop the car when he noticed in the window of a suburban house a star signifying the loss of a family member in combat. He walked to the front door and knocked. The door was answered by an elderly woman whose grandson had been killed. Pinochet embraced her, thanking her on behalf of the Chilean people for her sacrifice.[53] "The fight against communism elicited an echo in the colonel's heart," wrote Vial.[54]

Throughout those years, Pinochet closely followed the great battles of the worldwide war on communism. As he rose to deputy director of the War Academy and then to chief of staff of the army's Second Division, Pinochet was informed of Ernesto *Che* Guevara's capture and execution in Bolivia. Father Camilo Torres, the Colombian priest who had joined guerrillas, was also killed. In Paris, leftist students took to the streets and dominated public dialogue about the future. In Santiago, students emulated their European cohort by occupying the Cathedral of Santiago. Frei had begun nationalizing Chile's copper mines. Chile's radical MIR—the group with which Allende's sister sympathized—had been forced underground, but continued robbing banks. And, finally, the Chilean military was especially chagrined when President Frei opened discussions toward returning to Bolivia its corridor to the sea lost in the nineteenth century War of the Pacific. Chilean generals and admirals saw their grandfathers' legacy being frittered away.

In 1969, the year he rose to general and was given a succession of administrative posts, Pinochet grew personally perturbed at what he saw as Frei's reluctance, at the end of his term, to govern with a firm hand. A presidential election was coming—when Allende would run for the fourth time—and Frei was nudging his Christian Democratic Party to the left. It was a particularly bitter pill for Pinochet when a national police unit refused orders to evict a group of squatters occupying private lands. The authorities turned a blind eye because of the pressing need for housing. "Pinochet believed that this was 'suicidal softness' and a political mistake, leading to a loss, not a gain, of votes."[55]

The whole issue of how to govern ultimately popped out at Pinochet like a Jack-in-the-Box when rebellious students in the district under Pinochet's command occupied their school building in a protest. There was considerable sentiment to evict them forcibly, and the army was the chosen instrument of that policy. Pinochet hesitated, however, and finally yielded to the wishes of President Frei's office. He stepped aside and let the secretary of education negotiate with the students. The tactic, Pinochet was told, would help the administration garner needed votes in Congress. "What is of interest about this episode was that it was typical of Augusto Pinochet. Carrying out his public, civic duties, he acted not as a military man but according to legal norms. But—exactly as in the Army—he acceded to his superiors: Frei ordered him to retreat. [He did so] without getting excited, without thought for himself (visibly, at any rate), and without scruples."

Pinochet also found that he was damned whichever way he went. Despite his lenience, communists in Congress continued to excoriate him. They accused him of being implacable in his desire to punish the students and described him as "a true danger to the public."[56] Pinochet would later reveal that his initial respect for Frei lasted only to that time. While he was grateful for Frei's patronage, Pinochet blamed Frei for allowing the Christian Democrats' liberal wing to split off, gravitating toward Allende. "They tied him in knots and immobilized him," Pinochet complained. "He tried to hold onto the left, but it got away from him."[57]

Of one thing Pinochet was right. By that time civic order had disintegrated. While the Chilean middle worried about shrinking family budgets, the radical left and right fought it out in the streets. In June 1970, when former Interior Minister Edmundo Pérez Zuvojica was machine-gunned in his car in Santiago, Pinochet and his fellow officers were observing chaos. The killing of the young leftist who might or might not have been carrying a white flag of surrender brought thousands into the street. At about the same time, at least 40 members of the right-wing Fatherland and Liberty organization were arrested. Though they were released after questioning, suspicion persisted after arms-and-ammunition caches were uncovered in three cities. The organization was girding for battle, and one of their leaders insisted that the military join them. He told a news conference that "the price of liberation is civil war" and that "the military knows very well the responsibility that falls to them."[58] Hearing the call, a tank unit in the Santiago garrison rebelled—it was dubbed the *tanquetazo*—and had to be forced back into their barracks.

In Pinochet's view, the presidential election of 1970 demonstrated the extent to which all Chileans had lost to the left. He was not alone. Allende's victory set many elements within the military—quite accustomed to aiming their weapons at striking miners and disruptive fellow citizens—stirring. An artillery general, Roberto Viaux, aroused the troops that were billeted in the north near Tacna and led them into the streets—the *tacnazo*—as part of a comic opera in which drivers circled La Moneda in their large, lumbering garbage trucks. Viaux and no fewer than 300 officers and non-commissioned officers were threatened with courts martial for dreaming up their part in the affair.

Elements of the military, from crews in port at Valparaíso to garrisons outside the capital to pilots flying jet aircraft—were spoiling for a fight. When their generals tried to calm things down—and defend the constitution—troops sometimes greeted commands with derision. The time that President Allende tried to convey the idea that he had the support of the military by calling the four principal officers onto the balcony with him, it was, again, like comic opera. His supporters in the street chanted their approval with choruses of, *Soldado, amigo/El pueblo está contigo* (Soldier, friend/The people are with you). At the same time, however, hundreds of angry military wives showed up outside the home of the secretary of defense. They shouted that their husbands were being insulted for being forced to protect a Marxist government. In fact, even Allende's balcony showmanship failed: "The presence of the commanders caused vigorous disapproval in the ranks, from the generals and admirals down. It was seen as a case of the superior officers being used for political purposes...."[59]

While much of the discontent was focused in Santiago, Pinochet held himself aloof at his command post in Iquique. "Pinochet absolutely did not participate in any of the happenings. He returned to Iquique by plane on October 17 and stayed there. The Iquique Division gave not the least sign of indiscipline or unrest. Neither the division nor its commander was mentioned in the rumors circulating in the Defense Ministry, the Army, or the press."[60]

Allende, of course, was at war with the Chilean Congress. By early 1973, the Chamber of Deputies was rebelling against the administration's appointments of provincial administrators. The deputies fired appointees either for showing too much lenience toward leftists or for arbitrarily arresting right-wingers. The out-of-control partisanship of the streets was translated to the halls of Congress as leftists extolled Allende programs and opponents trashed them. Christian Democrats suggested that Allende resign, clearing the way for a new election.

The pressure extended to General Carlos Prats, Allende's chief of the army and defense minister, and the result was bizarre behavior. Riding in the front seat of his staff car one day in the crowded streets of the capital, he saw a car pull up beside him. In the car he saw — and heard — two people shouting obscenities at him. Surely, the thought of his predecessor's assassination under similar circumstances flashed through his mind. He asked for his driver's pistol — overlooking the submachine gun on the seat between them — and pointed it at the offending driver. When the driver ignored a command to stop, Prats fired, hitting a rear fender.

Both cars stopped, as did others crowding around them. The general got out and approached the other car. The driver got out and came toward him. Only then did Prats see that the driver was a woman — and unarmed. Soon, the police and the press were there, and the incident became a *cause célèbre*. The general offered his resignation, which Allende refused. In fact, a commission of generals effectively exonerated him and expressed indignation at the state of things in the capital and the people's contempt for the army. Prats could take it no longer, however, and resigned his posts of chief of the army and defense minister. In the atmosphere of animosity, other top officers resigned as well.

Allende was running out of alternatives. He had already — in January 1971 — named Pinochet a major general and brought him down from his post in the north to serve as chief of the crucial Santiago garrison. "A dangerous Pinochet was more dangerous in the capital than in the north," Vial wrote. "Why did Salvador Allende trust him?" Pinochet's own later evaluation was that he was chosen, though not yet 60, because he was "old." Vial disagreed. "Undoubtedly, the reason was his accepted image as a general: the image of the underling, faithful, compliant, without goals or ideas of his own ... 'one hundred percent soldier.'"[61]

Now, however, with Prats gone, Allende appointed Pinochet to Prats's position of chief of the army, leaving the defense minister's position open. Pinochet later said he assured Allende he, Pinochet, was "not 'General Vicente Rojo,'" a reference to the general who turned on Francisco Franco and supported Franco's enemies. His "responsibility as a soldier," he told the president, was "to calm the public and stop any disturbance." Furthermore, he would make sure other officers agreed with that view.[62] Allende appointed Pinochet to the top army post on August 23, 1973, a mere 19 days before Pinochet struck.

*   *   *

Pinochet had made sure other officers were with him. Those who were not paid dearly. Isabel Allende, the noted author who was Salvador Allende's cousin, asked: "Who was Pinochet, really? This military man who so deeply marked Chile with his capitalist revolution and two decades of repression?... Why was he so feared? Why was he admired?... He was a crude, cold, slippery authoritarian man who had no scruples or sense of loyalty other than to the army as an institution — though not to his comrades in arms, whom he had killed according to his convenience...."[63] Isabel Allende compared Pinochet to the tragic protagonists of Mario Vargas Llosa's *Feast of the Goat* and Gabriel García Márquez's *Autumn of the Patriarch*, classic Latin American strongmen who controlled everything and understood nothing.

Pinochet and his fellow generals did understand, however, that Chile was clearly in deep political trouble. "Both left- and right-wing opposition hardened their positions in the final months of the Allende administration. Senator Carlos Altamirano, secretary general of the Chilean Socialist Party, threatened to expose the president as a weakling or traitor to the revolution if Allende did not move more swiftly to carry out political and economic reforms demanded by the extreme left wing. Southern Chile had become a political no-man's land, as farms were taken over.... Industrial plants, both large and small, began to fall under state control as credit disappeared." Middle-class support evaporated "as standards of living began to fall, food shortages developed, and political liberties eroded. After Allende began to ignore the Supreme Court and the Congress, he found himself forced to call in the Chilean military to shore up his regime."[64]

"Chile's Christian Democrats had had serious confrontations with socialism, and in 1973 they supported Pinochet's coup," wrote Argentine journalist Torcuato Di Tella. "Chilean socialism during Salvador Allende's tenure had committed more than one abuse and had failed to respect the interests of sectors represented by his rivals."[65] Eduardo Frei, the Christian Democratic president and Allende's predecessor, agreed. He blamed Allende's downfall squarely on Allende's shortcomings: "The military was called and complied with its legal obligation because the Executive and Judicial branches of government, Congress and the Supreme Court, had publicly accused the President of violating the Constitution, of breaking agreements reached with Congress and dictates issued by judges."[66]

Pinochet's takeover was roundly applauded in Washington, especially within the Nixon administration and its ideological commander, Henry Kissinger. Fundamentally, Allende and the Chilean left — like Castro before them and Ortega since — had strayed beyond the permissible. "Events essentially followed a principal objective," wrote Joan Garcés, an associate and friend of Allende, "*to keep the nation-state within the same powerful international system that held other countries. To reach that goal, there was a coalition among and coordination between local conservative forces and international representatives of the dominant country. The phenomenon is as old as the history of international relations.*"[67] Of Pinochet's regime, biographer Vial wrote: "The Western countries of most economic importance, especially in Europe, managed to forget easily — at least for the most part — the human rights abuses. A case in point was China ... the Iran of Khomeini and the Iraq of Hussein. 'Business is business.'"[68]

Novelist Allende, too, believed that the coup was engineered less to protect the national economy from the excesses of Marxism than to keep Chile under the sway of a military serving the interests of several huge U.S. corporations. "Thus the months went by," Allende wrote, "and it became clear to everyone ... that the military had seized power to keep it for themselves and not to hand the country over to the politicians of the right who had made the coup possible. The military were a breed apart, brothers who spoke a different dialect from the civilians and with whom any attempt at dialogue would be a conversation of the deaf, because the slightest dissent was considered treason in their rigid honor code."[69]

However, there was resistance to the coup within the military. Non-commissioned officers in training at a national police school in Santiago held out for three days. "Several regiments supporting the Allende government ... fought bloody engagements." Two weeks after the coup a Pinochet spokesman conceded that several armed groups in the south of the country were holding out. Most chilling, however, were reports that Pinochet supporters had paved their to future promotions with the bones of potential adversaries. Details gathered by Sobel included that "several hundred officers thought likely to oppose the coup had been shot *the night before* it occurred, and much of the fighting during the first three days after the takeover was among military units.... [M]any officers were killed or detained the night before the coup, including the then navy commander, Admiral Raúl Montero, and air force General Alberto Bachelet."[70]

* * *

Because of the almost unbelievable extent of the Pinochet regime's reign of terror, which is documented by those lucky enough to escape and by Chilean and foreign investigative commissions, a review of its economic and social reforms tends to stick in the throat. Nevertheless, a fair account was made by Chilean historian Carlos Huneeus.[71]

Huneeus condemned the excesses, cruelties, and abuses of the Pinochet government, but pointed out that the economic system engendered by Pinochet's administration grew out of the failures under Allende and provided a foundation for growth — despite its own failures— that has lasted into the return to democracy.

The Pinochet government's economic reforms were largely designed by the "Chicago Boys." They were a group of Chilean economists who, after graduation from Chile's Catholic University, attended the University of Chicago, the home of neoliberal economic theory. Neoliberal thinking encourages the maximum return on private investment while holding down labor's cost and influence. The economic successes of neoliberalism, Huneeus pointed out, can be seen in the industrial growth of Germany under Hitler and of Spain under Franco. Both examples created conditions for *post-dictatorship* industrial growth and political democracy.

"Economic insecurity and discontent with Popular Unity among much of the public caused many to support the authoritarian regime, with the hope that it would bring back order and growth.... So the [Pinochet] government not only stressed the totalitarian nature of the Popular Unity parties, but also kept alive the negative image of their economic management, particularly its effect on the working class and women."[72]

Pinochet's economic successes were a long time coming, even though the administration set up make-work projects and doled out benefits to the poor. A docile populace is easier to crush. "The new rulers sought the backing of the poor through political means, for in economic policy they gave priority to business interests." Still, unemployment rose to 15.7 percent in 1975 and went down only slightly in succeeding years. In 1983, the figure had risen to 19 percent unemployed, or 740,000 Chileans out of work. "The recovery was slow, and only in 1989 did the figure fall to a single digit (8 percent). Wages fell and stayed below 1970 levels until 1992."

The major difference between Allende and Pinochet was that the latter was able to combine rigid control of the population with unimaginably brutal oppression of enemies. It was no surprise that immediately after the coup, Chilean truckers called off their national strike. "Economic problems had hastened the political crisis of the Allende government and provoked massive protests in the streets of middle- and working-class neighborhoods, but under Pinochet things were different, with the military harshly repressing any sign of public protest."[73]

With the workers on their knees, the Pinochet regime began building for the future. "[T]he regime's reforms radically changed Chile's production infrastructure and laid the foundation of subsequent growth. Other Latin American dictators failed to manage their economies successfully, but Pinochet set up conditions friendly to growth, and his main economic institutions continued to function in Chile today." However, Huneeus continued: "Examined over the long term, the results were modest in terms of growth, employment, and inflation compared with the achievements of democratic governments in the 1960s and 1990s. The results were also uneven: neoliberal policies led Chile into its worst recession of the century, when in 1982 and 1983 the financial system collapsed and GDP dropped by 14.5 percent."[74]

In the end, no society can grow by bread alone, except fatter and more docile. "Authoritarian modernizations are partial," Huneeus concluded. "They do not affect the economy as a whole, or the social system since they maintain the components that benefit the interests of the dominant players.... Sweeping modernization can only be achieved in a democratic setting in which different interest groups have equal opportunities to make their demands, and in which the economic system becomes institutionally complex. Labor policy, for example was designed to favor the employers, curtailing worker rights and weakening the union movement. In the private sector, preference was given to larger companies at the expense of medium and small enterprises, and regulatory consumer protection institutions were reined in."[75]

* * *

Right after the coup, Decree 527 of the military junta vested all power in Pinochet, and he stamped his iron seal on the government. No longer was he fulfilling the wishes of a superior; he was superior to all and he unleashed the dogs of hatred. Between 1973 and 1976, Pinochet was a military dictator. Records of the 1970 election were burned; approximately 130,000 people were jailed; at least 3,000 people disappeared; thousands fled the country. Within weeks of the coup, Prats and his wife were killed when their car was bombed. Prisons were set up in Pisagua, where Pinochet had guarded communists; in Chacabuco; and on the formidable Dawson Island, in the Magellan Straits. An estimated 7,000 were imprisoned at the National Stadium, where those who managed to get out told of hearing the tortured screaming in agony, their cries often silenced by gunshots.

Critical to Pinochet's reign of terror — by comparison, a relatively modest 1,500 people were guillotined in the first eight, anguished weeks of the French Revolution — was his organization of DINE, the *Dirección de Inteligencia del Ejército*, the army's feared unit charged with identifying and dealing with enemies of the state. In all, during Pinochet's regime, the armed services and national police operated at least seven intelligence agencies, an agglomeration of spies, informants, and, when necessary, assassins. "It serves no purpose to detail the rapid expansion of DINA — its operations, its budget, its personnel, its management, its prisons, etc.," wrote Vial, who served on Chile's Rettig committee, which tried to sort out the carnage of the Pinochet years. "It became a monster with tentacles throughout the country and abroad, employing thousands — 50,000 by Contreras's account — of employees and informants."[76]

Manuel Contreras was the man chosen by Pinochet to direct DINE. A lieutenant colo-

nel from the engineer corps, Contreras was apparently picked by Pinochet not for his expertise in intelligence, but because of his well-known right-wing sympathies. DINA got right to
work. The Chilean writer Ariel Dorfman, who fled Chile, described the highly efficient operation that set up military courts throughout the land. Commanders responsible for those
courts were punished if they were not sufficiently harsh. On September 30, just three weeks
after the coup, Dorfman wrote, DINA officers, led by General Sergio Arrellano Stark, "in full
battle gear," set out to make sure operations were proceeding as ordered. They went to every
military prison before reaching the one at Calama. "Taking off from Santiago's Tobabalaba
airport on September 30, Arellano and company had gone first south and then north. In each
city where there had been no sentences and no political prisoners, the commanding officer
had been relieved and, later, arrested and sent to Santiago; and in cities where there had been
military tribunals but the results had been judged to be lenient or compassionate, a series of
prisoners already serving sentences had been illegally hauled out of their cells and executed.
Calama was the last stop of an itinerary of mayhem."[77]

At the top of DINA's target list were pro–Allende groups purported to have organized
cordones, or militias, and stashed weapons. "DINA undertook a systematic campaign of exter-
minating successive targets— one after the other — who'd belonged to Allende's security forces,
were members of the [ultra-radical] MIR, or Socialists, or Communists, targeting their commanders. The object was to infiltrate, identify, and kill them, in combat or after they'd been
disarmed — it was all the same.... The task of eliminating leftist strongholds continued until
late 1976, a total of some 1,200 murders: about 60 from the security force, 400 from the MIR,
an untold number from the Socialist Party, and 350 from the Communist Party. In many
instances, the bodies were never found."[78]

Setting the itinerary was Pinochet. "The authoritarian regime cannot be explained without taking into account the role played by General Pinochet.... He was head of state, of government, and of the army, jealously exercising each role simultaneously, aware that his
authority stemmed from his being at the top of the hierarchy of the most important, most
powerful branch of the armed forces.... Pinochet was the undisputed leader."[79] The consequences flowing from Pinochet's single-mindedness in Chile's heated political atmosphere
suggest the portrait of Nazi Germany drawn by Hannah Arendt: "Evil ... need not be committed only by demonic monsters but — with disastrous effect — by morons and imbeciles."[80]

Pinochet's personality made him grasp every lever of power, and his domination drove
him ever deeper into atrocities: "Pinochet was incapable of changing his political style once the
regime gained a firm hold and was about to enjoy the achievements of economic reforms. He
remained glued to the confrontational, aggressive style he had adopted early on, and supported
the actions of the DINA and CNI [secret intelligence agencies], protecting General Manuel
Contreras right up to his conviction by the Chilean Supreme Court in 1995 for his role in the
murder of ambassador and minister Orlando Letelier in Washington, D.C., in September of
1976. This support involved a high cost, as it rendered Pinochet responsible for every one of
the atrocities committed by the agents of these bodies, which explains his arrest in London."[81]

In 1980, Pinochet had engineered a rewriting of the national constitution, and in March
1981 he was sworn in as president. A list of 5,000 Chileans not allowed to re-enter the country was published in, appropriately enough, 1984. When Chileans organized street protests,
the army and the national police put them down. In 1986, Carmen Gloria Quintana and
Rodrigo Rojas were arrested by the military, splashed with kerosene, and set afire. Rojas
burned to death; Sta. Quintana lived despite 60 percent of her body having been burned. For
his part, Pinochet escaped an assassination attempt with minor injuries. The next year Pope
John Paul II visited Santiago.

In 1988 the agonizing path to the end began. Pinochet lost a plebiscite that would have kept him in power, and in 1989 Chileans altered the constitution, setting up the election of Patricio Aylwin, the candidate of 14 parties, as president. Pinochet refused to leave office until he was assured that he could continue as commander in chief of armed forces and be named Senator for Life. The latter designation made him immune from prosecution. Pinochet warned Aylwin not to make any promotions in the military that might displease him, and, from time to time, soldiers in camouflage would appear on Santiago streets as Congress debated. Pinochet also warned against prosecuting one of his sons, who had been accused of fraud. "In subsequent months, Pinochet tried to exert political influence, aiming to cultivate the image of an old statesman."[82]

Thus Pinochet remained safe as Chileans reclaimed their country. In March 1998 Pinochet relinquished his post as commander and chief of the armed forces and in October traveled to London for back surgery. There he was placed under house arrest at the request of a Spanish judge who was responding to charges that included 94 counts of torture of Spanish citizens living in Chile. The Spanish court had to focus its pursuit on the last fourteen months Pinochet was in office, because that was after Great Britain signed onto an international agreement against torture. For the rest of 1998 and into the next year, the attempt to bring Pinochet before a court stuttered, stopped, started, and stopped again.

Pinochet's lawyers argued that he was immune as head of state. Eventually, the case went, on appeal, to the English House of Lords, which voted that he was not immune. When it was found that a peer had ties to Amnesty International, there was yet another hearing. It was found that Pinochet could be extradited to Spain, but only for crimes after 1998. Before that could happen, however, British Home Secretary Jack Straw ruled Pinochet unfit for extradition after he suffered two minor strokes. By that time Canada had quashed charges by a Canadian nun that she had been tortured in Chile, and Straw had to dismiss warrants filed by Spain, Switzerland, Belgium, and France trying to bring Pinochet to trial. In March 2000 Pinochet flew home. He was greeted at Santiago's airport by thousands of supporters, including senior commanders of the armed forces.

Now, in Chile, the frustrating courtroom drama was played out again. Under consideration were 57 murders and 18 kidnaps for which the victims had never been found and were presumed dead. Although Pinochet was placed under house arrest, the Chilean military did its best to keep him out of a courtroom, and his lawyers argued that he was too feeble, mentally and physically, to stand trial. After the Supreme Court ruled him incompetent to stand trial, Pinochet, apparently feeling safe, yielded his Senate seat. However, charges mounted, and the courts reconsidered and stripped him of his immunity. Underscoring the ignominy, investigative committees produced evidence that between 1994 and 2002 Pinochet had hidden millions of dollars at the District of Columbia's Riggs Bank. A U.S. Senate subcommittee found he accumulated $8 million dollars in Washington, D.C., and misappropriated a grand total of more than $26 million. Thus, as bills of indictment finally began to be handed down, the charges included torture (23 cases), kidnappings (36), tax evasion, and corruption.

On November 25, 2006, on his 91st birthday, Pinochet took responsibility for his failures. Two days later he was again placed under house arrest on kidnapping charges. A week later he suffered a stroke, and a week after that he was dead.

*   *   *

By that time, there had been the most thorough accounting that Chile could manage. In 2003, on the 30th anniversary of the coup, Chilean President Ricardo Lagos formed the National Commission on Political Imprisonment and Torture, and late the next year a commission report documented 28,000 cases of torture. The list was the basis for reparations to be paid to victims and their families. At least seven top national officials suffered at the hands of the Pinochet regime, including Allende's interior minister, José Toha, who died from physical and psychological torture while held on Dawson Island. Human rights groups have since estimated that the total number of people killed as a result of Pinochet's coup was approximately 4,000.

22

César Chávez

Hispanic Spartacus

1927–1993
(United States)

"Now farming became industry, and the owners followed Rome, although they did not know it. They imported slaves ... although they did not call them slaves: Chinese, Japanese, Mexicans, Filipinos. They live on rice and beans, the business men said. They don't need much. They wouldn't know what to do with good wages. Why, look how they live. Why, look what they eat. And if they get funny—deport them."[1]
— John Steinbeck, *The Grapes of Wrath*, 1939

The tragedy of those lines is not just in the circumstances they portrayed—the plight of thousands of down-and-out migrants—but that they are today read only as "literature," or, worse, as "literary history," and not as persistent reality. The words helped seal the reputation of a Nobel laureate, but, sadly, they failed to have the effect their author wanted—to lead Americans toward solving the complex equation of migrant labor in the United States. Today, camps from Long Island to North Carolina to California crowd migrant farm workers together during planting and harvest seasons, often under unsanitary conditions. Some ten million migrant illegal immigrants are hidden in plain sight, awaiting services for themselves, education for their children, and some reasonably intelligent discussion from Congress. Perhaps the greatest tragedy is that the person who did most to hold up the plight of North America's migrant labor to the world, demonstrating in word and deed how to solve the problem, has almost completely disappeared from our historical memory.

* * *

In keeping with Steinbeck's imagery of slavery, César Chávez used to speak of his grandfather's having "escaped" from the Chihuahua hacienda where he worked in the 1880s. "On the hacienda," Chávez said, "they were slaves. The moment a baby was born, they would give him a tag and start keeping a book on him of all his expenses. By the time the child grew old enough to start working, he already was sold, he already owed a lot of money."[2] On the hacienda, if a worker got into trouble with co-workers or was disobedient, the owner would let the government know and the worker was immediately drafted into the Mexican army. In fact, it was to avoid conscription that Cesario Chávez—after a rift with the hacienda owner's son—fled to Texas. There, he earned enough money working on the railroad and on the farms to bring over his wife and their fourteen—there would be one more later—children. That was about 1888, when César Chávez's father, Librado, was two years old.

Eventually, "Papa Chayo," the grandfather, settled his family in Arizona's Gila Valley. "My grandfather developed a hauling business around Yuma, Gila Bend, and the mining towns," Chávez told Jacques Levy, a biographer who spent six years learning the story of Chávez and his movement. "As my dad got older, they worked together as long-line skinners, driving as many as twenty-two horses or mules hitched to one cart to haul their loads."[3] Eventually, Cesario got a contract to haul firewood to the crews building Laguna Dam. He put his earnings into homesteading a hundred-acre farm on the Colorado River three years before Arizona entered the union in 1912.

When he took title to the land, grandfather Chávez was asked if he was a citizen. Well, he replied, a dozen years earlier, not long after arriving in Texas, he got five dollars to vote for a particular candidate in a local election. That answer satisfied the authorities; and the story meant enough to his son Librado that he, too, figured he was a citizen until the 1950s, when the Walter-McCarran Immigration Act told him he was not. "Perhaps," César recalled, "because of the five dollars my grandfather received and what it later meant, our relatives in Yuma took their political activity very seriously."

As grandfather Cesario's numerous offspring grew up and married, they moved into homes of their own, but Librado stayed to work the farm. Then he, too, married when he was 38 years old. His wife was Juana Estrada, another native of Chihuahua who was six years younger. "My mother was then a very tiny woman, little more than five feet tall, with a slender waist and delicate features framed by long black hair that fell over her shoulders. Her hands were small, and her fingers long and thin and agile. She talked a lot, her tongue skipping as fast as her mind from one thing to another, while my father was very quiet." Chávez described his parents as having been tolerant of their children's behavior, which he attributed to their being older, thus more patient, as the children came along. Librado made many of their toys— sardine-can cars, and tractors of sewing spools—though he was usually too busy to spend time with the children. Doña Juana was the one who was there, insisting that the girls do "women's work" like washing and ironing because "they had to get trained" for marriage.[4]

Librado Chávez seemed resigned to his fate as a worker. Despite fainting at least once while working on the ranch under the scorching Arizona sun, Librado decided to take on more responsibility. He bought a business on the valley floor, a mile below the ranch. There were three buildings, a grocery store behind which the family lived, a garage, and a pool hall with a counter for sweets and cigarettes. "The grocery store was small, but it had all the major items people needed, and my dad had a ready-made list of customers. Our family isn't tiny. My aunts and uncles each had a dozen or more children; there were at least 180 nieces and nephews."[5] Because all those families got mail, Librado was eventually appointed an official U.S. postmaster. In addition, as befitted a man of so much standing in the community, Librado became something of a political boss. His opinion was respected, and he and his neighbors, all Hispanic, voted as a bloc in Arizona elections, some of which were close.

*   *   *

Cesario Estrada Chávez was born on March 31, 1927, in the house behind the store and named after his grandfather. His sister, Rita, who was born two years earlier, and his younger brother, Ricardo, would accompany César through his career. There were two other sisters, Helena and Eduvigis, or "Vicky," and another brother, Librado, or "Lenny." Their father's business prospered, but in order to provide for his growing family, he decided to increase his holdings yet again. He agreed to clear an 80-acre plot—pulling stumps with field horses— for the man who had sold him the store. In return, he would get the deed for half the cleared land.

However, the owner welshed on the deal. He sold all 80 cleared acres to another man, one Justus Jackson. "My dad was never afraid to stand up for his rights. He was not cowed because the neighbor was an Anglo, a white man. He went straight to a lawyer, ready for a court battle. But the lawyer, who was also an Anglo, advised him to borrow money and just buy the land ... when my dad couldn't pay the interest on the loan, the lawyer bought the land from him and sold it back to the original owner. It was a rotten deal all around."[6]

By then, the nation had descended into the Great Depression, and Librado was providing for his ailing mother in addition to extending credit to all those relatives. Eventually, faced with mounting debt, he sold his store for $2,750, which was enough to pay off creditors, but not the tax man. In 1937, the state foreclosed on the ranch. By that time the family had moved in with Chávez's grandmother, who by then was blind; the six kids were packed into one room. Among the things that Librado had been unable to sell was the pool table, so César and brother Ricardo threw a thin mattress on it and slept there. "The house, of course, had no electricity and no running water, but the canal was only about five feet from the front door ... its water clay-red with mud. We would put that water in big tanks, two fifty-gallon drums, and in a week's time, after two or three inches of dirt settled at the bottom, we could use it."

Sister Helena, who was born about a year before the family had moved into the ramshackle house, died of some undiagnosed childhood ailment. Doña Juana's knowledge of herbs was to no avail. "It was a time when everything seemed wrong. The air turned heavy, the usually dry desert heat became muggy, and the clear skies fill with dark clouds. Though a storm is very unusual in Arizona, there was lightning and thunder that shook the adobe walls.... As the rain grew more intense, Helena seemed to shrivel and shrink.... She died in my mother's arms."[7] Because the intense rain continued, the child could not be buried for several days.

Prospects in the area briefly improved when work began on a federal dam in 1936. Librado was able to rent back the pool hall and gas station he'd once owned. Ricardo—now known as Richard—and César helped, pumping gas and cleaning up. Their career as shopkeepers almost was ended when they were caught stealing cigarettes that they gave away to schoolmates. Among them were an increasing number of Anglos, their parents having moved into the area to work on the dam. Most came from the especially impoverished southern states, and tension rose. "Nearly every noon now there were fights with the Anglos in school. I don't remember exchanging blows.... But there were some heated arguments."[8]

As the Depression went on, even Librado's heroic work ethic could not keep up. In the summer of 1938, Librado left home with several relatives to look for work in California. "The odds against him were enormous. California was experiencing one of the greatest invasions in its history. Thousands of people were streaming into California then, uprooted from the Dust Bowl or destitute because of the Depression." Librado was among some 300,000 Americans driven to California by drought and the Depression. He found work threshing beans and saved up enough to pay for a shack in the small town of Oxnard. Librado sent for his family, and the family set out from Arizona in an 11-year-old Chevy with a rumble seat. There were Doña Juana, who spoke no English (nor did the two youngest children); two girls; three boys; and two cousins who did the driving. On the way, they stopped to rest in the desert. It was after midnight.

"The highway was quiet," Chávez recalled, "and the sand stretched out into the night. Nothing could have been more peaceful. Suddenly two cars bore down on us, their floodlights shattering the dark. Uniformed men piled out of the cars and surrounded ours. We were half-asleep, all scared, and crying." The only thing Doña Juana had to prove that they had not just come across the border was the letter from Librado, postmarked Oxnard. "Nothing we said seemed to satisfy them, and the harassment continued hour after hour. My mother must have died a hundred times that night. She was praying hard. Finally, after about five hours, they let us go."

Their father's plans for work in California did not work out, much to César's relief. "There were fences everywhere, too many people, and too much fighting."[9] They returned — in a 1930 Studebaker that had, to César's wonderment, a speedometer and an oil gauge! — to the ranch that Papa Chayo had homesteaded. Before long, however, it was lost for non-payment of taxes. "Landownership is very important," Chávez said of the experience, "and my dad had very strong feelings about the land. If we had stayed there, possibly I would have been a grower. God writes in exceedingly crooked lines."[10]

So it was back to California. One of the family's homes was a 10-by-12 room with 11 people living in it, including an uncle, an aunt, and cousins. The family chased after each harvest, be it peas, cherries, string beans, prunes, or, among César's least favorites, walnuts. Even though they were hard to harvest, however, walnuts were the basis of a business for César and Richard. Because walnut meats fetched the best price in unbroken halves, the two brothers set themselves up at a table each night, carefully opening walnut shells that another worker brought them.

César told Studs Terkel, the oral historian: "When we moved to California, we would work after school. Sometimes we wouldn't go. Following the crops, we missed a lot of school. Trying to get enough money to stay alive the following winter, the whole family picked apricots, walnuts, prunes. We were pretty new. We had never been migratory workers. We were taken advantage of quite a bit by the labor contractor.... In some pretty silly ways.... We trusted everybody that came around."[11]

The family was met by occasional kindness, but more often by cheating labor contractors. "I would say without hesitation that the most evil of all evils in the system is the farm labor contractor." A contractor would spot the family squeezed into its Studebaker, give them his card, promise a wage, and send them off. The contractor got $20 for each family of workers, and if the family arrived to find that the wage had been exaggerated, or there was no place to live with dignity, or no prospects for more work beyond planting or harvest, there was nothing to be done for it. "Labor contracting is nothing more nor less than a remnant of the system of peonage."[12] And there was prejudice. One of Chávez's strongest memories of those days was of stores with signs in their windows: "White Trade Only."

Family life followed an erratic path of uncomfortable and often unhygienic accommodations, at times with the parents and girls sleeping inside a tent, the boys outside. Labor in the fields was still back-breaking, and the most desirable farms were those that allowed children to work alongside their parents. Rita, the oldest child, stopped going to school in order to work beside her mother. "My mother and I used to tie carrots in the field. We would leave about 3:00 in the morning in order to get a space to go to work. We would start work with headlights from cars and tractors."[13]

Their fortunes improved somewhat when they met one Natividad Rodríguez. Rodríguez was a landlady with a punishing sarcasm and the proverbial heart of gold. She took the Chávez family in out of the rain after they'd made their way back to Oxnard and gave them a place to stay. Each morning, after their parents and Rita went to work, the children trudged off to school whether or not they had shoes to wear or socks that matched. If there were complaints about sock colors, Doña Juana offered, helpfully, "They're not that much different."

César quit school after the eighth grade, taking up farm work fulltime. By the time he was sixteen or so, he was big enough to do the job of an adult, including the odious task of topping sugar beets, some of which grew to 15 pounds and all of which were caked with mud.

But Chávez recalled that despite being tired to the bone from work, living in miserable conditions, and constantly having to find work, the workers around him typically stood up to abusive supervisors. "Once, in Wasco, we were picking cotton when another farm worker started arguing he was being shortchanged in weight. We argued for the worker, and when he quit, we quit, too. We quit many jobs over such arguments...."[14]

The plight of migrant farm labor had come to the attention of others, too. In 1942, a left-leaning faction of the American Civil Liberties Union, calling itself the American Committee for the Protection of the Foreign Born, split off from the ACLU to work on improving migrant workers' rights. Chávez told biographer Levy of an evening when his father talked to a CIO organizer who came to their home. Also there that night was an uncle who worked with his father at a dried-fruit operation and two older cousins. Because his mother was nervous around organizers — presumably because they were associated with strike violence — Librado sent his son out of the house while the organizer was there. Chávez recalled being impressed that his father was impressed with the man. That stuck in a young mind despite the fact that Chávez was at an age when he was generally alienated from adults. He gave short shrift to the church and its parishioners' quaint habit of praying to particular saints. Nor did he share his parents' belief in the folk medicine practiced by *curanderos*. He was not even particularly fond of *ranchero* music. Like his age cohort, Chávez adopted the pegged pants and duck-tail haircut of the *pachucos*. He was, that is to say, cool.

*   *   *

Young Chávez certainly seemed to appear so to Helen Fabela, a pretty girl who worked in a malt shop in her native Delano, California. "I remember she had flowers in her hair," Chávez told Levy.[15] He also remembered that she saved cigarettes, then very hard to get, for him. Alas, Fabela, when asked by Levy, could not recall exactly when she met her future husband, only that "César used to migrate and come by Delano every year."

In 1944, when he was 17, Chávez joined the Navy. "I don't know why I joined the Navy in 1944; I think mostly to get away from farm labor. I was doing sugar beet thinning, the worst kind of backbreaking job, and I remember telling my father, 'Dad, I've had it.'" He preferred the Navy to being drafted into the Army. "Those two years were the worst of my life: this regimentation, this super authority that somehow somebody has the right to move you around like a piece of equipment. It's worse than being in prison. And there was lots of discrimination. Before the war the navy had blacks and Filipinos who were given kitchen jobs, but no Mexicans. The only black man I ever saw who was better than a steward was a painter. The Mexican Americans were mostly deck hands. That's what I was."[16]

Once when he was home on leave, out of uniform, Chávez and a few buddies went to the movies. At the time, racial segregation in public places was practiced throughout the San Joaquin Valley. Chávez and his buddies knew and accepted that. But, for Chávez, the acceptance was wearing thin. "In Delano, the quarter-section on the right was reserved for Mexicans, blacks, and Filipinos, while Anglos and Japanese sat elsewhere. It had been like that since the theater was built, I guess. But this time something told me that I shouldn't accept such discrimination.... I decided to challenge the rule, even though I was very frightened. Instead of sitting on the right, I sat down on the left. When I was asked to move to the other section, I refused, and the police took me to jail." After an hour, he was released without charge. "It was the first time I had challenged rules so brazenly, but in our own way my family had been challenging the growers for some time."[17]

After serving in the Pacific theater, Chávez returned to farm work — and to civil disobedience. In 1948, while picking cotton alongside his father and others, a caravan of strikers rolled by. His father called out, "Let's go," and a group walked off the job. "As I recall, we struck for a few days.... Pretty soon there were just a handful of us, and the strike was over."[18]

What was just beginning was his marriage to Helen Fabela. He remembered that they were married during the cantaloupe harvest. Because he was interested in the missions established by Spanish colonists, they toured them for their honeymoon. Then it was back to work. Chávez worked the grape harvest, then picked winter cotton — "a horrible experience" — and sharecropped strawberries. Two children, Fernando and Sylvia, were born, and then Helen was pregnant with Linda. Chávez found work in a lumber mill.

Jobs came and jobs went. Chávez worked when he could, spent time with his family when he could, and, always, as a natural leader, organized. He went door to door and held his own meetings, keeping as low a profile as possible. "It's not at all dramatic. It's long and drawn out. Most of it is anticipation. The victories come much later."[19] In the early years of their marriage, Helen worked in the fields to help support the family.

There were strains. Chávez's weight dropped from 152 to 127 pounds; he was averaging four hours' sleep a night. When their son "Birdy" was two weeks old, he fell ill with a serious case of diarrhea. Chávez would remember years later that he "was too busy to take him to the doctor. Finally, Helen walked with him to an osteopath, who misread the symptoms." When Helen's tearful desperation finally stirred Chávez to action, they rushed the boy to a hospital, where they were told he would not live. Finally, in another town, they found a pediatrician who saved the child's life. Later, when Birdy was a toddler, Chávez kept him close, taking him in the car on organizing trips. "I would just take a pillow and some blankets for him, and then I'd teach him to tell from the car what kind of field it was."[20]

All around him Chávez saw why working people were too concerned with survival to rebel. They worked at futureless jobs in the hope of a better education and higher prospects for their children. But that, Chávez came to believe, was just what "the system" of growers and politicians and merchants wanted. As long as the working class kept on pulling itself up by the bootstraps, it was too tired to fight. People would focus on saving themselves and their families, leaving their neighbors to look out for themselves. Nothing would change. The world that Steinbeck described in 1939 would look the same in 1949 and 1959: "That's the trap most poor people get themselves into. It's easier for the person to just escape, to get out of poverty, than *to change the situation.*"[21]

Chávez began to get what he called his "education" when he met two Anglos, both of whom worked in the Hispanic barrio *Sal Si Puedes*, which means Get Out If You Can. The first was Father Donald McDonnell, a missionary priest who served mass in the barrio, which had no church. It was a ghetto of hundreds of Mexican American families, and most of those families were riddled with unmet needs. When a woman in the barrio died, her daughter went to Chávez for help with the burial. Chávez thought first of going to Catholic Charities, but Father McDonnell encouraged him to organize his own burial service.

Chávez was put off by the idea, but, with the priest's guidance, he relented. He borrowed an old Army litter and spent three hours talking the county hospital into releasing the body. It was a process that went all the way up to Pat Brown, then California's attorney general. State law allowed a family to bury its own, so the good father's idea prevailed. Everything was accomplished even though they were not allowed to use the hospital elevator, causing Chávez to throw his back out helping to lift the corpse down the stairs. They rolled the litter into the back of a station wagon on water pipes. The whole process would be repeated several times as Chávez conducted more burials, and in doing so he learned the value of funerals as an organizing tactic. Later, if a funeral home refused to bury someone, Chávez would get people together, and they would get it done.

Father McDonnell also talked Chávez into reading the lives of the saints, starting with St. Francis. With that, the priest did all that was required to push Chávez down a long road of reading everything he could get his hands on, including the writings of Martin Luther King, Jr., and Gandhi.

Chávez's second memorable teacher was Fred Ross, an organizer and recruiter for the Industrial Areas Foundation. All that reading was fine, but the time had come to get into the streets, and Ross, an experienced organizer, saw that Chávez had promise. Chávez was picking apricots at an orchard outside San Jose when Ross recruited him. "[T]he first practical steps I learned from the best organizer I know, Fred Ross," Chávez would say. "He changed my life." In 1952, then 25 years old, Chávez heeded Ross's urging and took a part-time organizer's job with the Community Service Organization. CSO was a civil rights organization involved in voter registration and combating discrimination. It was headed by the legendary community and labor organizer Saul Alinsky. The CSO concentrated its efforts mostly on cities, working the streets in barrios like *Sal Si Puedes*.

Ross taught Chávez the tactic of "house meetings," which kept gatherings small, protecting the identity of people lest they be intimidated. It became Chávez's job to show Ross his way around Hispanic neighborhoods, but soon Chávez was looking for something a little more dynamic.

"Well, he was hooked," Ross recalled. "[E]specially when the meeting was relatively small so that they could open up without being embarrassed to say what was on their minds.... At the very first [voter registration] meeting I was very much impressed with César. I could tell he was intensely interested, a kind of burning interest rather than one of those inflammatory things that last one night...." Chávez began to work on a voter-registration drive. Just as in the South, where state legislatures had enacted Jim Crow laws, California relied on hostile registrars to keep Hispanic voters away from the polls. "Although they were nonpartisan offices," Chávez said, "deputy registrars throughout California were Republicans. They were organized to prevent Chicanos from voting. There were restrictions on everything.

"We couldn't speak Spanish when we were registering; we couldn't go door to door; we couldn't register except in daylight hours; we could not register on Sundays." So Chávez became a "bird dog." The precinct organizer sent the bird dog along the street to turn out people. "I'd never done that before, and when I knocked on the first door and a Chicano lady came out, I was so frightened I couldn't talk. She stared at me. She hardly knew me, but she knew my mother. 'Well?' she said, looking at me. Finally, she smiled. 'Okay, we're going to register. We know you're registering people.'" Angry with himself for botching his simple job, Chávez moved on to a house filled with "rough characters" and found that they were people he could talk to. Chávez's career — supported by Helen, who continued to work in the fields — had begun.[22]

Chávez, working during the day at a lumber yard, got good enough at organizing that he asked the local CSO board for funds to pay for a small office. When the request was refused, Chávez decided to pay out of his own, shallow pocket. Ross, however, stepped in and talked Alinsky into giving Chávez a full-time job. Then Ross left the area to finish off a registration drive he'd begun elsewhere.

"It was tough following in my footsteps," Ross told Levy, "and he had to show them he wasn't just a young, dumb kid. He was very young then, only twenty-five, and looked younger, while I was nearly forty-three.... [A registration campaign] was his baptism, but he wanted to get into a place where he didn't have to follow anybody. Some way he fixed it with a priest, Father Gerald Cox, so that he would be invited to go into Oakland to start a voter registration drive." Chávez picked up the story: "Before I left for Oakland, Fred came to a place in

San José called the Hole-in-the-Wall where we talked for a half hour over coffee. He was in a rush to leave, but I wanted to keep him talking. I was that scared of my assignment."

When it came time for Chávez to conduct his first meeting by himself, he drove around the block, afraid to go into the house. When he got up the nerve, there were fewer than a dozen people there, so he went to a chair in the corner and sat in silence for ten, then fifteen, then twenty minutes. It was not until a woman wondered aloud where the organizer was that Chávez spoke up, by that time having driven his credibility deeper into the ground than his self-confidence. "That meeting was a disaster, really a disaster. I fumbled all over the place, I was so frightened." Then Chávez realized what others had long since recognized. "But toward the end of the meeting they were listening to me."[23] He got the people to come to more meetings, to commit themselves to help, to bring others.

In the next voter-registration drive, Chávez — now running his own pack of bird dogs — and others recruited so many prospective registrants that the authorities began to stonewall. Registrars kept short hours, wouldn't let registrants in the door, and refused to provide enough registration booths. "I soon realized that you can't do anything by talking, that you can't do anything if you haven't got the power. I realized that the first time I went to a public office to do battle. Fred was gone, and we needed more deputy registrars to get ready for the general election.... Although I was pretty frightened, I got mad right away and lost my fear. I got into a big argument with the registrar.... That's when I realized you can't do anything by talking. So we began to harass him with telephone calls. I got a lot of people, members of church groups, labor leaders, everyone I could to call him. Then every single day I called him, came to see him...."

By then, Chávez, though still a part-time organizer, had begun to impress people with his strong sense of ethics. He was creating not just a reputation, but something of a saintly aura. It would become more and more a part his image — not altogether appreciated by everyone — and the basis for his following. But for Alinsky, Chávez's saintliness was a source of amusement. Chávez had written to Alinsky in 1955 with a highly unusual request. Alinsky replied: "I have your note of September 2nd acknowledging your salary increase to $4,000 per year ... and for the first time in my association with you I find myself in sharp disagreement with your point of view about (a) You do not expect any more adjustments (b) That you are being overpaid.... If you want to have an argument with me on the basis of your convictions in this matter I suggest that you have a talk with your wife first.... Also, a point of personal curiosity. I note that there is absolutely nothing charged for meals. What were you doing in Fresno at the meeting? Were you on a diet, or did you carry a sandwich from home?... [T]his is a historic event because it is the first time that I have ever raised the question with an employee ... as to whether he did not forget to put things on his expense account."[24]

The CSO's efforts were drawing the attention of college students, many of whom spent their summers volunteering. Making a particular impression was Chávez's solemn sincerity. He related easily to plain people like himself, people with little education. His friends included "Okies," who, as Anglos, might otherwise be expected to keep their distance from Hispanics. They told him their personal and family problems. "The first one was an Anglo and older than I was, but he wanted to tell me that he and his wife were breaking up. I felt so bad and incompetent, as I didn't know what to do.... Since he wanted to tell me, I worked with him, and listened to all his problems.... Then others began coming to me."

Eventually, CSO organizers had registered so many working-class people that shocked registrars turned to intimidation; they insisted that Hispanic voters show that they could read English, including some very complicated prose. Ross was angered by the tactic, and asked the local CSO board to sign a protest to the U.S. attorney general, but Chávez was the only one who would sign. By then, however, Chávez was learning how to engage the news media. Newspaper and television reporters started to show up at meetings. "We also put a big blast in the paper. Then the Republicans accused us of registering illegals and dead people. We called them racists. It was a big fight, my first fight with this power structure, and my name started getting in the paper."

Eventually, the strains of prejudice that cut across U.S. society took their toll on CSO's momentum. When Chávez linked his efforts to those of a Pentacostal preacher, it drew fire from Catholics. "After a while an Italian priest in Madera started criticizing the CSO, complaining that there were too many Protestants in it. So I made a speech at the CSO meeting that no one on this earth was going to tell us whether there was too much of anything, that this was not a religious movement, and that if anybody wanted to make it so, then they had a fight on their hands. We lost a few Catholics, but we gained many Protestants."

Racial prejudice disrupted the CSO chapter where Chávez's sister Rita and her husband Ernie were organizers. Because Rita and Ernie had tried to get Anglo, Hispanic, and African American neighborhoods to consolidate their efforts, they were called "nigger lovers" by Anglos and Hispanics. Among the Mexican Americans who were less than receptive to CSO membership for African Americans was an owner who was a CSO board member. He refused to serve blacks in his restaurant, eventually tearing Rita's and Ernie's unit apart. "Well, it turned into a big, hot battle," Chávez told Levy. "Out of nine officers, seven walked out of the meeting and resigned. Only Rita and Ernie stayed. About 70 percent of the membership, if not more, walked out. It was the poor people, almost all illiterate, many of them from Mexico, who backed the constitution. But most of the middle class walked out."

Finally, even the Cold War took its toll. Every organizer of working class people was branded a communist. Almost from the beginning, Chávez was targeted. "These two young guys showed me their FBI credentials in front of everybody [at the lumber yard where he worked]. Everybody just stopped working and looked at me. The agents started asking me a lot of questions about Communism. I said, 'You know damn well I'm not a communist.'... From then on, every little place I went, I met the liberal lawyer, the liberal teacher, the liberal social worker. We would get together, and I got an education.... I also read in a more disciplined way, concentrating at first on labor, on biographies of labor organizers like John L. Lewis and Eugene Debs and the Knights of Labor."

As Chávez read, he became more and more convinced that passive, but tough-minded, resistance to injustice was the only way that had a prayer of success. Thus in addition to his perceived saintliness, Chávez's persistence became a hallmark of his style. If you don't know you're beat, you're not. And while others saw his behavior as inspired or exemplary or saintly, he insisted that it was just plain stubborn, and that being stubborn conferred power. "It's unfortunate that power is needed to get justice," he told Levy. "That suggests a lot about the nature of man."[25]

* * *

A signal event in Chávez's career — and his mythology — was his assignment to Oxnard, California, his old home town. He found a house outside of town for the family, then with seven — of an eventual eight — children. Helen Chávez told Levy: "The night before, César had gotten sick and was just burning up with fever. I said, 'Let's wait.' But we had everything packed, and he had a house meeting that evening. He said, 'No, we have to go.' I don't drive, so he had to. Here we get into our beat-up station wagon loaded with this huge rented trailer with all our belongings in it and the kids.... We had to stop along the way because he was really burning up with fever." Then their car broke down, and they paid a motorist who stopped to help them their last two dollars. Finally, after managing to cash a check to buy food for the kids, they arrived. "We went up to the little house we had rented, but it was dark, and there was no electricity.... We just threw a few mattresses on the floor so the kids could sleep. I fed them and put them to bed. César went up to this meeting, sick as he was."

So the Chávezes settled in, and in 1958 the Packinghouse Workers Union was organizing workers at the lemon-packing houses in and around Oxnard. Up to then, however, the owners had held the union at bay by negotiating for months without signing contracts. Frustrated workers were drifting away to find work in other places. The union, to bolster its effort, offered $20,000 to the CSO for help in organizing the community—registering voters, identifying neighborhood needs, and so on—and Alinsky agreed. Chávez pitched in, though he would later call Oxnard "probably my worst project of all.... I couldn't see how organizing by the CSO would help the plants organize." Nevertheless, Chávez remembered Oxnard from when he was a kid. "When we were migrants, Oxnard was an extremely bad place for us. In the back of my mind I thought that going back would be a little revenge. I just wanted to go back and fight."[26]

That taste for a fight did not jibe with Chávez's reputation for shyness, and the matter came to a head in Oxnard. The CSO board was split on the question of Chávez's effectiveness. If Chávez was a wallflower, as some said, how was he doing such a good job of organizing? On the other hand, things might be getting too rough for someone as mild-mannered as Chávez. At the time, Alinsky was still paying Chávez a part-timer's salary from Industrial Areas Foundation funds, so he asked the local CSO board to consider making him full time. One board member, a lawyer, balked. He argued that Chávez should submit *daily* reports on his activities and progress. After all, if the CSO was accepting from the $20,000 Packinghouse Workers Union, there needed to be accountability.

Dolores Huerta was at that meeting, which, though it was a "board" meeting, had drawn, as usual, onlookers from other chapters. "César was very quiet," she recalled, "very unassuming in every meeting. I mean he never spoke up, although he was an organizer like Fred [Ross] was. So he was kind of a hard guy to know. So Gilbert López, who was ... president of the Fresno CSO chapter, got up and made this big spiel asking how do we know what César's going to do and saying he would have daily reports sent in to the board of directors, and all of this junk. I remember I got really mad about it, although I didn't know César....

"There was this big fight about it, and I think López was finally outvoted. But that time César did get up, and he spoke about the kind of organizing that he would be doing. He also said that he would be willing to do whatever the board wanted him to do, but that it would probably be difficult to see results at first. I can't remember exactly all the things he said, but he impressed me very much because of the soft-spoken, very gentle way he had about him.... It was kind of like a lamb in the midst of a bunch of lions."[27]

Soon Chávez, too, was a lion, but that was not the most important transformation. Chávez was about to change from community organizing to the hard-nosed world of labor organizing. "When I went to Oxnard," he recalled, "I was sure the biggest issue would be a railroad crossing because when I was in school a lot of Mexicans got killed by the train.... Instead, they began to come at me with the *bracero* issue. That was an issue I didn't even suspect."[28]

In 1942 the United States and Mexico had agreed to alleviate the labor shortage in the Southwest United States resulting from World War by allowing Mexican nationals—*braceros*, or day laborers—across the border. The system served the interests of the growers, who paid next to nothing to get their crops planted, harvested, and packed. They did this in league with "contractors" who provided the hapless workers. Knowing a good thing when they saw it, the growers had influenced state legislatures and Congress to extend and expand the program in 1951. Before it expired at the end of 1964, the *bracero* program had brought in 4.5 million workers, with the single biggest year being 1956, when 445,000 *braceros* entered the country. That was two years before Chávez moved to Oxnard.

Local workers considered the *braceros* nothing more than "scabs"—unorganized workers willing to take minimum pay—and they wanted Chávez's help to stem the tide. "Finally I decided this was the issue I had to tackle.... *Braceros* didn't make any money, and they were exploited viciously, forced to work under conditions the local people wouldn't tolerate. If the *braceros* spoke up, if they made the minimal complaints, they'd be shipped back to Mexico." Indeed, it is worth noting that Chávez was operating in a world unchanged in the two decades since Steinbeck's book. Furthermore, it is clear that U.S. government policy had locked in place a system that benefited the owners of large farms. Finally, the contemporary reader might ask how much is different today.

The system had been in place so long that Chávez had trouble figuring out how to attack. He decided to step back into his role as a worker. "For the first couple of weeks I'd get up early in the morning, apply for work, and make notes." When he showed up for work at the *bracero* camp, he was sent to register at the Farm Placement Service, eight miles away. Because the office did not open until 8:00 A.M., he never got back to the camp before 9:00, by which time all the jobs had been handed out. Indeed, *braceros* were routed out of bed at 4:00 A.M. and were being assigned to fields by 4:30. So, the next day, Chávez sped straight to the camp, getting there between four and five o'clock. He was told he needed a referral from that day; the paper in his hand from the day before was no good.

Chávez did two things. First, he kept taking notes, building a memory, documenting every experience and making copies of all of the referral slips. Second, he designed a tactic that would become his trademark. He produced and directed a piece of street theater that showed how unfair the system was. "I tried to take others with me every day when I went to apply for work at the Farm Placement Service." At first, he couldn't talk anyone into joining him. Then a 17-year-old joined in the charade. "[H]e was my first follower, I guess." They "developed a little ritual going into the office." The office was way at the back of a big building, accessible by a narrow corridor. At the end of the corridor was one desk. "The guy behind the desk was going to sleep—no one had seen him in I don't know how many years. So we went and applied for work. It took one and a half hours to get through the application, there were so many questions." Where had they worked last? When? Each time Chávez and others went through the process, they asked for two copies of the form, filling out both and keeping one. Chávez stacked up the copies. "Little by little a few more guys joined me. And after we had gone about four or five times ... it began to work. The numbers who came to the office grew. I started making it into a sort of game." He got as many as ten out-of-work men to show up at 8 o'clock every morning. "We had to march through the entire office and then along one of the walls to the back. The ladies working here, the moment they saw us coming, turned around to look at us. It was a very funny scene."[29]

Chávez, who was reading Gandhi, was learning the pragmatic side of sainthood. By showing what injustice looked like when it was hung out like long underwear on a clothesline, people were appalled by the behavior of his opponents. "I always have had, and I guess I always will have, a firm belief that if you muster enough power, you can move things, but it's all on the basis of power. Now, I seldom like to go see my opponent unless I have some power over him. I'll wait if it takes all my life. And the only way you can generate power is by doing a lot of work."[30]

All of the fruit, vegetables, and flowers in the United States were—and are—moved from field to packaging to market by a vertically integrated system. Production, processing, cold storage, shipping, advertising, and retail sales—from farm to table — is controlled by big companies. The companies' size has made them powerful in dealing with legislatures and state agricultural agencies, but Chávez saw that they were vulnerable to the length of their marketing chains. Produce had to be delivered fast, and supermarket customers from Fresno to Syracuse had to believe in freshness as they eyed lettuce for rust and squeezed name-brand grapes. Chávez's public-relations campaign was to add the notion of fairness. He wanted consumers to read newspapers and see television reports that raised doubt as to whether what they were being asked to buy in the advertising section was being picked, prepared, and packaged by workers who were treated fairly.

The strategy was to show up at the right places at the right times for news cycles, with long — often very long — processions of workers carrying signs, marching, picketing, singing, and shouting. When Edward Hayes, director of California's Farm Placement Service, was keynote speaker at an installation ceremony of the Ventura County Farm Labor Association, Chávez and his cohorts were there. The Placement Service's role was to assure the flow of cheap, docile workers to growers statewide. "Hayes was a very powerful figure," Chávez said later, "a man who could keep thousands of people from getting jobs. It's amazing how you can hate a guy, but before I was through in Oxnard, that was one guy I hated."[31]

In anticipation of Hayes's appearance, Chávez had a leaflet distributed by perhaps a hundred volunteers, accusing Hayes of complicity with growers. The local Spanish-language radio station — where the announcer was a CSO board member — was alerted to cover the banquet. Chávez also called the governor's office, recently occupied by Pat Brown, the former attorney general and a popular Democrat. Chávez wanted everyone in Sacramento, especially officials at the California Dept. of Employment, which was over the Farm Placement Service, to know of the confrontation. News reporters loved the show, and pictures were run time and again.

Chávez's tactics, for all of his advocacy of passivity, could be harsh. He invited three state officials to one conference only to have their remarks drowned out by the crowd. "Fink!" workers cried. "We want jobs." Chávez recalled: "The people just lashed them. The three ran out of the meeting, visibly shaken."

When Chávez succeeded in getting three experienced workers hired the day after the conference, they were fired within, respectively, one, three, and five hours. So Chávez took their story to Bureau of Employment Security, which answered to the U.S. Department of Labor, and called for an investigation. To spur things along, he produced Farm Placement Service cards filled out by five of the most experienced workers he could find. Chávez's supporters filed so many formal complaints that the Placement Service opened an office in Oxnard to deal with them.

Still that was not enough. Chávez, like the smallest kid on the playground, knew he had to be the loudest. "Then we increased the pressure. We'd go over to the *bracero* camps and picket at night; then, after work, just shout at the people who administered the program, 'We want jobs!' for a half hour and drive them nuts. We had kids distribute leaflets in the stores saying, 'Dear Mr. Merchant, the reason we don't buy here is because the growers won't let us work. They have *braceros* working, and they take all the money to Mexico.'"

Chávez sent a list of fourteen demands to the head of the California Department of Employment. He got an answer that satisfied twelve. He immediately wrote back about the other two. "He answered something like, 'What the hell do you want? Blood?' Sometimes today I wonder how we ever did all that we did in Oxnard, because our fight for jobs was only part of the program. Of the other fights, one of the most dramatic was urban renewal—we once got five hundred at a city council meeting to protest an urban renewal project — but there were other fights, like getting deputy [voter] registrars, fighting the welfare department, and conducting citizenship classes. Thirteen hundred people came to class, and we had one class where over seven hundred became citizens in one day. We were holding the classes in schools, homes, on street corners...." More important to Chávez's long-range plans, attention from news reporters was multiplying the effect. The Hispanic community was emerging from the shadows of the American conscience. Also, as more CSO-backed workers got jobs, they were documenting conditions in the fields. "The authorities didn't know it," Chávez concluded, "but I had nineteen hundred signed affidavits by then, all notarized. Maybe together I had fourteen hundred people involved...."[32]

The CSO in general, and Chávez in particular, were being noticed. Still, however, the growers, when forced to hire local workers, would let them work for a few hours, then fire them; back came the *braceros*. If it was to be a war of toughness and patience, the growers were undaunted. So Chávez kept his foot on the pedal, and the state bureaucracy also took notice. State agents in the field felt the heat from their supervisors, who were on the phone with politicians, who were getting calls from their constituents, who watched the six o'clock news. At a meeting with a California official, Chávez recalled: "He told me, 'You know, these people don't want any investigations. They don't want anything public because this thing is a time bomb. They don't want any publicity on it, and you've got everybody shook up.' I didn't realize the magnitude of the situation, so I thanked him. I thought, if they don't want any publicity, fine. I knew what to do."[33] Chávez promptly turned out a crowd to march, as ostentatiously as possible, to the farm-employment office, registering people "until the guy ran out of cards and went to Ventura for more." Then they marched toward a ranch where they had been told there was work — and where they knew there would be police, reporters, and cameras.

* * *

In 1960, at the end of his assignment to Oxnard — after which his replacements fought among themselves, eroding what had been built — Chávez told the CSO board that he wanted to organize a labor union. Alinsky and the national board supported him; acknowledging the risk, Alinsky said that if CSO had to die on behalf of union organization, it would be "a very healthy death." But the general membership said no. Dolores Huerta was there. "We were all so sad. Fred and I were crying, and I guess the only one who was not was César. As the convention ended, he got up and said, 'I have an announcement to make. I resign.' He dropped the bombshell on the convention. He had so much guts. Everybody was pressuring him to stay; people were crying. But he didn't bow to the pressure. He left." Chávez said, "If I had the support of CSO, I would have built a union there. If anyone from [the U.S. Department of] Labor had come, we would have had a union. I think if the Union of Organized Devils of America had come, I would have joined them, I was so frustrated."[34]

Chávez agreed to stay on as national director for two more years, then formally resigned on his 35th birthday. By then he had helped organize nearly two dozen CSO chapters throughout California. Now he and a small cadre, including Huerta, Father Thomas McCullough, and Father Donald McDonnell set out to organize the farm workers' union that Chávez wanted. The good fathers tried, without success, to win the support of labor leaders Walter Reuther and George Meany. Then Father McCullough suggested they do it on their own, and in 1962 the National Farm Workers Association was born at a tiny convention in an abandoned movie theater in Fresno. Its flag, a stylized black eagle in a white circle on a scarlet field, would be seen in news photographs over the next fifteen years.

They set a goal of five years, by which time they hoped to be big enough to mount a successful strike on their own. Then they hit the road, organizing. Fred Ross recalled: "One hot summer night in 1962, César Chávez pulled up in front of his house in Delano, checked the mileage, and brought to an end the first leg of the long organizing journey that was to be called *La Causa*. In 86 days he had covered 14,867 miles, picked peas, staked grapes, suckered vines, and carried the message to more than 2,000 farm workers in the fields, the dirt roads, and the family rooms of hundreds of tiny barrio houses."[35]

Biographer Ilan Stavans wrote: "Chávez's strategy was first to establish a farm workers' organization and, in quick succession, to arrange a national convention in which its mission would be established.... By underlining the national, not the regional, Chávez sought to build a structure with far-reaching influence.... The term *la causa*, 'the cause,' was embraced. The motto of the convention became, *'Viva La Causa!'*"[36] As always, Dolores Huerta's enthusiasm led the way: "I made my husband, Ventura, quit his job to work for [NF]WA. Then my brother quit his job, and both worked full time without pay to organize the union." Father McCullough wouldn't let Huerta herself be an organizer. "He said farm labor organizing was no place for a woman. So I kind of worked under cover."[37] Chávez was glad to put her to work in Sacramento as a lobbyist, a job at which he considered himself a failure.

Fathers McCullough and McDonnell guided the writing of a constitution. Another guiding light was the Rev. C. Wayne Hartmire, head of the California Migrant Ministry, who coordinated much of the Protestant support. Within a year the AFL-CIO had set up a parallel effort, the Agricultural Workers Organizing Committee, AWOC. AWOC's first director was Al Green, an old-school guy who distrusted Chávez's unorthodox methods and his long-haired collegiate supporters. He was replaced, however, by William Kircher, a veteran of the automobile-workers' union, who became a believer in the farm workers' cause and trusted Chávez's management.

Distrust and differences of style among unions would continue, even after Chávez's union voted to affiliate with the AFL-CIO. This became clear almost immediately as Chávez led his new organization into the teeth of a big strike at the lettuce fields in California's Imperial Valley. Tough AFL-CIO organizers did not think they needed to be instructed in technique by Chávez, and some of the more aggressive even proposed beating up a few *braceros* so the Mexican government would intervene and call them home. Although the strike was being coordinated, once again, by the Packinghouse Workers, different factions and their leaders pulled in different directions. Chávez was headed toward credit unions, health clinics, voter registration, participation in politics, lobbying, and a movement that pulled entire families up by their bootstraps. Banging heads was not part of the plan.

And Chávez harbored misgivings about the traditional unions. As the leader of an affiliate, Chávez was offered a comfortable salary by the AFL-CIO. He turned it down. He did not — nor would he ever — trust or admire large organizations. He saw the AFL-CIO as too closely allied with grand notions like "the good of the country." By contrast, he saw himself and his followers as grunts, foot soldiers, toilers in the trenches. "I just knew that a big organization was not going to let a little organization get it into trouble. They had too many things at stake if we started raising hell with strikes and boycotts."[38]

*   *   *

Throughout the late 1960s and 1970s, Chávez built the union and his style, from national boycotts with lots of publicity to long days and nights of quiet fasting. That style made him, at least briefly, a legend. The times, of course, created many "legends," for it was the era of civil disobedience, marches on behalf of civil rights, and massive, sometimes violent, demonstrations against the Vietnam War. The assassinations of Martin Luther King, Jr., and Senator Robert F. Kennedy followed the assassination of President John Kennedy. Joan Baez and Pete Seeger and Bob Dylan sang of justice blowin' in the wind, but justice was to be found in precious few other places. And in September 1965 the strike that put the Chávez's union on the map began.

The Delano Grape Strike began when Philippine nationals who were grape pickers struck. Although the federal law allowing *braceros* into the country had expired in 1964, Governor Brown had won an extension for California. Thus the growers had created an unholy mixture of wages throughout the state, playing *braceros* off against other workers. Wage rates varied among regions, between growers, and even according to workers' ethnicities. The AFL-CIO called a strike to protest wages below $1.40 an hour in one area, while Mexican Americans were working for $1.10 in another area, and Filipinos worked for $1.25 in yet another.

At first, Chávez was reluctant to jump in because the NFWA still had only about 1,200 members, no more than 200 of them paying dues. His people certainly were not going to cross another union's picket lines, but joining the strike would require funds to pay participating workers; otherwise they would quickly be starved into returning to the fields at whatever wage they could get. "I said it was going to be a long struggle," Chávez said later, "and the only way we could win was by staying with it ... if we went up like a wave and then came down, at the point we came down we would have to start over with whatever we had left."[39]

There was an alternative. Chávez could play his strongest suit, a public demonstration designed to elicit widespread moral indignation. That would place growers where they least wanted to be, in the limelight. Chávez aimed for September 16, Mexican Independence Day. By October, there was the beginning of a national boycott of table grapes. Although the first strike was against the grower DiGiorgio, wine-maker Schenley was boycotted as well. Strikers pointed out that while California's Fair Trade Act set a minimum price for liquor, of great benefit to Schenley, there was no such minimum wage for the field workers picking the grapes destined for Schenley's wine. Four months into the boycott, Schenley signed. It was the first contract between a grower and a farm worker's union in the history of the United States.

So far, so good. Chávez had been coaxed into the DiGiorgio strike, and it paid off. "What had started six months earlier as an unplanned, ill-prepared farm labor dispute over wages in an obscure part of the San Joaquín Valley had developed into a burgeoning worker movement.... *La Causa* was like a runaway freight train."[40]

The simile was apt, for it would be five years before the Delano Grape Strike ran its sometimes violent course. DiGiorgio Corp. was huge. In California, it owned more than 15,000 acres in grapes and more devoted to pears, plums, and apricots. Chávez's researchers also discovered that DiGiorgio "owned W&W Fine Foods, TreeSweet Products, processing plants, and a sawmill. We learned later that in 1965 DiGiorgio made more than $231 million and that several of their directors ... were also directors of Bank of America and other corporations."[41] DiGiorgio had crushed big strikes in 1939 and 1947, calling on sheriff's deputies to beat up picketers and destroy their mobile kitchens while *braceros* were brought in to do the work. Union organizers were derided as communists. "In 1960," Chávez knew, "DiGiorgio not only broke another strike, they were able to get a judge to order the state to provide scabs."[42]

Chávez and his staff decided on a work "slowdown"—allowing workers to keep being paid while eroding the company's profit—and aimed boycotts at DiGiorgio's other companies. The staff set up their headquarters at a forlorn place called "Forty Acres" near the Delano city garbage dump. Volunteer organizers showed up in droves, willing to work for $5 a week plus meals and a place to sleep.

In its first week, the strike touched about 2,000 workers in some twenty camps. "In some places the growers locked the workers out of the camps, camps where they had been living for years. In others, the men refused to leave, and the utilities were shut off. Then the growers added armed security guards, one of whom took a shot at a striker." It was a shot that would echo across a thousand news broadcasts. Chávez called a meeting in Delano at Our Lady of Guadalupe Church. "By the time the meeting started the hall and balcony were jampacked and people were coming out of the rafters.... The meeting was very spirited, a band played, and every so often the hall rang out with cries of '*Viva La Causa*.'"[43]

That description, however, highlights the profound differences between Chávez and his supporters—a combination of middle-class Anglo idealists and Hispanic workers and intellectuals—and the rest of the union movement. In 1966, when Chávez's NFWA merged with the AFL-CIO—changing its name to the United Farm Workers Association, or UFWA—it happened only after it was made clear the new UFWA would march to Chávez's beat. Chávez had by then spent nearly two decades sculpting and cementing his ties with the Hispanic community. His people were looking for dignified treatment for themselves and needed services for their families. Of course, higher pay was part of it, but it was not everything by a long shot. Chávez was a leader of something beyond the imagination of most labor leaders. "If there was a big strike," recalled Jim Drake, "César *is* the picket line, he is there, with the people, reacting." Drake, a graduate of Union Seminary, showed up in California with his wife and an infant son and became Chávez's driver. Drake was among the many who attached themselves to *La Causa* as a moral imperative and was a sharp observer of conditions. "He is at his best when there is a lot of pressure; he is at his worst when there isn't much happening."[44]

The other unions were not quite the same. The Teamsters, who organized packers and shippers while ignoring field workers, had long satisfied themselves with "sweetheart contracts" that were favorable to the growers. The huge union was, according to historian Taylor, "bumbling through one of its periodic exercises of conscience" by joining the strike against DiGiorgio. But Levy called the Teamsters "the rogue elephant in the labor movement." They were big, well financed, and able to elbow aside other unions. Even after being expelled from the AFL-CIO in 1957 because of their ties to organized crime, the Teamsters never lost their ability to make or break strikes by other unions. They were not interested in a unified front against DiGiorgio; the Teamsters wanted all contracts for themselves. Their leader was William Grami, whom Levy described as "a smooth, soft-spoken, highly intelligent, and ambitious Teamster executive ... the chief strategist and leader of their move into the fields. Over the years, he would tackle César Chávez time and again."[45]

The Filipinos, on the other hand, looked more like an old-fashioned "anarchist-socialist movement; they struck like guerrillas, sought pay hikes but no union recognition." Neither the Teamsters' selfishness nor the Filipinos' anarchy interested Chávez. "Instead of drifting with the seasons, calling hit-and-run strikes that sometimes succeeded in pushing wages up, but more often ended in busted heads and jailed pickets, Chávez was attempting to build a permanent, broadly based organization. The UFWA had a credit union with $25,000 in worker funds invested; the union had rented offices in several farming towns and established service centers and a $1,000 burial insurance program."[46]

Most importantly, Chávez's flexible strategy flowed not from strategic calculations, but from the people's needs. Often, in fact, his tactics were chosen for him by his followers. During the DiGiorgio strike, the California authorities proscribed picketing, which reduced violence, but left farm workers without a voice. What Chávez lost were the photographs in the morning papers and video on the evening news of women with long, braided, black hair walking quietly with picket signs between cordons of burly sheriff's deputies or surly Teamsters thugs. Chávez needed to give sincerity a face.

One day, a few women approached Chávez. He thought they'd come to ask for money, which he did not have. No, they said, and they hoped he didn't think they were telling him — like nagging wives—how to run a strike. But if they couldn't picket, they said, how about a prayer vigil? Chávez recalled: "I got [his brother] Richard and had him take my old station wagon and build a little chapel on it. It was like a shrine with a picture of Our Lady of Guadalupe, some candles, and some flowers. We worked on it until about two o'clock in the morning. Then we parked it across from the DiGiorgio gate where we started a vigil that lasted at least two months. People were there day and night." The numbers grew and the media were there to count them. "It was a beautiful demonstration of the power of nonviolence."[47]

There were also, of course, less beatific moments. When DiGiorgio's public relations people suddenly called a press conference, the intent was to get the company's message across without union representatives present. Chávez's organizers, however, managed to push their way into the tent where the press conference was being held, shoving aside Teamster guards. A DiGiorgio spokesman rushed up, threatening to call sheriff's deputies. William Kircher, the AFL-CIO executive who was by then a Chávez ally replied, simply, "You'd better call enough of them."

But when elections were finally held, a victory by Chávez and his AFL-CIO allies was declared null and void because of DiGiorgio-Teamster chicanery. "Donald Connors, DiGiorgio chief counsel, said the 'results are inescapable.' The field workers preferred the Chávez-led UFWOC."[48] The courts, however, would not allow the results to prevail because there had been so much dirty dealing. The DiGiorgio elections were rescheduled, and right away the Teamsters spread their meddling to another Chávez-inspired strike against California's Perelli-Minetti Vineyards. So it went, but across the country, Americans were getting an unprecedented look at the owners, their techniques, and their lackeys.

In Washington, the U.S. Senate Subcommittee on Migratory Labor held hearings, and the senators listened in disbelief to Matt Triggs, a senior lobbyist for the American Farm Bureau Federation. The federation was a powerful growers' association that favored a whole host of union-busting measures. They wanted to outlaw boycotts or strikes at harvest time, and they supported laws that strengthened the growers' hand in labor relations. At the Senate hearings, the growers' goal was to thwart legislation to bring farm workers under the protection of the National Labor Relations Act, which prohibits child labor and guarantees minimum wages. "Whenever legislative proposals are advanced to help raise farm workers out of poverty," wrote historian Taylor, "Agribusiness is quick to appear in opposition, using the mythology of the family farm to cover its callous approach to labor relations."

But as Triggs testified, Senator Robert F. Kennedy and other liberals were astounded. Triggs repeatedly insisted that any problem should be seen as "created in part by the seasonal and short-run characteristic of agriculture employment, which we regret, but which we don't know what we can do about." Kennedy then ticked off proposals, including one for improved schooling for all children, including migrants' kids. To each program, Triggs said, the federation was opposed. Then what, Kennedy asked incredulously, was to be done? "[T]o be opposed to a minimum wage, to be opposed to legislation which would limit the use of children between the ages of 10 and 13 for working, to be opposed to collective bargaining completely ... to oppose all that without some alternative makes the rest of the arguments you have senseless."

When the hearings were moved to California in March 1966, Senator Kennedy met Chávez, who told the committee: "Hearings similar to these have been called for decades, and, unfortunately, things have not changed very much in spite of them. The same labor camps which were used 30 years ago at the time of the La Follette committee hearings are

still housing our workers. The same exploitation of child labor, the same idea that farm workers are a different breed of people — humble, happy, built close to the ground — prevails."[49]

In 1967, Chávez's UFWA widened its focus to Giumarra, the largest grower of table grapes
in the nation. A strike was called, but it failed after only a few days. So tactics were shifted
to a boycott in California, and Giumarra responded by having new labels designed, making
it harder for boycotters to associate the new label with Giumarra. The union took the challenge and expanded its boycott to all Giumarra brands.

Americans were being educated, and Chávez — advised by liberal aides who worked for
next to nothing and inspired a legion of leafleting volunteers who worked for even less — was
their teacher. He missed no detail. In the nation's first strike against rose growers, the lesson
was how grafters had to crawl along the rows, slitting stems and inserting buds. Promised $9
per thousand plants, the workers were getting $6.50 to $7.

Chávez called a strike at a rose farm that was small by the standards of grape growers.
There were only 85 grafters, so the decision was made not to employ a picket line. Instead,
each worker pledged not to go back to work until there was a settlement. Taking no chances,
Chávez aides enforced the pledge by driving around early in the morning, looking for houses
with lights on. When they found one, they knocked on the door and asked why anyone was
up so early if they were not going to work that day.

As time passed, however, the workers' resolve weakened, making more drastic measures
necessary. Dolores Huerta had time on her hands because, though named as lead negotiator,
the rose grower had called her a communist and refused to speak to her. So Huerta made herself useful on the snoop squad. One morning when a house occupied by three grafters had
its lights on, Huerta drove her truck into the driveway behind their car, got out, locked the
doors, and left with the key. The grafters stayed home.

Finally, the grower hired a labor contractor and brought in replacement workers — all
from the same town in Mexico. Chávez promptly wrote a letter to the mayor of the town,
who publicly condemned the strikebreakers and posted a public notice in the town square.
When the strike eventually ran its course, the grafters won a pay raise, but no contract.

* * *

The case of the rose grafters, however, demonstrated Chávez's dilemma. He could not
be everywhere at once. Advisers were telling him to look at the big picture; if he spent time
on tiny half-victories he would be playing the growers' game. No union had enough organizers, no cause enough adherents, no movement enough force to overcome the agricultural
establishment by going, field by field, through every farm in every county of California. But,
at the same time, Chávez knew that it was his personality, charisma, and commitment to
which the workers responded. So Chávez tried to have it both ways. He would couple his image
of concerned, saintly asceticism and sacrifice to grand, theatrical events. And one of his most
impressive was the 1966 march from Delano — the focal point of the DiGiorgio strike — to
Sacramento, the state capital.

For twenty-five days, newspapers' front pages and television stations' lead stories showed
thousands of demonstrators strung out along the highway, their righteousness for all to see.
Nevertheless, when they reached the capitol on Easter Sunday, Governor Brown refused to
meet with strike leaders. Chávez was realistic: "As it turned out, we had about ten thousand
there on the steps of the capitol on Easter Sunday.... But we knew that it was only the end of
the march. We still had an army of growers arrayed against us."[50]

Author Frederick Dalton, who focused on the moral implications of Chávez's career,
noted the power of his example. "The pilgrimage to Sacramento," Dalton wrote, "is a clear

example of the prayerful popular religiosity of farm workers spilling out into the public arena. Prayer was an integral part of the pilgrimage routine, and churches and church halls were essential to the success of the pilgrimage."[51] Author Marco Prouty, however, pointed to the division that Chávez caused in the church's thinking. "The Catholic clergy in California's Central Valley initially hesitated to endorse Chávez's union because the farm workers challenged the very growers who were *the Church's largest contributors*. Agriculturists were the major benefactors for many of the Central Valley's schools and churches, and in some of the smaller communities, an entire parish would be dependent upon the largess of one or two growers."[52]

Indeed, there was some skepticism about the place of prayer in brass-knuckle economics. "Not everyone in Chávez's union shared his enthusiasm for the Catholic Church or *La Causa*'s emphasis on faith," wrote Prouty. "Jerry Cohen, who for years headed the UFW's legal team, admitted, 'a lot of liberals and radicals were pissed' about Chavez's inclusion of faith in the union. They felt the prayer, fasting, and sacrifice were 'phony and ... taking away from work.' One exceptionally harsh critic of Chávez's faith, Antonio Orendian, the UFW's secretary-treasurer, described Chávez's fasts as 'an embarrassing religious display that indirectly supported the hierarchy of the Roman Catholic Church.'"[53]

Such criticism rolled off Chávez's back like water. "He was a devout Catholic," observed Pat Henning, a California organizer. "I'm not sugarcoating that at all. He was a tough cookie. But he went almost daily to Mass. He spent an hour each day in prayer." Often, after early mass, as the sun came up, Chávez lingered for long chats with neighbors who spoke no English. Quite simply, he found God in others. In addition, he found comfort in periods of solitary contemplation in the western mountains. "César drew inspiration, solace, and strength from attending morning Mass in a Catholic parish.... He also meditated and prayed on his own, drawing inspiration, solace, and strength from seeking God in solitude in the Tehachapi Mountains surrounding La Paz [California]."[54]

To emphasize the depth of his commitment, Chávez fasted three times. In 1968, as the glow of the Sacramento march faded and the DiGiorgio strike dragged on, Chávez fasted for 25 days to stress his belief in non-violence. The strike had been rough, and his own organizers contemplated giving the Teamsters some of their own medicine. To dissuade them, Chávez toured the locals, speaking of the need for nonviolence, and settled into his period of self-denial. When the fast ended, Senator — and presidential candidate — Kennedy was there to hand him a piece of bread and call him "one of the heroic figures of our time." Thus the ascetic and the theatrical were wrapped into a neat, photogenic package. Then Chávez, Kennedy, and 8,000 farm workers attended mass. If there was anyone in the United States who was still unaware of the farm workers' cause, it wasn't the fault of the celebrities—like Joan Baez and Martin Sheen — who beat a path to his door. Few, however, stayed to volunteer, and in tragic reminders of the times, Chávez would later be visited by the widows of Senator Kennedy and the Rev. Martin Luther King, Jr.

By 1970, most California table-grape growers had signed UFWA contracts, and Chávez turned his attention to lettuce. And as soon as they saw him coming, the lettuce growers knew what to do. "After nearly a century of fighting unions, lettuce growers stampeded to sign with the Teamsters. First to sign was a group in Salinas. Then others followed ... growers that procured the bulk of the nation's lettuce, a good share of its strawberries, and a salad of other vegetables."[55] California Governor Ronald Reagan weighed in with his opinion that it was "tragic" that Chávez's union was signing contracts that meant workers "had no choice" but to join his union in order to get work. Because the lettuce growers were linked to large, well-known companies, Chávez again called for a national boycott.

In the Salinas Valley, the UFWA began picketing the growers who were hiding behind sweetheart contracts with the Teamsters, and in December, Chávez was arrested for violating an injunction against picketing. His arrest was planned so the injunction could be tested in court and, presumably, found unconstitutional on appeal. News photographs of the period show a stark contrast between the diminutive Hispanic picketers and the big, often overweight Teamster "guards" surrounding lettuce fields. They had been placed there to prevent Chávez from going out into the rows to talk to workers.

As far as jail was concerned, Chávez had read Gandhi, King, and others who had made the most of being jailed. He recalled the experience with enthusiasm. Jail was just another place to organize. "I made a lot of friends," he told an interviewer, "inside with the inmates, did a little organizing and spread the word around quite a bit. I wasn't too successful in convincing anybody about non-violence inside, but they are all with us." While Chávez was in jail his supporters stood vigil outside. In the early hours of the morning they sang Mexican *mañanitas*, the traditional songs of workers to greet the day. "I never felt alone. For one thing, at night I could hear their singing. I heard the *mañanitas*. I thought, 'This is the first time they give me *mañanitas*.' Well, they were for the Virgin and the Chicanos who were all over the jail. Four-thirty in the morning *gritando, gritos de La Raza*. See the determination?"[56]

* * *

As spring arrived in 1972, the farm workers could claim they had a union. "What had been a ragtag coalition of Mexicano and Filipino farm workers in 1965 was now a bona fide union within the AFL-CIO."[57] The UFWA had 147 contracts covering as many as 60,000 jobs on farms in California, Arizona, and Florida. Some of the farms were family owned operations of 50 acres or so, but some were as big as 100,000 acres, owned by companies like Coca-Cola, United Fruit, and Hueblein. The UFWA had some 30,000 dues-paying members, a number that was swelled every spring by people arriving to look for work in the fields. At a system of "hiring halls," UFWA members were assigned based on seniority. Some parents objected to this system, wanting the whole family, including children, to work together. At the other end of the equation, the growers—and their allies, the Teamsters—objected to the hiring-hall system because it slowed down the more haphazard methods that increased the growers' and the labor contractors' power.

By now the UFWA was working out of a headquarters called La Paz, located in an old tuberculosis sanatorium in the Tehachapi Mountains near Bakersfield. The union had 26 field offices in three states and 33 "boycott houses" across the country. Volunteers earned $5 per week and expenses—a total cost of $300 a month for each volunteer family and $50 a month for each individual. "President César Chávez and the UFWA executive board were also paid $5 a week. Chávez's expenses for 1972 totaled $5,144, an average of $426 a month for him, his wife, and the three of his eight children who were still living at home.

But to suggestions that the UFWA had "arrived," Chávez demurred. In historian Taylor's view, "He was right. The UFWA had only captured control of a tiny portion of the total farm labor force, and that control was, at best, tenuous. The agribusiness employers in California, Florida, and Arizona were not accepting the inevitability of a Chávez-led labor organization's coming into their fields; if anything, the Chávez-led efforts from 1970 through 1973 had solidified the farmers' resolve to fight off the menace of organized farm labor."[58]

Because of that continuing pressure, in April 1972 Chávez fasted again. The stated purpose was to raise Americans' awareness that half a dozen farm-state legislatures were debating union-busting bills. In fact, Kansas, Idaho, and Arizona legislatures passed laws outlawing or inhibiting boycotts or strikes during harvest and narrowing unions' ability to bargain. At the same time, Chávez was embroiled in a recall campaign against the anti-union governor of Arizona, Jack Williams. Dramatically, he gave orders from his small room in a Mexican American barrio in Phoenix, where he was visited by George McGovern, the Democratic candidate for president.

The fast lasted 25 days and was ended after he spent the last five days in a hospital — where he was visited singer Joan Baez. Throughout, Chávez alternated between being the feeble spiritual leader and the fiery spokesman. He told the *Catholic Worker*: "Farm workers in Arizona tried to tell their legislators about the unfairness of this law. They collected letters and petitions and brought them to their representatives. They were met with cold indifference.... In many cases their letters were thrown into trash cans in front of their eyes." After Gov. Jack Williams signed an anti-union bill, Chávez continued, he "was asked by a reporter to comment on the farm workers who wanted to meet with him. He responded: 'As far as I'm concerned, these people do not exist.'"[59]

After the fast, thousands of people attended the celebratory mass, but, on balance, what was the result? asked historians Richard Griswold and Richard García. Most immediately, the recall petition fell short by more than 100,000 signatures, and anti-union legislation continued to sprout. California was setting up a plebiscite on an initiative to outlaw boycotts and restrict eligible union voters to full-time, non-seasonal workers. For the future, however, thousands of Mexican Americans were registering to vote for the first time, and in the following election four Mexican Americans and a Navajo were elected to state legislative seats. Arizona elected the nation's first Mexican American governor.

Away from the polling booth, however, the violence continued. In the spring and summer of 1973, table-grape growers avoided another three-year contract with the UFWA by signing with the Teamsters. Chávez traveled among the locals, trying to explain to nonplussed UFWA workers what had happened, and thousands of grape workers struck for three months. All during that time Chávez's strikers were arrested, beaten up, and shot for violating anti-picketing injunctions the courts had awarded to growers.

By any standards, 1973 was a violent year, and the farm workers' adversaries were not just the courts and sheriff's deputies. *Wall Street Journal* reporters documented the criminal connections (and convictions) of Teamsters' associates, including members of their image-building public relations firm. The Teamsters PR people stirred up a whole catalogue of rumors, including the story that William Grami, the Teamster organizer, had been shot in the head by UFWA picketers. "'The UFW-instigated violence that has occurred during the past two weeks must be stopped,' he says," the Teamsters newspaper noted. "'We don't want to be forced into a position of retaliation.'" The Teamsters were themselves torn by internal divisions, with headquarters often embarrassed by people like Grami on the front lines. After Frank Fitzsimmons, the Teamsters president, repudiated Delano contracts signed by Teamsters organizers in California, dissidents rebelled. Within days, two UFWA workers were shot and killed, and one of Chávez's sons, an intern in the California legislature who was observing picketing, was the target of a shot that missed.

In the meantime, Teamsters hurling 20-pound rocks attacked Chávez's car. Teamster goons stabbed a bystander in the neck and back with an ice pick, apparently having mistaken him for a UFWA picketer. A young couple and their two-and-a-half-year-old daughter were burned out of their trailer five months after the husband and wife joined Chávez's union. And of one particularly violent confrontation, Levy wrote: "On the picket line the next morning, 180 Teamsters charge into a UFW picket line with iron pipes, clubs, tire irons, and machetes. The four hundred farm workers and volunteers defended themselves, and the battle raged in an asparagus field beside the vineyard for more than an hour."[60]

No victory came easy. But in 1975 California Gov. Jerry Brown —former Gov. Pat's son —

outlawed use of the short-handled hoe, which had kept field workers bent over crops since time immemorial. Also, the California legislature enacted the unprecedented Agricultural Labor Relations Act. The act assured farm workers of the right to organize, helped the UFWA continue to win elections, and led to a Teamsters' agreement to withdraw from organizing in the fields.

*   *   *

With all of those victories on the outside, however, Chávez by the mid–1970s was losing his grip inside the union. He was accused by some of his closest associates of neglecting proper management. Even as the UFWA got bigger and more successful, Chávez was seen as failing to delegate authority, unrealistically expecting others to be as saintly as he was, and bogging himself down in details. Jack Quiggly, a business manager who quit after two years, told author Taylor: "[W]e ought to handle that stuff. He is far too important and far too capable in the larger issues to be tied up with paper clips and light bulbs."[61] With Quiggly gone, Chávez started getting up even earlier every morning to dive into the most minute issues. Others, arriving for work, would find accounts and records flagged by dozens of notes.

Chávez was seen as wanting others to work for the same low pay that satisfied him and perform at the levels of commitment of which he was capable. Some said he surrounded himself only with those who were awed by his charisma. And, some said, Chávez, who had worked so long at freeing migrant farm workers from oppression, did not encourage independence of thought within his own staff. "As *La Causa* atrophied, critics openly assailed Chávez's management style as inflexible and autocratic."[62]

It was as though success spoiled everything. "The union's deficiencies worsened as *La Causa* experienced its major victories during the late 1970s," wrote Prouty. "Apparently, the UFW could only find peace in war.... Instead of parlaying victories into better contracts for the farm workers, union officials fought bitterly among themselves and *La Causa* imploded."[63] Others followed Quiggly out the door: organizers, accountants, legal counsel. All unions had trouble in the 1970s, and, indeed, labor unions in the United States have never had the appeal of their European brethren, much less a union trying the organize the lowly migrant farm workers. But whatever the causes of the UFWA's troubles, most critics accused Chávez of choking the spirit of a charismatic movement by insisting that even the most petty details be handled through him.

Perhaps most unfairly, Chávez was blamed for internal arguments between men with highly aggressive personalities in a dog-eat-dog environment. Oddly, historian Prouty even suggested that if only Chávez had heeded the advice of Roman Catholic clergymen, he could have performed a kind of managerial miracle. Within the union, Prouty wrote, Chávez needed to create "a process that required an efficient administrative apparatus rather than marching or fasting. Despite the fact that [Monsignor George C.] Higgins and [Bishop James] Rausch had advised Chávez of the need for administrative reform, he did not undertake corrective action. Moreover, it appeared that Chávez did not wish to remedy the situation by becoming a conventional labor union; after observing traditional union officials "at the conventions in their gray pinstripe suits and red ties," Chávez noted with disdain that "they looked like the employers of their workers."[64]

Of course, Chávez was right to be skeptical of traditional union men. Some were economic quislings, who lost no opportunity to satisfy personal ambitions while ignoring the interests of their workers. Those were the men to whom Chávez had to point the way into the lettuce fields and grape orchards, which they had avoided for decades. They were the men who claimed the heritage of Samuel Gompers while nuzzling up to farm owners. Moreover,

Chávez had never disguised his intention to lead a movement toward social and economic justice for Hispanic workers and their families, not just patch together some union bureaucracy that trudged from paycheck to paycheck. "From the very beginning," wrote historian Taylor, "Chávez made it plain the NFWA was to be a totally independent, service-oriented worker movement, a movement built and controlled by the men and women who worked for wages on the farm."[65]

As for criticism of his fasting, Chávez insisted that it was "a very personal, spiritual thing, and it's not done out of recklessness. It's not done out of a desire to destroy yourself, but it's done out of a deep conviction that we can communicate with people, either those who are for us or against us, faster and more effectively spiritually than we can in any other way."[66]

* * *

By 1975, the results of the long, triangular battle — Hispanic migrants against both the Teamsters and the growers — were beginning to come in. After a first round of elections in August, the results showed 74 contracts won by Chávez's United Farm Workers and 73 taken by the Teamsters. By the end of the year, however, UFW had 198 contracts covering 27,000 workers; the Teamsters counted 115 contracts covering 12,000 workers. There were continuing challenges posed by the owners' inherent strength and the Teamsters' duplicity, but for the nonce Chávez was king of the mountain.[67] Harris Polls showed that grape boycotts were attracting millions of supporters.

The halcyon period did not last long. Internally, Chávez continued to have trouble holding his movement together. Top staff members drifted away. Some efforts failed. In California, although Chávez stalwarts gathered 700,000 signatures in less than a month to get Proposition 14 — assuring organizers access to workers in the fields — onto the California ballot in 1976, the initiative was defeated. The *Village Voice* printed a two-part article: "César Chávez's Fall from Grace." Chávez recalled of the time: "The world was really changing. Now we had to start planning. We had to talk about restructuring the union. We had to look at what we were doing." But events were overwhelming. In 1979, Chávez was on the losing end of a political battle to select a speaker for the California Assembly.[68] In 1980, Ronald Reagan — the man who called Hispanic farm workers "barbarians" — was elected president of the United States. "By the end of the 1970s," wrote historian Prouty, "the UFW appeared poised to become a major force in the AFL-CIO with a membership of more than one hundred thousand farm workers; instead, the union atrophied over the next decade, losing 80 percent of its organizational strength."[69] Historians Griswold and García, risking understatement, wrote: "[T]he next decade or so — with Reagan as the next resident of the White House — was to see a change in public mood."

Through the 1980s, conservative governors refused to enforce hard-fought gains in California's farm labor law. Thousands of farm workers were unceremoniously dumped from their jobs. In 1983, farm worker René López was shot after he emerged from casting his vote in a union election. In 1984, Chávez declared a third grape boycott, and later that year he told a California audience: "Today, thousands of farm workers live under savage conditions — beneath trees and amid garbage and human excrement — near tomato fields in San Diego County, tomato fields which use the most modern farm technology."[70]

* * *

With the organization weakening and membership fading, Chávez still had a role as the nation's conscience. His cause was the mounting evidence that herbicides and pesticides were damaging the health of field workers. In addition, when workers brought polluted dust home in their clothes and in their hair, the hazard extended to their families. In 1988, at age 61, Chávez went on his last and longest fast: 36 days. His purpose was to expose this most insidious jeopardy, the poisoning of children as their parents returned from work every afternoon and as dust blew across their playgrounds.

Chávez called it his "Wrath of Grapes" tour, a series of speeches in the 1980s and 1990s to sound the alarm. In many respects, it was Chávez at his best. He did not have to face down Teamsters goons or suffer the indignities meted out by sheriff's deputies. It was just Chávez and his audience. In March 1989, he told an audience at Pacific Lutheran University: "How do you measure the value of a life? Ask the parents of Johnnie Rodríguez. Johnnie was a five-year-old boy when he died after a painful two-year battle against cancer. His parents, Juan and Elia, are farm workers. Like all grape workers, they are exposed to pesticides and other agricultural chemicals. Elia worked in the table grapes around Delano, California, until she was eight months pregnant.... 'Pesticides are always in the fields and around the towns,' Johnnie's father told us. 'The children get them when they play outside, drink the water, or hug you after come home from working in fields that are sprayed.'"

Chávez's style had evolved into a combination of morality tale and policy lecture. "The chief sources of carcinogens in these communities are pesticides from vineyards and fields that encircle them," he continued. "Health experts think the high rate of cancer in McFarland [a small town] is from pesticides and nitrate-containing fertilizers leaching into the water system from surrounding fields. Last year California's Republican governor, George Deukmejian, killed a modest study to find out why so many children are dying of cancer in McFarland. 'Fiscal integrity' was the reason he gave."[71]

Some Chávez critics suggest that his speeches and published words were polished — like the clever words of Manuela Sáenz, Bolívar's mistress — by his coterie of admirers, many of whom were writers and editors. It should be borne in mind, however, that like all autodidacts Chávez was widely read. His eloquence frequently arose from his synthesis of others' ideas and took shape in humble settings, like his "house meetings" and jailhouse conversations and early morning chats in church courtyards.

Others acknowledge that Chávez rose well above any simple description. "There are those who maintain that it is a misrepresentation to think of Chávez as anything but a charismatic and effective labor organizer," wrote José-Antonio Orosco, a modern philosopher. "Peter Matthiessen writes that even though Chávez read and thought about the works of St. Paul, Niccolo Machiavelli, Winston Churchill, and Thomas Jefferson, he was 'a realist, not an intellectual'.... It is true that in the 1960s, during the height of *La Causa* ... Chávez often remarked that his sole objective was to build a union.... However, once the United Farm Workers came into existence and *La Causa* started to mature, Chávez's thinking on the nature of his work also started to change. By the 1980s, Chávez began to refer to *La Causa* not only as a labor struggle, but also as a social movement for the empowerment of new generations of Latinos/as."

Chávez had read the history of the American Southwest. It is a history of cultural theft, beginning when Anglo Americans removed children of the native tribes from Franciscan mission schools — where they were learning to farm — and condemned them to barren reservations. It continued when the land was subdivided into family farms for European immigrants who shipped their produce back East, and family operated *tiendas* gave way to Sears, Roebuck & Company "[O]ne sees," Orosco continued, "that modern agribusiness troubled Chávez not merely because of the difficulty in negotiating labor contracts with large corporations, but also because he believed it represented the loss of a way of life in which people and communities are connected to the land, and one another, as sources of intrinsic value."[72]

In the spring and summer of 1992, still trying to be active, Chávez accompanied UFWA vice president Arturo Rogríguez on a round of vineyard walkouts in the Coachella and San Joaquín valleys. They were the impetus for the grape workers' first industry-wide raise in pay in eight years.

* * *

On April 23, 1993, César Chávez died in his sleep in San Luis, Arizona, not far from the Gila River Valley farm that his parents lost to the Depression. He'd gone there on union business. There would follow the predictable praise. President Bill Clinton would call him "a Moses figure." Historian Marco Prouty brought the imagery into the New Testament: "César Chávez had led a revolution — a peaceful movement for social change — that, if only for a brief period during the early 1970s, prompted the American Catholic hierarchy to make social justice one of its highest priorities."[73] And one year after Chávez's death, Rodríguez, now the UFWA president, led a march from Delano to Sacramento to commemorate the 1966 march and to initiate yet another year of negotiations between field workers and farm owners. Seventeen thousand people walked with him.

Author Peter Matthiessen described the scene at Chávez's funeral. "On April 29th, in ninety-degree heat, an estimated thirty-five thousand people, in a line three miles long, formed a funeral procession from Memorial Park in Delano, California, to the burial Mass at the United Farm Workers field office north of town. With the former scourge of California safely in his coffin, state flags were lowered to half-mast by order of the governor, and messages poured forth from the heads of church and state, including the Pope and President of the United States.... Anger was a part of Chávez, but so was a transparent love of humankind...."[74]

Alas, historian Ilan Stavans pointed to a sad reality: "A poll conducted in 2005 suggested that the vast majority of young people in the country don't know who [César Chávez] was, what he stood for, what his legacy is. Even though his mission is part of the elementary school curriculum in most states, his words are easily reduced to sound bites."[75]

Matthiessen, however, found some faint hope that the ones who miss César Estrada Chávez the most are the ones who will best remember. Matthiessen wrote: "During the vigil at the open casket on the day before the funeral, an old man lifted a child up to show him the small, gray-haired man who lay inside. 'I'm going to tell you about this man someday,' he said."[76]

23

Vicente Fox
Breaking the Political Mold
1942–
(Mexico)

Between 1500 and 1850, two distinct cultures, the Spanish and the English, colonized the New World from the Great Lakes to Yucatan. Upon arriving, they looked upon the land, God, and the indigenous inhabitants in very different ways. They looked at each other, however, the same way: with dismay, even disgust. Neither accepted the other's way of living or, especially, his religion. But they settled down, cheek by jowl, and looked to the future.

The Spanish intermarried with the native tribes, creating the *mestizo* culture. They built a stratified, feudal pyramid of families, with those at the top controlling mining, large-scale ranching, and the cultivation of cash crops. For those enterprises they employed local labor, first from the native tribes, then from boatloads of African slaves. Spanish clerks dutifully kept land records on parchment, and Catholic clerics opened mission schools to teach tribal children how to love the Spanish God.

The English, on the other hand, brought their own women from Europe, drove away the forest tribes, and opened their Atlantic ports to European immigrants. Then Anglo Americans stormed across the continent, burned the parchment records, squeezed the native tribes onto segregated reservations, and hired the Spanish-Americans as workers in the mines, as laborers in the fields, and as clerks in general stores. They linked east and west with railroads and transformed their cities into markets.

Thus did Spain's—and, later, Mexico's—feudal economy sleep beside Anglo America's restless capitalism, the two separated only by a border that was quickly erased by sandals scuffing across the sand in the search for work. Over the decades, as the market for chaps was replaced by the one for designer jeans, it became clear that prosperity paid little attention to nationality. All capitalism needed to grow stronger and stronger and bigger and bigger was, at the top, organization, and, at the bottom, workers. Looking out upon these realities early in the twentieth century, the Mexican president Porfirio Díaz uttered one of the region's most memorable phrases:

"Poor Mexico. So far from God and so close to the United States."

Late in the same century, there arose from the land another Mexican president, Vicente Fox, whose specialty was the well-turned phrase, a characteristic that sometimes landed him in the soup. Decades had passed between the presidencies of Díaz and Fox, and the economic imbalances that had grown up between Mexico and the United States were reflected in Fox's career. Born on the land in Guanajuato, he rose to president of Coca-Cola Mexico. Then he returned to his roots to enter politics, beginning what became a full, frontal assault on the rigid political system Mexicans had devised and maintained for seventy-one years. Fox's capture of the presidency in 2000 promised a political pluralism that Mexico had never known.

* * *

Vicente Fox Quesada was born July 2, 1942, in Mexico City. While he was still tiny, the family moved San Cristóbal Ranch in San Francisco del Rincón, Guanajuato, founded by his paternal grandfather. Vicente was the second of nine children, six of them boys, of José Luis Fox, a farmer, and Mercedes Quesada. There are unusual aspects to both sides of Fox's family, which, taken together, gave him the personality on which he staked his career. In fact, there was one detail in his family background that almost kept him from the presidency.

In 1916, as Mexico's long and bloody revolution ground its way through the sixth year, Joseph Louis Fox, the grandfather, wandered down from the United States in search of work. He settled in the tiny village of Irapuato. "Like the dispossessed Mexicans he passed going the other way," Fox recounted in an autobiography, "Joseph was hungry."[1] Joseph spoke no Spanish then and never learned, but he went to work as night watchman for a carriage company. He saved his wages and bought out the owner. His business prospered, and Joseph bought a 10,000-acre ranch called San Cristóbal.

His grandfather's enterprise and pertinacity made a lasting impression on Vicente Fox. Fox is quick to point out that San Cristóbal had been the smallest of seven ranches owned by a rich Mexican family. That family spent its time in the capital, squandering its wealth rather than working the land. Fox saw in the difference between his grandparents' toughness and the dissolute Mexican family's profligacy a metaphor for Mexico's failure to match the industry of the United States. Fox almost lost the ranch he'd just bought in 1916 when an unruly band of revolutionaries approached San Cristóbal, determined to steal it. Joseph and his workers armed themselves and, quite literally, held the fort until the raiders drifted away. For Vicente Fox, the incident was far more than mere metaphor because his father — and, later, he and his brothers — would have to go through essentially the same thing.

Grandfather Joseph's wife was Elena Pont, the daughter of a French soldier and "an indigenous peasant girl."[2] The soldier — Fox's great grandfather — had been stranded after the 1864 execution of Maximilian, the "emperor" Napoleon III tried to impose on Mexico. Fox described Elena as an "elegant and French-speaking" girl who married an Englishman and was widowed before marrying the rough-hewn American, Joseph.

Fox's parents were José Luis and Doña Mercedes Quesada de Fox. His father's three sisters included one who became a nun and lived to a ripe old age in an Ohio convent. The international aspects of Fox's background influenced his view of the world, but in the case of his mother, Mercedes, they almost cost him his run at the presidency. Because of Mexico's deep-seated feelings about *gachupines* — the native-born Spaniards who worked their will on Mexico's proud *mestizos* — the constitution requires not only that a presidential candidate be born inside the country, but his parents as well. Doña Mercedes was born in her parents' native Basque region when her father — a warehouse owner who started as a grocer's boy in the capital — returned to Spain on a business trip. His pregnant wife accompanied him so she could give birth in the bosom of her family. Mercedes came back to Mexico as an infant, was given a religious schooling, and set the tone for her family by attending mass every morning for the rest of her life. In 1938, she met José Luis in Mexico City, and no one would question her place as a quintessential Mexican until her son's race for the presidency.

It was also in 1938 that José Luis, Fox's father, had to defend ownership of San Cristóbal for the second time. The president was Lázaro Cárdenas, who expropriated Mexican oil production, theretofore controlled by U.S. investors. That single act remains the prime symbol of Mexican independence in the face of U.S. dominance. In addition, Cárdenas's term is sometimes cast as "the perfect dictatorship" for defining the long reign of the *Partido de Revolución Institucional*, the PRI. Cárdenas also tackled the age-old Mexican problem of the *ejidos*, the traditional farmland of the native tribes that was communally cultivated. Over the long, dictatorial presidency of Porfirio Díaz, government mapmakers stripped the *ejidos* from their rightful native owners. Díaz distributed the land to his cronies, assuring his continued presidency and making them rich. By 1910, when the revolution exploded, 3,000 families owned half of Mexico's arable land. Cárdenas intended to redistribute that land to the tribes, and José Luis was informed that San Cristóbal would be reduced to 250 acres. Angry, José Luis took his case directly to the president's office, where he argued that he was not the only family member living at San Cristóbal. There were three others, and each should be entitled to 250 acres. His argument prevailed, and San Cristóbal held firm at 1,000 acres—at least for the time being.[3]

*   *   *

Fox has said that San Cristóbal, because of its history and his own growing up there, formed his view of life. "For my brothers and me," Fox said of his early years, "Mexico was a paradise: a warm and friendly macho world where men milked cows, broke horses, and drank tequila straight up, fought bulls in the ring, hunted ducks, and generally ruled the roost. The only mild irritant was that the woman in charge occasionally yanked you out of this halcyon Eden, put you into a uniform, and packed you off to the Jesuit *preparatario* in León."[4]

"The woman in charge," of course, was Doña Mercedes, his mother and the occasional warden over young ne'er-do-well cousins who were turned over to her as a last recourse. "The ranch was the anchor of my family," Fox recalled. "Any cousin who was not keeping up with his studies, or was behaving badly, or had problems with his parents, was sent to the ranch to work, as if it were some kind of reform school."[5] Doña Mercedes never missed a mass or a step.

Products of that rustic environment were not all that desirable, however, in the eyes of Fox's schoolmates. He and his brothers went to school with kids who looked out on a world, at least in their own minds, from a lofty perch. "When José, my older brother, and I enrolled in first grade in the La Salle School (in León) we were considered lowlifes, not only because of the way we talked, but for the way we dressed. Until we were ten years old my mother dressed us in short pants, which meant that many times we got beat up by other kids.... José and I stayed at La Salle until fifth grade and then went to the Jesuits' Lux Institute in 1954. Although José is older we always studied together, and because we were so far from home, everything, including our first communions, were arranged in tandem by our mother, who was killing several birds with one shot. From the time we were toddlers José and I stuck together...."[6] Back at home, the Fox boys' playmates were native children from nearby *ejidos*, and, as they grew up, the *muchachos* hanging out at local bars.

It was apparently Fox's appreciation for a relaxed style of life that led Doña Mercedes to clamp down a bit. Fox has described himself as having been "banished" to Campion Jesuit High School in Prairie de Chien, Wisconsin. There, he spent a year of high school.[7] During that year, he bused tables in the school cafeteria and learned the bitter lesson that he would never be invited to his classmates' homes because he was a Mexican. Despite such knowledge, however, it is clear he had not learned modesty: "I was good at sports, even American sports, but I always hated physical violence. Give me a bat and a glove, the soccer field, and the basketball court; I ran track, hurled the shotput, fought bulls at home in the *corrida*, even played American football. I'm the one you want as your matador or your tight end, whether it means facing a quarter-ton bull or one of the mighty Norwegian linebackers of Prairie de Chien, Wisconsin."[8]

Returning to San Cristóbal, however, Fox began to understand the complexities of life. One of his childhood friends had been Antonio Valdivia. What had become of Valdivia while Fox was off at an expensive school made Fox realize that what the Jesuits had been telling him was true: Social inequalities are plain to see, if you look. When he got back to Guanajuato from Wisconsin, Fox wrote, Valdivia was no longer there. He had "finished school at age twelve, barely knowing how to read.... I watched my boyhood pals leave one by one to wash the windows of cars they could not afford in Mexico City, to build houses their future wives would enter only as maids in Houston, to pave roads they were not legally allowed to drive in Arizona." Those who stayed in Guanajuato "were earning the pesos that bought barely enough corn for their families to scrape by, with never enough to pay for a doctor for a grandmother's diabetes or a fine new suit of clothes, much less the tuition fees of the *preparatario* in León."[9]

In the same dramatic language that reveals what a Mexican can do with a background in U.S.–style marketing, Fox continued, "This was the beginning of my rebellion as a proud *hijo desobediente*, the disobedient son of the mariachi song. It would be thirty years before I joined the opposition National Action Party, the PAN, but my opposition to the System began the day I came back from Wisconsin to find the gap widening between me and Antonio Valdivia."[10]

In 1960, Fox and brother José Luis went off to Universidad Iberoamericana, a Jesuit university in Mexico City where he was, once again, kidded about his clothes, this time for their "ranchero" style. The two brothers stayed with their aunt at her apartment in Mexico City. Fox studied business administration, but left after four years without graduating. (He later, at age 56, completed his final exams the year before he ran for president.) His reason for leaving was a job at Coca-Cola Mexico, where he would learn the art and science of selling.

At Coke, Fox was among those who led the charge against the soft-drink dominance in Mexico of archrival Pepsi-Cola. "My first job was to make friends with the old guys, the veterans of the cola wars, who knew every dirty trick in the book to beat the opposition. It was a friendly combat. You drank tequila with the Pepsi drivers in the rough trucker bars until dawn. At 5:00 A.M. you stumbled into the parking lot.... Then you reached into the front seat to grab an ice pick and spiked the tires of the Pepsi truck ... because the first guy through the door got to fill the empty icebox with his brand." Fox was a route supervisor, training for management. By his count, he rode 2,500 routes, though he doesn't offer the number of times he actually risked stabbing another man's tires.

For several years, Fox, a tall, handsome, and gregarious man, lived the high — it was, after all, the Sixties— life of a bachelor. He and his pals had seen the James Dean movies and instructed themselves well in the mechanics of being "cool," once pushing that concept to the point that Fox and three others rolled Papa Fox's brand-new Volkswagen. Now earning a good salary and rising through the ranks of Coca-Cola Mexico, Fox was not in the least interested in anything like politics. Nor was he interested in marriage until the late 1960s, when he met his boss's beautiful, blonde secretary, Lilián de la Concha, whose father was an oil company engineer. Fox changed his view of himself from madcap bachelor to half of "the model young executive couple of the era, like one of those American television programs we still couldn't get on Televisa."

Describing the early 1970s, when he and Lilián were childless, their vacations were in a pick-up truck, driving from Guanajuato to Texas to British Columbia. The world they saw,

Fox believed, opened to the future. "These were the heady years of American globalism. The United States led the way in every field ... Americans built it, bought it, invented it, designed it, refined it, mined it, grew it, improved it, created it, invested in it, sold it."[11] Back at home, things took a less hopeful turn, and the Foxes were called upon once again to rally around the family homeplace.

As part of President Luis Echeverría's program of nationalizing large estates and expropriating industries, PRI agents cast their eyes, in Fox's words, on "what was left of San Cristóbal." That was still 1,000 acres, and in truth it had not been fully farmed. It was thus a part of Mexico's continuing inability—exacerbated by U.S. agricultural import and export policies—to rationalize its farm economy. Fox got a phone call at his Coca-Cola office, jumped in his car, and headed for San Cristóbal, where PRI officials had informed their supporters that there was farmland for the taking. By the time Fox got to San Cristóbal, a band of surly men was hanging around the periphery of the farm. They were waiting for the Foxes to cut and run. Instead, Fox, along with José and the other boys and their 59-year-old father, did what family lore expected them to do. As in 1916 and 1938, they held the fort.

"They came through the gates," Fox wrote, "fifty or sixty *campesinos* from other states, a rough-looking bunch wielding shotguns and rifles, pistols and machetes. They seized the warehouse and the barns, the fields and the old irrigation works...." The Foxes decided that what was needed was to show that they most certainly were owners of an operating farm. So they and their workers hefted picks and shovels and started working the land by overseeing the digging of irrigation ditches and construction of new fences. José led the effort and Vicente drove to the farm on weekends. Eventually, the strategy worked. "The invaders grew bored after months of occupation."[12]

In 1974, at age 32, Fox was made president of Coca-Cola Mexico. As such, he was full of himself later that year when he attended his university class reunion. In a grand ballroom at an expensive hotel in Mexico City, friends and acquaintances, many of whom had also done well for themselves, crowded around, showing off their beautiful wives and praising their shiny automobiles. "It seemed a farm boy's American dream, this celebration of my brilliant rise to become the youngest Coca-Cola president in the company's global empire at age thirty-two." But at that gala affair, surrounded by scions of some of Mexico's richest families, he listened to the principal speaker, Father Schiefler, who had once thrown Fox out of school. The good father chose not to pay tribute to his former students' good fortune, but rather reminded them of the teaching of St. Ignatius: Bring happiness to others. Through tears, Father Schiefler made it clear he was ashamed of them. He expressed regret for having wasted four years of his life on them when now they lived lives of greed and self-aggrandizement, even as they were surrounded by Mexico's miserable poverty. "I sat there," Fox recalled, "stunned."[13]

He stayed at his job, however, and Coca-Cola sent him off to an executive-training program at Harvard Business School. In 1978, Fox was offered a promotion to Miami, en route, potentially, to further promotions up the ladder of a worldwide corporation. He would decide, however, to leave Coca-Cola and turn his hand to Fox family businesses.

At home, four important changes were coming into his and Lilián's lives. Discovering that they would not be able to have children, Vicente and Lilián flew to Costa Rica to meet the director of an adoption agency. They quickly flew home after being offended by the babies-for-profit atmosphere. Subsequently, they discovered a Mexican philanthropist whose mission was to provide childless couples with children, and with her help they built their family. Fox has written of the experience in the vocabulary of all adoptive parents, one of unparalleled wonder. Fox recalled walking past suggestions that he choose this or that one because of eye color or hair color or some such attribute. He was too far gone from the instant he entered the nursery. "The moment we walked in, I saw two black eyes staring at me from a crib in the far corner, and I *knew*.... It happened to us four times, and the blessings of our four children were sublime."[14] The first was Ana Cristina, followed by Vicente, Paulina, and Rodrigo.

Before long, Fox followed his family's call to entrepreneurship, a call, not incidentally, that allowed him to live in a Paris loft. He left Coca-Cola to help with Fox Boots, a family company selling stylish cowboy boots in the United States and Europe. Out of offices established by their father, the Foxes sold not just broccoli from the farm, but boots made trendy in American movies. He, Lilián, and Ana Cristina spent a year and a half in Paris taking care of business, which included occasionally unloading boxes of out-of-style boots. Fox liked the bohemian life, but it also put him in mind of his mother's influence. "It was at this time, making regular pilgrimages to the sanctuary at Lourdes ... that I discovered what a refuge one finds in religion in hard times."[15]

Fox was formulating his political beliefs. In Europe, he observed hundreds of thousands of immigrants working on factory floors, making consumer goods sold in the countries whence the immigrants came. They were the engine of the European Union's success, and Fox grew impatient for "trade, trade, and more trade. The Americas simply must have our own answer to the European Union and the mighty economic tigers of Asia."[16] Fox also was looking at the manufacturing operation at Fox Boots. The company was born of a clever reading of the market for Mexican styles, of course, but it also depended on intelligent, reliable labor. The Fox family found that intelligent, reliable labor force in Guanajuato. Why, Fox asked himself, are so many in the United States unable to accept the intelligence and reliability of the typical Mexican worker?[17] That inability was, and remains, a major obstacle to improving relations between the United States and Mexico. Fox's business sense was transforming itself into political ideas. Fox the Harvard-trained salesman was edging toward Fox the stump orator.

Up to then, Fox had been contemptuous of Mexican politics, which were dominated — some would say oppressed — by the PRI. But the same personality that drove him to defend San Cristóbal moved him to get involved. "In the 1980s," he wrote, "I was just another small-time entrepreneur trying to get by, suffering the consequences, struggling alongside my five brothers to keep our family *changarros* [small enterprises] afloat. Inside, my anger grew, like that of the Mexican people."[18]

His anger manifested itself as neoliberalism, a philosophy in which the strong — business owners, landowners, investors — are freed to "create value," in the phrase of the day. Private investment is re-introduced to nationalized companies, business and personal tax burdens are eased, and businesses, especially small businesses, are encouraged by government policies. Those ideas had particular resonance in Mexico in the early 1980s after President José López Portillo, in the last months of his term, nationalized the banks, devalued the peso, and imposed currency-exchange controls. The peso's official value dropped from about 4 U.S. cents to 2.2 cents and on Mexico's hyperactive black market went as low as 0.7 cents. Under López Portillo's PRI successor, Miguel de la Madrid, there was little improvement. The peso's value fell even farther and Mexico reneged on its international debt. In the meantime, virtually every Mexican knew López Portillo "had plundered the public coffers in a way extreme even by Mexico's tolerant standards."[19] With Mexicans who voted for him still living in hovels, López Portillo retired to a compound that included five huge houses.

"The nationalization of the banks in 1982 provoked a serious conflict inside the system," Fox wrote, "and weakened one of its key parts: the entrepreneurial sector. What happened to the banks make it very clear that no sector would be safe from the caprice of the system and its operators. Business owners throughout the country, especially owners of middle-size and small businesses, recognized that it was not possible to remain aloof ... vis-à-vis the power brokers."[20]

An example of how power was brokered was in the operations of the news media. Television and radio operating licenses were placed in the hands of a few supporters, protecting an inefficient industry from competition while guaranteeing a smooth ride on the airwaves for PRI officials. Fox asserted that "*priista* businessmen paid the official party's bills and bribed its politicians — elected officials even bribed one another — to get contracts and permits, erect barriers to competition, and suffocate any entrepreneur from outside the System with red tape. Sold to the public in the name of nationalism, the whole scheme was really about *control....* Finally, there was the PRI's political machine itself, which feared U.S. dominance and seditious foreign notions like economic mobility, classless democracy, and freedom of expression. So our national leaders censored the press, bought off reporters, defrauded voters, and set up crippling barriers to keep foreign companies from investing in Mexico."[21]

While his philosophy might have come straight from the neoliberal rack, Fox showed true originality as a politician when he called on his exuberance as a natural salesman. Though he wasn't always effective, he was always noticed. "A group of small- and medium-business owners who later would be dubbed 'the Northern Barbarians' ... decided to join the National Action Party."[22] Barbaric behavior, however, had to be moderated. "My first political act was an act of entrepreneurial mutiny." He showed up at a meeting of businessmen and farmers in León. "Everyone was there in fine suits and silver cuff links. But here comes Vicente Fox, clumping up to the podium in cowboy boots, carrying two volumes of government regulations, each one the size of a small hog.... 'We have to comply with all of the damn rules in these two books just to get an export permit to sell broccoli in McAllen [Texas],' I complained. 'How the hell do you expect us to compete in the U.S. market with all this bullshit?' I was not invited back."[23]

Despite that impolitic debut, Fox found himself part of an increasingly broad front challenging PRI's dominance. On the right, PAN candidates were winning scattered, but impressive, state and local elections. On the left, candidates from PRD, the *Partido de Revolución Demócrata*, led by Cuauhtemoc Cárdenas — son of the legendary President Lázaro Cárdenas — were winning in some cities, especially Mexico City. Fox was recruited to run for the national Chamber of Deputies' 3rd district of León. But because so many PAN movers and shakers looked at him askance, it was clear that he would not get their help. He would have to recruit a small cadre of friends and family members. Furthermore, politics in Mexico can be a very rough game. The stress would cost Fox his marriage to Lilián; the loss of his mentor to a mysterious and violent death; gunpoint threats by PRI henchmen; and criticism from the press that he was, at best, a wise-guy, and, at worst, a toady for the United States.

*   *   *

By joining PAN, Fox found himself a member of a party that often fielded candidates who won elections, but were denied office by PRI chicanery. "The party had occasionally, over its long history of opposition to PRI rule, fielded local candidates in town mayoral elections who proved sufficiently popular to attract a majority of votes," wrote historians Julia Preston and Samuel Dillon. "But when that happened, PRI authorities as often as not stole the elections."[24] Fox also knew PAN candidates often held onto their posts by collaborating — not to say selling out — to the PRI majority. "Over fifty years of constant work," Fox wrote, "PAN's members had developed and refined their doctrine, and during that time traditionalists in the party had concluded that in order for them to achieve power it was first necessary for Mexican society to undergo a process of cultural and political transformation. Some even despaired that they would never, realistically, reach a position of power and so saw their role as simply criticizing the system. Thus over the years, PAN was sustained by men who had good ideas but lacked *the hunger to win*."[25]

One *panista* who exemplified the necessary hunger, however, was Luis Álvarez, whose persistence helped pave the way for Fox. Álvarez, a prosperous manufacturer of jeans, had been trying to beat PRI's odds since Fox was in grammar school. Preston and Dillon wrote: "By 1986, Álvarez had been jousting with the PRI for thirty-two years." Not only was Álverez getting beat, his supporters risked getting beat up, as in a 1958 run for the presidency: "In Jalpa, Zacatecas, Álvarez was delivering a speech in the town plaza when he saw several local police, pistols in hand, detaining one of his campaign aides. Álvarez left the microphone, elbowed his way through the crowd, and confronted the police. 'Why are you arresting *him*?' Álvarez asked them. 'I'm the candidate.' 'Are you running for President of Mexico against the PRI?' one of the policemen inquired. 'Yes, I am,' Álvarez confirmed. 'Right. You're under arrest,' the officer said, and led him off to jail." Álvarez was held for four hours and released only after PAN leaders back in Mexico City protested to PRI headquarters.[26]

But the more PRI stole elections, the greater grew the discontent of Mexicans. "Mexicans refer to the years 1970–1982 as the 'tragic dozen,' during which dreams of greatness and autonomy were continuously shattered."[27] Parties to the left and right of PRI stumbled along on the outside, while the PRI mismanaged the government.

Even during the Echeverría years, 1970–76, which were fueled by oil-boom income, Mexico borrowed too much in order to finance social reforms. All the while, the PRI tried to disguise its failures behind a mask of technocratic expertise. The problems persisted into the 1980s.

In 1983, Álvarez finally won an election, along with several other PAN candidates. Álvarez was elected mayor of Chihuahua City with the support of the local bishop, who reflected the church's growing disillusionment with PRI's corruption and broken promises. In fact, PAN candidates took six of the state of Chihuahua's seven biggest cities, with the seventh falling to another non–PRI candidate. Preston and Dillon called it "the most jolting election defeat the official party had ever suffered." Even PRI candidates seemed to be learning humility. The candidate defeated by Álvarez, rather than fretting and asking PRI headquarters to bail him out, stepped forward with an uncharacteristic concession speech. Mexican politics were still tough, but the stage was being set for Fox to make his entrance. "PAN had to confront the authoritarianism of the regime," Fox wrote, "and put the brakes on its plans to improve its position through a series of frauds even more crude than those we were accustomed to, some tainted by outright violence."[28]

Encouraged by the liberalized atmosphere of "the Chihuahua uprising," losing PAN candidates in other states made public — loudly — the circumstances of their losses. They cried fraud in eight states and mounted public demonstrations of their anger, sometimes finding earthy ways to demonstrate discontent. "After a fraudulent election in Chemax, Yucatán, a mob of one hundred local men seized a PRI official who had attempted to steal a ballot box and, one by one, urinated in his face."[29] Mostly, however, confrontations favored PRI thugs, who were more likely to be armed. In sum, while the pushing and shoving continued, the PRI quietly settled back into its technique of scouring the countryside for voters, mostly among the poor. But PAN was learning.

The person who talked Fox into getting serious about politics was Manuel Clouthier, a Sinaloa farmer, who ran as a PAN candidate for governor and president. Fox was trying to get farmers organized to protect their interests and had grown very frustrated, but Clouthier told him to take heart. Clouthier was, Fox recalled, "magnificent: a *toro* charging straight at the matador no matter the danger, railing against the PRI's economic failures and corruption, the repression of the authoritarian government that had walled Mexico off in poverty, crisis and despair." Fox compared Clouthier to Ghandi and Martin Luther King, men who persevered against the odds. Men like Álvarez and Clouthier, successful in business before turning to politics, would wake up the Mexican middle class after its having "endured seventy-one years of the PRI's benign neglect." For too long, Fox believed, the middle class had been griping "at cocktail bars in Polanco or neighborhood barbecues in Guanajuato," after which "they are ready to put on their best smile the next day for the government official who decides whether they get the permit to dig a well." Working people, who were "being squeezed out of existence by the System" needed leadership. "The great mass of people feel only hopelessness ... beneath it all seethes the anger of the true democrats: the students and the intellectuals, the labor activists, the fed-up housewives who take to the picket line."[30]

On New Year's Day 1988, Fox launched his run for Congress. Well, perhaps "launched" is too ambitious a verb. In downtown León, he stepped up to make his first speech before "quite a following, maybe ten idlers in the square and two dogs who barked incessantly as I hemmed and hawed at the microphone, wondering what I'd gotten myself into." It was Fox's first experience talking seriously to anyone not beholden to him for the next paycheck. He was discouraged, but Clouthier remonstrated with him for his lack of determination after one setback. "For the first time in my life ... I was taking a microphone with a political goal, and if today we were to look at a videotape of that meeting I would be a laughingstock. It would show me as completely speechless, embarrassed, and with nothing to say that would possibly move those twelve souls. Experiences like that reaffirmed my conviction that the world of politics and the world of private enterprise cannot be compared. To be in politics requires a long, difficult apprenticeship, and it's not enough to have good ideas, it requires talent, but, more than anything, leadership."[31]

Meanwhile, Fox's brothers and father were concerned that going up against the PRI "system" would only hurt their farming and boot businesses. They told him there would be recriminations, and they were right. The next month, the government closed the vegetable-packing plant for alleged breaches of sanitation regulations. The month after that at Fox Boot Company there was a strike. After 70 years of good labor relations, Fox wrote, "word went out from the PRI-controlled leather workers' union; 'Fox is against the System; he needs to be punished.'" Eventually, the problems were ironed out, and Fox, having faced down those challenges, adopted an even more dramatic campaign style, emulating the emotional Clouthier, who had once staged a hunger strike to protest the PRI's electoral fraudulence. "Mexico was a dictatorship," Fox wrote. "It had always been a dictatorship, and it seemed that Mexico would always be a dictatorship — until people of courage stood up to change that."

Fox won his election in the spring of 1988. With a seat in the House of Delegates, he now played an active role in PAN politics. He was minister of agriculture in Clouthier's "shadow cabinet," and supported Clouthier's campaign for the presidency against the PRI's Carlos Salinas de Gortari. That support required monitoring election booths to prevent, insofar as possible, PRI thugs from tampering with results. This was Fox's first experience in on-the-street politics, and he appreciated his fellow *panistas*, "the freedom fighters who stood beside me when the PRI men stuck a pistol in my belly and demanded a ballot box that was stuffed full of their forgeries. (I gave them back. We also burned a few.)"[32]

The 1988 presidential election was crucial. PRI officials, after six decades of having their way with the Mexican electorate, were concerned that the colorless technocrat Salinas might lose. "The selection of the PRI's presidential candidate for 1988 was seen as the most critical point in the history of the regime since the departure of Lázaro Cárdenas."[33] Within the PRI, the choice of Salinas alienated the left wing by making it painfully clear that the right wing was in charge. Outside the party, Salinas's candidacy was about to create the kind of sensation from which Fox could only benefit.

Salinas had been hand-picked because he was a technocrat, showing off the PRI's competence. But he also showed PRI's varicose veins; he was boring. Salinas's performance on the stump confirmed everyone's misgivings about the ability of a technocrat to manage a political campaign. The popularity of the other candidates—PRD's Cuauhtémoc Cárdenas and PAN's Manuel Clouthier—and their access to considerable resources, as well as their well-managed political organizations, made Salinas's task even harder.

So, on July 6, as vote tallies came in to the Federal Election Commission in Mexico City from around the country, the count proceeded into the night. Tension rose. And rose. Until, late at night, when the lights, quite literally, went out. Without electricity, the commission delayed announcement of the final tally for a week. "It is likely that the problem had little to do with technical difficulties and much more to do with the results in the capital, where Cárdenas was beating Salinas by at least a 2–1 margin. While Salinas had probably intended to reduce the degree of electoral fraud, he was not prepared to lose the election."[34]

The commission declared that Salinas had won with 50.3 percent of the total vote, besting Cárdenas's 30 percent and Clouthier's 17 percent. In response, Cárdenas and Clouthier mobilized their supporters to protest what they believed was an egregious election fraud. Clouthier went on a hunger strike, and Fox, who is well over six feet tall, joined his mentor's cause without changing his diet. "I grew a fierce black beard in solidarity," he wrote. "Now I was bigger and rougher-looking at 110 kilos—220 pounds—no longer a skinny youth with his big brother to do his fighting for him, but a full-blown revolutionary in the best tradition of Latin American guerrillas and U.S. hippies. As usual, we got things late in Mexico— we didn't get the sixties until the eighties."[35]

The PRI's methods, Fox came to understand, were brutally efficient. The government declared certain districts overwhelmingly, if not totally, in the Salinas column, counting more ballots for Salinas than could possibly have been cast. Then officials prevented successful contradiction by locking ballots away in the basement of Congress under armed guard. Faced with that reality, PAN stalwarts were split between those who were satisfied with continued passive resistance, and the firebrands. Fox, of course, was among the latter, some of whom stormed the building where the locked ballot boxes were under guard in the basement. After some tense moments, during which soldiers were ordered to aim their loaded rifles at the invaders, temperance prevailed. Fox and the others tramped back up the stairs "out into the cool air of Mexico City at midnight, found the nearest bar, got stinking drunk on tequila ... and lived to fight another day."[36]

* * *

In Congress, Fox made himself, quite deliberately, a spectacle. Charging that ballot boxes in his district had been stuffed with Salinas votes, Fox demanded that his own election to the House of Deputies be annulled. He claimed that he and others had hidden boxes of fraudulent ballots, which he dragged onto the floor of Congress. Then he decked himself out in ballots with holes torn in them so they would hang over his ears, transforming himself into a tall, bearded Mickey Mouse. The erstwhile Coca-Cola salesman was doing his best to ridicule the election results and mock Salinas's sizeable ears. As with his high-jinks of the past, his protest had no immediate effect, but Fox cast himself as one candidate who could express Mexico's widespread outrage. "It was political street theater at its best: Mexicans are a fun-

loving people; we enjoy a good carnival.... It was a national sensation, and it put Vicente Fox
on the map." Fox insisted: "This was war — or civil disobedience at least. We came in spoiling for a fight, 240 newly elected democratic revolutionary deputies from left and right, united
in our determination to reject the results of the PRI's election fraud."[37]

War, indeed. On October 1, 1989, Clouthier and his driver were killed in a head-on crash
with a truck on the open highway. Fox was among those who did not fail to see the mystery
in the circumstances, but there was nothing to be done. The driver of the truck, who survived with only minor injuries, was never charged.

Nevertheless, across the country, in the middle of Salinas's presidency, PAN candidates
began to advance. They not only won congressional seats, the first PAN governor was elected —
in Baja California, a state far from PRI-controlled precincts in the heart of the country. As
part of that wave, Fox ran for governor of Guanajuato and clearly beat Ramón Aguirre, the
PRI candidate. But PRI election officials, unwilling to let Fox take the election, claimed victory. They said Aguirre had won more than 70 percent of the vote. Fox later wrote that if the
government had declared a close, 51–49 win, Mexicans might have swallowed it. They were
accustomed to PRI's manipulation. But this time "the official party had overreached. Everyone in Mexico knew that Vicente Fox had been elected governor of Guanajuato."

President Salinas, locked in his own political contest to put the North American Free
Trade Agreement into place, could not afford "a fight with some cowboy over the governorship of a small state in central Mexico, raising questions about whether his government was
corrupt and undemocratic." So Salinas and the PRI relented, sort of. They declared the
reported voting results invalid, but rather than naming Fox the winner, they chose another.
The PRI pushed Aguirre overboard and named an "interim" governor, PAN's Carlos Medina, a personal friend of Salinas. Throughout the sordid affair, PRI's performance was so inept
that Mexican leftist writer Gregorio Urías believed that PRI had guaranteed Fox's reputation
as a feared maverick.[38] When the dust settled, Fox had been established as a leading *neopanista*,
a renegade who believed in free-market capitalism, but one unfettered by stodgy old men in
three-piece suits.

Battles against PRI tactics continued. Salinas had made pronouncements about reforming PRI that historian Centeno believed to be sincere. "There were, however, significant limits to the reform." While President Salinas accepted opposition victories in two states, he
disavowed fraudulent election counts in two others — including Fox's in Guanajuato — and
replaced governors in two more. But Salinas seemed less interested in reform than appearances, Centeno speculated, in a "search for international legitimacy rather than a newfound
respect for democratic norms."

Fox agreed. The PRI had tricks suitable for every occasion. When Fox helped a friend in
a local election later that year, the two of them got into line to vote the night before, wanting to beat PRI thugs to the punch. But when the doors opened "we found the ballot boxes
already full, just as they had been in the July national elections." They went back that evening after the polls closed to commandeer the ballot boxes and disclose the ruse to authorities, but they were stopped by PRI hooligans. "The meanest-looking of them stuck a pistol
in my belly.... I would like to tell you that I faced them down.... But we surrendered the box."[39]
Those realities would continue until there was such widespread indignation that it overwhelmed the guns.

＊　　＊　　＊

In 1994 — as Fox tells the story — his sister Mercedes persuaded him to run again for governor of Guanajuato, even though he was tired of being in the public eye. She showed up with

a bunch of PAN supporters who appealed to his ego. "*Shit*, I thought. *I'm back in politics....* Six months later I was governor of Guanajuato, in a landslide this time, a victory even Carlos Salinas couldn't steal."[40] This time Fox's victory was not part of a wave. Events conspired to make him stand out in a crowd. "[I]t had not gone well for PAN in the congressional elections of August 1994, or in the municipal election in December of that year. Fox had somehow been separated from the party; nevertheless, many skeptics saw him as the only option if PAN hoped to hold onto the governor's office in Guanajuato."[41]

Holding onto a governor's office was but one of the events of 1994, however. PRI presidential candidate Luis Donaldo Colosio was murdered; the party's general secretary was shot down on a Mexico City street; and Raúl Salinas, the president's brother, was arrested for corruption. Though acquitted, his wife was picked up in Switzerland while withdrawing funds from a bank account that reportedly held more than $100 million. In addition, there was a family tragedy in store for the Foxes.

For Fox personally, there was a series of tragedies. "It was about this time that Lilián left me for another man," Fox wrote in his straightforward style. "So I plunged myself into a custody battle in the courts, a business battle to save the farm, and a democracy battle on the streets." He wrote of "pour[ing] myself into love. Every waking hour I could find, I spent loving Ana Cristina, Paulina, Vicente, and little Rodrigo. I made sure I was there to take them to school and pick them up, have dinner and help with their homework." Problems, however, multiplied. There were business pressures, the death of this father, a whispering campaign about his failed marriage, the need to spend time with his children — it all took time and energy. During the campaign he often took his children along and speeches took on an emotional tone, even "a religious fervor as I waved the banner of the Virgin, calling on Mexicans to rise up for freedom with tears in my eyes and anger in my voice."[42]

By the time of the divorce, he and Lilián had been married twenty years. Their eldest child, Ana Cristina, would later attribute the divorce to "different outlooks." Insight into that general description, however, might be gained from a remark Ana Cristina made to a Mexican magazine, a remark that speaks volumes about Mexican politics. "My mother couldn't see him involved in politics because she was afraid he'd have the same luck as 'Maquío,' Manuel Clouthier ... whose death, according to some, was not an accident. What I don't know is why they decided that we should live with my father."[43]

In the 1994 presidential race, the PRI replaced the murdered Colosio with Ernesto Zedillo, who, predictably, won. By that time, however, global economic conditions had left Mexico in a financial swoon. As usual, outstanding international debt had built up, and to make matters worse the *zapatistas* — taking their name from the legendary Emiliano Zapata — began their violent upheaval in the southern state of Chiapas.

In Fox's Guanajuato, however, things were going relatively smoothly. He decided that his prominence was sufficient to launch an initiative toward his across-the-border partner, Gov. George W. Bush of Texas. Governor Fox, therefore, walked straight through the brambles that separated northern Mexico from Texas and raised the question of illegal immigration. Fox asked Bush to agree to a plan: For every million dollars Texas investors sent south toward economic development in Guanajuato, Mexico would "guarantee" creation of a thousand jobs. Fox called it a "cohesiveness fund," tamping down illegal immigration while turning a profit. Bush turned Fox down flat, declining even to suggest such a thing to the Texas legislature. "'It's a great idea, but that's not going to happen,' he said firmly. 'Down deep in their hearts, people here in Texas just wouldn't support a deal like that.'" In fact, Fox recalled, talking to Bush about emigration-immigration issues made him feel as if he were back "selling onions door-to-door in McAllen again." Rejected by Bush, Fox settled for a kind of international road trip, setting up Guanajuato trade centers in major U.S. cities. "From Austin, I moved on to other cities, new leaders, more ideas. Now more than ever before, Fox was in a hurry."[44]

Fox's term as governor produced gains. General Motors Corp. created jobs for 3,400 workers in Guanajuato, and the state's economy took off. Author Muñoz Gutiérrez listed no fewer than 34 elements of Fox's "leadership style" that comprised the backbone of his administration. Indeed, the book brings together the mottos and "mission statements" and measurements—or in managerspeak, the "metrics"—of how the Fox administration focused every thought, attitude, and action on "adding value" to the state of Guanajuato. The stuff of precinct politics is sliced and pureed into pie charts, line graphs, and algorithms worthy of an MBA term paper.

Whatever the form, however, the substance was impressive. Value was, in fact, added to the lives of Guanajuatans in several important ways. Industrial investment broadened income distribution. The delivery of health services was expanded. The number of classrooms built in 1996 was 204, a figure that grew in 1997 to 1,651, and in 1998 to 4,600.[45] Fox was also expanding his own experience. He attended his first World Forum, in San Francisco, where he learned the wonders of microcredit—the notion of lending small amounts to entrepreneurs in poor countries—and met Arnold Schwarzenegger at a dinner party, where Schwarzenegger introduced him as "the next president of Mexico."

* * *

When the time came for his presidential run, Fox needed no encouragement from his sister. On December 11, 1998, a year and a half before election day, he announced his candidacy. This was a wily move not only because Fox was a good campaigner; he had some obstacles to get past.

First, Mexicans take their xenophobia seriously, and Article 82 of their constitution prohibits not just that a presidential candidate be native born—as does the U.S. Constitution—but that his or her parents also be native born. The restriction reflects both Mexican pride in its "*mestizo* revolution" of 1917 and continuing vigilance against interlopers. Fox, for all of his roots in the Mexican countryside, had to concede that his mother, the formidable Doña Mercedes, was born in Spain. Article 82 was clear. He was disqualified. Fox argued, of course, that his mother had been brought back while still an infant to her home in Mexico City—where she had been conceived. So Fox set about making his case. "Like a Coca-Cola salesman looking for new grocery stores," he recruited others to lead the charge to set Article 82 aside. It would be a battle because the PRI, on its own, would never accede to "the mad bearded farmer of Guanajuato.... By now I was a well-known troublemaker who had cultivated my own brand image as a tough guy who shot from the lip."[46] The effort was successful, and Fox was allowed to run, but he still had problems in his own party.

PAN's Old Guard had not changed its mind that Fox was an upstart. They didn't trust him. "Individual PAN-istas were as smart and as switched on as any Mexican politicians," wrote Jeffrey Davidow, then U.S ambassador to Mexico, "but, taken together, the party was stuck in a rut. It had been in the opposition for so long it really did not know how to win." When Fox told them he knew how, he still was not greeted with open arms. "The PAN leadership saw Fox as an outsider who had come to the party late in life after a career in business."[47] So, in the spring of 1999, Fox met with PAN leaders. They still were not convinced. Only after he beat challengers in a September intraparty election was Fox accepted as PAN's man.

Still, Fox knew that to run an effective national campaign he needed a U.S.–style campaign staff. Mexican politicians had for years been crossing into the United States to buy "inside-politics" books, so he hired people to form "Friends of Fox." One his closest Friends would be Marta Sahagún Jiménez, who had worked in Fox's second gubernatorial campaign. The wife of a Guanajuato veterinarian and ten years Fox's junior, she was an ardent worker for PAN, which reserved a third of its candidacies for women. She joined Fox's presidential campaign as a media spokeswoman — not as a potential cabinet minister, as Fox at first imagined. "[F]or years our relationship was strictly business, no love at all."

That changed when "one day in 1998, Marta came to me in tears." Her marriage, she said, was falling apart. Still stung by his own divorce, Fox counseled her to work it out, and so she tried. "Over time we began to see each other in a different light: as something more than just coworkers and comrades in a political crusade, still professional in public but growing closer and closer in private. Finally, I dared to ask her on a trip to Buenos Aires. I don't know if it was the heady music, the splendid architecture, or the Malbec wine, but since that magic week in one of the world's great romantic cities we have been a couple.... Love can move mountains, and now we were two on the move, together with our little band of friends, to bring democracy to Mexico."[48]

On a less romantic plane, PRI's technicians were portraying Fox as inexperienced. His support appeared limited to wealthier and upwardly mobile Mexicans and those who were tired of PRI's unfulfilled promises and corruption. To the criticism of Fox, Mexican writer González Ruiz added his distaste for Fox's style: "Throughout the campaign Fox has repeatedly used insulting language that abounded with vulgar expressions. In addition, he has emphasized that his winning will be thanks to the 'vote to punish' PRI."[49] Both Fox and his PRI opponent, Francisco Labastida, looked to Washington for a benevolent smile from U.S. President Bill Clinton, neither with any success.

Ambassador Davidow was also keeping his fingerprints off the election — and trying to stay out of the newspapers altogether — though he met briefly with each candidate: "Without high expectations, I invited Fox for breakfast at our residence. The press play had led me to expect an ego in cowboy boots, with few thoughts beyond the script of his election strategy. Instead, I encountered a man who has obviously thought carefully about Mexico's future. He was committed to pursuing liberal economic reform and serious about changing the country's political dynamic to give the people faith in their government. He was also humorous, sometimes in a self-deprecating fashion, and possessed the greatest gift a politician can have, the ability to see himself from a distance."[50]

Fox was also a blunt observer of the political scene. Of his predecessor, elected after the assassination of Colosio, Fox wrote: "Here we have President Zedillo, who has, frankly, none of the qualities of a leader; he may be very smart, of that I have no doubt, but that is a quality that only works in private enterprise. In politics, there are other qualities, and none of them works when you've got *atole* [a bland corn drink] in your veins; what must happen is a chemistry, a direct communication, with the community, and both parties must understand precisely the work and the compromises that will be necessary."[51] Of his opponent, Fox said, "In fifteen years on the road with Coca-Cola, I met all of [Mexico's] cultures. Francisco Labastida, the man who would be anointed as the PRI candidate in the 2000 presidential election, had not."[52]

The campaign, of course, was about personalities. Rare is the presidential election in modern Latin America — or anywhere else, for that matter — in which one candidate has more potent ideas than another. As a most perceptive observer of Mexico remarked twenty-five years ago: "Improving management of its assets, generating jobs for the 800,000 men and women who enter the work force each year, and creating opportunities for the 40 percent of the population who live in hardscrabble poverty at the base of an ever more distended social pyramid are preconditions to Mexico's becoming a more influential state."[53] Labastida intended to continue PRI's nationalistic industrial policy, and Fox intended to open up private investment as much as Congress would allow. Beyond those precepts, the rhetoric was predictable.

"For the economy to be viable and sustainable," went one of Fox's pronouncements, "it's necessary to cultivate our human capital ... broaden the instruments of personal savings, encourage Mexicans to invest in their own country, substitute our manufacturing for imports, increase exports and attract foreign investment ... included the excluded ... assure basic civil rights." He concluded: "I hope that as Mexicans we can forge, through dialogue and consensus, a Mexico with a bright, hopeful future. I believe, along with millions of Mexicans, in a different and better Mexico. I have full confidence within a generation we can make our dream a reality. We will overcome whatever barrier is in our way."[54]

On the stump, things were more lively. Part of what made them lively was the PRI's hiring of U.S. political hired-gun James Carville, a veteran of campaigns fair and foul. Because Labastida had been governor of Sinaloa, a northern state long troubled by drug gangs, he was saddled with the rumor that he collaborated with drug lords to keep them out of his state, though there was apparently no truth to the story. More to the point was the support Sinaloa got from Mexico City because of Labastida's PRI connections. By contrast, Fox said, Guanajuato "ranked dead last in federal government largesse ... critical in a nation where 95 percent of all fiscal income is doled out by the presidency..."[55]

Fox created a stir by referring to Labastida, a significantly shorter man, as *chaparrito*, or "shorty." He suggested that to stand "toe-to-toe" in debate, Labastida would have to use the stool his handlers always placed behind his lectern. When Labastida called Fox out on the insult, Fox replied that he could stop being rude, but PRI politicians could not stop being corrupt. As the news media recycled the exchange, superficial attitudes of the public were reflected in almost daily polls. It was just the sort of campaign that lent itself to the merits of a tall talker.

And Fox made sure his voice was heard as far afield as possible, for Mexican emigrants in the United States would be able to vote. "Candidate Vicente Fox promised voters at home and the millions of Mexicans living in the United States that once elected he would speak for them all. He painted a new vision of a Mexican diaspora with continuing and strong ties to the motherland. He vowed to be its protector and advocate."[56]

In April 2000 the first debate was held, and polls and editorials suggested that Fox did well. The next month, major polls showed him ahead for the first time. Then, on May 23, a day Fox's campaign workers dubbed "Black Tuesday," the candidates griped in a televised debate over nothing more than the conditions of a second debate. No one looked good, but Fox looked worst. Then, after he'd started to fight his way back in the polls, there were more problems. Fox insisted that the government was tapping his cell phone calls, including those to his wife. The PRI, meanwhile, wanting to show that it was really an open party, not a monarchy, held a "primary" election to give exposure to Labastida. The PRI—advised by Carville—also produced "those hatchet-job commercials that are surely the worst export of the United States ... the ads warned that Vicente Fox was a dangerous radical whose election would lead to revolutionary overthrow of the established order. What Carville & Company missed was that the Mexican people *wanted* to overthrow the system."[57]

The subject of a second debate remained stalled as the PRI held out for a bland, moderated, no-interchanges format. Eventually, with Fox and Labastida essentially tied in the polls, the notion of a second debate was jettisoned. However, Cuauhtemoc Cárdenas, the leftist candidate, still had a trick up his sleeve. He invited the other two to a debate about a second debate. Fox and Labastida were to join him at his home, where, Fox later wrote, he "walked straight into an ambush."

First, Cárdenas succeeded in looking statesmanlike by calling the other two together. Second, when Fox arrived at the house there were dozens of reporters and cameramen who'd also been invited. He felt as if he'd been thrown into a lion's den. Third, Labastida and Cárdenas had prepared notes, and Fox had not. To start the discussion, Labastida and Cárdenas stated their positions calmly while Fox, when his turn came, reverted to type. He banged the table impatiently and demanded a debate that day —*Hoy! Hoy! Hoy!*— thereby confirming the notion that he was a bit of a madman. Then the other two revealed that, sure, they were ready to debate at the end of the week. Suddenly Fox was seen as unreasonable; he fell behind in the overnight polls.

Some advisers counseled Fox to apologize. One even called his mother, the formidable Mercedes, to ask her to discipline him. But another adviser recalled that Mercedes, a long time ago, had remonstrated with her son for precisely that kind of temperamental display. He recalled her saying at the time that Vicente was too stubborn to be president. "'He is what he is,' she said, 'and you'll never change him. He uses bad language that embarrasses the family....' And here's the thing, Vicente — she said that with pride!" So, in the debate, Fox did not apologize, but recounted his mother's warning. Then he added, "But you need firm character and true leadership to end seventy years of corruption, poverty, and desperation. Do you think a weak and gray person could stand up to the PRI and its allies?" He pounded the table again. "I had no idea whether I had achieved a feat of political judo and turned our biggest negative into a strength — or just sealed the lid on my political coffin."[58] He found out soon enough. At a rally a few days later a crowd of thousands chanted *Hoy! Hoy! Hoy!* The polls gave Fox 49 percent to Labastida's 17.

*   *   *

On election day, July 2, exit polls showed Fox up by seven points, a figure confirmed by incumbent President Zedillo's own poll. Nevertheless, it was uncertain whether the margin was enough to spur Zedillo to concede that the PRI, after seven decades, had lost, or would fall prey to the PRI operatives who had stolen elections before. Zedillo did the former.

The count was Fox, 16 million votes, or 42.5 percent of the total. The PRI's Labastida garnered 13.5 million votes, or 36 percent. The leftist Cárdenas won 6.2 million votes, or 6.6 percent.

"On his fifty-eighth birthday, Vicente Fox had swept to the Mexican presidency," wrote Ambassador Davidow. "The rural vote had declined as a percentage of the total vote. But more importantly, Fox had successfully challenged the PRI's hold over the countryside.... Fox had obtained 5.3 million rural votes to Labastida's 6.3 million."[59] Thousands of people flowed into the streets, singing the national anthem and chanting *Hoy! Hoy! Hoy!* President Zedillo wanted Labastida to make a concession speech when the polls showed him decisively out of the race, but he refused.

Fox and his supporters did not care. When Fox, surrounded by aides and supporters, arrived at a victory rally, he could not see up ahead and asked an aide what it was that he was hearing. He was told: "That's the sound of a hundred million people who just got their freedom."

*   *   *

In the heady aftermath of the historic election — less than two weeks after inauguration day, Popocatetl, near Mexico City, would erupt, as if in recognition — all eyes were on this novel phenomenon, a non–PRI president. Over the rest of the summer and into the fall, Fox, as president-elect, took aim at the real issues that followed the tinsel of campaigning. He made an overture to the rebels in Chiapas, still holding on from their 1994 uprising. He said he was willing to talk. He traveled abroad, visiting the United States, the European Union, and Canada. He proposed gradually opening borders with United States and Canada. He even managed to talk his way past a stumbling block after a Mexican newspaper found kids as young as fourteen picking vegetables at San Cristóbal in violation of Mexican law.

Also during the transition period, the religious issue raised its mitered head. In Mexico, the Roman Catholicism brought to the Americas by the Spanish during the Inquisition is in the care of an ultraconservative church. Clerics keep a wary eye on the secularists who fought and won the 1910–17 revolution. In fact, the 1929 rebellion of the *cristeros*— Roman Catholics who objected to the church-state separation embodied in the 1917 constitution— led to as many as 100,000 *cristeros* being killed by government troops and their sympathizers. That history burns in Mexico's collective conscience, and in the 2000 presidential race, Fox was the only serious contender who wore his Catholicism on his sleeve. "Many people outside Mexico," Fox wrote, "do not realize that our revolution was also a war against the power of the church.... After [President Francisco] Madero's death and the founding of the Institutional Party of the Revolution [the PRI], a series of anti–Catholic PRI presidents sought to rein in the church, which they saw as keeping Mexico on its knees ... priests were murdered ... church altars were desecrated and sacked by government soldiers." Fox placed himself firmly on the church's side: "I have gathered one of the largest private collections of Cristero literature. These were the stories of my childhood."[60]

What brought religion to the fore during the transition period was a successful vote in August by PAN members of the Guanajuato legislature "to repeal the law granting a right to abortion to women who had been raped." Although the bill was vetoed by the governor, "it caused immediate, overwhelming demonstrations of protest by various sectors," according to Mexican author González. Fox, however, pulled the fat out of the fire by showing that he was more than a crazy cowboy. He counseled patience and civility on both sides. "In that case, Fox himself showed the capacity for listening to popular demand over and above sectarian interests and old ideologies."

The abortion issue arose in different ways, demonstrating — like an earlier effort in Jalisco to ban miniskirts— that followers of Our Lady of Guadalupe were going to be heard in Mexican politics. The entire issue of religion, in fact, illustrated another similarity between elections north and south of the Rio Grande. If modern Mexican politicians acknowledge their debt to U.S. books about winning elections, Mexico's conservative Roman Catholics must have been studying the tactics of their fundamentalist brethren in the United States. On balance, concluded González, Fox handled the issue well. He appeared to be "[a] person who could decide for himself between designing a good government — one that left behind authoritarian practices and trying to renovate tired institutions— or yielding power to clerics and the extreme right."[61]

On broader questions, however, González wondered about a Fox presidency because his campaign lacked substance and focused on bashing the PRI. "In his campaign for the presidency, Fox placed his emphasis on being the champion of 'change.' But the banner of generic 'change' doesn't work as a rhetorical strategy. On the contrary, many of the concrete changes that Fox advanced, like the so-called 'Fox Decalogue' and others in his pamphlet, 'Fox Proposes,' were not in line with popular demands but rather with the interests of the extreme right and the Catholic hierarchy....

"There was an aggressive 'lynching' rhetoric directed generically against members of the

PRI and their sympathizers that caused doubt during the campaign of the possibility of a truly plural nation. That rhetoric appealed to an emotional level, not to a serene evaluation of possible futures. Among those possibilities is a government controlled by the Catholic hierarchy and allied with conservative groups and the far-right-wing of the PAN."

President-elect Fox fueled those concerns when, in October, he proposed extending Mexico's 15 percent value-added tax to food and medicine, an idea that caused a sharp and immediate backlash. Revenue-raising proposals are always controversial, and because of its effect on Mexico's poor it was quickly dubbed the "tortilla tax." Fox stuck to his guns.

Delaying as long as he could, in November Fox chose a cabinet that was essentially conservative. But by then even critics like González were ready to concede that Fox's affiliation with PAN and his own conservative statements during the campaign should be set aside because "during his time as president-elect Fox has shown a spirit of forming a plural government."[62]

Even Davidow, whose view of Latin America seems constricted by his years in the U.S. Foreign Service — including service in Chile during the overthrow of President Salvador Allende — conceded that Fox was doing reasonably well. "Fox did have some success in his first months in office," he wrote. "His handling of the Chiapas conflict demonstrated political courage and a willingness to take risks. He had bombastically declared during his campaign that as president he could solve the Chiapas problem in fifteen minutes." When the *Subcomandante* Marcos, the charismatic Zapatista leader, responded to Fox's election by announcing a public-relations march into the capital, it threw many Mexicans into a panic. Many officials — hired over the preceding three fourths of a century by the PRI — were against the trip. Those officials, Davidow wrote, "tended to see government as a necessary and organized conspiracy against chaos." But in the end, although Marcos scored a public relations coup, so did Fox. "[W]ith his display of moderation and tolerance, Fox had boldly secured a significant victory."[63]

Fox remembers the period with more wit. "We'd had a good first year," he recalled. "In late August 2000, just after the presidential election but before I took office, our opposition movement had even ousted the PRI from its stronghold in Chiapas, forming a joint PAN-PRD coalition to elect as governor indigenous-rights activist Pablo Salazar, who brought peace to the jungles of the Zapatista rebellion." When Marcos upped the ante by announcing "that he, too, would take advantage of the new era of freedom," one public-relations specialist was about to meet another. "Marcos unveiled plans to march the rebel Zapatista army to the nation's capital and seize the streets to protest the previous government's policy of ignoring the people of Chiapas. The rebels were coming, Marcos said, to back Vicente Fox's bill for indigenous rights. With friends like this, who needs enemies?"[64]

*   *   *

On December 1, 2000, Fox was inaugurated as Mexico's sixty-second president. During the ceremony his daughter Ana Cristina — in an unprecedented act for a Mexican president — approached the podium and handed her father a crucifix. By that time, Fox had already broken tradition by going to morning mass, something that Mexican presidents had studiously avoided.

From that point, events moved from the symbolic to the realistic. "Fox's political problems began on the day he was elected," wrote Davidow. The PRI held a dominant number of seats in Congress and was willing and able to collaborate with the [leftist] PRD in opposition. Behind Fox were only PAN members of Congress who had skulked on the periphery of his campaign. And, finally, Fox's own cadre of supporters "was not sufficiently well schooled in the dirty arts of politics to succeed in Mexico's tough public arena." Beyond that, opponents bred like mice. "The PRI had been traumatized by its electoral defeat. Mutual recriminations were the order of the day and factions were multiplying."

Fox could have capitalized on the PRI's internal dissension, forming new alliances, but, to his credit, did not. "Fox could have moved aggressively to split it and draw some of its elected representatives to his banner. But Fox chose not to. It was not his style."[65] Author Urías reached the same conclusion. Fox was setting the tone for Mexico's future. "Later, as we understood elements of [Fox's] governance better it was clear that there were fewer differences between PAN and PRI.... For example, a National Development Plan was moving political and economic leaders toward a general acceptance of neoliberalism — as in the addition of the value-added tax to food and medicines — and both parties were swimming in that stream."[66]

If PAN and PRI were drawing closer, familiarity was, in some respects, breeding contempt. "The very structure of the Mexican political system added to Fox's difficulties," Davidow wrote. "The constitutional prohibition against re-election for all public officials means that members of Congress generally do not have to be concerned about their constituents' views or about paying a price for obstructing a popular president."[67] In addition, Fox found that the cooperation PRI had built with different groups was hard to reverse. Teachers' loyalty to the PRI, for example, provided support at all electoral levels and protected them from being weeded out of the classroom even if incompetent. "If you were one of Mexico's 1.5 million teachers, you belonged to a PRI teachers' union, and your job was protected."[68] To his surprise, however, Fox found that teachers and other groups, frustrated by seven decades of realities that the PRI couldn't erase, met him halfway.

In short, Fox was discovering what all candidates find out if they win. "Vicente Fox," Davidow wrote, "found it was easier to become president of Mexico than to be president of Mexico. The euphoria ... began to evaporate quickly, and within a few months of his inauguration newspaper pundits and others were expressing disappointment in his government. Fox, a man of warmth and obvious good intentions, maintained high personal popularity in public opinion polls. But as it became increasingly apparent that he could not deliver on his bold campaign pledge of change, disillusionment with his administration began to sink in."[69]

That evaluation is unfair. Rare is the president of any nation who lives up to the illusions created during campaigning. Davidow was in a unique position as U.S. ambassador to hear the gossip and learn the substance of Fox's presidency. But denizens of the U.S. Foreign Service often exaggerate the former — and their own importance — and have less to do with the latter than they would have people believe. Any Mexican president must guide his citizens past the prejudiced and generally selfish policies of its neighbor to the north, and in Fox's case U.S. policy was especially difficult to swallow. The Bush administration had launched a war in Iraq, and it expected everyone to follow it down the barrel of U.S. misstatements. Right after Fox's election had raised him to international prominence, and just as an American president, a Texan, appeared to understand Mexican issues, all hell broke loose.

Fox was the first Mexican president invited to address the U.S. Congress. He won plaudits for his remarks, but they were soon drowned out by the clamor of war. "My speech to Congress, carefully crafted by my foreign minister, Jorge Castañeda, focused on trust — a term I used over and over in that address. 'I am aware that for many Americans and for many Mexicans, the idea of trusting their neighbor may seem risky and, perhaps, unwise. I am sure that many on both sides of the border would rather have stuck to the old saying that 'good fences make good neighbors'.... These perceptions have deep roots in history. In Mexico, they derived from a long-held suspicion and apprehension about a powerful neighbor. And in the

U.S. they stem from previous experience with a political regime governing Mexico, which for the most part was regarded as undemocratic and untrustworthy." Fox later said he was resigned to the prospect that that last remark would "cause a firestorm in Mexico, where politicians hated any mention of our country's sordid past of corruption, narcotraffic, and economic crisis."[70]

Fox was ushered into closed-door meetings with U.S. congressional leaders ranging from liberals Senator Ted Kennedy and Rep. Richard Gephardt to conservative Sens. Trent Lott and Jesse Helms. After the meetings, Fox was convinced he was making friends. "'We're with you on this, Mr. President,' said the lawmakers, even anti–NAFTA union Democrats and the same right-wingers who would later oppose Bush on our guest-worker proposals." Making a campaign-style appearance in Ohio, Fox and Bush talked mostly about immigration, and Bush told Fox his optimism about the chance for reform was growing. But four days after Fox returned to Mexico, the 9/11 attacks occurred. "Overnight the world changed. America's borders clanged shut. Our revolution of hope came face-to-face with the walls of fear."[71]

The Bush administration's enthusiasm for its new, best Mexican friend cooled after world leaders, though saddened by the loss of life in the 9/11 attacks, were skeptical — to say the least — about the war in Iraq. President Bush, laboring to build a "coalition of the willing," was dismayed when Mexicans, initially sympathetic, began to turn away, taking Fox with them. Mexican intellectual Carlos Fuentes rejected any suggestion that Mexico was obligated to support the Middle East ventures of the Bush administration. "Fuentes argued that the United States had brought the attacks on itself by recklessly pushing its own power throughout the world.... He told his countrymen not to act as America's *achinchicles* — a wonderful Mexican word meaning 'minions' and full of the onomatopoeia of clanking prisoners' chains. His defiant assertion that 'we are not lackeys' became the battle cry of the Mexican 'this is not our war' crowd."[72]

When Fox joined the crowd of U.S. critics, it was seen in the White House as a betrayal. "Just a week earlier," Davidow complained, "as Washington feted Fox like a hero for the stunning electoral triumph in 2000 that had ended seventy-one years of one-party rule in Mexico, he had issued a stirring call for a new era of understanding."[73] Davidow obviously felt that "understanding" was the same as "support." But Mexicans' collective memory includes many U.S. invasions of Latin America for trumped-up reasons, including the one in 1845 that cost Mexico half of its sovereign territory.

Moreover, as the United States went into its border-to-border defensive crouch, the Mexican economy suffered. "Closing the borders hurt us the most," Fox wrote, "and for the longest duration." With nearly two thirds of U.S. goods sold to Latin America headed for Mexico, transshipment was slowed to a crawl; tourism was scared away. Fox tried every trick of the political trade. "With our proposed economic reforms already facing stiff resistance from an opposition-controlled Congress, I decided at our first January 2002 cabinet meeting to focus on what we could do by ourselves. The United States had its own problems." Fox rejected a plan to direct Mexican buying toward certain, friendly, U.S. congressional districts, but he concluded that doing nothing was not wise, either. "The only course remaining was to make incremental changes in those areas where we could ... and bold changes in areas we controlled directly, through executive action. The most dramatic — and politically costly — of those moves was to raise electricity rates, which we did in January 2002." His personal popularity fell in the polls from the 80s to the 50s. "This mattered little to a guy who couldn't run for re-election, but it would allow the PRI to regain ground."[74]

In foreign affairs, Fox continued to shoot from the hip, and allowed his cabinet to do the same. This sometimes led to left-right cooperation that suited both Fox and Mexico. Fox chose as ambassador to Cuba a PRD leftist. But when Fox made his first official visit to Cuba — in February 2002 — he publicly raised the question of political prisoners on the island and even met with a group of dissidents. When U.S. officials groused about Fox's continuing Mexico's close relationship with Cuba, Foreign Minister Castañeda reacted by giving the entire hemisphere a sprightly lecture.

A former leftist with an independent turn of mind, Castañeda set things straight in "a long press interview on his return to Mexico City. He talked more sense about the Cuban-Mexican relationship than any Mexican government figure had ever dared to do publicly. The old days are gone, he asserted. 'In a world without a cold war, in a democratic hemisphere now with no dictators, in a Mexico without a regime that utilizes the romantic identification with Cuba in its own shadow game, it is time to recognize reality. Cuba is a country, not a protest song. Our relations with the Cuban Revolution are over and our relations with the Republic of Cuba have begun.'"[75]

During 2002, Fox led the government to begin to resolve its own history of civil-rights abuses. Investigations during the year uncovered a mountain of files related to torture and killing of political victims in the 1960s and 1970s. The 2002 proceedings included the dramatic interrogation of former president Luis Echeverría, who had earlier been in charge of national police as interior minister. In September — after Fox canceled a trip to Texas to protest the execution there of a Mexican national — a court in Mexico City indicted three army officers with first-degree murder in connection with no fewer than 134 killings.

*   *   *

Early on President Fox's social agenda was to make an honest woman of Marta. After complaints from reporters that she was not the best spokesperson for the administration — Fox said they were angry because she refused to pay the usual subsidies for friendly reportage — Fox took action. He fired her as press secretary, he said at the time, in order to make her first lady. They were married a year to the day after the election — at Los Pinos, the former presidential mansion outside Mexico City. The happy couple lived in a Mexico City hotel while the government renovated "an old gardening shack" near the National Palace. Fox thus had an unpretentious residence for himself and Marta and a spare bedroom for visiting children.

Davidow portrayed Fox's term as generally successful. "Fox did a credible job as president. He deepened Mexico's fiscal stability. He attracted new foreign and domestic investment. His fiscal policies allowed interest rates to fall and millions to buy houses with mortgages at fixed rates. He decreased significantly the number of Mexicans living in abject poverty. He presided over a major decentralization of government authority. And, he ran an administration that was considerably more honest than most of its predecessors. He accomplished all of this without a legislative majority, without a truly effective political party of his own, and against the opposition of the former ruling Revolutionary Institutional Party (PRI) and the leftist Revolutionary Democratic Party (PRD)."[76]

Fox summed up things with his customary wit. "[T]o make a hundred-year leap and lead Mexico into the twenty-first century (after having missed the twentieth century altogether), we needed a sweeping fiscal-reform package to help government pay for itself. The goal was to balance the budget and get Mexico out of the deep hole of debt the old regime had handed over with the keys to Los Pinos — yet still fund the ambitious education, housing, health care, and antipoverty programs we envisioned as the fruits of our new democracy."[77] Looking to Mexico's future, Fox supported the plan for a much-needed new airport at Atenco, outside Mexico City and away from the two-runway facility there. The idea, however, fell under the weight of public protests because an extensive residential area would have to be destroyed.

And despite the predictable charges that he was selling Mexico's patrimony, Fox — using administrative techniques copied from British planners — opened up state-owned companies that control the petroleum, natural gas, and electrical industries. Fox was able to bring in outside investment without full privatization. Fox pointed out that when he took office, Pemex — the oil company that provides a third of Mexico's annual budget — was spending $8 to bring up each barrel, compared to a $6.49-per-barrel cost for Shell Oil Company. Although Pemex was second in size only to Saudi Arabia's Aramco and half again the size of Exxon, inefficiencies rendered Pemex much less profitable than either one. New investment opened up deep drilling for oil in the Gulf of Mexico and was responsible for building 36 power plants, increasing electrical supply by more than a third. During Fox's six-year term, 2000–2006, Mexican per-capita income rose 60 percent, to the highest in Latin America.

* * *

In sum, Fox found himself in the position of every elected chief executive, standing on the bridge of the supertanker that he had promised to sail like a skiff. Watching from the shore are many, like former Ambassador Davidow, who believe that every election is a new voyage, and every campaign promise is to be parsed for its lasting effect on the human condition. "Perhaps history will judge Fox harshly," Davidow wrote. "He may be criticized for failing to understand the role of the Mexican president, for not using the powers available to him, or for being too timid or absent in the battle to reform the country's institutions.... But, clearly, for most Mexicans, at the end of his *sexenio*, Fox, though appreciated as a decent man, was seen as having failed to fulfill the promise that propelled him to office ..." In this view, "Fox did not bring about the kind of fundamental change of the social, political, and economic systems that he seemed to have promised, or, at least, so many Mexicans thought he had promised."

The reality was more nuanced. On the key issue of Mexico's petroleum industry, Fox won a partial victory. After suggesting that Pemex, the national oil company, should be sold to private investors, Fox had to back down. It was clear that Mexicans would not stand for the loss of their national treasure to foreigners. But the industry, studies showed, still needed $120 billion worth of modernization over the first decade of the new century. So, pointing out the many inefficiencies of Pemex as a state-owned entity, he settled for a public-private solution. He found ways to channel in private investment. He tiptoed — in cowboy boots — along the divide between an outright sale and letting Pemex rust to death. The result was national income, also bolstered by revenue from the tortilla tax, that flowed into Mexican coffers.

* * *

In the important area of U.S.–Mexican relations — that is, as half of the New World's Odd Couple — Fox scored gains that even Davidow couldn't ignore. "Even before Fox took office, he made clear that he was determined to press the United States government to deal seriously with the issues of illegal immigration. When he bluntly said that it was time for the United States to 'get real,' he meant that Washington should acknowledge the country's dependence on Mexican migrants and stop forcing them to live in a shadow land of illegality, uncertainty, and vulnerability. A decent, religious man, Fox was motivated by a real concern for the lives of his countrymen. In recognition of their willingness to sacrifice for their families back home, he called them 'heroes.' His rhetoric constituted a significant change in

Mexican political discourse. In his outspoken advocacy of immigrants, Fox was not encumbered by the inhibition that had muffled the PRI's concerns."[78]

Fox has, in fact, been at his most eloquent and his most blunt in discussing emigration/immigration. "The enemies of immigration," Fox has written, "will cite statistics showing that 40 percent of Mexicans would come to the United States if they had a chance. They warn of a 'Third World invasion' of swarthy, mustachioed Mexicans who look and talk like me and the good-hearted, hardworking, dark-skinned indigenous and *mestizo* kids I grew up with at San Cristóbal. But I have been that exiled farm boy, if only for a year, and then only to go to a Catholic school in Wisconsin with three square meals a day. Even then I can tell you that a Mexican farm boy who crawls across the barbed wire at the Rio Grande desperately loves his homeland and desperately wants to stay."[79]

Emigrants, Fox said, are fed up with a country in which only 5 percent go to college, and some never go to school at all. Ten percent of Mexican adults cannot read or write, and the Mexican average for years in school is five. Mexican emigrants are looking for and generally finding work even if their entry is illegal. And many will say, as Fox bluntly did in May 2005, Mexicans are often in the United States to work at jobs "that not even blacks want to do." Fox erupted in public in the spring of 2006 when Bush ordered 6,000 National Guard troops to "protect" the border and chase illegal immigrants farther underground. "'We need to find a way to bring these folks out of the shadows and into the legal system, so we know where they are, educate their children, collect the taxes and keep people safe on both sides of the border."[80]

* * *

Fox has also spoken with honesty on the other insoluble problem along the border, the flourishing drug trade. Drugs were never an issue in the Fox-Labastida campaign, perhaps because Mexicans considered drugs a U.S. social problem. In fact, the National Institute on Drug Abuse of the National Institutes of Health offers the following explanations why cocaine — typically shipped from Colombia and South America — and heroine — now being grown by Mexicans to meet increasing demand — have attracted so much illegal entrepreneurship in the hemisphere.

1. In 1997, an estimated 1.5 million U.S. citizens — 0.7 percent of the population age 12 and older — were heavy users of cocaine. An additional 682,000 (0.3 percent) were "frequent" users, meaning they got high at least 51 days a year. Children were catching on. "The use of cocaine powder rose steadily in 8th, 10th, and 12th graders throughout the first half of the nineties.... In 2006, 6 million Americans age 12 and older had abused cocaine...."

2. Heroin was used by 68,000 Americans in 1993, 117,000 in 1994, 196,000 in 1995, 216,000 in 1996, and 325,000 in 1997. "The rates of heroin use in the student population remain quite low, but they have risen significantly among 8th, 10th, and 12th graders.... By some measures, heroin use is growing as a problem in many cities."[81]

Fox found Mexico caught between two realities. Mexicans did not want to own up to their inability to capture and prosecute drug cartels, and the United States was tongue-tied when the conversation turned to its responsibility for the drug consumption that brings criminality in its wake. Thus the image of Mexico as a drug capital persists, even though Mexicans are at least as outraged by the problem as U.S. citizens. Mexican citizens cheered as loudly as anyone when the notorious Tijuana cartel leader Francisco Javier "The Wildcat" Arellano Félix was captured. "[Yet] anti–Mexico voices in the United States often seize on these high-profile busts as evidence that ours is a dangerous, drug-infested country whose government is run by corrupt drug lords. In fact, the opposite is true: Mexican drug cartels are in the news primarily *because* administrations like [his successor] Felipe Calderón's and mine worked so closely and publicly with U.S. authorities to crack down, arrest cartel leaders, and extradite these thugs. To suggest otherwise denigrates the courage of the police chiefs who have been slain, the prosecutors whose families have been kidnapped, the crusading journalists whose offices are bombed."[82] "The Fox administration achieved some improvements in law enforcement," conceded Davidow, "but the lack of trust and cooperation among the different agencies continued to be a big problem.... Under Fox, The Mexican army started to work more closely with his attorney general's office, also headed by an army general. Old problems remained.... But there was impressive progress nevertheless."[83]

* * *

As for the hemisphere's biggest political *fútbol*, NAFTA, Fox took a pass from his predecessors and was lucky just to keep it on the field of play. Fox saw NAFTA as a mixed blessing. Mexico's northern cities took advantage of NAFTA's promise. So did many U.S. companies. "But NAFTA was not so kind to Mexican farmers. "The United States came to Mexico, convinced us to open our markets, and taught us to compete American style — to make better products at lower prices, to use computers and cell phones, to show up on time, to work through lunch so that we could be more efficient.... We traded some of our lifestyle for this progress.... So I ask the antiglobalists in the United States: Now that you have won and the world is competing the American way, how can you throw up walls of tariffs, string barbed wire around your borders, and turn back Mexican eighteen-wheelers at the Rio Grande?" Fox reserved his sharpest words for "the highly efficient and *richly subsidized* agribusiness of the United States, where the economic insanity of farm-price supports for millionaire growers and billionaire-run corporations persists even today."[84]

* * *

At the end of his term, and aside from all the issues of controversy and the statistics of progress, Fox's legacy as an agent of change rested on whether he could make change stick. "Beginning in 2000," wrote the Argentine journalist Juan Tokatlian, "the hemisphere underwent some democratic advances and several retreats. Among the former, the case of Mexico stands out as a triumph of the conservative Vicente Fox and the defeat of the PRI, which had been the only governing party for seven decades. Even so, one must continue to watch the political evolution of the country because a change in party in the executive branch does not signify a radical transformation of the deeply rooted culture of authoritarianism."[85]

If the Mexican electorate returned the PRI to the presidency, or if Fox were deemed such a failure that a leftist were chosen to follow him, Fox's presidency would count for little. Those considerations made the 2006 election crucial, and it was surrounded by a new crowd of troubles. This time the regional unrest was not in Chiapas, but Oahaca. Corn produced by subsidized corporate giants in the United States, dumped on the Mexican market, made it impossible for Mexican farmers to get a decent price. Their revolt was joined by doctors, teachers, and other non-farm workers, who demanded that NAFTA be corrected.

Furthermore, despite anti-narcotics efforts—Fox took credit for the arrests of 20 narcotics chiefs, 50 of their lieutenants, and a total 70,000 criminals—the problem got worse. A *New York Times* article decried the U.S. side of the border as a "Vast Arms Bazaar for Mexican Cartels." A total of 6,600 gun shops stocked military-style submachine guns more powerful than those carried by Mexican police. "In 2008," the article concluded, "more than 6,000 Mexicans were killed in drug-related warfare, and most of the 20,000 weapons that have been seized by the Mexican government originated in the United States."

Into that maelstrom was cast the PAN candidate selected as Fox's successor. He was Felipe Calderón, a forty-three-year-old former PAN party chairman, a leader in Congress, and, briefly, Fox's secretary of energy. Fox — and wife Marta, who would be criticized for trying to influence the choice — preferred Santiago Creel, Fox's minister of the interior. But the party Old Guard chose Calderón. They still did not cotton to the upstart in cowboy boots. Fox, however, accepted Calderón as a worthy successor. "Felipe won the primaries by promising to take the PAN back to its roots and be a more aggressive agent of change — more Fox than Fox."[86]

In the election, Calderón carried PAN's — and Fox's — banner forward. "July 2, 2006, precisely six years to the day after Vicente Fox's impressive victory," wrote Davidow, "Mexico elected his successor in an election as dramatic and as historically important as the one that gave Fox his triumph."[87]

24

Néstor Kirchner Ostoic and Cristina Fernández de Kirchner
Peronist Pair
1950– and 1953–
(Argentina)

It is not just that Néstor and Cristina Kirchner spent time in jail—a fairly common experience for modern Latin American leaders—that separates them from their peers. Beyond imprisonment, it must further be kept in mind that many of their fellow students, their colleagues, and their most intimate friends "disappeared," their earthly remains never to be found, their murderers never to be punished, their promise never to be fulfilled. Indeed, before either Néstor or Cristina Kirchner rose to the presidency of Argentina, they lived through extremely perilous times. Such is the tragedy of recent Argentine history that the Kirchners first had to survive a harsh military dictatorship—Argentina's "dirty war"—before they could join efforts to lead their nation into a more hopeful future.

* * *

Carlos Néstor Kirchner, the president's grandfather, was a descendant of German immigrants. The Kirchner family background, in fact, speaks volumes about the ethnic mixture that makes up Argentina and the southern countries of South America—they were German, Spanish, Swiss, and Croatian, and some Kirchner antecedents came to the New World by way of South Africa. They made their way to Patagonia, Argentina's southern frontier of sheep and cattle ranches, which by the end of the nineteenth century was becoming what its sparse population still likes to call "a land of strong men and free spirits."

Carlos settled in the frontier town of Río Gallegos, Santa Cruz, and married a merchant's daughter, Margarita Cönning. Kirchner inherited the store and, along with his brother and sister, prospered as a wholesaler and retailer. Their success paralleled the growth of Río Gallegos from a small town into the provincial capital after the discovery of gold nearby. The brothers' signatures are on the act of founding the Santa Cruz wing of the national *Unión Cívica Radical,* the Radical Party, which exists today.

Of Carlos's and Margarita's marriage were born four children, the eldest of whom was Néstor Carlos—originality with male names was not a family characteristic. Néstor Carlos completed secondary school and went to work for the post office, a coveted career. After his work at the post office taught him to use the telegraph, he met and courted a counterpart across the border with the Chilean post office, María Juana Ostoic. She was the daughter of a Croatian immigrant, a furniture maker, and their Morse Code romance led to marriage in

1946. The couple lived in Río Gallegos, where Néstor Carlos, during the day, worked as an accountant for the post office and kept his association with the family store. In the evening, he cast gold teeth for a local dentist. At night, he walked to the local movie theater, where he sold tickets. In addition, he operated a small accounting business.

The Kirchners had driven their stake into the Patagonian future. Historian Walter Curia quotes the Argentine economist Horacio Lafuente to describe Santa Cruz in the early part of the twentieth century: "In 1920, it was a society of recent arrivals from different parts of Argentina and the four corners of the planet, of unknowns almost without pasts. There were no traditions, no ancestry, no family fortunes, just people existing beneath a very thin coat of varnish that could not always hide the fact of their recent and, in many cases, doubtful origins."[1] That mixture, Curia notes, pitted the owners of land and the operators of factories against their workers in "the bloodiest fight between capital and labor in Argentine memory." Argentina was the world's second largest exporter of wool, generating a profit stream that brooked no interruption. Although Radicals dominated national politics, Santa Cruz politics were in the hands of the Rural Society, a creation of the region's large landholders. They were stoutly opposed by the Workers Society, and in the early 1920s the conflict was sometimes punctuated by gunfire. Various members of the Kirchner family managed to end up on both sides of the owner-labor disputes, but family fortunes survived and grew.

For three generations, the Kirchners invested in the market for housing in a region that retained its frontier appearances even as its sparse population struggled to demonstrate sophistication. Into the twentieth century, Río Gallegos had not grown beyond 2,200 residents, and all of Santa Cruz numbered fewer than 10,000 residents. Nevertheless, historian Curia wrote, "the society was acquiring its own physiognomy: young men dressed in the English style mixed on street corners with groups of Indians wrapped in cloth blankets."[2]

*   *   *

At the end of World War II, Néstor Carlos and María Juana began their family. They had three children. The eldest is Alicia Margarita, whose intelligence and assertiveness followed the family pattern and whose political career has been just half a step behind her brother's. Contributing the sort of historical memory that motivates ambitious families, Alicia has said of her Swiss grandmother, Margarita Cönning: "She had a deep-seated sense of family. She was a symbol for us, her perseverance, her forcefulness, her desire, her constant enthusiasm. She was a natural investigator, a reader...."[3] The second child was the future president, also Néstor Carlos, born February 25, 1950, thus sharing the birthday of José de San Martín, the nineteenth century Liberator of Argentina.

The history of the contemporary Kirchners, then, is interwoven with Argentina's archetypal founding families, like that of the legendary—and barbarous—*gaucho* Juan Facundo Quiroga. Such families were known for their single-minded pursuit of wealth and power. The backdrop of Patagonia would shape their political ideas, and Patagonia was no place for the inhibited. It should be borne in mind that grandfather Carlos Kirchner, so lovingly remembered by his family, had a reputation as a ruthless usurer. It took the efforts of his son, Nestor Carlos, the president's father, to restore the family's reputation for fair-dealing.

He did so with the help of his brother, the president's uncle, Carlos Santiago Kirchner. Carlos Santiago built one Kirchner enterprise upon another, providing the prosperous platform from which his nephew would launch his quest for public office. More importantly, he helped build the family's prominence in Santa Cruz to a point that one day, during the darkest times of military oppression, the family name would save his nephew's life.

* * *

In 1951, just a year after Néstor Kirchner was born, his father got his first chance to vote for Juan Domingo Perón. Perón, a charismatic army officer, was elected for the first time in 1946. Perón was the author of the vague political ideas labeled *justicialismo*, or, more simply, *peronismo*. Peronism, though it gave lip-service to a "heterogeneous nature," tried to satisfy four principal constituencies: those who craved *caudillo*-type leadership; the industrialists who needed protection for their economic power; right-wing, authoritarian intellectuals; and trade-union leaders.[4] At bottom, Perón's electoral strength derived from working-class nationalism, the bedrock of Argentine political life. His government was one of corporate fascism, in which social, political, and economic leaders defined broad policies and Perón delivered the muscle. For all the controversy Peronism caused, it is still admired by many Argentines, and for the Kirchner family, the ascent of Juan Perón signaled the beginning of an enduring belief system.

The balloting in 1951 was the first time residents of the Argentine territories— not yet populous enough to be provinces—could vote in national elections. The elder Kirchner, then 28, became part of a groundswell of *peronist* support in the provinces. Perón won nearly 69 percent of the Santa Cruz vote, above his average in the rest of the country. That support would survive despite Perón's overthrow by the Argentine military in 1955 and throughout his exile. Indeed, Peronism, declared illegal in Argentina for nearly 20 years, provided a political banner that was eagerly taken up by generations of students, including Néstor Kirchner and his wife-to-be, Cristina Fernández.

Six years later, when he was seven years old, young Kirchner began to undergo a series of physical problems that would hamper his development but, ultimately, strengthen his abilities. He had to deal head-on with his afflictions and in doing so emerged respected by his mates and confident in himself. The problems began when a contagious disease caused in little Kirchner a convulsive cough; at the same time, a "lazy" left eye put him behind thick, horn-rim glasses. In addition, dental problems affected him for years during his youth and caused problems with his diction. Those setbacks, which left him struggling in school, had little effect on his childhood happiness. He and his playmates— who devised a rich variety of nicknames to mock each other — enjoyed carefree fun in the streets of Río Gallegos. They played a game called *la chueca*, a cross between soccer and sledding, on the rough, snow-covered streets of the town. The Kirchner family sled, in fact, was the envy of the neighborhood.

Kirchner began school in 1955, and his youth would be relatively sublime in spite of the fact that Argentina's political divisions were deep and constantly erupting into violence. It was in 1955 that Perón was overthrown after naval aviators bombarded the Buenos Aires' Plaza de Mayo in an attempt to assassinate him. The attack killed 156 people and wounded 846. Uprisings would continue to roil public affairs, but Kirchner was safe in the small school that was near his home. It operated on the Patagonian calendar from May to September so children didn't have to walk to school in the snow. Kirchner is remembered by friends as quiet, cautious, and observant. He seemed not so shy as simply biding his time. From his paternal grandfather he learned chess and, apparently, adopted aspects of his personality. The grandfather was known as a formidable chess opponent who blew disdainful smoke in the eyes of those he was beating, but stomped angrily away from the board when the game went the other way. Critics, and not a few friends, would describe the future president as behaving in much the same way.

Kirchner's relationship with his older sister, Alicia, has been strong since their childhood days. It was she who helped engender in him a love of politics, and it was her nurturing that helped him deal with academic problems. Alicia was a year ahead of her brother when he, at age 12, joined her at *Colegio Nacional República de Guatemala* in Río Gallegos. She was an exceptional student who won the chance to go north to La Plata to study social work when she was only 17 years old, an unusual freedom for that place and time. (She would later earn her Ph.D. in social work.) Meanwhile, at the school Nestor used his height — he was the tallest in his class— to make up for limited ability as a basketball player. He also employed his boundless enthusiasm. A substitute, young Kirchner once bolted off the bench and *tackled* a member of the opposing team who had broken away for an easy basket. Kirchner was thrown out of the game, but, of course, he wasn't playing anyway, and the opposing team was stopped from scoring.

After a good beginning at the school — when he was 15 Kirchner decided he wanted to be a teacher — his studies bogged down. For one thing, there was his tendency to argue in class with history teachers; for another, he built quite a record of demerits for behavior. In addition, problems with diction continued. Withal, the young Kirchner revealed the sort of backbone that one develops through adversity, not easy success. He was taken out of the *Colegio* and sent to an agricultural school in Tierra del Fuego, originally a mission school for now-depleted native tribes. That was a come-down of no small proportions for a son of privilege. When he was allowed to return to Río Gallegos, Kirchner continued to battle academically and behaviorally. He repeated a year and had to take a pre-test to satisfy the authorities in Buenos Aires that he could master a high school curriculum before he was allowed to continue. He did so and returned to school, but he still struggled to improve his diction.

It was during high school that his friends gave him his nickname, "Lupín," for his ungainly appearance. The name was conferred upon him because they thought he looked like the hero of a history-based comic book popular at the time. It is said that while Kirchner could bristle at adolescent slurs as easily as the next boy, he took the nickname in stride. Better to be popular and the brunt of an affectionate joke than to be ignored. He surely earned his peers' respect, and was elected president of the Student Center. "That clumsy adolescent, the target of jokes of his friends, was voted by the students to represent them."[5]

Curia added: "Timid among the boys of his group, insecure and nervous during exams, Néstor was a fragile kid. He spent mornings making deliveries for his father's store in a Citroen and, when alone, he could be found comfortably hiding himself in the pages of *The Cisco Kid*, *The Lone Plainsman*, and *El Gráfico*."[6] But by his fourth and fifth years of secondary school, according to a friend, Kirchner had his share of friends, including girlfriends, the sort of lasting companions with whom he continued to get together at their old Río Gallegos hangouts. And, as he entered his twenties, he demonstrated considerable dynamism. "By that time Lupín was no longer the kid who was sent out to buy cigarettes."[7]

Kirchner earned his high school diploma when he was almost 19 years old, and whatever might be said of his academic performance, his family's patience and support — as well as his own persistence — were remarkable. After graduation, he turned his attention to working for his father, making deliveries for the store, and helping his uncle open a book store. When he turned his direction toward further schooling, it was to study law at the University of La Plata. His environment changed from gaucho-rural to urban-sophisticated. His circle of friends widened, and he immersed himself in political activism.

Kirchner walked onto a campus that was at the center of Argentine political ferment. La Plata was where, only a few years before Kirchner's arrival, students and faculty members had founded FURN, the *Federación Universitaria de la Revolución Nacional*. It was the first Peronist university group, which saw itself as "the Peronist revolutionary wing."[8] FURN's formation was a signal event for many reasons, not least of which was that Peronist dogma — Perón was living in exile in Spain — had been officially banned. Also, La Plata is next to Buenos Aires, known for its hostility to Peronism, so FURN was casting down the gauntlet before anti–Perón forces. Thus FURN gave Peronist students a place to hang out, to shape their political views, to begin splitting into the several intramural cliques that Peronism engendered, and from which to spill out into the streets with flyers, manifestos, and screeds shouting their views. The group's first goal had been to hang a portrait of the late Eva Peron on a wall at the entrance of the law school, but they quickly turned to more substantive matters. Those included encouraging the government to allow Perón to return from exile, repealing the law that prohibited Peronist expression, and modifying the oppressive policies of the regime of General Juan Carlos Onganía.

Onganía was a tough conservative. He had overthrown the government of Arturo Illía in 1966, seeing it as weak after Peronists tried — twice — to bring their leader back from exile. Calling his government the "Argentine Revolution," Onganía cracked down on student organizations and instituted a list of right-wing initiatives. The same month that Kirchner entered the university, April 1969, Onganía, then in his third year in office, took his entire cabinet to Patagonia, Kirchner's birthplace, and grumbled about how many "foreigners" lived in the region. And, in fact, it was a melting pot, then with a population of nearly 87,000, some 22,000 of whom were born outside Argentina. Eighty-five percent of them were Chilean, as was Kirchner's mother. Rather than reading the numbers as a signal of regional progress, Onganía saw the immigrants as a threat.

Onganía saw as an even more immediate threat to his regime the demonstrations by students over rising university costs. Students grew more and more disruptive until a riot in Córdoba led to more than 20 deaths. FURN, which originally supported the Onganía government, joined the opposition. A FURN manifesto averred: "Neither the coup of the elites nor the continuation of the 'Argentine Revolution' will provide a national solution. The program that unifies us is a revolutionary fight. The blood of our martyrs will not be negotiated."[9]

For all of their bluster, however, Peronists were divided against themselves and were neither as numerous as they were loud nor as well regarded as they were self-centered. Kirchner was one of only about a dozen at La Plata's law school, where he was still trying to convince his Peronist comrades that he was trustworthy. But by the end of his first year, in the eyes of companions, he had grown. A Río Gallegos friend thought he was tougher. "For him, La Plata was a tremendous change ... he was thinner, looser, more open, and even more attractive. Néstor had always been timid, and well short of a genius. But he was always a good person.... Maybe even too good."[10] A former high school teacher who ran into Kirchner about that time was surprised when Kirchner handed him a circular espousing the views of the *montoneros*. That was a group so radical and with tactics so drastic that they formed the most serious armed threat to the Argentine military. Surely, the teacher thought, this was not the Lupín of old.

But Kirchner had been swept into the hot-headed temper of the times. Arguments turned into confrontations, and ardor disintegrated into fistfights. Hundreds of students of one group might climb onto a train to show up at another group's demonstration, there to shake their fists and, if one side or the other didn't retreat, trade blows. Moderate Peronists looked to their right and found, with disdain, Catholic student groups. To the left they saw only "hippies" who were more concerned with getting stoned than seeking justice. All the while, they fought among themselves over tactics, possible alliances, and a whole range of ideological positions. Their stances ranged from collaboration to armed resistance. All the while, the number of Peronist sympathizers at the law school grew and spread to other faculties.

Kirchner eventually worked his way into the Peronists' layers of management, which ranged from a directory of three or four members at the top, to a middle-management group of ten or fifteen, and on down to a cadre of, perhaps, a hundred militants. Below them were up to two hundred and fifty followers. "Lupín was between the third and the second circle," recalled a colleague, "where he made himself available. You could count on him; he was always there. He wasn't one of the principal leaders, the ones who were always talking, the notables. But he was always involved in what was happening. If he wasn't a director, neither was he, as some people have said, some anonymous chump. He was a militant."[11] Journalist Olga Wornat, who was a contemporary, remembered the times as filled with students' fighting against the authorities and among themselves. "The years '68 and '69 were known for 'lightning acts,'" she wrote, referring to the spray-painting of slogans and scattering of inflammatory pamphlets, "and street fights with the mounted police. University debates pitted reformers against non-reformers, and clashes between leftist radicals and Peronists were often violent."[12]

Kirchner had entered a world in the company of thousands of students and activists who were led by their beliefs. But that world would change to one in which thousands of his schoolmates would die at the hands of a paranoid dictatorship. The military government saw threats everywhere, and Argentines were arrested and would abruptly "disappear" into torture, murder, and hasty burial in shallow, unmarked graves. Some dissenters, evidence would later reveal, were dropped into the sea from military helicopters. Early in his college career, Kirchner shared a room in a *pensión* near the railroad station with Juan Carlos Conochiari, known as "The Rat." Conochiari would later join the *montoneros* and die in a 1975 firefight with army troops near Córdoba. The number of Kirchner's friends and associates who would also be lost was legion.

Kirchner and his mates fulfilled academic requirements as necessary, continued their political activities, and made their way toward political effectiveness. Kirchner remained a relatively anonymous figure, despite his unusual appearance and idiosyncrasies. After the *pensión*, Kirchner moved in with three new roommates who would remember him as disheveled, with his long hair tied back in a ponytail, and his spectacles as thick as bottle bottoms. His habit of sleepwalking, they said, meant that sometimes they found him standing by his bed cheering for his favorite soccer team, or out in the street, wandering in a dream. It is probably just as well that about that time he was introduced to Cristina Fernández.

* * *

Cristina Elizabet Fernández was born February 19, 1953, six months after the death of Eva Perón, who would become her idol. Cristina's family was not like Néstor Kirchner's, but rather of more modest means, a middle-class family lost in the urban, relatively sophisticated precincts of northern Argentina. Cristina's paternal grandfather, Pascasio Fernández, had arrived in Buenos Aires in the early 1920s after serving as an enlisted man in the Spanish army. Fernández quickly learned the trade of tailor, and soon his sweetheart, Amparo, the daughter of a well-to-do Spanish family, also came to Argentina. They married, built a middle-class life in La Plata — still a small town, though a provincial capital, next to Buenos Aires — and began their family. Amparo, it is said, never started preparing the noon or evening meals until she'd read the morning newspaper cover to cover.

Amparo had a reputation for being good at math, though she'd ignored early advice to study economics. It was she who, by carefully keeping the books for her husband, improved the family's prospects over the years. Pascasio eventually left tailoring to find work in the countryside, starting a country store and, later, a nursery. He bought a farm and made it prosper. They were not particularly interested in politics. A daughter, Sara, recalled: "They often called us oligarchs, but we weren't. We broke our backs working to achieve what we achieved." Amparo bore eight children, two of whom died very young; the oldest surviving child was Eduardo.[13]

Eduardo was Cristina's father, and Ofelia Wilhelm, her mother. After Cristina was born, Ofelia, who had been living with Eduardo for years, married him. They took in Ofelia's younger, unmarried sister, Sara, to live with them, and she helped rear Cristina and her younger sister, Giselle. The girls' early life was one of ballet lessons, Catholic catechism, and political talk at the dinner table, to which Eduardo brought a stubborn anti–Peronist view. Ofelia later described her family as a bit crazy. "However," wrote journalist Olga Wornat, "between arguments, exits and returns, differences, conciliation and conflict, they produced two daughters, built a family, and overcame the torments of many years."[14]

Eduardo became the first driver hired for a bus line that ran between La Plata and City Bell. Over time, he acquired his own buses and founded a company. Although remembered as "distant" and "laconic," Eduardo was reasonably well liked. However, his time with his family was limited because his working hours kept him away, and his personality tended toward the unaffectionate. Two of his brothers became dentists, and one, Osvaldo, was killed in one of those bizarre occurrences that characterized the early twentieth century in the Americas. Driving home from a professional meeting, Osvaldo heard shots and the loud cries of a street fight. Panicking, he turned the wrong way — into the line of fire. He was killed in a rain of bullets. Uncle Osvaldo had been close to Cristina's family, and Cristina did not quickly recover from the loss.

Aunt Sara described the family as one in which strong personalities clashed from time to time: "My brother Eduardo was a good man, a fighter.... He loved his sisters, and he did everything he could to support them. He had a difficult marriage with Ofelia; she was a very complicated woman with a strong character. And, in reality, they lived together, but apart."[15] Strong temperaments produced sturdy offspring. Giselle grew up to become a physician; Cristina grew up to become the first woman in history to be elected president of Argentina.

Ofelia's combative personality and political inclinations translated directly to her daughters. Ofelia was one of the original Peronist militants and also an avid football fan. Eduardo bought a place on the board of directors of *Club Gimnasia*, and Ofelia's cheering was loud enough to be identifiable in a crowd. Nevertheless, while friends remembered Cristina's relationship with her mother as close, in later years Cristina was guarded in comments and her visits home with Néstor would be brief and rather formal. For her part, Ofelia, who had always done her own shopping in a society in which cooks and maids were common, remained a modest homemaker even after her daughter reached the very heights of Argentine leadership and celebrity.

If mother Ofelia provided a view of the politics of Peronism, the image of Eva Perón gave both her daughters a vision of the romance. She was their heroine, embodying strength, femininity, and, of course, a strong will. "The first time I ever saw a picture of Eva was when I was very small," Cristina told journalist Wornat. "I found it in a book of keepsakes... My maternal grandfather, who lived with us, had saved it along with his identification card from the Peronists.... In the black-and-white photos she appeared with workers, and there was Eva at a gala in Colón, wearing her best jewels. Beautiful, wise.... Eva the fairy, Eva in Dior dresses; with her jewels she was the image of the beneficent, the provider. But, the Eva that I most appreciate? The one I incorporate into my activism? She is the one shown in a spectacular mural that my sister had in her room. She is the militant, with the pillbox hat, stern and austere in her cloth suit, tense in front of a microphone. She has taught me that each of us takes part in the narrative of her time. History doesn't begin when I arrive nor end when I leave...."

[W]e are merely instruments of history. That is the image I've had of Eva since I was a very young girl."[16]

La Plata, however, was a conservative town, where young women were supposed to think about getting married. If they thought about politics at all, they were certainly not to think about the Peróns. Nevertheless, the allure was strong. When Cristina was ten years old, the First Congress of Peronist Youth was held, and Revolutionary Peronist Youth groups began to be formed around the country. Cristina's adolescence would mix her mother's interest in the political with her father's affluence. She was enrolled in a proper school, and her father joined La Plata's exclusive Jockey Club. She would later tell Wornat that she shared with her new, sophisticated teen-age friends the usual adolescent anxieties. And, despite a thorough grounding in Roman Catholic catechism, God went in and out of favor in her eyes. She was left, in the end, as a believer, but one who recognized that human enterprise is the answer to most problems. Like her grandmother, Cristina read voraciously, including the girlie stuff favored by cousins and friends. But as she grew older, she came to resent the need to counteract her beauty by constantly insisting that she wasn't dumb. "It always bothered me that if you were attractive, you had to demonstrate that you were very, but *very*, intelligent. If you don't, you're treated as stupid and frivolous."[17]

At the university, some acquaintances did, indeed, whisper that Cristina was just a bit too pretty and clothes-conscious to be a true political activist. Others decided she "did not fit the profile of the student militant. Nevertheless, she ignored those who underestimated her. Nothing strengthened her resolve like confrontation."[18] Seeking a career of confrontation, Cristina gave up her studies in psychology after her first year and switched to law.

From the beginning, Cristina attended meetings of the *Frente de Agrupaciones Eva Perón* and joined *Juventud Universitaria Peronista*, JUP, a newer group representing the leftward end of the Peronist spectrum on campus. Her romance with a high school sweetheart, Raúl Cafferata, was ending, a result accelerated by his lack of interest in going to political meetings. "Her private, petite-bourgeois world of having an 'official' boyfriend and a predictable future as 'Mrs.' was colliding with another, unpredictable, dangerous, and fascinating one. Politics suddenly appeared in her life, not in books, but in pure reality, like a blow, like an instrument changing reality."[19] Cristina was thick into the JUP's effort to organize Bureaus of National Reconstruction in every department of the university. It was then that the political princess was introduced to the political frog.

*   *   *

She saw Kirchner as disheveled and ungainly, with his long hair tied back in a pony tail. He was from the sticks. They were introduced by a classmate, the girlfriend of a friend of Kirchner, and Fernández immediately set about improving him. She had ideas about his appearance, insisted that he study harder, and tried, without much success, to get him interested in music. They studied together, but Kirchner was one of those students who could not sit still for long and was continually jumping up to pace about.[20]

Many Argentines were edgy. In their view, the passion of Peron's years had given way to a torpid conservatism. One student of that time sneered to Wornat that "even workers' sons who came to the university were following the oligarchy." Peronist students were trying to break through the torpor by making speeches, building burning barricades of tires in the streets, and short-circuiting the wires of trolleys, trying desperately to be noticed. As confrontations became more frequent, they resolved nothing except to get students beat up and, at times, shot. Hugo Bacci, a student leader, remembered: "Lupín was a significant militant — made of iron; he was in everything, doing everything, and debating everything — but he wasn't a leader. We were mostly men because in the (law) school there were more men than women.... Everything was painting slogans and lightning actions with leaflets, and Lupín was always there."[21]

Increasingly, Fernández was at his side. The governments they fought were puppets with the generals holding the strings. The military alternated between allowing civilian governments, administered by compliant, "elected" presidents, and taking over themselves. By the time that Onganía had established his "Argentine Revolution," the country was well settled into a pattern: anti–Peronist leaders, protected by the military, demonstrated how little capacity for leadership they had. Peronists, for their part, shouted at the top of their lungs, arguing that only an aging exile living in Spain could save the country from itself.

Finally, in a testament to how bankrupt was Argentina's leadership, Onganía gave in. In November 1972, Juan Perón was to be allowed to return — but, at first, just for a month. Then the electoral ban on Peronist parties was lifted. Then obstacles fell until, in early 1973, Perón, now 76 years old, was allowed to run again for president. Though still in Spain, Perón was elected by a landslide in March with 62 percent of the vote. The old warrior insisted that the vice president be his wife, María Estela Martínez de Perón, known as "Isabelita." She had been an exotic dancer whom Perón married while in exile. All of this seemed to Peronists not tawdry but reason for celebration. So they converged on Ezeiza Airport outside Buenos Aires to welcome their savior back on June 20. It was a cold, rainy day of Argentine winter, but local police estimated the crowd at three and a half million people, including Kirchner and Fernández.

The young couple, along with classmates and comrades, had ridden commuter trains to the airport the day before. They spent the night at a nearby construction site, protected by Peronist labor union members. The students needed protection because murderous adherents of both left and right would be in the crowd. A right-wing militia, the Argentine Anti-communist Association — or "Triple A" — was shooting *montoneros*, who, in turn, were exploding bombs, kidnapping, and shooting their own victims. During this period, fifteen supermarkets owned by the Rockefellers were blown up by *montoneros*, who also managed to kidnap and kill an Argentine general. On a single day, 21 bombs exploded in Buenos Aires.

At the airport that day, the atmosphere was triumphant, but cautious. "I remember Lupín in Ezeiza," one of Kirchner's comrades would say. "He was walking at the side of a column with his red and black bracelet, with others who today are dead and disappeared. It is impossible to erase from my memory his thin figure, that hook-nose and wall-eyed look, which he then hid behind those dreadful glasses with thick rims and triple-strength lenses."[22] The dangers were heightened by angry divisions within Peronism, where advocates of armed conflict disparaged their moderate classmates. Both Kirchner and Fernández were well aware that if they knew the classmate standing beside them, they could not be so sure of that other one, the anonymous face in the crowd over there in a slouch hat and raincoat. Comrades and antagonists looked just alike, and they were aware that many of their friends carried sidearms. Of course, the danger was part of excitement. "Never mind the army, the repression, the tanks, and even less the cold, the rain and the mud," wrote journalist Wornat. "It was a date not to be missed."[23]

It was also a day of infamy in modern Argentine history. Firing broke out with devastating effect. Members of the infamous Triple A took aim at both *montoneros* and known Peronists. At least 13 people in the crowd were killed and 365 injured, though estimates of both went much higher. The senseless carnage of Ezeiza was a turning point for Fernández. She had no stomach for what she considered rabble-rousing without fixed, achievable ends. The camaraderie and the analytical vigor had given way to excess. "There's no doubt," wrote Wornat. "In the middle of that intellectual richness and the dominant values of stern discipline — transcending criticism — there were times when power and insensitivity prevailed over the law and over reason; years of craziness and violence."[24]

After Ezeiza, some Peronist youth groups re-organized themselves and tried to regain more moderate bearings. To head Fernández away from that course, a left-wing Peronist student and *montonero* went to see her. He questioned her commitment. Fernández told Wornat that she only knew the young man's *nom de guerre*—"Fox"—and that he "disappeared" four years after their conversation. But she remembered his disappointment in her insistence on being outspoken publicly, her willingness to debate, rather than going underground into some clandestine cell. Fernández felt that she was changing, withdrawing from the ranks of her more radical friends because she doubted their methods. "'He was furious with me because I didn't like what was happening,'" she told Wornat. "'The Fox' was not mistaken. He had seen that something was happening to Cristina Fernández. She was not conforming to the Stalinist line of conduct of the JUP, and she wanted to debate freely. Nothing in the world annoyed her more than someone trying to clip her wings. It didn't matter who.... Without explanation, Cristina quit the JUP.

*   *   *

The need Fernández felt to reshape her world view would evolve into something more than just youthful malaise. She would recognize, and later help effect, the change needed in Argentine politics in general and Peronism in particular. She would be at Kirchner's elbow as he and their friends designed programs that were aimed at attracting popular support — programs that could be implemented without exciting acrimony.

Perón died a year after the debacle at Ezeiza Airport and was succeeded by his vice president and widow. As might be imagined, she proved to be even more of a disaster than her late husband. Because Perón had identified himself with the right wing of his party, Isabelita continued to encourage the murderous right-wing militias in their pursuit of leftists. This was the Argentine manifestation of a hemisphere mired deeply on the Cold War. U.S. policy, defeated in South Vietnam and unable to break its fixation with Fidel Castro's Cuba, was taking aim at defeating Sandinistas in Nicaragua. Chile was headed toward a right-wing military government of the kind that already existed in Brazil. In Argentina, the fist of the military was felt in various ways throughout the country, and Kirchner was among those who resented the army's oppressive incursions into his native province of Santa Cruz.

For Fernández and Kirchner, tension peaked in 1974 when they learned the fate of their friends Rodolfo Achem and Carlos Miguel. Achem and Miguel, charismatic and widely respected administrators at the La Plata campus and among the founders of FURN, were kidnapped and killed. The news came at a time when both Kirchner and Fernández had tempered their public statements, but Achem and Miguel continued their outspoken ways. The murders were attributed to the Triple A.

"The kidnapping of Achem and Miguel provoked a commotion in the city. Hours later, their bodies, riddled with bullets, were found.... More than anyone, Kirchner, who had begun his militancy in FURN under the leadership of Carlos Miguel and "The Turk" Achem, was shocked. The two murdered were his most precious political and ideological referents, and the brutality of the assassination was a tough blow to the future of the Peronist University Youth and the Justicialist Party."[25] Fernández remembered: "I felt a fear, an outrageous fear. Contrary to some friends who saw things another way, I saw everything as ending, that we would be crushed, that an indescribable tragedy was coming. I felt it, and always I had good intuition. I saw it coming. I wasn't wrong."[26]

A cloud descended of their lives and the lives of their closest comrades. Even Kirchner's and Fernández's marriage could not escape the temper of the times. They were married May 9, 1975, though Kirchner's suit was not well received by Cristina's conservative father, who by that time was a wealthy investor. Kirchner's proposal was, however, welcomed by her mother and sister. The ceremony took place at the civil registry in Río Gallegos, and they were fond of telling people later that they, as poor students, could not afford anything more elaborate. Both families attended the civil ceremony along with a few friends, and, with no other music available, they all — or, all except Señor Fernández — sang the "Peronist March."

A later ceremony was performed at her family's house, which was so small that only a few friends were invited. At that time, neither had completed law school. So, for a while they lived in an apartment while Kirchner worked at the economic ministry. His mother-in-law, who was employed there, helped him get the job. In journalist Wornat's image: "Néstor Kirchner got a haircut and decided that, before anything else, he was going to go to work. They lived austerely, and Cristina devoted herself to housework and cooking. The reality that surrounded them did not let up, but before long they were able to move into a house that Cristina's father lent them."[27]

They continued their studies, and Kirchner kept up his way, despite the political tension that surrounded the campus, of arguing with professors as if he considered himself on an equal footing. He stayed clear of the *montoneros* and friends who espoused armed revolt, but that was no guarantee of safety. Danger lurked on every street corner. A friend remembered a night at the end of 1975 when Néstor and Cristina studied at the friend's house until midnight, when he drove them across town to their place. On the way, three cars pulled up beside them and forced them to the curb. "Some guys from the civil guard with rifles got out, shouting, 'They're the ones. They're the ones.' Néstor said quietly, 'Stay cool, Pal,' but I didn't get it. I got out of the car and said: 'What's going on?' They stuck the muzzle of a pistol in my chest and pointed their machine guns at me. The tension was terrible. They began to shout at each other until one said: 'No, they're not the ones.' I got back in the car and drove to their house in absolute silence. No one spoke the whole way. I always wonder how we all survived; it's a miracle, or I don't know what to call it.... But I will always remember that the night they killed 'Negrita' [Mirta Aguilar, an activist student and close friend of the Kirchners] we had been studying together."[28]

If it seemed that Argentina's night could not be darker, it was not so. In March 1976, as small armed uprisings continued in the countryside and protests troubled the cities, the military came down hard. The army placed "Isabelita" under house arrest and condemned Argentines to the worst seven years of their troubled history. General Jorge Rafael Videla led a three-general junta that took charge of the government. There would be three such juntas over the course of the dictatorship, but the world would come to know their members as "the generals." They were the authors of Argentina's ignominious "Dirty War," seven years of terror. Kidnappings were perpetrated by the government and its thugs; there was widespread, systematic, and brutal torture; children of the state's many enemies were cruelly placed for adoption by parents approved by the military; their parents and others were kidnapped and killed, to be known forever after as *los desaparecidos*, "the disappeared." Although the official finding of a subsequent investigative commission was that 8,961 Argentines had gone missing, unofficial and widely accepted estimates were that there were many, many more.[29] There is, in fact, common speculation that as many as 30,000 Argentines "disappeared."

Throughout that grisly period, according to author Susana Kaiser, who was a witness to the times, too many Argentines averted their eyes, swept up as they were by the country's economic prosperity: "They did not ask who was paying for their pleasures — the trips to

Miami, the vacations ... and the needless shopping that obtained them the nickname 'I'll take two.' Whether it was for condominiums in Brazil or Ray Ban sunglasses, the affluent upper middle class went on mad shopping sprees because they had more expendable income than ever, thanks to the economic policies implemented during the terror." Infants of women captured as enemies of the government, including those born in captivity, were often taken and given to childless couples who collaborated with the regime. "Human rights violations ranged from torments of pregnant women that included the torture of the fetus to torturing individuals in the presence of their relatives to make them speak, including mutilation, torture, [the] killing of children, and impalement."[30]

Aware of the dread all around them, the Kirchners returned to Río Gallegos in 1976 to visit his family; they wound up in jail. They had gone out to dinner with friends at a restaurant in town. An army officer walked in and arrested the Kirchners and their friend, "Chacho" Vázquez. They all knew that when the sons and daughters of Argentina's leading families were taken into custody—and many were—it was always touch-and-go as to whether their offenses against the regime were relatively simple—like rabble-rousing public statements—or amounted to treason. Being a member of an affluent family helped, but it did not always mean release. "During the month we were imprisoned," Cristina Kirchner remembered, "the entire Kirchner family rallied to help us. That protected us." She was confident enough to use the experience as an education: "I remember that I did exercises and talked with the other prisoners. I became their buddy. One of them was there because she had poisoned her husband with cyanide in his *mate* [an herbal drink]. Another one had been raped, but stabbed the rapist to death. They knew that I had almost completed my studies, so they asked for legal counsel for their defense."[31]

The Kirchners were released from jail, but it was as if they had begun down a slope from which there was no honorable return. Buenos Aires of this time has been compared with Belfast, Northern Ireland, during "the troubles." Between 1975 and 1979, some 2,000 Argentines disappeared in and around the environs of Buenos Aires and La Plata alone. All around the Kirchners student and legislative leaders, officials of many stripes, and even governors—Peronists and others—were being forced out of office or were quitting their posts because of arbitrary actions by the military government or because of threats and intimidation. The Kirchners' position was ameliorated only by their having been soldiers of the resistance, not field marshals. It was the activists of higher echelons—especially those who had joined more radical Peronist wings—who were forced underground. Moderates were left with a relatively toothless opposition. "Kirchner was outside the organic militancy and was among an unclassifiable group, made up of young men who had remained in the middle of the road, between campus groups on one side and armed organizations on the other. In open resistance to the secrecy and paramilitary strategy, they had left behind the armed groups in order to return to nothing."[32]

Which is not to say that Kirchner was docile. In May 1976, he was among those who risked arrest by helping to slip Peronist leader Carlos Negri, in disguise, past authorities and into hiding in Brazil. In fact, in the six months leading up to July, when they left La Plata to live in Río Gallegos, the Kirchners moved their residence five times. Looking back, Fernández has said that if her father had known some of the dumps where Kirchner asked her to live he'd have killed Kirchner before the army got him. Only a block away from one of their apartments, the army raided a house occupied by several of their friends and some other people they did not know. All of the occupants were killed, and the house was leveled by a bulldozer. Given the military government's paranoia, no Argentine was safe.

That was clear the second time Kirchner was arrested, again in Río Gallegos. He was taken into custody along with his friend, Rafael Flores, and the two were held in isolation. Out of contact with each other or the outside world, they feared they would be transferred to military custody in Buenos Aires, beyond the influence of their families.

The arrest came after Kirchner had earned his law degree and opened a practice in partnership with a judge. They represented several influential clients, including a national labor union, but it was clear that the military government had Kirchner in its sights notwithstanding his position in the community. Their interrogators wanted to know about events that had occurred years before, and Kirchner and Flores were taken to the office of the colonel in charge of the military district. There, a captain conducted the interrogation in an atmosphere of tension. Each was asked if he had been in the central plaza of Buenos Aires on May 25, 1973, when Héctor Cámpora took office as president. Yes. Had he carried a banner of the *montoneros*? No. Had he seen such banners? Of course, the banners were huge.

After three days and nights, with the Kirchner and Flores families bringing pressure on the army, both were released. Cristina and others later said that if the arrests had been made in La Plata, where neither of their families had influence, they would not have come out alive. In fact, Kirchner, after being elected president, inquired as to the circumstances of the arrest. He was told that they were lucky to have had one Enrique Gentiluomo, an intelligence officer, as their interrogator. Not only did Gentiluomo have a reputation as a reasonable man, he later told historian Curia that he had hoped to one day get a personal interview with President Kirchner. "It is one of those pathetic turns in the Argentine tragedy," Curia wrote, "the old interrogator manifesting enthusiasm for the remote possibility of again meeting the President."[33] Ironically, Flores was one of those who fell out with Kirchner over the latter's later attempt to change Santa Cruz's provincial constitution to allow himself to be re-elected indefinitely. In Argentina's Byzantine politics, no corridor ran straight.

A few days after his father's release, Máximo, the Kirchners' first child, was born. All the while, Cristina, who still lacked three courses for graduation from law school, had been working at the firm and taking care of the house and, now, would care for their baby. After returning to La Plata to be close to her family for Máximo's birth, she returned to Río Gallegos and told Néstor, not for the first time, that they should leave the country for their own safety. They decided to stay.

*   *   *

Such fear was not unwarranted. The world was just beginning to learn, through the bravery of a few women, that Argentina was being held hostage by its own government. In April 1977, the *Madres de la Plaza de Mayo* were born when fourteen mothers marched to government offices in Buenos Aires. They demanded to know where their children were. They had disappeared, the mothers said. Thrown out of the office of the Minister of the Interior, the mothers retreated to the plaza and agreed to meet a week later. When the military would not allow them to congregate, they decided to stroll around a plaza monument to Argentina's 1810 rebellion against Spain. News of their quest, and photographs of marching Argentines, went out to the world.

A few weeks later, three mothers returned to the ministry while sixty waited outside. They were again thrown out after being told their children were probably off on sexual escapades. By late that year, an advertisement in the daily *La Prensa* listed 237 names of the children of *las Madres de la Plaza*. To dramatize their anguish, the women banged saucepans—*cacerolas*—and to identify each other they wore diapers as white kerchiefs. However, it was not until the World Cup in January 1978 drew 80,000 soccer fans and hundreds of journalists to Buenos Aires that the women were able to focus the world's attention. Prohibited from congregating, one hundred mothers filtered into the plaza, then, on a signal, donned their kerchiefs as they made for the monument and waiting reporters and cameramen. The mothers' bravery was unquestioned, but it did little to remedy the oppression. The military junta lasted another six years, during which at least three of the mothers disappeared.

In those times, the Kirchners built, with the help of his father's friends, the law practice in Río Gallegos. Cristina got her degree in October 1979, and the firm prospered by representing mortgage holders who were trapped by Argentina's sometimes meteoric inflation. The turbulent economy meant that yesterday's agreed-upon prices bore little relation to the value of tomorrow's peso. Lenders holding mortgage paper, like many of Kirchner's father's friends, were especially interested in how debts would be settled. The courts decided on "indexing," meaning that settlement would be closer to the most current exchange rates. That was necessary, judges agreed, to resolve Argentina's housing shortage by spurring builders to get active again. The need for borrowers to pay at inflationary rates led, of course, to thousands of foreclosures. But among the winners were the lawyers, like the Kirchners, whose fees multiplied with their clients' collections. Néstor Kirchner and his family, according to historian Curia, benefited from inflated income and increased legal fees when Argentine courts accepted the indexing solution. "In that moment, he was revealed as a very active collector, including frequently charging the maximum [fees]."[34]

National affairs were expanding Kirchner's prospects in other ways. By that time exploitation of oil in the Magellan Strait and Tierra del Fuego had begun, enormously increasing the wealth of Argentina and, especially, its southern provinces. The future of Santa Cruz brightened. Older sister Alicia had married Armando "Bombón" Mercado, a powerful man whose fortunes were also on the rise. Mercado was a close friend of the secretary general of *Sindicato Unido Petroleros del Estado*, the powerful oil workers' union, and he would later lead the Peronist bloc in Congress. In turn, he became a close friend of Carlos Menem, a future Peronist president. The Kirchners' law firm became the union's legal counsel, and the Kirchners became thoroughly enmeshed in national politics.

In the telling of historian Curia, these events and arrangements constitute an environment of dealings, favoritism, and questionable practices that were not greeted with universal admiration. Two attempts were made to blow up or burn down the Kirchners' law offices in Río Gallegos. The first attempt, because the office's natural gas supply had been turned off, was unsuccessful. The second, however, completely burned out the suite of offices. Cristina, always the fiery one, led the charge to get the incident thoroughly investigated by police. She had a suspect, who was the military chief of the district, Andrés Antonietti. She tried, but never succeeded, to get him indicted for the crimes.

The arson attacks, however, were little more than a heated footnote during a period in which Argentina was locked in half a dozen torments. The war with Great Britain over control of the Malvinas (or Falkland) Islands was widely seen as the generals' attempt to divert attention from Argentina's worsening economic plight. Thus, by the time Carlos Menem became president, his task was to bring order, not settle old debts like Cristina's. "In the Menem years," Cristina said, "when that man (Antonietti) appeared and did all that he did, it gave me the shivers to see him. He disgusted me. He held himself above everyone in a government that was said to be democratic. I can't forget the years in Santa Cruz and the bombing of the offices. I know it had to be him."[35]

However, neither local arson nor Argentina's predilection for self-destruction kept the Kirchners from relative prosperity. By 1987, when they closed the law firm, they owned twenty-two properties in Río Gallegos. Máximo, who studied journalism and law but did not graduate from college, took up a career of minding the family's business affairs, including the rental properties. "Kirchner was finished forever with the age of innocence," declared Curia. "For in that time, right after the war in the Malvinas, the country was preparing itself to return to democracy, and he was working intensely in politics."[36]

*   *   *

The noun "politics" cannot do justice to what had to occur in Argentina in the 1980s. The generals—itself a term that pales beside the perversity of men who turned their guns, their insecurities, and their savagery on their fellow citizens—left a shambles. The criminal idiocy of having gone to war with Great Britain, trampling on fifteen years of United Nations' mediation, left Argentina inert. The small, barren islands are largely populated by the descendents of English colonists, and British arms outgunned the poorly trained and equipped Argentine soldiers, 625 of whom were killed. Humiliated and angry, Argentines finally insisted on a return to democracy. In 1982, in their last ignominious act, the generals exonerated themselves for "mistakes" during their seven-year reign of terror. In 1983, the democratically elected government of Raúl Alfonsín took office.

The administration imprisoned some generals for terrorist acts and began to investigate crimes of the dictatorship. The National Commission for the Disappearance of People issued a report called *Nunca Más*, "Never More." At the same time, however, the Alfonsín government decreed pardons for many offenders and generally reined in efforts toward vengeance. History would not be so kind, revealing widespread treachery. In her book, *Postmemories of Terror*, Susana Kaiser noted the complicity of the Argentine Roman Catholic Church: "Only four bishops, of eighty, publicly denounced the dictatorship." One of those four dissenters was killed in a suspicious automobile accident. "There are even reports of some priests witnessing torture sessions to encourage confessions of guilt for political crimes or giving information about other activists."[37] Kaiser speculated that present-day Argentines continue to feel the emotional weight of the dictatorship because of their "two devils theory." Many ordinary Argentines, she wrote, felt themselves caught between leftist radicals and right-wing assassins, both undesirable. Nonetheless, she pointed out, the Draconian methods of the generals were responsible for thousands of deaths, while the leftist radicals caused few. In the end, the silence imposed through fear lingers even *today*, as some modern Argentine history books omit any discussion of the era, and some teachers ignore it in their classes.

With the return of democracy, the traditional parties and their factions circled each other warily, and Kirchner joined other professionals in forming a Peronist group called *Ateneo Juan Domingo Peron*. It was a vehicle for reaching out to voters, and it set up community centers in working-class barrios. That was an idea straight out of the book written by Juan and Eva Perón. Any claim to wear the mantle of the Perons, however, was going to be instantly questioned by people who had had enough of dictatorship. Political nerves were frayed. An indication of animosities erupted when the vice president of the Peronist party, Deolindo Bittle, made a 1982 trip through the southern provinces. His mission was to pay homage to Argentine soldiers and renew contacts with local Peronists. But when he reached Río Gallegos, Bittle, accompanied by other party dignitaries, was confronted by a long-haired, angry Kirchner. As he entered a hotel, Bittle came face to fact with Kirchner, who—as if he were a protesting student—shouted in Bittle's face. Kirchner praised the name of Isabel Perón and questioned Bittle's ability to bear her torch. It was hardly an auspicious display, but out of just such intra-party and inter-regional disputes were political careers being shaped, and it was no different for the Kirchners.

In the 1983 presidential election, Kirchner supported a fellow *santacruceño* who finished well behind the resurgent Radical Party's candidate, Alfonsín. Nevertheless, Peronist prospects were on the rise. Alfonsín's victory margin was a spare 51.74 percent, and Peronists ran well enough nationally to take their place, along with Radicals, as one of the country's two dominant parties in Congress. Also, because of factionalism and Argentines' continuing fascination with personal leaders—*caudillos*—coming elections would depend on who percolated to the top as groups split and individuals built their own cadres.

Kirchner had plenty of competition. He was still unknown nationally and less than dominant regionally. In Santa Cruz, in fact, when the Peronists chose among three lists for party leadership, Kirchner's list finished third. However, in 1983 he supported Arturo Puricelli for governor of Santa Cruz and thus won a post in his administration. Kirchner was named head of the Office of Social Security for the province. That gave him a chance to demonstrate management skill and gain recognition. And that, coupled with self-promotion financed by his own funds, fueled his career. Kirchner's flair for dramatic confrontation also helped. The Puricelli administration, using an accounting technique common to feeble governments, covered a budgetary shortfall until the end of the fiscal year by using social welfare funds for other purposes. Kirchner protested loudly to the national government. Then he dramatized his position—defending the poor, the feeble, and the jobless—by abruptly resigning his post. National news coverage launched his career, but Cristina told Wornat that her husband's actions were substantive. Times were tough—Argentine state employees went for three months without salary—and somebody had to speak up. "[T]he province was devastated, there was no health care, no schools, and the province was heavily in debt...." Kirchner's term at Social Security, however, had "left a public health system that was a source of pride for us and with $550 million in deposits outside the country."[38]

Cristina's defense of political tactics reflected the fact that she—despite a 1984 miscarriage after six months of pregnancy—never excluded herself from participation in the design of the Kirchner political future. Kirchner would step into a race for another provincial post, but he and Cristina were looking beyond the limits of Santa Cruz. One evening in 1986, having invited another couple for dinner, Kirchner suddenly asked the husband to abandon his own campaign for legislative office to help Kirchner run, first, for governor, and, within 20 years, for president. The friend laughed, declined to buy into Kirchner's wild idea, and went on to lose his bid for the legislature. The Kirchners continued their ambitious planning.

With Kirchner vying for the Santa Cruz administrative position—as *intendencia*—he and Cristina again invited friends over for dinner and planning. They felt they had to distinguish themselves from other Peronist factions and appeal to a wider electorate. As various opinions were offered in the living room, Cristina—in the kitchen in her tripartite role as mother, wife, and political theorist—was not going to be excluded. "The *Frente para la Victoria Santacruceña* (the Santa Cruz Front for Victory) was born in '87," their friend and ally Dante Dovena told Olga Wornat. "I had proposed *Frente para la Victoria Justicialista*, but Cristina, who was in the kitchen ... called out, 'Not Justicialism. Better *Santacruceña*.' And Néstor liked it. We had the feeling that Peronism by itself no longer cut it, and we had to open the field to other ideas. Néstor won the *intendencia* and from then on didn't stop."[39]

Nor did Cristina, who was stepping out of Néstor's shadow and entering the political arena herself. Once again she was juggling careers as mother, wife, Kierchner's alter ego, strategist, and now, player, as she ran a successful campaign for the Santa Cruz legislature. She was already identified as an active Peronist and an architect of her husband's emerging career, and some observers quickly identified Cristina as headed for national office.

The Kirchners, withal, were a political package. A March 1989 column in *La Opinión Austral* noted: "Regarding political strategy and internal decisions, Cristina Fernández has not been high on the political marquee recently, but few doubt the influence she has exercised in affairs of the State and even the appointment of functionaries. Of a direct, straight-ahead style — frequently exercised in confrontations with the opposition and in internal party wrangling — Dr. Fernández has been at Dr. Kirchner's side during his first years as Intendent and surely now would prefer her own place in government....

"The arrival of Dr. Nestor Kirchner ... is not a result of chance or political alchemy, but the result of admirable work with an almost obsessive dedication to the realm of political recruitment. That erstwhile young student of [the University of] La Plata took his first steps in politics in the JP [Justicialist Party] when he was studying law, and translated, with a great feel for practicality, all of the generational changes that were transforming Peronism....

"Néstor Kirchner did not take that road alone. His wife and the present provincial deputy, Dr. Cristina Fernandez, has been a decisive factor in his political career.... The governor himself has pointed out: 'She's not just the wife of Dr. Kirchner, but occupies her own political space in the *Frente para la Victoria*.'"[40]

With Cristina's election to the Santa Cruz provincial legislature, Peronist Carlos Menem was elected president of Argentina. Peronism had redefined itself and was flourishing. Political scientist Torcuato De Tella noted that Peronism, with its base in the working class and the disenfranchised, was broadening its support among Argentine conservatives. That would be the path the Kirchners would follow. "[F]or the first time in its history, practically all important organized groups had a legitimate representation in the system, with no one being barred from attempting to influence it. Paradoxically, this happens at a moment when the marginalization of the poorer strata, who are bearing the brunt of the conversion from a statist to a competitive market economy, is most severe."[41]

When Menem succeeded Alfonsín to the presidency, it was the first time in six decades that a candidate of one Argentine party had peacefully succeeded that of another. Over the course of those long years, Argentina had isolated itself. The principal task of the Menem presidency was to demonstrate that now better judgment prevailed, and the nation had learned from its mistakes.[42] At least during the early years of his administration, Menem accomplished that task, and the Kirchners benefited. Menem's popularity in Santa Cruz enhanced their prospects. In 1990, Kirchner launched his campaign for governor of Santa Cruz.

That fact, however, might seem paltry by comparison with his wife's accomplishment ot the same year. Their daughter, Florencia — "Florita" — was born on August 6, and her mother was back in the Chamber of Deputies the day after the delivery. In fact, Cristina's strength of purpose — or, perhaps, several purposes — was taking on mythic proportions in the press. News reporters doted on her assertiveness. At one point in Kirchner's campaign for governor, his aides told him of a policemen's strike, suggesting that he get over to where the police were meeting so he could talk to them. He agreed, and hurriedly called his wife to accompany him. When she wasn't ready to go on the spot, he asked why. Lupín, after all, was not a man to be delayed. He waited, however, while his wife put on her make-up.

In 1991, Kirchner was elected governor of Santa Cruz in a "crushing victory" over his Radical opponent, despite the fact that Menem was defeated (by Alfonsín) in his campaign for re-election. The stage was set for Kirchner to further his ambition, but first there was provincial business. He established himself as an administrator with such no-nonsense measures as lengthening provincial employees' work days by one hour, changing from 8:00 to 3:00 to 9:00 to 5:00. He imposed controls on what doctors could charge under provincial medical programs. In the meantime, Cristina's status in the Santa Cruz legislature strengthened as she took a lead role in investigating allegations against a former Santa Cruz governor. That same year, however, politics were upstaged by a volcano in the southern core of the country. Its eruption blocked the sun and spread ashes over 40 percent of Santa Cruz.

The lingering ash cloud killed a million and a half sheep and destroyed the entire year's crop of fruit.

Through the 1990s and into the new millennium, the Kirchners' political careers flourished. He was re-elected governor twice, holding the office for 12 years. Cristina also continued to win elections, advancing from the provincial legislature to the national Senate. Into the national spotlight, Cristina brought her interests, her family name, and her passion. "Cristina had been fighting for the cause of the glacial islands in the Santa Cruz legislature" wrote Wornat, "and that cause was transformed into her principle theme when she was elected to the national Senate." She also brought her pugnacious personality and her husband's prospects. "But from her arrival at her office on the second floor of Congress she began collecting enemies. With her confrontational style and contentiousness she was rising to star status and inserting into public notice her husband's name. The press was not referring to her as "Cristina Fernández," but as "Cristina Kirchner" or "Fernández de Kirchner."[43]

The Kirchners broadened their political focus to include Peronist efforts at rewriting the Argentine constitution as delegates to a national convention. It gave them a chance to both demonstrate their independence and present themselves as thoughtful rebels. Either way, news reporters loved it. "It was an arena that allowed enemies within and without the party to take aim at her, as well as a forum in which she could display her intelligence and equality. Eduardo Menem, another delegate, found that being the president's brother was not nearly as interesting to the press as Cristina's logic, much less her looks. She waded into the debate over the question of Argentina's arms sales to Ecuador. She took after the minister who was his boss, and she separated herself from the errant policy of the administration of Carlos Menem, a Justicialist and one of the most powerful politicians in Argentina." When she had the audacity to ask for the resignation of the minister of defense, Carlos Alasino, over the illegal arms sale, some delegates were appalled. Cristina shot back: "This is not a barracks, Alasino is not a general, and I am not Private Fernández."[44]

When Menem was returned to the presidency, it was in the midst of economic turmoil, and his leadership was called into question. "The new Menem government was inaugurated in the midst of an economic crisis that had been kept hidden from the public. In July, Argentines learned that the unemployment rate had reached 18.6 percent, an unheard-of level for a country with a long history of full employment."[45] Unemployment was a reflection of other problems. Between 1980 and 1993, Argentina's annual gross domestic product had been shrinking, some years by as much as seven percent. Inflation was almost always in triple digits and got as high as 3,297.5 percent.

Moreover, Menem and his cohorts were seen as clumsy in their attempts to build a majority in Congress by attracting minor parties, and he was losing support in the provinces. Provincial officials, including in Santa Cruz, were demanding a bigger share of oil revenues. As on a see-saw, Menem's fortunes fell when the Kirchners' rose. "[T]he strong offensive of the governors from the 'little' provinces in the Constitutional Convention in Santa Fe had shown Kirchner as a Peronist rebel. The national media didn't ignore the Kirchners appearance on the scene, as Cristina, both in the Convention and in her role as a critic within the Justicialist bloc, confronted the party leadership and guaranteed them thorough exposure in the daily newspapers."[46]

As Kirchner's star rose, however, so did others'. Aging Peronist Eduardo Duhalde returned to prominence by winning the governorship of Buenos Aires province, making him a rival of Menem. "[O]pposition to the government increasingly came from within the ranks of Peronism itself, more than from other political parties," asserted political scientist De Riz. "Succession within Peronism is at the heart of these struggles." Of course, struggles over succession had in the past often been serious enough that they brought the military back on the scene. De Riz continued: "Twelve years after the restoration of democracy in Argentina, is the commitment to reconstruct democratic institutions strong enough to prevent a return to the past?.... In Argentina, as in other new democracies, differences between the parties exist, but clear profiles are not generated to help the public discriminate among them; politics becomes personalized, the leaders are increasingly discredited, and the number of citizens who do not identify with a political party grows."[47]

So by the time Kirchner was into his third term as governor, Argentina was well along its troubled path to the past. As the millennium dawned, 40 percent of the ballots cast in legislative elections were blank, signaling voters' disenchantment. At the presidential level, incompetence and confusion were manifest. Fernando de la Rúa, elected president, spent only one week in office before stepping down. During that week he reneged on Argentina's foreign debt and declared a bank holiday. He was followed by *three* interim presidents, none of whom was up to the job. Finally, a desperate Congress appointed Eduardo Duhalde to the job. "At the end of 2001 came the dizzying crash," wrote American novelist Maxine Swann, who was living in Buenos then. "For some time, the economy had been deteriorating; the peso's one-to-one convertibility with the dollar was an artificial paradise. Economic measures known as the *corralito*, or 'little corral,' were introduced, essentially cutting off people's access to their savings."[48]

The exchange rate dropped to three-to-one, making pesos that had been worth $1 worth 33 cents. Argentine historians Garrone and Rocha tell the story that during this time Kirchner was asked to serve in the cabinet of Duhalde, his old Peronist mentor. Kirchner refused. So Duhalde, desperate for help, offered him the job of chief of staff. Kirchner's staff advised against that, too, preferring to let Duhalde sink on his own. So Kirchner refused that post, too, but called Cristina — who had just turned down the education portfolio — to joke that he had taken the job. There was a long silence before she told him she didn't believe it. However, if it were so, she said calmly, she would demand a divorce.[49]

The campaign toward the next presidential election began in chaos and ended in, well, chaos. On top, however, would be Néstor Kirchner. Looming over the election were forces of a global economy that baffled everyone and had chewed up five presidents in one month. At the outset, the Peronists were split among at least ten potential candidates, with Kirchner, according to a poll, running a distant sixth. The Santa Cruz governor's mansion served as campaign headquarters, and Cristina was continually on the phone, recruiting, haranguing, cajoling. Kirchner eventually rose to the top of the polls with the help of, ironically, Duhalde. The old Peronist was intent upon denying his archrival Menem a third term, and Kirchner exploited the opening, ending up the official candidate of the Justicialist Party. Menem, complaining that he'd been hoodwinked, withdrew.

An indication of how leftward future policies would be under President Kirchner appeared at his May 2003 inauguration. Prominent among a jolly group of friends were Presidents Hugo Chávez of Venezuela, Luís Inacio Lula da Silva of Brazil, and Fidel Castro of Cuba. At 53 years old, Néstor Kirchner was Argentina's 52nd president.

Adoring journalists were by now describing Kirchner in glowing terms. "As methodical as a Swiss watch," wrote Argentine journalists Garrone and Rocha, "tenacious in the tradition of the Basques, with a capacity for work and an unbelievable force of will, but also authoritarian, autocratic, and, above all, forceful."[50]

"But is he 'truly Peronist?'" asked Torcuato di Tella in 2003. "I don't know, but what I do know is that Peronism is a very diverse force, an overwhelming torrent that transformed the nation, that made many things better and many things worse, and that Argentina has changed in the last 50 years, for the worse in many respects, but for the better in others that are more profound and that do not allow for a simplistic view, but without doubt are going to begin to flourish as soon as we escape from this pit."[51]

*　*　*

Argentine political history might be seen as the nation's periodically falling into, and struggling out of, pits. The fate of the Kirchners, like that of all modern political leaders, has been to avoid the menacing pits of a viciously competitive global economy while holding onto the confidence of the electorate with improved services. In Argentina, that means equal parts of playing the *caudillo*, tending to the nation's bookkeeping, satisfying the expectations of the world financial markets, and staying a step ahead of critics. Kirchner was deficient in several areas as he began his term. Never known as a strong administrator, he had to pull together an administration recruited from the shambles of the election. Kirchner won the presidency with the weakest electoral mandate in Argentine history, 22 percent of the vote, after Menem, winner of the first round, enigmatically withdrew his candidacy and "fled the balloting, calling the result fraudulent.[52] Menem's sudden departure confirmed many Argentines' view that he was too weak to have been president during troubled times in the first place.

In the early months of his administration, Kirchner had to deal with two-year-old questions about more than half a million dollars in Santa Cruz campaign funds. The funds had been deposited in foreign banks through the good offices of a Kirchner family friend. The question hovered without resolution while funds floated outside the provincial government's reach. Finally, a successor governor insisted on access. Kirchner was also dealt a blow by a serious, life-threatening recurrence of his gastrointestinal condition. Almost 20 years earlier, Kirchner had suffered a hemorrhage and other complications resulting from a bleeding ulcer; this time he was hospitalized while Cristina spent long hours at the hospital, resolutely refusing to speak to reporters. Both critics and journalists insisted that this time his illness was a matter of state. Cristina told journalist Wornat why she wouldn't talk. "I didn't want to. Beyond his being president, he's my husband."[53] Kirchner recovered, but he also went through a later bout with cancer, the disease that killed his father.

With regard to Argentines' questions about their political future, Kirchner was never reluctant to state his view. At the outset of his term, he spent hours with political scientist Torcuato di Tella, discussing his thinking, especially in terms of the economy. At the outset of his term, the planets were aligning for emerging economies around the world: almost endless credit, eager markets, and competition between the United States and Asian countries to strengthen their ties with Latin American resources and productivity. Kirchner foresaw continuing demand for Argentine oil, beef, grain, and other commodities, and he could count on domestic enthusiasm for Peronist governance. Argentina's relatively well-educated people and extensive middle class—the class derided by journalist Wornat as enjoying prosperity under the generals—were ripe for the new millennium. On most analysts' minds was the broad, general question as to whether the emerging nations' leaders would kowtow to U.S., European, and World Bank ideas of laissez-faire capitalism, or institute their own "industrial policies." The latter choice suggested that emerging nations like Argentina would maintain close control over mineral resources and emphasize providing services to the lower classes. An industrial policy tightened control and sought electoral popularity.

"Yes," Kirchner said, "an 'industrial policy' is definitely necessary: a model for production and employment. I'm a partisan of active policy for productivity.... In the 1990s, the markets and the economy broke free of the State and its policies in a tacit acceptance of 'the end of history' and in explicit acceptance of the 'trickle down theory'—that economic freedom and the free play of markets will provide benefits that eventually reach everyone.... I say that the only thing that trickled down from that theory was misery."[54]

Kirchner decried the kind of "prosperity" that did not spread beyond industrialists, investors, and the management class. Politicians were left to bear the brunt of mass dissatisfaction. "The markets assuredly are organized economically," Kirchner continued, "but they don't express themselves socially. Only the presence or the absence of the State constitutes a coherent policy. That policy ought to be expressed by the State and the markets, trumping the pendulum that has in the past swung between an omnipresent State to an absent State — allowing us to arrive at *an intelligent State*." Kirchner said he especially regretted the privatization of Argentine railroads and the country's having given up control of its petroleum industry. "In Argentina," Kirchner asserted, "the obtuse policy of privatization and indiscriminate opening to foreign investors has destroyed the country."[55] Such sentiments spelled out Argentina's future and sent shivers up the spines of every member of the Bush administration in the United States.

Kirchner based his argument on history. Between 1960 and 1980, Argentina promoted import substitution and subsidized industrial growth. Per-capita production increased three percent annually. In the next 20 years, a "neoliberal" opening of markets, privatization, and free-market competition — all wildly applauded by the World Bank and the United States — shrank per-capita production increases to just over 1 percent. "The State," Kirchner continued, "must recapture control of macroeconomic instruments and encourage a model of production and work. But, notice that I'm not saying we must re-nationalize or re-impose state control, as some are suggesting I do."

After two and a half years of Kirchner's term, *The New York Times* evaluated Kirchner's and Argentina's progress. "Just four years ago," wrote Latin American correspondent Larry Rohter, "Argentina's economy was prostrate and its politics in chaos after a financial crisis resulted in bank deposits' being frozen, the government's defaulting on more than $100 billion in debt and five presidents' holding office in two weeks. But on Tuesday the country is expected to pay off the last of its debt to the International Monetary Fund (IMF) and simply walk away from further negotiations with the group." Although Argentina still owed a huge amount to international lenders, Rohter called the $9.8 billion installment "an important symbolic milestone."[56]

By Kirchner's third year in office, he had taken important steps in leading Argentina toward the left. There were price controls, and there was collaboration with other left-leaning Latin American leaders in putting together a trade alliance known as Mercosur. It was to be independent of the U.S.–dominated proposal, the Latin America Free Trade Association (LAFTA). And, in an ominous prelude to the kind of troubles that would plague his successor, Kirchner barked at supermarket owners for raising prices and urged a boycott of Shell Oil for the same thing. He got away with such presidential actions because he had support in the Argentine Congress, which expanded executive control over economic policy. More dangerously, Congress also enhanced executive control of the judiciary. Kirchner's power was consolidating, and he surrounded himself with advisors unlikely to engender original ideas. He found more opportunities for bonding with Chávez of Venezuela, Evo Morales of Bolivia, and Lula of Brazil, lacing up a united front against the United States.

Importantly, Kirchner also tightened the executive's reins on the armed forces and cleared the way for prosecutions; he apologized publicly to the families of "the disappeared." Commentators described his having "faced down" the military and "stood up to" the International Monetary Fund. By his third year in office, a polling firm found that Kirchner was favorably viewed by 87 percent of respondents. Riding the crest of a strong economy, Kirchner fashioned a role for himself as a modern *caudillo*. "What Kirchner likes is to be absolutely in charge," said Joaquín Morales Solá, political columnist for the conservative Argentine newspaper *La Nación*, "so he has become his own economic minister. Even more than moving left there's a turn toward a personal style of governing, with a dose of authoritarianism and ... confrontation."[57]

As for how "personal" his style was, it looked a bit like that of his hero, Perón. Cristina was at his side, happily bridging the legislative-executive divide, sharing the same political interests, issues, and instincts. On a fact-finding trip through the southern provinces, Cristina was a formidable presence in his entourage. "She monitored the organization from her space, she handled telephone calls, she spoke with functionaries, she passed on to her husband the essential information, and she discussed with him the responses the government would have."[58] As it turned out, Cristina was serving an apprenticeship. She would need all the training she could get, for as the Argentine economy tailed off and international credit markets crashed, Kirchner was forced to hand over a troubled economy to his wife and successor. The country still staggered under a debt burden of more than $90 billion.

* * *

"May the best woman win," was the headline on the *Buenos Aires Herald*. Cristina Kirchner took 45 percent of the run-off vote over Elisa Carrio, a center-left former congresswoman, who got 23 percent. Roberto Lavagna, a former finance minister, was a distant third with 17 percent. In late 2007, Cristina Fernández became the first woman elected president in Argentina's 191-year history. At her inauguration, she paid tribute to "the women in the white handkerchiefs," the mothers, grandmothers, and sisters who had defied the generals with their protest marches and their calls for an investigation into "the disappeared" from Argentina's "dirty war." She also recalled the memory of Eva Perón as her role model.

Cristina Kirchner brought onto the world stage the personality that had been admired — or avoided — by Argentines throughout her career. Journalist Wornat thought Cristina Kirchner's shoot-from-the-hip tendency, expressing her distaste for many things and her impatience with others, made her a woman "who doesn't know the meaning of the word 'hypocrisy.'"[59] The result was both admirable and lamentable. One anonymous Argentine politician complained: "Cristina is as smart as she is unbearable. I worked with her on various projects and came to know her pretty well. She is brilliant, but I left because she is impossible to put up with."[60]

Shortly after her election, there was a bizarre indication of how close her husband had gotten with Venezuela's Chávez. In August 2007, during the campaign, Franklin Durán, a Venezuelan-American businessman, was arrested in Buenos Aires with a suitcase stuffed with $800,000 in cash. The money had allegedly been sent by the Chávez government to help finance Mrs. Kirchner's campaign. In a 2008 federal trial in Miami, testimony told a story of threats, bribes, kickbacks, and illicit — but highly remunerative — dealings between Durán and the Venezuelan government. "The case has drawn angry reactions from Mr. Chávez and Mrs. Kirchner," said *The New York Times*, "who accused the Bush administration of trying to drive a wedge between Argentina and Venezuela, which have grown close in recent years."[61]

Because Cristina Kirchner walked into a global economic meltdown, her presidency would be substantially more challenging than that of her husband. Kirchner had led a turnaround in the Argentine economy, but now the country faced a growing list of problems related to inflation and shrinking government reserves. In addition, because of drought and other ravages of nature, and owing to worldwide speculation that ran commodities prices through the roof, Argentina, like other nations, had to balance the impulse to earn cash by exporting commodities or sacrifice the income to provide for its own population. In the very first year of Cristina Kirchner's term, she ran head-on into angry farmers who wanted to ship their production abroad. When her administration refused to allow it in order to keep Argentina's stores stocked, the battle was on.

Angry farmers staged four strikes in three months. In March 2008, farm groups ended a three-week strike by jamming up roads with trucks and tractors after causing nationwide food shortages. Cristina Kirchner, making four speeches in eight days, forced farmers into negotiations by surrounding herself with the support of consumers. On April 1: "Tens of thousands of Argentines marched in downtown Buenos Aires in support of President Cristina Fernández de Kirchner," said *The New York Times*, "as she confronted a 20-day farm strike that has provoked food shortages and a political crisis. The rally, a week after thousands of middle-class Argentines banged pots and pans in the capital's streets in support of the farmers, was a show of strength for Mrs. Kirchner, who urged the farmers to end their strike. She still refused to roll back a new tax on some farm exports, the farmers' main demand."[62]

Her accomplishments often, however, reflected her abrasive personality. "Mrs. Kirchner's approach to resolving the crisis has often been to fan the flames of conflict," noted reporter Alexei Barrionuevo. In fairness, Barrionuevo pointed out, the farmers' holding back needed food further stoked the crisis.[63] And, in fact, it was Cristina Kirchner's persistence that led to tactical success. She got Congress—controlled by Peronists—to vote yea on her agricultural policy, taking the heat, to some extent, off her.

She had been left no choice. It was estimated that food prices had risen 30 percent since the end of 2007, while the country's growth rate of 8 percent over the preceding five years was slowing. That enviable rate of growth had been built upon her husband's decision to subsidize Argentine purchases of Bolivian natural gas. That kept natural gas prices for Argentines low, and drove up productivity all the way through the first year of Cristina's presidency. Once again, the favorable conditions that allowed her husband's presidency to soar, came crashing down on Cristina's term.

* * *

Political scientist Tokatlian and his collaborators have suggested that for Argentina, globalization presents special challenges. "In the case of Argentina," Tokatlian writes, "entry into 'high globalization' and 'high democratization' suggests potential problems and continual internal changes." Because its economy is so strong and its democratic institutions are so weak, the minority that controls the economy is constantly at loggerheads with cantankerous consumer/voters.[64] It is along that tightrope that the Kirchners have had to walk. Watching with rapt attention have been Argentina's 40 million citizens—and two other groups. "In the case of Argentina," Tokatlian adds, "the two principal external actors to which it subordinated its foreign policy—by conviction, not conspiratorially—were the United States and international lenders."[65]

The Kirchners, by choice and circumstance, have cast themselves in the modern Latin American role of leaders hewing to their own course, free of U.S. domination, but struggling. They have had the unusual ability to ride the crest of Argentina's strengths, yet always looking straight down into the depths of Argentina's many weaknesses. "Today's Argentines are socially a lot like those of 50 years ago," historian Di Tella wrote, "although with more poor, but with similar indices of urbanism, education, and cultural development. Therefore, their historical memory is better. Someone always has an uncle or a grandmother who saw Evita come out on the balcony and who recalls the experience with emotion.... For that reason, and not because of some supposed geniality of Perón, Peronism has survived in Argentina."[66]

And, one must add, because of Néstor and Cristina Kirchner. But in the summer of 2009, the realities of global economics and domestic politics continued to torture the Kirchner legacy. Ex-President Néstor Kirchner, who had always had a strong hand in his wife's presidency, was forced to give up his post as leader of the Peronist Party. President Cristina Fernández de Kirchner soldiered on alone.

25

Daniel Ortega Saavedra

Sandino Redux

1945–
(Nicaragua)

Even the most fervent defender of U.S. foreign policy since 1900 must concede that no people have more reason to dislike that policy than Nicaraguans. Their distrust is the understandable result of a rich variety of brigands who have trampled Nicaragua in pursuit of their own selfish ends. In the nineteenth century, filibusterer William Walker led his private army onto shore, and in the twentieth century U.S. Marine Col. Ollie North provisioned his mercenaries with illegal funds from the administration of U.S. President Ronald Reagan. And for four decades of the twentieth century, U.S. interests were ignominiously served by Nicaragua's oppressive Somoza family, which was finally overthrown in 1979 by the *Frente Sandinista de Liberación Nacional*, the Sandinistas.

Rising from the cadre of nine men who led the Sandinistas was Daniel Ortega. Impelled by other Sandinista leaders—and, at times, restrained by them—Ortega carried their leftist banner from jungle warfare into competition among democratic political parties. It must also be said of Ortega's rise that it would have been little more than that of any other despot had it not been for those other brave Nicaraguans—the merchants, journalists, and civic leaders—who also opposed the Somozas. They, indeed, have stood tall during Nicaragua's democratic elections to insist that Sandinistas put away their rifles and their arrogance and behave like democrats, not leftist thugs. Throughout, it has been Ortega who, with singular determination, has overcome his shortcomings as a public speaker and his confusion as a policy maker to emerge as the first among Nicaraguan equals.

* * *

In the early nineteenth century, Nicaragua excited the interest of the United States and England as a possible passage for an interoceanic canal. Spain had tried and failed to build such a canal in 1814, and by 1850 the United States and England were ready to sign the Clayton-Bulwer Treaty. They agreed, cavalierly, that neither would claim exclusive control over the canal, if built, or over Central America in general. Their plans were supported by the wealthy merchants and ranchers of Nicaragua who pulled the strings of puppet governments. Of course, the very largest companies growing, packing, and shipping coffee and fruit were controlled by U.S. investors.

Nicaragua's development could not have been so thoroughly shaped by the nation's plantation owners and merchants had they not enjoyed the enthusiastic support of the Roman Catholic Church. "The Church was an essential part of colonial society," wrote historian

Perez-Brignoli. "Not only did it represent the spiritual dimension of the Conquest and function as an instrument for ideologically controlling the colonized Indians, its economic power, with its resources and properties, was immense." Indeed, the church itself was a land owner. The diocese that covered Guatemala and Nicaragua owned more than 50,000 head of cattle; clerics impressed women to gather food and cook for them; and the church recruited almsmen to collect taxes among thousands of parishes.[1]

Notions of nationalism — an ability to see oneself as sharing interests with neighbors— were virtually nonexistent. Nicaragua was at the mercy of foreign investors and invaders. An example of the latter was Tennessean William Walker in 1855. Walker was a graduate of the University of Tennessee who had earned medical and law degrees abroad. He had already (in 1853) declared Baja California and Sonora — two sparsely populated Mexican provinces— to be an independent republic before Mexican forces easily drove out his rag-tag, mercenary army. Undeterred, Walker then sailed for Nicaragua with 56 men armed with a new model of rifle. He joined his little army with Nicaraguan Liberals who were fighting to overthrow the Conservative government.

For a time, Walker had his way. "Walker easily took over," wrote Perez-Brignoli, "and quickly set up a phantom government in Nicaragua controlled in reality by the mercenaries. The U.S. State Department recognized it in May of 1856 to the considerable alarm of the other Central American countries and also of Great Britain. In reality, Walker was preparing to annex Nicaragua to the United States, a move backed by growing investment, weapons, and men drawn from the slave-owning [U.S.] South."[2]

The case of Walker illustrates not just the swashbuckling antics of a nineteenth century renegade, but the strong inclination on the part of Anglo-American industrialists to treat Central America in general, and Nicaragua in particular, as a convenience. Walker got himself elected president, suspended the Nicaraguan law against slavery, and curried favor with investors in the southern U.S. states. With his sovereignty recognized by the United States, Walker led his army in an attack on a town in the Guanacaste region of today's Costa Rica, intending to expand Nicaragua's borders. But when Walker seized a Lake Nicaragua steamer owned by Cornelius Vanderbilt's Accessory Transit Company he awoke serious opposition. Walker took over the company and gave it to two Nicaraguan friends, thus pitting himself against Vanderbilt, a man with friends in the White House. More ominously, Vanderbilt was a man with considerable resources. Vanderbilt promptly financed an army recruited by the other Central American governments and equipped by England. The hastily assembled army made short work of Walker, who in May 1857 surrendered to the U.S. Navy to avoid capture by the Central Americans. Alas, even this defeat did not keep Walker, the following November, from trying again. He sailed from Mobile to Graytown, Nicaragua, with yet another expeditionary force. This time, he was arrested and sent home like an errant schoolboy. (In 1860, Walker again sailed from Mobile, this time for Honduras. The English navy arrested him en route and handed him over to Honduran authorities, who tried and executed him.)

Walker, of course, was a piker compared to other U.S. investors, who would end up owning vast tracts of Nicaraguan land and numerous Nicaraguan politicians. Walker's bellicose style, though, would serve as a model for later U.S. efforts, including serial invasions. In 1901, the Hay-Pauncefote Treaty with Great Britain gave the United States exclusive right to build a transoceanic canal over a Nicaraguan route, an arrangement to which a compliant Conservative president of Nicaragua agreed. Two years later, of course, Nicaragua was let off the hook as a canal site when President Teddy Roosevelt — declaring "I took Panama" by arming a rebellion against Colombia — redrew the map of Central America. That led Nicaragua's new Liberal president, José Santos Zelaya, to declare his own intention to build a canal in

Nicaragua. And that occasioned invasions by U.S. Marines in 1909 and 1912. The United States was not going to let some upstart Nicaraguan dig a competing canal.

Every time the U.S. Marines invaded, they left behind trainers for the Nicaraguan soldiers who were expected to protect puppet Conservative governments from being overthrown by their own people. As far as a canal was concerned, the United States engineered the Bryan-Chamorro Treaty of 1916. It gave the United States the right—in perpetuity—to build, if one was ever to be built, a canal across Nicaragua.

The treaty also extended to the United States a 99-year lease on the Corn Islands in the Caribbean and the right to build a permanent naval base. To pay for these privileges, the United States floated a loan to Nicaragua, exacting as collateral future customs income. Then, to protect what had been turned into a branch office of U.S. investments, the Marines came back, again and again. "The United States converted Nicaragua into a virtual protectorate: it controlled the customs collections, the railways, and the National Bank—all the while the U.S. Marines assured internal peace."[3]

Which is not to say that Nicaraguans were completely docile. Between 1913 and 1924, there were no fewer than ten popular, armed insurrections. Each time Nicaraguan presidents called in the U.S. Marines. This unrest finally resulted in violent uprisings by United Fruit Company workers on the Atlantic Coast and a revolt led by Augusto Sandino. Of all of Nicaragua's rebels, the most indomitable was Sandino. When a pact was offered in 1926, Sandino refused to agree and fought on. Then, in 1932, the Marines, without having captured or killed Sandino, gave up and withdrew. It was only in 1934, after five years of fruitless attempts to track Sandino down, that the Nicaraguan government signed a truce and succeeded with treachery where it had failed at arms. Sandino was invited to dinner with government officials in Managua. After dessert and coffee, he was arrested. Along with his lieutenants, Sandino was driven into the countryside and gunned down. Nicaragua descended into the black years of the Somozas.

The Somoza family's reign was rigorously abetted by President Franklin Roosevelt, who forswore any U.S. intention of continuing U.S. intervention in Central America. Grandly announcing his "Good Neighbor Policy," Roosevelt was careful to leave enough Marines in Nicaragua to train the National Guardsmen then under the command of Anastasio Somoza García. Somoza García would parlay his command of the National Guard into the presidency. His Guardsmen would protect the Somozas' villainy for four decades. He enjoyed telling of his close relationship with Roosevelt, proudly saying that Roosevelt had once said of him: "He's an SOB, but he's our SOB."

* * *

José Daniel Ortega Saavedra, the future president, was born November 11, 1945, in the gold-mining town of La Libertad, in Chontales, a region of cattle ranches east of Lake Nicaragua. The frontier flavor of La Libertad and the social realities of rural Nicaragua were caught in an interview with Daniel's mother, Lidia Saavedra de Ortega, by biographer Denis Lynn Daly-Heyck. "I was the natural child of *Don* Benjamín Saavedra Montiel," she said, "a successful businessman who decided to recognize me as his own, so he asked my mother, *Doña* Mercedes Rivas, if I could come live with his other five daughters in order to receive a good education. My father was in the dry goods business, but he also helped obtain credit for individuals and businesses. Unfortunately, his North American associate swindled him, and he was broke for a while. This sort of thing happened all the time in La Libertad because of the gold mines, the speculation, and all the foreigners who had come to seek their fortune."[4]

Saavedra, who was mayor of La Libertad, was a supporter of the rebel Sandino, and young Lidia formed her political thought at his dinner table. He sent her off to Managua for secretarial training, then brought her back to manage his store, selling supplies to mining companies and their employees. "I sold everything from fine cloth to cigars," she recalled. "I also taught elementary school for a few years in La Libertad, but I was too intense."[5] Such was the intensity of her support for Sandino that she was briefly clapped in jail.

Don Daniel Ortega, her future husband, came to La Libertad to work as an accountant for one of the mining companies. He, too, had been an illegitimate child reared in the family of his father in Granada, a more sophisticated city founded by the Spanish in 1534. *Don* Daniel matched *Doña* Lidia's support for Sandino, having served as a rebel soldier. After Somoza García ordered Sandino murdered in 1934, Ortega sent a letter of protest, including his photograph so there would be no mistake about who sent the letter. It got him arrested and almost got him shot. Later, when Somoza García was trying to bribe ex–Sandinistas into supporting him, he sent *Don* Daniel an envelope stuffed with cash. Ortega returned it, including a personal note: "Eat shit." Lidia recalled: "He was a Sandinista; he was very intelligent; he read a lot, and he was bold, even fearless, you might say."[6]

His son Daniel, the future president, was the third child of their marriage, but the first to survive. Their first two children died of malaria. Daniel's brother, Humberto, who would become chief of Sandinista armed forces, was born two years later. Their little brother, Camilo, also a Sandinista rebel, would be killed in battle with the Somozas' National Guard. A sister, Germania, died before she was three years old, and a later child, Sigfrido, also died as an infant. The younger children's given names, Lidia would explain, arose from the elder Daniel's admiration for the foreigners who operated La Libertad's mines. "My husband gave the children German names because he was very fond of German culture," *Doña* Lidia recalled, "and also because many of the engineers excavating the mines were German, and my husband admired their ability."[7]

The family had to leave La Libertad as ore veins played out and foreign investors departed, leaving behind a virtual ghost town. The Ortegas moved to Juigalpa, closer to Managua, the capital, where *Don* Daniel started an import-export business and *Doña* Lidia opened a bakery. The Ortega boys attended Catholic schools, and young Daniel was an altar boy who taught Bible classes in Managua slums.

"[W]e were able to send Danielito and Humberto to the *Colegio Pedagógico*," *Doña* Lidia said, "which was private and run by the Christian brothers. Danielito loved to read...." He won oratorical and essay prizes awarded at the 150th anniversary of independence of Central America from Mexico. "Do you know that he was such a diligent, serious student that the brothers invited him to join their order?" *Doña* Lidia asked proudly. However, always the realist, she conceded that a religious career was never in the cards: "After a while, however, my sons' political activities were too much for the school to deal with, so many marches and demonstrations."[8] Ortega would graduate from high school and briefly study law at the Central American University of Managua, but he had made up his mind. He was a boy who insisted on growing into manhood as a rebel.

*   *   *

All around Ortega were rebels, as opposition to the Somoza regime was widespread, if ineffective. Even after 1956, when Somoza García was assassinated — despite the efforts of President Eisenhower's personal physician, hurriedly sent to his bedside — the Somoza dynasty was carried on seamlessly by, in turn, his two sons. Between 1958 and 1961, there were no fewer than 19 revolts, each of which was, in turn, suppressed. In that political climate Ortega, in 1959, joined student demonstrations as a member of Nicaraguan Patriotic Youth. The next year, at age 15, he was arrested, imprisoned, and tortured for the first time.

Once he was released, Ortega helped organize urban cells for an organization now called the Nicaraguan Revolutionary Youth. Arrested again, he was thrown in jail, where he studied law, history, and geography. He also wrote poetry and won an essay contest, managing to get his entry into the mail from his cell. During his imprisonments, his father and mother militated to try to improve the miserable conditions of Somoza prisons, which at one time or another held both of their older sons. There were so many Somoza opponents in prison, in fact, that it was there that Ortega, by the time he was eighteen years old, was recruited by the *Frente Sandinista de Liberación Nacional*, the FSLN, the Sandinistas.

The FSLN was founded by Carlos Fonseca, Silvio Mayorga, and Tomás Borge, whose goal was the same as Sandino's had been. That, fundamentally, was to establish a popular government that would distribute opportunity across class lines and, especially, rid Nicaragua of foreign domination. That meant overthrowing the Somoza dynasty, an idea that many Nicaraguans applauded. It also meant bringing to heel those elements of the Nicaraguan bourgeoisie that helped prop up the Somozas, a notion that gave many middle-class Nicaraguans pause. It smacked, quite simply, of Marxism. "The principal Sandinista theme was, and is, autonomy," wrote Daly-Heyck. "This theme has strong Marxist, nationalist, and Christian components that are sometimes in conflict, but that on the whole are seen as contributing to the objective of national self-determination."[9]

Fonseca, Mayorga, and Borge formed the FSLN from members of other groups that had for years been trying to bring down the Somozas. Their strategy, implemented from 1962 to 1969, was to assemble a guerrilla army in rural areas. That changed, eventually, after early defeats by Somoza's National Guard. Fonseca, in fact, would later be killed in combat in the countryside, by which time the Sandinistas had learned that Somoza's dominance in the *campo* meant they had to build a core of support in the cities.

Whether inside or outside the cities, the struggle young Ortega joined was beginning to reflect the profound changes occurring in Latin America. Fidel Castro became the rebels' role model and mentor after emerging from a successful rebellion that identified itself as Marxist. Castro had also withstood the forces of the United States by repelling the invasion at Cuba's Bay of Pigs. At the same time, the Second Vatican Council, from 1962 to 1965, was encouraging Roman Catholic priests to elevate the church's mission above hearing the confessions of the wealthy and counseling the poor to be patient. "Liberation theology" was aimed at organizing governments and society to attend to the needs of poor and working class people. But while Liberation Theology espoused tactics of non-violence, many advocates of change found it possible to carry both a rosary and a rifle.

New groups were finding their voices, and as their voices rose to a clamor, oligarchs were terrified. According to historian Perez-Brignoli, the Central American privileged class "tended to view any concession as the first link in a chain that would end up in social revolution." In Central America in general and Nicaragua in particular, U.S. policy had long been to protect U.S. investors' interests. "[P]articularly in the international context, there was a readiness of the United States in its foreign policy to sacrifice any declaration of good intentions in the service of strategic interests."[10]

Only in a few, brief instances were reformers able to push aside the heavy hand of Washington to produce change. In Guatemala, Juan José Arévalo, a teacher and philosopher, spoke of "spiritual socialism" and led a progressive movement that would last for more than a decade. Also, Central American nations created *MERCOMUN*, a common market that encouraged industrialization, created a regional free-trade zone, and subsidized the formation of new businesses.

In Nicaragua, hope for a better economic future flowered as new markets opened, better fertilizers and techniques for pest control were developed, and prices—except for coffee—rose. The country's economic planners, spurred by Central American integration, entered a hopeful era of import-substitution. Before long, however, it was realized "that the overall cost of industrialization ha[d] been borne by the great majority of the population, whereas its greatest benefits ha[d] been enjoyed by a narrow group of business owners and middle sectors."[11]

The number of Nicaragua's urban poor rose dangerously, and Washington and Managua watched nervously as students rioted from Paris to Berlin to San Francisco. They saw a worldwide tide of rising expectations that was out of control. Throughout Central America, Perez-Brignoli wrote, "this 'imminent and menacing conspiracy' was no more than an ideological cover-up of an undeniable fact: the system of social relations ... was simply bankrupt. United States policy had an astonishing duality.... Technical experts and study missions were unequivocally aware of the need for structural changes and reforms. Nonetheless, in the end the hand of the U.S. State department always obeyed strategic considerations. This is why there was unconditional support for all the region's repressive regimes such as that given to Somoza."[12] Indeed, the Somozas still commanded 7,500 disciplined, well-armed National Guardsmen, their officers trained by the U.S. Central Intelligence Administration and the U.S. Army.

Even President John F. Kennedy's vaunted Alliance for Progress, whose wonders were touted by fresh-faced legions of Peace Corps Volunteers, was suspect. Its support for agricultural improvements and democratic reforms papered over the United States' real goals, Perez-Rignoli insisted: "Behind those ambitious reforms lay hidden, in reality, a counterinsurgency operation using notions of modernization and practical democracy. The effort was to reverse the Cuban Revolution and the guerrilla movements that threatened to multiply wherever there were fertile conditions."[13] No conditions were more fertile than Nicaragua's.

Ortega joined the FSLN in 1963—his brother Humberto two years later—and the next year he was fighting alongside insurgents in Guatemala. He was captured, extradited to Nicaragua and imprisoned, and, again, tortured. Released in 1965, Ortega founded and edited *El Estudiante*, the publication of the Students' Revolutionary Front. He also directed the Popular Civic Committees that he helped organize in Managua and was chosen to be a member of the national directorate of the FSLN. Party operations were financed by bank robberies in Managua in which the Ortega brothers played prominent roles. Together they also gunned down Gonzalo Lacayo, a known Somoza torturer, in the street.[14]

In November 1967, Ortega was arrested by the Somoza National Guard and imprisoned for seven years. During that time, he and his fellow prisoners turned the cellblocks into halls of recruitment to the Sandinista cause. But they were also tortured. A fellow prisoner, Doris María Tijerino, a Sandinista commander, provided a dark view of what imprisonment by the National Guard meant., "[I]n '67, in November, I was captured again in my home," she said. "They conducted a series of raids in the city and captured various clandestine houses of the *Frente*. That's when they captured Daniel Ortega and gave him that scar on his forehead.... Besides beatings, at times with the hand, at times with objects, they made me do exhausting physical exercise, such as maintaining impossible postures for a long period.... Directly underneath my buttocks they placed a bayonet, so that if I fell, I would be run through. This was a physical torture, but the psychological aspect was terrifying and degrading. They made a big show of placing the bayonet, and they would have me touch it to see how sharp it was. Then, when I could not see, they would take away. The mental aguish was terrible."[15]

While Daniel was in prison, his brother Humberto dropped out of sight, making his way to Cuba for military training. In 1969, Humberto was among those who tried to help Carlos Fonseca escape from a prison in Costa Rica, but the plan went awry. Humberto, injured in both arms, lost the use of the right one and ended up in prison with Fonseca. They were released the next year in exchange for prisoners taken in an airliner hijacking orchestrated by the FSLN. For Humberto, there followed military training in North Korea and more time in Cuba with Fonseca. The long period of exile led critics like Tomás Borges to accuse Humberto of having little experience as a rebel other than fetching coffee for Fonseca. Others, however, see his exile as the time that Humberto conceived the *tercerista*—"third way"—ideas that his brother would adopt and that would allow Sandinista guerrillas to pull together Sandinista factions.[16]

In 1974, Daniel Ortega's turn came. Two days after Christmas, the Sandinista commander Juan José Quezada led a dramatic raid on a holiday party at the Managua home of a prominent backer of the Somoza regime. Twelve of the wealthy revelers were taken hostage, and in exchange for their release the Sandinistas demanded that fourteen of their own be set free. Daniel Ortega was among them.

The streets of Managua into which Ortega emerged were much changed. One of his poems, in fact, noted that his imprisonment was during some very important style changes for a young man in his twenties. Its title: "I Never Saw Managua When Miniskirts Were In Style."[17] More generally, the streets showed the enormous physical wreckage that was a result of the devastating earthquake that had struck Managua two years earlier. Because of the government's unwillingness to pay for rebuilding, grumbling had multiplied, fingers were pointed at Somoza, and there was tension. "In the wake of widespread unrest following the earthquake, the government cracked down on criticism, whether it came from unemployed laborers, displaced farmers now reduced to squatter status, increasingly vocal student groups, opposition leader Pedro Joaquín Chamorro's newspaper *La Prensa*, or the fledgling guerrilla band of the Sandinistas."[18] All dissidents tried to capitalize on the grumbling by recruiting. Chamorro, for his part, set about extending his influence beyond the pages of the newspaper to the founding of the Democratic Union of Liberation (UDEL). It brought together a range of moderates.

The Sandinistas, however, were convinced that moderation was not the answer. They were following the Cuban model, training raw recruits in their camps in the countryside with the intent to take on Somoza's well-trained, well-equipped National Guardsmen head-to-head. A picture of those times was provided to interviewer Daly-Heyck by Manuel Calderón Chévez. Calderon was a former seminarian (he was expelled) who joined the Sandinistas in the mountains when he was 21 years old. He called the time "an odyssey." After three weeks of military training, he joined a force that was small, but, as far as the people knew, large. "From the political point of view, the most important thing about the *montaña* was to have maintained alive the hope of the FSLN. That, to a certain extent, helped us win people to our cause because everyone thought that in the *montaña* there was a big army. But we weren't big at all; we were small, very small. Counting the groups I knew about, there were about 100 to 125 of us, and most of the time we were divided up in groups of 10, 15, or, occasionally, 30."[19]

At that time Daniel Ortega was in hiding in Costa Rica, but he was called back to Managua in the spring of 1976. It was dangerous, and the person assigned to cover his back was Leticia Herrera: "I was reassigned to Managua even though it was very dangerous for me there, but I knew the city and all the cells we had created. Also, I was very well acquainted with all the collaborators because of my years community-organizing. This was an important assignment for me because I worked directly with Commander Daniel Ortega."

Herrera was herself a *comandante* and a valuable member of the FSLN who would later rise to vice president of the National Assembly. A rebellious teenager, she had studied in the Soviet Union, where she met her first husband. By the time she was assigned to assist Ortega, her husband had been killed by the Nicaraguan National Guard and their child was in the care of her mother in Costa Rica. Because of Ortega's long imprisonment and the earthquake's destruction, Ortega was in special need of help because he was essentially lost in the streets of Managua. "I became indispensable for him, for he had to depend on my knowledge of the groups, neighborhoods, support systems, and so forth that we had developed in Managua, because he no longer knew the city ... all his familiar landmarks and points of reference were now gone.... I felt a strong sense of responsibility for Daniel's security; he could leave the safe house for only a few hours at night, so I was the one who always went out."

The rebellion see-sawed between urban actions like the kidnapping of Somoza's friends for ransom and rural ambushes of National Guard outposts. The former periodically kept the Sandinistas in the public eye, but the latter demonstrated how far they had to go to claim anything like victory. Throughout the 1970s, many Sandinistas did not survive, either because they were killed like Fonseca in the hills or rooted out of hiding in Managua, and discovery was nearly the fate of Herrera and Ortega. Three of their companions were killed within blocks of where Ortega and Herrera were headed to pick up cash intended for the Sandinistas. "The next day, about 6:30 or 7 A.M.," Herrera recalled, "I was supposed to take Daniel to a house where he was going to meet with Eduardo Contreras. He was now dead, but we still didn't know because the National Guard, in order to catch the rest of us, did not publish the news right away.

"This house was near where Carlos Roberto had just been killed. Daniel wanted to go alone and wanted me to let him off at a distance from the house, but I told him I didn't think he knew the territory well enough." Sure enough, Ortega stayed in the car while the driver walked ahead to check. He ran into a National Guard antiterrorist unit that was poised, waiting, around a corner from the house. He talked his way out of the area and walked, carefully, back to the car."[20]

*   *   *

It became clear to the Sandinistas that their ideas—ideas on which their recruitment, survival, and eventual governance depended—were not well understood by the people at large. So Sandinista leaders tried to reach across the divide between themselves and, on the one hand, illiterate farmers, and, on the other, sophisticated members of the merchant class. First, however, they had to thrash out their own differences. "The Front had to overcome its internal problems," Ortega believed, "which manifested themselves most sharply from 1975 to October 1977. This was when the division of tendencies polarized us with regard to revolutionary strategy and tactics."

The goal was "consolidation into a political and military nucleus involving farmers and farm laborers, industrial and construction workers, secondary and university students, artists, intellectuals, technicians, and progressive professionals, teachers, journalists, clerics, and workers in both production and service industries."[21] Such inflated rhetoric is the stock in trade of revolutionaries, but it reflected an undeniable reality. The illiterate were not stupid, and the sophisticated were not going to be duped. Failure to unseat the Somozas up to that point reflected not just failure at arms, but an inability to advance a cogent philosophy of governance to replace them; Sandinista leaders were split into three camps, which they called "tendencies."

The nine *comandantes* were evenly divided among the three tendencies. Jaime Wheelock, Carlos Nuñez, and Luis Carrión were of the Proletarian Tendency. While Marxist-Leninist in its focus on the needs of the urban working class, this tendency accepted the need for cooperating with major capitalist powers.

Tomás Borge, Henry Ruiz, and Bayardo Arce were of the more hard-nosed Prolonged Popular War Tendency, which has been described as Maoist. Their goal was the recruitment and education of a peasant army in the countryside. Although their ideas followed what had become the classic strategic thinking as developed by Ernesto *Che* Guevara in Cuba, problems were always clear to see. When Sandinista founders Fonseca and Eduardo Contreras came back from hiding in Honduras to try to bring the two factions together, they were both killed in combat in the countryside. Tomás Borge, a third founder, was taken and imprisoned. The National Guard was, quite simply, on top of Sandinista efforts to create the "revolutionary foci" Guevara had called for. By 1977 only a few dozen Sandinista leaders were left. And although they had thousands of sympathizers, they could count on no more than 200 fighters.

Into that strategic breach walked the Ortega brothers and Victor Tirado. They called their tendency *Tercerista*—literally, "third way"—but it was often called the "Insurrectional" faction. Primarily, the *terceristas* foresaw cooperation among Sandinista factions. "In reality, it did not represent an entirely new approach; rather it served primarily as a mediator between the two existing tendencies."[22]

Equally important would be the necessity of mediating between the Sandinistas and other Somoza opponents, especially the many members of the bourgeoisie who had opposed the Somozas. Thus, Ortega would be cast in a role, that of mediator, for which he was not particularly well prepared. The threat of prison and torture and constantly risking death are not the best ways to settle the mind. However, no other Sandinista was any better prepared. Close observers of Ortega noted that even though he was more rigorous in his Marxist thought than, for example, his brother Humberto, Ortega had taught himself to accept others' views. That served him well in bringing together disaffected individuals and competing factions, and, in the process, elevating his own prospects. "Daniel was more disciplined and a better mediator, often effectively rebuilding political fences that Humberto (or others) had knocked down ... there are many other examples of his finding a compromise or getting his way."[23]

In late 1977, the Sandinistas got important support from an urban group of intellectuals, professionals, and business leaders who called themselves the "Group of Twelve." They acceded to the view that armed resistance was the only way to overthrow the Somozas and that the FSLN represented the best hope for successful guerrilla warfare. They backed the *tercerista* tendency, seeing it as "a faction that espoused political pluralism and a democratic constitution."[24] The political stage was now set, and 1978 proved fateful.

*   *   *

In January, Pedro Chamorro, the newspaper publisher, was murdered. His intelligent, brave, and forceful criticism had finally proved to be too much for the Somozas. It would later be shown that the fatal command came directly from the Somoza family, but if the family's intent was to squelch growing discontent, it didn't work. The outrageous act misfired. It brought together groups of Somoza opponents that had never gotten along with each other; demonstrators poured into the streets.

Some 120,000 middle-class and working-class people turned out, and a workers' strike paralyzed much of the nation. South of the capital along the western shore of Lake Nicaragua, Sandinista uprisings erupted in Rivas and Granada. On the Atlantic side of the lake, the tribal community of Monimbó took its cue in February and fought the National Guard with primitive weapons that included boiling water, hand-made knives, and rocks. The Guard responded with tanks and aircraft.

In the battle, young Camilo Ortega, the younger brother of Daniel and Humberto, was killed. The day was carried by a special unit led by Major Anastasio Somoza Portocarrero, the president's son. With crushing effect, the National Guard regained control.

Nevertheless, in some quarters the tide seemed to be turning. Watching from Washington, the administration of President Jimmy Carter, spurred by liberals in Congress, denied Somoza any more right to purchase U.S. arms. Latin American governments went further, raising their voices in support of the rebellion and encouraging the United States to do the same. "The inconsistent U.S. policy under Carter suddenly found itself without allies or choices," wrote Perez-Rignoli. "The Sandinista Front received abundant help from such important neighbors as Mexico, Venezuela, and Cuba, along with others that were strategically situated, such as Panama and Costa Rica."[25]

At that time, Daniel Ortega was reassigned from Managua to the northern front, and Herrera went with him. She later slipped across the southern border into Costa Rica — where Ortega's mother was, for safety's sake, living — to give birth to their child, whom they named Camilo.[26] Ortega later married Rosario Murillo, a poet, who had studied in Switzerland and England. A pretty, diminutive woman who was known as a stylish dresser, Murillo would accompany Ortega during presidential campaigns in the manner of a U.S. political wife. There were also later *affaires de cour*, fodder for Nicaragua's hyperactive media.

Daniel's reassignment was part of a surge by the Sandinistas to try to deprive the National Guard of the momentum it had gained in early spring. By July 1978, even as his lieutenants were assuring him that he was in control, Somoza got a rude awakening. He allowed the Group of Twelve to return from exile, whereupon they were greeted at the Managua airport like rock stars. Then, in August, Sandinista Edén Pastora — whose *nom de guerre* was *Comandante Cero*, Commander Zero— led a foray right into the National Palace. He secured the building and took captive some 500 government workers. Among those taken were high officials and several members of the Somoza family. Pastora's band took away $5 million, won allowance to post a Sandinista tract stating the movement's intentions, and guaranteed that 83 Sandinistas, including Borge, would be released from Somoza jails. Pastora became a folk hero and a prominent rival of Daniel Ortega.

In September, Sandinista raids on targets in Managua and half a dozen other places met with some success, and many Nicaraguans concluded that the rebels, if they persisted, actually had a chance of winning. Somoza did his part to foul up his own plans by employing the insane tactic of bombing Managua neighborhoods. As a result, retreating Sandinistas were joined by long lines of frightened, fleeing non-combatants. Then, in the aftermath of the bombing raids, the National Guard would enter the target neighborhoods looking for survivors. Boys more than 12 years old were killed. The barbarity, which left more than 6,000 Nicaraguans dead, finally broke the bond the Somozas had had with the Catholic Church and emboldened more Nicaraguans to rebel. A broad coalition of opponents was formalized, protected by the Sandinista army.

By the spring of 1979, the Sandinistas were strong enough to mount attacks on a broad front, stretching thin the National Guard's forces. In May, students called a national strike, and it was followed the next month by another one. Sensing the end, Nicaraguan leaders formed a five-member Government of National Reconstruction, including Ortega and two fellow Sandinistas and two democrats, one of whom was Violeta Chamorro, the widow of *La Prensa*'s slain owner, Pedro. On July 19, Anastasio Somoza Debayle resigned as his supporters fled to Honduras, El Salvador, and Costa Rica. Many *somocistas*, including former National Guardsmen, took their weapons with them as they fled across the border to Honduras, where they formed heavily armed bands. Somoza himself would shortly be assassinated in Paraguay, to which he had fled, by a bomb that was more powerful than his armor-plated Mercedes.

Daniel Ortega and the other Sandinista commanders, who had established a provision capital in León, moved into Managua.

By the time it finally was driven from power, the Somoza family had accumulated ownership of a third of all Nicaraguan assets. The family had held power since shortly after Sandino was killed in 1934, surviving countless uprisings. Over the 18 years leading to the Somozas' downfall, an estimated 50,000 Nicaraguans were killed. Now the world waited to see what would follow.

* * *

After the overthrow, Ortega was cautious about a future with all those National Guardsmen hiding in Honduras and all that history of U.S. intervention in Nicaraguan affairs. He had heard, he said, ominous remarks from right-wing members of the U.S. Congress. "We must realize that there are powerful enemies watching this process," he continued. "There are reactionary forces that are opposed to this victory." President Carter defended his administration's support for the new government. "It's a mistake," he said, "for Americans to assume or to claim that every time revolutionary change takes place in this hemisphere, or even an abrupt change takes place in this hemisphere, that somehow it's a result of secret, massive Cuban intervention.... I think that our policy in Nicaragua is a proper one."[27]

Ortega's policies, however, drew fire. By the end of 1979, Ortega, who was named "Coordinator" of the new government, had overseen the seizure of all of Nicaragua's television stations. His government denied a democratic critic of Somoza his request for a license to open a new station. The administration announced that television broadcasting would henceforth be the province of the Sandinista-dominated government. Brother Humberto was given control of the army. Virtually every Sandinista minister of the new government, constantly surrounded by television, radio and print reporters, took the opportunity to make clear that Nicaragua's No. 1 priority should be to serve as a model for anti-imperialist causes around the world. "You can be certain," Ortega assured everyone who was listening, "we will never betray the revolution."[28] Nor would they brook much opposition. In the months following the coup, at least 2,000 opponents found themselves in Sandinista jails.

And as is so often the case, the new leaders, proclaiming a future of equal opportunity for all, were first in line to expropriate the best property. Ortega moved into the house of Jaime Morales, a banker and businessman, in a wealthy Managua neighborhood. It did not matter that Morales had been an opponent of Somoza. Ortega's example was part of a pattern. Sandinistas seized all they could find of the thousands of weapons left behind by National Guardsmen, seized for themselves the largest homes, and turned their eyes toward Moscow. "When Somoza fell, the FSLN, which by then had most of the guns in the country, proclaimed itself the vanguard of the people and immediately and deliberately tilted toward the Soviet bloc."[29]

The "tilt," as one might imagine with a small Central American nation that the United States had such a long record of dominating, would remain a topic of discussion. Eventually, Bayardo Arce, a Sandinista, would express his exasperation at the way stereotypes persisted. Asked to clarify the oft-stated affinity that Sandinistas felt for Marxism-Leninism, said, yes, the attachment was real "as long as we leave [aside] the essential problem of the arbitrary connotations of language.... When you say 'Marxism' or 'Marxism-Leninism,' everyone grabs his mental register—meagerly supplied, of course, with facts—and, 'click-click-click,' out comes the Kremlin. That is nonsense."[30] Historian Dennis Gilbert provided an important modification: "The evidence ... leaves little doubt that Marxism is the basic source of Sandinista thought. However, the Sandinistas have not treated Marxism as a fixed canon, but as a body of insights that they can adapt to their own needs and Nicaraguan conditions."[31]

Vanden and Prevost added their view: "The arrival in power of the Sandinistas and their allies in July 1979," they wrote, "brought the first possibility of real constitutional government to Nicaragua because the revolutionary forces were bound to the principle of political pluralism supported by popular participation. However, the Sandinista commitment to political pluralism was a complex one and was not based primarily on the concept as it is articulated in liberal democratic ideology.... Nevertheless, one aspect of the Sandinista concept of pluralism was the construction in Nicaragua of a governmental system based on constitutional principles and the rule of law."[32]

To establish the new government, the nine Sandinista *comandantes*, including the Ortega brothers, proclaimed themselves the National Directorate. The Directorate — its membership was later enlarged — would keep a stranglehold on power for a long time. After four years, Ortega could still boast that the "National Directorate is the supreme leadership body and central authority of the FSLN and of the Sandinista People's Revolution."[33] He continued to stake that claim for eleven years.

To include non–Sandinistas in affairs, a five-member Junta of National Reconstruction was formed, and of that group Daniel Ortega was the only *comandante*. He served alongside Sergio Ramírez, one of the Group of Twelve, and Violeta Chamorro, who had replaced her late husband as director of *La Prensa*. Ortega was demonstrating his skill at a serious game of King Of The Mountain. As egos pushed and shoved, trying to knock each other off the hill, Ortega held his ground. After years of warfare, imprisonment, and torture, Ortega was not going to be pushed aside in the organization of peace. But in many respects he was an ugly duckling — surrounded by a gaggle of geese.

Historian Daniel Gilbert saw this as an important attribute: "Ortega is an uninspiring speaker," he wrote, "with a humorless public demeanor. On the record, he is something of a political mystery. In speeches and interviews he typically speaks *ex officio*, for the party and state. During the struggle against Somoza, he rarely published anything under his own name or spoke for attribution, allowing his younger brother and political ally Humberto to assume a more salient role. But in a party suspicious of personalistic leadership, Ortega's colorlessness and discretion were virtues and probably contributed to his emergence as first among equals on the Directorate and his nomination in 1984 as the FSLN's president candidate, a role Borge is said to have coveted."[34]

In fact, Borge, the oldest Sandinista and the only survivor of the founders of the movement, was the one most often described as the engaging idealist. He was known for his charm, his natural ability to identify with the poor, and his capacity for arousing a crowd with his eloquence. He was the ideologue, the idealist, always interested in finding solutions for the problems of the poor. It was Borge who could discuss a range of ideas from Marxism to Liberation Theology. But for all those reasons the other *comandantes* considered Borge a threat to their advancement. Ortega? Well, Ortega was a pragmatist, something of a plodder.

As the Sandinistas set up a formal structure for the new government, they made clear that whatever its organization, it was they who held all the guns and would advance all their ideas. "This reorganization fixed power in the hands of the Directorate and ... it was impossible to separate the state, the army, and the mass organization from the top Sandinista leadership," wrote Miranda and Ratliff. "For example, one day Humberto Ortega would meet with the most important chiefs of the army and give directions as minister of defense, and the next day he would appear as a member of the Directorate to approve political programs for army officers that would guarantee their loyalty to the Sandinistas, educate them in the principles of Marxism-Leninism, or direct them on what the army would pay Sandinista cadres. It created a labyrinth."[35]

Personal relationships were often stormy—*Doña* Violeta Chamorro, feeling blocked from important decisions, eventually quit the Junta—and hardly established precedents for cooperation. In the day-to-day conduct of government business, Sandinistas turned administrative departments into fiefdoms. Other former *comandantes* were not welcome in their offices. They set up Sandinista Defense Committees, the National Union of Farmers and Cattle-raisers, the Sandinista Workers' Federation, the Rural Workers' Association, and the Luisa Amanda Espinosa Association of Nicaraguan Women. Sandinistas called them "schools of democracy" and set about trying to reform an economy that had been operated like a franchise for foreign investors by the Somozas.

* * *

"The first characteristic of the Nicaraguan revolution that we believe should be taken into account," stressed historians Richard Harris and Carlos Vilas, "is the backward and underdeveloped nature of the forces of production in revolutionary Nicaragua, which is a product of its past history of neo-colonial and dependent capitalist development." The Sandinistas were confronted with the need to build a modern economy atop a medieval society. "In many important ways, the revolutionary transformation of Nicaraguan society has been conditioned by its relatively unskilled workforce, its technological backwardness ... and ... its export-oriented economy."

Under Somoza, as long as landowners could count on dirt-cheap labor to harvest crops, operate elementary processing machinery, and move products to the ports, they saw no need to build schools. They were unmoved by any need for the delivery of medical care. Least of all did they encourage civic organization. Coffee, sugar, cocoa, and beef were destined for foreign tables. Little else need be considered.

Given that background, the Sandinista government achieved considerable progress early in its life. By the early 1980s, productivity figures had regained pre-revolutionary levels, and investment was returning though a burdensome foreign debt required attention. It was at that point, however, that the administration of U.S. President Ronald Reagan identified Nicaragua as the principle arms supplier to nearby Salvadoran rebels and cut off U.S. aid to Nicaragua.

Moreover, the United States made available $19 million in aid to the Contras, the anti–Sandinista guerrillas, meaning that agrarian reform was severely hampered by roaming armed bands determined to undermine the new government. Using the arms and aid they got from the United States, the Contras employed sabotage and frequent attacks inside the country. From the outside, the U.S. Central Intelligence Agency mined Nicaraguan ports and bombarded fuel depots. In cities, anti–Sandinista elements were encouraged—and funded—to do all they could to disrupt economic and political recovery, including resign from governing bodies.

The Sandinistas, no matter how well they had educated themselves during long nights in the jungle or in exile, were ill-prepared for that kind of harsh political reality. It was not debate, it was sabotage. Of course, the population whose hearts and minds the Sandinista wished to win did not make up a congenial audience. They wanted results, though they had trouble articulating their needs after decades of strangulation by the Somozas. The result was a drumbeat of criticism, including from a bourgeoisie that had either cooperated with the Somozas or kept their political views to themselves.

Interviewer Daly-Heyck captured the cavalier attitude of middle-class Nicaraguans who had cooperated with the Somoza regime. "To be frank," said Gilberto Cuadra, a businessman, "working for the [Somoza] government had its advantages. [The 1960s] was when

Nicaragua really began to develop.... For an engineer, modernization on that scale was an exciting adventure."[36]

Others, selfishly, agreed, and they were around to torment the Sandinistas. Cuadra was a founder of COSEP —*Consejo Superior de Empresas Privadas*— which was a kind of Chamber of Commerce organized under the Somozas in 1974. Its members had admired U.S. business practices and saw no reason those practices should not be allowed by the Sandinistas. "COSEP has tried to cooperate with the revolution," Cuadra said. "In 1979, we felt that the revolution would benefit everyone.... We thought, well, these are young, inexperienced *muchachos* ... straight from the mountains.... Our relations, while not friendly, were not tense either. So, for about a year and a half we tried to work together. But they began to regard us as a class that should disappear, as one that had exploited workers and, of course, this was true of some individuals, although it was not the common denominator. So our relations became cooler and cooler, until finally they became cold."[37]

Cold, indeed. Because the Sandinistas were unready to trust their revolution to being picked apart by others, they canceled the national election that was planned — naively — for 1980. As a concession to pluralism, the Sandinistas increased the Council of State to 47 members, but they firmly held onto a majority of votes. Before the year was out Nicaragua's banks had been nationalized, Somoza family properties were designated the property of the people, and many small enterprises were organized under government control. The distribution of sugar was nationalized, and many export commodities were subjected to state planning. Before 1981 closed, Ortega announced the nationalization of 14 companies, and more were being cleared for takeover.[38]

The bourgeoisie responded through COSEP. Merchants asked — also naively — that the Sandinistas give up control of the army and the national police. At least, they said, give us opportunities for electoral politics, with competition among parties. COSEP even offered those "*muchachos*" advice on how Nicaragua should be managed. "Then," recalled Cuadra, "we wrote them a letter — I was vice president of COSEP at the time — saying that the economy was in terrible shape and that we saw their clear alignment with Russia, that there was no pluralism, that there was too much emphasis on the army.... We wrote Daniel Ortega a letter October 20, 1981. He was coordinator of the junta at that time, and immediately, that same night, we were taken prisoner and each kept in separate, solitary cells for twelve days, all of us who signed the letter, the six presidents of COSEP. Then we were condemned by the tribunals to seven months in jail for public agitation and provoking chaos in the society."[39]

Ortega was, none too subtly, letting Nicaraguans know that the Sandinistas did not welcome "advice" from Somoza collaborators. He did, however, commute the sentences the following February. This back-and-forth, however, was a harbinger of continuing conflict. To his left, Ortega could hear Jaime Wheelock, one of the *comandantes*, threatening to nationalize all industry that didn't cooperate. To his right, COSEP leaders found a thousand criticisms. Between the two, Ortega was treading a narrow path. Real reform required an autocratic hand; pluralism would be based on cooperation among people of different views. The Sandinistas were implementing policies that were completely untried in the Nicaraguan context, and while they were sure COSEP's capitalism didn't work, they were not having a lot of luck with their newly organized collective farms.

In 1981, Ortega publicly admitted that collectivization was not going well. More than half of the productive farming and cattle land remained in the hands of large and middle-size owners, and impatient peasants had been seizing land. Once they had the land, however, the poorly educated peasants were unable to work it with any efficiency or skill. Furthermore, the state-operated farms were also producing poorly despite large investments in expensive, imported machinery. The new technology was crippling the national budget without producing results. Ortega told Nicaraguans that the time had come for easing back on agricultural policy and encouraging small, individually owned, farms. Productivity had to take precedence over ideology.

Nevertheless, Ortega warned, such accessions to reality should not suggest that the Sandinistas were turning back the clock. He still considered it treason to suggest that Sandinista plans should be set aside. He was convinced that COSEP and its members were trying to retard the economy by failing to re-supply inventories, choking off investment, and refusing to offer credit. Ortega warned that this "decapitalization" campaign, intended to make the Sandinistas' economic ideas fail, had to stop. "This is a private sector," Ortega declared, "that is consciously playing with fire and that wants to destroy popular power in order to impose its own power to rob and oppress workers."[40]

To achieve success in the agrarian economy, the Sandinistas had to find a better balance among several competing forces. Throughout Nicaraguan history, indigo, cocoa, and, later, coffee, all contributed to the country's total output, but cattle was king. Nicaragua had long supplied cattle to all of Central America, and, as a result, was stuck in a ranching culture that inhibited the development of other agricultural commodities. To break that stranglehold, the Sandinistas' first task was to change attitudes and land-distribution patterns that were centuries old. And if that wasn't enough of a challenge among Nicaragua's westernized, *mestizo* community, the Sandinistas also had to deal with tribal cultures living in the Atlantic Coast region. When the Sandinistas tried to seize tribal lands in the east, it led to armed resistance and the flight of thousands of refugees into Honduras. Tribal leaders were jailed, and more than 50 Miskito villages were destroyed. Eventually, the tribes would win designation of semi-autonomous regions, but that came only after years of confrontation and negotiation. All their study of Marx had ill prepared the Sandinistas for dealing with the Miskitos.

At bottom, the Sandinistas' dilemma was that they could not give the peasants what they wanted and still feed the rest of the country. "In its initial incarnations," wrote historian Gilbert, "the Sandinista agrarian reform favored the state farm and protected the (non-*somocista*) agrarian capitalist. But it offered little to the peasant." So Ortega—who, in effect, got his job because of his ability to juggle conflicting ideas—talked and talked. He announced plans that were really nothing more than an attempt to buy time. If owners used their land acceptably, he assured productive farmers, they could continue to farm their land with his good wishes. However, he said loud enough for all peasants to hear, "land unused except for contemplation by its owner" was going to be seized. "Therefore, by expropriating [only] idle land we are protecting the good producer, the efficient producer, protecting him in this way from the natural pressure of the landless peasants."[41]

On the other hand, peasants had to be schooled in the methods and equipment of large-scale farming, and that took time. "Ultimately, agrarian questions had to be fought out in the National Directorate.... The collegial character of the Directorate may have contributed to the indecisiveness of Sandinista agrarian policy, which tended to drift with changing tides of political circumstances. Even when decisions were made, basic issues were often left unresolved and policy remained ambiguous."[42]

Yet for all of the headaches of agrarian reform, between 1979, when Somoza fell, and 1983–84, Nicaragua's total acreage in agricultural production increased slightly. More importantly, however, acreage devoted to the domestic market—feeding Nicaraguans—jumped by about 10 percent, from 842 acres to 944 acres.[43]

*   *   *

That the Sandinistas made any progress in the countryside was all the more remarkable for having been accomplished while holding their new arch-enemies, the "Contras," at bay. The Contras—an appellation from the Spanish word, *contra*, meaning "against"—began as a militia of former National Guardsmen. The militia took on a variegated profile as more farmers, unwilling to accept the loss of their land, took up arms. In 1980 the Contras were a corps of perhaps 120 fighters; over the next two years they were joined by a small force led by former Sandinista Edén Pastora and the men of several native tribes from the Atlantic seaboard. Importantly, the Contras were funded, trained, and equipped by the U.S. Central Intelligence Agency.

The Contras' disruption of Sandinista agrarian programs was severe. Moreover, when the Sandinistas responded to the threat by impressing young Nicaraguan men into the army, it was not popular, especially in the countryside. In effect, the Contras turned Nicaragua's interior into a war zone with all of the attendant economic disruptions. "The shortage of labor and the destruction occasioned by the continuing civil wars," Perez-Brignoli wrote, "decidedly conspired against developing a plantation-style agriculture and reinforced the traditional preference for cattle ranching."[44]

Throughout its early years, the Sandinista government was forced to govern with one hand while defending its very existence with the other. Typical of Contra tactics was a raid in which a squad slipped across the border into Nicaragua and detonated explosives beneath a 400-foot bridge over Rio Negro. The attack fouled commerce by interrupting traffic on the Central American Highway. When Ortega accused the CIA of complicity, Washington pulled out photographs of Soviet and Cuban ordinance being shipped into Nicaragua for the Sandinista army. This tit-for-tat continued, with the United States arming the Contras and criticizing the Sandinistas for defending themselves. Indeed, the Sandinistas frequently had to take extraordinary measures to win a war being waged within its own borders. At one point, the Brazilian navy intercepted a Libyan ship delivering arms to the Sandinistas. The ship's bill of lading showed it was delivering medical supplies.

In March 1981, Ortega took the opportunity of a speech before the U.N. Security Council in New York City to explain his view of the conflict. "When our revolution triumphed," he said, "we felt that it was necessary to normalize relations with the United States within a new framework of respect and cooperation, despite the historical fickleness of U.S. policy. In this spirit, I met in Washington in September 1980 with President Carter, and we must acknowledge that an effective dialogue then became possible.

"This mutual disposition to readjust and improve relations between Nicaragua and the United States was brusquely affected in January 1981 when the new administration [of Republican Ronald Reagan] assumed the presidency of the United States.... The new administration had proclaimed in its electoral platform action aimed at, among other things, destroying the revolutionary process in Nicaragua and halting, at all costs, the process of change in the Central American region."[45] He went on to elaborate nine points where agreement might be reached, citing a willingness to "begin direct and frank conversations" with the Reagan administration if the United States would stop its support for the Contras. Such talks were not to be. In April, Edén Pastora, the erstwhile Sandinista hero who was now a critic, declared that the Sandinistas had betrayed their own revolution, and the Contra attacks continued. When the attacks finally tailed off, it was less because of the Sandinista army's strength than the Contras' inherent weaknesses. The CIA simply was not getting the job done, and Reagan administration got tangled up in its own duplicity. When the CIA went so far as to mine the

Nicaraguan coasts, some members of Congress were appalled. Congress held back a $21 million allocation to the CIA-Contra operation. At the same time, the governments of Honduras and Costa Rica lost patience with cross-border raids from their territory that were sullying their countries' reputations in Latin America.

In 1982 and 1983, other Latin America nations heightened their efforts to curb the war, which the Sandinistas refused to call a "civil war" like the one raging next door in El Salvador. President José López Portillo of Mexico, invited to Managua to accept a "Sandino Prize," used the occasion to ask the United States to give up its clandestine campaign. Then Colombia, Mexico, Panama, and Venezuela suggested 21 principles of mutual respect between the Contras and the Sandinistas, a list known as the "Contadora" proposal. When Jerry Brown, the former governor of California, and a delegation from the United States sat down with Ortega to explore the usual questions, they tried his patience with questions he felt were impertinent and irrelevant. Wasn't he Marxist-Leninist? That was "secondary," Ortega replied, to being a Sandinista. Wasn't Nicaragua a threat to its neighbors? "How can anyone with even a minimum of intelligence," Ortega replied impatiently, "believe that Nicaragua would want to invade its neighbors?... Wouldn't the United States love to see us do that?" Well, Brown persisted, "If you are not a threat to your neighbors, then why did even the Carter administration, which had originally aided the revolution, withdraw support?" Ortega shot back: "On the contrary, Carter continued to defend aid to Nicaragua until he left office.... Perhaps $55 million of that $75 million was disbursed. The rest of the aid was canceled by the Reagan government."[46]

In fact, at this time the Reagan administration was approaching a low point in international guile. Congress, trying to prevent the administration from interfering in Nicaraguan affairs, specifically passed legislation prohibiting the movement of U.S. arms or equipment to the Contras. It was later disclosed in congressional hearings, however, that the administration had secretly sold U.S. arms to an otherwise hostile Iranian government in order to invest the profits in further arming the Contras. Alas, the deceitfulness did nothing to strengthen the Contras, and only contaminated the Reagan administration's reputation. "The contra army sustained by the [Reagan] administration's creative financing was no closer to defeating the Sandinistas in 1988 than it had been in 1982," wrote historian Gilbert, "but the war did impose enormous social and economic costs on the revolution. Over 20,000 had died in the fighting; thousands of others had been left maimed or crippled. By 1985, the war had generated 5,000 orphans."[47] A 1990 summary by the United Nations that accompanied the eventual disarmament agreement documented that there had been a total Contra army of 21,863 guerrillas, several times the size of the Sandinista army that drove Somoza from power.

* * *

As the Contra threat subsided, it left behind strong anti–Sandinista sentiments that would find expression in electoral politics. Nicaragua's economic prospects were troubled by shrinking global markets and the protectionism of other countries. At the same time, the Reagan administration, having lost its surreptitious war, kept trying to dissuade international lenders from extending credit to Nicaragua. Nevertheless, a "surface calm," to use historian Gilbert's phrase, settled over the country. Nicaragua was approaching its first democratic election since Sandino himself lived. That calm was occasionally interrupted by Ortega's inability to rein in his cantankerous personality.

In early 1983, Pope John Paul II flew into Nicaragua for a visit. The atmosphere was tense because Catholic clerics were still deeply split over whether to cooperate with the Sandinistas. The Pope used his appearance to publicly admonish a Nicaraguan cleric who was serving as a Sandinista government minister. He even jerked away his pontifical hand when the priest knelt to kiss his ring at the airport. Ortega — a long way past his alter-boy youth — was miffed. Rather than make what was supposed to be a welcoming speech, he delivered a lecture. He reminded the Pope of Nicaragua's long, tortured history of having been picked on by outsiders, especially the United States, without benefit of protection by the church. The Pope flew away, leaving behind the formidable Nicaraguan Archbishop Miguel Obando y Bravo — whom he elevated to cardinal — as his spokesman and rabid opponent of the Sandinistas.[48]

The incident only highlighted the continuing social and political divisions. On the eve of the revolution's fourth anniversary, Ortega continued his refusal to embrace a conciliatory stance toward opponents. Asked if approaching elections would require the Sandinistas to depart from at least some of their original goals, he replied sharply. Those policies, Ortega snapped, were "proposed, drafted, developed, and then made public and guaranteed by the Sandinista National Liberation Front. It's important to make clear that the program which we are calling the 'original' program was entirely prepared, discussed, and approved by the FSLN.... That is to say, at no time was any agreement or political pact made with another political force."

The Sandinistas, he continued, had reached out to Nicaragua's leading individuals, including Violeta Chamorro, and persuaded them to go along with Sandinista goals. "They were asked, 'This is the Sandinista front's program. Do you support it?'" If his opponents had since changed their minds, well, the election would be their chance to do something about it.

"A campaign was developed to portray the revolution as betrayed," Ortega maintained, "as having cast aside the spirit of the original programs and as having radicalized the process to its own detriment. In reality, the original program *demands* a radicalization of the process— that is, a deepening of the process. Measures such as nationalizing exports and banks are radical; striking blows at the large economic holdings of *somocistas* and at large landholders with idle land by means of the agrarian reform — all these are profound measures that logically come into conflict with the interests of those who had another type of program in mind. The FSLN has consistently applied the original program. It has not been diverted from its course for a moment."

Yet for four years, Ortega lamented, teachers sent to rural schools to implement Sandinista improvements were assaulted by Contras; young men impressed into self-defense battalions were resentful; and the United States had continued to block international lenders from providing needed credit. Throughout these travails, Ortega said, the Sandinista government had been seen by the world at large as a moderate, non-aligned, viable nation. "How else," he asked his interviewer rhetorically, "could you explain Nicaragua's election to the United Nations Security Council in spite of U.S. opposition and its campaign to block that election?"[49]

Ortega's remarks, however, were all about pressures from outside the Sandinista fold. There was also trouble inside, where personalities chafed. Once the decision was made to go ahead with the election, Sandinistas faced the equally important task of choosing a candidate. That candidate, on the one hand, had to win the votes of moderates, and, on the other, build upon the Sandinistas' hard-won legacy. Miranda and Ratliff offered a look inside the intramural wrangling, their view perhaps colored by Miranda's own place in the pecking order. The *comandantes* were particularly wary of the possibility of the candidacy of Edén Pastora, the fabled Comandante Cero, because they were jealous of his popularity and distrusted his being "an uncontrollable social democrat." Another possible contender was Tomás

Borge, the last surviving founder of the FSLN and a man whose reputation was burnished by his having been subjected to brutal treatment by the Somozas. But Borge could not get over his animosity toward Humberto Ortega, who had been safe in Europe during much of the Somoza years. Miranda remembered that "Borge often described Humberto as 'a petty-bourgeois opportunist who only knows how to talk about revolution in foreign cafés.'" For his part, Humberto dismissed Borge, a short man, as "a vainglorious dwarf who thinks that revolutionary merit comes only at the point of a pistol."

Nevertheless, Borge was a man whose opinion had to be respected, and he looked with affection on Daniel Ortega, who had both fought shoulder-by-shoulder with the Sandinista army and also suffered torture in Somoza's jails.[50] In fact, Miranda and Ratliff also disparaged Humberto Ortega as a manipulator, describing him as "prepared to ally himself with anyone if that suited his needs at the moment...."[51] As petty as these observations may seem, they demonstrate something of the slippery ladder that Daniel Ortega had to climb, and did.

In May 1984, Nicaraguans made their choice. They chose 61 Sandinistas to a 96-seat National Constituent Assembly, and they elected Ortega president. After the election, however, animosities continued to run deep. Not only were Sandinistas still nose-to-nose with COSEP and the merchant class, tension continued between the government and religious and labor leaders. In the countryside, a three-month campaign to forcibly relocate more than 50,000 rural families began in an attempt to institute land reform. As late as autumn 1985, Ortega announced a suspension of Nicaraguans' civil rights. It was necessary, he insisted, to protect the nation against agents of U.S. subversion who were "within certain political parties and the press and religious institutions."[52]

Criticism of Sandinista tactics came even from the Socialist International, the vice president of which declined an invitation to speak at Ortega's inauguration. The Socialists grumbled that "those of us who believe we have done so much for the Sandinista revolution feel cheated because sufficient guarantees were not provided to assure the participation of all political forces."[53] The Roman Catholic Church kept up its criticism, and the relatively broad internal opposition led by *La Prensa* caused Ortega to censor and then temporarily close the newspaper.

In response to criticism, there was movement toward toning down some economic programs, including in agrarian reform. "In 1985, Daniel Ortega won new stature in both state and party, leading some to conclude that the collegial rule of the FSLN was breaking down. In addition to becoming president of Nicaragua, Ortega was named 'coordinator' of a newly created 'Executive Committee' of the National Directorate."[54] Ortega met with foreign mediators—including Costa Rican President Oscar Arias Sánchez, who would win a Nobel Prize for his efforts—to resolve once and for all the conflict with the Contras.

It became clear that despite damage to the treasury caused by the war and the U.S. trade embargo, the Nicaraguan economy was progressing. Improvements were possible in healthcare delivery and education. But social and economic gains came at a political cost, and Ortega proved himself still capable of wielding an iron hand. "The Somozas closed *La Prensa* many times," Violeta Chamorro complained, "but they didn't confiscate it like the Sandinistas. Ortega says we were financed by the CIA. That's the pretext they used to close the paper from June 16, 1986, to September 19, 1987, when they allowed us to reopen only after intense pressure by the international community."[55]

Also, Ortega tended to answer critics by defining the Sandinistas in relation to the social analysis of Marx and Engels, weaving in assertions that were more rhetorical than real. By this time, his long experience in making his way through the jungles and among the egos of the other *comandantes* stoked his inclination to say just about anything. Asked about his philosophy, he would cite the usual pantheon of Latin American heroes—Venezuelan Simón Bolívar, Cuban José Martí, and Mexicans Hidalgo, Morelos, Zapata, and Villa—as worthy disciples of Marx and Engels. Such men had not been bound by dogma, he said, but inspired by the obvious needs of the poor and the working class. Augusto Sandino, of course, was cut from the same cloth. "The Sandinista movement understands revolutionary ideology," Ortega said, "and it doesn't ignore Marxism or fail to treat with respect the Great October Revolution. [But] our movement never set out, at any time, to elaborate an ideology. Its actions are determined by very specific goals: To expel invaders; to promote social change on behalf of workers and farmers; and, in order to achieve these goals, to depend on the workers' vanguard, the Army of Defense of National Sovereignty...."[56] Now that the formerly shy and unassertive Ortega had talked his way to the presidency, it was hard to get him to be quiet.

Indeed, for all of his philosophizing, Ortega was not overcoming an image as a kind of international brat, the little guy from the little country who caused capitalists such big headaches. In January 1988, Ortega made an official visit to the Vatican for an audience with Pope John Paul II. The Pope, who no doubt remembered Ortega's lecture at the Managua airport, promptly turned the tables, admonishing Ortega to loosen civil restrictions and broaden democracy. The Pope's manner, treating the diminutive Ortega a bit like a schoolboy, was, according to observers, "more abrupt" than they'd ever seen him display with a foreign leader.[57] Despite such public conflict with the church, however, Ortega was careful to keep his religious obligations in order. Historian Dennis Gilbert pointed out that Ortega had "quietly baptized his [seven] children—perhaps to satisfy his very Catholic mother."[58]

As Ortega's first presidency drew toward a close, he hardly needed to pick fights with the Pope to find problems. The Soviet Union, a Sandinista sponsor, was crumbling. In public, Ortega sounded nervous, scolding Nicaraguans "not to overstep their right to criticize the government.... Everything has its limits.... He who sows the wind reaps the storm." From the border came reports that several Contra leaders and their Honduran supporters had been murdered. The inflation rate was put at 36,000 percent, and the Nicaraguan *córdoba* was said to be without real value. A Sandinista austerity program called for the elimination of 35,000 government jobs, including 10,000 men and women in the army and 13,000 members of the national security force. To garner what approval it could, the Ortega government eased controls on the media, liberalized election statutes, and released political prisoners, including former Somoza supporters. Within weeks, 1,894 former National Guardsmen were set free and re-entered Nicaraguan society.

In the United States, Democrats and Republicans were still divided, with former President Jimmy Carter talking to Sandinista leaders while Vice President Dan Quayle, representing the new administration of President George H.W. Bush, visited Contra field emplacements. Bush himself seemed to want it both ways, continuing the U.S. embargo and calling Nicaragua "an unusual and extraordinary threat" while asking Congress for $9 million to promote fair elections. Liberals condemned the request as interference in Nicaraguan affairs, and conservatives criticized giving money to the pro–Sandinista Supreme Electoral Commission.

*   *   *

Attention was focused on the commission as people inside and outside Nicaragua asked the same question: Would Ortega allow a fair election, and, if so, would he step aside if defeated? The first three days of voter registration filled the books with 1,336,342 names out of a total population of 1,970,486 eligible voters. A poll sponsored in part by *Nuevo Diario*, a pro–Sandinista newspaper, predicted in late October that Violeta Chamorro was leading Ortega by 11 points.

Ortega, attending a conference in Costa Rica that included Latin American leaders and President Bush, intemperately said he was revoking a 19-month-old truce with the Contras. The announcement was like a bombshell. Bush called Ortega "that little man" who was like an "unwanted animal at a garden party." Indeed, Ortega's abrupt remark flew in the face of international reports suggesting progress in Sandinista-Contra talks. Even the oldest Sandinista of all, Tomás Borge, said the Contras were winding down operations. Cynics saw in Ortega's behavior evidence that he, too, had seen the polls and was desperately trying to rally support. He even threatened to attack Honduras. The episode passed when Central American presidents reached an agreement by which the Sandinistas stopped helping the Salvadoran rebels and both the Salvadorans rebels and the Contras would stand down.

Despite Ortega's histrionics, he, too, stood down after Violeta Chamorro thrashed him in the election. Fears to the contrary proved unfounded. Ortega announced the Monday morning after the weekend election that his government would abide by the results. There was a collective sigh of relief when Ortega stepped aside and Chamorro stepped to the microphone for her inaugural speech. Ortega and the Sandinista had made the important transformation from armed rebels to defeated democrats. In fact, authors Miranda and Ratliff noted wryly that during the electoral campaign even Ortega had learned to smile like a politician. He was less of a scowling soldier and more of a statesman. He "became much more at ease in public during the course of the 1980s and even smiled a lot and became 'hip' during the 1990 presidential campaign."[59]

Chamorro, who continued her opposition to Sandinista policies through the years, had won the presidency with 55.2 percent of the popular vote. Ortega got 40.8 percent. Nicaraguans had pulled off that *sine qua non* of modern rebellions, the peaceful transition from a military regime to a democratic one. A transition agreement negotiated between Chamorro and the Sandinistas assured that certain Sandinista programs would be preserved. They were also allowed to keep the property they had acquired. "The Sandinista decision to accept the electoral result also was influenced strongly by the bright international spotlight then on Nicaragua," added the realists Miranda and Ratliff, "deriving in large part from the presence of thousands of pre–election and election day observers.... So the Sandinistas accepted the vote on the negotiated terms and tried to make the most of it by securing for themselves, while they were still in office, an enormous chunk of property and power for the years ahead."[60]

Chamorro's victory had required cooperation among some 20 partisan groups from across a wide political spectrum. They banded together into a coalition of 14 parties. Approximately 86 percent of Nicaragua's eligible voters participated. In the National Assembly, Sandinistas won 38 of 90 seats, and in local elections their power was similarly diminished.

All of those numbers added up to an enormous political accomplishment by Nicaraguans. Because the 1990 election bridged the chasm between a military movement and electoral politics, it was "possibly more important for the future of Central America than any other elections in the region's history," according to a report published by the University of Pittsburgh. The report concluded: "The principal technical characteristics of the elections, including successful negotiation by all parties over electoral rules, highly competent and even-handed administration of the election by the *Consejo Supremo Electoral* (CSE), a low degree of systematic coercion by any of the contending parties, a basic level of human rights protections, the broad ability of the parties to participate in the process, albeit with unequal resources, has led the Latin American Studies Association (LASA) Commission to a judgment that the process, although occasionally problematic, was fundamentally democratic."[61] Observers speculated that a big part of the Sandinistas' defeat was their agrarian policy.

During her administration, Chamorro drastically reduced the size of the army, which had been built up to counteract the threat posed by the Contras. The army was reduced from 96,000 to 15,000 soldiers even as peace brought a major reduction, if not elimination, of violence in the countryside. A devastating inflation of 13,500 percent was brought under control. And, not surprisingly, the abrasive and debilitating friction between the National Assembly and the Office of the President that raged during the Ortega term abated.

Nicaragua's democratic successes did more than call attention to the tiny country. It also shone a light on U.S. policies and attitudes over the decades. The University of Pittsburgh report noted the "long-standing pattern of U.S. interference in Nicaraguan affairs."[62] That interference included public statements, right up to election day, that the balloting would be flawed. "Owing to the presence of so many international observers, however, the United States was forced to accept the validity of the election, in contrast to its behavior in 1984, when in the view of the LASA delegation ... the Reagan administration used a combination of diplomatic, economic, and military instruments in a systematic attempt to undermine the Nicaraguan electoral process."[63] In 1990, there were still plenty of problems to go around, including Nicaragua's lack of experience with civil discourse. "Violence at campaign rallies increased during November and early December," the report said, "and loomed as a very serious problem."[64] There were threats against officials at all levels, an unfortunate characteristic of Nicaraguan politics that continued. Importantly, however, not only was Nicaragua changing for the better, so were the Sandinistas. They were recognizing the need for a change in attitude from one of armed arrogance to political persuasion. "The FSLN has made a transition in recent years," the University of Pittsburgh noted, "from a more elitist style to a more inclusionary one."[65]

After the election, Nicaraguans asked each other the same questions heard in all democracies. How could the polls that predicted an Ortega victory have been so wrong? The answer, it seemed, was that as many as 10 percent of poll respondents who said they were voting for Sandinista candidates did not. Fears of reprisal were set aside in the secrecy of the voting booth. Responses to pollsters made clear that many Nicaraguans blamed the Sandinistas for economic problems, for the military draft, and for being unable to get beyond the sterile hostility with the United States.[66]

Post-election analysis also allowed for calm reflection on the accomplishments of Ortega's presidency. Renaldo Antonio Téfel, an original member of the "Group of Twelve," saw progress: "From my vantage point, I see many concrete achievements of the revolution. Certainly, doubling the student population from 500,000 to one million, the literacy campaign, the enormous proliferation of unions and cooperatives and community organizations, the neighborhood CDSs— Sandinista Defense Committees— throughout the country, the participation of the people, the fact that the people have learned to speak. *That* is the more important thing. It's extraordinary! The humblest people are not frightened in front of the TV."[67]

* * *

When the presidential election of 1996 loomed, Nicaraguans' capacity for democracy was again tested. Hard feelings— indeed, periodic violence —continued to raise the fundamental question as to whether Nicaragua would slip backward. Outside observers, like a volunteer fire department, were called to the scene. Ortega was again a candidate, and Nicaraguans were still capable of dividing their political thought a dozen ways. "Lingering distrust and continued political polarization influenced Nicaraguans again to look to external actors to provide the guarantees and confidence to carry out the October 20, 1996 elections," said a report by the Carter Center in Atlanta. Identification of eligible voters, registration, verification to the satisfaction of all political factions, transportation of voters from remote villages, and secure, accurate, and verifiable counting of ballots all were issues. "[T]he fact that between 11 and 12 percent of the votes were nullified in the various elections and that a dozen parties submitted appeals indicates the need for a serious evaluation of the process."[68]

This time, the elections were described by the Carter Center's report as "extremely complicated." Once again, there were the simultaneous, often conflicting, never gentle, forces of a small nation. Nicaragua continued to be rent by new factions and ancient hatreds. There were actually six elections, a new election-law-and-oversight commission, and provision for twice as many polling stations as there had ever been. "The fact that the two largest parties [a new coalition called *Alianza Liberal* and the Sandinistas] together won 88 percent of the vote reflects an emerging biparty system, but one that is polarized around two ends of the ideological spectrum."

In the balloting for the National Assembly, no party captured 60 percent of the seats that would have been necessary to change the constitution. For the Sandinistas that meant they would be able to deal themselves in on any fundamental change only by cooperating with other parties. In addition, according to the Carter Center, "The 1996 elections also demonstrated a greater commitment of the Nicaraguan society to the rule of law. The campaign was an improvement over 1990, free of violence and harassment of political parties ... a remarkable achievement for a country with its history of divisions and traumatic conflict."[69] The *Alianza*'s presidential candidate was José Arnoldo Alemán Lacayo, who was never mistaken for being anything like the agent of compromise that Violeta Chamorro had been. Alemán was a dyed-in-the-wool rightist. Thus the race between Alemán and Ortega was a clear choice between right and left.

Or was it? "Sandinista Daniel Ortega, professing himself now *an ex–Marxist*, is one of the two major presidential candidates," noted the *Washington Post*. "The other, playing right to his left, is the former Managua mayor Arnoldo Alemán. Each characterizes the other as irredeemably authoritarian...."[70]

Alemán won about 896,200, or 51 percent, of the votes; Ortega took 665,000, or 38 percent. The other 11 percent of the votes for president were spread among 17 minor candidates. "Mr. Alemán's apparent victory," concluded *The New York Times*, "completes a stunning transformation of the political landscape in this country."[71]

If Nicaragua's political pendulum had swung to the right, however, it would not stay there long. As democracy opened the political environment to free expression, Nicaraguans were taking full advantage. Parties sprouted and split. In 2000, the Sandinistas and their principal opponents— the Constitutionalist Liberal Party, or PLC— agreed to change the election law to allow the president to win without a majority. The law now allowed a 40-percent victory, or, if the leader had at least a 5-percent lead, a 35-percent total. The agreement anticipated, as had been predicted, the nation's becoming a two-party system and allowed for some loss to minor parties. What happened, however, was that the PLC itself split.

Ortega won the presidency with a bare 38 percent of the vote. The PLC candidate got 27 percent, and the candidate of its erstwhile allies, the Nicaraguan Liberal Alliance (ALN), took the other 28 percent. The few percentage points remaining were peeled off by minor candidates, including the hapless Edén Pastora, the man once known as *Comandante Cero*, who got 0.29 percent.

However, the important story was not to be told in a neat tally of presidential percentage points. In the twenty-first century, rare is the political leader who can claim to be the captain of his or her country. Drought, evaporating international credit, disappearing water supplies, lack of food — every kind of discomfort known to man, and many only recently discovered, has visited executive mansions in search of solutions. By the summer of 2008,

Nicaraguan news media were filled with headlines of woe and stories of despair. "The food crisis passed being a threat to become a daily reality," said the Managua daily newspaper *La Prensa*. "one that strikes countries like Nicaragua with great force, according to the farmers appealing yesterday for help from the government."[72]

Under such pressure, Nicaraguans, like many others, have tended to take to the streets to protest practically anything. In the summer of 2008, Nicaraguans could not understand how President Ortega had reached an agreement with former President Alemán, who was being investigated for corruption. Ortega, they cried, was letting Alemán off the hook. The agreement reinforced their conviction that the government was incapable of either honesty or effectiveness. Ortega, aware of their discontent, had warned them not to demonstrate. The people ignored his warning. *La Prensa* described the result: Under the headline, "Who said fear?" and "Thousands march in defense of democracy, against Ortega, hunger, and the value of life," the article began: "The Government over which Daniel Ortega presides was shown yesterday that his mandate of the night before [when the agreement was sealed] was rejected. Thousands of people of different social classes marched in Managua to demand respect for democracy and to protest against his government, hunger, the dearness of necessities, and the 'institutional dictatorship' that they believe exists thanks to his agreement with the Liberal ex–President Arnoldo Aleman, who has been accused of corruption. Enough! We want democracy! Was the cry in chorus."[73]

Unable to provide solutions—if, indeed, there were solutions—Ortega and the Sandinistas responded with more ham-handed politics, and their opponents replied in kind. In November 2008, elections were held in cities and towns across the nation. Sandinistas were, again, accused of stealing those elections. Robert Callahan, the U.S. ambassador, immediately threatened to withhold $64 million in antipoverty aid until Ortega could prove that Sandinista mayors were legitimately chosen.

Demonstrations followed, street fights erupted, and shots were fired. The conflicts continued into December as anti–Ortega marchers converged on downtown Managua, only to be attacked by Ortega supporters throwing rocks and ripping up the marchers' paper signs. The *Washington Post* carried an article that began: "MANAGUA — The U.S. Embassy has been accused of counterrevolutionary subversion. A nervous Catholic Church is appealing for calm. The opposition party is crying electoral fraud, while roaming gangs armed with clubs are attacking marchers. The mayor here has called it anarchy. And everyone is asking: What is President Daniel Ortega after? This sounds more like the Central America of the 1980s."[74] Perhaps, but at least it did not sound like the 1880s, or even the dark years of the Somoza regime, and that was progress.

Luís Inacio Lula da Silva
Brazil's Diminutive Giant
1945 –
(Brazil)

The election of Luís Inacio Lula da Silva as president of Brazil in 2002 has been compared to the election of Salvador Allende, a communist, to the presidency of Chile more than three decades earlier. Allende, of course, was killed in a military overthrow of his democratic government, while Silva's election proved to be a testament to Brazil's civic stability. That stability has only been found, however, after centuries of political turmoil — including military overthrows — that continued well into Silva's early life. Both Silva and his older brother, José, spent their share of time in jail for political activity. Yet Brazil's institutions — and its military's forbearance — allowed Silva to be re-elected in 2006 with 61 percent of the vote. In fact, the biggest obstacle to Silva's re-election was a corruption scandal that reached deep and wide into his own administration. Withal, Silva is still widely seen as a true hero of the left. He is a man with almost no formal education who was raised to his lofty stature on the shoulders of his country's organized laborers, who are themselves the basis for one of the world's fastest growing economies.

*   *   *

On October 6, 1945, Luís Inacio da Silva was born in Garanhuns in the state of Pernambuco, in the northeast of Brazil. That area, it is said, is filled with Silvas, a veritable chorus of proud cousins. Luís was the seventh of eight children born to Eurídice Ferreira de Mello and Aristides Inacio da Silva. Aristides owned a small plot of farmland and also worked as a laborer. He left the home when Luís was an infant to look for work on the docks of Santos, forty-five miles down the coast from São Paulo. Thus Aristides was part of a migration that took millions of Brazilians out of the hinterland in search of jobs. Luís did not meet his father until he returned home to visit when Luís was five years old.

In 1952, when Luis was seven, Eurídice piled her eight children into the back of a wooden-frame truck to join Aristides at the coast. The trip took 13 days. When they arrived, Eurídice found her husband living with another woman, his second cousin, and their four children. No doubt disheartened, but undaunted, Eurídice settled her family into a poor neighborhood of Guarujá, a beach resort. By this time, the family had grown. With Luís and his mother were not only seven brothers and sisters, but three cousins as well.

Almost from the time he could first walk, Luís contributed to the family income by selling peanuts, oranges, and coconut tapioca in the streets. He also, at his mother's insistence, got enough schooling to complete several elementary grades, which none of his brothers did.

According to historians Emir Sader and Ken Silverstein, Luís did not learn to read until he was ten years old, and then only after his mother kept sending him back to school every time he "escaped."

In 1956, Eurídice took the children to São Paulo, a city that was in many respects the very heart of Brazil. Paulistas, a proud people, have provided a great deal of the energy that has shaped Brazil into a force in the hemisphere. In São Paulo, Eurídice moved her family into the neighborhood of Ipiranga. They lived in one room behind a bar, where they shared the bathroom with patrons. Luís worked the streets as a peanut seller and left school behind forever after fourth grade in order to hold jobs as shoe shine boy and office messenger. By age 12, Luis had found his first full-time job with a dry cleaner.

He later worked at a warehouse in São Paulo before getting a job at a screw-manufacturing factory. It is said that his excitement at this "real" work was so great that after his first day at work, Luis wore his dirty overalls home and showed his mother his hands, artfully soiled.

* * *

By entering his country's working class, young Silva was enrolling for a priceless education. He would learn not just a trade — steel worker — but the art of politics and the science of leadership. He would become part of the history and drama of an elephantine nation in which the country's other poorly educated workers had been deprived of their rightful place for 470 years. For if Silva's time as a leader was coming, it was because Brazil was finally evolving into an industrial power that could no longer ignore the demands of its workers.

From its beginning in 1500, Brazil's enormous size — it is to Portugal as the United States is to Maine — exhibited forces that constantly threatened to pull it apart. Its self-reliant regions exerted a powerful centrifugal force, at first against the designs of Portuguese planners, and later in defying the centralizing efforts of its own government. The Portuguese were not even able to organize Brazil's shipping resources sufficiently to transport sugar to eager European markets, depending instead on Dutch bottoms. Brazil's unmanageable size continually tipped its future away from fulfillment of its enormous potential. In addition, Brazil's rambunctious mixture of peoples frequently had trouble agreeing on common goals. Gilberto Freyre, a harsh observer of his country's character, attributed the erratic nature of Brazil's centuries to its original settlers, whom he found incapable of setting a firm course if it meant missing their siesta. The Portuguese colonizer, he wrote, was "a vague figure ... [w]ith no absolute ideas ... inclined to a voluptuous contact with exotic women.... No one was less rigid in contour, less strict in the lineaments of his character.... rather a clinging tradition of ineptitude, stupidity, and salaciousness."[1]

When Brazil's sugar industry faltered in the late seventeenth century because of slackening world demand, Brazilians sought ways to broaden their economy. The first choice was trading, and a merchant class developed in coastal cities. It rose as the power of large landowners waned, and the landowners, in an attempt to protect their prerogatives, launched a campaign of violence and prejudice. They condemned the merchant class as "New Christians," or, that is, crypto-Jews. The landowners' campaign was in vain, however, as during the early eighteenth century the merchants found alliance with gold and diamond miners from the interior. Then mining, in its turn, made its own contribution to chaos as a flood of immigrants searching for minerals invaded the interior, the traditional land of native tribes. It was in this environment that Portuguese authorities had trouble collecting taxes or exercising control. Economic power shifted from northeastern farmland toward the southeast coast, and civil control evaporated in both places.

"Portugal had never governed, nor could it rule, by force," observed historian Colin MacLachlan. "At the end of the eighteenth century only 2,000 regular troops scattered along the coast, most officered by Brazilians, provided an illusion of strength.... When the relationship [between Portugal and Brazil] came under a significant stress the cause was economic. In the latter part of the century the mother country ran a huge trade surplus with Britain and an equally large deficit with its colony."[2] Portugal had become a middle man, a broker, and a weak one at that. MacLachlan, in fact, described Portugal's role as "parasitic." At the beginning of the nineteenth century, Napoleon Bonaparte's invasion of Portugal hastened the inevitable. The invasion put to flight the Portuguese crown and 10,000 Portuguese citizens with whatever wealth they could carry. They were protected across the Atlantic by the English navy as they hastily relocated to Brazil. The colonizer was seeking refuge in his own colony, a colony that henceforth would chart its own course.

Brazil was self-sufficient when Crown Prince Pedro's father returned to Portugal. So Pedro, left as regent, quietly ushered the nation into independence as a constitutional monarchy in 1822. Thus the gargantuan offspring, with huge expanses unexplored and unexploited, began its struggle toward political maturity, a process that would stretch into the present. Brazil's political adolescence has been manifest in many ways. In the realm of religion, the constitution of 1824 both declared Roman Catholicism the official religion of the state and protected freedom of worship. Historian MacLachlan suggested that the result was less than rigid: "In colonial Brazil," he wrote, "under frontier conditions clerics became ever more lax, a tradition that carried over into the empire. Clerical celibacy remained an idea, but a highly theoretical one.... A folk Catholicism emerged unimpeded by dogma."[3]

Socially, Brazil's huge African population has labored to fully integrate itself. In 1831, the emperor was pressured by enlightened advisors to sign a treaty ending the slave trade, but not slavery itself. The landed aristocracy was outraged, especially when some slaves saw the end of slavery as near and ran. By 1885, the number of fugitives was legion, but the authorities, including the army, refused to enforce laws enacted to hold slaves on their plantations. Moreover, the economy at that point was so vibrant that runaways easily found work in cities and seaports as free men and women. Even in areas where diehard slave owners held out, some of them were forced to hire freed Africans to work alongside their slaves. Slavery thus atrophied before an 1888 law ended it altogether. When the royalty was ousted a year later, many landowners supported republicans against the monarchy that had freed their slaves.

So the republic was born with a social and ethnic chasm that still exists, despite Brazil's reputation as an ultraliberal society. While some former slave owners delighted in the fall of the monarchy that freed their slaves, others envisioned an economy in which freed slaves would be cheap farm labor. For their part, former slaves were trapped. They had "lost the perceived paternalism of the empire and gained much less than they hoped."[4] Indeed, devotion to the hand that freed them was so strong that black monarchists' organizations lasted at least into the 1930s.

This racial division invites comparison with the United States. "Both Brazil and the United States endure the self-inflicted stain of slavery and its lingering consequences. Shared experiences, from the relatively static condition of bondage to the fluid one of race in a free society, challenge both countries. The Brazilian myth of a racial democracy, now on its last legs, sharply contrasted with the now defunct American myth of 'separate but equal.'"[5] Brazil's freedom from monarchy and its slaves' emancipation came fully seven decades—two generations—after Latin America's other peoples had won their independence and their slaves had been freed. Which is to say it came at about the same time that Reconstruction ended in the United States, with Union troops leaving behind a conquered Confederacy. Thus both Brazil and the United States trudged toward the final years of the nineteenth century — and beyond — dragging with them the heavy prejudices that are the detritus of racial oppression.

Another aspect of their similar histories, however, has had very different consequences. That is in the realm of military participation in government. Despite the shaping of U.S. history by its armies in the Civil War and during Reconstruction, civilian government has prevailed. Not so Brazil. The Brazilian military first earned the gratitude of republicans by supporting their overthrow of the monarchy. Subsequently, the military has periodically saved Brazil from civic chaos. But, in general, from the early days of the republic right up to the 1970s, the Brazilian military has loomed over democratic institutions, holding the whip hand in the country's political development. It was, after all, a military government that would throw Silva and other labor leaders in jail in 1980.

* * *

The imprisonment of Silva and his comrades was the inescapable result of Brazil's history of laborers on one side of the ramparts, and oligarchs and (most) military officers on the other. Brazil's military has never been far from the elbow of presidents, choosing them, throwing them out of office, shaping their policies, and protecting them from the wrath of workers. The first president of Brazil, Marshal Deodoro da Fonseca, reshaped his iron allegiance to the crown into a strong central government, and the military made short work of turn-of-the-century rebellions. When the army put down a small proletarian movement among shoe makers and textile workers that was organized by Bolsheviks, attitudes on both sides were hardened for centuries to come.

Because Brazil's imperial tradition lasted well into the Industrial Revolution years, it left a legacy of scorn for laborers that historians describe as feudalism. In inland agricultural areas, medieval practices — like holding laborers to the plantation that first hired them — persisted even as farm laborers propelled the economic growth of the mid–nineteenth century. Even when the Brazilian government began to provide interest-free loans to attract European immigrants, contracts were written not for workers, but for vassals, who were bound to their employers. Many immigrant farmers had to share the production of individual plots with landowners. Immigrants finding jobs on coffee plantations were oppressed despite the fact that it was those very laborers who helped preserve Brazil's coffee economy, which had been in decline.

Although government-sponsored contracts worked in recruiting laborers, leading to some 60 inland colonies of European immigrants, most Brazilian landowners dismissed the arrivals as second-class. Between independence in 1822 and 1880, 400,000 immigrants flooded into Brazilian ports, four of ten of them Portuguese. Many others were Italians, who flooded into Buenos Aires, Argentina, to the south, and Germans. But later, as more immigrants were Asians, ethnic prejudice deepened, exacerbating labor's position in Brazilian society.[6] Brazilians had been hoping to emulate Argentina, Chile, and Uruguay, where the arrival of substantial numbers of European immigrants had enhanced prosperity.

At the time, Brazil's leading Europhile "social scientists" were touting an imagined value of European immigration. This contention was met head-on by spokesmen for the Afro-Brazilian community, setting up a confrontation that persists to this day. Indeed, after programs were mounted to attract immigrants — from as far away as Japan — continued well into the twentieth century, it became clear that ethnic prejudice would create turmoil even as Brazil acquired an international reputation for being a relatively tranquil melting pot. More to the point, the wide variety of cultures making up Brazil's working class made it all the easier to keep divided. In general, workers remained unorganized and cheap. While other Latin American countries spawned labor movements, Brazil did not.

Even Brazil's coffee economy was diminished early in the twentieth century when over-production lowered prices, sending coffee workers—with their reputation for docility—into the job market. When Brazilian rubber plantations looked like a substitute, English companies in India and Malaya burst that balloon. Over time, the elites of the three principal coffee states—Minas Geráis, São Paolo, and Rio de Janeiro—parlayed their management skill, their infrastructure, and their aggressiveness to remain Brazil's most powerful areas. Between quarrels—some of which could be called wars—the Paulista coffee oligarchy united with the agricultural elites of São Paulo and the dairy farmers of Minas Gerais to dominate, under the wing of the military, national politics. The combination, known to Brazilians as *café com leite*—or, coffee with cream, because of the ethnic combinations—laid a stone wall of control that would only be breached by the labor unions and their political movement at the beginning of the twenty-first century.

Historian Mauricio A. Font has written that Paulistas led elites to dominance of Brazilian politics by not allowing other groups to weave themselves into the fabric of change. The strategy was superior to that of their counterparts in Colombia, where the coffee-growing elite allowed itself to be divided into two parties, Liberal and Conservative, which were susceptible to infiltration by other groups. "In Colombia," Font wrote, "a polarized and conflict-ridden two-party system ... amplified localized demands and conflicts, [but] that of São Paulo tended to absorb and fuse them, something which reinforced centralization." Paulistas pressed elite demands, co-opting journalists and intellectuals. Paulista elites even accentuated their uniqueness as leaders by stressing their descent from the robber barons who built Brazil. "It is true that Big Coffee elites looked at the past glories of the *bandeirante* for a powerful and energizing myth to clothe their naked claims to ascendancy.... The goal was control in every sense, and it was achieved.[7]

Though it may be hard for modern observers of Brazil to understand, elites fortified their position with a certain Puritanism. Inhibited by a colonial lack of self-confidence, Brazilians tightened up social rules. In 1886, for example, it was the actress Sarah Bernhardt who had shocked Brazilians into recognition of the beauty of Copacabana Beach. Theretofore, bathing in the ocean had only been a practice of the poor. Bernhardt got Brazilians' attention not only with her "bathing suit"—which must have impressed every young man fortunate enough to glimpse it—but actually wore it into the water. "Bathing" began to attract a higher class of practitioners and became so popular that in 1917 Rio de Janeiro's city fathers wrote stict rules of seaside protocol. Civic boosters began improving the appearance of their cities and building the infrastructure—from trolley lines to sewer lines—suitable for a growing industrial power. The advent of World War I brought "a booming wartime export economy [that] increased the middle class and expanded employment opportunities at all levels."[8]

After the war, a series of barracks revolts, led by young officers, were aimed at opening government to broader participation. Also, industrial growth added to the pressure as people like the Silva family flowed in from the hinterland to crowd the cities looking for work. The economy grew enough to allow a reduction in imports as Brazilians learned to make their own goods for domestic consumption. The flowering of these political and economic shoots was the election of Getúlio Vargas, the candidate of the masses. In 1930, Vargas displaced the oligarchs' president, Washington Luís, ushering in a new day. Such was the fervor of the day that though Vargas actually had lost the election to Julio Prestes de Albuquerque, 1,000,000 votes to 700,000, Vargas's muscular masses declared the election a fraud, threw Prestes out of office, and put their man in.

The Vargas presidency would become a touchstone for political activism in Brazil, and the "Revolution of 1930" was an effervescent time. Labor organizers arrived from Spain, Portugal, and Italy. Anarchists, communists, and socialists joined Brazilian intellectuals in declaring that the people's day had come. Ominously, however, a series of regional revolts during the 1930s demonstrated just how strong the centrifugal urge among Brazil's states was. The revolts were upsetting to centralists, and they raised a loud alarm in the barracks. In 1932, São Paulo state was in an armed conflict with Minas Gerais, which was allied with Rio Grande do Sul. For the most part, the battle was over each powerful state's rotating right to choose the national president. Then, in 1935, rebels in three cities demanded establishment of soviet republics. They were led by Luís Carlos Prestes, an army officer and a communist. Security forces under President Vargas discovered their plan and stopped them, but just three years later the presidential palace was attacked, this time by a band of fascists! To add to the ideological confusion, the Vargas regime first tried to emulate Germany's Nazis, and Brazilians' general pro–Axis sympathies caused the English navy to blockade the Brazilian coast. Eventually, Brazilians changed their minds and cooperated with the Allies, leading to organization of a strong steel industry that supported the Allied war effort; the government finally declared war on Germany.

The Vargas regime lasted until 1945, the year Silva was born, and by then, at the beginning of the Cold War, Brazilian communists had grown in electoral power. They were publishing their own newspapers and showing concentrated strength in Rio de Janeiro local elections. Though communists still represented less than 10 percent of the Brazilian electorate, Brazilian leaders, dutifully accepting their assignment from the capitalist powers, outlawed the Communist Party in 1947. Nonetheless, the party was able to capitalize on its widespread acceptance among Brazil's working class and remained organized. It went underground, and its members supported Vargas's return to the presidency in 1950.

Although his second term would end in tragedy, Vargas oversaw a significant broadening of the electorate, raising the hope that Brazil's masses would one day choose their own political future. In 1930, two million Brazilians had voted; by 1945 that figure had tripled to six million. Industrialization was enfranchising a wider range of middle- and working-class voters. In 1954, the end of Vargas's presidency came when a political rival was almost assassinated — and his bodyguard was killed. Although Vargas had not been informed, the assassination attempt was arranged by one of his friends, and Vargas was blamed. Humiliated, Vargas committed suicide.

His spirit lived on, however, in the continuing string of left-leaning leaders who followed, and, in fact, in Brazilian democracy in general. The next president was Juscelino Kubitschek (1955–60), a man who managed to toe the military's line. Then came João Goulart in 1961–64, who stepped over it. Both Kubitschek and Goulart sprang from Brazil's irrepressible populism, a full-spirited, infectious, exuberant view of political possibilities. By then, in spite of the dour tone of the Cold War, millions were falling in love with the Brazil's signature musical style. In fact, Kubitschek was dubbed "the bossa nova president." Brazilian workers began manufacturing automobiles—first, Mercedes cars and Scandia trucks—on a scale that drove the country's economic recovery. This combination of determination and style is the tradition from which Silva would emerge, but Kubitschek and Goulart were not so fortunate. In the view of the United States government, they were dangerous leftists. Kubitschek met fear of his liberality head-on, launching ambitious plans, including round-the-clock construction of Brasilia, the inland capital. Brasilia would open the unpopulated interior and a network of highways to allow exploitation of Brazil's otherwise inaccessible resources. Just as importantly, a capital in the interior would finally create a counterbalance for the powerful coastal cities.

Finally, a measure of Goulart's importance to the labor movement was that during his tenure, unions, though still weak, began to show strength of purpose. Brazilians were exercising an independence of thought that ran contrary to what conservatives—domestically, the Brazilian military, and externally, the United States—found acceptable. Goulart took a well-publicized trip to the People's Republic of China, which U.S. policy at that point refused to recognize as a legitimate government. The Brazilian military, no doubt prodded by its foreign patrons, lost its patience with Goulart and overthrew him in 1964. The country slid back toward political darkness. Its working class faced further oppression. The evolution of Brazilian syndicalism was over, wrote historian Leonicio Martins Rodrigues. "The government intervened and union directors were arrested; others were exiled or went underground. Their positions were occupied by replacements or governing councils named by the government. Cooperative organizations—like the Workers General Command and the Pact for Unity and Action and so on—were dissolved.... Political activity by unions was severely prohibited and the activities of professional organizations had to be strictly limited to the protection of their own interests."[9]

* * *

At the time, young Silva was unable to find steady employment. Such was his luck, indeed, that he lost the little finger of his left hand in an industrial accident in 1964, when he was 19 years old. In January 1966, he finally found a job at Villares Industries, a large metallurgical company, and succeeding years would transform him from a callow, shy, apprentice tradesman into a leader. He was proving popular enough among his fellow workers that they gave him the nickname "Lula"—the Portuguese word for "squid." Lula's enthusiasm and abilities were clear enough for his supervisors to usher him into a training program at a local technical school. For three years, he studied mechanics and lathe operation, and although he would later acquire a high-school equivalency diploma, Lula would disparage such schooling as meaningless compared to his training as a metal worker.

He had found his calling, but he wasn't interested then in union membership, much less a role as a leader. Lula had long heard his brother José, known familiarly as "Friar Chico," extolling the virtues of labor solidarity. His words were ignored by brothers and cousins alike. "All the rest of my family was anti-union," Lula would later recall. "Union members were seen as only thieves [and] all their leaders were crooks." Whenever José cranked up one of his speeches about the importance of unions during family discussions, "everyone would be against him."[10]

With developing skill and steady work, Lula was headed toward marriage and family. He was focused on improving his own and his family's lot in life and ready to let others fend for themselves. He wanted to work at an automobile factory because "people in the automobile industry got something like ten raises a year ... they had houses, they were the first to buy televisions, the first to buy cars." He saw them at Christmas, he recalled, "loaded with boxes of toys for their kids."[11] It was at this point that Lula married, but lost his wife, Maria de Lourdes, to hepatitis during childbirth only months later. He was remarried three years later to Maria Leticia, the widow of a murdered taxicab driver. They have five children.

Lula's lack of interest in union membership persisted even after he went to work for Industrias Villares on the outskirts of São Paulo. It was a union shop, but Lula worked there for four years without joining. Finally, brother José, by this time a member of Brazil's underground Communist Party, talked him into investigating syndicalism. "It was in 1968, at the beginning of the year, when he invited me to accompany him, and it was my first union meeting." His first, perhaps, but more than a decade later he remembered the issue under discussion and his strong view on the subject.

Nevertheless, Lula's joining of the Metalworker's Union was undertaken casually, and once he was in the union he was lackadaisical about his position. Nevertheless, presumably because of his intelligence and vigor, he rose quickly in the ranks. It is probable, in addition, that his diffidence was a simple matter of caution. He was conscious of his lack of formal education, and his opinion had not changed that most, if not all, union leaders were, like politicians, full of hot air.

That view was not far off the mark. During that period all of Brazil's recognized unions, including the Metalworkers, were shot through with hypocrites. Since the 1930s and the Vargas government, unions had worked hand-in-hand with the government. The Consolidated Labor Law of 1943 formalized a system in which union members were protected, but much as domestic pets are protected. The law, amended over the years but not eliminated, authorized only those unions that carried the imprimatur of the national Labor Ministry. By defining rules of recruitment, membership, and size, the nation's nearly 5,000 labor organizations were kept fragmented and docile. It was the ministry that collected the workers' periodic dues— the all-important "check-off"— imposed yearly taxes, and controlled union bank deposits. All workers, whether union members or not, paid a day's wages every year. The ministry hired and fired union officials and ruled on the legality of strikes. No union organizers were allowed on factory floors, and limp-wristed negotiations were conducted between management and representatives of the Labor Ministry. Union officials, protected in their sinecures, were of no mind to challenge their protector. It was, to say the least, a paternal system. It included social and health-care programs, but an individual's chance of advancement in the union hierarchy depended on his kowtowing to government officials. When union people showed too much independence, they were sacked. Strikes were almost completely banned.

In the first six years of the military government, the labor minister intervened in 536 labor cases, more than 400 of them in the regime's first two years. The ministry expelled from their jobs more than a hundred union leaders and their supporters in Congress. Illegal strikes were harshly repressed. "For virtually the next decade, unions rarely challenged the regime, either on ideological or financial grounds."[12]

This was Lula's classroom. His rise as a leader would only be possible on the shoulders of his comrades insofar as they were able, as a class, to modify Brazilian law and reform Brazilian politics. That task would last for decades, during which several of his comrades would be killed. The Metalworkers Union would have to grow beyond the confines of its members' own, relatively narrow concerns— higher pay and better conditions— in Brazil's burgeoning economy. Its leaders would have to extend their reach into wider social movements, leaving behind the tools of the factory floor and taking up the causes of farmers, native tribes, Catholic activists, and the poor. Their final destination would be a brand-new political party, one that would transform Brazilian political life.

The metal workers' journey traversed a landscape affected by two other broad conditions of the day: Liberation Theology and the Cold War. On the left, the papal encyclical *Pacem in Terris* had set in motion thousands of small struggles by Catholic clerics and laypeople to relieve the problems of the poor and accomplish social injustice. On the right, industrial barons and the traditional Catholic hierarchies of many Latin American nations, including Brazil, were discouraging any opening toward liberality because of their fear of godless communism. The result was a period of conflict that lives on in Brazil's collective memory as the "dirty war." The Metalworkers Union was expanding its appeal right into the teeth of those conflicting philosophies.

Brazil's workers had been restive since the Kubitschek and Goulart administrations failed to deliver on programmatic promises. Under the military regime, however, there was little they could do to express themselves. In government circles, the meritocracy once encouraged by Vargas had long since yielded to cronyism, and the military government pulled the reins still tighter. For the overall economy, that was good. The generals' continual intervention in union affairs held wages down and added to productivity. Between 1968 and 1974, Brazil's gross national product grew at an astounding average annual rate of 11.2 percent. Its rate of industrial expansion was even higher. During the same period, the percentage of Brazilians in poverty was being cut in half, to one out of four. "Not coincidentally," noted historians Emir Sader and Ken Silverstein, progress "was accomplished during the time of the most rigorous repression."[13]

Critics spoke up at their peril. Dissenting members of Congress were sent home. The constitution was suspended. Demonstrations were squelched, and virtually all political and civil rights were suspended. Student protestors in the cities were repressed, guerrillas operating in the countryside were pursued, journalists were found dead, and enemies real and imagined were imprisoned or killed. To justify its wage-suppression, the government ginned up statistics that were totally false and misleading, but the ruse would not be uncovered for years.

In the late 1960s, Lula, later saying that it was only a lark, accepted nomination to a minor position in the union. He would serve as a substitute member of the board. Still in his twenties, Lula had earned a reputation as a good guy, but he was not considered a firebrand. It may be — he later speculated — that he was put in the seat because he was considered easily manipulated, like others who were trading their integrity for a chance to rise in the union ranks. Whatever the circumstances of his choice, however, he was on his way up in the officialdom of the 140,000-member São Bernardo Metalworkers Union. In 1972, he was chosen First Secretary. Diminutive, modest Lula, the man who'd aspired only to be the best metal worker in Brazil, had found a new calling. "Lula, whose personal background was integral to his success as a union and political leader," wrote historians Sader and Silverstein, "played a crucial role in labor's early stirrings."[14]

The task the union assigned to Lula was to explain to members their government benefits. It was a singularly bland assignment, seen as a dead-end. Lula, however, used the post as a way to learn what was on union members' minds. The most important thing he learned was how little the union hierarchy knew of workers' goals. The workers were timid about speaking out in an environment of government oppression and general upheaval. Leftist guerrillas' tactics included kidnapping, bank robberies, and the assassination of Brazilian soldiers. Many of those guerrillas operated from bases across the border in Chile until 1973, when General Augusto Pinochet led a coup that deprived them of their territory. Similarly, it was three years later that Argentine generals overthrew the troubled government of Juan Peron's widow, locking the southern core of the continent in military dictatorships.

In Brazil, however, conditions began to improve, if tentatively. Ernesto Geisel, serving as president under the watchful eye of the military, indicated the beginning of a gradual liberalization. Historians have compared the Brazilian military's task to the slow, thoughtful release of a tiger's tail. "The length of transition was notable," wrote historian Margaret Keck, "as were the military's attempt to maintain control throughout much of the process and the unwillingness of key democratic political forces to precipitate a decisive rupture with the authoritarian regime...." The role of Brazil's military had become so ingrained in the country's consciousness, and the fissures running through society were so deep, that the population remained hesitant, watchful. "Studies of the Brazilian transition have produced a somewhat schizophrenic view of the past several decades of the country's history," Keck continued. While civil restrictions were somewhat relaxed, and the upward flow of suggestions, complaints, and demands increased, also obvious were "the persistence of clientelist and patrimonial relations."[15] Brazil's military, even as it smiled and reached out the hand of fellowship, kept its other hand on the hilt of its sword.

At that juncture in Brazil's history, Lula, too, was at a crossroads. On the one hand, he was popular with his mates in the Metalworkers Union, but in the larger world outside union halls, events were unfolding swiftly. As he rose to the top of the Metalworkers Union, he had to show he was up to handling more complex, more dangerous affairs.

In 1975, Lula was elected president of the Metalworkers with 92 percent of the vote. That lopsided margin, however, must be judged in light of Lula's suspicion that he was being made president because he was a good guy, easy to slap on the back and then ignore. His predecessor as president and the man who had nominated Lula as his successor, Paulo Vidal, was just such a man. He had run the table of union jobs and was now moving into a sinecure in the government's bureaucracy, where he would help oversee unions. Vidal likely figured that Lula would be quietly incompetent, shy, and trustworthy. That would allow Vidal to continue his domination of metalworkers' affairs on behalf of the government. "At that time I had never spoken over a microphone," Lula has said. "I had to read my acceptance speech — the only speech I've ever written — which I could hardly do because I was shaking so.... [A]lthough we'd won the election it was really hard to preside over the union. Paulo Vidal was still the secretary general, much more experienced, much better known among union leaders, a much more experienced orator, and a much better communicator."[16]

As president, however, Lula learned. He traveled, he talked to people with much more schooling, and he listened. When brother José was jailed for his organizing activities, Lula started losing his insecurity. "After my brother went to jail I stopped being afraid. If struggling for what he was struggling for were a reason to be imprisoned and tortured, then they would have to arrest and torture a lot of people.... It was good in that it awoke a very strong class consciousness in me."[17] Lula opened discussions with union members and other leaders as to possibilities for concerted action. The government, wary of this new-found aggressiveness, kept an eye on him, but Lula had no provable connections with subversive groups.

To force Lula's hand, Vidal put him to a test. Metal workers were tangled in a dispute with Ford Motor Company. Vidal acceded to Ford managers' proposal that an assembly be convoked inside the main plant. Lula wouldn't buy it. He believed that the setting would intimidate his workers. He issued a contrary order, adding the admonition that from then on if there were decisions to be made relative to the metal workers, either he or his vice president, not the secretary general, would speak for the union. "It was Lula's declaration of independence," wrote historian Keck.[18]

Not all solutions were so simple. The military government and the labor movement were at loggerheads even as they tried to find some way to coexist. Union leaders knew who had the guns, and the generals had no stomach for endless confrontation. Both knew that while they were butting heads, the global economy was knocking at Brazil's door. Industrial employment had reached almost five times what it had been in 1950, and jobs in the service sector were multiplying almost as fast. The progress was admirable, but union leaders knew that even as employment had risen, wages had fallen. Per capita income was rising, but income was unevenly distributed. Brazil's economic train was chugging along, but not everybody had a ticket. By the time economic growth slowed in the mid–1970s, fully 13 percent of the people in inner cities, 26 percent of the residents of surrounding areas, and 44 percent of Brazil's rural families were still stuck in poverty.[19]

It was time for some plain talk, and in mid–1977, the Metal Workers Union sharpened the terms of debate. The union published the results of a study it had commissioned. How, the study asked, had wages continued to stagnate even as the economy flourished? The study made the answer brutally clear. Put simply, government economists had been falsifying national statistics, especially in the measurement of inflation. Workers' demands for more money had been regularly brushed aside by specious arguments. The workers' pockets had been picked.

The union's study explained the hoax. It was clear that metalworkers' wages, over the preceding decade, should have risen by 34.1 percent more than they had been allowed to. When the union petitioned for redress from the government, however, its members were disappointed. They took their case to the courts, but failed there, too.

For many working-class Brazilians, however, what the study showed transcended statistical charts or even the court's decision. The study was hard evidence that government and business leaders were crushing their hopes for justice. To turn the tables, they concluded, the labor movement had to transform itself into a political party. Emotions were running high, allegiances were being formed, and Lula recognized the sea change in Brazilian affairs. "The 1977 campaign definitively transformed Lula into a leader," wrote historian Keck.[20]

But political machinations did not come easily to him. Lula had always believed that workers lived in one world, politicians another, and his world, he believed fervently, was the former. But student and worker movements were growing in numbers and organizing themselves to take advantage of the government's announced intention to "open" the system. The old Left was fading in importance and new groups, spurred by human-rights advocates, were trying to find their places. Exiled labor leaders, intellectuals, and even guerrilla commanders were being allowed to return. Many of them were contributing to an increasingly dynamic dialogue in newspapers and magazines. The metal workers were being called upon to do their part in forming a workers' party.

"1977 was a year in which various sectors of society screamed out to find a little bit of oxygen," Lula would say later, "to breathe a little more. Everyone complained, including the workers. But the workers did not publicly protest. A number of times we were called to take part in other movements, but we were always suspicious, worrying about getting involved in something that wasn't directly related to workers...."[21]

These years were critical and eventful. Labor showed it could hold together, attract the sympathy of many other Brazilians, and mature into a political force. When Lula's São Bernardo union struck Saab-Scania, the truck maker, it "was Brazil's first large-scale strike in a decade — and it was also the first time Lula ever spoke to a strike assembly."[22] The union demanded a 20 percent pay raise and the right to direct — as opposed to following government-named spokesmen — negotiations with the company. The strike attracted 80,000 workers by the end of its second week and spread to Ford, Volkswagen, Chrysler, and Mercedes. The final settlement won a 24.5 percent raise. "The great victory," Lula said, "even more than the wage increase, was that we forced the companies to negotiate an agreement directly with the union without government interference."[23]

The strikes spread. When the metal workers called for a general strike in 1979, a huge soccer stadium had to be rented to hold the 80,000 workers who showed up for its organizational meeting. "When we arrived," Lula said, "the fences, the stadium, the grass—everything — was occupied.... The sound didn't work, and I was alone like a clown on top of the table. The "clown" made himself heard for four hours, even holding onto his audience when it started to rain. Later, when the government declared the strike illegal, Lula wasn't deterred. "The strike can be considered illegal, but it is just and legitimate because its illegality is based on laws that weren't made by us or our representatives."[24] When the government closed down union offices in three cities and blocked assemblies at the soccer stadium, the strike was over, but workers still won a 15 percent raise — less than they wanted.

After the strike, despite their pledges, companies fired some returning workers, and the unions could do nothing about it. Pro-government members of Congress declined to help, and opposition members were impotent. Moreover, the government was showing that it would not hesitate to strong-arm strikers. An important union leader was shot and killed during a disturbance at a São Paulo factory. "[S]trikers should be prepared to confront increased violence from the regime," wrote Sader and Silverstein. "Whereas in 1978 there were few direct clashes, as most strikers remained on workplace premises, 1979 saw state and capital working hand in hand. Companies forced workers on to the street, and police were soon on hand to repress pickets and other strike activity." Which is not to say the workers gave up and went home. In 1979, there were 113 strikes involving 3.2 million workers in 15 states, "one of the biggest strike waves in Brazilian history."[25]

Lula, like other union officials, was targeted for smear campaigns designed to shake workers' confidence in their leaders. "The problems were enormous after 1979," Lula would remember. "Already at the end of the year, members of the directory were talking among themselves, and everyone understood the following: Lula was finished helping the workers and was becoming an obstacle for them. Why? Because all of the conservative forces in the country and everyone who wanted to hold onto power was going to prevent Lula from moving forward."[26]

To the dismay of Brazil's conservatives, however, worker solidarity was building. In addition to learning to trust their leaders, union members—and, for the first time, Lula—were beginning to accept the necessity of *political* action. The strikes began over wages, "but in struggling for wages, the working class won a political victory.... Second, I think these fourteen years during which strikes were prohibited left not only bosses but also union leaders unprepared ... I, for example, had never been in a strike, had no experience. And, finally ... I think the worker realized how much his work is worth."[27]

Against this backdrop of tension, the military government undertook its plan to reshuffle political parties in preparation for the return to free elections. Although the armed forces intended to hold onto power until 1991, the chartering and registration of official parties began. The new parties would replace the old, token two-party system that pitted the promilitary *Alianca de Renovacão Nacional* (ARENA) against the toothless *Movimento Democrático Brasileiro*. The new array called for six parties, including the labor unions' *Partido dos Trabalhadores*, or PT. The biggest party, by far, was the *Partido do Movimento Democrático Brasileiro* (PMDB), a presumed middle-of-the-road party. The PMDB has been described by Argentine scholar Torcuato S. Di Tella as "the great organization that battled the dictatorship and, because it was the biggest party in Brazil, eventually exploded into a thousand pieces, some ideological and some simply regional."[28] As the military government tried to tiptoe offstage, the PMDB immediately proposed a constitutional amendment allowing direct presidential elections. The proposal, at first rejected, would eventually prevail.

In their design of the new party system, pro-government thinkers surely hoped that leftist forces would do what leftist forces had so often done—divide and conquer themselves with internal arguments. But this time leftists were not so naive. Sorely disappointed in the watery support they'd gotten from "opposition" members in Congress under the military regime, leftists realized they had to squelch internal wrangling, pull together, and send stiffer spines to Congress. Lula's position in all of this was as an *autentico*, one of the labor leaders whose forthrightness had bonded them with workers. Too many other leaders had been willingly manipulated by the government, and *autenticos* joined in the call for a truly independent workers party.

At the time, although laws regulating civic activities were being liberalized, the government still laid a heavy hand on civil liberties. Habeas corpus was restored, but the president retained the power to declare a "state of siege" and suspend Congress if he declared the state imperiled. The president also continued to dominate all financial issues; his authority overrode Congress in budgetary matters. Public workers, including bank employees, still could not strike. If the military was allowing reform, it was doing so in the tiniest of increments. As a result, Lula and other labor organizers, social activists, and progressive clerics were not so much marching to a new beat as easing their way through a minefield.

Later, Lula would look back on the work of inspiring workers to take up politics as made easier by the obstacles placed in their path. "In fact, it was civil resistance that gave birth to the PT," he said. "We went on strike when it was forbidden to do so. We created the PT against the advice of most of the left...."

Indeed, elite antagonism was not the only thing that brought workers together. The left also failed to understand the need to reach out to groups historically dismissed as hopelessly bourgeois. "The Left has learnt a lot about politics from the PT," Lula continued, "but it still seems not to have realized that you can't make politics without the participation of the people. Not enough attention is paid to the whole issue of people's awareness. Today there are thousands and thousands of small entrepreneurs, shopkeepers, taxi-drivers, and people of all kinds who do not feel that the PT represents their interest. It is not enough any more to talk to the worker at the factory gate.... We must broaden our discourse to address his various interests, as a citizen, as a consumer, as a family man."[29]

On May Day 1979, the *Partido dos Trabalhadores* was ready to issue its first first manifesto. The document declared that "the exploited and oppressed have the permanent necessity to maintain organizations to offer resistance ... to the oppression and privileges of the dominant class." By early 1980, the party was a reality. Historians Sader and Silverstein called the PT "the first political party in the country's history that was not formed at the behest of the elite."[30] Organizationally, the PT's most radical characteristic was that it required cooperation among its branches in Brazil's historically inner-directed cities and states, which often pursued goals at cross-purposes. To meet the requirements as a national party and qualify for participation in the coming transitional election, PT formed 627 municipal commissions and built its certified membership to nearly 300,000 voters. PT's central board expected every local and regional branch to contribute to the formation of national policy and, once that policy was formed, unite behind it.

"The Worker's Party is a historical innovation in this country," Lula said. "It is an innovation in political life and an innovation in the Brazilian left as well.... It is a party born out of the consciousness that workers won after many decades of serving as a mass to be manipulated by bourgeois politicians ... Only the workers can win what they have a right to. No one ever has and no one ever will give us anything for free."[31]

In the spring of 1980, 200,000 metalworkers from across the São Paulo area kept up the pressure for change by striking for higher wages, a cut in the work week from 48 to 40 hours, and job security. When 100,000 strikers gathered again at the soccer stadium, army helicopters hovered overhead, and troops with submachine guns menaced them on the street. Fully 1,600 labor activists were arrested, among them Lula. The State of São Paulo was put under military control, and the government seemed to be pursuing a policy of crushing the life out of the labor movement. Lula was convicted and sentenced to three and a half years in jail, but the judgment was reversed on appeal.

The immediate criticism of the *Partido dos Trabalhadores* was that it would be hijacked by traditional leftist — that is, European — ideologies. Lula rejected that argument with his usual direct language. "It's time to finish with the ideological rustiness and self-indulgence of those who sit at home reading Marx and Lenin," he said. "It's time to move from theory to practice. The Workers Party is not the result of theory, but the result of twenty-four years of practice."[32] Historians Sader and Silverstein agreed. "The thorough rupture with Brazil's 'old left' is crucial to understanding the PT's birth and future trajectory," they wrote. "In addition to its political and generational distance from previous leftist organizations, there was also a general distrust of and disagreement with those elements of the left that survived the early years of repression.... Both wings of the reborn Communist Party were thoroughly different from the PT ... the PT consciously avoided too rigid a definition in terms of socialist ideology

Lula was being educated by Brazilian thinkers even as he'd once been schooled by metal workers. He was being convinced that the working class had to reach out in all directions, but never assuming that others would join them for anything so watery as "moral convictions." Brazilian Fausto Cupertino, drawing on the work of American economist James Burnham, rejected the facile notion that the power of industrial "owners" is diluted by legions of corporate shareholders who can be counted on to have workers' interests at heart. Rather, Cupertino argued, it is technicians "who control the corporate economy, who make the decisions not only as 'proprietors' in the strict sense of that term, but as technicians, or managers, and directors—people who don't function as simple salaried workers."[33] Lula, like many others, thought of Marx as outdated; the task was to find all workers, including managers and technicians, whose interests could be represented alongside those of the workers. Still pundits kept comparing the Brazilian movement with Eastern European, Cuban, and other socialist systems. Lula sarcastically dismissed the comparisons. Polish socialism "no longer interests the Poles," he said. And when the silliest of comparisons was drawn between Brazil, one of the world's great emerging economies, and Cuba, one of the world's smallest, Lula was similarly sardonic. "I've been to Cuba," he said, "and there all the bars and taxis are state-controlled. I think that's a lot of responsibility for the state."[34] Out on the street, Brazilians were less concerned with such ideological rumination. They saw in the headlines every day that production was falling and inflation was soaring. While reporters and their editors conjured idle comparisons, workers and their families were suffering. And they were concluding that new leadership was needed. At the First National Conference of the Working Class in São Paulo in 1981, a poll was taken among delegates. They were asked to choose their ideal leader. Nine percent gave their vote to traditional union leader Joaquím dos Santos Andrade; 46.5 percent picked Lula.[35] The military was not assuaged. Fifteen PT officials were arrested, organizational records were stolen from one regional party headquarters, another regional headquarters was destroyed by fire, and 30 party leaders, including Lula, were arrested.

*   *   *

Although the military did not intend to give up control totally until 1985, the election of 1982 was supposed to form the bridge from dictatorship to democracy. The campaign would be an early, national test between PT and its rough-hewn followers, and the PMDB, a larger, more sophisticated organization with a reputation for progressive thought and sophisticated analysis. PT members saw PMDB's leadership as having sold out to elites; PMDB intellectuals saw Lula and other PT leaders as a bit too rough around the edges to guide Brazil's future.

It was at that point that Silva became "Lula" in order to flaunt his popularity with his working-class mates—rough-hewn though they may be. Luís Inacio da Silva formally adopted Lula as part of his name, and the squid stepped up to the podium. Enthusiastic crowds chanted "Loo-lah, Loo-lah, Loo-lah." For them, the name change was a superfluous formality. They had their man; now it was up to Lula to lead them where he would — which, in 1982, was into a campaign to become governor of the state of São Paulo.

By then PT had enrolled 400,000 members. Although Lula lost his gubernatorial bid, the party reaped eight seats in the national congress, 12 state congressional seats, and 78 city council positions. Despite those achievements, however, the '82 elections were seen as a national failure by party loyalists because PT fell below the minimum 5 percent needed to be on the next national ballot and the 3 percent needed to be eligible in nine states. Only in two places did PT meet the legal criteria. In São Paulo, where Lula was on the ticket, the party got nearly 10 percent; and in Acre PT took more than 5 percent of the vote. Brazilians have a joke that Brazil is a nation of the future — and always will be. That possibility loomed for the *Partido dos Trabalhadores*.

Lula acknowledged the problem with his characteristic honesty. "In 1982, when I was a candidate for governor in São Paulo, I made a big mistake.... We created a narrative where I said, 'Lula, candidate for governor Number 13, ex-dye factory assistant, ex-lathe operator, ex-trade unionist, ex-prisoner, ex-I don't-know-what-else: a Brazilian, like you.' I imagined that the working class would understand by this: 'Wow, this guy is all this and is a candidate; we could do this, too.' But it seems that workers understood exactly the opposite: Nobody wanted to be a Brazilian like me. They wanted to be Brazilians with a university degree; they wanted to be Brazilians with better living conditions, with better schooling, with a better quality of life. Because of this mistake, I began to understand that we couldn't just assume that everyone would understand ... we can't be isolated, we can't speak only to each other."[36]

*   *   *

Tancredo Neves, elected president to oversee Brazil's return to civilian rule, died on the eve of his inauguration. That left the nation to plod ahead under Vice President José Sarney. Rampant inflation, which had been briefly brought under control, returned. It was pushed upward by overall economic growth and the rising wages it inspired. Within two years, the inflation rate was up to 1,038 percent. It reached 2,500 percent. A measure of the madness of the times was that President Sarney had to step in to defuse a nuclear-arms race, of all things, between Brazil and neighbor Argentina.

On a more sane plane, the PT had work to do. Lula and others inaugurated an educational campaign to convince politicians of the legitimacy of workers' goals. They took congressional leaders on fact-finding missions. They put their message before activist groups — even some illegal ones — in a broad effort to explain the labor movement to the middle class. Lula was among those who argued that leftist groups had a place at the side of workers. Assimilation, he insisted, would moderate leftists' tactics and make their goals more acceptable to a broader swath of Brazilians. In the sort of "big umbrella" strategy employed by the major parties in the United States, PT sought to reflect the interests of other progressive parties. All of this reaching out found some success, but it also made some politicians skittish about PT's efforts to attract leftists. In the middle of all that, there was an internal dispute. Leaders from São Paulo — accustomed to being the smartest guys in the room — insisted that they should define the party's future. Others rejected that idea if, they said, PT was truly a national party.

Thus, the PT was not only building itself into something brand-new, it was struggling against Brazil's old, old problem of regional divisions. Historian Keck believed that Lula's leadership helped turn the tide toward the broader view. After the 1982 election, "Lula and the union redoubled their efforts to develop a new relationship with the union's rank and file." To do it, they discarded the colorless prose Brazilians were accustomed to. In its place, they unleashed their Brazilian personalities. An artist devised the cartoon figure "João Ferredor," John Ironworker. Economic tracts were drawn as comic books. Caricatures voiced the zeal of labor organizers. The central purpose was to convince industry and the government that Brazil's workers' wages had been left behind when the economy found its way again. "With the wage-recovery campaign," Keck wrote, "Lula became a national figure."[37]

In the process, the party found new voices among its middle leadership, blending disparate, often contentious, forces and modulating somewhat the cantankerous world of economic debate. It was a task that would have tried the patience of a diplomat dealing with other diplomats, and Lula was dealing with working-class people, intellectuals, politicians, and rights activists who all shared a history of distrust and impatience. "In spite of widespread dissatisfaction with the inadequacy of internal political education and cadre development," Keck continued, "the amount of leadership renewal in the PT has been unusual by Brazilian standards. While the party's original leadership was mainly composed of people who had made a name for themselves in other organizations or as intellectual leaders, an increasing number of new party leaders have come up through the ranks. Although Lula remains the symbolic leader of the PT ... the party has had two other presidents, and there has been significant turnover.... Debates in *diretório* meetings and national party meetings are heated, and the position supported by party leaders (including Lula) is voted down with some frequency."[38]

The building of the party continued, and by 1986 Brazil was on the cusp of returning to full democratic government, replacing the military charter that had been in place for two decades. That year Lula was elected a PT member of Congress from the State of São Paulo, polling the highest number of votes in the nation. He was perfecting his role on the stage of Brazilian politics, but it was a stage that was changing from hard-handed military oppression to sleight-of-hand civilian chicanery. This meant Lula could no longer be leading man just by standing tough against the system. Now he had to figure out how to make the system work.

* * *

In 1987 Brazilians were awaiting the consequences that would flow from the nationwide Cruzado Plan. The plan created a new currency to stem inflation and ease the transition to civilian government. At the plan's core was a freeze on wages and prices, and at first it worked. Rising prices slowed, and domestically produced goods, better able to compete, began to replace imports on store shelves. Then, however, exports faltered, and Brazil's trade surplus had shrunk from $1.3 billion in May 1986 to a measly $136 million in March 1987. As the nation's holdings of foreign currency fell, so did its ability to pay down international loans.

The problems at first fell relatively evenly on all Brazilians, but as time went on the weight was shifted to the shoulders of the working class. Brazilian manufacturers figured out a way to beat price controls by holding their products off the market, knowing that limited supplies would drive up prices. Thus workers' wages were stuck in place while prices were not. Moreover, rising prices strained the government's ability to finance the economic and social programs that were needed to assure the people's allegiance; popular dissatisfaction grew.

Before affairs got really bad — and before the problem of inflation fully revealed itself — national elections arrived. The polling was set for November, and, true to form, the government continued to mislead Brazilians about the state of the economy right up to the wire. Most importantly, the government kept quiet about what was planned in response. The idea was to give the government's favored candidates time to ensconce themselves in power before turning the lights on. Potential candidates were still tightly controlled, and as the election approached, the generals and the industrialists revealed their presidential candidate, who was embraced, as if on cue, as an "honorary member" of PMDB, the middle-of-the-road party. In other words, he was rushed in from the wings. Predictably, he won, and his coat-tails pulled a PMDB majority into Congress.

"Then, in an amazingly cynical move," wrote historians Sader and Silverstein, "even by the shameful standards of Brazil's political elite, the Cruzado Plan's price freeze was ditched even before all the votes had come in." Eliminating the price freeze meant that workers' paychecks were devalued before the ink on them dried. Brazilians were furious. "The move provoked a flood of phone calls to electoral centers, with outraged citizens asking if it was too late to change their votes."[39] It was too late, but the high-handed policies of the government guaranteed continued conflict because Brazilians knew they faced more years under an incompetent administration. "Inflation for 1988 was close to 1,000 percent, a historical high, and wreaked havoc for all but the wealthiest. Between 1986 and 1989, three different national currencies were used."[40]

The shenanigans of 1987, however, jolted Brazilians into action. By the next year, broadened voting laws enfranchised all adults, including illiterates. As a consequence, in local elections Lula's Workers Party won 1,000 municipal council seats and 36 mayoralties. "In November 1988 the Workers' Party sent shock waves through the Brazilian political elite by winning the mayoral races in three state capitals (São Paulo, Porto Alegre, and Vitória) and twenty-nine other cities in Brazil (including many of the major industrial centers in São Paulo)."[41]

Because the Workers Party victories were spread across the country, party leaders decided it was time to launch Lula's first run at the presidency in 1989. The notion humbled Lula, he said later, conjuring thoughts of his mother, who had died in 1980. "She cried when I was able to get a job as a metalworker," he recalled. "Imagine if she could see me now."[42] Because of the liberalized voting laws, the election would be the first chance in thirty years for Brazilian parties to nominate their own candidates. It was also, however, the first presidential election that did away with plurality winners. To win the presidency required a majority. In multiparty systems, that typically required a run-off between the two top vote-getters. Thus both candidates go after losing candidates' voters, and often there are enough right-wing parties to patch together a majority for the conservative contender. So it was for Lula. He made the runoff, but ultimately fell short of election, drawing 47 percent.

Nevertheless, the campaign defined a classic challenge for a working class candidate to stand against a traditional elite candidate: the young and charismatic Fernando Collor de Melo. Brazilian political observers have noted that during the campaign Lula exhibited his learned ability for building coalitions that stretched beyond factory workers. That is, he was becoming a politician. By the time of the run-off, Lula had eased himself to the right to try to offset claims that a Lula victory would mean PT officials would be able to walk into Brazilians' apartments and take them for themselves. A Lula victory, Collor charged, would cause unrest that would end in "a bloodbath." Miriam Cordeiro, an old girlfriend of Lula and mother of his then-15-year-old child — whom Lula had long acknowledged — was hauled before the television cameras. She accused Lula of having offered her the money for an abortion. Later, a female Collor aide told reporters that Cordeiro had been paid $23,000 by the Collor campaign for her dreary performance. After Collor's election, however, there came a moment of cosmic balance. Before two years of his regime had passed, Fernando Collor de Melo was himself removed from office for corruption.

So Lula and the Workers Party returned to the fray again in 1994 and 1998, losing both elections to Fernando Henrique Cardoso. Lula's losses did not spoil his sense of humor. After losing in 1994, Lula was interviewed in his office at union headquarters by journalist Bernardo

Kucinski. He was described as "good humoured and lively. Telephone calls came in from all over Brazil." Lula was asked the central question of the day: Was socialism not dead in Brazil, given that some of its staunchest supporters had given up the ghost? He acknowledged that the question had split Workers Party members, but added: "Personally, I never supported what was called 'real socialism;' that is, the socialism that existed in eastern Europe until 1990. So I have no reason now to wring my hands and say I got it wrong.

"In fact, I feel more socialist all the time. If you can accept the fact that 80 percent of our wealth is concentrated in the hands of only 20 percent of the population, while the other 80 percent of Brazilians get only 20 percent of the wealth, then you can support the capitalist system of production. But I don't accept it." Such questions reflected most Western journalists' fascination with "socialism," not as it exists in Scandinavia or Belgium, but in its harsh permutation as Soviet communism or as it is portrayed by iron-eyed capitalists. Lula took another view. "Socialism was not the issue in the 1994 campaign; there was no ideological debate. The decisive issue was the new, stable currency, the *Real....* In fact, though the Soviet Union doesn't exist any more, anti-communism hasn't ended."

Then he turned his attention to another view of Latin America's emerging reality: "The Left is advancing in Latin America," Lula continued. "There was an extraordinary advance in Uruguay.... In Argentina the left opposition is growing. In Venezuela the social democrats won, but the Left is playing an increasingly important role. In Mexico, new forms of opposition are emerging. These are big steps forward for the Left. We must remember that until 1990 the Latin American Left didn't even meet to talk to each other."[43]

Commentators, however, were wondering if Lula's inability to get over the top in presidential elections did not mean it might never be possible for a union organizer — the unspoken subtext being a union organizer with limited education — to be elected president of Brazil. Lula, in his pragmatic way, was undaunted. "[M]embership in a union," he said, "can be taken as evidence — the same as membership in organizations that are overtly political — of one's interest in and connection to electoral politics ... one's relationship with electoral politics goes beyond objective conditions and takes on its own meaning."[44] Democracy — the campaigning and sloganeering and half-truths and sound bites — are a learned skill, Lula maintained. During his 1989 race, Lula said: "When I remember how the average São Bernardo worker thought ten years ago and how he thinks today, I realize my struggle may have been tiring, but it was worth it."[45] Lula, it seemed, was learning not just the art of politics but the science of political psychology.

That learning process was multiplied by the legions of workers who followed him. Through the years of the political campaigning, Brazilian workers were broadening their knowledge and effectiveness. They were also getting the encouragement and hard-nosed assistance of progressive members of the Catholic Church and other advocacy groups. With their organization, the workers brought warm bodies to a crusade that some priests and social activists had been conducting since 1964 and imposition of the military dictatorship. Then, when the unions were at their weakest, liberal priests and others had been the first to protest, passively but resolutely, against the conditions of their poor and working-class parishioners. Their cause was a natural fit with the Workers Party representatives who were spreading out to local labor disruptions. While those representatives did not recruit every disgruntled worker in the land to the Workers Party, they made sure every Brazilian knew where the union offices were. The union recruiters did well in areas where Catholic activists were organizing, where rural organizers were working with farmers, and where the poor were trying to find their voice. The movement flourished as a result of solidarity.

In the early 1980s, Workers Party influence had largely been restricted not only to factory workers (245,000), but to Paulistas (64,000, nearly twice as many as in any other major city). Catholic activists drew the party's efforts toward the north and northeast, where they were organizing the human dregs of Brazil's feudal past, the landless peasants. Those peasants' needs had gone virtually unnoticed by labor organizers, and the Catholic Church had at first supported the military for its restoration of civic order. But the church began its lean to the left — when the labor movement was still under the thumb of the government — in its battle to improve conditions in the countryside. The military government first promised to expropriate enough of Brazil's vast, largely unproductive plantations to settle 15 million peasants on the freed land. Then it got cold feet. When landowners objected, the grand plan fell on its face. "As is usual in Brazil, the powerful won the battle. The government never came close to meeting even its reduced targets for land reform."[46]

In the aftermath, the Workers Party lent a hand to church activists, helping form small nuclei that educated the people in preparation for local elections. Church activists had set up "Base Communities," and party organizers joined them. They focused on the Parrot's Beak region of the southeastern Amazon Basin. Lula, not wanting to scare off his new partners, stressed that the party's role was collaborative, not dominant. "The Workers Party doesn't intend to assume the tasks of the Church or of the union movement," he said. "Nor do we want to transform the Base Communities, the neighborhood associations, student groups or unions. In terms of effective organization, every sector of society should be organized.... And the political party has its own role to bring together these organizations at a regional and national level."[47]

Lula brought them together again in the 1998 election, edging still closer to the magic number, though his campaign style was still rough. "Lula was a charismatic figure," wrote historian Ted Goertzel, "and many people saw him as a savior who would lead them out of their misery. [But] Lula sometimes got swept up in the enthusiasm, and his rhetoric became more radical. At one rally in a remote Amazonian community he remarked, "Imagine if Christ came back to earth today ... what would he have been called? ... A communist, a communist.... [T]hose who would call me a communist would have said the same about him."[48]

* * *

What more than anything else was keeping Lula's electoral hopes alive was other leaders' inability to deal with Brazil's—and the world's—economic problems. Chaos was counting for more than campaign rhetoric. Most other leaders were flirting with, and succumbing to, right-wing notions of "privatization," the favored response of international lenders. Lula argued, on the other hand, that doing what international lenders asked did not keep them from leaving borrowers in the lurch without a backward glance. His opponent in 1994 and 1998, Cardoso, on the other hand, was glad to march in step with foreign lenders. "Cardoso's vision of Brazil's future included a proposal to convert state industries, like the telephone system, to private companies," wrote Goertzel. The idea ran afoul of the monumental decision by Russia in August 1998 to declare a moratorium on its payments to foreign creditors and to devalue the ruble. "The next day a billion dollars of investment capital left Brazil. The money kept flowing at about the same rate, day after day, until the government stemmed the flow by offering 49 percent interest rates to investors who would leave their money in Brazil. The Brazilian stock exchanges plunged with others around the world.... Lula and his supporters believed that the crisis confirmed everything they had been saying for years."[49]

That Lula was unable to turn his vision of Brazil's future into electoral victory had something to do with his style. Even some sympathetic observers called his campaign rhetoric a combination of naiveté and confusion. Also, Lula as a public figure elicited hostility from a certain sort of Brazilian voter. Many Brazilians were angry, and he presented himself not just as a candidate but as a target. "In his rhetorical style, Lula often seemed more angry than reassuring or empathetic," wrote Goertzel. "To many voters, it seemed as if he was cheering for Brazil's failures."[50]

Cardoso, however, eventually helped Lula make his case. Cardoso was an erstwhile leftist who had been forced into exile in the late 1960s. By the late 1990s, he had shifted to the right, and in doing so let his country down, in the eyes of many Brazilians. "By the time Cardoso ended his eight years in government," wrote journalist Sue Branford, "international capital had taken over huge areas of the Brazilian economy and the country was caught in a foreign debt trap of unprecedented proportions. Unemployment — and crime — had reached record levels."[51] Even supporters of Cardoso, an intellectual who spoke six languages, accused him of an inability to speak Portuguese in the plain words of the Brazilian worker. His policies, so warmly supported by international bankers, brought inflation under control, but led the economy knee-deep into mediocrity. Cardoso spent eight years presiding over policies that drove Brazilians to a level of impatience that cried out for change. In the meantime, Lula matured. He was ready for his fourth run at the brass ring.

* * *

For the campaign, Lula convinced his Workers Party brain trust that his platform — like those of President Bill Clinton in the United States and Prime Minister Tony Blair of Great Britain — must be more moderate. He was trying to bring into camp that last three or four percent of Brazilian voters who had eluded him. Cardoso had been elected on a promise that he would lead Brazil away from domination of the United States and toward leadership of Latin America. But despite two full terms, he'd failed. Journalist Branford noted: "Although it is by far the largest country in Latin America and has borders with ten countries, Brazil has never assumed the leadership role commensurate with its geographical size and economic might."[52]

In 2002, it was Lula's turn to take the helm. In November, Lula — with José Alencar as his vice president — was elected president. On his fourth try, he won 60 percent of the 52.7 million votes cast in the in the runoff. His platform — uniting Workers Party ideas with those of a coalition of parties — was one of independence. There was to be no crumpling before the wishes of the United States. That long-sought goal, if it was to be accomplished, had to balance the fact that the United States is a huge and desirable market for Brazilian products as well as the producer of goods and services that Brazilians want. U.S. policy tends to tip the resulting imbalance in its own favor by locking in agreements through the Free Trade Area of the Americas, or FTAA. Lula, leading a nation with an impressive array of natural resources and industrial capacity, must keep from getting caught in the U.S. net. His strategy has been — as his electoral campaign promised — to help build regional cooperation among Latin American countries. This puts him on many a stage smiling and shaking hands with U.S. bugaboos like Venezuela's Hugo Chávez. In general, however, Lula has taken a centrist line, stressing the necessity of Brazil's finding its own way without alienating any country. He has vowed to enlarge social programs and eradicate hunger in Brazil.

In one important way, Lula's presidency immediately fulfilled a promise that Brazilian liberals made to themselves long ago: enfranchising huge numbers of new voters. From the inception of its democracy, Brazil's oligarchs strangled popular participation in elections. Long after Brazil's First Republic took form, the oligarchy kept its thumb on the electorate. By 1894, only 2 percent of the population could vote — not by secret ballot. By 1930 and the election of Getulio Vargas, the figure had risen only to 6 percent. Away from the coastal cities, local politicians' control of polling places cemented their power, a situation parallel to that of the Jim Crow South in the United States. Brazilian women first voted in 1932, but free-and-fair national elections eluded Brazilians until after World War II.

Even then, the franchise was enlarged only slowly. From 1946, when only 16 percent of Brazilians were voting, the count crept up to 22 percent in 1961 and to 34 percent in 1974. In 1989, the year Lula began his quest for the presidency, illiterates were first allowed to vote and eligibility was lowered to age 16. The vote rose to 56 percent. That opening of the electorate was matched by democratic stability. Cardoso was the first Brazilian president since Vargas to serve his terms and pass the sash of the presidency to a successor. At the beginning of the twenty-first century, nearly two thirds of Brazilians—106 million people — were voting.[53] Like its economy, Brazil's democracy came of age with Lula as leader.

*   *   *

In the first months of Lula's tenure, Brazilian banks' earnings grew and the São Paulo stock exchange set records for continued growth. Tax revenues resulting from economic expansion were allowing Brazil to pay down its foreign debt, including to the ever-demanding International Monetary Fund. Social programs were being funded. Then, 15 months after he'd taken office, Lula's first administration was very nearly blown apart. "After February 2004," wrote Brazilian journalist Lucia Hippolito, "Lula's administration would never be the same."[54]

For any other president, jaundiced Brazilian voters might have seen what happened as just another scandal. But for Lula's presidency, it was a profound betrayal of trust. The Worker's Party had always been more than just another political party. It was to be a community of mutual respect and interdependence. "The ethos associated with the party since its creation," wrote journalist Sue Branford in 2002, "has become the party's indelible trademark." Its 1981 statement of principles stressed the importance of individuals' attitudes, of relationships among members, of loyalty to the party platform, and of exemplary conduct toward the rest of society. "By the first principle," the manifesto stated, "we mean individual political integrity that, for example, does not allow anyone holding office to advance his or her own personal position through political patronage, even though this may be common practice in the bourgeois system."[55] It would become painfully clear that the tarnish of corruption was not limited to the bourgeoisie.

Brazilian journalists, like sailors long at sea, sniffed something in the wind that smelled of corruption in Lula's administration in January 2003. There followed a series of rumors that turned into revelations, stories that became scandals, and, finally, a congressional investigation and formal charges. Key officials in Lula's administration were forced to resign, and from February 2004 to February 2005, the Workers Party lost its majority in Congress.

The allegations were varied, the proofs always embarrassing. At one end of the spectrum of shame was the postal worker filmed accepting a small bribe during a discussion of government contracts. At the other, uncovered by congressional hearings and the continued attention of news reporters, was evidence of tens of millions of dollars' worth of corruption. Payments were said to have gone to members of Congress and to have financed Lula's campaign for the presidency. The result, continued Hippolito, "shows us a government paralyzed, apathetic, without initiative. A government wrecked by the political situation.... Its base of support in Congress having imploded, denounced for an extensive pattern of corruption, including abuses of the State and the national treasure, of buying deputies' votes in favor of government policies—all of that having taken place during Lula's administration that took office in January 2003."[56]

By late August 2005, two Workers Party officials in the administration stood accused. One was Lula's chief of staff, José Dirceu de Oliveira e Silva, who resigned in 2005 and returned to Congress, but was expelled from his seat before the year was out. De Oliveira was accused of controlling a secret multimillion-dollar slush fund that financed party members' election campaigns and was used to buy votes in Congress. Other important administration figures followed him out the door.[57]

Antonio Palocci, the minister of finance, resigned in March 2006 as the revelations dragged on. Palocci was a medical doctor and a Trotskyite who had converted his thinking to fiscal conservatism. He had been accused of accepting a bribe in the 1990s when he was the mayor, but he had recovered his reputation to become a principal architect of Lula's successful policies for attracting foreign investors, including the International Monetary Fund. Fortunately for Lula and Brazil, Palocci's malfeasance did not derail Brazil's powerful economy. Palocci himself said: "Brazil's economy has nothing but clear skies ahead, even though the finance minister is going through hell."

Lula, amid the turmoil, was preparing another presidential campaign. After the Palocci resignation, *New York Times* reporter Larry Rohter summarized the precarious situation: "Mr. da Silva himself has not been directly implicated in the accusations of accepting payoffs, and he has denied any involvement. But his chief of staff resigned in June, shortly after congressional hearings began, and the president, secretary general and treasurer of the governing Workers' Party were also forced to step down because of their involvement in the scandal."[58]

Throughout, Lula adamantly denied that he was personally involved, but eventually his story was dented by disclosure that he was a frequent visitor to the luxury apartment in Brasília where bribes were asked for and received and the spoils of corruption were divided. Among the seamier details of the divvy-up-the-money meetings was that prostitutes were sometimes there to help with subsequent celebrations. "The PT spent 20 years building an image as an ethical party," wrote Hippolito, "preoccupied with public trust, a fierce defender of transparency in the handling of Brazilians' money. But after rising to power, it forgets everything and acts just like that decadent elite that it has spent the last 20 years criticizing."[59]

Lula, in spite of all, survived the charges of corruption, hypocrisy, and incompetence. Brazil's economy was flourishing under his presidency, and Brazilians have, if nothing else, exhibited a kind of cultural élan, a national sense of self that is remarkable. Or, in the view of historian MacLachlan: "Social connectivity between the classes is weak," he wrote in 2003. Adding: "In a country with an ingrained patriarchal history, corruption may be inevitable."[60] Historian Robert Levine, writing well before the scandal, described Brazilians as, to say the least, unusual: "What is telling about the country's psychology — to the extent that there is such a thing — is the resilience of Brazilian culture and its ability to break out into new and dynamic creative directions ... both at the levels of elite and of popular culture. "[61] Brazilians have taken up European and North American fashions, ideas, and manners—from philosophy to industry to video silliness—and made them their own. What was already their own — from bossa nova to *futbol* to beauties on the beach to the ugliest of political excess— Brazilians flaunt like a Carmen Miranda headdress.

They survive. Lula won re-election in late 2006. Forced to another runoff, Lula took 61 percent of the vote. The result was better than he'd gotten four years earlier, before the scandal. He plunged into the task of extending his country's record of economic growth. He surrounded himself with some of the hemisphere's most interesting thinkers. In 2007, Lula picked as his minister of strategic affairs Roberto Magnabeira Unger, a 60-year-old Harvard Law School faculty member. Magnabeira had joined the Harvard faculty at age 24 and become its youngest tenured professor at 29.

Magnabeira is a prolific author, but his thinking defies simple description. It is "leftist" in a world in which self-described leftists have long since run out of workable ideas. Their good fortune is that their adversaries, "neoconservatives," preside over a global economy crippled by their mismanagement. Magnabiera rejects traditional economic analysis, which he dismisses as "shrunken pragmatism," a state in which economists debate while the poor — and especially poor children — await relief. Magnabeira suggests building a corps of middle-class entrepreneurs who both generate growth and insist on wide distribution of the benefits of that growth. "Chastened by the failures of bold transformations," he has written, "societies come to believe that the status quo is an inescapable fate."[62]

Magnabeira's thought is the more remarkable for having been brought to the forefront of Brazilian politics by a working-class party and a man who began his working career shining shoes and selling sweets on some of the meanest streets in the hemisphere. In the spring of 2009, that man, Luís Inacio Lula da Silva, was an organizer of a summit of Latin American leaders in Rio de Janeiro. His purpose was to lead Brazil into its rightful place, looking eye-to-eye with the United States. "I'm going to ask the United States to take a different view of Latin America," Lula said. "We're a democratic, peaceful continent, and the United States has to look at the region in a productive, developmental way, and not just think about drug trafficking or organized crime."

Hugo Chávez
Elected Leftist
1954–
(Venezuela)

In 2006, after Hugo Chávez had been elected president of Venezuela with a 56 percent major-ity, had overseen a redrafting of the national constitution that was approved by 72 percent of the people, and had been briefly overthrown, only to be returned to the presidency to the delight of cheering crowds, George W. Bush, the U.S. president, described him as "under-mining democracy." The remark was sadly reminiscent of the simplistic attitudes expressed by so many U.S. presidents toward Latin American leaders. Bush's concern was, if only briefly, assuaged by a 2007 plebiscite that denied Chávez the right to succeed himself. He accepted the defeat gracefully. Then, however, in a resounding illustration of democracy Latin Amer-ican style, yet another plebiscite in early 2009 gave the Venezuelan president the right to suc-ceed himself. The English magazine *The Economist* asked: "Chávez for ever?" Perhaps, but a more important question was whether Chávez would use the powers of the presidency to con-tinue his work as a reformer, or fall back into his unfortunate tendency for empty bombast.

* * *

Hugo Chávez Frías was born July 28, 1954, in the mud-brick house of his grandmother, Rosa Inés Chávez. Mama Rosa lived in Sabaneta, Barinas, a tiny town of dirt streets on the *llanos*, a vast grassland that spills into Colombia. The land is the equivalent of Australia's "outback," a region that has never outgrown its image as "the frontier." Chávez's mother, Elena Frías de Chávez, lived with her husband, Hugo de los Reyes Chávez, in an even smaller vil-lage, Los Rastrojos, two miles away. They had gone to Sabaneta because there would be a mid-wife and minimal services there, taking precautions that are necessary in rural Latin America, where fully half of all children born die before reaching their fifth birthdays.

Little Hugo and his brother Adán, a year older, grew up in Sabaneta. Mama Rosa, a devout Catholic who had been deserted by her husband years before, reared the boys while their parents worked. They commuted to their jobs as teachers by bicycle every weekday. Although Chávez's parents had only minimal schooling — the father graduated from sixth grade — they made careers for themselves and saw to it that their children got full educations. Six of Doña Elena's children — all boys— lived to maturity. One child, another boy, died at six months from leukemia.

As is so often the case among the poor, family stories revolved around the humiliations of poverty. Hugo would tell of showing up at elementary school in rope sandals and being razzed by his classmates. Well, Mama Rosa was having none of it, so she sallied forth into the dirt streets of the village. There, she basically begged until she had enough money to buy proper shoes. As the children grew, Mama Rosa included them in her business, which was making candy at home. She sugar-coated slices of orange, mango, and guava, and the boys sold them house to house. Although Adán didn't much cotton to the idea, young Hugo loved it. He easily developed the skills of a politician, selling sweets and promising more.

Hugo's sport of choice was not the predictable *futbol*, but baseball. He and Adán played with a homemade bat and a ball fashioned from wound-up cloth. That was all it took to conjure dreams of one day playing in the big leagues. Chávez would later describe this period as idyllic, a time when he also sketched, painted, and memorized poetry. Elena and Hugo Sr. eventually moved to a house on the same street as Mama Rosa's in Sabaneta, but that was not all good news for the boys. Their mother, busy with her job and rearing the other children, proved to be more strict. She meted out harsh punishment — unless Mama Rosa hid the boys.

In fifth grade, Chávez's teacher was his father, who was active in local politics. In 1958, when little Hugo was four years old, a revolt overthrew Venezuela's then–President Marcos Pérez Jiménez, who had himself seized power six years earlier. In the shifting sands of partisanship, the elder Chávez managed always to find himself a place. He worked first on behalf of *Movimiento Electoral del Pueblo*, later switching to COPEI, the Social Christian Party. It was an astute move, for COPEI would later share political dominance in Venezuela with *Accion Demócrata*, or AD. Thus was little Hugo being prepared to enter political life, surrounded by political talk and the examples of an assertive family. Importantly, his head was also filled with romantic yarns of the region's frontier history and of *llanero* bravery.

Chávez developed a keen interest in history and his family's place in it. Col. Pedro Pérez Pérez, an officer in the forces of Ezequiel Zamora, a nineteenth century rebel, was Chavéz's great-great grandfather. His son, Pedro Pérez Delgado, was Chávez's great-grandfather. After his father's rebellion was quelled, Pérez became a bandit and a well known brute, detracting somewhat from his political image, but enhancing the romance.

More political instruction was to come. In the mid–1960s, Adán and Hugo moved with Rosa to the city of Barinas to attend Daniel O'Leary School, the only high school in the state. They took a house across the street from José Esteban Ruíz Guevara, a founder of the local Communist Party and owner of an extensive collection of books about Simón Bolívar. Since that time, Chávez has made Bolívar, a Venezuelan, the focus of his historical studies and a recurrent symbol of his programs.

Chávez has dismissed the facile notion that Ruíz, the communist, influenced his thinking during his vulnerable teenage years. At that point, Chávez has recalled, he and Ruíz's sons were more focused on grand themes like teenage girls than on the future of the nation. Indeed, while Chávez was a student at O'Leary School, he never joined the Communist Party chapter there. It was later, Chávez has said, after graduation from military school, that he welcomed Ruíz's counsel on such things. Chávez has, however, counted among his role models Douglas Bravo, a well-educated product of the landowning class and a dashing member of Venezuela's 1950s — legal — communist party.

However Chávez may have portrayed these choices of counselors and heroes, they suggest the intensity with which Chávez's political education was conducted. Venezuela has historically had difficulty finding its way along a path of moderation, much less democracy, and the events unfolding around Chávez were typical. Overthrows alternated with free elections, without Venezuelans' ever being completely clear on which was better. Even the harsh regime of Pérez Jimenez had accomplished some remarkable feats of infrastructure building, including road and bridge projects. Then, when his administration's record of corruption caused his fall, his successor, democratically elected Romulus Betancourt, was swallowed by mediocrity.

Although Betancourt's election was a model for participatory democracy, his governance foundered. A man of the middle, he was disliked by both the liberal and conservative extremes and quickly discovered that Venezuela's centrists were too weak to protect him. In the second year of his term, a car bomb, apparently set at the request of right-wing military men, nearly killed him. Less than two years later, leftist naval officers instigated two bungled overthrow attempts. All the while, guerrilla bands were forming in the countryside and demonstrators were appearing in city streets. His own party, *Acción Demócrata*, pulled itself apart as some leftist members joined the protests.

By that time, Venezuelans had the example of Fidel Castro to ponder, and in the early 1960s, a small force of armed leftists thought themselves strong enough to confront the Venezuelan army. The violence of their tactics, however, turned away moderate elements and divided the left. Thus by the late 1960s, Venezuela, as if exhausted, settled into a period of democratic elections carefully controlled by the two dominant parties, the AD and the more conservative COPEI. A broad amnesty brought all but the most recalcitrant guerrillas in from the mountains.

Among the holdouts was Bravo, who, forced into exile, wandered through Europe and as far as China. By leftists everywhere, Bravo was feted as harbinger of imminent world revolution. His charisma was considerable, and back at home he organized a political arm called the *Partido Revolucionario de Venezuela*, the PRV. The idealistic platform of the PRV attracted the political conscience of older brother Adán, who was a student at the University of the Andes, in Mérida. By that time Adán was fully embroiled in national politics; he had considered himself a Marxist-Leninist from the time he was sixteen years old.

In 1971, little brother Hugo, who might still not have fully comprehended the depth of Adán's radicalism, surprised friends—and horrified his protective grandmother—by enrolling at the national military academy. He did so, he would later say, not to prepare himself for a military career, but because it offered him a ticket to the big city. Caracas was where the best baseball was played, and Chávez, seventeen years old, wanted to be seen by scouts for the professional leagues. When a recruiter came to O'Leary School, Chávez decided to enter military school, where he would excel on the school team, and from there move into Venezuela's celebrated winter league. There, at games frequented even by scouts from U.S. major league teams, Chávez would show them what he could do as a left-handed pitcher. As it turned out, his academy tryout as a pitcher went badly, but when he was given a turn at bat he hit the ball well. He was accepted as a first baseman and into the academy as a plebe. In August, Chávez stepped onto the campus of white-washed buildings at Fort Tiuna in Caracas.

Venezuela's officer corps was not made up of the sons of oligarchs, as was the case with most Latin American nations, where light-skinned, upper-class cadets are graduated to command ranks of dark-skinned sons of the barrios.[1] Moreover, by the time that Chávez became a cadet, the academy had instituted its Andres Bello Plan, named for the nineteenth century Venezuelan intellectual. The purpose of the Bello Plan was to produce an even more enlightened officer corps schooled in the liberal arts. Reading assignments ranged from Karl Marx, hero of the proletariat, to Karl von Clausewitz, model of the Prussian aristocracy. Venezuela, given its armed forces' propensity for meddling in government, hoped to develop a corps of officers suited for nation-building.

So for Chávez, already interested in literature, history, and politics, the academy was a godsend. He could get all the Simón Bolívar he could read. And it was none too soon, for all around Latin America government was being shaped by military men. In 1968, General Omar

Torrijos led a coup in Panama, and General Juan Velasco Alvarado directed a military overthrow in Peru.

Torrijos sent his son to Venezuela's military academy, and he and Chávez became friends and teammates. Chávez was invited to the Torrijos home. He also got a chance to visit Peru when he was chosen among a small group sent to attend the Lima celebration of the 150th anniversary of battle of Ayacucho. That trip, in 1974, was during Chávez's last year at the academy, when he was mature enough to blend his understanding of history with the realities of modern governance. In that 1824 battle, a Bolivarian army delivered the crushing blow to Spanish forces in South America. However, Bolívar floundered when it came to governing the newly freed republic, and 150 years later Velasco was having no better luck organizing a stable government than Bolívar had had. Velasco's regime, after overthrowing the democratically elected Francisco Belaunde Terry, stumbled into a mire of corruption and mismanagement. Velasco had, however, instituted several populist initiatives that impressed the young Chávez, and when he flew back to Venezuela, he took Velasco's writing with him.

In addition, those years provided Chávez with two more important lessons in the unruly school of Latin American governance. General Augusto Pinochet had in the fall of 1973 overthrown the popularly elected president of Chile, Salvador Allende. It was clear that the right-wing Pinochet acted with firm support from the Nixon administration and the U.S. Central Intelligence Agency, and Chávez was able to observe in the first years of his military career the carnage that Pinochet oversaw. Similarly, Argentine generals overthrew President María Estela, the widow of former President Juan Perón, in 1976 and imposed a draconian military government that assassinated — the infamous *desaparecidos*, or "disappeared"— some ten times the number killed in Chile, a staggering 30,000 Argentines.

*   *   *

That was the hemispheric political environment into which Chávez was graduated from the academy in July 1975. When he had entered four years earlier, he was one of a class of 374; only 67 made it. Chávez ranked seventh. As a second lieutenant, Chávez was assigned to a counterinsurgency unit, one of those formed in the 1960s to combat guerrilla bands operating from jungle redoubts. Since then, however, the army had systematically squeezed the threat out of them. Nevertheless, the guerrillas still had appeal as the romantic armed wing of a dissident movement that encompassed students, intellectuals, and some labor unions, and they were still recruiting, including among the armed forces.

Lieutenant Chávez, named communication officer, joined a unit in Barinas, close to his family, including Mama Rosa — who was still not enthusiastic about her grandson's career choice. It seems that neither was Chávez's commanding officer, who made it known he didn't much like the only "college boy" in his outfit. Chávez's assertiveness did not help, nor did his insistence that he be allowed to play baseball for a local professional team. There were games scheduled when, in the commander's view, Chávez ought to be in the barracks. The two resolved matters when Chávez argued that it was better for him to be staying in shape during his time off rather than boozing and whoring like his fellow officers. It also helped that Chávez could still hit a fastball low and away, to the delight of the soldiers listening to radio broadcasts back in the barracks.

Chávez parlayed his popularity into opening up other off-duty activities for the battalion, including a sports program in which townspeople were recruited to help in the construction of a baseball park. Whether one considered it a "gift for gab" or an annoying unwillingness to shut up, Chávez's personality was irrepressible. So his commander turned him into a recruiter. He continued for two years in Barinas before being posted to a front that was less upbeat.

In 1977, Chávez's unit was transferred to a more active guerrilla front in Anzoátegui, to the east. Now he was not only in an active war zone but brought face to face with his own political ambivalence. This close to the guerrillas, Chávez was forced to think about whose side he was on. He was put to his first test when, named to command a remote position, an intelligence officer showed up at the campsite with three captured *campesinos*. The officer said the three were guerrillas. Chávez had them held in a tent but felt compelled to intervene when he heard their cries. He went to the tent, took away the baseball bat the intelligence officer was using, and ordered him to stop or be thrown out of the camp. The man took his prisoners and left, later complaining to headquarters about the way he was treated. Chávez was threatened with, though never brought before, a court martial.

Chávez had other concerns, like the corruption he observed among top officers. Among other things, they were selling government equipment and pocketing the cash. When Chávez spoke of these concerns, his friends introduced him to dissidents. They, in turn, pressed him to expand his reading from the romanticism of Bolivarian history to the practicalities of leftist politics. It had been ten years since Ernesto "Che" Guevara, Fidel Castro's principal lieutenant, was captured and killed in Bolivia, and Chávez was reading Guevara's revolutionary writing even as he was supposed to be hunting the Venezuelans who were Guevara's disciples. "How long can I be like this?" he later recalled asking himself.[2]

By that time, Chávez's recollections suggest, his thinking was plodding toward resolution. When the oppressed recognize the extent of their oppression, he was being told, a cadre of individuals must be prepared to lead. And, importantly, when established institutions begin to lose authority, and the oligarchy reveals the depth of its corruption, that was the point that the hot-headed egotist, which Chávez seemed to be, had to transform himself into a leader. But like all revolutionists, from Bolívar to Lenin, Chávez was skeptical of the masses' ability to recognize their own interests. Chávez compared the Venezuelan masses to wet wood, unlikely ever to catch fire.

*   *   *

Chávez's heart, however, had no such problem. While stationed in Anzoátegui, Chávez acknowledged that back in Barinas was a young working-class woman named Nancy Colmenares. He asked her to marry him, though it was a staple of the Barinas rumor mill that her prospective mother-in-law, Elena, disapproved. Their first child, Rosa Virginia, was born in 1978, followed by María Gabriela in 1980, and Hugo Rafael in 1983.

As his own family grew, Chávez was unimpressed with the political maturity of Venezuela's 16 million people. Social divisions deepened even as the nation's fortunes rose and fell according to global oil prices. Although there were frequent street demonstrations of discontent, the people always dissolved into a leaderless mass. In 1976, President Pérez took the progressive step of nationalizing the petroleum industry, but the move meant little more than rearranging the furniture at headquarters. Maladministration persisted, and U.S. companies continued to control production and distribution. "Internally," wrote historian Norman A. Bailey, "oil development took place in a chaotic fashion, and the revenues were misused in various ways." Externally, Bailey continued, between 1932 and 1973: "Questionable Venezuelan energy policies were reciprocated in spades by the United States. Preferences were given frequently to Canada and Mexico, but never to Venezuela." Nevertheless, "Venezuela has always, without exception, supported the United States whenever a crisis of oil supply occurred.... Even the formation of OPEC, often blamed on Venezuela, took place only after then oil minister Juan Pablo Pérez Alfonzo's suggestion of a North American energy community was ignored by the United States."[3]

Through it all, Venezuelans, rather than using oil to control their own destiny, meekly cashed in on periodic booms to go on spending binges. In 1970, oil had sold at $1.76 a barrel, and by 1976 the per-barrel price had risen to $10.31. Thus in the decade leading up to 1983, petroleum earned Venezuela $150 billion, providing prosperity that was squandered. Revenues were not used to expand educational opportunities, improve health care, or fund agrarian reform. The government simply papered over problems, calming unrest and assuring that U.S. leaders would continue to portray Venezuela as an island of democracy among Latin American dictatorships.

Chávez was being instructed by dissident economists in the basics of governance: create manufacturing jobs, build housing, broaden opportunities for schooling, and reform Venezuela's archaic system of land tenure. They also told him that across Venezuela was a loose corps of dissident leaders, and, waiting to be inspired, a goodly number of followers. Some of Chávez's closest friends—the brothers Ruíz and their father, for example—knew of his restlessness and introduced him to every radical thinker they knew. Finally, during the 1977 Christmas holiday, Chávez learned of the depth of his brother Adán's political discontent while voicing his own complaints about the army. Adán counseled patience. He told his younger brother not to jeopardize his place in the ranks with foolish talk. When Chávez was transferred to a post in Maracay, he asked for reassignment from information officer to the tank corps. He figured that if action was imminent he would be of more use commanding heavy armor than manning a portable typewriter.

In 1978, meetings were arranged between Chávez and Alfredo Maneiro, a long-time Communist guerrilla leader, and Pablo Medina, who had experience in organizing labor unions. Maneiro also cautioned against impatience. Nevertheless, Chávez prevailed upon an old friend and fellow officer, Jesús Urdaneta Hernández, to help form a clandestine unit, the "Venezuelan People's Army." Two other officers, Miguel Ortíz Contreras and Felipe Acosta Carles, were also recruited. By the following year, Adán felt the group was ready to hold a highly dangerous meeting with the old revolutionary romantic, Douglas Bravo. Bravo, though still on the government's most-wanted list, was living in disguise in Caracas.

That meeting led to others, and the threads of conspiracy were drawn tighter. Because Bravo was distrusted by non-communists, meetings with him were kept secret except within a small circle. To reconcile this awkward union between an army officer and a communist guerrilla, Chávez began to speak of the coming revolution not as socialist, but "Bolivarian." This inclination to put lipstick on a pig would lead Chávez's critics—especially those who lost power struggles to him—to accuse him of being manipulative.

As Chávez and his friends plotted, so did others. A parallel conspiracy was being hatched by an air force officer, William Izarra. As with Chávez, Izarra's thoughts of rebellion ran all the way back to his training in anti-guerrilla warfare. In the late 1960s, Izarra became convinced that the guerrillas' views made sense, and during a fellowship at Harvard University in 1978–79, Izarra read Karl Marx and other leftist thinkers. Back at home, Izarra's continued association with leftist intellectuals led to his being exposed and forced to give up his commission. In fact, Chávez's behavior was also beginning to attract the notice of his superiors.

At that time, Venezuelan governments had good reason to worry about dissidents. Presidents tended to be so inept and their administrations so corrupt that they effectively overthrew themselves. Billions in oil revenue meant that millions flowed into their pockets. Then, when prices fell, the government paid for public services and infrastructure by borrowing, doubling down on the problem. Luis Herrera Campins was elected president on the promise that he would stabilize accounts, but then international events caused so much oil money to come in that Campins practically choked on it. Between 1981 and 1983, Iran, first, underwent its revolution, and then went to war with Iraq. A large portion of the world's oil supply was bottled up, and prices soared. Campins forgot all his promises of austerity and went on his own spending spree. Of course, as night follows day, oil prices fell, and Herrera was forced into drastic action to try to stave off insolvency.

Prophetically, in December 1982, small currents of history converged. The citizenry was in turmoil as Campins floundered toward an emergency devaluation of the Venezuelan *bolívar*. At the same time, the commanding officer of the Maracay military base in Caracas needed a speaker for the annual commemoration of the death of Bolívar. As luck would have it, Chávez, acknowledged as an expert on the life of The Liberator, was on the base.

He was there to take a class, and he was selected to make the speech. He would later say that he stepped to the lectern thinking not only of Bolívar, but of Mama Rosa, who had died earlier in the year. If his grandmother was a source of tenderness, Chávez said, her spirit and determination were also an inspiration to rebel. So, in his speech, Chávez, then 28 years old, envisioned Bolívar looking down from heaven on his native country awash in insolvency, corruption, and incompetence. In a thirty-minute delivery, Chávez averred that something had to be done. He did not spell out what.

As the formation was dismissed, a furious major in the audience brought everyone back to attention. He excoriated Chávez for sounding like a politician, the worst insult he could think of. The tension was allayed only when a colonel stepped forward, ordered quiet, and told the major that Chávez had cleared his remarks with him the night before. The incident demonstrated the extent to which the military was split. When Chávez got back to the barracks, he was agitated, and three old friends—Urdaneta, Acosta, and Raúl Isaías Baduel—suggested a jog to settle them all down. Before the four returned to the base, they had formally sworn to form the core of a revolt. With a proper sense of drama, Chávez adapted their oath to conform to the one Bolívar devised in 1805 when he swore that one day he would drive the Spanish from South America.

* * *

The plotters still had the problem of blending nationalists with socialists. In Venezuela, the former were inspired by the figure of Ezequiel Zamora, a *llanero* who cut a fine figure on horseback, but was not good at organization and administration. For socialists, on the other hand, there were examples from Lenin to Castro of how to organize, but their humorless insistence on rigor and discipline were unattractive to most Venezuelans. Those models had to be resolved as they spoke to potential recruits, but they also had a more immediate challenge. That was the possibility of discovery, so they adopted a clandestine protocol, complete with codes and passwords. Then Chávez, chosen to be an instructor at the academy, wrapped all of that planning into a determination to recruit rebels in the heart of the army's education system.

Despite the gravity and danger of his situation, Chávez biographers insist, he never lost his ebullience. He pushed aside initial misgivings about teaching and adapted himself to that role for four contented years. He called his oldest students his "second graduating class," and, at home, doted on his three children as they grew into their teenage years. Over time, however, the domesticity gave way to amorous pursuits more like those of his hero Bolívar. In 1984, Chávez met Herma Marksman, a school teacher with two children who was in the midst of a divorce. She became Chávez's mistress and a follower of his cause with her own code name. She occasionally served as his driver for secret meetings with other conspirators and as a sounding board for his ideas. Their affair lasted nine years.

Chávez rose to the rank of captain and was reassigned to the *llanos*. He was sent to command a remote outpost in the village of Elorza, on the border with Colombia. It was late in the summer of 1985, and, on the surface, Chávez seemed content with his lot. He continued to give free rein to his personality, encouraging and supporting baseball teams for local children. He staged parades and saint's day celebrations for their parents. He organized *días civico-militares*, when the army brought doctors and nurses into the area. Chávez enjoyed playing the hero—the *capitán* in tailored fatigues—and students at the Elorza high school named him *padrino*—honorary godfather—two years in a row. Only occasionally, he would later say, was he depressed for being cut off from his friends and fellow officers.

Those friends were busily plotting as the government rode its usual merry-go-round. The series of devaluations of the *bolívar* that had begun in the early 1980s continued to breed dissatisfaction. Dissatisfied voters threw out COPEI and brought back the AD. But the new AD president, Jaime Lusinchi, did no better. He oversaw a disastrous scheme to set several values for the *bolívar* and frittered away the national treasury. Lusinchi also caused considerable embarrassment by leaving his wife at home and taking his private secretary on an official visit to Spain. Back in Caracas, his wife divorced him, while in Madrid the Spanish government refused to let him and his sweetheart stay at a state-sponsored residence. They were sent to a hotel.

In 1985 and 1986, Chávez and his co-conspirators tightened their plans. They organized the first of what they hoped would be a series of organizational meetings in different parts of the country. They recognized that government agents were on their collective trail—by that time, rumors about Chávez were rampant—but they also knew there were so many clandestine groups that they hoped the government wouldn't know whom to round up first. All the same, when Chávez and the others held the meetings, they took such precautions as carrying repelling ropes to escape from rear windows, hiding guns to hold off the authorities, and storing food to withstand a siege. However, the greatest threat they faced was the result of their own success. They were winning converts at such a pace that some recruits had trouble coexisting with others, and others couldn't keep their mouths shut. Also, Chávez's was encouraging a rebellion consisting of sabotage and subversion—as opposed to a frontal assault—that was seen as hopelessly out of date. In fact, Chávez did not altogether disagree with his critics. His naiveté was partly rooted in his isolation on the frontier, but he was reading voraciously and trying to think clearly. "I feel," he later said, "that in Elorza I finished finding myself."[4]

Soon, however, army investigators found him. Chávez was promoted to major in the summer of 1986, but by that autumn his entire career was jeopardized. A young officer who was being drawn into the conspiratorial fold reported his experience to superior officers. Names were named, personnel files were pulled, and investigations were launched. Rebels who at had at times looked like the Keystone Kops suddenly got very serious. Chávez and his friends were alerted only because a fellow conspirator stole a look at the investigative file and put out the word.

Flushed like a covey of quail, the conspirators scrambled to let everyone know. Chávez happened to be in Caracas for minor eye surgery and he got word to Herma Marksmen to burn the incriminating papers, of which there were many, at her house. Her incendiary effort hearkened back to the Keystone Kops days. She drove the papers to a remote spot on the beach, soaked them with kerosene, and dropped them into a crack in the rocks. The she threw in a match. The ocean wind blew out the match. She kept striking and dropping matches and the wind kept blowing them out. When she finally ran out of matches, she walked back to the road, got the car, and found a store in the early hours of the morning. Finally, she got flames. Chávez, in the meantime, his face swollen from eye surgery, drove through the night warning his friends and his brother Adán.

The episode, hardly a testament to the cleverness of the conspirators, blew over because the government was no more astute. It was unable to make a case, which suggests that it was too incompetent even to protect itself. Chávez's superior officers, however, were sure he was guilty of something, even if they couldn't prove it. They decided to send him off to a kind of internal exile. He was dismissed from his command and put in charge of an even smaller, almost non-existent post that was still farther afield. Thus Chávez was reduced to commanding a down-at-the-heels unit of ten soldiers and a few native tribesmen he recruited to fill out the ranks. It was clear he was being watched.

* * *

Watching Chávez, however, was like watching a clown holding a machine gun. One was never sure whether he was funny or deadly. His unit was the next thing to a military joke. He and his soldiers were ill clad, poorly housed, and undisciplined. Chávez vegetated, informed that back in Caracas the movement for which he had risked so much was losing its leaders, failing to recruit at anything like its former pace, and generally dissipating. Its remaining members mostly spouted revolutionary clichés and plastered walls with posters of *Che* Guevara. Chávez retreated into clown mode.

One day at his government-forsaken post, Chávez was sleeping away the morning when a soldier knocked at his door. A military helicopter was approaching, he was told. Major Chávez, dressed like a day laborer, walked out to see what was up. From the helicopter stepped a smartly uniformed general who realized he was surrounded by men wearing rubber boots because their military-issue footwear had worn out and not been replaced. He saw infantrymen on horseback. The general was Arnoldo Rodríguez Ochoa, and he had heard about Chávez's unusual personality. The major offered the general a cup of coffee. The general decided he liked this young military misfit.

In 1988, when General Rodríguez was appointed head of national security, he brought Major Chávez to headquarters as an aide. Oddly, Chávez was allowed to make the move without serious opposition from the officers who had so recently been looking into his personnel file. Chávez moved from commander of an almost lost platoon of hapless soldiers on the frontier into a Caracas office across the street from Miraflores, Venezuela's presidential palace.

* * *

At Miraflores was Carlos Andrés Pérez, elected in December 1988. Pérez was a leading actor in Venezuela's presidential drama. He was first elected president in 1974, when Chávez was a nineteen-year-old cadet marching in the inaugural parade. Pérez had remained a charismatic leader despite his mixed record in office. He was a disciple of the grand old man of Venezuelan democracy, Rómulo Betancourt, and as such was a champion of the people. He'd opposed Venezuelan dictators with enough vigor that he was once forced into exile for nearly a decade. During his 1975-to-1979 term, Pérez demonstrated his leftward tilt by opening relations with Castro and shipping guns to the Sandinista rebels of Nicaragua. He also nationalized Venezuelan oil producers. What brought him into disfavor, including with his own party, was a record of corruption that filled the pockets of a handful of oligarchs. Now, with Chávez across the street, he was back.

This time he was saddled with the problems Lusinchi left behind. The national debt exceeded $4 billion. Foreign lenders were calling for austerity until they got their money back; services had to be reduced throughout Venezuela; and the currency was revalued. Pérez also decided early in his administration to let gasoline prices, which had been among the lowest in the world, rise radically. Thus every consumer item that was carried on a truck went up, food shortages followed, and bus companies couldn't cover expenses. The anger of farmers, workers, and consumers led to street riots at the end of February 1989.

In Caracas, the chaos set a wretched example for the nation. It was known as the *caracazo*, a word suggesting social explosion. Residents of nearly twenty cities demonstrated, and from the countryside came peasants eager to share the turmoil. As disruptive as the riots were, however, they represented only the amorphous rage of people who couldn't find leaders to fix complex, ancient problems. Nothing serious was being done. Newspapers of the period carried photographs of rioters on one page, winners of beauty contests on another. Eventually, the Pérez administration, still only a few weeks old, called into the capital nine thousand troops to quell the riots. The force included tanks, their cannons pointed at unarmed civilians. The most serious disruptions lasted five days. Atrocities were committed on both sides. Newspaper accounts detailed one particularly egregious massacre, apparently committed by government officers who buried sixty-eight bodies in an unmarked grave. Some showed signs of torture and mutilation. In response as many as a thousand Caracas businesses were looted, burned, or both. Across the country, nearly 3,000 businesses were damaged. The government placed the death toll at fewer than 300, though more objective estimates ran past a thousand killed.

Chávez himself missed the entire affair because he'd been diagnosed with chicken pox and was quarantined, but events of those days had a profound effect on him and many Venezuelans. Francisco Arias Cárdenas, a respected leader among those plotting with Chávez, had commanded soldiers putting down the riot. He was appalled by the suppression of people whose only crime was being poor. Felipe Acosta Carles— one of those who calmed Chávez down after his speech — was shot and killed by a rioter. Several officers who had to impose order during those days and who had fired on their fellow Venezuelans were forever changed. They approached Chávez and other Bolivarians in the aftermath, and if they were not already members of the conspiracy, they enrolled then and there. The government's harsh repression did the recruiting that the conspirators had been neglecting, but tumult also affected Chávez's personal life. As the 1990s began he and Nancy were divorced.

As Venezuelans continued to talk about the riots, more officers made known their dissatisfaction with the government. In turn, investigators began picking them up for questioning. By the end of the year, about a dozen officers, including Chávez, were interrogated. All the government had to go on were rumors, but the rumors had been numerous and the questioning was heated. One general, agitated by the rumor of a plot to kidnap his son, challenged Chávez to a duel. Chávez declined, and, in the end, investigators could prove nothing. His and others' suspicious behavior was attributed to their being Bolivarianos, intense nationalists who held Venezuelans, including themselves, up to idealized, romantic standards. While troublesome, they did not seem traitorous. Only after they were released did the government begin to see the seriousness of their threat.

Because of the lingering suspicion, Chávez felt that his career had begun to suffer. He, like other officers, had been preparing for higher command in a course of study. Although Chávez had flunked his first attempt, he'd retaken some tests and passed the second time. He got his promotion to lieutenant colonel, but was concerned that he was not assigned his own battalion.

The same problem faced two of his fellow Bolivarianos until no less a figure than the defense minister intervened. In 1991, all three got their assignments: paratroop battalions, seemingly perfect duty for carrying out a coup. Whether this was intrigue or not was uncertain. Perhaps generals were playing a chess game of their own. Or perhaps Venezuela's armed forces were so shot through with conspiracies and counter-conspiracies that everyone was manipulating someone. It has been suggested that Chávez's reputation was such that his potential for disloyalty had been discussed with President Pérez. It is said that Pérez dismissed the danger out of hand, perhaps believing that no one as outspoken as Chávez was capable of surreptitious behavior. Whatever the case, Chávez's promotion and battalion command left him with a more immediate problem. It had been years since he last jumped out of an airplane.

*   *   *

The conspirators were now awaiting their opening. They planned to use an innocent mobilization as a cover for storming into power. Their first chance popped up when Venezuela — along with the United States and France — was asked to send troops into Haiti to staunch a coup attempt on the new Haitian government of Jean-Bertrand Aristide. That was canceled. Next came an airshow, allowing the paratroops to float down to an open field, then pluck Pérez out of the reviewing stand. That plan was beset by several problems. Air force support for the conspirators fell through; civilian rebels talked about taking the revolution into their own hands; and it became clear that government investigators had again picked up the conspirators' trail. As plans were made and abandoned, in fact, loose lips were making the conspiracy an open secret.

In addition, normal military training assignments were spreading rebellious officers across the country, making coordination impossible. In order to strike while the Bolivarians were in place, the leaders decided to get on with it. The coup would be on February 3, 1992, when there was another air show. Pérez would just have returned from a trip abroad, and the plan was to capture Pérez when he arrived at the airport. If he got away from the airport, a tunnel on the road to Caracas would be blocked and he would be taken there. If both of those plans were thwarted, the plotters were prepared to go into Miraflores.

Other units, including civilian groups, were to take control of radio and television stations. Information released to citizens was to include pictures of the captured president. Chávez was the overall coordinator, communicating with elements throughout the country from a military museum in Caracas. After the country was under the control of the rebels, a *junta* of civilian leaders and military officers would become the acting government. Elections and the drafting of a new constitution were to follow.

The bulk of troops scheduled to occupy and hold various strategic places were not to be told they were helping overthrow their government until assembly on the morning of February 4. Many junior officers were also kept in the dark, being told that they must give up their side arms and restrict themselves to barracks until it was all over. When they did find out, however, many eagerly joined the cause.

Although some conspirators got cold feet at the outset, others moved efficiently to control barracks locations and military bases. At first, things went well, and by 7 P.M. the rebels had captured two small bases. Then, however, the young captain charged with seizing the military academy in Caracas had second thoughts. He was dating the daughter of the commandant and he spilled the beans to his prospective (and future) father-in-law. That put the government on alert, and the rebels began to meet resistance.

At the airport, there had been too many loyal troops for the rebels to make their move anyway, and Pérez was hustled away by his guards. On the road into the capital, a burning vehicle did indeed block traffic, but loyal troops quickly grasped the situation, cleared a path, and waved the presidential caravan through safely. Those with Pérez later said he was more angry than frightened. In fact, he seemed glad that the long-rumored coup attempt was afoot, and said in the car that he was eager to begin planning how to isolate the rebels and bring the armed forces back under control. Before 11 P.M., Pérez climbed into bed at the presidential residence.

At about that time, however, rebels were storming police stations and military posts in Maracaibo, a city of two million that is the heart of Venezuela's oil industry. They took control of the city without meeting resistance and practically without firing a shot. When the news got back to Caracas, Pérez, after a first attempt failed to rouse him, had to be awakened and informed by his daughter that the rebellion was real. He threw on clothes over his pajamas and fled the residence just ahead of the rebels' arrival. The attack so terrified his wife and children that they all hid in her bedroom.

For Chávez and the other leaders in Caracas, matters had come down to the last, worst possibility. There would have to be an all-out assault on Miraflores. That raised the possibility of many more dead and wounded than they'd hoped. Nevertheless, they had been successful in neutralizing nearby air force planes, depriving the government of help from the air, and most of the presidential guard was still asleep — it was just after midnight — in their barracks across the street from Miraflores. Pérez's car sped through the entrance of the nearly empty Miraflores minutes before the arrival of the rebels' column of tanks. A couple of party and government officials had arrived before him, and Pérez excoriated them for letting the revolt reach this point. Pérez was told that the leader of the revolt was Lt. Col. Hugo Chávez, but recrimination would have to wait; rebel tanks were crashing onto the palace grounds.

The rebels were able to surround Miraflores and cut off the palace guard from getting back into place. Then, with automatic fire from the street shattering windows, they broke down doors. Calls for relief from inside Miraflores either did not get through or only reached commanders who were themselves under attack. All exits seemed to be covered, and Pérez apparently was trapped.

The man who saved the day for the president was his director of security, Vice Admiral Mario Ivan Carratú. Carratú at first told Pérez that there was no escape; surrender was their only recourse. But Pérez, sixty-nine years old, was full of fight and would hear nothing of it. He and his body guards had armed themselves with Uzi machine guns, and Pérez wanted to fight. Instead, Carratú ran through secret, underground tunnels to the palace car park, broke a hole in the thick glass of a locked door, and went back to collect the president. After leading Pérez to a car, Carratú found that the large, metal garage door would not open without a key he did not have. Two garage attendants, shot through a window, lay wounded on the concrete floor and were of no help. The admiral, showing the skill of an electrician's mate, tore open the door's control box and crossed the appropriate wires to open the door. Pérez was driven away, once again just ahead of the rebels, who were fifty yards away in a tank.

Pérez wanted to go on television to tell the nation that he was still in charge. So Carratú phoned the Miraflores operator and discovered that the rebels had not yet reached the government switchboard. She put the admiral through to the studios of Venevisión, where Carratú persuaded the head of security, whom he knew, to arrange for an appearance by the president. So, at 1:15 A.M., after Carratú told Pérez to tuck his pajama collar beneath his dress shirt, Venezuela's president addressed a nation that was mostly still sound asleep. The tape was rerun continually as Venezuelans woke up, and from his shaky command post at the television station, Pérez pulled the fat out of the fire. He kept insisting on camera that his forces were in control — even though rebels had taken Maracaibo, Valencia, and Maracay. Faced with Pérez's stolid certainty, however, enough rebels lost heart that rebellion lost its momentum.

*   *   *

During the long night, Chávez had been, in effect, a no-show. Critics have roundly crit-icized him for a failure of leadership. Indeed, Chávez was responsible for communication among rebel groups throughout the country, and it was their isolation that left rebels in the dark and dispirited. They were never able to evaluate how successful they had been outside of Caracas. On the other hand, it can be said that Chávez, by accepting responsibility for the coup and negotiating a surrender, prevented further bloodshed. And, in his customary fash-ion, Chávez emerged from the failed coup as something of a hero, the popular face of oppo-sition to a regime many Venezuelans despised.

All the same, there were foul-ups aplenty. With every rebel officer's watch synchronized to strike at midnight, Chávez did not even arrive in Caracas until after 12:30 A.M. He still had to make his way to his command post: a military museum within sight of Miraflores. More-over, the communication apparatus required for coordinating the revolt had not been installed because the signal-corps soldiers who were to do the job earlier in the night had been held on their base by suspicious commanders. Finally, Chávez arrived at the museum only to learn that it was in the hands of loyal troops, who fired on him and his companions as they drove up. Chávez has told interviewers that he called out that he and his men were "reinforce-ments," calming things for the moment. But the ruse soured when the colonel commanding the troops at the museum turned on the television and saw Pérez making his frantic announce-ment that he was still in charge. Pérez said the coup was led by the paratroop unit from the Maracay base. The colonel turned from the television and looked at Chávez, whose uniform bore the insignia of that very unit. The colonel asked the lieutenant colonel to explain.

Chávez, quick on his feet—and desperate—told the colonel that, well, yes, he was, indeed, part of the revolt and that the colonel should surrender because he and his men were surrounded by rebel troops. And, in fact, two buses full of rebel soldiers did pull up to the museum. Such was the gentlemanly ambiguity of the situation that the colonel surrendered. That, however, did nothing to remedy the fact that the revolt was careering through the long night without its central command. Foot soldiers, many of whom had first heard of the revolt that afternoon, were risking their lives. Without central control, the cause was lost. Fernando Ochoa Antich, the minister of defense who that night also flew back to Caracas to find him-self in the middle of a rebellion, would later say it was Chávez who could have saved the day. Had he simply taken his troops at the museum down the hill to Miraflores he could have turned the tide in that battle. Because he did not Caracas and the coup were lost. Chávez would dis-miss speculation as to his lack of courage or resolve by pointing out that his decision to capit-ulate saved many lives. "To launch an attack with one hundred men against a regiment is a suicidal thing," Chávez said, "and without knowing what was happening, it's craziness...."[5]

As news of the coup attempt spread over the world, eliciting statements of support for the Pérez regime, Pérez and his advisors insisted on a statement of surrender. They wanted it broadcast on television, and they wanted it delivered by a humbled Chávez, wearing civil-ian clothes and in handcuffs. If Chávez did not submit to those conditions, rebel positions—which were several and still strong—would be bombed by the Venezuelan air force. Chávez was hardly in a position to refuse, but refuse he did. Negotiations ensued.

Eventually, Chávez talked himself into a fairly strong position. There would be recrim-inations galore among the conspirators as to what went wrong, but in those last moments of the coup attempt Chávez pulled a rabbit, albeit somewhat tattered, out of his beret. Taken to the Defense Ministry at mid-morning, Chávez saluted, handed over his sidearm (and his rifle and hand grenades), and said he had come to surrender. Although he had agreed for his statement to be carried on radio, officers at the ministry suggested that television stations be called, too. That delayed proceedings while the stage was set. During the delay, Chávez sat on a couch smoking. Perhaps because of confusion among the officers carrying out Pérez's orders, or perhaps because of residual support for the rebels among the officer corps, when Chávez appeared before the cameras, contrary to Pérez's explicit orders, he was in full uniform, including the paratrooper's maroon beret. He was not in handcuffs. He looked defeated, but proud.

He was also composed, partly because earlier in the morning he'd been given a chance, after agreeing to surrender, to speak by phone with small clutches of rebel leaders. He told them the fight was over, saluting them and thanking them for their valor. From those conversations he patched together a kind of dress rehearsal for standing in front of the cameras. And in the end, of course, Chávez was a wordsmith. "First of all," began the man who had just been arrested after a failed coup, "I want to say good morning to all the people of Venezuela." That is something a master of ceremonies, not a humiliated brigand, might say. "This Bolivarian message is directed to all the courageous soldiers who are in the paratrooper regiment in Aragua and the tank regiment in Valencia. Comrades: unfortunately, for now, the objectives we had set for ourselves were not achieved in the capital city...."

"For now"? Supporters then and biographers since emphasize that phrase. He was stating his resolve and his belief that Venezuela's problems were not going to disappear just because the rebels had lost "for now." It was hardly "Let the ruling classes tremble," but it certainly was not a statement of humility from a man who faced trial for treason. It conveyed, in fact, more of the tone of Fidel Castro's "History will absolve me" speech, which was also uttered after his imprisonment for a failed uprising. Indeed, Chávez's complete remarks— which only lasted a bit over a minute—had the tone of a man who was hardly repentant. His message, as he promised his captors, was that it was time for the rebels to lay down their arms. Then he concluded: "Comrades, listen to this message of solidarity. I am grateful for your loyalty, for your courage, for your selfless generosity. Before the country and before you, I accept responsibility for this Bolivarian military movement. *Muchas gracias.*"

He took the blame, but Chávez also elevated himself to a symbolic stature that he, in truth, did not deserve in a fractured movement that included Bolivarians, leftists, nationalists, and discontented people of many stripes. He swept aside his fateful failure to coordinate the rebellion, wasting hard-fought battlefield successes—though others did not. Jesús Urdaneta Hernández, one of Chávez's original partners in the conspiracy, who commanded the troops that took the Maracay base and never wanted to surrender, felt betrayed by Chávez. Ronald Blanco de la Cruz, another conspirator, also held Chávez to blame for the coup's failure. Yet Chávez skillfully used 72 seconds of air time to turn a failed coup into a personal triumph. "Chávez appeared out of nowhere," wrote biographer Jones, "giving a face to a faceless rebellion."[6] He would continue to play that role.

*   *   *

From the standpoint of history, the attempted coup of 1992 was a predictable milestone on Venezuela's long road of political ambivalence. Venezuela has often been portrayed as a functioning democracy, if one periodically interrupted by the military. But that view overlooks Venezuelans' tendency to divide between one set of voters who elected oligarchs and another set of voters who elected other oligarchs. In the aftermath of Chávez's attempt, critics were quick to point out that the masses had hardly flooded the streets in solidarity with the rebellion. Some called for Chávez's execution. On the other hand, there was residual support. There were speeches defending the coup attempt's legitimacy in the eyes of common

people. Venezuela's record of handing the presidency back and forth between the two dominant parties meant that democracy had not been, in the words of former president Rafael
Caldera, "capable of feeding them and stopping the exorbitant rise in the cost of living. [I]t
has not been able to put a stop to the terrible cycle of corruption."[7]

The scholar Juan Carlos Navarro wrote: "The coup attempt ... created excellent conditions for [Chávez and other rebels] to emerge from the shadows, accelerating the pace and
commitment of several and creating conditions for others to become public. Second, it
reopened a forgotten dimension of Venezuelan politics, the struggle between democracy and
authoritarian rule that filled the first century and a half of Venezuelan history."[8] Chávez spent
the next two years in prison. From his cell, however, he was able to participate in the national
discussion much as Castro had nearly four decades before. At first depressed by the failure of
a conspiracy that had been years in the making, Chávez was told by his first visitor—a priest
who was allowed to see him after a week incommunicado—that he was seen as a hero by
many Venezuelans. Later, when Chávez and his fellow conspirators were transferred from the
basement interrogation rooms of military intelligence in Caracas to a jail in the city, they could
see for themselves. The coup attempt—in which fourteen soldiers on both sides, five policemen, and one civilian were killed—was not the failure they had feared. Approximately a
thousand enlisted men and a hundred and thirty officers had been recruited to the cause, and
they remained a base of support, tested on the field of battle.

In the following weeks, Venezuelans were so interested in the jailed *golpistas* that enter-
prising news reporters made their way to Chávez's cell. There, of course, he was more than
ready to talk. Because he was allowed to keep his uniform and paratrooper's maroon beret,
news photographs suggested not a traitor but a fallen hero. When adoring stories continued
to appear, the Pérez administration finally responded by heavily censoring news outlets, intimidating editors, and, when articles kept coming, seizing magazines off loading docks. Editors
responded to censorship by publishing editions with gaping, white, empty holes in their pages
that taunted the government with its lack of popularity. Sixty-two retired military men added
their voices to the tumult in a signed, full-page newspaper advertisement critical of the Pérez
government. It was a confrontation the government could not win, and eventually, despite
scattered support from the oligarchy and U.S. spokesmen, Pérez backed off.

In the enflamed imaginations of Venezuelans, the revolt took on a life of its own. Flyers
and poems and even a prayer—*Chávez Nuestro* in the meter of The Lord's Prayer—spread
through the streets. Supportive graffiti appeared on building walls. To squelch the hero-wor-
ship, the government transferred Chávez to a prison outside the city, but admirers simply
made the trek to the new site. All the attention to Chávez, however, had an effect on his fellow inmates. Disciplined military men, already appalled by some of the behavior of the common criminals imprisoned around them, began to resent the hoopla for Chávez, who was no
more committed to the cause than they. His biggest contribution, in fact, had been drawing
attention to himself, just as he was doing now. Ronaldo Blanco de la Cruz, an army captain
who had sacrificed his career to join the cause, spoke of trying Chávez in prison before a jury
of his peers for his failure of leadership the night of the revolt. Francisco Arias Cárdenas, the
air force officer whose dignity and intellectual depth had won him a wide following among
conspirators, saw in Chávez the characteristics that had split conspirators before and would
continue to do so. In a paradoxical pattern that would continue throughout Chávez's career,
his popularity built a following even as his personality divided it.

Furthermore, a more sober approach to national affairs was being put together on the
outside. Venezuelans were trying again an old response to political division: the "patriotic
front." It was a committee of elders formed to analyze what led to the strife and seek to resolve

differences. It was a perfectly logical technique in a nation that had been divided against itself since its founding, and it had particular resonance when the winning side was as unpopular as the Pérez government. For Chávez and his colleagues, it was a chance to better understand national issues, and they turned their cells into schoolrooms.

On the outside, Chávez supporters, including his brother Adán, opened up lines of communication between the Bolivarianos and the front. Independent intellectuals initiated their own analysis of what Venezuela needed and how to achieve it. Media attention to all of that activity increased popular awareness, and some spoke of another armed revolt; others calculated the chances of breaking Chávez out; still others spoke of assassinating President Pérez; civilian dissidents grew restless again; and military cabals devised new codes. Because the navy and air force had been largely absent from the February uprising, there was pressure on both sides within their ranks to play more of a role. In fact, pressure within the military for another coup attempt pushed the level of leadership up to generals and admirals. Admiral Hernán Gruber Ódreman was chosen to lead.

In the summer of 1992, the rumbling on the outside brought Chávez into conflict with Arias Cárdenas, the imprisoned air force officer whose standing among dissidents equaled that of Chávez. Arias Cárdenas, who had butted heads with Chávez before, felt that the time for another coup was not yet right. Chávez did, and his allies on the outside made known their view that Chávez, because of his iconic position in the eyes of the masses, should make the call. These people included an element that referred to Chávez as *El Comandante,* an indication of their romantic, if narrow, view. They were the sort of people who chose not to go through the arduous process of forming a political party—defining policy positions—but were eager for armed revolt. They prevailed, meaning that their move would have to be mounted before December, when state and local elections were scheduled. They picked the last week in November. As events unfolded, the conspirators found that Arias Cárdenas had been right.

Once again, the rebellion went well at first. Launched at daylight on November 27, the rebels captured major air bases and took charge of antennae serving three television studios. In jail, the February conspirators, including Chávez, clustered around a radio that had been smuggled into their prison. They were waiting to be freed. By noon, however, events had taken a tragic turn.

Battles on the ground were often bloody, and in the skies Venezuelan air force pilots fought each other. But when rebel planes dominated air space, rebel troops failed to secure the sector beneath it. Videotapes, including one that featured Chávez speaking from his prison cell, were broadcast. They called on the people to rise, which, once again, failed to happen. Loyal troops recaptured bases, and President Pérez reprised his February appearance on a television station controlled by loyalists. The second rebellion in a year collapsed in disarray. This time, one hundred and seventy-one Venezuelans were killed, more than eight times the toll of the February attempt. The result, though, was exactly the same: failure.

* * *

However, if rebellion had failed to remove Pérez from office, democratic institutions did the job instead. A newspaper columnist accused Pérez and his friends of stealing millions by misusing government funds and illegally trading currency. Government investigators picked up the scent. They brought to light that Pérez and his oligarchic buddies had turned Banco Latino, an otherwise nondescript Venezuelan bank and the nation's central bank, into a giant scheme to line their pockets. The Venezuelan Supreme Court ruled that Pérez could be brought to trial, and the Senate immediately barred him from office.

The experience so aroused popular discontent that national politics showed signs of institutional reform — Venezuelan style. In the December elections, a candidate from the leftist *Causa R* (for Radical) party was elected mayor of Caracas. *Causa R* had been around for years, but not until Pérez's disgrace had it been able to break through the AD-COPEI monopoly. Another new face — a very pretty one — emerged when Irene Sáez, a former beauty queen, was elected mayor of Chacao, a wealthy jurisdiction on the edge of Caracas. And in state after state, gubernatorial candidates of AD, Pérez's party, lost. Venezuelans appeared to be fed up with corruption, incompetence, and lack of concern for social progress, but what pushed them over the edge was more immediate. Because of Pérez's mismanagement, the International Monetary Fund was demanding that foreign creditors be paid back, an effort that, in spite of high oil prices, seriously depleted Venezuela's resources.

The stage was set for the next presidential election, and Chávez was intensely interested in how it would play out. The contest was among four people, some new, some very old. One of the oldest was 78-year-old Rafael Caldera. He was remembered by Venezuelans as a righteous and honest man from his previous presidency in the 1960s. More importantly for Chávez and his friends, Caldera was also remembered for granting amnesty to rebels of the day. Running as an independent, Caldera won — despite an allegation that a goodly portion of the *Causa R* candidate's ballots were thrown in the trash. As far as most Venezuelans were concerned, once again an establishment candidate had won. On the night of Caldera's victory, Chávez, using a telephone smuggled into his cell, called Caldera to offer his most sincere congratulations. Within weeks of Caldera's inauguration in early 1994, the February rebels were being released. Chávez insisted on being the last one out, but he, too, was back on the street by late March.

Chávez stepped out of jail and into an enthusiastic welcome by his many admirers. However, his record as a leader had been thoroughly discussed over the two years of his imprisonment. Not only was his behavior in the February coup attempt at issue, but some faulted him for meddling in the November attempt only to burnish his own image. The harshest criticism came, predictably, from Arias Cárdenas. Joining in, however, was Herma Marksman, Chávez's erstwhile mistress. Marksman accused Chávez of seeing himself not just as a political leader, but a messiah. Even President Caldera was criticized for not prohibiting Chávez — who could have been held for thirty years—from participating in electoral politics. Over the next three years Chávez prepared to do exactly that.

*   *   *

At first, Chávez dismissed any notion of a political career, continuing the contempt he'd long shown for politicians. But he was too much of a performer and a student of history to continue in that vein. He had come out of prison to find crowds of adoring people, with children wearing play fatigues that matched his uniform. Some women wore expressions of rapture suitable to his image as a *macho*, and some men were tired of the traditional parties' reeling from one crisis to the next. By comparison, Chávez appeared to be something of a savior. Through 1995 and into 1996, Chávez listened to advisors and admirers. Among the latter was one Marisabel Rodríguez, who found ways to express her admiration that led to the birth of their daughter, Rosinés, in late 1997. They were married two months later.

Marisabel accompanied Chávez on his path of testing the political water, moving among the people and currying their favor. He visited Bolívar's tomb, walked the streets of poor barrios, and traveled to farming villages. He made a trip to Cuba, where Castro, a man who could work a crowd as well as anyone, greeted him at the airport and showed him around. They made joint appearances and compared notes on what was necessary to turn imagery into policy. Throughout this period, at home and abroad, wherever Chávez went, he talked. He made formal speeches, held conversations with common people, and made offhand remarks to reporters. Newspapers, magazine, and television reporters dogged his steps, though there was so little substance to what he said that traditional politicians tended to dismiss him as a charismatic, but fleeting, phenomenon.

Chávez, too, saw himself as stuck in a rut, criticizing politicians rather than beating them at their own game. His old friend-turned-foe Urdaneta had not waited so long. He accepted a diplomatic appointment from the Caldera government as soon as he was released from prison and went on to be elected governor of Zulía, an important oil state. Chávez, without gainful employment and without serious direction, was still wandering. Importantly, the mainstream media were ignoring him. Eventually, his friends and financial supporters began to construct a serious strategy, bolstering his appeal to the crowds with an organization. They put together support of both leftists and more traditional politicians, soft-pedaling the fire-eyed nationalism Chávez had espoused for so long. And they employed the *sine qua non* of modern electoral politics: the demographic survey conducted by a public relations firm.

By the spring of 1997 the threads of a political campaign were woven. Because Venezuelan law prohibited political parties from exploiting The Liberator's name, Chávez and his associates changed MBR-200 — their original *Movimiento Bolivariano Revolucionario*, or the Bolivarian Revolutionary Movement — to MVR, the *Movimiento Quinta Republica*. (Venezuela has instituted five republics since independence from Spain.) The new party was registered and Chávez's presidential campaign was launched. *El Comandante* became *el candidato*, and he would demonstrate much more devilish talent as a politician than he ever had as a military commander.

The political climate was still turbulent, common folk were unhappy, and guerrilla bands had been increasing their recruitment efforts in the countryside. Not only had the sins of the Pérez years not been expiated during the Caldera years, they had grown worse. Inflation soared; price controls inhibited business growth; civil freedoms were restricted, and the IMF still loomed over the national budget, glowering. To top off matters, by autumn petroleum prices had dropped. Indeed, the election campaign of 1998 encompassed so many idiosyncrasies of Venezuelan politics that it explains how a candidate of Chávez's eccentricities could win.

The Caldera administration, feeling the heat of public discontent, was suppressing expression, and Chávez and his Bolivariano cohorts were among those the government clamped a lid on. With the national police harassing him, watching him, and tapping his phone, Chávez played a cat-and-mouse game. He sometimes disguised himself and he often held meetings in out-of-the-way places. He managed, despite the pressure, to bring together leftist dissidents and form an amalgam of parties and splinter groups to make up the "Patriotic Pole" as the foundation of his presidential campaign. Chávez brought his popularity to the table, and the groups he recruited provided their legitimacy and organization. Given the confusion of his opponents, that combination quickly propelled Chávez to frontrunner in national polls.

Chávez's principle opponent — and surely the most eye-catching — was the lovely Irene Sáez, whose career as mayor of an upscale suburb had ill prepared her for a national campaign. Her popularity was such that she won endorsement of COPEI, but she eventually turned into a Venezuelan blonde joke. AD, on the other hand, nominated and then abandoned a 76-year-old candidate. Eventually, AD and COPEI, traditional opponents, patched together a cooperative campaign vehicle at the last minute, throwing yet another candidate into the breach in a frantic effort to head off the Chávez juggernaut. The panic spread to Congress, where the traditional parties, fearing a landslide and the loss of their majority, passed a last-minute law separating congressional and presidential election days to minimize the effect of Chávez's coattails. Even the administration of U.S. President Bill Clinton got into what was looking like a political circus by making a clumsy attempt to thwart Chávez's campaign. The State Department denied Chávez a visa before his planned pre-election trip to the United States. Chávez—employing a style that would become his trademark—laughed off the snub, holding up, instead, his VISA credit card for the cameras. In the materialistic United States, he said, that was the important visa. And in Latin America, nothing had more currency than tweaking the nose of Uncle Sam.

On the other hand, Chávez, presumably at the insistence of his braintrust, showed that he could calm his manic behavior when necessary. He shed his fatigues—too Castro—in favor of sweaters and sport shirts—oh, so Jimmy Carter. He tried to assure international investors that he was not going to run roughshod over them. After all, he implied, Venezuela's oil industry had been nationalized 20 years before, so what harm could Chávez possibly do? He even compared himself to the moderate British Prime Minister Tony Blair, who had modeled himself on the easy-going President Bill Clinton. In dulcet tones, Chávez explained that with him at Miraflores, Venezuela would be just another member of the happy hemispheric family. As photogenic confirmation of his family instincts, Chávez brought before the cameras wife Marisabel—also a fetching blonde—and their tiny daughter, Rosinés.

Chávez won the election handily. He took about 56 percent of the more than 5 million votes cast. That was well ahead of the 40 percent won by Enrique Salas Romer, the last-minute compromise candidate the establishment had clumsily rallied behind. Irene Sáez wasn't able to garner 185,000 votes. So stunning was Chávez's victory that the United States reversed course, issued a visa, and President Bill Clinton met briefly with Chávez in Washington. Thus when Chávez accepted the sash of his office in February 1999, his detractors were prepared for him to show himself an oaf, and his supporters waited anxiously for him to live up to their image as a hero.

True to form, Chávez gave a performance. Although inaugural tradition called for his predecessor, Caldera, to administer the oath of office, that denizen of the Old Guard couldn't bring himself to do it. Instead, the job fell to long-time Chávez supporter Luis Alfonso Dávila, the former air force officer who had been elected president of the Venezuelan Senate. Then, Chávez, speaking to the gathered heads of state, a crowd of legislators and officials, a mob of supporters jamming the streets, and, of course, the television cameras, ignored the traditional pledge to uphold the constitution. Instead, he resolved to propel "over this moribund constitution ... the democratic transformations that are necessary so that the new republic will have an adequate magna carta for our times."[9]

He then spoke for an hour and forty-five minutes, delighting supporters and confirming the worst fears of opponents. How, he asked, could a nation with the greatest oil reserves in the world still have eighty percent of its population weighed down by abject poverty? The immediate result of his speech, laced with literary references, was to send his approval ratings in opinion polls through the roof. Even the official line of the U.S. State Department softened to give Chávez a chance. He was especially praised for his eloquence. Less clear was how Venezuelans would respond to his demand for a popular convention to rewrite the constitution.

Chávez's silver tongue was forgotten as his administration became more characterized by its iron hand. His supporters needed little incitement to take to the streets, so rowdy crowds became a manifestation of public policy. Were international news organizations critical? Supporters would organize sit-ins, interfering with their operations. Were legislators unenthusiastic about Chávez initiatives? Street crowds were led in shouts for Congress to be dissolved.

When the constitutional convention was planned and citizens sued the Chávez government over how delegates would be chosen, President Chávez threatened to dissolve Congress and the courts. Crowds of his bullying supporters turned out to shout their approval of his bluster.

Chávez continued to find ways to delight a populace denied competent government for so long. His trips to friendly capitals enhanced Venezuelans' pride. His regular appearances on radio and television, and the initiation of his own show, "Aló, Presidente," allowed him to answer phoned-in questions, which he did sitting before a large portrait of Simón Bolívar. His performances included singing and playing the xylophone. Yet Chávez also confirmed critics' misgivings. An egregious example was when Chávez sent a sympathetic letter to the infamous terrorist, Illich Ramírez Sánchez. A Venezuelan known as "Carlos the Jackal," Ramírez was serving a life sentence in France for hijacking an airliner. Such behavior, recycled endlessly in the news media, served as a sideshow while Venezuela slouched through 1999 toward an uncertain future. While oil prices nearly tripled, the economy shrank. The unemployment rate rose to a record high. The national deficit grew.

Another aspect of Chávez's behavior that troubled critics was his insistence on often wearing a uniform, including the paratrooper's maroon beret. It carried more than a whiff of the sort of militarism that marked the country's past. In addition, Chávez had appointed to high office, including his cabinet, more than a few of his former fellow officers from the February insurrection. Furthermore, Chávez ordered the army into the streets in "Plan Bolívar 2000." Seventy thousand soldiers were sent into the barrios to fix roads, set up medical clinics, cart away garbage, and sell food acquired by the government at bargain prices. He said he was simply enlisting the help of the armed forces in a national *civico-militar* campaign to make friends between sectors that had been arch enemies.

The problem with Plan Bolívar, though, was not that it was militarization, but that it was a simple-minded attack on endemic problems. Rather than a substantive effort to improve public services with higher taxes, or increase resources through competent management, it was show-time. In fact, for all of Chávez's speeches—sometimes pre-empting television airtime of immensely popular *telenovelas*—the economy went backward. During the first year of Chávez's presidency, gross national product fell and employment faltered. Skittish foreign investors cut back, and nearly $5 billion in Venezuelan capital was moved offshore. Chávez's histrionics were costing him the opportunity to turn popularity into leadership.

Real reform, he insisted, would only be possible after the coming constitutional convention. The convention, Chávez and his supporters said, would allow popularly elected delegates to take over the role of Congress, with all of its cronyism. Further, convention delegates would reconstitute Venezuela's notoriously corrupt court system. The powers of Congress and the courts would be brought into check, and the powers of the president would be broadened. Like so many Latin American leaders, Chávez advanced the tired idea that the solution to every national problem lay in hardened presidential power. Whether Chávez had the wisdom to conceive the solutions or the skill to implement them were open questions. Congress and the Supreme Court and their supporters fought to retain their prerogatives, but Congress eventually gave up the ghost and adjourned. For its part, the Supreme Court first ruled that the convention had no power over it. In the end, however, the court reversed itself. The field was left wide open, and onto it charged Chávez's reformers.

In the beginning, the debate over the constitutional convention was restricted to leaders of the executive, legislative, and judicial branches. The first hint of popular discontent followed Chávez's insistence on a nationwide referendum on whether the convention should be held at all. The referendum seemed to confirm Venezuelans' mass ambivalence. Six of every ten Venezuelan voters abstained. That lent credence to those who said it was a bad idea, but by abstaining, rather than voting against the convention, the majority left the decision to supporters. Nearly nine of every ten Venezuelans who went to the polls approved the idea. So the convention was on, and there was nothing to be done but gather signatures on petitions for the choice of delegates. More than 1,100 citizens gathered the required number of names, of whom only about a fourth were outright Chávez supporters. But by the time the convention's 131 elected delegates were called to order, however, Chávez partisans—including wife Marisabel—had an overwhelming majority, 125 to 6.

The first order of business was to attack the established order. Luis Miquilena, a long-time Chávez mentor who was president of the convention, asserted that it had "originating character;" that is, fundamental legal powers. That interpretation was contested by the traditional institutions, but to no avail. The Supreme Court, which had first ruled against such a broad reading of the convention's authority, reversed itself, yielding to Chávez's forces. The chief justice of the Supreme Court resigned in protest, but that only strengthened the hand of Chávez's forces. Then convention delegates effectively disbanded Congress, the members of which decided to take a vacation. What was called a "peaceful revolution" was underway. There were roars of disapproval at home and abroad, but Chávez listened for, and got, even louder roars of approval from many Venezuelans. This continued Venezuela's democracy by decibels.

The convention promptly initiated reforms of the court system, long known for corrupt and lazy judges, and passed improvements to prisons, which were overcrowded and dangerous. Those moves were met with widespread approval. Then the delegates took aim at Congress, and that was another matter. Members of Congress came back to Caracas from their forced vacation ready to fight. To demonstrate their disapproval, some burned military berets, Chávez's symbol. Yet when they and their supporters marched toward the national legislative building, their way was blocked by police. The resulting melee between police and the stick-wielding crowd featured legislators climbing over the iron fence surrounding the building and tear gas, rubber bullets, and water cannons fired by police.

By the autumn of 1999—still in the first year of Chávez's term—the convention had made good on its pledge to clean up the court system. Several judges had been dismissed and several dozen publicly named as corrupt, incompetent, or both. A new transparency in the selection of judges was guaranteed. Work had begun, with the help of international human rights agencies, on improving prison conditions. Native tribes won recognition of the collective ownership of land they had long been promised. There were new guarantees of human rights. Importantly, the new charter combined the two chambers of Congress into a unicameral National Assembly. And it allowed, more or less in line with other Latin American democracies, the president, under extreme circumstances, to force legislation through the National Assembly. It made recall possible for all elected officials—national, state, and local. Most controversial were the changes to the legislative branch, and members of Congress, a den of entrenched interests, remained opposed.

Chávez, all the while, never lost his predilection for showmanship. He embarked for Asia to meet national leaders and, more to his liking, to appear before Asian crowds. He returned to take Marisabel on a junket to Cuba, where he—and she—joined Fidel Castro for a crowd-pleasing game of baseball. Chávez returned to Venezuela with the December 15 ballot looming. And as the vote approached, opponents—including the Catholic clergy—pulled out all the stops. They warned that because members of the military were enfranchised to vote in elections—a common practice in modern democracies—Venezuela would be militarized. Because the president's term was increased from five to six years and allowed for two sequential terms, there were dire warnings that Chávez would turn his presidency into the beginning of a dictatorship.

Venezuela's hyperactive news media, covering a seemingly endless series of elections, was alive with charges and countercharges. Many of them were about as dignified as the pushing and shoving outside Congress only a few months before. But when the final tally came in, it approved the new constitution with a 70 percent margin. That result would establish Venezuelan institutions into the future, despite the horrible effect on the Venezuelan national consciousness of the natural disaster that occurred the same day.

In the two weeks before the vote, an unseasonal rain had soaked Mount Avila, the peak of which rises more than a mile and a half above the Caribbean coast. Then, during the 48 hours before the night of the vote, the equivalent of twice the year's average rainfall drenched the mountainside. The land gave way. Mud, boulders, and forests slid down the steep face of the mountain, devastating entire villages and killing thousands of men, women, and children. One boulder that hurtled down the mountain was estimated to weigh 840 tons. Because so many of the villages inundated by mudslides and destroyed by debris were ramshackle affairs, the death toll could only be estimated: The number of those killed was put anywhere between 5,000 and 20,000. Displaced were some 140,000 men, women, and children.

After weeks of political wrangling, Venezuelans united in an outpouring of sympathy and aid. Chávez bolstered his image as a man of action by taking a risky helicopter ride to the scene when wind and rain conditions were still severe. He also added to his reputation for unpredictability by refusing part of the U.S. aid that was being sent at the expressed request of his administration. Apparently, Chávez feared the arrival of U.S. soldiers accompanying the bulldozers slated for reconstruction.

*   *   *

As Venezuela dealt with its tragedy and began implementation of its new constitution, criticism of Chávez mounted. He could still count on the support of roughly half of the electorate, but that is a fraction fraught with danger. Every issue rallied one friend for every one opponent. The equation begged whether or not the controversy was of the Chávez administration's making. The Caldera government had agreed to open a huge area of Venezuelan jungle on the border with Brazil for the mining of gold and diamonds and construction of an electrical power line. Environmentalists complained about destruction of the forests, and advocates for indigenous tribes decried the intrusion into their ancient province. Chávez, who insisted on living up to the agreement, found himself in the unusual position of being showered with praise by the business community. Other issues were more predictable.

In dire need of reform was a public school system that had never enrolled nearly the proportion of children that a developing nation needs and provided only minimal, outdated materials for the pupils who got in the doors. Half of its pupils left before completing high school. The situation had long festered as past governments averted their eyes from the need for taxes, and upper and middle class families paid tuition to private and parochial schools. Quickly, the Chávez government made sound changes that were popular. The changes were so popular, in fact, that more parents than could be accommodated lined up, only to be turned away. Fees the public schools had used to augment meager budgets were eliminated, but when taxes were proposed in their stead they were, predictably, controversial.

So the Chávez government established five hundred "Bolivarian schools." The schools—which provided free breakfast and lunch, uniforms, and, in some cases, computers—were a dramatic first step toward reform. Chávez took reform a step further when he sent administrators into public and private schools to recommend improvements, including the dismissal of incompetent teachers from public schools. The imposition of government standards on private schools excited a hue and cry from middle and upper class parents, who exaggerated the power of the administrators. Newspaper headlines then exaggerated the exaggerations. The brouhaha over schools and a brawl with a labor union — pitting Chávez's insistence on free election of leaders against continued domination by *Acción Demócrata* — exemplified the first years of Chávez's tenure. Heated rhetoric, hyperventilating headlines, and heavy-handed tactics made every attempt at reform an exercise in futility. More ominously, in early 2000 several of his allies-turned-critics — including Urdaneta and Arias — called a press conference to tell Venezuelans that they could no longer abide Chávez's tactics.

Singled out for particular criticism was Chávez's *personalismo*, cozying up to advisors who pleased him personally and freezing out officials whose intellect and integrity were widely acknowledged. Chávez, they felt, was either on a podium, making speeches, or in a cocoon, hearing praise. And the very corruption Chávez had railed against was creeping back into his own administration. Over the months, harsh words were traded while policy concerns were ignored. Though oil prices rose, national obligations went unmet. Even though U.S. ambassador to Venezuela, John Maisto, declared that the Chávez regime had been relatively open and democratic, others blasted Chávez with sometimes hysterical commentary. The American magazine *Newsweek*, for example, headlined: "Is Hugo Chávez Insane?"

Eventually, a furious Arias declared himself a candidate in the approaching presidential election, ordered by the new constitution. Predictably, the campaign was as nasty as it was all-encompassing. Under the new constitution, more than 6,000 offices — national, state, and local — were to be filled, and some 35,000 candidates would present themselves. But if the enormity of the task weren't enough, the computer-backed voting system stumbled under the strain; voting, scheduled for the spring was put off until late July. When the election was finally held, Chávez ran up an even greater margin of victory in the presidential race than he had the first time. He won nearly 60 percent. Parties that supported him took 105 of the 165 seats in the new unicameral National Assembly, an impressive number, but short of the two-thirds Chávez would need to ratify his choices for important posts and to approve his budget.

Installed in the presidency, Chávez set about making good on plans he had been formulating for some time. He wanted to stabilize world prices by bringing Venezuela and other members of the Organization of Petroleum Exporting Countries (OPEC) back into mutual agreement on goals. The OPEC countries, each pursuing its own national interest, had been divided, weakening their resolve to control supply and keep prices high. So Chávez set off on a whirlwind tour to the other ten OPEC nations, inviting leaders to a summit, which would be their first in 25 years. Venezuelan news reporters traipsed along like courtiers, assuring that the journey would be seen, if not understood, by all. U.S. officials especially agonized over Chávez's stop in Iraq to meet to Saddam Hussein, but Chávez had more in mind than twisting Uncle Sam's nose. The high-level contacts and the subsequent conference in Caracas represented more than just headline-grabbing. Venezuela's status in world affairs was enhanced. Besides, if Chávez wanted to make the White House agonize, all he had to do was invite Fidel Castro over for a state visit and another baseball game — which was exactly what he did after the oil summit.

* * *

By late 2001, Chávez was secure enough in his presidency to issue forty-nine executive decrees aimed at reform. It was a grab-bag of populist measures, including channeling credit to farmers; protecting offshore areas from incursion by large fishing interests; reforming, for the second time, land tenure; and restructuring management of the oil industry. The last two, modifying the way a nation exploits its land above and below the surface, go to the very heart of reform in Latin America. Since Spanish colonists took the land and its riches from native tribes, those two issues have determined whether Latin America's sovereign nations advance or stagnate.

Venezuelan liberals had been trying since the early 1960s to break large tracts of farm land —*latifundia*— into viable family farms—*minifundia*. This was an enormously complex problem, requiring that ancient farming methods be modernized, idle land energized, and entrenched owners pacified. The process was accomplished in the southwest United States after the Mexican War only by a combination of strong homestead laws, hordes of arriving immigrants, and a burgeoning market back East. In Venezuela, the '60s reform program went full circle, granting small plots and then allowing rich investors to recapture the land. The Chávez program also had calamitous results, including small-scale warfare in the country-side, but still managed to effect some reform.

Landowners in the incendiary region along the Colombian border — where dissidents persist to this day — rose up in arms. They formed militias that were reportedly trained by infamous Colombian paramilitary groups. Reform advocates were shot in cold blood. In the first four years of the program, an estimated 130 land-reform organizers were killed. In sum, the violent response was successful in protecting the large landholdings; not an acre was ever expropriated. Nevertheless, while private land had not changed hands, 130,000 families were moved onto their own farms on 4.5 million acres of public land that had lain unused.

Needless to say, the program united landowners in opposition, and Chávez's rhetoric did the rest, driving away even former supporters. By 2002, Chávez was mixing his enthusiasm for land reform with remarks and activities that made some old friends blanch. He voiced support for the *Fuerzas Armadas Revolucionarias de Colombia* (FARC), the political-turned-bandit army that had waged a thoroughly unproductive rebellion since the early 1960s. FARC had turned its early politics into organized drug-running, kidnapping, and pointless mayhem. Yet Chávez applauded their efforts, and many of his former allies in the Venezuelan military found his support ill-informed and insulting. They appeared before television cameras in full uniform — despite attempts to silence them — and denounced his reckless policies. At the same time, material evidence of Chávez's support surfaced in the form of e-mails and computer records, further exposing his poor judgment.

His efforts at reforming the oil industry were similarly stormy. Since first elected, Chávez had signaled his intent to rein in the industry's operations. Once again, he was not the first to think reform was necessary. President Pérez nationalized the oil fields, organizing Petróleos de Venezuela S.A. (PdVSA), owner of Citgo, the chain of gas stations operated in the United States. But the Pérez plan allowed foreign managers to continue to operate with a freedom Chávez distrusted. PdVSA's computer systems, for example, were designed and maintained by a San Diego technology company with ties to the U.S. military. Chávez felt the arrangement risked exposure of geographic details of strategic oil reserves, including unexploited deposits.

Of more immediate concern was the degree to which foreigners influenced Venezuela's share of petrodollar profits. Between 1976 and 1993, 66 cents of every petrodollar had been retained by the Venezuelan government. From 1993 to 2002, however, that proportion was cut in half by a business plan adopted by Venezuelan authorities. The point of the plan was to increase production by bringing in capital investment from foreign companies, a process called *apertura*, or "opening." Volume increased straightaway by 1 million barrels per day, to 3.6 million by 1997, but profits were shared in exchange for the investment.

The plan also placed PdVSA under a board of directors controlled by retired executives of foreign oil companies and called for Venezuela's petrochemical company, *Pequiven*, to be sold to private buyers. None of that loss of state control sat well with Chávez. Some Venezuelans were calling OPEC quotas "obsolete." Chávez railed about PdVSA executives drawing fat salaries and running up big expense accounts.[10] Chávez wanted more of his, Venezuelan, appointees on the board of directors and more of the profit brought home to the Venezuelan treasury. The debate raged until there was a walkout by PdVSA white-collar workers, inflammatory stories in the newspapers, televised antics by Chávez — he blew a referee's whistle and raised his arm in a *futbol* referee's "Offsides" signal — and a summary dismissal of PdVSA executives. Field workers responded with a strike, the effects of which Chávez tried to ameliorate with soldiers working on oil rigs.[11]

By the spring of 2002, discontent had developed into conversations about an overthrow. Street protests got bigger. Finally, on the morning of April 11, a Thursday, a crowd gathered in what would become the biggest demonstration since the first Pérez presidency half a century before. The crowd in Caracas was estimated at half a million people. Among them was a businessman and former diplomat, Pedro Carmona, who was being encouraged to run for president against Chávez. Events, however, would not wait for that. Confrontation could not be avoided, for far from being a spontaneous expression, the uprising had been planned for months; its military wing was well organized and almost open. The U.S. Central Intelligence Agency had been reporting the probability of an attempted coup, and the National Endowment for Democracy was channeling U.S. public funds to Chávez's opponents.

Once protesters massed outside of Miraflores, Chávez was, in effect, trapped inside. Soon, a second group of dissidents was marching to join the first. But as the crowd of Chávez opponents grew, radio and television reports spread the word to the *barrios*, where Chávez supporters began to mobilize. Although military supporters of Chávez had made known their willingness to throw themselves into the equation, before they could act effectively Miraflores was encircled by civilians, and dissident troops blocked access by parking heavy equipment in the streets.

By mid-afternoon, confrontations — rocks thrown, tear gas canisters launched, shots fired — began and went from bad to worse. Chávez, barricaded in the basement at Miraflores, asked television stations to stop broadcasting tape of the street confrontations and broadcast his own appeal for calm. Some stations defied his request by continuing satellite broadcasts of the violence, even showing split-screen images: on one side men were shooting at each other; on the other Chávez called for calm. Late in the afternoon, Chávez returned to his office, donned his maroon beret and fatigues and strapped on a pistol. The worm had turned.

Television screens were filled with carnage. Leading figures of both the opposition and *chavistas* contributed to the fighting. A massive confrontation at a Caracas bridge became a symbol of the day's atrocities. Perversely, the uprising blended the oldest forms of violence with the modern technology of television, thoroughly confounding the truth. Footage showed atrocities that had been altered to support the editor's point of view. For example, broadcasters distributed around the world pictures that supposedly showed Chávez supporters killing protesters at the bridge, pictures the other side condemned as distorted. On the sidewalks around Miraflores, however, there was no mistaking reality.

Marisabel de Chávez and four-year-old Rosinés were escorted out of Caracas. Even Chávez's other three children by his first wife were sent to safety. Fidel Castro telephoned, counseling Chávez, whose flair for drama Castro knew well. Castro warned against doing something drastic like killing himself. He also discouraged Chávez from donning a helmet and taking up a submachine gun the way Chilean President Salvador Allende had nearly thirty years before. Live to fight another day was the advice, and Chávez confidante José Vicente

Rangel, who was at his side through the tense night, later said that Castro's call was profoundly helpful. Other expressions of support came in, including from military officers who could have mounted a counter-coup. Chávez had no stomach, however, for a bloodbath—which might have included the bombing of Miraflores—and sent two generals to parlay with the rebels.

Negotiations droned on, and Chávez and his lieutenants discussed options until three o'clock the next morning. At his aides' insistence, Chávez did not resign, but rather submitted to capture. When that was announced to the crowd outside Miraflores, his supporters shouted their support in the signature chant: "Hu-go, Hu-go, Hu-go." When Chávez surrendered his pistol and walked into the hallway, his staff sang the national anthem. And when his captors refused Chávez's ministers' request to accompany him into confinement—fearing that, alone, he would be assassinated—the possibility that he would indeed be killed seemed even more stark.

Pedro Carmona, the choice of those who planned the overthrow, assumed the presidency before dawn. Chávez, who was removed to Fort Tiuna nearby, began an uncertain wait. It had to be like the hours he spent as a captive after the failure of the February coup—hours that led to two years in prison. While he was being held, Chávez was allowed to watch television, which was filled with talking heads making clear that the coup had been well planned and holding Chávez responsible for all manner of atrocities. The tone of their remarks convinced Chávez that he would be murdered. Indeed, once when he was taken out of his room, he was convinced that the two soldiers who escorted him were going to kill him but were talked out of it by their comrades. Tempers were running high throughout the country, and the depth of Chávez's plight was directly related to his isolation. A sudden shot in the temple could be portrayed as suicide. Angry pro–Chávez crowds, anxious about his whereabouts, turned to looting.

In captivity, however, Chávez was permitted to telephone his family. He asked Marisabel to get word to the rank and file of his supporters that he had not resigned. He gave the same message to his daughters. Although his eldest daughter, the twenty-four-year-old María Gabriela, broke down upon hearing her father's voice, her younger sister, Rosa Virginia, took the phone. Her father's instruction: Call Castro. It will be difficult to get a call through, but figure it out. And that is what Rosa Virginia did.

She called the switchboard at Miraflores, still attended by faithful staffers, who got the call through. Castro immediately set up a telephone interview on live Cuban television for María Gabriela. He also called back every half hour with reassurances. Venezuelan broadcasters, however, were allowing nothing but criticism of Chávez to be shown. It would take some clever artifice to get out the news that Chávez had not resigned, but was being held captive.

Oddly, Chávez was interviewed by his captors; he was asked formalistic questions sent by the legal department of Venezuelan military forces. His health was checked, and he signed a form attesting to his status. Chávez told the women who performed the duties that he had not resigned, though the women did not record the remark. Later, however, they noted his claim on the form and sent a copy to the office of Attorney General Isías Rodríguez. Rodríguez, understanding that he would not be allowed to convey this information to Venezuelans, scheduled a news conference to announce his own resignation. On a live broadcast, before the news editor could cut him off, Rodríguez blurted out that Chávez had not resigned, an act that could legally be performed only before the national legislature. As that news spread, several Latin American capitals issued condemnations of the coup; contrarily, Washington offered its warm congratulations.

As the imprisonment went on, street disruptions continued, and the authors of the coup seriously overplayed their hand. Squads were sent to round up Chávez supporters, though it was unclear that they were guilty of anything but support for a constitutional government. They were blamed for killings that occurred during the anti–Chávez demonstrations, but it was clear to objective observers that many of those arrested were perfectly innocent. In addition, anti–Chávez mobs in Caracas continued to create bedlam, including an attack on the Cuban embassy. Carmona laid a heavy hand on a government he only tenuously controlled, appointing coup leaders to posts and anointing himself a defender of democracy. He was unaware that the presidential guard, which had stayed at its post, would be part of a swift counter-coup. He was also oblivious to the fact that the high-ranking officers who engineered his ascent to the presidency did not command boots on the ground.

Throughout the ordeal, Chávez could do nothing but wait. When his captors took him by helicopter to an island off the coast, he smuggled a note to a friendly soldier —"To the Venezuelan people ... I have not renounced the legitimate power that the Venezuelan people gave me"—who tried to get it to loyal forces at the Maracay base. When he was visited by a nurse who told him that her mother was one of his fondest supporters, he was moved to tears. "I had a lot of things bottled up inside me," he would later say. "She left, and I went into the bathroom and cried and cried and cried."[12] The next morning, April 14, his guards at Miraflores had enough confidence to begin denouncing the coup and calling him *Presidente.*

Just two days after the coup was completed, it was crushed. With pro–Chávez crowds ringing Miraflores, army officers loyal to Chávez simply marched their men through entry tunnels and occupied the building. Carmona fled, his supporters in the military in no position to help. For the most part, military officers were confused by a stalemate between a past president who had not resigned and a current one who did not even enjoy broad support among leaders of the rebellion. The officers who recaptured Miraflores first looked for Chávez's vice president, who'd gone into hiding. He was needed to take office until Chávez could be brought back to Caracas. Then they arrested Carmona. By early morning on April 15th a helicopter hovered over the city bringing Chávez back. He was all in one piece, but his country was more divided than ever.

* * *

The year 2002 was rent by three general strikes. Opponents were trying to force Chávez from office by disrupting the economy. Street protests became as popular as beauty contests. Plaza Altamira, a park in Caracas, became a kind of Opposition Central as dissidents mingled there day after day. Leaders of the failed rebellion were their idols, and it was to Plaza Altamira that opponents of the regime went to reassure each other. Venezuela was like two countries: one angry, the other hopeful. What looked like progress to half the nation — in 2003, spending on education rose to 20 percent of the national budget, double the year before — was anathema to the other half. With only rare exceptions, what pleased supporters infuriated detractors, and Chávez's strident personality only exacerbated the rift.

The linchpin of the opposition was the petroleum industry. Some oil workers and most industry managers walked off the job. Oil exports dropped precipitously. The captain of an oil tanker anchored his ship's 280,000 gallons of gasoline in the Lake Maracaibo channel, blocking others. Banks were reduced to opening a few days a week. Foodstuffs had to be imported. As the threat from the oil industry worsened, with service stations shut and distribution facilities jeopardized, Chávez deployed soldiers to guard facilities and imported oil. Wherever they could do the jobs of striking workers, soldiers were ordered to pitch in.

In that political environment, it was only through Chávez's hard-headed persistence, reinforced by mass demonstrations of supporters, that got him through. The series of crises lasted into 2003, with the Venezuelan business community doing all it could to strangle the economy. All the while, anti–Chávez forces were rooted on by the news media. "Without exaggeration, never has a Venezuelan leader been so criticized and lambasted by the media."[13] Eventually, business leaders weighed their loss of profit against putting up with a president they so deeply detested. The economic rebellion ground to a halt, and the adoring crowds of Chávez supporters flowed into the streets. Chávez chided the oligarchs that the opposition had "failed." Beginning in 2003, his government used oil revenues to establish the Robinson Mission, a network of programs providing health services, subsidized food markets, and literacy classes. The effort cost nearly $2 billion over its first few years.

Next, the opposition held up the new constitution, pointing to its unusual provision for recall of the president. First, a petition approving the recall vote had to have signatures from a fifth of registered voters: 2.4 million people. Once balloting was approved, a successful recall required (1) more votes than supporters of the president, and (2) more votes than he got when last elected: 3.8 million. Still, it was not clear whether, even if recalled, the president could simply run again at the next national election. But whatever the legal details, Chávez's opponents were willing to give recall a try. A prominent figure among opponents was Marisabel, from whom Chávez was divorced in 2003.

When an oversight commission ruled that the first petition fell short of the required number, Venezuelans fell into one of their periodic fits of protest, and it was eventually agreed that the petitioners should get another chance. The second petition stretched into early 2004, and, even though thousands more signatures were collected, a commission ruled in March that 1.9 million of the 3.4 million signatures shown on petition sheets were still invalid. Again, street protests were mounted, and this time eight people were killed. In April, another compromise was reached, clearing a definitive recall vote. Chávez jauntily predicted he would win with 5 million votes.

On August 15, a Sunday, the recall election was held under the watchful eye of former U.S. President Jimmy Carter and other international observers. Nearly 10 million voters—of 14 million registered—went to the polls. Chávez supporters exceeded his prediction, giving him 5.6 million votes. However, the fact that his opponents got 3.9 million votes meant that 40 percent of Venezuelans voting still wanted Chávez to go away.

* * *

It should have been clear, however, that Chávez, supported by a broader electoral mandate than most U.S. presidents enjoy, was not going away. The discourse surrounding him was not getting any more substantive, just louder and, often, more embarrassing. Chávez, an admirer of Fidel Castro, was annoying the same people who had had trouble accepting Castro for the past half century. And every time Chávez tweaked the noses of his critics in "the colossus of the North," the United States, they embarrassed their country with their responses. In the summer of 2005, for one egregious example, Pat Robertson, a Christian evangelist on U.S. cable television, raised the possibility of assassinating Chávez, concluding that "we really ought to go ahead and do it." Felix Rodríguez, a CIA operative who served as an advisor to the American president George H. W. Bush, implied at the time that plans were prepared for just such an attack if an opportunity presented itself. And by February 2006, then–U.S. Secretary of Defense Donald Rumsfeld was comparing Chávez to Adolf Hitler. It was in that context that U.S. President George W. Bush—whose election in 2000 was by a minority of U.S. votes cast—described Chávez as "undermining democracy."

Chávez, of course, continued to return such favors. At the United Nations in 2007, he took the podium of the General Assembly the day after President Bush had been there. Chávez remarked: "Yesterday, the devil came right here ... and it smells of sulfur still today." Then he made the sign of the cross and rolled his eyes heavenward. The remark, unpopular in the United States even among Bush's critics, nevertheless was part of a 23-minute speech that brought applause that stretched for four minutes before it was gaveled to a close.

On the other hand, the performance probably cost Venezuela a temporary seat on the U.N. Security Council. Once more, Chávez's unfortunate style had trumped substance. Yet that December Venzuelans re-elected him president, but denied him, in a plebiscite, the right to succeed himself indefinitely. It was as if Venezuelans were reminding him that his temporal popularity did not guarantee electoral immortality. Undaunted, however, in the spring of 2007 the Chávez government took majority control of four foreign oil companies operating in the Eastern Orinoco valley — Conoco, Total, ExxonMobil, and Chevron — in order to strengthen its hand over the industry. The government also denied RCTV, a television station that supported the coup five years earlier, its operating license. Venezuelans' war against themselves went on.

*   *   *

Beneath the racket, Chávez has managed to advance programs that are sometimes substantial and lasting, and sometimes flashy and fleeting. With Castro, Chávez proposed a Bolivarian Alternative of the Americas, which he described as an alternative to the United States–led Free Trade Association of the Americas. Venezuela also drew its neighbors closer by selling oil to them at discount prices. Chávez has proposed a Latin American "OPEC" and a 5,600-mile, $20 billion natural gas pipeline from eastern Venezuela to Argentina with feeder lines into Peru, Bolivia, and Chile. On a continent jaundiced by centuries of disarray, such ideas invite skepticism, but they are ideas floated over governments too long in the sway of U.S. policy and dominated by unimaginative oligarchies. Even opponents eventually acknowledged the value of Robinson Mission health services, food markets, and literacy classes. And of Chávez's approach to the thorny issue of land reform, one U.S. expert, Peter Rosset, noted in 2005 that "Venezuela right now has the only serious government-administered land reform in Latin America. In the United States, Chávez is often painted as a villain or crazy, but this land reform, small and incipient as it is, shows that he is much more on the side of the poor than other presidents in the region."[14]

On the other hand, some Chávez programs are criticized as limited in their effect. In 2004, insisting that Venezuela's public health system was in "disarray," Chávez invited 20,000 Cuban physicians into rural areas. The effort sparked the seemingly inevitable protest marches by opponents, but the program has continued, incorporating Venezuelan physicians, flying some patients into Havana, and even treating patients in nearby countries. The Chávez government claimed that by 2008 the program had provided care for more than 400,000 patients, costing from $16 million to $20 million a year. "Those who call Chávez a vulgar populist are wrong," one of 96 Nicaraguans who underwent eye surgery told the *New York Times*. The president of the Venezuelan Ophthalmology Society, however, noted that while the results for individuals were admirable, Chávez's priorities were political — helping a relative handful of patients outside the country while ignoring systemic health-care needs in Venezuela.[15]

This two-sides-to-every-story aspect of Venezuelan politics is characteristic of Venezuela's political history, but is magnified by Venezuela's highly developed news media. Newspaper, magazine, and television companies have provided a national platform for every confrontation. In such a sophisticated — and excitable — media environment, Chávez's politics have been well served by his skill in self-promotion, but the spirit of compromise is submerged in a sea of acrimony. "For the past three years," wrote media analyst Marcelino Bisbal in 2002, "the practice of journalism hasn't been able to extricate itself from the maniacal thinking of 'Chavism' and 'anti–Chavism.'"[16] Chávez's contribution to that history, wrote Vladimar Villegas Poljak, has been to make "plain a strategy of frontal, personal combat with some media outlets and some individual reporters."[17] Chávez has responded to antipathy with animosity, trading blows, not changing behavior.

Bisbal added the observation that Chávez's style has accentuated the fact that popular revolutions in Latin America find their supporters largely among poor people, who are disproportionately dark-skinned. As in Cuba and, indeed, in the United States, the dark are disproportionately poor. The sometimes vicious exchanges between Chávez and his antagonists in the media "have made possible and even predominant personal and ethnocentric values."[18] Finally, there is the charge that Venezuela's media conglomerates have contributed to an environment of contempt for the underclass. "[T]he private media ought to set aside their partisanship and political partiality and dedicate themselves to their fundamental function, that of trying to recover the status and credibility that they have lost among the greatest part of civil society, which they have stigmatized because of social condition and cultural level, never allowing themselves any descriptive term better than 'rabble,' or 'mob,' or 'horde.' Those 'mobs' also have a right to information, to see their reality reflected and their points of view represented in the mass media."[19]

* * *

Thus the flames of social class and ethnicity burn at the edges of Venezuela's continuing political conflict because they have never been stamped out, not because Chávez lit them. That would explain both the conflict's ferocity and Chávez's popularity. He is seen not just as a president, but as a champion. That explains why, in February 2009, thousands of red-shirted Chávez supporters marched en masse throughout the nation. They were showing their support for his attempt, yet again, to win a plebiscite allowing him to succeed himself indefinitely as president. This time, Chávez won the plebiscite, carrying 55 percent of the vote — a narrow majority, but a democratic one, and one he could truly claim as his. It seemed that Hugo Chávez might be around to annoy his enemies and delight his followers as long as his hero, Fidel Castro.

Chapter Notes

Sources for Chapter 1 through 20 can be found in the text and in the Bibliography.

Chapter 21

1. Eduardo Labarca, *Salvador Allende: biografía sentimental* (Santiago: Catalonia, 2007).
2. *Ibid.*, p. 21
3. *Ibid.*, pp. 21–22.
4. *Ibid.*, p, 24.
5. Jordan M. Young, in the Introduction to *Chile & Allende,* ed. Lester A. Sobel (New York: Facts on File, 1974), p. 11
6. Labarca, p. 40.
7. *Ibid.*, p. 41.
8. Hugh O'Shaughnessy, *Pinochet: The Politics of Torture,* (New York: New York University Press, 2000), p. 16.
9. Labarca, p. 64.
10. *Ibid.*, p. 313.
11. *Ibid.*, p. 61.
12. Salvador Allende, *"Defensa permanente de la democracia. Projecto que declara fuera de la ley al Partido Comunista,"* in *Obras Escojidas, 1933–1948,* pp. 460–61.
13. Labarca, p. 196.
14. *Ibid.*, p. 215.
15. Quoted in Ozren Agnig, *Allende, el hombre y el politico,* (Santiago: RIL, 2008), p. 61.
16. Joan E. Garcés, *Allende y la Experiencia Chilena* (Barcelona: Editorial Ariel, 1976), pp. 94–95. Italics in the original. Author Garcés was quoting the official record of a U.S. Senate investigation, *Alleged Assassination Plots,* p. 231.
17. Sobel, p. 31.
18. *Ibid.*, p. 1.
19. Quoted in Les Evans, "The Victory of the *Unidad Popular,*" in *Disaster in Chile,* ed. Les Evans (New York: Pathfinder, 1974), p. 16.
20. *Ibid.*, p. 10.
21. Quoted in Sobel, p. 31–33.
22. *Ibid.*
23. Agnig, p.188.
24. *Ibid.*
25. Quoted in Labarca, p. 229.
26. Gonzalo Vial Correa, *Pinochet, la biografía,* Vol. 1 (Santiago: Aguilar, 2002), p. 143.
27. *Ibid.*, Vol. 1, p. 144.
28. James D. Cockcroft, Henry Frundt, and Dale L. Johnson, "Multi-national Corporations and Chile," in *The Chilean Road to Socialism,* ed. D ale L. Johnson, (Garden City, NY: Anchor, 1973). Cited in Evans, *Disaster in Chile,* p. 267.
29. Peter Kornbluh, ed., "Chile and the United States: Declassified Documents Relating to the Military Coup, September 11, 1973," *National Security Archive Electronic Briefing Book No. 8, nsarchive@gmu.edu.* The archive is an independent, nongovernmental research institute at George Washington University.
30. Quoted in Sobel, p. 43.
31. *Ibid.*, p. 5.
32. *Ibid.*, p. 95.
33. *Ibid.*, p. 113.
34. *Ibid.*, p. 118–20.
35. Agnic, p. 278.
36. Quoted in Vial, Vol. 1, p. 219.
37. Quoted in Sobel, p. 141.
38. Quoted in Sobel, p. 142.
39. Labarca, p. 343.
40. Vial, Vol. 1, p. 12.
41. *Ibid.*, p. 11.
42. *Ibid.*, p. 12.
43. *Ibid.*, p. 28.
44. *Ibid.*, p. 39.
45. O'Shaughnessy, p. 17.
46. Vial, pp. 63–64.
47. *Ibid.*, p. 44.
48. *Ibid.*, p. 61.
49. *Ibid.*, p. 90.
50. Quoted in Vial, *ibid.,* p. 94.
51. *Ibid.*, p. 98.
52. *Ibid.* p. 102.
53. Vial, Vol. 1, p. 98.
54. *Ibid.*, p. 101.
55. *Ibid.*, p. 108.
56. *Ibid.*, pp. 109–110.
57. Quoted in Vial, *ibid.,* p.111.
58. Quoted in Sobel, p. 125.
59. *Ibid.*, p. 178.
60. *Ibid.*, p. 115.
61. *Ibid.*, p. 140.
62. *Ibid.*, pp. 192–93.
63. Isabel Allende, *My Invented Country* (New York: HarperCollins, 2003), p. 169.
64. Sobel, pp. 2–3.
65. Torcuato S. Di Tella, with Néstor Kirchner, *Después del derrumbe* (Buenos Aires: Galerna, 2003), p. 18.
66. Quoted in Agnic, p. 266.
67. Garcés, p. 132. Italics added.
68. Vial, p. 282.
69. Isabel Allende, *The House of the Spirits,* trans. Magda Bogin (New York: Alfred A. Knopf, 2005), p. 440.
70. Sobel, p. 145. Emphasis added.
71. Carlos Huneeus, *The Pinochet Regime,* trans. Lake Sagaris (Boulder, CO: Lynne Reinner, 2007).
72. *Ibid.*, p. 271.
73. *Ibid.*, pp. 272–4.
74. Huneeus, p. 272.
75. *Ibid.*, p. 275.
76. Vial, p. 235.
77. *Exorcising Terror,* (New York: Seven Stories, 2002), p.147.
78. Vial, Vol. 1, p. 238–39.
79. Huneeus, p. 13.
80. Amos Elon, in the Introduction to Hannah Arendt's *Eichmann in Jerusalem: A Report on the Banality of Evil* (New York: Penguin, 2006). Arendt's reporting of the trial of Adolph Eichmann was first published in book form by Viking in 1963.
81. Huneeus, p. 14.
82. *Ibid.*, p. 456.

Chapter 22

1. John Steinbeck, *The Grapes of Wrath* (New York: Penguin, 1999), p. 232. Originally published in 1939.
2. Jacques Levy, *César Chávez: Autobiography of a Movement* (New York: Norton, 1975), p. 7.
3. *Ibid.*, p. 7.
4. *Ibid.*, p. 34.
5. *Ibid.*, pp. 8–9.
6. *Ibid.*, p. 9.
7. *Ibid.*, pp. 11–12.
8. *Ibid.*, p. 30.
9. *Ibid.*, p. 38.
10. *Ibid.*, pp. 35 — 42.
11. Studs Terkel, "César Chávez, 1970," in Richard W. Etulain, *César Chávez: A Brief Biography with Documents* (Boston: Bedford/St. Martin's, 2002), p. 47.
12. Levy, p. 63.
13. *Ibid.*, p. 71.
14. *Ibid.*, p. 63.
15. *Ibid.*, p. 86.
16. *Ibid.*, p.84.

17. *Ibid.*, p.84–85.
18. *Ibid.*, p. 79.
19. *Ibid.*, p. 160.
20. *Ibid.*, pp. 143, 159.
21. *Ibid.*, p. 89. Emphasis added.
22. *Ibid.*, pp. 103–04.
23. *Ibid.*, pp. 101–116.
24. *Ibid.*, p. 125.
25. *Ibid.*, p. 105–124.
26. *Ibid.*, 126.
27. *Ibid.*, pp. 126–27.
28. *Ibid.*, p. 126–39.
29. *Ibid.*, pp. 125–144.
30. *Ibid.*, pp. 109–10.
31. *Ibid.*, p. 132.
32. *Ibid.*, p. 135–37.
33. *Ibid.*, p. 139.
34. *Ibid.*, p. 144–47.
35. *Ibid.*, p. xxi.
36. Ilan Stavans, ed., *César Chávez: An Organizer's Tale* (New York: Penguin, 2008), p. xv.
37. Levy, p. 145.
38. *Ibid.*, p. 147.
39. *Ibid.*, p. 183.
40. Ronald B. Taylor, *Chávez and the Farm Workers* (Boston: Beacon, 1975), p. 120.
41. Levy, p. 221–22.
42. *Ibid.*, p. 219.
43. *Ibid.*, p. 184.
44. Quoted in Taylor, p. 181.
45. Taylor, *ibid.*, p. 219.
46. *Ibid.*, p. 129–30.
47. Levy, p. 227.
48. Taylor, p. 202.
49. *Ibid.*, pp. 11–12.
50. Levy, pp. 218.
51. Dalton, p. 43.
52. Marco G. Prouty, *César Chávez, The Catholic Bishops, and the Farmworkers' Struggle for Social Justice* (Tucson: University of Arizona Press, 2006), p. 31. Emphasis added.
53. *Ibid.*, p. 24.
54. Dalton, pp. 45–46.
55. Levy, p. 327–28.
56. Quoted in Stavans, p. 107.
57. Taylor, p. 13.
58. *Ibid*, p. 14–15.
59. Quoted in Dalton, p. 9.
60. Levy, p. 490–92.
61. Taylor, p. 321–22.
62. Prouty, p. 133.
63. *Ibid.*, p. 134.
64. *Ibid.*, p. 133.
65. Taylor, p. 130.
66. Quoted in Richard Griswold del Castillo and Richard A. García, *César Chávez: A Triumph of the Spirit* (Norman: University of Oklahoma Press, 1995), p. 121.
67. *Ibid.*, p. 129.
68. *Ibid.*, pp. 132–33.
69. Prouty, p. 132.
70. Quoted in Jerome R. Adams, *Greasers and Gringos* (Jefferson, NC: McFarland, 1993), pp. 292–93.
71. Stavans, p. 198.
72. José-Antonio Orosco, *César Chávez and the Common Sense of Non-*

Violence (Albuquerque: University of New Mexico Press, 2008), p. 4.
73. Prouty, p. 139.
74. Peter Matthiessen, "César Chávez, 1993," in *César Chávez: A Brief Biography with Documents*, ed. Richard. W. Etulain (Boston: Bedford/St. Martin's, 2002), p. 116.
75. Stavans, p. xxiv.
76. *Ibid.*, p. 118.

Chapter 23

1. Vicente Fox with Rob Allyn, *Revolution of Hope* (New York: Viking, 2007), p. 1. The book, a kind of out-sourced autobiography, documents Fox's understandable pride in his family and personal accomplishments while reading a bit like advertising copy.
2. *Ibid.*, p. 5.
3. *Ibid.*, p. 17.
4. *Ibid.*, pp. 44–47.
5. Vicente Fox, *Vicente Fox a Los Pinos* (México, D.F.: Editorial Oceano, 1999), p. 24.
6. *Ibid.*, p. 18.
7. Fox, *Revolution, op. cit.*, p. 128.
8. *Ibid.*, p. 36.
9. *Ibid.*, p. 44–47.
10. *Ibid.*, p. 46.
11. *Ibid.*, pp. 57-60.
12. *Ibid.*, p. 74–75.
13. *Ibid.*, p. 52.
14. *Ibid.*, pp. 86–87.
15. *Ibid.*, p. 98.
16. *Ibid.*, p. 101.
17. Fox, *A Los Pinos*, p. 25.
18. Fox, *Revolution*, p. 96.
19. Julia Preston and Samuel Dillon, *Opening Mexico* (New York: Farrar, Straus and Giroux, 2004), pp. 123–24.
20. Fox, *A Los Pinos*, p. 59–60.
21. Fox, *Revolution*, pp. 38–39. Italics in the original.
22. Fox, *A Los Pinos*, p. 60.
23. Fox, *Revolution*, p. 97.
24. Preston and Dillon, p. 118.
25. Fox. *A Los Pinos*, p. 60. Emphasis added.
26. Preston and Dillon, pp. 122–23. Emphasis in the original.
27. Miguel Ángel Centeno, *Democracy Within Reason* (University Park, PA: Pennsylvania University Press, 1994), p. 9.
28. Fox, *A Los Pinos*, p. 61.
29. Preston and Dillon, p. 127.
30. Fox, *Revolution*, pp. 104, 96–97.
31. Fox, *A Los Pinos*, pp. 61–62.
32. Fox, *Revolution*, pp. 109, xx.
33. Centeno, p. 11.
34. *Ibid.*, p. 14–15.
35. Fox, *Revolution*, p. 116.
36. *Ibid.*, pp. 117–121.
37. *Ibid.*, pp. 113–121.
38. Gregorio Urías Germán, *La*

democracia en México después de la alternancia (México, D.F.: Grupon Editorial, 2003), p. 79.
39. Fox, *Revolution*, p. 117.
40. *Ibid.*, p. 137.
41. Ramón Muñoz Gutiérrez, *Pasión por un Buen Gobierno* (México, D.F.: Ediciones 2000, 1999), p. 16.
42. Fox, *Revolution*, pp. 132–34.
43. Quoted in Édgar González Ruiz, *La Última Cruzada* (México, D.F.: Grijalbo, 2001), p. 166.
44. Fox, *Revolution*, p. 150.
45. Muñoz, p. 16.
46. Fox, *Revolution*, p. 130–31.
47. Jeffrey Davidow, *The Bear and the Porcupine* (Princeton, N.J.: Markus Wiener, 2007), pp. xvi, 133.
48. Fox, *Revolution*, p. 172–73.
49. Fox, *Revolution*, p. 172–73.
50. Davidow, p. 73.
51. Fox, *A Los Pinos*, p. 61–62.
52. Fox, *Revolution*, p. 59.
53. George W. Grayson, *The United States and Mexico: Patterns of Influence* (New York: Praeger, 1984), p. 195.
54. Fox, *A Los Pinos*, pp. 165–66, 214.
55. Fox, *Revolution*, p. 180.
56. Davidow, p. 129.
57. Fox, *Revolution*, p. 186. Emphasis in the original.
58. *Ibid.*, pp. 188, 190.
59. Davidow, p. 144.
60. Fox, *Revolution*, p. 17.
61. González, p. xiv.
62. *Ibid.*, p. 153.
63. Davidow, pp. 159–62.
64. Fox, *Revolution*, p. 221.
65. Davidow, pp. 163–65.
66. Urías, pp. 81–82.
67. Davidow, p. 165.
68. Fox, *Revolution* p. 90.
69. Davidow, p. 159.
70. Fox, *Revolution*, pp. 228–229.
71. *Ibid.*, pp. 229–30.
72. Davidow, p. 4.
73. *Ibid.*, p. 2.
74. Fox, *Revolution*, pp. 234–36.
75. Quoted in Davidow, p. 181.
76. *Ibid.*, pp. xix-xx.
77. Fox, *Revolution*, pp. 202–03.
78. Davidow, p. 209.
79. Fox, *Revolution*, p. 33.
80. *Ibid.*, p. 208.
81. National Institutes of Health, Institute on Drug Abuse, http://www/drugabuse.gov/DrugPages/Cocaine.html.
82. Fox, *Revolution*, p. 326. Emphasis in the original.
83. Davidow, pp. 171–73.
84. Fox, *Revolution*, pp., 61–69, 151. Emphasis added.
85. Tokatlian, Juan Gabriel, *Hacia una nueval estrategia internacional* (Buenos Aires: Grupo Editorial Norma, 2004), p. 37.
86. Fox, *Revolution*, p. 330–31.
87. Davidow, p. xix.

Chapter 24

1. Quoted in Walter Curia, *El ultimo peronista* (Buenos Aires: Editorial Sudamericana, 2006), p. 21.
2. *Ibid.*, p. 2.
3. Cited in Curia, p. 29.
4. Torcuato Di Tella, "Evolution and Prospects of the Argentine Political System" in Joseph S. Tulchin and Allison M. Garland, eds, *Argentina: The Challenges of Modernization* (Wilmington, DE: Scholarly Resources, 1998), p. 128.
5. Valeria Garrone and Laura Rocha, *Néstor Kirchner: Un muchacho peronista y la oportunidad del poder* (Buenos Aires: Planeta, 2003), p. 34.
6. Curia, p. 33.
7. *Ibid.*, p. 34.
8. Garrone and Rocha, p. 46.
9. Quoted in Curia, p. 39.
10. Quoted by Curia, p. 40.
11. Cited in Curia, p. 43
12. Olga Wornat, *Reina Cristina* (Buenos Aires: Planeta, 2005), p.132.
13. *Ibid.*, p. 62.
14. *Ibid.*, p. 59.
15. *Ibid.*, p. 62.
16. *Ibid.*, p. 40.
17. *Ibid.*, p. 67. Emphasis in the original.
18. Garrone and Rocha, p. 75.
19. Wornat, p. 79.
20. Garrone and Rocha, p. 75.
21. Quoted in Wornat, p. 82.
22. *Ibid.*, p. 147.
23. *Ibid.*, p. 84.
24. *Ibid.*, p. 92.
25. *Ibid.*, p. 101.
26. *Ibid.*, p. 106.
27. *Ibid.*, p. 108.
28. *Ibid.*, p. 109.
29. Susan Kaiser, *Postmemories of Terror* (New York: Palgrave Macmillan, 2005), p. 2.
30. *Ibid.*, pp. 1, 3.
31. Wornat, p.109.
32. Curia, p. 49.
33. *Ibid.*, p. 54.
34. *Ibid.*, p. 56.
35. Wornat, p. 169.
36. Curia, p. 58.
37. Kaiser, p. 34.
38. Wornat, p. 174.
39. *Ibid.*
40. *La Opinión Austral*, March 11, 1989, cited in Wornat, pp. 174–75.
41. Di Tella, in Tulchin and Garland, p. 131.
42. Juan Gabriel Tokatlian, *Hacia una nueva estrategia internacional* (Buenos Aires: Grupo Editorial Norma, 2004), pp. 161–62.
43. Wornat, p. 183.
44. *Ibid.*
45. De Riz, Liliana, "From Menem to Menem" in Tulchin and Garland, *op. cit.*, p. 147–48.
46. Curia, *op. cit.*, p. 83.

47. De Riz, in Tulchin and Garland, *op. cit.*, p. 148.
48. Swann, Maxine, *The New York Times*, June 19, 2008, p. D1.
49. Garrone and Rocha, *op. cit.*, pp. 120–21.
50. Garrone and Rocha, *op. cit.*, p. 9.
51. Di Tella, Torcuato S., with Kirchner, Néstor, *Después del Derrumbe*, Buenos Aires, Galerna, 2003, p. 9.
52. Wolnat, *op. cit.*, p. 20.
53. Wornat, ibid., p. 20.
54. Di Tella, *op. cit.*, p. 33.
55. Di Tella, ibid., p. 54.
56. [Rohter, Larry, "Dwindling debt boosts Argentine leader," *The New York Times*, Jan. 3, 2003, http://www.nytimes.com/2006/01/03/international/americas/03 argentina. html]
57. Quoted by Rohter, *ibid.*
58. Wornat, op. cit., p. 13.
59. Wornat, *ibid.*, p. 13.
60. Wornat, *ibid.*, p. 42.
61. Barrionuevo, Alexei, "Venezuelan says Chávez ordered cover-up of suitcase of cash," *The New York Times*, Sept. 9, 2008, p. A18.
62. "Argentina: Huge March for Kirchner," *The New York Times*, April 2, 2008, p. A10.
63. Barrionuevo, Alexei, "Conflict With Farmers Takes Toll on Argentina," *New York Times*, June 24, 2008, p. A14.
64. Tokatlian *et al.*, *op. cit.* p. 164.
65. Tokatlian, *ibid.*, p. 158.
66. Di Tella, *op. cit.*, pp. 54–55.

Chapter 25

1. Hector Perez-Brignoli, *A Brief History of Central America*, trans. Ricardo B. Sawrey A. and Susana Stettri de Sawrey (Berkeley: University of California Press, 1989), p. 50.
2. *Ibid.*, p. 82.
3. *Ibid.*, p. 112.
4. Denis Lynn Daly Heyck, *Life Stories of the Nicaraguan Revolution* (New York: Routlege, 1990), p. 244.
5. *Ibid.*
6. *Ibid.*
7. *Ibid.*
8. *Ibid.*, p. 247.
9. *Ibid.*, p. 12.
10. Perez-Brignoli, pp. 127–28.
11. *Ibid.*, p. 142.
12. *Ibid.*, p. 143.
13. *Ibid.*, p. 144.
14. Roger Miranda and William Ratliff, *The Civil War In Nicaragua* (New Brunswick, NJ: Transaction, 1993), p. 46. Miranda was a major in the Sandinista army and from 1982 through 1987 during the war against the Contras. He was chief of staff and an aide to the Sandinista defense minister, Humberto Ortega.
15. Quoted in Daly Heyck, p. 64–65.

16. Miranda and Ratliff, p. 46–47.
17. Dennis Gilbert, *Sandinistas: The Party and the Revolution* (New York: Basil Blackwell, 1988), p. 44.
18. Daly Heyck, p. 11.
19. Quoted in *ibid.*, p. 114–15.
20. Quoted in *ibid.*, p. 97–98.
21. Daniel Ortega, *El Sandinismo: El Más Alto Grado de Organitión del Pueblo* (Managua: Universidad Nacional Autónoma de Nicaragua, 1987), pp. 13–14.
22. Harry E. Vanden and Gary Prevost, *Democracy and Socialism in Sandinista Nicaragua* (Boulder, CO: Lynne Rienner, 1993), p. 44.
23. Miranda and Ratliff, p. 48.
24. Daly Heyck, p. 12.
25. Perez-Rignoli, p. 150.
26. Daly Heyck, p. 99.
27. David A. Ridenour and David Almasi, *Nicaragua's Continuing Revolution, 1977–1990* (Carrboro, NC: Signal, 1990), p. 47–48.
28. Quoted in Miranda and Ratliff, p. 3.
29. *Ibid.*, p. ix.
30. Quoted in Gilbert, p. 23. The remark was made in 1984.
31. *Ibid.*
32. Vanden and Prevost, p. 72.
33. Quoted in Gilbert, p. 42.
34. *Ibid.*, p. 43.
35. Miranda and Ratliff, p. 21.
36. Daly Heyck, p. 125.
37. *Ibid.*, p. 132–33.
38. Ridenour and Almasi, pp. 47–48.
39. Daly Heyck, pp. 132–33.
40. Quoted in Gilbert, p. 114.
41. *Ibid.*, p. 90.
42. *Ibid.*
43. Eduardo Baumeister, "The Structure of Nicaraguan Agriculture and the Sandinista Agrarian Reform," in Harris and Vilas, p. 28.
44. Perez-Brignoli, p. 80.
45. Marcus, Bruce, ed., *Nicaragua: The Sandinista People's Revolution* (New York: Pathfinder, 1985), p. 8.
46. Peter Rossett and John Vandermeer, eds., *Nicaragua: Unfinished Revolution* (New York: Grove, 1986), pp. 8–9.
47. Gilbert, p. 168.
48. *Ibid.*, p. 142
49. Marcus, pp. 193–200.
50. Miranda and Ratliff, p. 25.
51. *Ibid.*, p. 48.
52. Quoted in Ridenhour, p. 146.
53. Quoted in Ridenhour, p. 135.
54. Gilbert, pp. 47–48.
55. Quoted in Daly Heyck, p. 38.
56. Ortega, *El Sandinismo*, pp. 7, 9.
57. Ridenhour, p. 209.
58. Gilbert, p. 44.
59. Miranda and Ratliff, p. 37.
60. *Ibid.*, p. 275.
61. *Electoral Democracy Under International Pressure*, The Report of the Latin American Studies Association

Commission to Observe the 1990 Nicaraguan Election (Pittsburgh, PA: Latin American Studies Association, University of Pittsburgh, March 15, 1990), p.1.

62. *Electoral Democracy Under International Pressure*, p. 2.

63. *Ibid.*, p. 4.

64. *Ibid.*, p.29.

65. *Ibid.*, p.15.

66. *Ibid.*, p. 40.

67. Quoted in Daly Heyck, p. 32.

68. *The Observation of the 1996 Nicaraguan Elections*, Special Report of the Council of Freely Elected Heads of Government Latin American and Caribbean Program (Atlanta, GA: Carter Center, 1996), p. 12.

69. *Ibid.*, p. 12.

70. *Washington Post* editorial, October 14, 1996, quoted in *ibid.*, p. 67.

71. Larry Rohter, *The New York Times*, "Rightist is Victor over Sandinistas in Nicaragua Vote," October 22, 1996, cited in *ibid.*, p. 12.

72. Luis Núñez Salmerón, "*Agricultores Presionan*," *La Prensa*, July 3, 2008, p. 3B.

73. Arlen Cerda and María José Uriarte, "*Quién Dijo Miedo?*" *La Prensa*, June 28, 2008, p. 1A.

74. William Booth, "Democracy in Nicaragua in Peril, Ortega Critics Say," *Washington Post*, November 20, 2008, p. A12.

Chapter 26

1. Gilberto Freyre, *The Masters and the Slaves*, trans. Samuel Putnam (New York: Knopf, 1946), pp. 161–162.

2. Colin M. MacLachlan, *A History of Modern Brazil* (Wilmington, DE: Scholarly Resources, 2003), p. 4.

3. *Ibid.*, p. 31.

4. *Ibid.*, p. 45.

5. *Ibid.*, p. xx.

6. *Ibid.*, p. 42.

7. Mauricio A. Font, *Coffee, Contention, and Change* (Oxford, England: Basil Blackwell, 1990), p. 276.

8. MacLachlan, p. 75.

9. Leonicio Martins Rodrigues, *La clase obrera en el Brazil* (Buenos Aires: Centro Editor de America Latina, 1969), p. 13.

10. Altino Dantas Junior, ed., *Lula Sem Censura*, 4th ed. (Petrópolis: Editora Vozes, 1982), p. 19.

11. Cited in Margaret E. Keck, *The Workers' Party and Democratization in Brazil* (New Haven: Yale University Press, 1992), p. 73.

12. Emir Sader and Ken Silverstein, *Without Fear of Being Happy: Lula, the Workers Party and Brazil* (London: Verso, 1991), pp. 37–38.

13. *Ibid.*, p. 21.

14. *Ibid.*, p. 39

15. Keck, p. 1.

16. Dantas, pp. 27, 28.

17. Quoted in Keck, pp. 74–75.

18. *Ibid.*, p. 75.

19. *Ibid.*, p. 77–78.

20. *Ibid.*, p. 76.

21. Quoted in Sader and Silverstein, p. 42.

22. *Ibid.*

23. *Ibid.*

24. *Ibid.*, p. 43.

25. *Ibid.*, p. 44.

26. Quoted in Dantas, p. 64.

27. Quoted in Keck, p. 65.

28. Torcuato S. Di Tella, *Después del derrumbe* (Buenos Aires: Galerna, 2003), p. 12.

29. Sue Branford and Bernardo Kucinski, *Brazil: Carnival of the Oppressed* (London: Latin American Bureau, 1995), p. 105.

30. Sader and Silverstein, p. 51.

31. Quoted in Keck, p. 126.

32. Quoted in Sader and Silverstein, p. 50.

33. Fausto Cupertino, *Classes e Camadas Sociais no Brazil* (Rio de Janeiro: Civilisacão Brasileira, 1978), p. 43.

34. Quoted in Sader and Silverstein, p. 95.

35. *Ibid.*, p. 47.

36. Quoted in Keck, p. 227.

37. *Ibid.*, pp. 75.

38. *Ibid.*, pp. 121–22.

39. Sader and Silverstein, p. 29.

40. *Ibid.*, p. 96.

41. Keck, p. 237.

42. Quoted in Sader and Silverstein, p. 35.

43. Branford and Kucinski, pp. 98.

44. Quoted in Odaci Luiz Coradini, *Em Nome de Quem?, Recursos Sociais no Recrutamento de Elites Políticas* (Rio de Janeiro: Nudeo de Antropologia da Política, 1998), pp. 190–91.

45. Quoted in Sader and Silverstein, p. 35.

46. *Ibid.*, p. 61.

47. *Ibid.*, p.74.

48. Quoted in Ted G. Goertzel, *Fernando Henrique Cardoso: Reinvigorating Democracy in Brazil* (Boulder, CO: Lynne Rienner, 1999), p. 117.

49. *Ibid.*, p. 171.

50. *Ibid.*, p. 173.

51. Sue Branford and Bernardo Kucinski with Hilary Wainwright, *Politics Transformed: Lula and the Workers' Party of Brazil* (London: Latin America Bureau, 2003), p. 76.

52. *Ibid.*, p. 4.

53. Robert M. Levine, *The History of Brazil* (Westport, CT: Greenwood, 1999), p. 147.

54. Lucia Hippolito, *Por dentro do governo Lula* (São Paulo: Editora Futura, 2005), p. 9.

55. Branford, *Politics Transformed*, pp. 21–22.

56. Hippolito, p. 10.

57. *Ibid.*, p. 10.

58. Larry Rohter, "Brazil's Finance Minister Quits Amid Continuing Political Scandal," *The New York Times*, March 28, 2006, http://www/nytimes.com/2006/ 03/28/international/ americas/28brazil.html.

59. Hippolito, p 72.

60. MacLachlan, p. 234, 35.

61. Levine, pp. 147–8.

62. Dee Hon, p. 41, "A New Kind of Capitalism," in *Adbusters*, Vol. 77 (April 2008) pp. 40–1.

Chapter 27

1. Bart Jones, *Hugo! The Hugo Chávez Story from Mud Hut to Perpetual Revolution* (New Hanover, NH: Steerforth, 2007), p. 39.

2. Cited in Jones, p. 62.

3. Norman A. Bailey, "Venezuela and the United States: Putting Energy in the Enterprise," in Louis W. Goodman, Johanna Mendelson Forman, Moisés Naím, Joseph S. Tulchin, and Gary Bland, *Lessons of the Venezuelan Experience* (Baltimore, MD: Johns Hopkins University Press, 1995), p. 391.

4. Cited in Jones, p. 103.

5. *Ibid.*, p. 150.

6. *Ibid.*, 158.

7. Cited in Jones, p. 159.

8. Juan Carlos Navarro, "Venezuela's New Political Actors," in Goodman, et al., p. 128.

9. Nicolas Kozloff, *Hugo Chávez: Oil, Politics, and the challenge to the U.S.* (New York: Palgrave Macmillan, 2006), p. 10 ff.

10. *Ibid.*, p. 106.

11. *Ibid.*

12. Cited in Jones, p. 359.

13. Vladimir Villegas Poljak, "*Medios Vs. Chávez: la lucha continua*," in *Chávez y los Medios de Comunicación Social*, ed. Marinellys Tremamuno, (Caracas: Alfadil Ediciones, 2002), pp. 54–5.

14. Quoted in Jones, p. 314.

15. *The New York Times*, February 26, 2008, p. A4.

16. Marcelino Bisbal, "*El dilemma de lost medios y los comunicadores — o armando el rompecabezas*," in Tremamunno, p. 129.

17. Villegas Poljak, in Tremamunno, p. 53.

18. Bisbal, in Tremamunno, p. 118.

19. Tremamunno, in Tremamunno, pp. 58–9.

Select Bibliography

Chapter 1

Baudot, Georges. "Política y Discurso en la Conquista de México: Malintzín y el diálogo con Hernán Cortes." *Anuario de Estudios Americanos* 45 (1988).

Cantu, Caesar C. *Cortés and the Fall of the Aztec Empire.* Los Angeles: Modern World, 1966.

Díaz del Castillo, Bernal. *The Discovery and Conquest of Mexico, 1517–1521.* Trans. Alfred Percival Maudslay London: George Routledge and Sons, 1928. (From the copy by Génaro García.)

Long, Haniel. *Malinche (Doña Marina).* Santa Fe, N.M.: Writer's Editions, 1939.

Morris, J. Bayard, trans. *Hernando Cortés, Five Letters.* New York: Robert M. McBride, 1929.

Padden, R. C. *The Hummingbird and the Hawk.* Columbus: Ohio State University Press, 1967.

Prescott, William H. *History of the Conquest of Mexico.* 2 vols. London: Richard Bentley, 1849.

Rodríguez, Gustavo A. *Doña Marina.* Monograph, Imprenta de la Secretaria de Relaciones Exteriores, Mexico, D. F., 1935.

Solis, Antonio de. *Historia de la Conquista de México.* Buenos Aires: Espasa-Calpe Argentina, 1947.

White, Jon Manchip. *Cortés and the Downfall of the Aztec Empire.* New York: St. Martins, 1971.

Chapter 2

Alexis, Stephen. *Black Liberator.* Trans. William Stirling. New York, 1949.

Beard, John R. *The Life of Toussaint L'Ouverture, the Negro Patriot of Hayti.* Boston: Wendell Phillips, 1863.

Heinl, Robert Debs and Nancy Gordon. *Written in Blood.* Boston: Houghton- Mifflin, 1978.

Korngold, Ralph. *Citizen Toussaint.* New York: Hill and Wang, 1944.

Chapter 3

Bushnell, David, ed. *The Liberator, Simón Bolívar.* New York: Knopf, 1970.

Collier, Simon. "Nationality, Nationalism and Supranationalism in the Writings of Simón Bolívar." *Hispanic American Historical Review* 43/1 (February 1983).

Lecuña, Vicente. *Crónica razonada de las querras de Bolívar.* New York: Colonial, 1950.

Madariaga, Salvador de. *Bolívar.* New York: Schocken, 1952.

Masur, Gerhard. *Simón Bolívar.* Albuquerque: University of New Mexico Press, 1948.

Sherwell, Guillermo A. *Simón Bolívar, Patriot, Warrior, Statesman, Father of Five Nations.* Clinton, Mass.: Colonial for the Bolivarian Society of Venezuela, 1951.

Trend, J. B. *Bolivar and the Independence of Spanish America.* Clinton, Mass.: Colonial for the Bolivarian Society of Venezuela, 1951.

Chapter 4

Ballesteros de Gaibrois, Mercedes. *Manuela Sáenz, El Ultimo Amor de Bolívar.* Madrid: Fundación Universitaria Española, 1976.

Rambos, Humberto. *Bolívar Intimo: Cartas.* Caracas: Talleres de B. Costa-Amic, 1967.

Rumazo Gonzalez, Alfonso. *Manuela Sáenz, La Libertadora del Libertador.* Bogotá: Ediciones Mundial, 1944.

Von Hagen, Victor Wolfgang. *The Four Seasons of Manuela.* New York: Duell, Sloan and Pierce Little, Brown, 1952.

Chapter 5

Metford, J. C. J. *San Martín the Liberator.* Oxford: Basil Blackwell, 1950.

Mitre, Bartolomé. *Historia de San Martín.* 3 vols. Buenos Aires: Editorial Universitaria, 1968.

Orfila, Alejandro. *The Liberator General San Martín.* Washington, D.C.: Organization of American States, 1978.

Chapter 6

Amunátegui Reyes, Miguel Luis. *Don Bernardo O'Higgins: Juzgado por algunos de sus contemporáneos.* Santiago: Imprenta Universitaria, 1917.

Archivo de don Bernardo O'Higgins. Tomos 1–31. Santiago: Editorial Nascimento, 1946.

Balbontín Moreno, Manuel, and Opazo Maturana, Gustavo. *Cinco Mujeres en la Vida de O'Higgins.* Santiago: Arancibia, 1964.

Cabello Reyes, Carlos. *Genio y Figura de Bernard O'Higgins.* Santiago: Editorial Cultura, 1944.

Carrasco, Adela. *Pensamiento de O'Higgins*. Santiago: Editorial Nacional Gabriela Mistral, 1974.

Clissold, Stephen. *Bernardo O'Higgins and the Independence of Chile*. London: Rupert Hart-Davis, 1968.

Kinsbruner, Jay. *Bernardo O'Higgins*. New York: Twayne, 1968.

O'Higgins Pintado por Si Mismo. Santiago: Ediciones Ercilla, 1941.

Chapter 7

Alberdi, Juan Bautista. *Proceso a Sarmiento*. Buenos Aires: Imprenta la Industrial, 1910.

Anderson Imbert, Enrique. *Una Aventura Amorosa de Sarmiento: Cartas de Ida Wickersham*. Buenos Aires: Editorial Losada, 1969.

Bunkley, Allison Williams. *The Life of Sarmiento*. Princeton, N.J.: Princeton University Press, 1952.

Guerrero, César H. *Mujeres de Sarmiento*. Buenos Aires: Artes Gráficas Bartolomé U. Chiesino, 1960.

Rojas, Ricardo. *El Profeta de las Pampa*. Buenos Aires: Editorial Tosada, 1945.

Sarmiento, Domingo Faustino. *Facundo ... Civilización y Barbarie*. Mexico, D.F.: SEP/UNAM, 1982. (*Facundo* was first published in 1845).

_____. *Obras Selectas*. Buenos Aires: Editorial la Facultad, 1944.

_____. *Recuerdos de Provincia*. Buenos Aires: La Cultura Argentina, 1916. (Originally published in 1850).

_____. *Viajes en Europa, Africa i America*. 3 vols. Buenos Aires: Libreria Hachette, 1958. (Originally published in 1851).

Chapter 8

Bernstein, Harry. *Dom Pedro II*. New York: Twayne, 1973.

Burns, E. Bradford. *A History of Brasil*. 2d ed. New York: Columbia University Press, 1970.

Calogeras, João Pandiá. *A History of Brazil*. Trans. Percy Alvin Martin. New York: Russell and Russell, 1963. (Originally published in 1939.)

Corréa da Costa, Sérgio. *Every Inch a King*. Trans. Samuel Putnam. New York: Charles Frank, 1950.

Drescher, Seymour. "Brazilian Abolition in Historical Perspective." *Hispanic American Historical Review*. 48/3 (August 1988).

Oliveira Lima, Manoel de. *The Evolution of Brazil*. New York: Russell and Russell, 1966. (Originally published in 1914.)

Reichmann, Felix. *Sugar, Gold and Coffee*. Ithaca: Cornell University Press, 1959.

Simmons, Charles Willis. *Marshal Deodoro and the Fall of Dom Pedro II*. Durham: Duke University Press, 1966.

Tarquinio de Sousa, Octavio. *José Bonifacio, emancipador del Brasil*. Mexico, D.F.: Fondo de Cultura Económica, 1945.

Williams, Mary Wilhelmine. *Dom Pedro the Magnanimous*. Chapel Hill: University of North Carolina Press, 1937.

Worcester, Donald E. *Brazil: From Colony to World Power*. New York: Charles Scribner's Sons, 1973.

Chapter 9

Foner, Philip S., ed. *José Martí, Major Poems*. Trans. Elinor Randall. New York: Holmes and Meier, 1982.

Gray, Richard Butler. *José Martí, Cuban Patriot*. Gainesville: University of Florida Press, 1962.

Kirk, John M. *José Martí, Mentor of the Cuban Nation*. Tampa: University Presses of Florida, 1983.

Lizaso, Félix. *Martí, Martyr of Cuban Independence*. Trans. Esther Elise Shuler. Albuquerque, N.M., 1953.

Mañach, Jorge. *Martí, Apostle of Freedom*. Trans. Coley Taylor. New York: Devin-Adair, 1950.

Chapter 10

Cadenhead, Ivie E. *Benito Juárez*. New York: Twayne, 1973.

Roeder, Ralph. *Juárez and His Mexico*. New York: Viking, 1947.

Smart, Charles Allen. *Viva Juárez!* Philadelphia: Lippincott, 1963.

Solana y Gutiérrez, Mateo. *Psicología de Juárez*. Ed. B. Costa-Amie. Mexico City, 1968.

Chapter 11

Herrera, Celia E. *Francisco Villa ante la Historia*. Mexico, D.F., 1939.

Lansford, William Douglas. *Pancho Villa*. Los Angeles: Sherbourne, 1965.

Mason, Herbert Molloy *The Great Pursuit*. New York: Random House, 1970.

Peterson, Jessie, and Thelma Cox, eds. *Pancho Villa: Intimate Recollections by People Who Knew Him*. New York: Hastings House, 1977.

Torres, Elias L. *Twenty Episodes in the Life of Pancho Villa*. Trans. Sheila M. Ohlendorf. Austin, Tex.: Encino, 1973.

Vives, Pedro A. *Pancho Villa*. Madrid: Ediciones Quorum, 1987.

Chapter 12

Black, C. E. *The Dynamics of Modernization*. New York: Harper and Row, 1967.

Dromundo, Baltazar. *Vida de Emiliano Zapata*. Mexico, D.F.: Editorial Guarania, 1961.

Newell, Peter E. *Zapata of Mexico*. Sanday, Orkney, U.K.: Cienfuegos, 1979.

Parkinson, Roger. *Zapata: A Biography*. New York: Stein and Day, 1975.

Reyes, H. Alonso. *Emiliano Zapata, Su Vida y Su Obra con Documentos Inéditos* Mexico, D.F., 1963.

Womack, John. *Zapata and the Mexican Revolution*. New York: Knopf, 1969.

Chapter 13

Cockcroft, James D. *Intellectual Precursors of the Mexican Revolution*. Austin: University of Texas Press, 1968.

Hahner, June E. *Women in Latin American History.* Los Angeles: UCLA Latin American Publications, 1976.

Macías, Anna. *Against All Odds: The Feminist Movement in Mexico.* Westport, Conn.: Greenwood, 1982.

Mendieta Alatorre, Angeles. *La Mujer en la Revolución Mexicana.* Mexico, D.F.: Talleres Gráficos de la Nación, 1961.

Phelan, John Leddy. "México y lo Mexicano." *Hispanic American Historical Review.* 36 (1956): 309–18.

Reed, John. *Insurgent Mexico.* New York: Simon and Schuster, 1969. (Compiled from dispatches to *Metropolitan* magazine and the *New York World,* this volume was first published in 1914.)

Romero, Ricardo. *La Mujer en la Historia de México.* Mexico, D.F.: Costa-Amic Editores, 1982.

Turner, Frederick C. *The Dynamic of Mexican Nationalism.* Chapel Hill: University of North Carolina Press, 1968.

Chapter 14

Bermann, Karl, ed. *Sandino Without Frontiers.* Hampton, Va.: Compita, 1988.

Campos Ponce, Xavier. *Sandino.* 3d ed. Mexico, D.F.: Editores Asociados Mexicanos, 1979.

Macauley, Neill. *The Sandino Affair.* Chicago: Quadrangle, 1967.

Selser, Gregario. *Sandino.* Trans. Cedric Belfrage. New York: Monthly Review, 1981.

Vives, Pedro A. *Augusto César Sandino.* Madrid: Ediciones Quorum, 1987.

Walker, Thomas W. *Nicaragua, The Land of Sandino.* Boulder, Colo.: Westview, 1981.

Chapter 15

Alexander, Robert J. *The Perón Era.* New York: Columbia University Press, 1951.

Baraguer, Joseph R., ed. *Why Perón Came to Power.* New York: Knopf, 1968.

Cowles, Fleur. *Bloody Precedent.* New York: Random House, 1952.

Scobie, James R. *Argentina.* New York: Oxford University Press, 1964.

Chapter 16

Barnes, John. *Evita: First Lady.* New York: Grove, 1978.

Boroni, Otelo, and Roberto Vacca. *La Vida de Eva Perón.* Buenos Aires: Editorial Galerna, 1970.

Flores, Maria. *The Woman with the Whip: Eva Perón.* New York: Doubleday, 1952.

Fraser, Nicholas, and Marysa Navarro. *Eva Perón.* New York: Norton, 1981.

Taylor, J. M. *Eva Perón: The Myths of a Woman.* Chicago: University of Chicago Press, 1979.

Chapter 17

Acuña Valerio, Miguel. *El 48.* San José: Lehmann, 1974.

Ameringer, Charles D. *Don Pepe: A Political Biography of José Figueres of Costa Rica.* Albuquerque: University of New Mexico Press, 1978.

Baeza Flores, Alberto. *La Lucha Sin Fin.* Mexico, D.F.: Costa-Amic, 1969.

Bonilla, Harold H. *Figueres y Costa Rica.* San José: Editorial Sol, 1977.

Figueres Ferrer, José. *América Latina: Un Continente en Marcha.* San José: EIDED, 1966.

Gleijeses, Piero. "Juan José Arévalo and the Caribbean Legion." *Journal of Latin American Studies.* 45 (1988).

Chapter 18

Boorstein, Edward. *The Economic Transformation of Cuba.* New York: Monthly Review, 1968.

Farber, Samuel. "The Cuban Communists in the Early Stages of the Cuban Revolution: Revolutionaries or Reformists?" *Latin American Research Review.* 18/1 (1983).

Franqui, Carlos. *Family Portrait with Fidel.* New York: Random House, 1981.

Matthews, Herbert. *Fidel Castro.* New York: Simon and Schuster, 1969.

Meneses, Enrique. *Fidel Castro.* Trans. J. Halcro Ferguson. New York: Taplinger, 1966.

Sutherland, Elizabeth. *The Youngest Revolution.* New York: Dial, 1969.

Szulc, Tad. *Fidel: A Critical Portrait.* New York: Morrow, 1986.

Yglesias, José. *In the Fist of the Revolution.* New York: Pantheon, 1968.

Chapter 19

Guevara, Ernesto. *Reminiscences of the Cuban Revolutionary War.* Trans. Victoria Ortiz. New York: Monthly Review, 1968.

James, Daniel. *Che Guevara, A Biography.* New York: Stein and Day, 1969.

_____, ed. *The Complete Bolivian Diaries of Che Guevara.* New York: Stein and Day, 1968.

Rojo, Ricardo. *My Friend Che.* New York: Dial, 1968.

Chapter 20

Brockman, James R. *The Word Remains, A Life of Oscar Romero.* Maryknoll, N.Y.: Orbis, 1982.

Delgado, Jesús. *Oscar A. Romero: biografía.* Madrid: Ediciones Paulinas, 1986.

Erdozain, Plácido. *Monseñor Romero, Mártir de la Iglesia Popular.* San José, C.R.: Editorial Universitaria Centroamericana, 1980.

Keogh, Dermot. *Romero, El Salvador's Martyr.* Dublin: Dominican, 1981.

Walsh, Michael J., trans., *Archbishop Oscar Romero, Voice of the Voiceless. The Four Pastoral Letters and Other Statements.* Maryknoll, N.Y.: Orbis, 1985.

Chapter 21

Agnic Kostulovic, Ozren Nikola. *Allende, el hombre y el politico.* Santiago de Chile: RIL, 2008.

Allende, Isabel. *The House of the Spirits,* trans. Magda Bogin. New York: Alfred A. Knopf, 2005. Originally published as *La Casa de los Espíritus* (Barcelona: Plaza y Janés, 1982).

Allende, Isabel. *My Invented Country,* trans. Margaret Sayers Peden. New York: HarperCollins, 2003. Originally published as *Mi País Inventado* (Madrid: Areté, 2003).

Allende Gossens, Salvador. "Defensa permanente del la democracia: Proyecto que declara fuera de la ley el partido comunista." In *Obras Escogidas, 1933– 1948,* Vol. 1, ed. Patricio Quiroga Zamora. Santiago de Chile: Ediciones Lar, 1988.

Dorfman, Ariel. *Exorcising Terror.* New York: Seven Stories, 2002.

Evans, Les. "The Victory of the *Unidad Popular."* In *Disaster in Chile,* ed. Les Evans. New York: Pathfinder, 1974.

Garcés, Joan E. *Allende y la Experiencia Chilena.* Barcelona: Editorial Areal, 1976.

Huneeus, Carlos. *The Pinochet Regime,* trans. Lake Sagaris. Boulder, CO: Lynne Reinner, 2007.

Labarca, Eduardo. *Salvador Allende: biografía sentimental.* Santiago de Chile: Catalonia, 2007.

O'Shaughnessy, Hugh. *Pinochet: The Politics of Torture.* New York: New York University Press, 2000.

Sobel, Lester A., ed. *Chile & Allende.* New York: Facts on File, 1974.

Vial Correa, Gonzalo. *Pinochet, la biografía.* 2 vols. Santiago de Chile: Aguilar, 2002.

Chapter 22

Dalton, Frederick John. *The Moral Vision of César Chávez.* Maryknoll, NY: Orbis, 2003.

Griswold del Castillo, Richard, and Richard A. Garcia. *César Chávez: A Triumph of the Spirit.* Norman: University of Oklahoma Press, 1995.

Levy, Jacques E. *César Chávez: Autobiography of La Causa.* New York: Norton, 1975.

Matthiessen, Peter. "César Chávez, 1993." In *César Chávez, A Brief Biography with Documents,* ed. Richard W. Etulain. Boston: Bedford/St. Martin's, 2002.

Orosco, José-Antonio. *César Chávez and the Common Sense of Nonviolence.* Albuquerque: University of New Mexico Press, 2008.

Prouty, Marco G. *César Chávez, the Catholic Bishops, and the Farmworkers' Struggle for Social Justice.* Tucson: University of Arizona Press, 2006.

Stavans, Ilan, ed. *César Chávez: An Organizer's Tale — Speeches.* New York: Penguin, 2008.

Taylor, Ronald B. *Chavez and the Farm Workers.* Boston: Beacon, 1975.

Terkel, Studs. "César Chávez, 1970." In *César Chávez, A Brief Biography with Documents,* ed. Richard W. Etulain. Boston: Bedford/St. Martin's, 2002.

Wathen, Cindy, ed., George Elfie Ballis, photographer, and Ann McGregor, compiler. *Remembering César.* Clovis, CA: Quill Driver, 2000.

Zinn, Howard. *A People's History of the United States.* New York: HarperCollins, 2005. Originally published in 1985.

Chapter 23

Centeno, Miguel Ángel. *Democracy within Reason.* University Park: Pennsylvania State University Press, 1994.

Davidow, Jeffrey. *The Bear and the Porcupine.* Princeton, NJ: Markus Wiener, 2007.

Fox, Vicente. *Vicente Fox a Los Pinos.* México, DF: Editorial Oceano, 1999.

_____ with Rob Allyn. *Revolution of Hope.* New York: Viking, 2007.

Gonzálo Ruiz, Édgar. *La Última Cruzada.* México, DF: Editorial Grijalbo, 2001.

Grayson, George W. *The United States and Mexico: Patterns of Influence.* New York: Praeger, 1984.

McKinley, James C., Jr., "U.S. Is a Vast Arms Bazaar for Mexican Cartels." *The New York Times,* February 26, 2009, p. A1.

Muñoz Gutiérrez, Ramón. *Pasión por un Buen Gobierno.* México, DF: Ediciones 2000, 1999.

Preston, Julia, and Samuel Dillon. *Opening Mexico.* New York: Farrar, Straus, and Giroux, 2004.

Urías Germán, Gregorio. *La democracia en México después de la alternancia.* México, DF: Grupo Editorial, 2003.

Chapter 24

"Argentina: Huge March for Kirchner." *New York Times,* April 2, 2008, p. A10.

Barrionuevo, Alexei. "Conflict with Farmers Takes Toll on Argentina." *New York Times,* June 24, 2008, p. A14.

_____. "Venezuelan Says Chávez Ordered Cover-Up of Suitcase of Cash." *New York Times,* September 9, 2008, p. A18.

Curia, Walter. *El ultimo peronista.* Buenos Aires: Editorial Sudamericana, 2006.

De Riz, Liliana. "From Menem to Menem: Elections and Political Parties in Argentina." In Tulchin, Joseph S., and Allison M. Garland, eds. *Argentina: The Challenges of Modernization.* Wilmington, DE: Scholarly Resources, 1998.

Di Tella, Torcuato. "Evolution and Prospects of the Argentine Party System." In Tulchin, Joseph S., and Allison M. Garland, eds. *Argentina: The Challenges of Modernization.* Wilmington, DE: Scholarly Resources, 1998.

_____ and Néstor Kirchner. *Conversaciones: Después el derrumbe.* Buenos Aires: Galerna, 2003.

Garrone, Valeria, and Laura Rocha. *Néstor Kirchner: Un muchacho peronista y la oportunidad del poder.* Buenos Aires: Planeta, 2003.

Kaiser, Susana. *Postmemories of Terror.* New York: Palgrave Macmillan, 2005.

Rohter, Larry. "Dwindling Ddebt Boosts Argentine Leader." *New York Times,* January 3, 2003, *http:// www.nytimes.com/2006/01/03/international/ americas/03argentina.html.*

Swann, Maxine. "At Home Abroad: Crisis and Renewal." *New York Times,* June 19, 2008, p. D1.

Tokatlian, Juan Gabriel. *Hacia una nueva estrategia internacional.* Buenos Aires: Grupo Editorial Norma, 2004.

Wornat, Olga. *Reina Cristina.* Buenos Aires: Planeta, 2005.

Chapter 25

Baumeister, Eduardo. "The Structure of Nicaraguan Agriculture and the Sandinista Agrarian Reform." In Harris, Richard L., and Carlos M. Vilas, eds. *Nicaragua: A Revolution Under Siege.* London: Zed, 1985.

Booth, William. "Democracy in Nicaragua in Peril, Ortega Critics Say." *Washington Post,* November 20, 2008, p. A12.

Cerda, Arlen, and María José Uriarte. "*Quién Dijo Miedo?*" *La Prensa,* June 28, 2008, p. 1A.

Daly Heyck, Denis Lynn. *Life Stories of the Nicaraguan Revolution.* New York: Routlege, 1990.

Electoral Democracy Under International Pressure. The Report of the Latin American Studies Association Commission to Observe the 1990 Nicaraguan Election. Pittsburgh: Latin American Studies Association, University of Pittsburgh, March 15, 1990.

Enciclopedia de Nicaragua, Vol. 2. Barcelona: Grupo Oceano, 2003.

Gilbert, Dennis. *Sandinistas: The Party and the Revolution.* New York: Basil Blackwell, 1988.

Harris, Richard L. "Epilogue: A Revolution Under Siege." In Harris, Richard L., and Carlos M. Vilas, eds. *Nicaragua: A Revolution Under Siege.* London: Zed, 1985.

Marcus, Bruce, ed. *Nicaragua: The Sandinista People's Revolution.* New York: Pathfinder, 1985.

Miranda, Roger, and William Ratliff. *The Civil War in Nicaragua.* New Brunswick, NJ: Transaction, 1993.

The Observation of the 1996 Nicaraguan Elections. Special Report of the Council of Freely Elected Heads of Government Latin American and Caribbean Program. Atlanta, GA: Carter Center, 1996.

Ortega Saavedra, Daniel. *Combatiendo por la paz.* Mexico City: Siglo Veintiuno Editores, 1988.

_____. *El Sandinismo: El Más Alto Grado de Organización Del Pueblo.* Managua: Universidad Nacional Autónoma de Nicaragua, 1987.

Perez-Brignoli, Hector. *A Brief History of Central America,* trans. Ricardo B. Sawrey A. and Susana Stettri de Sawrey. Berkeley: University of California Press, 1989.

Ridenour, David A., and David Almasi. *Nicaragua's Continuing Revolution, 1977–1990.* Carrboro, NC: Signal, 1990.

Rosset, Peter, and John Vandermeer, eds. *Nicaragua: Unfinished Revolution.* New York: Grove, 1986.

Salmerón, Luis Núñez. "Agricultores Presionan." *La Prensa,* July 3, 2008, p. 3B.

Schmidt, Blake. "Nicaragua: Rights March Assailed." *New York Times,* December 11, 2008, p. A20.

Toriello Garrido, Guillermo. *A Popular History of Two Revolutions: Guatemala and Nicaragua,* trans. by Rebecca Schwaner. San Francisco: Synthesis, 1985.

Vanden, Harry E., and Gary Prevost. *Democracy and Socialism in Sandinista Nicaragua.* Boulder, CO: Lynne Rienner, 1993.

Chapter 26

Branford, Sue, and Bernardo Kucinski. *Brazil: Carnival of the Oppressed.* London: Latin American Bureau, 1995.

Branford, Sue, and Bernardo Kucinski with Hilary Wainwright. *Politics Transformed: Lula and the Workers' Party of Brazil.* London: Latin America Bureau, 2003.

Conniff, Michael L., and Frank D. McCann, eds. *Modern Brazil: Elites and Masses in Historical Perspective.* Lincoln: University of Nebraska Press, 1989.

Coradini, Odaci Luiz. *Em Nome de Quem? Recursos Sociais no Recrutamento de Elites Políticas.* Rio de Janeiro: Nucleo de Antropologia da Politica, 1998.

Cupertino, Fausto. *Classes e Camadas Sociais no Brazil.* Rio de Janeiro: Civilisacão Brasileira, 1978.

Dantas Junior, Altino. *Lula Sem Censura,* 4th ed. Petrópolis: Editora Vozes, 1982.

Font, Mauricio A. *Coffee, Contention, and Change in the Making of Modern Brazil.* Cambridge, England: Basil Blackwell, 1990.

Goertzel, Ted G. *Fernando Henrique Cardoso: Reinvigorating Democracy in Brazil.* Boulder, CO: Lynne Rienner, 1999.

Hippolito, Lucia. *Por Dentro do Governo Lula.* São Paulo: Editora Futura, 2005.

Keck, Margaret E. *The Workers' Party and Democratization in Brazil.* New Haven, CT: Yale University Press, 1992.

Levine, Robert M. *The History of Brazil.* Westport, CT: Greenwood, 1999.

Martins Rodrigues, Leoncio. *La clase obrera en el Brazil.* Buenos Aires: Centro Editor de America Latina, 1969.

Chapter 27

Bailey, Norman A. "Venezuela and the United States: Putting Energy in the Enterprise," pp. 387–397 in Goodman, Louis W., Forman, Johanna, Mendelson Naím, Moíses, Tulchin, Joseph S., and Bland, Gary, eds., *Lessons of the Venezuelan Experience,* Baltimore, MD: Johns Hopkins University Press, 1995.

Bisbal, Marcelino. "El dilema de los medios y los comunicadores—o armando el rompecabezas." In *Chávez y los Medios de Comunicación Social,* ed. Marinellys Tremamunno. Caracas: Alfadil Ediciones, 2002.

"Chávez for Ever?" *The Economist,* February 21, 2009, p. 39.

Díaz Rangel, Eleazar. "Fragmento de un discurso." In *Chávez y los Medios de Comunicación Social,* ed. Marinellys Tremamunno. Caracas: Alfadil Ediciones, 2002.

Golinger, Eva. *Bush vs. Chávez.* New York: Monthly Review, 2008.

Guevara, Aleida. *Chávez, Venezuela, and the New Latin America.* Melbourne, Australia: Ocean Press, 2005.

Harnecker, Marta. *Understanding the Venezuelan Revolution,* trans. Chesa Boudin. New York: Monthly Review, 2005.

Jones, Bart. *Hugo!* The Hugo Chávez Story from Mud

Hut to Perpetual Revolution. New Hanover, NH: Steerforth, 2007.

Kozloff, Nikolas. *Hugo Chávez: Oil, Politics, and the Challenge to the U.S.* New York: Palgrave Macmillan, 2006.

MacLachlan, Colin M. *A History of Modern Brazil.* Wilmington, DE: Scholarly Resources, 2003.

Martins Rodrigues, Leonicio. *La clase obrera en el Brazil.* Buenos Aires: Centro Editor de América Latina, 1969.

Navarro, Juan Carlos. "Venezuela's New Political Actors." In *Lessons of the Venezuelan Experience,* ed. Goodman, Louis W., Forman, Johanna, Mendelson Naím, Moíses, Tulchin, Joseph S., and Bland, Gary, eds. Baltimore, MD: Johns Hopkins University Press, 1995.

Nuez, Sebastian de la. *Marisabel: La historia te absolverá.* Caracas: Editorial Exceso, 2002.

Rohter, Larry. "Brazil's Finance Minister Quits Amid Continuing Political Scandal." *New York Times,* March 28, 2006, http://www.com/2006/03/28/ international/americas/28brazil.html.

Romero, Simon. "Porlamar Journal: Free Eye Care from Chávez, All the Better to See Him." *New York Times,* February 26, 2008, p. A4.

Sader, Emir, and Ken Silverstein. *Without Fear of Being Happy: Lula, the Workers Party and Brazil.* London: Verso, 1991.

Schoen, Douglas, and Michael Rowan. *The Threat Closer to Home.* New York: Free Press, 2009.

Villegas Poljak, Vladimar. "Medios Vs. Chávez: la lucha continua." In *Chávez y los Medios de Comunicación Social,* ed. Marinellys Tremamunno. Caracas: Alfadil Ediciones, 2002.

General

Anna, Timothy E. "Spain and the Breakdown of the Imperial Ethos: The Problem of Equality." *Hispanic American Historical Review.* 42/2 (May 1982).

Blomberg, Pedro. *Mujeres de la Historia Americana.* Buenos Aires: Librarías Anaconda, 1933.

Connell-Smith, Gordon. *The Inter-American System.* London: Oxford University Press, 1966.

Herring, Hubert. *A History of Latin America.* 2d ed. New York: Knopf, 1961.

Lewis, Oscar. *Pedro Martínez: A Mexican Peasant and His Family.* New York: Random House, 1964.

Martin, Cheryl E. "Reform, Trade and Insurrection in the Spanish Empire." *Latin American Research Review.* 19/3 (1984).

Rock, David. *Argentina, 1516–1982.* Berkeley: University of California Press, 1985.

Wilkie, James W., and Albert L. Michaels, eds. *Revolution in Mexico: Years of Upheaval, 1910–1940.* Tucson: University of Arizona Press, 1969.

Williams, Eric. *From Columbus to Castro: The History of the Caribbean, 1492–1969.* New York: Harper and Row, 1970.

Index

abolitionists 21
ACLU (American Civil Liberties Union) 235
Adams, John 14
Adams, John Quincy 101
AFL-CIO (American Federation of Labor–Congress of Industrial Organizations) 244–253
Aguilar, Jerónimo de 8
Alberdi, Juan Bautista 72, 104
Alessandri, Arturo 205–206, 209
Alinsky, Saul 237–238, 243
Allende, Isabel (author, and cousin of Salvador) 225–226
Allende, Salvador 203–230; first three campaigns for president 209; overthrow 217–219
Arbenz, Jacobo 170, 185
Ayala, Plan of 122–124
Aztec people 6–7

Baptiste, Pierre (Toussaint's tutor) 15
Batista, Fulgencio 174–177
Battle of Ayacucho 37
Battle of Boyacá 29
Battle of Caseros 103–104
Battle of Chacabuco 52
Battle of Junín 31
Battle of Maipu 54, 70
Battle of Ocotal 136–137, 139
Battle of Trafalgar 48
Bolívar, Simon 1, 25–33; inspiration to Hugo Chávez 358; meets San Martín 30–31; political philosophy 28; saved by Sáenz 32
Bonifacio de Andrada e Silva, José 88–91
Bowles, Chester 170
boycotts 245–248
Braganza, House of (Brazil) 87
Brazil 85–95, 329–351; slavery 331–332
Bush, George W. (Texas governor and U.S. president) 267, 275

Cárdenas, Lázaro 257–258
Carlos V 10
Carlotta (queen of Brazil) 112
Carranza, Venustiano 117–119; 124–126
Carter, Jimmy 2, 320–321

Castro, Fidel 173–182; Sierra Maestra campaign 177–179
Castro, Raúl 182
Catholic Church: and Argentina's "dirty war" 295; and César Chávez 243, 249, 252; and Daniel Ortega 322, 324; and Nicaraguan history 305–306
La Causa 244, 252, 254
Chamarro, Violeta 314, 317, 323; election to Nicaraguan presidency 325
Charles III 47
Charles IV 26, 48, 58, 62, 77
Chávez, César 231–255; Catholic Church 243, 249, 252; Delano Grape strike 245ff.; fasting as tactic 249–251; Great Depression 233–234; NFWA (later UFWA) formed 243–244
Chávez, Hugo 352–381; beats 2004 recall 379; coup attempt of 1992 362–365; elected president 1998 369–370; overthrown, restored 2002 376–378; wins 2009 plebescite 381
El Chipote 137–138
Christophe, Henri 18, 20, 23
CIA (Central Intelligence Agency) 171–172, 217
Civil rights movement 250
Clouthier, Manuel 263–267
Cochran, Lord 54–56, 89
Codex Florentino 7
Colombia 27
Community Service Organization (CSO) 237–243
Comonfort, Ignacio 107–108, 110
Congress of Tucumán 76
Congress of Vienna 86
Constant, Benjamin 95
Contras (Nicaragua) 320–321, 325
Coolidge, Calvin 134, 135
Córdoba, Gonsalvo de 12
Córdoba, Gen. José María 32, 39, 40
Cortés, Hernán 6–13
Cortéz Castro, León 162–163
Cruz, Sister Juana Inés de la 127
Cruz, Tomás Godoy 53
Cuba, economy 174, 180–182

Deodoro, Gen. Manoel 95
Dessalines, Jacques 18, 21, 23

Díaz, Porfirio 99, 105, 112–113, 114, 121, 129–130, 256
Díaz del Castillo, Bernal 3–10
Dorfman, Ariel (Chilean author) 228
Drug violence (U.S.–Mexico) 278–279

Ecuador 35
Eisenhower, Dwight D. 180
encomienda 7
Enlightenment 15, 25
Environmental pollution (herbicides, pesticides) 254
Ernst, Isabel 155

Farmers, farming (agrarian reform) 374–375
Farrell, Edelmiro 144, 146
feminism 128
Ferdinand II 15
Ferdinand VII 15, 26, 29, 49, 54, 62, 86
fermage, system of 20
Figueres, José 161–172; in Boston and New York 162; businesses 162; Caribbean Legion 164; "Generation of '40" 163
First Feminist Congress 132
Fox, Vicente 256–280; president of Coca-Cola Mexico 260; president of Mexico in 2000 271; programs 276–280
Franco, Francisco 157, 226
Frente Sandinista de Liberación Nacional (FSLN; Nicaragua) 309, 310–317, 319, 322–324, 327
FSLN see Frente Sandinista de Liberación Nacional

Gadsden Purchase 106
Gaitán, Jorge Eliécer 174, 208
Galindo, Hermila 128, 131–132
Gaou-Guinou 14
Gardia, Calixto 101
Garibaldi, Giuseppe 116
George III (king of England) 14
González Ortega, Beatriz 128
Goulart, João (Brazil) 334–335
Gran Colombia 30, 57
Grau San Martín, Ramón 174
Great Depresión 233–234
Guadelupe Hidalgo, peace of 106

Guajardo, Jesus 126
Guevara, Ernesto "Che" 2, 183–
    193; in Bolivia 186–193; Sierra
    Maestra campaign 186–187; trav-
    els 184–185
Gutiérrez de Mendoza, Juana Belén
    123, 128, 130–131

Haiti 14–24
Havana Peace Conference, 1928
    137–138
Haya de la Torre, Victor 138, 170
Hispaniola 20
Hoover, Herbert 138
Huerta, Victoriano 116, 117, 121–
    123
Hughes, Charles Evans 137
Hugo, Victor 94, 99
Huilzilopoctli 6
Humboldt, Alexander, von 26

Isle of Pines 176
Iturbide, Agustín de 105, 110

Jaramillo, Juan 13
Jean-François 18
Jefferson, Thomas, on slavery 22
Jesuits 47, 195
Jiménez y Muro, María Dolores
    127–130
João VI (king of Portugal) 85–87,
    90
Juárez, Benito 104–113

Kennedy, John F. (U.S. president)
    171–172
Khrushchev, Nikita 180–181
Kirchner, Cristina 286–304; arrest
    292; election to provincial legis-
    lature 297; first female president
    of Argentina 302; national senate
    298
Kirchner, Néstor 281–302; arrests
    292, 293; governor of Santa Cruz
    (three times) 297; presidency
    299–302; programs 301–302
Kissinger, Henry (U.S. national se-
    curity advisor) 214
Kubitschek, Juscelino 334

La Pena, Rosario 99
Las Heras, Juan Gregorio 52, 53–
    55, 69
Laveaux, Etienne-Maynard 18–19
LeClerc, Victor Emmanuel 23
Leopoldina, María 87–88
Liberation Theology 309, 316
Lienzo de Tlaxcala 7
La Llorana 13
Locke, John 49
Lodge, Lautaro (secret organiza-
    tion) 49–51, 53, 68, 69
Louis XIV 16
Louis XVI 18, 48
Louis Phillip 59
Lula da Silva, Luís Inacio 329–351;
    corruption in administration
    349–350; elected president 2002
    348

Macandal, François, burned to
    death 15
Maceo, Antonio 101, 103
Machado, Gerardo ("the butcher")
    174
Machiavelli, Niccolo 9
machismo 128, 154
Madero, Francisco 115–117, 121–
    122, 129, 131
Maitland, Thomas 20
La Malinche see Marina, Doña
Mann, Horace 80
Mantilla, Carmen de 101
Maria I (queen of Portugal) 85
Marina, Doña 5–13
Martí, José 96–103
Maximilian 110–112
Mayas 5–6
Mendive, Rafael María de 97
Metalworkers Union (Brazil) 335–
    342
Miranda, Francisco de 27, 61, 71
Mitre, Bartolomé 80, 82–83
Moctezuma 8–9, 12
Moncada, José María 101, 134–135
Monteagudo, Bernardo de 56, 71
Montesquieu, Charles Louis 49
Montoneros (Argentina) 285, 286
Mulattoes, status in Haiti 16
Muñoz Marín, Luis 170

NAFTA (North American Free
    Trade Agreement) 279
Nahuatl language 6
Nahuatl tribes 6
Napoleon Bonaparte 14, 22, 85, 86;
    and the exploitation of Haiti 15–16
Nixon, Richard (U.S. president)
    214

Oaxaca 104–105, 279
Obregón, Alvaro 118 119, 124, 132
Oduber, Daniel 162, 172
Oge, Vincent 16
O'Higgins, Ambrose 60
O'Higgins, Bernardo 60–72
Orlich, Francisco 162–163, 168, 171
Oro, José de 74
Ortega, Daniel 305–328; career as
    subversive soldier 308–316;
    elected president in 1990 325;
    elected president in 2000 327;
    rises in Sandinista hierarchy
    315–325
Ortega, Umberto (Daniel's
    brother) 308, 310, 313, 316, 323
Ortíz de Domínguez, Josefa 127

Páez, José Antonio 28
Palacios, José 33, 44
Palafox, Manuel 122, 124, 125
Panama Conference 38
Partido de Acción Nacional (PAN;
    Mexico) 259
Partido de Revolución Demócrata
    (PRD; Mexico) 262
Partido de Revolución Institucional-
    izada (PRI; Mexico) 258
Partido dos Trabalhadores (PT;

Brazil) 340
Paz, Gen. José María 75
Paz, Octavio 1
Peace of Basel 48
Pedro I (king of Brazil) 85–91; ab-
    dication 90
Pedro II (constitutional monarch)
    90–95
Peñalosa, Angel Vicente "El Cha-
    cho" 83
Perón, Eva 151–160; enfranchise-
    ment of Argentine women 157;
    fatal illness 157–160; meets Juan
    Perón 152; radio career 152; re-
    sentment among Argentines 155,
    157; social programs 155
Perón, Juan 142–150; affection for
    Nazis 146; "the blue book" 147;
    justicialismo 148; meets Eva 145;
    military career 142–144
Pershing, Gen. John 119, 125
Petión, Alexandre Sabes 17
Picado, Teodoro 164
Pinochet, Augusto 203–230; ac-
    counting of murder and kidnaps
    227–230; in Allende's cabinet
    214; overthrow of Allende
    217–219
Pont, Marshal Marco del 51–52
Puertocarrero, Alonzo Hernandez
    8
Pueyrredón, Juan Martín 51, 68, 71

Quetzalcoatl 6, 9
Quiroga, Juan "Facundo" 75–79

Reagan, Ronald 305, 321, 326
La Reforma 99, 107, 111, 122
Reyes, Cipriano 146
Rigaud 19–21
Rodríguez, Simón 25
Romero, Bishop Oscar Arnulfo
    194–202
Rosas, Juan Manuel de 75–77
Ross, Fred (union organizer) 237–
    238
Rousseau, Jean-Jacques 25

Sáenz, Manuela 2, 34–46; exile to
    Jamaica 44; marriage 35; meets
    Bolívar 36
Sandinistas see Frente Sandinista
    de Liberación Nacional (FSLN;
    Nicaragua)
Sandino, Augusto 2, 133–141
San Martín, José de 30–31, 47–59;
    crossing the Andes 63–64; free-
    ing Chile 51–53; meets Bolívar
    30–31, 57–58; in Peru 51; resigns
    as Protector 58
Santa Anna, Antonio López de
    105–107
Santander, Francisco de Paula 29;
    exiled 43
Sarmiento, Domingo Faustino 73–
    84; first major essay 79; first
    publication of El Facundo 79;
    "Generation of 1837" 78
Schlesinger, Arthur M., Jr. 170, 181

Serna de Guevara, Celia de la 183
Socialist Party (Chile) 206, 208
Soler, Gen. Miguel Estanislao 52, 68–69
Somoza, Anastasio 165, 187, 189
Somoza family 305, 307, 308, 314, 317, 323
Sonthonax, Léger-Félicité 18, 19
Spanish Inquisition 61
Stimson, Henry 135
Sucre, Gen. Antonio José de 32, 36, 44

Tacubaya, el complot de 129, 131
Teamsters (Union) 246–253
Tehuelche Indians 51
Tenochtitlán 11–12
Thereza (queen of Brazil) 92, 95
Thomas, Norman 170
Thorne, Dr. James 35, 43
Toltecs 6

Toussaint L'Ouverture 2, 14–24
Treaty of Lircay 66
Treaty of Tehuantepec 109
Treaty of Tordesillas 86
Treaty of Utrecht 1
Trujillo, Rafael 165, 171, 174

Ulate, Otilio 165, 167, 169
United Farm Workers Association (UFWA, formerly the National Farm Workers Association) 243–246, 248–253
United Provinces of la Plata 51
University of Havana 173–174
Urdaneta, Gen. Rafael 33, 45
Urquiza, Gen. Justo José de 81, 82, 84

Valdés, Firmín 98, 99
Vance, Cyrus R. 202
Vargas, Getúlio (Brazil) 333–334

Velásquez, Diego 7, 11
Vera Cruz, siege of 109
Vesco, Robert 172
Villa, Pancho (Doroteo Arango) 2, 114–119; gathers army 117
Volman, Sacha 171

Walker, William (filibusterer) 306
Washington, George 19
Wilson, Woodrow 117, 122, 125

Xicotenga 11

Ypiranga, Grito do 89
Yrigoyen, Hipolito 138, 185, 143

Zapata, Emiliano 1, 2, 120–126; meeting with Villa 124; women in army 125